THE
IMMORTALITY
KEY

THE
IMMORTALITY
KEY

The Secret History of the
Religion with No Name

BRIAN C. MURARESKU

Foreword by
Graham Hancock

St. Martin's Press
New York

First published in the United States by St. Martin's Press,
an imprint of St. Martin's Publishing Group

www.stmartins.com

Frontispiece © Pontificia Commissione di Archeologia Sacra; courtesy of Archivio PCAS

Library of Congress Cataloging-in-Publication Data

Names: Muraresku, Brian C., author.
Title: The immortality key : the secret history of the religion with no name /
  Brian C. Muraresku ; foreword by Graham Hancock.
Description: First edition. | New York : St. Martin's Press, 2020. | Includes
  bibliographical references and index. |
Identifiers: LCCN 2020017251 | ISBN 9781250207142 (hardcover) |
  ISBN 9781250270917 (ebook)
Subjects: LCSH: Christianity and other religions—Greek. | Christianity—Origin. |
  Greece—Religion. | Hallucinogenic drugs and religious experience. | Mysteries,
  Religious.
Classification: LCC BR128.G8 M95 2020 | DDC 204/.2—dc23
LC record available at https://lccn.loc.gov/2020017251

First Edition: 2020

10 9 8 7 6 5 4 3 2 1

For Julieta Belén and Alexa Paz
without whom this book never would have been born
and because of whom it was almost never finished

And my PJ, the *formosissima causa sine qua non*

Contents

Foreword by Graham Hancock   *xi*

Introduction: A New Reformation   *1*

Part One

BREWING THE PSYCHEDELIC BEER

1. Identity Crisis   25
2. Fall from Grace   37
3. Barley Meal and Laurel Leaves   54
4. Secret of Secrets   69
5. The Beatific Vision   83
6. Graveyard Beer   106
7. The *Kukeon* of Catalonia   129
   Epilogue to Part One   157

Part Two

MIXING THE PSYCHEDELIC WINE

8. The Drug of Immortality   167
9. Vineyards of Heaven   190

10. Holy Elixirs in the Holy Land   204
11. Drunk with the Nectar of Eternity   226
12. All This Was Not Just Picnicking   253
13. The Holy Grail   267
14. A Gnostic Eucharist   291
15. Mystery Coast Highway   318
16. The Gospel of Infinity and the Toad Eucharist   333
17. Our Eyes Have Been Opened   356

Afterword   *376*
Notes   *393*
Index   *443*

αν πεθάνεις πριν πεθάνεις,
δεν θα πεθάνεις όταν πεθάνεις

If you die before you die,
You won't die when you die.

Foreword

Like Brian C. Muraresku, author of the excellent *Immortality Key* that it is my pleasure to introduce to you here, I was raised in a Christian household. My family was Presbyterian, whereas Brian's upbringing was Roman Catholic. There are many doctrinal differences between these two denominations but both practice the rite of Holy Communion and until as late as the eighteenth century both advocated and pursued horrific deaths by burning at the stake for "heretics"—particularly those accused of witchcraft.

My mother and father met in church in Edinburgh in the 1940s and my father went on to qualify as a surgeon, subsequently taking up a post as a medical missionary at the Christian Medical College in Vellore in the south of India, which he held from 1954 until 1958.

Born in 1950, I was my parents' only child and our four years in the "mission field," embedded in a devout Christian community, were undoubtedly formative in my life—although certainly not in the way that my father in particular had hoped. His efforts to fill my head with Christian ideas, buttressed by regular readings from the Old and New Testaments, only fueled my growing dislike of attending church and being forced to listen to long, boring sermons.

By the time I was fourteen that feeling of dislike had crystallized into detestation. The year was 1964; I'd been back in Britain for six years and

I was having a miserable time at a boarding school in the city of Durham. Affiliated to the Church of England (which has its own doctrinal differences from Catholicism and Presbyterianism, but with both of which it shares the rite of Holy Communion), that school, at that time, was horrible and sadistically violent in ways I won't even begin to describe here and was overlooked by a chilly stone chapel where regular services were held—services that we, as pupils, were required to attend.

I remember actively dreading those services for being so remorselessly boring, and actively resenting them for their stupidity and irrationality. Why should I believe in this "God" and in his "son" Jesus, and why should I believe in Heaven and Hell, angels and Satan, just because the Bible, ministers of the church, and my parents told me that these things were real?

They weren't real to me!

Expressing my rebellion—in my teenage way—by refusing to kneel, pray, or sing hymns during chapel services, I determined that henceforth I would question everything and never again take anything on trust just because some authority figure, or some musty book, said it was so.

By my late teens I was already a committed atheist—indeed atheism seemed to me to be the only reasonable and rational position to hold in response to Christian dogma. Then in the early 1970s I attended university where I studied sociology, at that time a radical and questioning discipline, and my views hardened further.

I've stayed an atheist ever since, in the strict sense of the word—which derives from the Greek *átheos* and means literally "godless." Fifty years have gone by and I still see no reason to believe in a deity or deities of any kind. Nevertheless certain experiences that have come my way during this past half century have changed my outlook profoundly and, while "god" remains an unproven hypothesis, the experiences I speak of have persuaded me of the existence of realms and realities other than our own that coexist with ours, and exert influence upon every one of us, but that largely go unseen and unrecognized in modern technological societies—particularly those that have suffered long exposure to Christian teachings.

Experiences

If I listen to a sermon in church, the experience I have there (almost need-less to say) is the experience of listening to a sermon in church, plus the experience of whatever reactions the sermon evokes in me.

The "experience" in this case, therefore, is akin to the experience of lis-tening/reacting to a lecture or to any other kind of teaching. I may learn something new, or I may be confronted by material that I am already fa-miliar with. And I may react with any of a broad range of emotions from crushing boredom at one end of the scale to enthusiastic engagement at the other, and with varying degrees of agreement or disagreement with what the speaker is saying.

Likewise if I listen to a lecture or read a book or academic paper on the human sex act, I may experience the lecture or book or paper as boring, or stimulating, or intriguing, or disconcerting, or informative, or redundant, etc. One thing is for sure, however: hearing the lecture or reading the book or paper is categorically *not* the same as the experience I would enjoy if I were actually having sex.

We can hopefully agree, therefore, that—as experiences—teachings, ser-mons, books, lectures, and papers are separate, distinctly different from, and of a lower order than, whatever it is they seek to describe, analyze, or elucidate. Just as to hear a lecture on sex is not the same as having sex, so to hear a sermon on the Kingdom of Heaven is not the same as visiting the Kingdom of Heaven and experiencing it directly.

Which brings me to the subject of psychedelics and the experiences they unleash.

My first encounter with psychedelics was in 1974 in England when I took LSD on impulse at a festival and was rewarded with twelve hours of bliss, revelation, scary challenges, time travel, and mystery. The experience was so powerful, however, that I felt afraid to seek it out again—suppose the second time went wrong to the same heightened level as the first time went right?—and over the next thirty years I declined several opportunities for further "trips."

Until, that is, I found myself writing a book that I originally intended to be about the mystery of Stone Age cave art but that ended up being about so much more than that. The book, published in 2005, was *Supernatural: Meetings with the Ancient Teachers of Mankind*, and in 2002 during the preliminary stages of research, I came across the work of David Lewis-Williams, professor of anthropology at the University of Witwatersrand in South Africa. Newly published that year, David's book *The Mind in the Cave: Consciousness and the Origins of Art* came as a revelation to me. It presented reams of evidence supported by cogent arguments to make the case that the characteristic features of cave art all around the world, and the remarkable common themes in this art created by people who could have had no direct contact with one another, are best explained if the artists, wherever and whenever they lived, had all experienced deeply altered states of consciousness—specifically those trance-like altered states sought out by shamans in tribal and hunter-gatherer cultures through the consumption of powerful psychedelic substances. In brief, David's "neuropsychological theory of cave art" proposes that shamans of the Stone Age used a variety of means—notably psychedelic plants and fungi—to enter trance states in which they experienced powerful visions. Later, returning to the "normal," everyday state of consciousness, they remembered their visions and painted them on the walls of caves.

I quickly discovered that the shamans of tribal and hunter-gatherer societies still extant in the world today all likewise embrace trance states, in many cases brought on by psychedelic plants and fungi. Many subsequently make paintings of their visions and—remarkably—this modern shamanic imagery, said to depict the "spirit world" and its inhabitants, is strikingly similar to the imagery of Stone Age cave art.

Being a hands-on researcher I knew that the time had come for me to renew my acquaintance with psychedelics. For my first research "trips" I chose to travel to the Amazon rain forest of South America to sit down with shamans and drink with them the sacred visionary brew known as Ayahuasca—"the Vine of Souls" or "Vine of the Dead"—in which the active ingredient is dimethyltryptamine (DMT), the most potent hallucinogen known to science.

All in all I had eleven Ayahuasca sessions in the Amazon in 2003, enough to provide me with the authentic firsthand experiences I felt needed to write my book. But since *Supernatural* was published in 2005 I have taken part in more than seventy further Ayahuasca sessions, the four most recent of which (at time of writing) were held in Costa Rica in December 2019. My practice is not entirely consistent but I try to make an Ayahuasca pilgrimage once a year, on each occasion, wherever in the world I choose to go, joining with small groups of fellow seekers (usually in the range of five to twenty people but sometimes—rarely—with as many as a hundred), to experience the brew in a ceremonial setting. Typically these ceremonies are facilitated by Amazonian shamans or by Westerners who have undergone apprenticeships with Amazonian shamans and—with increasing frequency in the Western context—it is women, not men who lead and guide the ceremonies.

Drinking Ayahuasca is hard work. The brew tastes obnoxious—a mixture of battery acid, rancid socks, raw sewage, and just a hint of chocolate—and routinely induces diarrhea, intense sweating, and projectile vomiting followed by exhausting bouts of dry retching. The visions that accompany all this can sometimes be terrifying, and sometimes deeply comforting. Extraordinary swirling, scintillating geometric patterns provide an otherworldly backdrop, but the visions also routinely include encounters with intelligent entities, sometimes in human form, sometimes in animal form, and sometimes in the form of part-animal, part-human hybrids—known technically as therianthropes (from the Greek *therion*, meaning wild beast and *anthropos* meaning man).

Despite having to brace myself for the discomfort of the experience, it is these visions that draw me back to Ayahuasca year after year—this sense of gaining entry to a seamlessly convincing parallel universe and of being offered the opportunity to participate there in intriguing, meaningful, and sometimes life-changing encounters with seemingly otherworldly entities.

Very commonly these entities appear as serpents or as serpent/human hybrids, and "Mother Ayahuasca" herself, the entity believed by many to be the supernatural intelligence behind the brew, is frequently depicted in shamanic art as a serpent or as a serpent therianthrope. I have met "her" in this form many times. On one memorable occasion, for example, "she" appeared to me as a great boa constrictor twenty or thirty feet in length. She wrapped her coils gently around my body, laid her huge head on my shoulder, and gazed into my eyes for an infinity. She seemed very real to me—indeed more real than real—and her presence (despite the "natural" horror that we humans are supposed to have of serpents) was that of a deeply compassionate, utterly beautiful goddess who simply loved me for the longest while during which "she" repeatedly beamed into my mind what felt like a telepathic message—a very simple, very basic message delivered nonetheless with astonishing, breathtaking power—that I needed to be kinder and more nurturing to others.

I emerged from the session with the clear knowledge that although I could not go back in time and correct past mistakes and past unkindnesses, I could choose never to repeat those mistakes and to be a kinder, more positive, compassionate, and constructive influence on the lives of others.

I do not know whether Mother Ayahuasca is "real" in the way that we normally mean when we speak of real people or things, but what is interesting is that at the level of phenomenology (sources thoroughly documented and footnoted in my book *Supernatural*), many thousands of people have undergone encounters with "her" during Ayahuasca sessions and have had their behavior and their outlook profoundly changed as a result. Those changes are real even if materialist science would like to reduce the entity who inspires them to a mere epiphenomenon of disturbed brain activity.

Very often this entity (who, I repeat, may or may not be real but is experienced as real) gives us profound moral lessons in the depths of the Ayahuasca journey. We may be shown episodes from our lives in which we have behaved unkindly or unjustly to others, or been mean-spirited and unloving, or have failed to live up to our own potential. And we will be shown these things with absolute clarity and transparency, with all illusions and excuses stripped away, so we are confronted with nothing more nor less than the cold, hard truth about ourselves. Such revelations can be very painful. Frequently people cry during Ayahuasca sessions because of them. But they bring insight and give us the chance to change our behavior in the future: to be more nurturing and less toxic, to be more considerate of others, and to be more aware than we were before of the incredible privilege the universe has given us by allowing us to be born in a human body—an opportunity for growth and improvement of the soul that we absolutely must not waste.

Perhaps this is one of the reasons why Ayahuasca has been so very successful in getting people off addictions to harmful hard drugs. For example, Dr. Jacques Mabit has for many years been offering heroin and cocaine addicts incredibly effective treatments with Ayahuasca at his Takiwasi clinic in Tarapoto, Peru, where they might typically undergo twelve sessions with

Ayahuasca in the space of a month. (See here: www.takiwasi.com/docs/arti_ing
/ayahuasca_in_treatment_addictions.pdf.)

A very high proportion of participants have such powerful revelations
about the roots of their own problems and behavior during the sessions that
they leave Takiwasi completely free of addiction, often without withdrawal
symptoms, and never resume their habit. The success rate is far better than
for any of the conventional Western treatments for drug addiction.

Meanwhile in Canada, Dr. Gabor Mate was offering phenomenally successful Ayahuasca healing sessions to his drug-addicted patients before the
Canadian government stepped in and stopped his work on the grounds that
Ayahuasca itself is an illegal drug. (See here: www.theglobeandmail.com
/life/health-and-fitness/bc-doctor-agrees-to-stop-using-amazonian-plant
-to-treat-addictions/article4250579/.)

As Brian Muraresku documents in the pages of *The Immortality Key*,
however, Western science, so long recruited to justify the harsh punishments
called for by the "war on drugs," is increasingly recognizing the positive, life-
changing benefits of psychedelics—in ridding individuals of post-traumatic
stress disorder, for example, or, in the case of those with terminal cancers,
of their fear of death. The potential of psilocybin (the active ingredient in
"magic mushrooms") is presently being investigated at the Johns Hopkins
Center for Psychedelic and Consciousness Research and it is striking, as
Brian reports, that "about 75 percent of the research volunteers consistently
rate their one and only dose of psilocybin as either the single most meaningful experience of their entire lives, or among the top five."

Likewise, I am here to attest that in several (though by no means all) of
my many Ayahuasca sessions I have been blessed with experiences of such
extraordinary power, yielding such penetrating insights, that I unhesitat-
ingly rank them among the most meaningful of my life. Indeed they have
been so meaningful that they have changed my entire outlook on life and
on the nature of "reality." I'm still an atheist, and I still accept that those
scientists who seek to reduce consciousness to matter may be right. But my
experiences with Ayahuasca have convinced me, as no amount of reading
or studying or listening to lectures or sermons ever could, that materialist-
reductionism is a profound error, that to be alive and conscious at all is a
mystery of enormous, immeasurable proportions and, in brief, as Shakespeare

put it in *Hamlet,* that "there are more things in heaven and earth" than are presently dreamed of in our philosophy.

When I first embraced atheism I embraced the interlinked ideas that there is no transcendental meaning or purpose to life, that there's no heaven and no hell, and that when our bodies and brains die it's absurd to imagine that some "spiritual" part of us—the "soul"—survives.

After my Ayahuasca experiences I'm no longer so sure that logic and reason can effortlessly reduce us to our bodies in this way. On the contrary, I've seen much to convince me that although consciousness manifests in the body during life it is neither made by the body, nor confined to the body, nor inevitably extinct on the death of the body. One outcome of this is that I no longer fear death as I once did; rather I regard its approach with curiosity and a sense of adventure.

I think I can say, therefore, that my experiences with Ayahuasca have been *persuasive,* perhaps in very much the same way that the experiences of pilgrims to the ancient Greek sanctuary of Eleusis were persuasive and for very much the same reason—namely, as you will learn in the pages that follow, that a likely psychedelic brew, the *kukeon,* was drunk by participants at Eleusis after which they experienced visions that banished all fear of death. The specific psychedelic compounds involved in Ayahuasca are closely related to those in the *kukeon* but by no means identical. The effects of the "beatific visions" and deeply meaningful experiences induced in both cases, however, appear to be quite remarkably the same.

Ancient Teachers

Throughout much of Western history, until the fourth century AD when early, "primitive" Christianity began to be systematically stamped out beneath the jackboots of the Roman Catholic Church, "beatific visions" were the primary recruitment tool of the enormously ancient and influential "religion with no name" that is the subject of *The Immortality Key.* This religion could shift and morph into multiple forms—the Eleusinian and Dionysian Mysteries are among the examples Brian gives, and to these I would add the much older religion of the painted caves that I explored in *Supernatural*—but the common factor in every case was a psychedelic sacrament (sometimes food, sometimes drink, sometimes both) consumed by all participants.

"Primitive" Christianity, as Brian convincingly argues here, started out around two thousand years ago as merely the latest form or incarnation of this archaic religion, and—at least in some cases—seems to have made use of bread and wine infused with psychedelic plants and fungi as its sacrament. At that time, because Christianity was persecuted under the Roman Empire until the reign of Constantine (AD 306–337) it was normal practice for its adherents to meet secretly in small groups to eat the bread and drink the wine of Holy Communion, and afterward experience powerful and deeply meaningful beatific visions. And more often than not, these secret ceremonies of direct experiential communion with the divine were led by women with men playing a secondary role.

Then, from the second half of the fourth century AD onward, came the rise of Roman Catholicism, dominated by men who took decisive steps to marginalize the role of women in the Church and to remove the psychedelic elements from the sacrament, reducing Holy Communion to the empty symbolic act, devoid of powerful experiential content, that hundreds of millions of Christians continue to perform.

My friend, the visionary artist Alex Grey, whose work has been much influenced by Ayahuasca, describes the Old Testament story of the serpent, the forbidden fruit, and God's expulsion of Adam and Eve from the Garden of Eden as "the first psychedelic slapdown."

Pursuing that thought, Roman Catholicism's persecution of "primitive" Christians and the extirpation of their visionary Communion wine might be described as the second psychedelic slapdown.

And then, in the twentieth century, just as we seemed to be freeing ourselves from the loveless iron grip of the Church and opening up to new spiritual possibilities, governments around the world waded in with the so-called "war on drugs"—the third psychedelic slapdown.

Over the centuries, therefore, enormous and often deadly forces (with the power, for example, to burn people at the stake or imprison them for decades) have repeatedly been unleashed to prevent people from experiencing direct contact with realms and realities other than the mundane. At the same time, however, even when it must have seemed that the "religion with no name" had been deleted completely from the human record, there were always—if I may extend the metaphor—multiple "backup disks" in the form of psychedelic plants and fungi growing all over the planet. There might be long gaps, lacunae of centuries even, but the moment would always come when certain curious individuals, either by accident or by design, would sample the plants and mushrooms that serve as the permanent Hall of Records of the religion with no name, thus setting in motion the experiences and subsequent processes of social organization that would ultimately allow it to be restored in full force.

It is not an accident that the Mazatec shamans of southern Mexico refer to the psilocybe mushrooms used in their ceremonies as "little teachers," and, in a sense, that is what all psychedelic plants and fungi are—literally the ancient teachers of mankind. Whether we engage with Ayahuasca, or with Psilocybe mexicana, or with peyote, or with LSD (which is itself derived from the fungus ergot) we are dealing with the biological agents of the religion with no name and with their numinous capacity to reawaken our spiritual appetites and potential.

Brian tells us that he has never in his life had a psychedelic experience—nor is there any reason why he should since The Immortality Key offers hard factual data and empirical argument rather than a trip report. Moreover, the author's decision to remain a psychedelic virgin is, in my view, a wise strategic move since it denies self-styled skeptics—of whom there are legions—any lazy ad hominem dismissal of this important book as the "ravings" of a "druggie" or other similar slurs.

My own approach is different. I could not have written Supernatural without direct experience of psychedelics and the resulting skeptical backlash has been large, sustained, and obvious. Indeed, to this day, more than fifteen years after Supernatural was published, my engagement with psychedelics remains one of the main tools that skeptics use to ridicule and dismiss my work.

I have no regrets.

Despite my persisting, undiluted atheism, and the many years in which I distanced myself from anything and everything that looked like religious faith, the psychedelic ceremonies in which I have participated all around the world—ceremonies often led by women and held in secret like the Communion of the "primitive" Christians—have reintroduced spirituality into my life.

For this I am deeply grateful.

—Graham Hancock

Introduction

A New Reformation

"I'm an atheist, I don't believe there is a God," she affirms. "But then I began to feel this love. Just overwhelming, all-encompassing love." There is a long silence. "And the way I describe it is being bathed in God's love," she goes on, her voice cracking, "because I find no other way to describe it. I felt that I belonged, that I was part of everything and had the right to be here. How else do I describe it? Maybe what your mother's love felt like when you were a baby. This feeling of love was suffusing the entire experience."

I'm talking with Dinah Bazer—New Yorker, grandmother, survivor. And unrepentant nonbeliever. She was diagnosed with mixed-cell ovarian cancer in 2010 at the age of sixty-three. Ordinarily more than half the women in Dinah's position don't outlive the dreaded five-year window past their diagnosis. But Dinah was one of the lucky ones. She caught her tumor early at stage 1C, ensuring much better odds of winning the battle. After six rounds of chemotherapy and two years of follow-up appointments, the cancer was in remission, and Dinah should have been feeling optimistic. But she couldn't shake her paralyzing fear of the disease that is never cured—only contained—and could always return with a vengeance.

In 2012 Dinah confessed her existential crisis to one of the nurses from the Perlmutter Cancer Center at New York University during a routine checkup. It was suggested she enroll in a first-of-its-kind study that their psychiatric team was conducting with Johns Hopkins University. On its face, the researchers were trying to determine if psilocybin, the active compound in magic mushrooms, could ease depression and anxiety in cancer patients. According to the findings of the randomized, double-blind, placebo-controlled trial released in the respected *Journal of Psychopharmacology* in November 2016, the vast majority found clinical relief—with 87 percent of NYU's twenty-nine volunteers reporting increased life satisfaction or well-being for months afterward.[1] Like Dinah, a full 70 percent rated their one and only dose of psilocybin as either the most meaningful experience of their entire lives, or among the top five. The numbers were consistent with the fifty-one volunteers from the Hopkins study, the results of which were published simultaneously.[2] Altogether, eighty tormented people dove into the unknown. Most left with a new lease on life, forever changed. The outcome is characterized as "unprecedented within the field of psychiatry."[3]

While the new batch of data was eye-catching from a therapeutic perspective, the researchers weren't necessarily looking for the next Prozac or Xanax. There's not much money in a single-dose wonder drug. The pharmaceutical industry tends to prefer long-term users who get hooked on a steady regimen of renewable prescriptions. Instead the NYU team had joined their colleagues at Hopkins on the hunt for something far more valuable. The real question wasn't *whether* psychedelics might work for those confronting death, but *why*? And the initial answers had already led the scientists down a rather unscientific path, trespassing into corridors of the mind that once interested students of religion alone.

A decade earlier, in 2006, the Hopkins team completed the first psilocybin project since the 1970s, when research into the forbidden substance became largely impossible during the War on Drugs. Under tightly controlled conditions the psilocybin unleashed a profound, mystical experience that seemed to anchor the lasting emotional and psychological benefits recorded by the thirty-six volunteers. They had no life-threatening illness, and were otherwise free of the debilitating angst that consumed Dinah. But these early results were shockingly similar to the 2016 collaboration with NYU: one-third of the participants rated their experience "as the most spiritually significant of their lives," comparing it to the birth of a child or the death of a parent. Two-thirds placed it among the top five.[4] When friends, family, and coworkers were interviewed, they confirmed the remarkable transformations in the volunteers' mood and behavior for months, even years, following their single dose.

From that moment on, Dr. Roland Griffiths upended his career to focus almost exclusively on psilocybin, creating what is now called the Johns Hopkins Psychedelic Research Unit. More than 360 volunteers and fifty peer-reviewed publications later, he's ready to call a spade a spade.[5] In his 2016 TED Talk, Griffiths said the drug-induced ecstasy he routinely witnesses in the laboratory is "virtually identical" to that reported by natural-born prophets and visionaries throughout human history. The underlying experience itself, whether activated by psilocybin or some spontaneous internal flood of neurotransmitters, must be "biologically normal."[6] If we are essentially wired for mystical experience, it raises the intriguing prospect that, under the right mind-set and environment, any curious soul can be instantly converted into a religious savant.

Griffiths's colleague, Dr. William Richards, has been testing that hypothesis since the 1960s, when he codeveloped the very scale to measure these peak states of consciousness, the Mystical Experience Questionnaire. Richards himself holds the dubious distinction of administering the final dose of psilocybin in 1977 at the Maryland Psychiatric Research Center, the last legal refuge for this research before an extended hiatus. Together with Griffiths, he was the first to get the ball rolling again in the early 2000s, once the federal government was persuaded by the "high standards of scholarly competence" at Hopkins, one of the top medical schools in the country.[7]

In his 2015 book, *Sacred Knowledge: Psychedelics and Religious Experiences*, Richards maps out the essential features of the perfect psilocybin journey: transcending time and space, intuitively sensing the unity and sacredness of all things, accessing knowledge that is normally not available. Oftentimes there is a merging of the everyday personality with a larger, more fundamental whole. Words fail to capture the unsinkable conviction that the experiencer has somehow glimpsed the ultimate nature of reality, an insight that seems "blatantly obvious" at the time, and is usually accompanied by intense feelings of joy, tranquility, exaltation, and awe.[8]

On the ineffability scale Dinah is certainly no exception. I'm wondering why an avowed atheist would appeal to "God" to describe the infinite love that "bathed" her as the psilocybin supercharged her biochemistry. "Why not the love of the 'universe,' or the love of the 'cosmos,' or the love of 'na-ture'?" I ask.

"Because 'God' is as good as the 'universe' and the 'cosmos' and 'nature.' These are all things we really don't know. I've always thought heaven and hell were absurd ideas. I am not interested in mysticism at all. I tend to think of it as a bunch of baloney. And I don't think there's any meaning to life. But it doesn't matter to me, because my own experience is all I have. I've had very religious people ask me, 'You don't believe in God?' And I say: 'No, I believe in Love.' And I can still feel it sometimes."

"Even now . . . seven years later?"

"Oh yes."

But words don't always fail. Dinah can dredge up poignant specifics about the visions, now indelibly tattooed on her psyche, that unfolded during the psilocybin session in 2012. Lying comfortably on a couch, with her eyes under a sleep shade and headphones pumping a soothing mix of classical and instrumental music, she tackled the therapeutic portion of her six-hour journey in pretty short order. In her mind's eye Dinah saw what she immediately recognized as her fear and anxiety: "a big, black lump like coal under my rib cage, on the left-hand side, which was not where the cancer was. It was not my cancer." Enraged, she yelled some colorful language at the inky intruder like a proper New Yorker. And in an instant it was gone. For good.

The nasty part out of the way, Dinah had nothing left to do but enjoy the playlist that had been skillfully cobbled together by the NYU team. "So I just drifted away. I was living in the music, like a river." That's when the love of "God" entered Dinah's life, staying with her for the remaining hours on the couch, and the many years since. But something else happened too. And the researchers believe it holds the key to the whole experience.

The sequence is tricky to verbalize. Dinah is keen that I not misquote her by writing something as sentimental and clichéd as "being at one with the universe." So she describes a process in which there was a "dissolution of the self" and a "melting away of barriers." She remembers the moment when concepts like "internal" and "external" no longer held true. "I'm not just standing there, looking out at the world anymore. I'm part of the world." After a lengthy pause while she harvests the right phrase, Dinah refers to this fleeting moment as "a state of pure being." She recalls taking several deep breaths, exhaling with force, just to hear the air escape her chest. She needed to prove that her physical body was still there, that it still existed somewhere in time and space. The source of her awareness, once so easy to locate, was suddenly everywhere and nowhere at once. And then it all made sense. In that unsettling, parallel reality—wading effortlessly to the violins—Dinah arrived at the realization that "birth and death actually don't have any meaning." When forced to clarify, she adds, "It's more of a state of always being."

"Always being?"

"Always being. So being now and always. There's no beginning or end. Every moment is an eternity of its own."

A poetic breakthrough from a skeptic. That's precisely what Dinah's guide, Dr. Anthony Bossis, was hoping for. As a professor with NYU's Department of Psychiatry and its director of palliative care research for the psilocybin study, the clinical psychologist's professional specialty is the "existential spiritual and psychological distress" that preys on so many Americans as they approach death. Recent statistics show that depression is up 26 percent for those at the end of life.[9] In a culture that generally avoids the topic, subcontracting the gritty details over to a ballooning hospice-care industry, Bossis believes we simply "don't end well" in this country.[10] Instead of "a bad death marked by needless suffering," he sees psilocybin as a "meaning-making medicine" with enormous potential.[11] Not just for the dying, but for everybody.

The historic partnership with Hopkins gave Bossis a front-row seat to the cutting-edge research of Roland Griffiths and William Richards that had fascinated him for years. His unforgettable sessions with Dinah and dozens of other volunteers brought home the real-world consequences of the seemingly unreal experience at the mystical core of these psilocybin trials. For Bossis, Dinah is the ultimate example of the sustained positive impact that can be triggered by an unexpected rendezvous with "God's love." Even for an atheist. While language can never do justice to what Dinah experienced, she undoubtedly made contact with what Bossis calls a "timeless dimension" that fosters "non-attachment" to all the pain, despair, and stress of being human, allowing a connection to something "more enduring" within. In a personal email Bossis explained why such an irrational event can reliably generate so much meaning for those on the verge of death:

Participants in our study often described this experience with the new-found knowledge that consciousness survives bodily death—that we are not only our bodies—which is a profound gift to a person with a body that is failing, and will soon stop functioning due to advanced disease. It has been described as a transcendence of past, present, future. Timelessness in the moment. I've heard participants speak about feeling "outside of time." The insight that we are not bound by the material world is a powerful one. It is psychologically, existentially and spiritually liberating.

In order to identify with that grander, more expansive aspect of themselves—the part that might never die in Dinah's "state of always being"—a shedding of the familiar has to occur. Surrendering the physical body and losing all sense of time and space can feel disorienting, like a little death all in itself. "As if a foreshadow of what's to come," Bossis writes, "some of the volunteers say 'this is what death will be like, this is death.'" William Richards has been documenting the same phenomenon since the 1960s, using the identical words as Dinah to describe the transition into "mystical realms of consciousness as 'melting' or 'dissolving,' even as being deliciously seduced by a divine lover." In *Sacred Knowledge: Psychedelics and Religious Experiences*, he further adds:

The mind may undergo one or more intense experiences of death and rebirth and awareness of the ego (that is, that part of your mind that functions with your name in everyday life) may ebb and flow. Similarly, awareness of the body lying on the couch may come and go as one might expect to experience in a state of deep trance.... This threshold between the personal (that is, the everyday self) and the transpersonal (that is, more fundamental or universal dimensions of consciousness) is conceptualized by different people in different ways. Most commonly, the term "death" is employed as the ego (everyday self) feels that it is quite literally dying. Though one may have read that others have reported subsequent immersion in the eternal and experiences of being reborn and returning to everyday existence afterward, in the moment imminence of death may feel acutely—and for some terrifyingly—real.[12]

And right there, plain as can be, is the stated goal of every mystic or saint who has ever tried to put any of the world's religions to the ultimate test. To die before you die. Or rather, to psychologically maim the ego—even for a brief instant—in order to be initiated into an understanding of what lies beneath all the thoughts, feelings, and memories that have gone into the lifetime construction of our false, or at the very least incomplete, sense of self. The little ego (Latin for "I") that seems so firmly in control is just an elaborate illusion. And only half the story, as brilliantly narrated by the Harvard-trained neuroanatomist Jill Bolte Taylor in her 2008 book, *My Stroke of Insight*.

With minute attention to every detail, Bolte Taylor recounts the cerebral hemorrhage she suffered in 1996, when the rupture of a blood vessel in a very strategic area of her left hemisphere sent all "calculating intelligence" out the window. The half of her brain responsible for categorizing and organizing sensory input simply went off-line. Suddenly there was no more "brain chatter." No dialogue with her inner voice—that adviser that helps us navigate the external world by comparing incoming data from the five senses to past experiences, and running split-second algorithms to determine the best course of future action. It's the kind of linear, rational thinking that reminds us to restock the refrigerator or put gas in the car before it's too late. It prompts us into the bathroom when nature calls, leaving infants and toddlers to soil their diapers. Before the ego has fully formed, this mental back-and-forth takes a few years to mature and lock in place. But once it does, the left hemisphere assumes daily command, forcing the right hemisphere's more immediate awareness of the present moment into the shadows of forgotten childhood.[13]

During Bolte Taylor's stroke, it wasn't about what happened before, or what comes next, but what's happening *now*. The same timeless *now* that awed Dinah with its endlessness: "every moment is an eternity of its own." Could this be how newborns see the world, before they even realize they're separate beings, independent of their mothers? Every parent gets a kick out of that developmental milestone when babies finally realize they have arms, staring in disbelief at the hands attached to their alien limbs. "Whoa, I'm a weird-looking thing," Bolte Taylor recalls reacting to her body during the initial stages of the stroke, while she mounted the Cardio Glide for her morning exercise routine. Like "a great whale gliding through a sea of silent euphoria," the scientist felt no worry, no concern, and no grief whatsoever. And with total contentment, she prepared to die.

But like Dinah and the hundreds of psilocybin volunteers ushered through a harrowing ego death in recent years, Bolte Taylor survived, reborn with fresh eyes and childlike wonder into the half of her brain that went missing with the pacifier. She calls it "the deep, inner-peace circuitry of the right hemisphere." Once it was reactivated, she could find solace in that "sea of silent euphoria" throughout the eight years it took to fully recover from the stroke. Similarly Dinah tells me she can relive the sensation of being "bathed in God's love" if she's just able to slow down. She doesn't meditate as often as she'd like, but whenever she does, that divine love wells up. The NYU playlist can trigger it too. Bossis gave her a copy after the psilocybin session, which Dinah particularly enjoys listening to on Thanksgiving. Whatever kind of "God" this is, it has nothing to do with tired doctrine or stale dogma. It's a felt presence that never judges, never condemns, never demands anything in return. Certainly not blind belief. When I visited William Richards at his oasis of a home outside Baltimore in the early summer of 2018, he distilled his decades' worth of research like a Zen master: "Once you've plunged into the ocean, does it really matter whether or not you *believe* in water?"

Dinah might not have been looking for it, but what she got was a genuine religious experience. And it's the kind of experience that just might speak to the rising tide of seekers who could spend a lifetime in the church, temple, or mosque and never once feel the rapture that is consistently delivered in a single afternoon at Hopkins and NYU. Over a billion people across the planet are now religiously unaffiliated, including one in five Americans and Europeans, and almost half the British public.[14] The "un-churching" of America is being driven especially by the 40 percent of millennials who don't identify with any faith whatsoever.[15] That figure is more than double what it was a generation ago. The God now rejected by America's largest generation, 73 million people, is not the God of Dinah Bazer. A God that you can actually *experience* in a direct and personal way is a God that makes sense. A God that erases depression and anxiety like a cosmic surgeon, obliterates the fear of death, and sends a shock wave of love through your fragile heart is a God that lives in high definition. And a God that could hardly be expected to start a war against nonbelievers.

More troubling is the God of organized religion and his army of spokesmen—those priests, rabbis, and imams who stand between superficial definitions of heaven and a common-sense public who have every right to demand proof. When the answer to their doubts is condescending moralism, contrived from an outdated and impenetrable holy book, it's time to cut out the middleman in the private search for transcendence. The result is the 27 percent of all Americans fueling the spiritual-but-not-religious (SBNR) phenomenon.[16] It has been called "the most important religious development of our time" because the trend is clear and will only surge in the years to come.[17] With unprecedented access to the teachings of the world's faiths, we are living in an age when the rallying cry of the SBNRs has never been more achievable: "to be the student and beneficiary of all traditions, and the slave to none."[18]

If there's a spiritual crisis in the West, it's because the defenders of the three great monotheistic faiths have forgotten their roots. When Yahweh appeared to Moses in a burning bush, it was a terrifying ordeal. The emancipator of the Israelites feared for his life and shielded his eyes from the God who would later warn, in Exodus 33:20, "You cannot see My face; for no man can see Me and live!" Christianity's greatest missionary, Saint Paul, was struck blind for three days on the road to Damascus by a flash of heaven-sent light, followed by an auditory hallucination of Jesus. Thereafter Paul would claim continued supernatural communication with the Son of God. The entire Qur'an was dictated to Muhammad word for word by the Angel Gabriel, who revealed Islam's scripture in a series of trances. One of Muhammad's earliest biographers, Ibn Ishaq, records the belief of family friends that the young prophet suffered a stroke. Modern scholars say he was prone to "ecstatic seizures."[19]

"There is no other way to start a religion," says the Benedictine monk Brother David Steindl-Rast.[20] "Every religion has its mystical core. The challenge is to find access to it and to live in its power." In what he calls the centuries-long "tension between the mystical and the religious establishment," the technicians who yearn for real experience are always butting heads with the authorities who are just trying to keep the house in working order. According to Brother David, "time has an influence on the system: the pipes tend to get rusty and start to leak, or they get clogged up. The flow from the source slows down to a trickle." When that happens, the experience of Dinah's

God recedes into the mists of history. The written word that tries to capture the original encounter inevitably replaces the personal experience of awe. So that "live doctrine fossilizes into dogmatism," and the ethics and morality that attempt to translate "mystical communion into practical living" are reduced to moralism.[21] But despite the dogmatism and moralism that inevitably muck up the system, the mystics have always come along with an embarrassing reminder for the self-appointed enforcers of the establishment's rules and regulations. When it comes to "God"—a word rarely used by the mystics—there is total unanimity on one crucial issue of paramount importance.

God does not reside in a holy book.

Whether it's the Bible or the Qur'an, the mystics have never found God by *reading* about God. There is no class, no lecture, no homily that will ever bring you closer to God. Because there is, in fact, absolutely nothing you could ever *learn* about God. For the mystics, the only way to know God is to *experience* God. And the only way to experience God is to *unlearn* everything the ego has been trying so vigorously to manufacture since our infancy. In order to stop wetting the bed and become productive members of society, that "deep, inner-peace circuitry of the right hemisphere" has been sidelined along the way. To bring it back online, say the mystics, the simplest and most effective method is to die before you die.

It's why the Sufis, the mystics of Islam, have been called "the impatient ones." Rather than wait until their actual death, the spiritual experts of the world's second largest religion rank one task more urgent than any other: recovering an "awareness of one's full identity" in this lifetime.[22] The twelfth-century Persian pharmacist Attar once said, "So long as we do not die to ourselves, and so long as we are identified with someone or something, we shall never be free."[23] His protégé, Rumi—the Sufi master and in recent years bestselling poet in America—was in total agreement: "If you could get rid of yourself just once, the secret of secrets would open to you. The face of the unknown, hidden beyond the universe, would appear on the mirror of your perception."[24]

It's why a fundamental concept for the Kabbalists, the mystics of Judaism, is *Ayin* (Nothingness). "When a man attains to the stage of self-annihilation he can thus be said to have reached the world of the divine Nothingness. Emptied of selfhood his soul has now become attached to the

march of science is winning converts at the local level, where the earliest buds of the psychedelic Reformation are beginning to flower. In May 2019 Denver became the very first city in the country to decriminalize the use and possession of magic mushrooms. Oakland and Santa Cruz soon followed in California, with their city councils extending the treatment to all naturally occuring psychedelic plants and fungi. As the first to legalize statewide cannabis for personal use in 2012, Colorado is already home to the International Church of Cannabis, which opened its doors in 2017.[33] The first psychedelic churches will inevitably be next.

Is this an artificial, get-God-quick scheme? Or, as Huxley predicted, are we witnessing the birth of a genuine Reformation, with the practical mystics of the twenty-first century leading the charge? For this movement to have any substance or merit, Huxley's vision must be based on rock-solid historical precedent. After all, the Reformation of the sixteenth century had some serious scholarship behind it. Martin Luther's fascination with the original Greek language of the New Testament was a product of the humanism that had engulfed Renaissance Europe. The humanists' chief motto was *ad fontes* ("back to the source" in Latin), which meant a return to the intellectual brilliance of the Greek and Roman ancestors, the midwives of the Christian faith. Luther based his German translation of the Bible on the Greek edition published in 1516 by the Dutch humanist Erasmus, who had meticulously compared the original New Testament with as many Latin manuscripts as he could find, in order to root out any discrepancies with the Greek source material. It has been said that "Erasmus laid the egg that Luther hatched"— the rediscovery of Christianity's true origins, and its real meaning, being the primary motivation of the entire Reformation.[34]

When Huxley wrote of a "revival of religion" in 1958, that's precisely what he had in mind as well. Except he wasn't looking to the New Testament. He was looking beyond the book, back to the original practices of the paleo-Christians that *surrounded* the New Testament. In *The Doors of Perception*, he entered sacrilegious waters: "In the early centuries of Christianity many pagan rites and festivals were baptized, so to say, and made to serve the purposes of the Church." Without getting into the specifics of a contentious debate, Huxley characterized the pre-Christian ceremonies as "soul-satisfying expressions of fundamental urges" that were incorporated "into the fabric of the new religion."[35] Strangely he didn't further pursue the so-called pagan continuity hypothesis: the theory that Christianity didn't magically appear from one day to the next, but inherited pagan elements from the Greco-Roman cults of the ancient Mediterranean world. It wasn't a new theory by any means. The debate between secular and ecclesiastical scholars over the Church's origins stretches back to the nineteenth century. In 1950 another Martin Luther—the Reverend Dr. Martin Luther King Jr.— would weigh in with an essay titled "The Influence of the Mystery Religions on Christianity." There was a time when people could discuss such things and respectfully disagree with civility. In 1954 the only thing Huxley added was a psychedelic twist.

By calling the foundations of Christianity into question, Huxley was prophesying not only the death of organized religion, but a return to its mystical roots. And a "revival" of something that, if the pieces could just be fit together, would not only rewrite the origins of Christianity but Western civilization at large. The task was too daunting for the British philosopher, however, and better left to the classicists, the specialists in Greek and Latin like Erasmus and Martin Luther, who would carry the torch in years to come. Only *they* had the *ad fontes* training to decipher what Huston Smith, author of *The World's Religions* and perhaps the preeminent religious scholar of the twentieth century, would later refer to as the "best-kept secret" in history. To this day it remains the greatest unsolved mystery of the ancient past— centuries of scholars working around the clock on the avid hunt for answers.

What was the original sacrament of Western civilization? And did it somehow sneak its way into the primitive rites of Christianity? If the experts ever turn up new information on the *real reason* why the universe of Greek-speaking pagans became the founding generations of Christianity, turning a Jewish healer from Galilee into the most famous human being who ever lived, it promises the Reformation to end all Reformations. Because the mystical core, the ecstatic source and true lifeblood of the biggest religion the world has ever known, will have finally been exposed.

Like this book, the pagan continuity hypothesis with a psychedelic twist is divided into two very simple questions:

1. Before the rise of Christianity, did the Ancient Greeks consume a secret psychedelic sacrament during their most famous and well-attended religious rituals?

2. Did the Ancient Greeks pass a version of their sacrament along to the earliest, Greek-speaking Christians, for whom the original Holy Communion or Eucharist was, in fact, a psychedelic Eucharist?

If the answer to the first question is "yes," and the roots of Western civilization were soaked in mind-altering drugs, then the recent experiments at Hopkins and NYU would appear to be anything but a modern fad. Indeed, it would force a massive reassessment of our current relationship with naturally occurring substances that were not only sacred, but indispensable to the architects of democracy and the world as we know it. If the answer to both questions is "yes," then the new Reformation is as well grounded and historically oriented as Martin Luther's Reformation, and it becomes an immediate reality for the tens of millions of SBNRs and religiously disillusioned. But more pressingly, today's 2.42 billion Christians (almost one-third of the global population) will have to decide whether they will continue sipping from a placebo amid "ninety minutes of boredom," or join the revolution that just might rescue a dying faith and a civilization on the edge of extinction. Two thousand years in the making, the crisis is real. And the stakes couldn't be higher.

Unfortunately the war for the soul of Western civilization has been neatly tucked away in dry academic journals and arcane conferences, where none of the learned in-fighting filters down to the general public. A little translation would go a long way. But just when they're needed most, all the interpreters seem to be disappearing, keeping all the controversy behind closed doors. And, until now, leaving this book unwritten.

The Classics are dying, and dying fast. Or maybe they're already dead. Who better than two very disgruntled Stanford-educated professors to assess the situation: "A mock epic struggle of nocturnal creatures croaking and scratching at each other for their tiny lily pad on an evaporating pond."[36]

Such was the judgment rendered in 2001 in *Who Killed Homer?: The Demise of Classical Education and the Recovery of Greek Wisdom*. In their bitter indictment of academia, Victor David Hanson and John Robert Heath eulogize the imminent death of our Greek intellectual heritage. They lay the blame squarely on spineless administrators and egg-headed, inbred Classics departments. On the one hand, there's the fear of leaving today's students unequipped with the kind of practical skills needed in a twenty-first-century economy. What college or university can honestly afford to push majors in dead languages? Once the school gets a reputation for graduating unemployed deadbeats, the jig is up. On the other hand, there are the classicists themselves. That "vast gulf between the vitality of the Greeks and timidity of those who are responsible for preserving the Greeks, between the clarity and exuberance of the former and the obscurity and dullness of the latter."[37]

A brutal combination. Between the bureaucrats and the bookworms, our institutions of higher learning have been sucked dry of the very thing that created them in the first place: Latin and Greek. For most of Western history, studying these ancient languages was the only thing you *could* do at a university. Since the Renaissance, higher education has largely been synonymous with fluency in the Classics. Just think of the "cult of antiquity" fostered by the first generation of Americans.[38] John Adams's opinion that Athens and Rome had "done more honor to our species (humanity) than all the rest" was far from unique in the late eighteenth century.[39] The principal drafter of the Declaration of Independence, Thomas Jefferson, looked to classical literature as "the ultimate source of both delight and instruction."[40] Historian Carl Richard explains that the "grammar" in grammar school actually refers to Greek and Latin grammar. The prevailing opinion of the time was that the classroom should be reserved for "serious academic subjects like classical languages," rather than wasted on things the child could easily learn at home, like English grammar.[41]

In the ensuing years, however, newer "utilitarian" subjects slipped into the curriculum for the very first time: the physical sciences, modern languages, history, and geography.[42] Noah Webster, the "Father of American Scholarship and Education" and the guy behind the famous dictionary, wanted to get down to brass tacks: "What advantage does a merchant, a mechanic, a farmer, derive from an acquaintance with the Greek and Roman tongues?" After World War II many universities dropped Greek from the core curriculum altogether, making it possible to graduate with zero knowledge of Western civilization's mother tongue. You can hear Hanson and Heath reminiscing about the glory days, bracing for the inevitable:

As long as literacy, polished written and oral expression, familiarity with politics and social systems, and a common set of unchanging ethical presumptions were the chief goals of a liberal arts education, as long as education itself demanded some memorization and structure from the student, Classics would not vanish—even if enrollments in the Classical languages took their customarily cyclical decline. . . . The study of Classics had always been at the center of Western education, had always risen to the challenge, answering the charges of irrelevancy, impracticality and pagan-inspired iniquity. The university itself, remember, was a Greek idea, its entire structure, nomenclature and operation Graeco-Roman to the core. . . . Twentieth-century minds as diverse as T.S. Eliot, Ezra Pound, Picasso and Winston Churchill proved the value of Classics for knowledge, expression and eloquence, for radicals and reactionaries alike.[43]

Then, according to the Stanford duo, came the "self-righteous" 1960s. The same countercultural movement that gave rise to antiwar protests, classic rock, and psychedelics, also put enormous pressure on an antiquated model of education—one well beyond its expiration date. Dead languages just didn't fit the times, with "personal growth and self-indulgence" leading more students to the arts or social sciences like politics, economics, and psychology—and less to the ancient past.[44] Authority and tradition were to be questioned at all costs. Nobody wanted to study useless grammar and syntax with a bunch of old white World War I vets. If the Vatican itself was about to remove Latin from the Mass, for God's sake, there was no hope for the American university.[45] And that's how, after more than twenty-five hundred years, Homer finally went the way of the typewriter.

In recent years enrollments in Ancient Greek have plummeted.[46] This is no "customarily cyclical decline." As it turns out, Hanson and Heath were on point. They saw the writing on the wall, and accurately predicted it back in 2001:

The Greeks, unfamiliar to the general public at large, are also now dead in the university itself. Today, Classics embraces a body of knowledge and a way of looking at the world that are virtually unrecognized, an almost extinct species even in its own precious habitat, the

academic department. We Classicists are the dodo birds of academia;
when we retire or die, our positions are either eliminated or replaced
with temporary and part-time help.

I was one of the lucky ones, I guess. I got to see the rare species, up close and personal, before it took a final, well-deserved bow. Founded in 1851, St. Joe's Prep was no place for a wiseass from the blue-collar enclave of Northeast Philadelphia whose only familiarity with such institutions came from watching *Dead Poets Society* and *School Ties*. I sometimes cursed the chance scholarship that ushered me into the fanciest all-boys high school in the city. But there were two things in the Jesuit playbook that quickly turned me into a bona fide member of the inner circle: Latin and Greek. It was love at first sight.

Four years later, absolutely convinced that I was destined to be a Classics professor or a priest, I was recruited by Brown University to continue my useless study of the ancient world. As the first person in my family to attend college, I decided to blow the opportunity on dead languages, picking up Sanskrit along the way. For four more years I traveled back in time, straight to the source: *ad fontes*. With nothing lost in translation, direct from the minds of the people who birthed Western civilization and penned the New Testament. My classes in the historic Macfarlane House on College Hill rarely saw more than five students. And yet it never once occurred to me that I was woefully unprepared for life in the real world. Not until I heard the graduate students grumbling about the job market, and mourning the grim reality summed up by Hanson and Heath: "so many Ph.D.s in Classics, so little employment . . . because there are almost no students—because there is really no interest in the Greeks in or out of the university."[47]

Chock full of useless knowledge and no marketable skills, I did the only other thing I was qualified for at that point. I joined the legal profession. After graduating law school and passing the New York Bar, I tried to settle into my new life on Wall Street at Milbank, Tweed, Hadley & McCloy. Hoping I'd actually learn something about international corporate finance, the partners made me subscribe to *The Economist*. In the summer of 2007 I randomly plucked an issue from the growing pile of unread magazines in the corner of my office. The title of the article that would forever change my life smacked me in the face: "The God Pill."

It was a brief write-up of the very first psilocybin experiment at Hopkins.[48] I'll never forget the moment when I read that statistic about two-thirds of the volunteers counting their single dose of the drug among the most meaningful experiences of their entire lives. An ethnomycologist by the name of R. Gordon Wasson was mentioned in the first line of the article—the inspiration behind the opening salvo of the psychedelic renaissance that would culminate in the fifty peer-reviewed papers from the Johns Hopkins Psychedelic Research Unit.

I instantly remembered a book titled *The Road to Eleusis*, first published in 1978. I had read it at Brown, in addition to every other book in the John D. Rockefeller Jr. Library that had anything to do with Ancient Greek religion. Together with coauthors Albert Hofmann and Carl Ruck, Wasson claimed a potent psychedelic was behind the life-changing vision universally witnessed over the millennia by initiates in Eleusis, the Greek spiritual capital, about thirteen miles northwest of Athens. From Boston University, Ruck would later suggest that Christianity itself was similarly founded on drugs. It was certainly an unconventional line of thought. At the time, however, there was very little scholarship specifically dedicated to drug use in Ancient Greece or early Christianity. With no way to dig deeper, that's where I had to leave the idea for many years. Until William Richards and Roland Griffiths, the chief researchers at Hopkins, brought it back on my radar in the most unexpected way possible: through the laboratory.

I logged straight on to my new Amazon account and used my law-firm salary to order everything Wasson, Hofmann, or Ruck had ever written. I then spent the next twelve years researching this book, as a thirty-year-old hypothesis became a forty-year-old hypothesis to which no one paid any attention. To this day I have never personally experimented with psychedelics, in the conscious effort to let the objective evidence guide the investigation that has consumed my adult life.

While the Hopkins and NYU data was compelling from a circumstantial perspective, hard evidence linking the Ancient Greeks or paleo-Christians to a psychedelic sacrament was pretty elusive. So I kept my nose to the grindstone on nights and weekends, when I wasn't practicing law, as additional data started coming in from other scientific disciplines like archaeobotany and archaeochemistry, which have now proven the existence of hallucinogenic beer and wine in the ancient Mediterranean. And its possible consumption for ritual purposes. Finally, sixty years after Aldous Huxley first issued his manifesto for a new Reformation, the pagan continuity hypothesis with a psychedelic twist is being put to the twenty-first-century test. And the public needs to know about it.

The problem is, this material is pretty dense. Take it from a onetime aspiring classicist: Google won't help. The original sources that inform the pagan continuity hypothesis are so niche, so obscure, and so damn hard to find that the only way to separate fact from fiction is to roll up your sleeves and track them down the old-fashioned way: in libraries, museums, and archives. Many are tucked away overseas, where ancient and modern language barriers make this stuff inaccessible to a fault. And then there are the archaeological sites scattered around the Mediterranean, some of which are holding on to clues that can be deciphered only in person. Perhaps most important of all are the experts themselves who dedicate their lives to the many disciplines with a stake in this quest. They don't always commit everything they know to writing. So simply paying a visit and tapping their brains can often yield incredible results.

Over the past year I journeyed to Greece, Germany, Spain, France, and Italy to get to the bottom of history's best-kept secret once and for all. If a psychedelic sacrament is essential for the birth of Western civilization and Christianity, where's the proof? I sat down with the government ministers, curators, and archivists whose mission is to guard precious relics that rarely see the light of day. I grilled the excavators, archaeobotanists, and archaeochemists who are in the field and laboratory right now, unearthing fresh evidence of our ancestors' ritualistic use of drugs and subjecting it to a battery of high-tech instrumentation. And I trekked through time with the classicists, historians, and Biblical scholars who are trying to make sense of it all.

This investigation has led me to conclusions I never could have anticipated twelve years ago. Not only is there evidence of psychedelic beer and wine at the heart of the Greek and Christian Mysteries, but also evidence of their suppression by the religious authorities. I spent a significant amount of time at the Vatican, developing a working relationship with the Pontifical Commission for Sacred Archaeology. I inspected the paleo-Christian catacombs controlled by the Pope, under the streets of Rome. I descended into the Vatican Necropolis under St. Peter's Basilica that is never discussed in Catholic school. I analyzed little-known artifacts with the curators of the

Vatican Museums. And I spent the better part of a year cultivating a genuine friendship with God's librarian at the Vatican Secret Archives, where I managed to root through manuscripts few have ever touched. The climax of my time in the Holy See was a behind-the-scenes appointment with the recently opened archives of the Inquisition—targeting key documents that have never before been translated into English. The result is a jarring confrontation with the pivotal role that women played in the preparation of the original Eucharist, and its survival among heretical Christian sects that the Vatican continues to battle to this day.

The following pages track my full immersion into the mystery. I explore an Ancient Greece that is in serious danger of vanishing from the university curriculum. And an early, secret form of Christianity that has been scrubbed from the record. I present every piece of evidence that, taken together, finally convinced me of the psychedelic reality behind Western civilization's original religion. A prehistoric ritual that survived for millennia, in the total absence of the written word, before finding a good home among the Greeks. A tradition that was later inherited by the first, Greek-speaking Christians, especially in Italy, where they came under attack by the Church Fathers. A vast knowledge of drugs that was kept alive through the Dark Ages by pagans and heretics. Until the witches of the world were hunted down for centuries, erasing all memory of the longest-running religion the planet has ever known. It doesn't have a name, and probably never had one. But one thing is certain: that storied tension between the mystics and the bureaucrats has reached a breaking point. In order to find our soul again, a popular outbreak of mysticism could be just what the doctor ordered.

And the prescription could be exactly what it was in the beginning: to die before we die, with a solid dose of the religion that started it all.

The religion with no name.

Part One

BREWING THE PSYCHEDELIC BEER

I

Identity Crisis

Though we are liable to forget, Western civilization was not founded as a Christian enterprise. The Ancient Greece that invented democracy, and birthed all the arts and sciences we now take for granted, never heard of Jesus. Before Jerusalem, before Rome, before Mecca, there was Eleusis. If Athens of the fifth and fourth centuries BC was the true source of Western life in the twenty-first century, then Eleusis was our first, undisputed spiritual capital. Throughout classical antiquity, the quaint harbor town was ground zero for generations of seekers. But its religion wouldn't last forever. In the battle for the sacred legacy of the West, Eleusis was a spectacular casualty. Its demise at the hands of the newly Christianized Roman Empire in the fourth century AD marked the beginning of an identity crisis that persists to this day.

Are we Greek or are we Christian?

Under the traditional view our Greek ancestors may have built the world as we know it, but Christianity saved its soul. Like the children of divorced parents, we try not to choose favorites or take sides. And we largely ignore the fact that the Greeks managed to find salvation long before Christianity showed up—a perfectly reasonable oversight, with the former center of the Mediterranean universe now scattered in ruins. Today the archaeological site of Eleusis is little more than crumbling bits of marble and limestone. And since 1882 the excavations have only turned up more questions than answers.[1] Why did the pilgrims flock to its temple for two thousand years, in search of life beyond the grave? Why was the age-old ritual performed under cover of darkness? Why was the magic potion hidden away? And why did the Christians shut it all down?

If you're not careful, the oldest unsolved riddle in the history of Western civilization has a way of getting inside your bones. When so much of their genius has survived, it just doesn't make sense for the religion of the people who created Western culture to simply vanish into thin air. There has to be more to the Mysteries of Eleusis, the longest running and most prominent spiritual tradition in Ancient Greece.[2] Unfortunately it was shrouded in secrecy from the very beginning, leaving nothing but hints and clues about what really took place within the holy precinct. Aristotle once said the initiates came to Eleusis not to *learn* something, but to *experience* something.[3] Whatever that experience was, it has successfully eluded scholars for centuries. That's how this puzzle was designed, after all. Fragments of the strange rites and ceremonies can be reconstructed, but the main attraction remains unknown. Year after year, how were the Mysteries able to consistently deliver on an impossible promise?

If you come to Eleusis, you will never die.

A bold claim, for sure. Hard to believe nowadays. But, for some reason, our ancestors believed it. In fact they couldn't imagine a world without the exceptional landmark. The Mysteries were said to hold "the entire human race together."[4] Life itself would be "unlivable" in their absence.[5] Among all the unanswered questions about Eleusis, one inescapable fact keeps researchers glued to the obscure corner of southern Greece that spoke to millions: it stood the test of time.

Well before Jesus walked the shores of Galilee, Eleusis was a beacon of hope in a nasty age of uncertainty, when the average life expectancy was much lower than today. Half the population might not reach the age of five.[6] For those who survived a traumatic childhood and managed to avoid enslavement, natural disasters, food shortages, violence, social unrest, deadly plagues, and infectious disease made for a far nastier existence than our own, with as much as 60 percent of the Greco-Roman world succumbing to the bacteria and viruses we have now largely managed to control.[7] If COVID-19 offers any insight on the past, it's the psychological and emotional toll of a pandemic, and the sense of helplessness that must have been excruciating for our ancestors. But as long as the Mysteries were celebrated once a year around the fall equinox, everything was in order. It was a fool-proof formula that ran uninterrupted from about 1500 BC until AD 392, when the annual festivities were abruptly outlawed by the Roman Emperor Theodosius, a die-hard Christian.

That's a long time for a lot of people to keep quiet, and for so little detail to leak into the historical record. But everyone who crossed the sacred threshold understood the price of admission. The word "mystery" comes from the Greek *muo* (μύω), which literally means "to shut one's eyes." Under penalty of death, all visitors were explicitly forbidden from revealing what they saw on the inside.[8] Whatever happened in Eleusis, stayed in Eleusis. Frustrating as it is for modern historians, that policy served the Mysteries well. The wall of silence only fed the mystique and guaranteed fans in high places.

In its heyday the temple attracted the best and brightest Athens had to offer, including Plato. To keep his experience classified, the godfather of Western philosophy used vague, cryptic language to describe the "blessed sight and vision" he witnessed "in a state of perfection"—the climax of his initiation into "the holiest of Mysteries."[9] Like all travelers, Plato was permanently transformed by whatever he observed in Eleusis. The latest in a long line of visionaries, men and women, with exclusive access to cosmic truths. Following their sip of an unusual elixir called the *kukeon* (κυκεών), and a night of spectacles in the temple, each pilgrim earned the honorary title *epoptes* (ἐπόπτης), which means something like "the one who has seen it all." Beyond any doubt, they claimed, death was not the end of our human journey. We do, in fact, survive the physical body. And underneath this mortal clothing, we are all immortals in disguise—gods and goddesses destined to the stars for eternity.

All that, after just one night at Eleusis?

From otherwise rational, sober people, it sounds like crazy talk.

To make sense of Plato, we have to remember how the Ancient Greeks ordinarily approached the afterlife. At the time, most people believed the soul went down to the bleak and nebulous regions of Hades. Whether it would live there forever or eventually fade away was not entirely clear, and it scarcely mattered. Death was nothing to look forward to. When Odysseus visits the land of the dead, his fallen comrade Achilles famously grumbles, "I would rather be a paid servant in a poor man's house, and be above ground, than king of kings among the dead."[10]

Unless you had been initiated into the Mysteries, of course, where seeing is believing. One inscription found on the site says, "death is for mortals no longer an evil but a blessing."[11] Pindar, perhaps the greatest lyric poet of Ancient Greece and a fellow initiate, wrote in the fifth century BC, "Blessed is he who has seen these things before he goes beneath the hollow earth; for he understands the end of mortal life, and the beginning [of a new life] given of God."[12] For Sophocles, one of the most renowned playwrights of the time, the world could be divided into those who had set foot in Eleusis, and those who had not. Just like Plato and Pindar, he stresses the visual nature of the experience: "Thrice blessed are those among men who, after beholding these rites, go down to Hades. Only for them is there life [after death]; all the rest will suffer an evil lot."[13]

Without divulging the big secret, much of the ancient testimony—what little remains—hails the sublime vision that proved to be a once-in-a-lifetime event for every pilgrim.[14] Clearly the Greeks had a profound religious system at their disposal. One that seems to match the grandeur and sophistication of their many accomplishments, the many gifts we happily inherited to build a civilization from the ground up. Eleusis was an enduring tradition, said to provide concrete answers to timeless doubts, and optimism in the face of oblivion. It's unavoidable: there was real religion before Christianity, which contradicts the running assumption that Greek spirituality was rather uninformed and idiotic.

If you were taught a cartoonish version of Greek mythology in high school, or even earlier, that's when the confusion may have begun. You were probably left wondering how the people who not only gave us the word "skepticism" (from the Greek skeptomai (σκέπτομαι), meaning "to look about carefully"), but actually practiced what they preached, could possibly believe in fairy tales. Zeus is in charge of lightning? Poseidon rules the seas? Everything evil came from Pandora's box? If the Greeks seemed too sensible for such things, it's because they were. Let's give credit where credit is due.

Like some cultural Big Bang, all the greatest hits suddenly burst on the scene some twenty-five hundred years ago. Where there was chaos, the Ancient Greeks gave us meaning through history, civics, and ethics. Where there was superstition, they created the first scientific disciplines, like physics, biology, and mathematics. Their stadiums and theaters became our sports and entertainment industries. They codified law, medicine, and finance, and laid the groundwork for the technology that consumes our life. The word "technology" itself comes from the Greek *techne* (τέχνη), meaning "skill," "cunning," or "handiwork." Social media has drawn us into a hyper-connected, global conversation that is entirely predicated on individual expression and the free exchange of ideas—fundamental rights that were virtually unheard of before the academies of Ancient Greece. Every time we open up Twitter, Instagram, or Facebook, we are tapping into that awesome legacy celebrated in Raphael's iconic *School of Athens*: Plato and Aristotle, surrounded by their fellow Greek luminaries, thinking our world into existence. Are we to believe the wisdom assembled on those steps got so much right, only to come up short on the most important questions of all? Why are we here? What happens when we die? What's the point of it all?

By and large, animal slaughter, endless libations, and formulaic prayers were the kinds of things that seemed to please the twelve gods on Mount

The School of Athens, painted by Raphael between 1509 and 1511, currently in the Apostolic Palace of the Vatican.

Olympus and keep disaster at bay. And for many Ancient Greeks, that was religion. But it didn't answer the big questions. For the level of brilliance on display in the *School of Athens,* bloody sacrifices to imaginary gods on far-flung hilltops wouldn't quite do the job.

That's where the Mysteries of Eleusis came in—just one of the many so-called mystery religions that fascinated the Mediterranean mind in the old days. For those curious souls in need of a little more substance and a little less nonsense, Ancient Greece had a full menu of spiritual alternatives that proved more satisfying than the traditional fare. At the core of the mystery religions was "an immediate or mystical encounter with the divine," involving "an approach to death and a return to life."[15] Like the mystics that would infiltrate Christianity, Judaism, and Islam in the millennia to come, the Greeks knew the ancient secret of dying before dying. However this one-on-one meeting with God was engineered, it's what Aristotle meant by the initiates descending on Eleusis not to *learn* something, but to *experience* something. Those inquisitive, cynical Greeks were after bona fide evidence: proof of the hereafter. They would never blindly settle for empty promises of a future life among the heavens. They had to peek behind the curtain to see for themselves whether there was any truth to the matter. For them and for us, how could authentic religion be anything less?

As one empire replaced another, the value of that experience was not lost on the Romans, who adopted the Greek temple in Eleusis as their own. Cicero, the great orator and statesman of the first century BC, recorded his take for posterity:

> For it appears to me that among the many exceptional and divine things your Athens has produced and contributed to human life, nothing is better than those Mysteries. For by means of them we have been transformed from a rough and savage way of life to the state of humanity, and have been civilized. Just as they are called initiations, so in actual fact we have learned from them the fundamentals of life, and have grasped the basis not only for living with joy, but also for dying with a better hope.[16]

In the second century AD, the emperor Marcus Aurelius studied in Athens and was later initiated in Eleusis.[17] He is reportedly the only lay person ever allowed inside the *anaktoron* (ἀνάκτορον), the holy of holies housed within the main temple, or *telesterion* (τελεστήριον). He earned the privilege. The Philosopher, as he was called, oversaw an extensive construction project to restore the site after it was nearly destroyed by the barbarian Kostovoks in AD 170. What the invaders sent up in flames, Marcus Aurelius methodically rebuilt to Roman standards, ensuring the Mysteries would never again suffer another desecration. Dwarfed chunks of the forty-two columns that once supported the 52-by-52-square-meter sanctuary can still be seen. Roughly three thousand people would have crowded onto the steps lining its interior to witness the secrets they had prepared up to a year and a half to observe.[18] Only on the second visit to Eleusis did a prospective initiate or *mustes* (μύστης) actually enter the sanctuary to become a full *epoptes*.[19]

To keep profane eyes off the sacred affair, the Philosopher also built a monumental gateway of Pentelic marble and a vast courtyard at the entrance to the site, now known as the Greater Propylaea. An imposing, larger-than-life bust of Marcus Aurelius has survived all this time, with the defaced im-

The colossal bust of Roman emperor and patron of the Mysteries, Marcus Aurelius (121–180 AD), beside the former Greater Propylaea at the modern-day entrance to the archaeological site of Eleusis. The four points of the Christian cross can be seen around the head of the Gorgon that once projected from the emperor's chest.

Courtesy of the Archaeological Museum of Eleusis, Ephorate of Antiquities—Western Attica (© Hellenic Ministry of Culture and Sports)

age of a serpent-headed Gorgon emblazoned on the Philosopher's chest. The decapitated monster was a common way of warding off evil in those days.[20] A stern warning to any future looters: this is sacred land.

For a time it worked. Until Christianity gathered enough steam to deliver the death blow. The Gorgon would eventually be smashed in, replaced by a giant cross, carved with pleasure directly into Marcus Aurelius's heart. The soldiers of Christ had a message of their own: this is godless land, polluted by demons. It is the tiniest example of a disturbing period in history that is only now receiving honest critical attention. Catherine Nixey's *The Darkening Age: The Christian Destruction of the Classical World* sets the stage for our investigation:

> In a spasm of destruction never seen before—and one that appalled many non-Christians watching it—during the fourth and fifth centuries [AD], the Christian Church demolished, vandalized and melted down a simply staggering quantity of art. Classical statues were knocked from their plinths, defaced, defiled and torn limb from limb. Temples were razed to their foundations and mutilated. . . . The violent assaults of this period were not the preserve of cranks and eccentrics. Attacks against the monuments of the "mad," "damnable" and "insane" pagans were encouraged and led by men at the very heart of the Catholic Church. The great St. Augustine himself declared to a congregation in Carthage "that all superstition of pagans and heathens should be annihilated is what God wants, God commands, God proclaims!"[21]

When the once hallowed walls of Eleusis were trampled in AD 395, the Visigoths may have placed the dynamite, but the Church lit the fuse. Following Constantine's blessing earlier in the century, Emperor Theodosius had already made Christianity the official state religion of the Roman Empire in AD 380. Twelve years later he proclaimed the Mysteries illegal, drawing a line in the sand. Civilization would eventually reap the secular benefits of all things Greek, but from then on, Christianity would serve as the default faith of the Western world. When it came to spiritual matters, best to pretend those Greek infidels and their satanic rituals never existed. For a secret religion like Eleusis that refused to keep written records, the extinction was swift and thorough. Before the end of the fourth century AD, total victory was declared by the early Church Father Saint John Chrysostom: "The tradition of the forefathers has been destroyed, the deep rooted custom has been torn out, the tyranny of joy [and] the accursed festivals . . . have been obliterated just like smoke."[22]

From the late fourth century AD until about two hundred years ago, the history of Christianity and the history of the West are essentially one and the same: the crowning of Charlemagne by Pope Leo III as the *Imperator Romanorum* and Father of Europe in St. Peter's Basilica on Christmas Day in 800, kicking off a long line of Holy Roman Emperors that would last until 1806; the East-West Schism of 1054 between the Orthodox Patriarch of Constantinople and the Catholic Church in Rome, forever dividing Europe in half; the Crusades that preceded the Renaissance, when the rediscovery of the Classics would lead to the Reformation and Counter-Reformation. In the Age of Discovery from the fifteenth to the end of the eighteenth centuries, Christianity left Europe and the Near East behind, becoming the indomitable global brand it is today. Missionaries were dispatched to every corner of the planet to convert local indigenous groups in Africa, Asia, and Latin America. Since there was no real separation between Church and state, the memory of Jesus and the hope for his imminent return were the guiding force behind it all. Especially in America, the ultimate blank slate for Christians. The colonies were flooded with Protestant denominations of every stripe, seeking the spiritual freedom to worship *their* version of Jesus. Well into the nineteenth century, the doctrine of Manifest Destiny declared Anglo-Saxons a superior race, chosen by God to bring "Christianity to the American continents and to the world."[23]

It's *this* legacy we see celebrated in Leonardo's *Last Supper*. The moment Jesus is said to have offered himself to his closest friends in the form of bread and wine. A foreshadowing of the crucifixion he would endure the following day, according to tradition, for the salvation of all mankind. This intimate dinner became Christianity's defining sacrament, the Eucharist. "Do this in memory of me," the Gospels record. It is a moment reenacted to this day, multiple times per day, in churches on every continent for hundreds of millions of faithful. For believers and nonbelievers alike, Jesus and his early followers single-handedly changed the course of history.

If only one image could tell the story of our humble origins, would it be *The School of Athens* or *The Last Supper*? Two of the most recognized paintings of all time. Two very different pictures of our past. Once again, are we Greek or are we Christian? Where does the Church end, and where does the state begin?

What better disconnect than the swearing in of an American president? In recent times all the pomp and circumstance takes place on the western front of the United States Capitol Building, an explicit homage to the Greco-Roman Pantheon in Rome. Its creator wanted to link "the new republic to the classical world and to its ideas of civic virtue and self-government."[24] At the far end of the National Mall, past the Egyptian obelisk, Abraham Lincoln monitors the inauguration from his gleaming replica of the Parthenon that sits atop the Acropolis in Athens. Again, the architect felt "a memorial to a man who defended democracy, should be based on a structure found in the birthplace of democracy."[25] Surrounded by neoclassical marble on all sides, the same pagan marble those Christian hordes tried to erase from memory over sixteen hundred years ago, the presidents raise their right hands and swear the oath of office . . . on a Bible. For good measure the last three presidents have actually used two Bibles. After Kennedy's assassination, Lyndon B. Johnson was sworn in aboard Air Force One on a Roman Catholic missal. Naturally none of this is mandated by the United States Constitution. It's just that old identity crisis rearing its head.

It may all seem insignificant, but at the root of this Greek vs. Christian

The Last Supper, painted by Leonardo da Vinci between 1495 and 1498, currently in the refectory of the Convent of Santa Maria delle Grazie in Milan, Italy.

debate are some really profound questions. Are we a people of reason or faith? Is our society founded on science or religion? Whether the issue is climate change, reproductive rights, or a global pandemic, that stark divide between *The School of Athens* and *The Last Supper* continues to frame the national conversation on matters of life and death. During protests over the unprecedented country-wide lockdown in April 2020, a green tractor-trailer pulled up to the Pennsylvania State Capitol, horn blaring, a defiant slogan freshly painted on the hood: "Jesus Is My Vaccine."

Over twenty-five hundred years into this experiment we call the West, is there any chance of reconciling the two competing worldviews that clashed so dramatically at the end of the fourth century AD? If so, then, as with any good compromise, there will be plenty of disappointment on both sides. People of reason may have to concede that modern science has its limits. Not everything of value can be weighed and measured. People of faith may have to admit that we can no longer afford legend over history, or obedience over curiosity. In a rapidly accelerating world Big Religion has failed to keep up with a younger generation that prefers fact over fiction. But Big Science and Big Technology may be going too fast, distracting us from the ancient search for meaning that defined the original religion of Western civilization. How do we bridge the gap?

The whole point of this investigation is to test a crackpot theory that has been widely ridiculed and even censored by the academic establishment. When one ill-fated classicist by the name of Carl Ruck at Boston University took charge of the pagan continuity hypothesis with a psychedelic twist in the late 1970s, he started by claiming that the sacramental potion known as the *kukeon* was a type of visionary brew. And that the inviolable secrecy surrounding the Mysteries of Eleusis had everything to do with protecting the psychedelic recipe that guaranteed immortality to the Greek-speaking world. When this hypothesis first appeared, in *The Road to Eleusis*, forty years ago, before I was even born, it was definitely the wrong idea at the wrong time. Exactly two decades had elapsed since Aldous Huxley's clarion call for the new Reformation in 1958. And during that time psychedelics had gone from a respectable subject of intellectual pursuit among British gentlemen like Huxley to one of the most polarizing issues in America. Not to mention the fact that they were completely illegal. Even the top universities in the country couldn't escape the long arm of the War on Drugs.

But that was only half the heresy. The Greeks had to invent the psyche-delic Eucharist. And then the Christians had to give it shelter. So to answer the second of the two questions baked into Huxley's revolutionary predic-tion about the "revival of religion," the same classicist at Boston University would later claim that some version of the Hellenistic sacrament had indeed been incorporated into the fledgling faith by Greek-speaking pockets of paleo-Christians all over the Roman Empire. And that their original Eucha-rist was therefore intensely psychedelic. Like Erasmus and Martin Luther's obsession over the Greek of the New Testament, this controversial analysis of the actual sacrament that sustained the earliest Christian communities was ultimately an attempt to rediscover the true origins of the world's big-gest religion, and the real vision of the most famous human being who ever lived. As the *Encyclopedia Britannica* makes clear, "Recovering the classics was to humanism tantamount to recovering reality."[26] And the modern-day attempt leads to a conclusion no less groundbreaking than the firestorm unleashed by Luther during the Reformation of the sixteenth century.

When we look at *The Last Supper*, maybe we're not looking at Christianity's founding event. Maybe we're getting a glimpse of the mysterious religion that was practiced by Plato, Pindar, Sophocles, and the rest of the Athenian gang. And just maybe this is how our identity crisis comes to a dramatic end: with a psychedelic plot twist. Rather than starting a new religion, was Jesus simply trying to preserve, or copy, the "holiest of Mysteries" from An-cient Greece? Or, more precisely, is that what his Greek-speaking followers wanted to believe? If so, that opens up a can of worms, making Jesus more of a Greek philosopher-magician than a Jewish Messiah. It means that the Jesus behind Leonardo's table really belongs on the steps of *The School of Athens* with his fellow initiates. Because the earliest and most authentic communities of paleo-Christians would have looked to the miracle worker from Nazareth as someone who knew the secret that Eleusis tried so desperately to conceal for millennia. A secret that could easily win new converts to the faith. But a secret the Church would later try to suppress, according to the theory. And a secret that would render all the infrastructure of today's Christianity virtually obsolete, uprooting 2.42 billion adherents worldwide.[27]

Back in the Garden of Eden, maybe the forbidden fruit was forbidden for a reason. Who needs the fancy building, the priest and all the rest of it— even the Bible—if all you really need is the fruit?

2

Fall from Grace

The hunt for the psychedelic origins of Western civilization has to begin with Eleusis. It was one of the oldest religious traditions of Ancient Greece and arguably the most famous. But timing is everything. Forty years ago the Classics establishment was in no position to seriously consider the controversial marriage of the Mysteries and drugs. Let alone the possibility that the earliest Christians inherited a visionary sacrament from their Greek ancestors. The one scholar who dared to question everything paid dearly for his original sin. A total pariah, he spies signs of redemption from a new generation of archaeologists and scientists. But the excommunication has been long and lonely.

It all started back in April 1978. Alarm bells were sounding from the towers of academia, as a motley crew of three misfits announced the unthinkable. The code had been cracked. What religious historian Huston Smith called history's "best-kept secret" was a secret no more. After centuries of false leads and dead ends, the unlikely team had finally breached the inner sanctum of the Mysteries of Eleusis. They had discovered what *really* made the Ancient Greeks tick. At long last they had unearthed the true source of our ancestors' poetry and philosophy. Perhaps the hidden inspiration behind the world as we know it. And the answer, they were quite assured, was a magic potion full of psychedelic drugs.

"As perverse as it is unconvincing will be the verdict of many," began one scathing review of *The Road to Eleusis: Unveiling the Secret of the Mysteries*. In a single paragraph, the learned critic quickly put the matter to rest, closing with a stiff punch: "Everything is wildly out of hand."[1]

Whenever you accuse the founders of Western civilization of getting stoned out of their minds, and then turning that hallucinatory event into their most cherished religion, a little pushback is to be expected. But the authors of the inflammatory charge couldn't have chosen a worse moment in American history to publish their findings. While most of the excess and hysteria of the 1960s had simmered down, the War on Drugs was just heating up. In a national press conference on June 17, 1971, President Nixon had stood before the cameras and declared drugs "public enemy number one," vowing "to wage a new, all-out offensive" across the country and around the world.[2] Drugs were scapegoated as a real and present danger—of greater concern, apparently, than the Soviet Union and the prospect of nuclear holocaust. Soon the fugitive LSD evangelist and countercultural guru, Timothy Leary, was "the most dangerous man in America."[3]

By the late 1970s, before the Reagan administration and the "Just Say No" campaign of my youth put crack, cocaine, and heroin in the crosshairs, psychedelic drugs had endured a decade in the media spotlight.[4] Of all the ways to fry your brain, nothing beat psychedelics. For a brief time "insanity due to LSD" became a popular criminal defense.[5] Not only was the drug seen as the chief threat to our public health and safety but also as the ultimate escape from reality. It was utter madness to suggest that these hazardous, potentially lethal compounds were the long-sought missing key to the Mysteries.

Even if the misfits offended the academic mainstream with their "perverse" hypothesis, it wasn't for lack of homework. In *The Road to Eleusis*, Gordon Wasson, Albert Hofmann, and Carl Ruck made a passionate and detailed argument for why the *kukeon*, the sacramental beverage of the Mysteries, must have been spiked with one or more psychedelics. And they did so in truly interdisciplinary fashion, which was basically unheard of in the stodgy field of Classics at the time.

Wasson was a J.P. Morgan banker turned amateur mushroom hunter. Or ethnomycologist, as he would prefer to be called—one who studies the relationship between people and fungi. His global anthropological fieldwork had convinced him that magic mushrooms played a pivotal role in the origin and development of humanity's spiritual awareness. It was one mind-bending experience, in particular, that sealed the deal.

In the heart of the Sierra Mazateca, a traditional healer or *curandera* by the name of Maria Sabina had agreed to guide Wasson on a healing journey, an initiation no outsider had ever attempted. Wasson was fixated on capturing the undocumented ceremony. At 10:30 p.m. one evening in 1955, he finally got the okay. According to custom, Maria cleansed and blessed some fresh *Psilocybe mexicana* that Wasson had handpicked earlier in the day. She instructed him to consume six of the mushrooms, which would flood his system with the psychoactive agent psilocybin. After a half hour of deafening silence amid total blackness, the adventure finally began.

Over the course of the next five hours, Wasson recalled, "the visions came whether our eyes were open or closed." He saw everything from "resplendent palaces all laid over with semiprecious stones" to "a mythological beast drawing a regal chariot." At one point he witnessed his spirit leave his body and shoot to the heavens. Oddly, the whole trip was seared into Wasson's memory as the *realest* thing he'd ever experienced. He recorded his grand epiphany in an article entitled "Seeking the Magic Mushroom." It would appear in the May 13, 1957, issue of *Life* magazine:

> *The visions were not blurred or uncertain. They were sharply focused, the lines and colors being so sharp that they seemed more real to me than anything I had ever seen with my own eyes. I felt that I was now seeing plain, whereas ordinary vision gives us an imperfect view; I was seeing the archetypes, the Platonic ideas, that underlie the imperfect images of everyday life. . . . The thought crossed my mind: could the divine mushrooms be the secret that lay behind the Ancient Mysteries?*[6]

A well-read individual, Wasson was very familiar with the testimony from Eleusis. He instantly identified with the ancient initiates, absolutely certain he had stumbled upon something that brought incredible meaning to our ancestors, but had somehow escaped the attention of modern scholars. How an echo of the Greek ritual had survived in the mountains of Mexico became a burning question that Wasson would dedicate the rest of his life to answering. In the meantime, however, the more immediate concern was having Maria Sabina's mushrooms scientifically catalogued. He sent some spores to Switzerland to be cultivated by his friend and future coauthor.

Albert Hofmann was already an internationally renowned chemist. In 1938 he had struck psychedelic gold at his research laboratory in Basel by extracting LSD from special cultures of ergot, a naturally occurring fungus. From Wasson's samples Hofmann was able to successfully isolate psilocybin as well, laying the groundwork for the experiments at Hopkins and NYU in recent years. Together, Wasson and Hofmann would unwittingly spark the pop-psychedelic revolution that was to come, thanks in no small part to Aldous Huxley and his eloquent marketing in *The Doors of Perception*. Millions of people would read Wasson's essay in *Life;* tens of millions would see him on the CBS news program *Person to Person*.[7] By the early 1960s hippies and beatniks were hopping down to Mexico to get their own taste of some Maria Sabina–style expansion of consciousness. Everyone from Bob Dylan to Led Zeppelin to the Rolling Stones is rumored to have followed in Wasson's footsteps.[8]

But it wasn't until July 1975, a full twenty years after his flash of insight in Mexico, that Wasson formally enlisted Hofmann to expose the mystery of the Mysteries once and for all. They had as good a chance as anybody else. In the absence of any hard data, all kinds of bizarre theories were put forward over the years. In the mid-nineteenth century, the great German classicist Ludwig Preller proposed that Eleusis was nothing more than an elaborate theatrical performance, complete with hymns, sacred dances, and stage props. By the late nineteenth century, Percy Gardner, professor of archaeology at the University of Cambridge, swore puppets were involved, "some perhaps of considerable size and fitted to impress the awakened nerves of the auditors."[9] That sublime vision reported by Plato, Pindar, and Sophocles? Nothing but smoke and mirrors. And Muppets. Under the right conditions, the imagination runs wild.

By the early twentieth century, the British classicist Jane Ellen Harrison struck a chord that would echo for decades to come. She saw Eleusis as a primitive fertility rite, a crude form of sympathetic magic. To ensure a proper harvest the initiate would undergo a long process of purification and fasting before partaking of the first fruits.[10] In this case it was barley grains, the principal ingredient of the *kukeon*. Like prehistoric folk before them, the Greeks would have abstained from the fruit of the fields until they were ripe and ready. At a harvest festival like the Mysteries, that taboo was apparently broken. The very first taste of the freshly cut crop "would easily come to be regarded as specially sacred and as having sacramental virtue."[11] Thus Harrison understood the *kukeon* as a ritualized potion. Out on a limb, she even suggested such potions could lead to "spiritual intoxication," with "moments of sudden illumination, of wider and deeper insight, of larger human charity and understanding."[12] But she got nowhere near psychedelic territory.

Unlike the many august scholars who preceded them, the ethnomycologist and the chemist went straight for the land of tangerine trees and marmalade skies. That sublime vision *had* to be generated internally, not externally, they reasoned. In a single line of Ancient Greek text from the seventh century BC, Wasson and Hofmann noticed something that had been largely overlooked for more than twenty-five hundred years. The *Homeric Hymn to Demeter* is one of those random clues that somehow made it past the wall of silence surrounding Eleusis. A beautifully crafted poem, it recounts the legend of Demeter's epic search for her daughter, Persephone— the two goddesses to whom the Mysteries were consecrated.

Once upon a time, young Persephone is out and about picking wild flowers when Pluto abducts her into his underworld kingdom. The innocent girl would have been damned to eternity as Queen of the Dead, were it not for her mother's grit and tenacity. After looking high and low for her missing daughter, the brokenhearted Demeter lands in Eleusis, where she continues to mourn. At Demeter's command, the king and queen of the archaic town erect the temple in her honor. But there is no consoling the Lady of the Grain. Furious, she hides every seed from the Greek plow, withering the fields and sending famine throughout the land. Humankind is on the brink of starvation when Zeus finally caves to Demeter's demands. He orders his brother Pluto to release Persephone at once. The King of the Dead obeys, but not before forcing a pomegranate seed down Persephone's throat as a kind of enchantment. Forever after, Persephone would still spend one-third of the year in the underworld, in exchange for two-thirds of the year above ground with Demeter.

When mother and daughter reunite, the Rarian plain adjacent to Eleusis is still "barren and leafless." But as springtime blossoms, the white barley "would be waving long ears of grain like a mane in the wind." Soon enough "the whole wide world became heavy with leaves and flowers."[13]

The almost perfectly preserved myth is an obvious tribute to the seasons, but it also contains a slew of rich elements that were already incorporated into the rites and ceremonies of the Mysteries. It's an origin tale, providing a nice precedent for the *legomena* (λεγόμενα) or "things said," the *dromena* (δρώμενα) or "things done," and the *deiknumena* (δεικνύμενα) or "things shown" during the initiation.

If you're on the lookout for ciphers, the barley comes through loud and clear. The *Hymn to Demeter* prizes the fields of Eleusis over any others on the planet. The Rarian plain is where life first returns to the earth after the drought. Its barley is truly one-of-a-kind, mentioned repeatedly through-out the 496-line poem. The most striking example is in line 209, where the famous *kukeon* is introduced.

The king and queen of Eleusis, Celeus and Metaneira, have just invited Demeter into their regal mansion to lift the grieving mother's spirits. The goddess hasn't eaten or drunk anything in days. Metaneira offers her some red wine, "sweet as honey," but Demeter refuses, claiming it would be a "sacrilege" to break her fast with the beverage that was more to the taste of Dionysus, the boundary-dissolving god of wine, theater, ecstasy, and mys-tical rapture. Appropriately, the Lady of the Grain was a beer woman. She requests the barley-based *kukeon*, which simply means "mixture" or "med-ley" in Greek. To avoid any ambiguity, she then rattles off the recipe of the magic potion that will be used in her rites for centuries: barley and water mixed with "tender leaves of mint" or *blechon* (βλήχων).[14]

The level of detail here doesn't really advance the plot, which makes the passage stick out like a sore thumb. Another peculiar feature is the gap in the original manuscript that cuts this section off in mid-sentence. As many as twenty-six lines are missing, the largest gap in the entire poem. Had the ancient author revealed too much, and did a later scribe try to correct the error? Were other, active ingredients of the *kukeon* originally included in the *Hymn to Demeter*? In the next chapter, we will explore the linguistic breakthrough that places the formulaic construction of this cooking lesson into a much larger, and much older context. The remnants of a liturgical ceremony that extends far beyond the Greek language into many parts of the ancient world.

But Hofmann was no linguist. He could only interpret the poetry through a scientific lens. And as a chemist he knew something few others

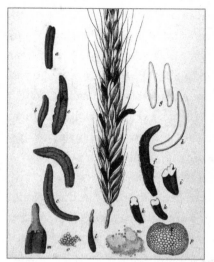 

Kernels of ergot (*Claviceps purpurea*) sprouting from a flowering spike of cereal grain. Once the slender, hardened spur known as the sclerotium falls to the ground, the fungus will begin its fruiting phase under warm, wet conditions—sending up tiny, purple-colored mushrooms. *Courtesy of the Biodiversity Heritage Library. After Sämmtliche Giftgewächse Deutschlands by Eduard Winkler, published in 1854. Illustration © Cameron Jones.*

did. Certainly no classicist or historian. Where there is barley, there is ergot, that fungal parasite mentioned above, also known as *Claviceps purpurea*. It regularly infects cereal grains like barley, as well as wheat and rye. But ergot is notoriously poisonous. It's more likely to give you gangrene and convulsions than launch a fantastic inner voyage to discover the meaning of life. Across Europe in the Middle Ages, as a matter of fact, contaminated bread would lead to routine bouts of ergot poisoning, or ergotism. It became known as St. Anthony's Fire, in reference to the monks of the Order of St. Anthony, who proved adept at treating the afflicted.

To avoid those unpleasant and often toxic side effects, could the Ancient Greeks have figured out some crude way to chemically isolate a pure, powerful hallucinogen from ergot? As far as Hofmann knew, he was the first to accomplish that delicate feat back in 1938. Interestingly, Hofmann hadn't been looking for psychedelics at all. He was just a boring scientist doing his boring job. He had accidentally synthesized LSD while trying to create new relief for circulation and respiratory disorders. Its psychoactive profile wasn't discovered until years later, in 1943, when Hofmann decided to self-experiment with 250 micrograms of LSD-25, his so-called "problem child."[15] How impossible would it be for a curious proto-scientist in the distant past to unlock the same secret Hofmann did in 1938? Especially when LSD-25 was far from the only mind-altering chemical at play. By the late 1970s, over thirty alkaloids had been isolated from ergot.[16] Found in plants and fungi, an alkaloid is any nitrogen-based organic compound that can interfere with the human nervous system. Some, like cocaine, caffeine, and nicotine, act as stimulants. Others can be psychotropic, producing a range of effects, including visions. That funky little fungus, ergot, was rife with possibility.

At Wasson's request Hofmann tracked down and analyzed the ergot of wheat and barley, both of which would have been plentiful on the Rarian plain so explicitly showcased in the *Hymn to Demeter*. He found they indeed contained two psychoactive alkaloids, ergonovine and lysergic acid amide. Both are soluble in water, meaning "with the techniques and equipment available in antiquity it was therefore easy to prepare an hallucinogenic extract."[17] Assuming, of course, that "the herbalists of Ancient Greece were as intelligent and resourceful as the herbalists of pre-Conquest Mexico."[18] Amazingly, Wasson's hunch twenty years earlier had been spot-on. There's no psychopharmacological reason why the ancient ergot of Eleusis couldn't have had the same effect as its chemical cousins, Hofmann's LSD-25 or the psilocybin resident in Maria Sabina's mushrooms. It's all fungus in the end.

But is this really why barley figures so conspicuously in the *Hymn to Demeter*? Until 1978 the crop had always been interpreted as a clear-cut symbol of fertility: Persephone's death in winter and resurrection in spring. Did the Lady of the Grain actually reveal the contents of the elusive potion that would lure pilgrims to Eleusis for two thousand years like moths to the flame? When Demeter said "barley," did she really mean ergotized barley, a coded allusion intended only for the initiates? Maybe this explains the three specific ingredients of the magic recipe: (1) ergotized barley, swimming with all kinds of alkaloids, some psychoactive; (2) water to separate the useful alkaloids from the toxic alkaloids; and (3) mint to cut the bitter, acrid taste known to accompany alkaloid admixtures.

With no scarcity of fertile fields, the Greeks could have chosen *anywhere* to host the Mysteries. Was Eleusis selected as the final site because its barley was uniquely prone to ergot infection? The kind of ergot that would produce *just* the right alkaloids, season after season, like clockwork? A solitary line of poetry from the seventh century BC seems like an awfully slim piece of evidence, but it's where this puzzle begins.

Wasson and Hofmann thought they had made a breakthrough, but they had to admit their shortcomings. They were up against the oldest and most pedantic discipline in the academy, and they needed every scrap of ancient literary and archaeological data that could possibly support their novel theory. Frankly, they were in way over their heads. The mushroom hunter and the drug maker would be laughed out of the room, unless they teamed up with a legitimate classicist to construct an air-tight case. When enough doors had been slammed in their face, they finally found their champion in the Harvard- and Yale-trained Carl Ruck, then chair of the Classics Department at Boston University.

In an age before Google or Wikipedia—before any computerized searching or digital library in fact—Ruck performed a masterful study of Ancient Greek literature that, until then, had received little attention. He also compiled an exhaustive record of neglected archaeological artifacts, some of which dated back to nineteenth-century digs. Within a few months, Ruck had enough evidence to complete *The Road to Eleusis*. Wasson wrote the first

Left: Albert Hofmann (left) and R. Gordon Wasson (right). Right: Carl Ruck (left) and his late husband, Danny Staples (right). Both images taken during the Second International Conference on Hallucinogenic Mushrooms in Port Townsend, Washington, October 1977. *Photos: © Jeremy Bigwood.*

chapter. Hofmann wrote the second. And Ruck filled the rest of the book with a staggering amount of well-sourced scholarship. There are a number of pages, maybe too many, where the minuscule footnotes dwarf the actual body of the text. At times it's like reading an annotated edition of Milton or Shakespeare.

Neither Wasson nor Hofmann had much to lose. Wasson, then seventy-nine, was independently wealthy, free from the politics and constraints of the university system. Hofmann, then seventy-two, had comfortably retired from the Sandoz Laboratories in Switzerland, which is now called Novartis—still a leading multinational company in the pharmaceutical industry. Ruck, the youngest member of the trio at forty-two, had everything to lose for consorting with "public enemy number one." And he lost it hard.

Nowhere in his published material or lectures could I find the actual details of Ruck's fall from grace, or what provoked such a vicious reaction from his colleagues. So after almost a decade of obsessing over his scholarship, I finally reached out to the reclusive professor in the early summer of 2018. Over fried clams and several rounds of cold beers, I met with Ruck at Jake's on Nantasket Beach, near his pre–Revolutionary War home in Hull, Massachusetts. We talked for hours past sunset until the busboys kicked us out. After bottling it up for forty years, the lanky classicist with fiery sapphire eyes and a brownish gray goatee spoke eloquently of his fraught relationship with an old nemesis. The one man who had the power and mettle to snuff out the psychedelic hypothesis before it even had a chance: John Silber.

"He was a kind of monster," Ruck chuckled into his beer with the gravelly baritone voice and refined accent of a vanishing New England. "John was very conservative. People had trouble dealing with him."

A no-nonsense Texan of conservative, Presbyterian roots, Silber led Boston University from 1971 to 1996. The one-time gubernatorial candidate would become one of the highest-paid college presidents in America, and took great pleasure in acting the part of boss man. He once referred to the gospel of psychedelic enlightenment espoused by Leary, its greatest prophet and America's most dangerous man, as "hedonism sweetened with nihilism."[19] That alone put Ruck's brazen theory among suspect company. But Silber also had a track record of punishing alternative approaches to history. Fans of Howard Zinn and his revolutionary *A People's History of the United*

States (1980) will recall the scholar's own time at Boston University, where he happily taught for twenty-four years alongside Ruck. Silber was known to routinely deny the self-described Marxist his sabbaticals, promotions, and pay raises.

Zinn's revisionist history may have put his patriotism in question, but Ruck's put his sanity up for grabs. He had exposed a fatal flaw in the foundation of Western civilization, and Silber didn't like it one bit. Though Ruck and Silber would never discuss *The Road to Eleusis* in any detail, the classicist is quick to paraphrase the president's sole commentary on the whole affair, "The Greeks just wouldn't have done that sort of thing." Tragically, Ruck himself had predicted this kind of response. On page 61 of *The Road to Eleusis*, he expresses his confidence in the evidence he painstakingly assembled to support Wasson and Hofmann. His bigger challenge, the biggest challenge of all, would be convincing people that "the rational Greeks, and indeed some of the most famous and intelligent among them, could experience and enter fully into such irrationality."[20]

There's the good ol' American kind of irrationality, like the cowboys' taste for whiskey and cigarettes. And then there are psychedelics. By the late 1970s few things were considered more irrational, un-American, or "perverse." For Silber they represented a complete rejection of the very things our Greek ancestors and Founding Fathers worked so very hard to establish. Purposeful things like law and order, common sense, and clean living. If it leaked that the greatest minds in the ancient world were avid drug users, wouldn't that give free license to all the LSD-loving, mushroom-eating, pot-smoking hippies out there? It would spell the end of civilization as we know it.

Silber instantly turned Ruck into a *persona non grata* by demoting the classicist and cutting him off from students and peers alike. It was a mark of distinction even Zinn had managed to avoid. Shortly after publication of the bombshell, Ruck was removed as chair of the Classics Department and forbidden from teaching graduate seminars. As a tenured professor, he couldn't be fired. But he could certainly be ushered away, far from the reach of the next batch of younger, open-minded classicists. And even farther from the public eye. Ruck's contacts in other departments were told to avoid him, blocking any cross-disciplinary efforts. If he wanted to follow this line

of pursuit, Ruck would have to do it alone. Seemingly overnight, the credentialed professor became an exile, a fate he never managed to escape.

Forty years later now, tempers have cooled. Every once in a while, another scholar will stop by to pour some salt in the wound, like this one-liner
from a recent textbook: "for the power of the Eleusinian experience, the
theater seems a better place to look than the kitchen or brewery."[21] But the
insults and intrigue have largely been replaced by more effective maneu-
vers, like silence. After all, there's not much to worry about at this point.
The provocative theory was pretty well contained a long time ago. Today's
students almost certainly have never heard of the incendiary book that once
rocked the Classics world. Plus, the original authors are all slowly fading
away. Wasson died in 1986 at the ripe age of eighty-eight. Hofmann died in
2008 at the even riper age of one hundred two. Ruck is the last man standing. He's eighty-four years old and poses little threat nowadays.

An eccentric at Boston University, Ruck is widely regarded as a harmless
old kook, safely stowed away in the back channels of the internet. The once
legitimate debate about our roots now passes as entertainment for amateur
historians on YouTube. Ruck still teaches one or two undergraduate classes
per semester, but remains off-limits to the future leaders of the Classics profession. He never attends conferences with his colleagues, rarely sees them
informally. They easily overlook the fact that instead of cowering into submission, Ruck has been churning out books and papers at a furious pace.
His CV, available on the Boston University website, runs eight pages.[22]

A man on a mission since *The Road to Eleusis* first debuted, Ruck has
spent the past four decades obsessively trying to prove that the Greeks
found God in a mind-altering cocktail brewed by witches. Yes, it was an
elite school of priestesses who prepared and dispensed the potion at Eleusis.
Would Demeter have it any other way? The Lady of the Grain who brought
the chauvinistic Zeus and his kidnapping, sex-offending brother to their
knees? The Mysteries were always the women's domain. At first, as a matter
of fact, women were the *only* ones who were eligible for initiation. This curious little detail might be connected to the birth and spread of Christianity,
Ruck soon realized.[23]

So when the classicists were beyond scandalizing, Ruck went after Jesus.
In the early 2000s, he started publishing years' worth of research into the
primitive origins of Christianity. Like Erasmus and Martin Luther during

the humanism movement of the sixteenth century, Ruck went straight to the source (*ad fontes*). There is simply no path to Jesus—and no way to understand his actual message—without dissecting the original language of the New Testament.[24] Each of the four Gospel writers—Matthew, Mark, Luke, and John—wrote in Greek. Saint Paul, who is almost single-handedly responsible for the success of the early Church, possessed total mastery of the language. He had to. From the mid-30s to the mid-50s in the first century AD, Paul founded a number of Christian communities around the Aegean Sea. His letters, or epistles, to these Greek or Greek-speaking pockets of faith account for twenty-one of the twenty-seven books in the New Testament. Their names may ring a bell.

Paul's First and Second Letters to the Thessalonians, who lived in today's Thessaloniki, now the second largest city in Greece. Paul's Letter to the Philippians, farther east in Philippi, a defunct city north of the Greek island of Thasos. Paul's Letters to the Ephesians, Colossians, and Galatians, just across the tide in modern-day Turkey. And Paul's First and Second Letters to the Corinthians, less than an hour's drive from the archaeological remains in Eleusis.

In Ruck's analysis of the Gospels, Paul's letters, and other Greek-language documents of the era, the earliest generations of Christians inherited a mind-altering sacrament from the Greeks, replacing Demeter's beer with Dionysus's wine as the vehicle for the psychedelic kick. For Christianity to compete with the eye-opening experience at Eleusis or the Dionysian ecstasy that had spread through the mountains and forests of the ancient Mediterranean, it needed a hook. At the time, what was more enticing than the legendary *kukeon* or the spiked grape elixir of Dionysus, to whom a third of all festivals in Ancient Greece were dedicated? Rather than restrict its use to a special pilgrimage site or the wilderness of Greece and Italy, did the early Church domesticate the ancient potion?

No longer locked up in Demeter's temple at Eleusis or splashed over the trees and rocks of the Dionysian backcountry, the proto-Mass could then be celebrated in the house churches and underground catacombs that defined early Christianity in the first three centuries after Jesus's death. It was there, in private homes and tombs, that the paleo-Christians used to gather to ingest their holy meal of bread and wine before the rise of the first basilicas in the fourth century AD. And it was there that the original Eucharist was nurtured in no small part by women, a new Greek sacrament to replace the old Greek sacrament. Not just once a year, but every week, if it so pleased the paleo-Christians. Sometimes every day. The mind-altering Eucharist would be an excellent recruitment tool for the pagan converts, who had grown up hearing about the Eleusinian and Dionysian Mysteries from their parents and grandparents. Mysteries they one day might aspire to see for themselves, especially if the would-be Christians in Greece could literally walk to Eleusis from Corinth! Or the would-be Christians in Rome could steal into the night to join any of the female-led Dionysian bacchanals that were still raging across southern Italy.

Ruck's psychedelic scholarship on the Ancient Greeks is not the only thing that makes him a fantastic anomaly among the dying species known as classicists. You might think his attempt to reconstruct the earliest and most authentic practices of Christianity's first generations would be a little easier for his colleagues to appreciate. The natural result of someone with lifelong expertise in the language and culture of Ancient Greece approaching the topic with fresh eyes. But in that pursuit Ruck is essentially a lone wolf. It's worth asking why so few classicists have picked up the challenge issued by Aldous Huxley in 1958 to assemble the kind of evidence that would historically support a new Reformation.

The fact of the matter is that classicists generally don't care about Christianity. Classics and Theology are different academic departments for a reason. The people who fall in love with Ancient Greek don't go to seminary to study the relatively simple Greek of the Bible or the Church Fathers. And they certainly don't become pastors and priests. They go to Harvard and Yale to study Homer, Plato, and Euripides, and to write increasingly esoteric articles about the *true* founders of Western civilization. They fight tooth and nail to land one of the rare remaining gigs at an elite university, because that's where the prestige has always been. As the classical philologist Roy J. Deferrari commented back in 1918,

> *Men of the church have always pored over Greek and Latin Christian literature, but only as the source of their theology. Classicists, on the other hand, have thrown them hastily aside as containing nothing but information for the theologian. The result has been that the literature and civilization of a very extensive part of the world's history has been very much neglected by the very ones best able to investigate it.*[25]

So even among classicists, Ruck is a refugee in the forsaken, disappearing field of dead languages. Even more old-fashioned today than it already was a generation ago. You couldn't hatch a better plan for obscurity if you tried. As Hanson and Heath detailed in *Who Killed Homer?* nobody learns Ancient Greek anymore, at least nobody who wants to pay the bills. And even if you did hop aboard the sinking ship, you could get a Ph.D. in Classics and never once run across Ruck's name. So all is well. The academic guard can breathe a sigh of relief as the disgraced scholar heads quietly into the night. And with him, a "perverse" and discredited idea that once had the potential to turn history on its head.

But what if he's right? What if Ruck's scholarship, scorned and sidelined for forty years, could finally answer the charges of "irrelevancy" and "impracticality" that threaten to scrub dead languages from the university curriculum altogether? What if this ultimate outsider, with no place in the academy, could once again demonstrate the critical importance of Classics at a time when the world might need it most? Improbable though it seems, history teaches otherwise.

At the end of the nineteenth century, when the social sciences were threatening to unseat the Classics, it was the self-made millionaire and high-school dropout Heinrich Schliemann who saved the day. He discovered the actual city of Troy, which until then most scholars had rejected as pure myth, a fantasy invented by Homer. Schliemann would become the "Father of Mediterranean Archaeology."[26] In the late 1920s, when postwar isolationism and a looming depression were challenging the old model of education, Milman Parry was forced to the Sorbonne in Paris when no American graduate school would finance his wild linguistic theories. But it was Parry who solved the riddle of Homer, proving the oldest "author" in Western civilization was really just an "illiterate bard." Dead by thirty-three, Parry demolished a previous century of classical scholarship.[27] Finally, in the 1950s, just before the downward spiral of the field, Michael Ventris was able to crack the exotic script known as Linear B, the first known Greek characters on record and the oldest writing system in Europe. The unknown architect from London was able in his spare time to solve what the paid professionals could not. Weeks before the publication of his masterpiece, Ventris was killed in a car accident at the age of thirty-four.[28]

And that's the way it has always been. It's the dreamers and romantics who keep rescuing Homer from the morgue. Every time a Schliemann, Parry, or Ventris comes along, the Classics receive an unexpected boost. The newspapers splash headlines of the latest discovery, the public shows interest, and the university administrators get their excuse to hire a new, wide-eyed classicist waiting in the wings.

The Road to Eleusis was clearly the wrong book at the wrong time. But times have changed. While psychedelics remain illegal at the federal level in the United States and much of the world, the clinical research is exploding at an unprecedented rate. In addition to the teams at Hopkins and NYU, scientists at Yale University, Harbor-UCLA Medical Center, and elsewhere are actively investigating the potential of substances like psilocybin, LSD, and MDMA to provide psychedelic-assisted relief for a slew of conditions, including alcoholism, nicotine addiction, PTSD, autism, anxiety, depression, and end-of-life distress.[29] In April 2019 the creation of the world's first dedicated institution for the rigorous study of psychedelics, the Imperial Center for Psychedelic Research, was announced by Imperial College London.[30] In September 2019 the Hopkins team launched the Center for Psychedelic and Consciousness Research, made possible by private donations to the tune of $17 million. And it's only a matter of time before more cities hop onto the psychedelic bandwagon that Denver, Oakland, and Santa Cruz got rolling from May 2019 to January 2020. Legalization at the state level will follow decriminalization at the local level, just as it recently did for cannabis, which is now legal for medical or personal use in thirty-three of America's fifty states. This was all unthinkable back in 1978.

Equally unthinkable was the fact that 27 percent of all Americans now identify themselves as spiritual but not religious (SBNR), including a full 40 percent of my generation. For the tens of millions already in the SBNR camp, and the millions more who might identify with an organized religion but haven't felt the rapture in years (if ever), Ruck's controversial scholarship on Christianity will fall on receptive ears. Even for the religiously devout, the hard archaeological evidence that helps put the sacramental practices of the earliest Christians into context could hardly be expected to provoke the same reaction it would have in years past. The younger generation is ready for something different, and the psilocybin experiments at Hopkins and NYU are pointing the way toward the responsible, practical mysticism that Huxley predicted would be made widely available by some future "biochemical discoveries." Like Watts and his "popular outbreak of mysticism," Huxley foresaw a time when large numbers of people would be able to "achieve a radical self-transcendence and a deeper understanding of the nature of things." By all accounts, that time is now.

But precedent matters. The revival predicted by Huxley is beginning to take shape. And it all feels strangely familiar. What if we've been down this road before? What if there are lessons to be learned from the religion with no name that spoke to the best and brightest in Ancient Greece and the earliest generations of Christians? Neither appears to have had a problem entering into the kind of irrationality that is illegal today. So I'm off to speak with the one person in modern Greece with the authority to tell me whether Ruck is in line to rescue the Classics by resurrecting an ancient faith. Or whether he and Homer are destined for the same inglorious finale.

3

Barley Meal and Laurel Leaves

One day in Athens can change everything.

It took weeks to arrange the meeting in September 2018 with Dr. Polyxeni Adam-Veleni, head of the General Directorate of Antiquities and Cultural Heritage in Greece. When it comes to the legacy of the civilization that shaped the modern world, she is the boss. The director is responsible for making sure nobody forgets about Ancient Greece, which has to compete not only with more practical subjects in universities across America and around the world, but also with the development of contemporary Greece, a country where ruins and relics can often get in the way of economic progress. An archaeologist and scholar herself, Adam-Veleni is the rare academic whose very job demands a daily balancing act, safeguarding the past while promoting the future. So if anyone could opine on Ruck's scholarship with common sense and a level head, it was her.

I called the director's office every day to reassure her staff I wasn't a crazy person, and that I had a matter of critical importance to discuss. We went through the same routine a dozen or so times before the appointment was booked. Adam-Veleni's assistant would politely inquire about the university or government institution I was representing. When I couldn't provide one, her tone would become uneasy, bordering on disbelief. "I'd like to discuss the Mysteries of Eleusis," I would say into the staticky line connecting Washington, D.C., and Athens. It's like calling the director of the CIA's office and saying you had a few questions about the Kennedy assassination you'd like to have cleared up.

After a series of similar phone calls and very earnest emails, however, I finally got the green light on the day I was boarding the Lufthansa flight to Athens. One sleepless overnight flight and a short nap later, I roll up in a taxi to the dilapidated office building housing the Ministry of Culture and Sports, just opposite the National Archaeological Museum. Security sends me to Adam-Veleni's corner office on the fourth floor. The director sweeps in from a board meeting that is taking place on the ground floor. She quickly explains how the Ministry's secretary-general recently placed her in charge of all the antiquities in Greece, which meant the Directorate of Museums, with its 242 archaeological museums, now answered directly to her. As did the country's fifty-three regional offices, which run the ground operations for each of Greece's ongoing archaeological digs.

"So you're busy?" I anticipate.

"I'm *very* busy." Adam-Veleni laughs. "Here, there are antiquities *everywhere*. There is great fear of the archaeologist in Greece, because if a developer wants to build something—like the metro, for example—they have to pay for the excavation first, which could last years. And cost millions of dollars. It's really quite expensive. But it's our duty to protect the antiquities and to show them to people."

With the ice broken, and the segue provided, I ask the director about the recent exhibition at the stunningly modern Acropolis Museum, ten minutes to the south of us. I had just missed a show there called *Eleusis: The Great Mysteries,* but the museum's website still featured a page explaining the choice to host it. "The Museum's goal is to present unusual subjects that will intrigue the current visitor and at the same time urge him to visit the places the exhibits originated from."[1]

"Why would one of your museums put on an exhibition like this?" I ask. "Is it just a historical exercise, for cultural preservation, or do you get the sense from your colleagues that the mystery is still alive? This was *the* religion that spoke to some of the greatest minds that this country, maybe the world, ever produced. And yet, we have no idea why. Even after all these years. Aside from the prohibition on speaking out, and all the shadows and secrecy, it seems like we've missed something in translation."

"Yes, we have. Thanks to Christianity," the director interrupts me with a total curveball. "That's the reason. It's that simple. It's nothing else. They changed everything."

This level of candor about Christianity's role in the death of classical civilization is rarely voiced back home, even among academics. For American classicists, Christianity is the elephant in the room. The clash of religions that took place at the end of the fourth century AD is perfectly accepted as part of the history of Western civilization, but it can be considered impolite to state the obvious. There's something about that reluctance to choose between the Constitution and the Bible—and wistful claims that the United States was founded as a Christian nation—that politicizes an undeniable reality. So instead of offending the theologians, American classicists generally retreat to their corner, leaving "a very extensive part of the world's history," as Deferrari put it back in 1918, "very much neglected by the very ones best able to investigate it." In Adam-Veleni I've found a kindred spirit willing to talk about events that weren't openly discussed in my entire time at university. As I try to think of a follow-up question, she launches headfirst, and unprompted, into two examples of what she has in mind.

"The destruction of the Great Library of Alexandria," she goes on. "This is a great loss, the greatest in the world, in my opinion. Things would be so different if we had all those sources, all those ancient texts. We have so little from antiquity."

In AD 392, the same year Emperor Theodosius outlawed the Mysteries, Bishop Theophilus of Alexandria led a rabid mob into "the most beautiful building in the world" and razed it to the ground.[2] It's unclear if Theophilus (Greek for "beloved of God") and the Christians he urged on were really after the glimmering statue of the Greco-Egyptian god Serapis, or the vast library collection that was cached in his temple precinct. Either way, Catherine Nixey's *The Darkening Age: The Christian Destruction of the Classical World*—which framed this investigation in the first chapter—lends exquisite detail to the annihilation of the "world's first public library" and its "hundreds of thousands of volumes."

The Christians "roared with delight" as a "double-headed axe" split Serapis's face. The body of the pagan statue was then barbecued in the central amphitheater as a form of "public humiliation"—"burned to ashes before the eyes of the Alexandria which had worshipped him." Insatiate, the "warlike" mercenaries for Jesus then tore the temple apart stone by stone, "toppling the immense marble columns, causing the walls themselves to collapse."[3] We don't know exactly what happened to the contents of the Great Library, but they were never seen again. As Nixey concludes,

> *A war against pagan temples was also a war against books that had all too often been stored inside them for safekeeping—a concept that from now on could only be recalled with irony. If they [the books in the Great Library] were burned, then this was a significant moment in what [Italian scholar Luciano] Canfora has called "the melancholy experiences of the war waged by Christianity against the old culture and its sanctuaries: which meant, against the libraries."*

After the destruction of the temple, the Christian rampage tore across town, attacking twenty-five hundred additional "shrines, temples and religious sites."[4] In Alexandria, as elsewhere, this kind of wanton mayhem was part of a wider campaign of spiritual—what today we might call "psychological"—warfare. Theophilus would replace the ancient temple of Serapis with a church to house some relics of John the Baptist that had been procured from Palestine. It was a "consciously planned provocation." The goal, "in unmistakable fashion," was to claim exclusive possession of "the physical and symbolic fabric of the city and capital of Egypt," which "now belonged to Christ and the God of the Christians."[5] Eunapius, a Greek historian of the era, said the Christians "boasted that they had overcome the gods, and reckoned their sacrilege and impiety a thing to glory in."[6]

The director and I are talking about events of the distant past, but it's hard not to make the obvious modern-day connection. In recent years, whenever ISIS henchmen ripped through an ancient Assyrian site or destroyed priceless artifacts in Iraq's Mosul Museum, Western pundits would hit the airwaves to bemoan the loss of cultural heritage. Our collective patrimony is at stake, they would say. "With a clean slate," one commentator opined, "ISIS seeks to present to future generations a new version of history, in which its binary narrative of ISIS heroes fighting evil will be able to flourish. Obliterating historic sites is an attempt to create a blank canvas for ISIS to build on: a new beginning."[7]

How different were the motives of the religious zealots in Alexandria, or Eleusis?

Adam-Veleni then cites her second example: the unbelievable amount of literature that has gone missing. "Just look at the theatrical tragedies we have. Only thirty-three and a half," she tells me. "But the production was much, much higher than that."

Sure enough, only nineteen of seventy-seven plays attributed to Euripides have survived. For Aeschylus, who was once prosecuted for revealing the Eleusinian secrets, it's seven out of ninety-nine. For the other Eleusinian mystic Sophocles, it's only another seven out of more than one hundred twenty. It's unknown if Euripides was initiated, but his plays contain tiny, possibly hallucinogenic details about the magical night in Eleusis.[8] Imagine how many other clues the playwrights may have embedded into the rest of their work? All of it, and countless other records from antiquity, just scrubbed from memory. The Christians can't be blamed for all of it, of course, but scholars estimate that "perhaps only one percent" of *all* classical literature has survived to the present day.[9] Think about that. Absolutely everything we know about the ancient world is based on the tiniest fraction of its actual output. For centuries classicists have been trying to reassemble a million-piece jigsaw puzzle with what Ezra Pound once called "two gross of broken statues" and "a few thousand battered books."[10] No wonder Eleusis refuses to reveal her magic.

While the numbers sink in, I cut to the chase. I reach into my brown leather pouch and pull out my prized copy of *The Road to Eleusis*, the black sheep of the Classics estate. Assuming the director has never heard of it, I explain the gist of the forty-year-old hypothesis that the *kukeon* was the central, psychedelic secret of the Mysteries. I tell her that Wasson and Hofmann are now deceased. But that Ruck is still plugging away at Boston University, still convinced he's right.

"Ruck . . . Ruck," the director mumbles out loud to herself, drawing a blank. She shakes her head to signal that she has, in fact, never heard the name.

"Okay. But without getting into the details, does the idea itself strike you as strange? Is it offensive for Ruck to say that the founders of Western civilization were doing drugs? Would it bother you if, perhaps once in their lives, the Ancient Greeks drank a psychedelic potion to talk to Persephone . . . to communicate with God?"

"No, no, no," the director quickly snaps, waving her hand in the air to dismiss the absurdity of the question. "Of course not!"

"But that seems to bother a lot of people." I am immediately reminded of a recent conversation with the eminent Swiss classicist, Fritz Graf, at Ohio State University. I spent the summer hounding any Greek scholar who would give me the time of day. Graf was extremely considerate from the very beginning, even if he completely disagreed with the psychedelic hypothesis. His very first email to me in July 2018 contained the unforgettable phrase, "Just to be open: I regard the Wasson-Ruck theory as rather farfetched."[11]

Despite that, Graf consented to a phone call, a rare opportunity to drink from the fountain of Central European wisdom that dominates the Classics. Graf earned his Ph.D. from the University of Zurich under the watchful eye of the German-born Walter Burkert, who is considered somewhat of a demigod in the field. In 1977, one year before the publication of *The Road to Eleusis*, he wrote *Griechische Religion der archaischen und klassischen Epoche*, published in English by Harvard University Press in 1985 as *Greek Religion*. It's the the gold standard for any would-be classicist. I had to read it twice. It's because of prowess like Burkert's that no serious student spends much time learning Greek without a basic comprehension of German. Burkert died in 2015. So in many ways, speaking with his mentee was my personal audience with the old school at its best. When I asked why he found the relationship between Eleusis and psychedelics "rather farfetched," Graf spoke slowly and deliberately to make sure I didn't miss a syllable. "The main thing is . . . there's not one shred of evidence in our sources."

Sitting with Adam-Veleni in Athens, however, that kind of skepticism is nowhere to be found. She skips right over the controversy: "In fact, I think they used drugs. Because they wanted to have, eh . . . how do you say, illusions."

"Visions?" I suggest.

"Visions! Yes. In antiquity, this was not so strange. For example, what is the name of this plant, the one with the morphine?"

"Morphine? Oh, the poppy."

"Yes, the poppy," the director repeats. "You see the poppy everywhere. And then there's Delphi. They say the Pythia has eaten leaves from what? From the laurel. This too provoked visions. Because it has oily leaves. And the oil is, in a way, a drug."

To this day the debate rages on about what inspired the famous prophe-
cies at the Oracle of Delphi, about a hundred miles northwest of this office.
What's certain is that women ran the show, just as they did in Eleusis. There
would be three Pythias, or high priestesses, at any given time, each having
dedicated her life to serving as a channel or mouthpiece for the god Apollo.
The petitioners gathered around the Pythia to learn their fate. The state con-
stitutions of Sparta and Athens were submitted for her approval by Lycurgus
and Cleisthenes, respectively.[12] In Sophocles's play, it was the Pythia who delivered the bad news to Oedipus that he would kill his father and marry his
mother. Walter Burkert includes this fascinating depiction in *Greek Religion*:

> *After a bath in the Castalian spring and after the preliminary sacrifice
> of a goat, she enters the temple, which is fumigated with barley meal
> and laurel leaves on the ever-burning hestia [Greek for "hearth"], and
> descends into the adyton, the sunken area at the end of the temple
> interior. There is where the Omphalos [Greek for "navel," it was the
> rounded stone thought to be the center of the world, allowing direct
> communication with the gods] and where, over a round, well-like
> opening in the ground, the tripod cauldron is set up. . . . Seated over
> the chasm, enveloped by the rising vapours, and shaking a freshly cut
> bay branch, she falls into a trance."[13]*

A number of theories have been proposed to explain how the Pythias'
trance was induced. Burkert agreed with the 1948 edition of the Oxford
Classical Dictionary, noting the fact that "volcanic fumes [rising] up from
the earth has been disproved geologically; the ecstasy is self-induced."[14] He
may have been one damn fine classicist, but Burkert was no earth scientist.
While past geologists attempted to disprove the "rising vapours" theory, a
fresh, interdisciplinary team came along in 2002 with two decades' worth
of evidence. The geologist, archaeologist, chemist, and toxicologist showed
that the priestesses of Apollo were likely under the influence of ethylene—a
"sweet-smelling gas once used as an anesthetic" that can produce feelings
of "aloof euphoria."[15]

In 1981 two hidden geological faults were serendipitously uncovered
when the Greek government decided to carve into the hillside east of Delphi
to make room for tour buses. In 1996, long after Burkert's *Greek Religion* had

been published, the new team finally surveyed the site, revealing that the sanctuary's "underlying strata were bituminous limestone containing up to twenty percent blackish oils."[16] It wasn't volcanism, but petrochemicals like ethylene that could do the job. The psychoactive gas would be released into the temple ground waters whenever the bitumen was heated by rather "simple geologic action."[17] In 2000 the team's toxicologist, Dr. Henry A. Spiller, lent further support to the theory after pharmacological analysis of a bedrock sample from the site. To him the effects of ethylene were well known: "In the first stages, it produces disembodied euphoria, an altered mental status and a pleasant sensation. It's what street people would call getting high. The greater the dose, the deeper you go."[18]

All this just to demonstrate three simple points. First, the Classics are at their best when the experts and specialists from a wide range of disciplines are able to converge on one thorny problem. That million-piece jigsaw puzzle needs all the help it can get. Second, as we saw in the last chapter with Heinrich Schliemann, Milman Parry, and Michael Ventris, it's not always the seasoned pros who get it right. New finds and new data are always just around the corner, and we never know where they're going to turn up next. And third, when it comes to drugs, classicists are simply out of their depth. Aside from the ethylene, there's no ruling out the "barley meal" or "laurel leaves" as additional tools for causing or enhancing the Pythias' altered state of consciousness. The plants were long associated with Delphi by Plutarch and Aeschylus. In a total blind spot, however, a scholar as formidable as Burkert fails to comment on the potentially psychoactive properties of Ancient Greek "laurel" the way Adam-Veleni just did—off the top of her head, no less.[19]

Not that Burkert wasn't generally open to the idea, by the way. On the immediately preceding page of *Greek Religion*, when discussing the ghostly visions reported at the Oracle of the Dead at Ephyra, he speculates that "perhaps the eating of certain kinds of beans had a hallucinogenic effect."[20] I like that word "perhaps"—a far cry from "the ecstasy *is* [emphasis mine] self-induced." That kind of absolutism can stifle creative solutions that bring all the evidence to bear. With that in mind, *perhaps* the thick, smoky incense of "barley meal" is yet another secret indication to initiates, like the one spotted by Wasson and Hofmann in the *Hymn to Demeter*. The LSD- and psilocybin-like magic of the relatively common ergot fungus might not survive the heat, but a witchy plant or herb that wound up in the barley meal could certainly make for hallucinogenic incense. Or *perhaps* it really was the laurel leaves that did the trick.

Speculation aside, so much remains unknown about drugs in the ancient world. Rigorous scholarship in this field is still largely absent from the Classics curriculum, and even considered taboo. One of the only classicists to pick up where Ruck left off is Dr. David Hillman, who also sports a master's degree in bacteriology. In order to complete his Ph.D. on the use of medicinal drugs in the Roman Republic, Hillman was instructed by his thesis adviser to delete all references to the recreational use of narcotics, stimulants, and psychedelics in antiquity. Hillman obeyed, later publishing his controversial findings in *The Chemical Muse: Drug Use and the Roots of Western Civilization* in 2008. The London *Times* referred to his study as "the last wild frontier of classical studies."

In personal correspondence Hillman explained that the medical and pharmaceutical texts that contain the evidence for ancient drugs are simply too complex for classicists, as they require a working knowledge of "biology, botany, anatomy, physiology, pathology, epidemiology, and pharmacology." As an example, Hillman cited Galen, the personal physician to Marcus Aurelius who wrote extensively about drugs. Born to Greek parents in Pergamon around AD 130, Galen's prolific output in Greek guided the practice of Western medicine up through the American Civil War, and was especially influential in the Byzantine Empire and Islamic world.[21] Despite the fact that there are more surviving works of Galen than of Homer, Pindar, Herodotus, Sophocles, Aristophanes, Euripides, Plato, and Aristotle combined, none of his pharmaceutical treatises has *ever* been translated into English.[22]

The blind spot that affected Burkert, and continues to plague most classicists to this day, doesn't seem to have clouded Director Adam-Veleni's thinking. When I ask why she believes drugs were involved at Eleusis or Delphi, she quips, "I'm Greek! It's common knowledge this."

"So it's not that controversial here?" I think of all the German and Swiss eyes that would be rolling if they could hear this. Aside from Albert Hofmann's, of course.

"No, not at all. Here, it's very natural."

Just then, the director's cell phone rings, and she attends to some urgent business. For the first time since we sat down, I remember where I am, and who I'm talking to. I deem it best to let Adam-Veleni get back to preserving the antiquities of the oldest cities in Europe, instead of answering random questions from a random American. But not without a parting gift of poetry.

While the director is chattering away at lightning speed in modern Greek, I reach back into my pouch and fish out my Homer from the plastic freezer bag that sheathes it. That Ancient Greek edition of *The Odyssey* with the baby blue jacket, first published by Oxford University Press in 1917. The only non-Greek letters in the entire book are the copyright page, in English, and the introduction by Thomas W. Allen, composed in Latin for no reason whatsoever. That's just how they did it in the glory days. There was no way I was going to Athens without my college textbook. I had been waiting too long to discuss a clue that I noticed in the Greek almost twenty years ago. And the director had just provided the long-awaited segue by referring to the use of drugs in antiquity as something that is "common knowledge" and "natural." Something that, perhaps, had been there from the very beginning. Something so ingrained in the way religion used to be practiced that it makes little sense to question, despite the unnatural bias that twenty-first-century American classicists and historians have about drugs.

I flipped *The Odyssey* open to Book 10, where the witches of Eleusis and Delphi would have found their idol, the rock star sorceress who started it all. Widely feared and respected for her encyclopedic knowledge of plants and herbs, the goddess Circe gets a leading role in the oldest surviving work of Western literature. A story that Milman Parry proved to be the written legacy of a deeper, oral tradition that stretched back long before the eighth or seventh centuries BC (the conventional dating for Homer). After a close call with the giant Lastrygonians, Odysseus and his crew wash up on the mythological island of Aeaea—which, don't worry, no classicist knows how to pronounce either. Circe drugs the hero's men and turns them into pigs, so she can have her way with Odysseus. With a little help from the god Hermes, who supplies an herbal antidote to shield the mere mortal, Odysseus manages to beat Circe at her own game of hocus-pocus. Impervious to her charms, he subdues the enchantress, releasing his friends from the wicked spell. For kicks, Odysseus spends a year on Aeaea as Circe's lover, drinking "sweet wine" with his mates.

Like the *Hymn to Demeter*, Book 10 of *The Odyssey* contains a recipe. Homer reveals the contents of the elixir that Circe concocted to make swine of the men, a key piece of evidence cited by Ruck in *The Road to Eleusis*.

10. ΟΔΥΣΣΕΙΑΣ Κ

ὅς μοι κήδιστος ἑτάρων ἦν κεδνότατός τε·   225

" Ὦ φίλοι, ἔνδον γάρ τις ἐποιχομένη μέγαν ἱστὸν
καλὸν ἀοιδιάει, δάπεδον δ' ἄπαν ἀμφιμέμυκεν,
ἢ θεὸς ἠὲ γυνή· ἀλλὰ φθεγγώμεθα θᾶσσον."

Ὣς ἄρ' ἐφώνησεν, (τοὶ) δ' ἐφθέγγοντο καλεῦντες.

ἡ δ' αἶψ' ἐξελθοῦσα θύρας ὤϊξε φαεινὰς   230
καὶ κάλει· οἱ δ' ἅμα πάντες ἀϊδρείῃσιν ἕποντο·
Εὐρύλοχος δ' ὑπέμεινεν, ὀϊσάμενος δόλον εἶναι.

εἷσεν δ' εἰσαγαγοῦσα κατὰ κλισμούς τε θρόνους τε,
ἐν δέ σφιν τυρόν τε καὶ ἄλφιτα καὶ μέλι χλωρὸν
οἴνῳ Πραμνείῳ ἐκύκα· ἀνέμισγε δὲ σίτῳ   235
φάρμακα λύγρ', ἵνα πάγχυ λαθοίατο πατρίδος αἴης.
αὐτὰρ ἐπεὶ δῶκέν τε καὶ ἔκπιον, αὐτίκ' ἔπειτα
ῥάβδῳ πεπληγυῖα κατὰ συφεοῖσιν ἐέργνυ.
οἱ δὲ συῶν μὲν ἔχον κεφαλὰς φωνήν τε τρίχας τε

A page from the author's college textbook. In this seminal passage of Ancient Greek from Book X of Homer's *Odyssey*, the witch Circe uses her drugs to transform Odysseus's men into pigs. Scribbled in 1999, the word "potion" is still visible in the left-hand margin.

The passage had always intrigued me. While preparing for class one day back in college, I had scribbled the word "potion" into the margin of the Ancient Greek text. My minuscule handwriting was an early suspicion that these few lines of poetry had something to do not only with Eleusis, but also with the bigger puzzle about the origins of religion in general. As the director wraps up her call, I alert her to a little-known line of research that implicates Ancient Greece in a web of drugs that may have once connected the entire ancient world.

"When you say 'natural' . . . this idea of drugs being 'natural.'"

"Yes, for us it's so familiar," Adam-Veleni adds.

"Well, I think it might be 'natural' or 'familiar,' because it comes from the foundational text of Western civilization. Circe mixing the *pharmaka*."

"Yes. *Pharmaka* . . . drugs," she chimes in, translating the Greek word φάρμακα that gave us the English word "pharmacy." As I pass her the distinct Oxford edition, the director scrunches her eyebrows, "So you speak Ancient Greek?!"

"Have a look at line 290 where Homer mentions the *pharmaka*. He even uses the noun *kukeo* for the 'mixed potion' that Circe uses to turn the men into pigs. Just like the *kukeon* from Eleusis."

The director knows exactly which passage I'm referring to and begins reading the ancient hexameter out loud. The music of the language transports me to younger days. In English, Hermes's classic warning to Odysseus goes like this: "she [Circe] will mix thee a potion (*kukeo*), and cast drugs (*pharmaka*) into the food." I ask the director to flip back another page, just to the right of my one-word note to self, "potion." She examines the fresh ingredients of Circe's *kukeon* embedded in lines 233 to 236.

There Homer tells us the Grand High Witch "mixed" (*anemisge*/ ἀνέμισγε) the "evil drugs" (*pharmaka lugra*/φάρμακα λύγρ') into the men's food, after having "stirred up" or "mixed up" a special potion for the occasion. The Greek verb *ekuka* (ἐκύκα) is used—from the same root as *kukeon*. That potion consists of cheese, barley, honey, and Pramnian wine (a dry, strong wine from the Greek island of Ikaria).[23] There's that barley again. Perhaps a significant clue, I thought, even a couple decades ago. In the process of reading *The Road to Eleusis,* I discovered Ruck's reference to a paper entitled "Let Us Now Praise Famous Grains," published in the *Proceedings of the American Philosophical Society* in February 1978 by Calvert Watkins. It immediately caught my attention because Watkins, Professor Emeritus of Linguistics and Classics at Harvard, had popped up in my Sanskrit studies. I hadn't known he was working on Eleusis as well.

Watkins's paper makes a brilliant case for the true origin of Circe's magic. Although it's virtually unreadable for nonspecialists, the "all-knowing" scholar, who died in 2013 a "towering figure," marshals an artillery of obscure comparative linguistic evidence across no fewer than twelve Indo-European languages.[24] Twelve! All in an effort to demonstrate why this and other passages from *The Iliad* and *The Odyssey* match, with "exact correspondence," the core features of a well-documented ritual from ancient India.[25] A ritual that certainly predates Eleusis and, in Watkins's opinion, influenced both Demeter's actual *kukeon* used in the Mysteries and Circe's mythical *kukeon* as portrayed by Homer.

The mysterious lost tongue that connects India to Greece is known as
Proto-Indo-European. Its exact homeland remains unknown. As it transformed over time and distance, however, the language retained certain core
links in vocabulary and grammar to its original source. This uncanny ability
of Proto-Indo-European to adapt to its environment made Indo-European
"the most successful family of languages in history," one or another of which
is natively spoken by almost half the planet today.[26] On the western front the
Indo-Europeans would spawn the Baltic, Slavic, Germanic, Hellenic, Celtic,
and Italic languages, which gave the ancient world Greek and Latin. Nowadays that branch of the family tree includes everything from Russian and
German to Spanish and English. Heading east from the Eurasian homeland,
the same Indo-Europeans would mix with entirely different populations to
produce the Indo-Iranian languages. Today those archaic roots have evolved
into Hindi, Urdu, Bengali, Punjabi, and Persian. In classical antiquity the
best-documented survivor of this eastern branch is the Sanskrit language
that made its way across the Himalayas into India.

On my very first day of Sanskrit class as an undergraduate, I was introduced to the following quote from 1785 by the Anglo-Welsh philologist Sir
William Jones:

> *The Sanskrit language, whatever be its antiquity, is of a wonderful struc-
> ture; more perfect than the Greek, more copious than the Latin, and
> more exquisitely refined than either, yet bearing to both of them a stron-
> ger affinity, both in the roots of verbs and in the forms of grammar, than
> could possibly have been produced by accident; so strong indeed, that no
> philologer could examine them all three without believing them to have
> sprung from some common source, which, perhaps, no longer exists.*

Sanskrit was a holy language with a mystical purpose, the earliest written
example of which is the Rigveda, a collection of sacred hymns composed
as early as 1700 BC. They may represent the oldest extant literature of *any*
Indo-European language. If *The Iliad* and *The Odyssey* are the mother texts
of Western civilization, then the Rigveda is our grandmother. And there
we find the original "mixed potion," a sacramental drink called *soma* (सोम).
In the Rigveda, *soma* is both a plant and the god residing in the plant. Just
like the *kukeon* of Circe and Demeter, the preparation of *soma* is often tied

to the "female presence."²⁷ It is referred to as the "elixir of life." And it is *explicitly* characterized as *madira*, the Sanskrit term that Watkins translates as "intoxicant" or "hallucinogenic." One particularly memorable line from the Rigveda reads: "We have drunk *soma* and become immortal; we have attained the light, the gods discovered."²⁸

After surveying the linguistic data, Watkins concludes that the similarities between the *soma* ritual of the Rigveda and "the ritual act of communion of the Eleusinian mysteries, by women for women" cannot be mere coincidence—"just too striking for a fortuitous resemblance to be plausible." And while the Circe passage above seems like a silly, little children's story about witches and pigs, Homer is in fact "describing a religious ritual"—"a liturgical act of Indo-European date, identical with the *soma* ritual of Vedic India."²⁹ For the spiritual language of the Ancient Greeks and Indians to be so profoundly interconnected, Sir William Jones's inkling about the "common source" of both Hellenic and Sanskrit must have been correct. Later on in this investigation, we will return to the hotly debated prehistoric origins of Proto-Indo-European, the mother tongue that seems to have introduced the religious use of drugs to both Greece and India, expanding outward over an ancient global triangle binding modern-day Iceland to Siberia to Sri Lanka. A secret pharmacology that somehow found its way into the subterranean catacombs we visit in Rome, now under the exclusive jurisdiction of the Vatican.

Is it possible that the linguistic success of Indo-European had something to do with this "religious ritual" or "liturgical act" that its speakers carried across the planet? If *soma* was undeniably "hallucinogenic," perhaps the *kukeon* was as well? Wasson certainly thought so. And if he could identify the unknown species behind *soma*, the *kukeon* might fall into place as well. Instead of a plant, however, Wasson suggested the visionary *Amanita muscaria* mushroom as the grandmother of all psychedelic rituals. Before he teamed up with Hofmann and Ruck, the ethnomycologist published his own breakout study in 1968, *Soma: Divine Mushroom of Immortality*. Right or wrong about the Indian sacrament, it's not the point. When Adam-Veleni says that the relationship between drugs and religion is "natural," I think this is what she's referring to. After all, *soma* and the *kukeon* have been around a hell of a lot longer than the War on Drugs.

The director agrees with me, and with the general thrust of Watkins's inquiry into the origins of the Greek sacrament. But if I'm in search of the roots of the Mysteries, she tells me there is only one person who can really help my investigation. So just as I'm about to leave, the director gives me the personal contacts for her friend and colleague Kalliope Papangeli, the chief excavator of Eleusis for the past many decades. After weeks of trying and failing to get in touch with the elusive archaeologist, I finally have my connection.

The second I leave the director's office, I stand at the corner of the National Archaeological Museum and call Papangeli's cell phone three times, hoping for a miracle. I then send her a text, begging to meet before I have to fly back to Washington. I make my way to a cozy little wine bar called Oinoscent, only a couple of blocks from my apartment back in the Plaka district. As I'm downing my second glass of Limnio from the Kikones vineyard, named after the ancient wine-making tribe that Homer placed in Thrace, my pocket buzzes.

My rendezvous with Papangeli is set for the next morning in Eleusis.

4

Secret of Secrets

I'm standing in front of the breathtaking Acropolis Museum. Brainchild of the Swiss-French architect Bernard Tschumi, the design received high honors from the American Institute of Architects in 2011. And rightly so. The whole structure floats majestically over existing excavations, all visible underfoot as you ascend a translucent ramp to the front entrance. Natural light floods the high-ceilinged interior of the ground level, the result of Tschumi using "contemporary glass technology to protect against excessive heat and exposure."[1] The effect is absolutely hypnotizing on the top floor, where forty-eight modern columns create a colonnade in the exact configuration that would have formed the original *cella* of the ancient Parthenon. Glistening in the sun are the original, pristine marbles of the temple's frieze, the half that weren't stolen by Lord Elgin and deposited in the British Museum in the early nineteenth century. Unfortunately I'm not here to enjoy any of it for long.

Before my meeting with Kalliope Papangeli in Eleusis, the only thing I've come for is a guidebook. I'm hoping for a little more background on the recent show I just missed, *Eleusis: the Great Mysteries*. I purchase a copy of the very elegant burnt-orange exhibition catalogue from the open-air museum shop and head to one of the long wooden benches in the spacious foyer. The cover features a 4-by-7-inch cardboard insert of a robed, scepter-bearing Demeter in profile, facing right. It's a close-up photograph of the marble

Demeter gracing the cover of the
Acropolis Museum's guidebook from
the 2018 exhibit *Eleusis: the Great
Mysteries. Courtesy of the Acropolis
Museum and the Archaeological Museum
of Eleusis, Ephorate of Antiquities—Western
Attica (© Hellenic Ministry of Culture and
Sports)*

stele in the National Archaeological Museum, dated between 470 and 450
BC. The goddess's right hand can't be seen in the image, but the original
holds a sheaf of grain stalks.

In his catalogue introduction Dr. Demetrios Pandermalis, president of
the Acropolis Museum, calls Eleusis "the most prominent" of all the visionary mystery cults, promising "personal bliss in life and happiness after
death." Even so, he includes the kind of perfunctory sketch of the *kukeon*
that would make Fritz Graf proud: "potential initiates would break their fast
by drinking the *kykeon* [an alternative English spelling], a mixture of water,
flour and royal mint." Full stop. Then, as Pandermalis closes his brief summary of the Mysteries, he grabs my full attention: "It is our hope that this
exhibition will be the herald for the celebratory year 2021, when Eleusis will
serve as the cultural capital of Europe. Within the captivating sacred silence
of that site we await the humming sounds of new initiates."

A quick tour of eleusis2021.eu confirms what, for me, is breaking news.
Director Adam-Veleni had mentioned something about this festival in passing, but I guess I was distracted by all the talk of the Great Library, the missing 99 percent of classical literature, and psychedelic witches. After more
than sixteen hundred years in the shadows, Eleusis is once again taking the

world stage. This time in a series of European Union–financed educational and arts initiatives across four main themes:

> The "Demeter—Mother Earth" programme focuses on our relationship with food. The "Persephone" programme focuses on our relationship with urban green areas, gardens and flowers. The "Ecoculture" programme focuses on climate change, energy and recycling. Finally, the "Feminine Nature" programme focuses on cultural heritage and femininity.

A letter on the website from the mayor of Eleusis, Giorgos Tsoukalas, laments the industrialization that overran the ancient city toward the end of the nineteenth century, leaving a "powerful footprint in the form of a series of derelict factories along the coastline" that now overlooks the otherwise crystalline Gulf of Elefsina.[2] As if the Church hadn't adequately wiped the sanctuary off the map back in the fourth century AD, Tsoukalas quotes Nikos Gatsos, a twentieth-century Greek poet, to capture the scope of the modern desecration: "Where the initiates joined hands reverently before entering the sanctuary / now the tourists discard cigarette butts / and visit the new refinery / Sleep, Persephone, in the earth's embrace / come out no more to the balcony of the world."[3]

Just when there was no hope for the deteriorating town, the diplomats in Brussels come bearing a quintessentially Eleusinian gift: resurrection. A public festival known as the "Contemporary Mysteries" is in the works, along with myriad events and activities centered on the very twenty-first-century theme of reconnecting to Mother Nature. It comes at a time of unprecedented planetary crisis, hastened by climate change. The decline of mammals, birds, fish, reptiles, and amphibians by an average of 60 percent since 1970 "threatens the survival of human civilization."[4] Some scientists are calling this the "sixth mass extinction event," the likes of which have only occurred five other times in the past 443 million years. In the past, such events could result in the disappearance of 95 percent of all life on Earth.[5]

We are a fragile species on a fragile planet.

The Ancient Greeks knew that. Death was always lurking just around the next corner. But Eleusis was there to defend them against whichever Greek word you prefer: cataclysm, catastrophe, holocaust, apocalypse. Scrolling through my phone in the museum foyer, I can't help but think of Vettius Agorius Praetextatus, a high-profile aristocrat of the fourth century AD. A prefect, consul and *hierophant* (literally, a priest who "shows the sacred things"), he held a number of respected political and religious positions in the Roman Empire. And like Cicero and Marcus Aurelius before him, Praetextatus was also initiated into the Mysteries. He was one of those cosmopolitan Romans who felt there was something truly extraordinary about Eleusis. Whatever the sublime vision revealed about the nature of existence, there was more at stake than just personal salvation. Much more.

In AD 364, the Christian emperor Valentinian abolished all nocturnal celebrations in an effort to shut down the Mysteries. The almost two-thousand-year march of pilgrims to Eleusis was in serious jeopardy of screeching to a halt. The Greek historian Zosimus credits Praetextatus with successfully convincing the powerful Valentinian to backtrack, permitting "the entire rite to be performed in the manner inherited from the ancestors." But it's what the initiate says to the emperor that, among all the strange things about Eleusis, always struck me as the strangest by far. It's a prophecy of sorts. Faced with the obliteration of "the most sacred Mysteries," Praetextatus declares that the shortsighted law "would make the life of the Greeks unlivable." Having drunk the *kukeon* and experienced the vision for himself, the priest points to Eleusis as the one place that "hold[s] the whole human race together."[6]

The Greek word for "unlivable" is *abiotos* (ἀβίοτος)—literally, the absence or opposite of "life" (*bios*). It's a rare, evocative word. The eminent Hungarian scholar Carl Kerenyi is fascinated by it in his seminal 1962 book on the Mysteries, written in German, *Die Mysterien von Eleusis*. Kerenyi concludes that the word was consciously chosen to inform later generations that the Mysteries "were connected not only with Athenian and Greek existence but with human existence in general."[7] The prophecy comes at a critical moment in the history of Western civilization when very little stood between Eleusis and the torches and pitchforks of the Christian mobs.

"Beyond any doubt," says Kerenyi, a distinct contrast is being drawn between the lovers of Demeter and Jesus: "the sharpness of the formulation of the significance of Eleusis, which has no parallel in earlier documents, springs from the conflict between Greek religion and Christianity."[8] In the epic battle of competing faiths that would erupt into the identity crisis we still suffer today, it was *only* the Mysteries that could guarantee a sustainable future for the human species, and the planet. According to Praetextatus, the temple of Demeter housed something indispensable that was utterly lacking in the Christian faith. Without that original sacrament, "inherited from the ancestors," we would all be doomed.

Why? How exactly did Demeter prevent not just Greek existence, but human existence, from becoming "unlivable"? How did the goddess whom Ruck refers to as the "Earth Mother" put our species in accord with nature? For the disgraced classicist, it's all about the Secret of Secrets, a phrase he coined to describe the archaic tradition of agricultural and biochemical expertise that was somehow able to manufacture the *kukeon* year after year. A vast trove of mysterious lore "passed on by word of mouth from herbalist to apprentice" throughout the long life of the Mysteries.[9] The harvesting of the ergot-infected grain and the mixing of the sacrament are believed to represent the "origin of all human science" that reveals the mystery of death and rebirth.[10] But because of the volatile properties of ergot, the production of the magic potion is only possible when the untamed lives in harmony with the domesticated. That trademark balance between yin and yang that the Greeks identified as *chaos* and *cosmos*. Literally, *chaos* (χάος) is the "infinite darkness" of "unformed matter" that existed in the "first state of the universe." While *cosmos* (κόσμος) is the "natural order" of the final product that we now glimpse in the night sky.

Trained by the female elders, the priestesses would have overseen the cultivation of the fields at Eleusis. Ruck sees that painstaking process as the thin line between the "wild, nomadic" ways of a prehistoric era and the "civilized institutions" rooted in the Greeks' biotechnology.[11] Grain itself is a curious creature, "carefully evolved from more primitive grasses."[12] When the crops are not "tended with proper care," a dangerous weed begins to grow. It is barley's evil stepsister, darnel. The scientific name is *Lolium temulentum*. In Ancient Greek, it was *aira* (αἶρα)—a plant associated with "divine frenzy." The funny thing about darnel or *aira* is that it serves as an excellent host for, what else, ergot. The job of the priestesses, Ruck contends, would have been to monitor closely the growth of the darnel and ergot so that neither got out of control. Too much, and the deadly weed and fungus can ruin the entire crop, threatening life itself. Too little, and there's no active ingredient for the *kukeon*. Only when chaos and cosmos work together do the raw psychedelic ingredients of the sacrament result. And only when the ordered, rational psyche is overwhelmed with a proper dosage of ergot-derived alkaloids does the disruptive, irrational vision result, "a sight that made all previous seeing seem like blindness."[13] What Ruck calls "the culminating experience of a lifetime."[14]

Under the visionary spell of the *kukeon*, Persephone is thought to have revealed the mystery of death and rebirth *directly* to the initiates. That's why Demeter set up the Mysteries of Eleusis in the first place, so Persephone could establish a personal relationship with each of the pilgrims. According to Ruck they would meet her face-to-face in that liminal space between this life and the next, convinced they had been given access to the true nature of reality. In the underworld that had invaded Demeter's temple, they would witness Persephone give birth to a Holy Child. It's unknown whether Persephone was there in the flesh, perhaps played by a Greek priestess, or wholly envisioned in the mind's eye. Maybe it was some special combination of the two that the ergot facilitated. The point is, the initiates *believed* it.

They apparently couldn't explain the vision away as wacky hallucinations, rattled brain chemistry, or wishful thinking. For those who had drunk the *kukeon*, it was a peek into another, freestanding reality. Similar to the one Gordon Wasson described back in the 1950s as crisper, sharper, brighter, and "more real" than the black-and-white, "imperfect" version we accept without question, day after day. In *The Varieties of Religious Experience* from 1902, psychologist William James used the term "noetic quality" to capture those rare moments of insight "into depths of truth unplumbed by the discursive intellect."[15] The mystic can experience "illuminations, revelations, full of significance and importance, all inarticulate though they remain; and as a rule they carry with them a curious sense of authority for after-time."[16] Perhaps what the Mysteries offered was the kind of ego-dissolving insight that was always cherished by the Christian mystics and suppressed by the Christian establishment. Once you become a mystic, there's no unseeing God.

After a brush with what Aldous Huxley calls the "unfathomable Mystery," things are never quite the same for modern initiates either. Across the board, volunteers in the Hopkins and NYU experiments report becoming better versions of themselves—more open, more compassionate, more forgiving, more loving.[17] "Bathed in God's love," atheist Dinah Bazer was finally able to appreciate and connect with people on a profound level for the first time in her life. When we spoke, she described falling in love with her family all over again. She recalled being surprised by the sheer goodness of others: "I don't think I realized how genuine people were until after this experience!"

But it wasn't an indulgent, self-obsessed New Ager that exited the psilocybin session, someone on the narcissistic hunt for *her* personal happiness and well-being. It was a "socially conscious" Dinah, who felt an innate sense of belonging as a fully-fledged member of the human tribe, passionately concerned about the future of the planet that her grandchildren's generation will inherit. Some have begun referring to this effect as the "science of awe." A recent article in *Psychology Today* explains the phenomenon as "a sense of embeddedness into collective folds and an increase in pro-social behaviours such as kindness, self-sacrifice, co-operation and resource-sharing. Experiences that arouse awe can help us to re-conceptualize our sense of self, our role in society and from a more cosmic perspective, our place in the universe."[18]

Clinical psychologist William Richards, the longtime collaborator in the Johns Hopkins psilocybin trials, concludes that ethics and morality are hardwired, "perhaps genetically encoded," within the human organism.[19] Psilocybin appears to unlock that code by tapping directly into what the mystics have been trying to mine over the history of Christianity with all their chanting, meditation, fasting, and prayer. And what the religious authorities try to beat into young children. As if decency and virtue were things to be *learned*, rather than natural impulses to be coaxed into expression.

Is this what Praetextatus meant by Eleusis holding "the whole human race together"? And life becoming "unlivable" in their absence? Did the transformational inner journey unleashed by the *kukeon* remind us how to care for one another and the planet? Was this the true technology on which Western civilization was built? Is a society that fails to incorporate this mystical experience fundamentally flawed, its institutions empty of the shared vision that made the world's first democracy actually work?

If so, that could very well explain the obvious distinction Praetextatus was trying to make between Eleusis and Christianity. By the fourth century AD the Church's mainstream Eucharist of ordinary bread and wine had replaced whatever heretical sacraments came before, as we will fully explore in the second half of this book. But another part of the campaign to rid the world of pagan influence, argues Ruck, was Christianity's exclusion of women from positions of leadership—the same women, the grandmothers, who were so integral to sustaining the Secret of Secrets in Ancient Greece.

Like many pre-Christian cultures, the Greeks revered the goddess in three principal forms: the young virgin (Persephone), the adult mother (Demeter), and the old crone (Demeter, once Persephone had given birth during the climax of the Mysteries). According to Ruck, Demeter's transition to grandmother brings her closer to death and confers on her a mysterious "power over plants." As she continues to mature, only *then* does the "female's ancient religious power" come to perfection "through her awesome compact with the terrible metaphysical sources of life."[20] Just like the Pythias at the Oracle of Delphi, whom the Greek historian Diodorus Siculus tells us were always over the age of fifty, Demeter in her new incarnation as the "prototypic witch" also inspired the Eleusinian priestess.[21]

Isn't it strange that the Christian holy family—Father, Son, and Holy Spirit—is an all-male ensemble? And isn't it even stranger that the only woman worshipped alongside the Trinity never becomes a grandmother? The Church would prize Mary's virginity and motherhood above all else. Instead of marveling at the grandmother's botanical know-how, the Church would demonize it. After the fourth century AD, Demeter and the old-crone archetype slowly disappeared. The same woman hunted by the Inquisition would eventually become the spooky lady stirring the bubbling green goop in the cauldrons of our Halloween books and Disney movies. The evil sorceress, up to no good. But according to Maria Tatar, who chairs the Program in Folklore and Mythology at Harvard University, "old women in fairy tales and folklore practically keep civilization together. They judge, reward, harm and heal. They're often the most intriguing characters in the story."[22] And they are the most intriguing real-life characters of this investigation, as we will see in detail in the Vatican's Archive of the Congregation for the Doctrine of the Faith.

I slip my phone back into my pocket and stare at Ruck's "Earth Mother" on the cover of the exhibition catalogue. So *that's* why the Acropolis Museum decided to host *Eleusis: the Great Mysteries*—to create a little momentum for the ancient sanctuary's metamorphosis into the European Capital of Culture in 2021. When the European Union talks about restoring our relationship with Demeter and Persephone, and reviving the "Feminine Nature" of Eleusis, I doubt Ruck's forty-year-old theory about a secret sisterhood of psychedelic priestesses is what they have in mind. No one in the "Contemporary Mysteries" festival is going to be throwing back an ergot-infused barley potion. Still, I can't quite grasp why *anyone* is paying attention to Eleusis, a small town of about thirty thousand people. Why now? A site once sacred to Mother Nature, today choked by oil refineries and cement factories. I get the metaphor. But for those of us stuck in the past, there's more meaning here.

I step outside into the blinding sun of a flawless Friday to continue meditating on Praetextatus's prophecy. And to visit the one place in Athens where the Ancient Greeks could never deny the awesome power of the Earth, or her unlimited supply of natural drugs.

I head a few yards north to the perimeter of the rocky citadel that juts from the ground, the Parthenon perched on its peak. The tourists are out and about now, making the walk a little less pleasant than this morning's. But as I reach the world's first theater, cut directly into the southern slope of the Acropolis, the crowds dissipate. I take a seat on one of the stone benches in the semicircular terrace facing the absent stage. Tufts of grass sprout between the marble thrones of the front row, where the priest of Dionysus and other VIPs may have enjoyed the performance in the same drugged stupor as the Greeks in the nosebleeds at the back.

Euripides, Aeschylus, Sophocles, Aristophanes—they all competed here to curry favor with the God of Ecstasy during the Great Dionysia at the beginning of spring. Unlike us today, the Greeks had no firm boundary between religion and entertainment.[23] The whole point of the performance was to "approach more nearly to the presence of their divinity."[24] No different from Eleusis. Dionysus wasn't *symbolized* by the wine . . . he *was* the wine. When a Greek celebrant ingested the fruit of the vine, she ingested the god himself. How else do we explain the concept of "enthusiasm" (derived from *entheos* (ἔνθεος), meaning "divine frenzy" or "god-possessed inspiration"), considered the "one quality . . . more than any other" that gave birth to tragedy?[25] The British scholar Peter Hoyle best described how "at that moment of intense rapture," Dionysus's maenads, or female devotees, "became identified with the god himself. . . . They became filled with his spirit and acquired divine powers."[26]

According to Ruck, "the nature of the theater experience was one of mass spiritual possession" that can be traced back to shamanic rituals "at the tombs of heroic persons, with the spirit of the deceased overtaking the priest and speaking through him or her to tell the dead person's story or myth."[27] The Greeks brought this "dangerous intoxication of the god" from the primordial countryside right here, to the very center of our ancient democracy, where the poetry of drama turned the unique Athenian dialect—known as *koine* (κοινῆ) or "common" Greek—into the language of the New Testament. Our ancestors could quote the Greek uttered in this amphitheater as easily as we might quote favorite lines from Hollywood. So *koine* persisted well past the Gospels, becoming the *lingua franca* of the Church Fathers and the early Byzantine Empire. To this day it remains the liturgical language of the Greek Orthodox Church.

Behind it all was the special wine that was served in this theater: *trimma* (τρῖμμα), which literally means something "rubbed" or "pounded." Ruck explains the drink took the name from whatever additives were "ground" into the potion to produce "a communal feeling of oneness" among the spectators, "with their shared cultural identity and with the spirits who were the city's metaphysical allies from the otherworld."[28] The "bewitching" that began with the actors, who drew down their ethereal characters through the magnets of makeup and wardrobe, would soon be transferred to the audience, "all attuned to the ghostly possession."

I can only imagine the atmosphere in 405 BC, when Euripides's *The Bacchae* debuted here, just after the playwright's death. How could he possibly have missed the show that would become the greatest tribute to the Dionysian Mysteries that antiquity ever produced? We know almost as little about the wine god's secret ceremonies—or the cryptic potions that nourished them—as we know about Eleusis. But like a bible for maenads who otherwise thrived in a world of hushed oral tradition, *The Bacchae* left behind a thick trail of clues that we will begin exploring later in this book. Clues that lead to a magical version of Jesus: equal parts natural healer, initiator of mysteries, and concoctor of drugged wine. Unknown to many faithful today, it's a version that places the founder of Christianity in the kind of detailed historical context that would have been self-evident to the earliest generations of Greek-speaking paleo-Christians.

Fortunately, our investigation is right on target, because one can hardly approach the God of Ecstasy without first unpacking the Mysteries of Eleusis. Before he seduced the fans of this very theater into the wild mountains and forests that would form his impromptu outdoor churches all across the Mediterranean well into the Roman period, Dionysus snuck his way into Eleusis as the child of Persephone. It hadn't always been that way, but the miraculous birth of the Holy Child, named Iacchus, who closed the Mysteries in the temple of Demeter, came more and more to be associated with the God of Ecstasy.[29]

In his doctoral dissertation from 1974, Fritz Graf himself penned the definitive study on how the delirium, frenzy, and madness associated with the God of Ecstasy made their mark on Eleusis.[30] Though he's no fan of the psychedelic hypothesis, Graf freely admits the irrational aspects of the rites that once belonged to Demeter and Persephone. During our conversation over the summer, he told me, "Indeed, it's undoubted that the initiates in Eleusis could have had, let's say, ecstatic experiences. Or something like that. For me, the most compelling argument is that Iacchus, the god who was leading the procession to Eleusis, is understood as a form of Dionysus already by Sophocles in the fifth century. So if Dionysus is present in Eleusis, that points to experiences that for the native initiate were comparable to what you would experience when undergoing the Dionysiac rites."[31]

Suddenly Praetextatus pops into my mind. Why did he schlep here, all the way from his lavish home in Rome? Would he really have trained for a year and a half, fasted for days, and walked the half marathon from Athens to Eleusis—for a second time!—just to meet a *metaphor*? Like every pilgrim, Praetextatus might remind us, he came to mourn with Demeter and spy Persephone and Dionysus in the flesh. And if Ruck is right, he didn't just come to sample an innocuous potion. He came to absorb divinity. Just as the *enthusiastic* Pythias might find Apollo in the mind-altering laurel, or Dionysus might slither through the *trimma* to possess his devotees. So Praetextatus might become one with the original Holy Family, the boundary between all living things forever dissolved with what William James would call a "curious sense of authority."

The classicist E. R. Dodds emphasizes the side effects of the original Dionysian sacrament that, very much like the *kukeon* of Eleusis, seems to have made life "livable" by drawing the human species and Mother Nature into a shared embrace:

> ... *a merging of the individual consciousness in a group conscious-*
> *ness: the worshipper* θιασεύεται ψυχὰν *["joins his soul to the group"],*
> *he is at one not only with the Master of Life but with his fellow-*
> *worshippers; and he is at one also with the life of earth.*[32]

Whatever happened to that sacrament? In the midst of our apparent global extinction event, would Praetextatus be having his "I told you so" moment? He warned us over sixteen hundred years ago that if the Mysteries ever died ... *we* would die. That whatever Christianity was offering, it was no match for the spiked-beer Eucharist of Demeter and Persephone or the spiked-wine Eucharist of Dionysus. How much longer can we afford business-as-usual until life becomes truly "unlivable"? We are sleepwalking toward the edge of a cliff, say the scientists, and no one seems to care.[33] Praetextatus might get a real kick out of all the climate activists and conservationists slamming their heads against the wall, trying to explain the gravity of the situation to the rest of us. The vulnerability of this lonely rock hurtling through space. The importance of Mother Nature.

Perhaps the founder of the National Resources Defense Council, Gus Speth, said it best: "I used to think the top environmental problems facing the world were global warming, environmental degradation and eco-system collapse, and that we scientists could fix those problems with enough science. But I was wrong. The real problem is not those three items, but greed, selfishness and apathy. And for that we need a spiritual and cultural transformation. And we scientists don't know how to do that."[34]

But maybe the Greeks did. Maybe the momentary annihilation of the ego that Praetextatus and his fellow initiates experienced at Eleusis, or the maenads found in the ecstasy of drugged wine, was enough to glimpse the big picture. To understand that the Earth is our solitary home for the moment. That we are all in this together. And that mistreating Mother Nature is more suicide than murder. I wonder how Praetextatus would react to the crown jewel of Ancient Greece being named the European Capital of Culture after centuries in history's landfill. Like any good initiate, on the constant hunt for omens and signs, would the Roman priest interpret 2021 as the muted dawning of a long-awaited comeback? Just when humanity is faced with the kind of threat that only comes along once every hundred million years, is this one last chance for a civilization in crisis?

For someone like Praetextatus who had experienced the visionary magic of Eleusis, it might all make perfect sense. Just as it did for Albert Hofmann, who a few months before his death in April 2008 left a concluding thought on the future promise of psychedelics:

> *Alienation from nature and the loss of the experience of being part of the living creation is the greatest tragedy of our materialistic era. It is the causative reason for ecological devastation and climate change. Therefore I attribute absolute highest importance to consciousness change. I regard psychedelics as catalyzers for this. They are tools which are guiding our perception toward other deeper areas of human existence, so that we again become aware of our spiritual essence. Psychedelic experiences in a safe setting can help our consciousness open up to this sensation of connection and of being one with nature. LSD and related substances are not drugs in the usual sense, but are part of the sacred substances, which have been used for thousands of years in ritual settings.*[35]

Among other precedents, Hofmann was of course referring to his long obsession with Eleusis. In the afterword to the thirtieth anniversary edition of *The Road to Eleusis*, also released in 2008, the Swiss chemist invoked the same God of Ecstasy as his countryman, Fritz Graf. "The Eleusinian Mysteries were closely connected with the rites and festivities in honor of the god Dionysus," he wrote. "They led essentially to healing, to the transcendence of the division between humankind and nature—one might say to the abolition of the separation between creator and creation. This was the real, greater proposition of the Eleusinian Mysteries."[36]

Where the chemist and the classicist radically diverge, however, is on precisely how that transcendence was achieved. When I spoke to Graf, he focused on the neurochemical power of the endorphins that would have attended the initiates' physical exhaustion after a ritual procession and several-day fast. He liked my buzz phrase, "an endogenously produced ecstatic experience." Hofmann preferred something more than a runner's high.

As we saw in chapter 2 when analyzing the main arguments of *The Road to Eleusis*, he claimed the hallucinogenic ergot potion would have been easy to prepare "with the techniques and equipment available in antiquity." Despite that conviction and several dogged attempts over the past forty years, however, nobody has ever been able to successfully reproduce the alleged psychedelic beverage in the modern-day laboratory. At least, nothing that produced the kind of experience attested at Eleusis. If one of those thirty ergot alkaloids really did the job, we still don't know which one.

The only way to determine which Swiss scholar is right is to trek thirteen miles up the Sacred Road to see if the original religion of Western civilization is finally willing to yield any of its precious secrets. According to Praetextatus and Albert Hofmann, the fate of the world depends on it.

5

The Beatific Vision

"The Eleusinian Mysteries and Christianity have so much in common. When I guide people through the threads of this archaeological site, I like to stress the similarities between ancient and modern," says Kalliope Papangeli in a lilting Greek accent. At last I'm sitting cross-legged on the chalky ground outside the Archaeological Museum of Eleusis with the woman who has spent more time among the ruins below us than any person living today. Known to some as "Popi," Papangeli is the chief excavator of Eleusis and the world's expert on the original religion of Western civilization. For the past hour she has been my personal escort through this forgotten, sprawling complex—ten times bigger than I ever imagined.

I was already winded by the acrobatic tour over massive blocks and boulders shaping our path across the craggy site. Now I'm dizzy from trudging up the steep hill that grips the museum. Wiry and rail thin, Papangeli has been doing this for decades. She is totally unfazed in her red polo shirt and navy blue khakis. We have taken shelter from the sweltering sun beneath a wooden pergola that becomes our shady retreat. Papangeli is settled on the bench beside a marble sarcophagus from the second century AD. An Ancient Greek master and pupil, I'm soaking in the view while the wise sage unloads a torrent of information. To my right the Gulf of Elefsina sparkles a magnificent shade of blue I can't recall seeing before. At the bottom of the steep incline to my left, the remains of Demeter's temple lie in silence,

whipped by passionate gusts of wind. Excavated earth surrounds the sanctuary on all sides in a massive, undulating footprint. If only these weathered
columns could talk.

I thought I journeyed here in search of answers to a very pagan Greek
riddle: did the initiates consume a psychedelic potion or not? And if so,
where did it come from? In order to prove the pagan continuity hypothesis right, we have to start with the Ancient Greeks and their prehistoric
ancestors. My conversation with Director Adam-Veleni and a close read of
the twentieth-century's giants in the field of Classics—Walter Burkert and
Carl Kerenyi—has convinced me that Ruck's scholarship is less controversial
than his reputation suggests. So I have been preparing for months to engage
Papangeli in a sober discussion, hoping to unpack forty years of academic
bias against drugs. Only after the visionary *kukeon* is established does the
possibility of the early Christians inheriting the biotechnology behind it
become fair game. But for some reason Papangeli keeps jumping straight to
the healer from Galilee. Completely untroubled by the obvious relationship
between the cult of Demeter, Persephone, and Dionysus on the one hand,
and the cult of Jesus on the other, the archaeologist has spent all morning
leading me through some of the most concrete examples on her site. She has
shown me up close how key elements of the Ancient Mysteries never really
disappeared. They merely stepped into the shoes of Christianity and kept
marching forward.

The first unprompted lesson in pagan continuity came at the very beginning of our tour, when Papangeli appeared in Marcus Aurelius's courtyard
in a sleek pair of sunglasses. As we crossed the Greater Propylaea, the monumental entrance to the more sacred areas of the precinct, the excavator
motioned to the well-preserved marble of another former gateway on the
right: the Lesser Propylaea. Carved in the first century BC, the architrave or
beam that once topped the double columns of the portal is now arranged in
bulky fragments on the ground. The symbols of the Mysteries are distinctly
recognizable in high relief.

From left to right on one chest-high chunk of white stone, I scanned
sheaves of grain, a rosette, and the sacred basket or *cista mystica*, as it's known
in Latin. On a more damaged piece to its right, I noticed the bucranium—a
skull representing the bull, sometimes associated with Dionysus, that would
be sacrificed in the all-night feast after the initiates had won their vision and

Marble architrave from the Lesser Propylaea, on the final steps of the Sacred Road connecting Athens to Eleusis. From left to right: the sheaves of grain, rosette, and sacred basket (*cista mystica*). *Courtesy of the Archaeological Museum of Eleusis, Ephorate of Antiquities—Western Attica (© Hellenic Ministry of Culture and Sports)*

completed the initiation. On a third and final piece of marble: another *cista mystica* and rosette. If there really was a psychedelic sacrament, it had to get from Athens to Eleusis somehow. And the containers carved in front of me are the prime candidates.

"In this *ciste* (κίστη)," explained Papangeli, using the original Greek word for a basket or hamper, "they carried the sacred things. They say that it was just some grain. Others believe inside the *ciste* were the small clay Mycenaean idols. Either way, it was something light. Because the priestesses had to transfer it to Athens and back, so it was something not very heavy."[1]

"It had to be portable, right?" I suggested.

"Yes," replied the archaeologist.

"A portable sacrament maybe?"

"Yes, perhaps."

"Do you think some of the ingredients of the *kukeon* would have been in there?"

"Maybe . . . maybe yes," conceded Papangeli. As the wind hissed through the cracks in the classical marble, I could sense a follow-up statement being prepared. "You know, in the Orthodox Church, we have a potion too."

The archaeologist was, of course, referring to the Eucharist. The more I thought about it, her casual link between the pagan and Christian sacraments wasn't all that random. It had never occurred to me before, but the fact that the *cista mystica* was ritually transported thirteen miles from Athens, to be presented here to the priestesses who would consecrate the *kukeon*, suddenly made me think of a super-sized offertory procession. It's that moment of the Catholic Mass when I would watch my nervous grade school friends present the Eucharistic "gifts" at the altar, amusingly marching up the middle aisle of the church with the unconsecrated Communion wafers and cruets of water and wine. Behind them, especially on Sundays, were the long-handled baskets full of money that the ushers had just collected in donations from the parishioners. The meaning is clear. In order for the priest to discharge his duties—transforming the bread and wine into the body and blood of Jesus—

The marble relief from the Archaeological Museum of Eleusis (above). The red-figure *skyphos* from the British Museum (following page). In both images, the divine missionary of the Mysteries, Triptolemus, is depicted riding his winged chariot of flying serpents. He is surrounded by both Demeter and Persephone. *Courtesy of the Archaeological Museum of Eleusis, Ephorate of Antiquities—Western Attica (© Hellenic Ministry of Culture and Sports)*

the people must first supply the raw materials and financial resources for the Mass's quintessential act. What good is a church without its congregation?

The idea settled here first, of course. The *cista mystica,* full of secrets, wasn't the only thing the initiates sent this way. They also paid their fees to the officiants, and dedicated their savings to the animal sacrifices that would take place throughout the affair, relegating participation in the Mysteries to "the less poor strata of the population."[2] In addition Papangeli pointed out the enormous grain silo to our immediate left. "Every city of Greece sent part of its production of grain to the Sanctuary of Demeter," she said, "because according to the legend, Demeter was the one who taught the people how to cultivate the earth."

In the *Hymn to Demeter*, the Lady of the Grain dispatches the royal prince and demigod Triptolemus to teach the art of agriculture to Greeks everywhere. More than a farming lesson, Triptolemus's travels across the ancient Mediterranean are referred to by Ruck as a "proselytizing mission" that was "analogous to that of Dionysus, as they both travel throughout the world on winged chariots drawn by serpents, spreading their respective gospels of the vine plant and the grain."[3] In the museum at our backs, there

Courtesy of the British Museum Images (© The Trustees of the British Museum)

is a marble relief from the fourth century BC depicting Triptolemus and his flying dragon cart.

A very similar scene appears on a red-figure *skyphos,* or drinking cup, from the early fifth century BC. Now in the British Museum, it was created around Athens but discovered in Capua, Italy—north of Naples. Triptolemus, holding five sheaves of grain in his left hand, is flanked by Demeter and Persephone, each bearing torches. The Holy Child Iacchus, clearly labeled as "Dionysos" (ΔΙΟΝΥΣΟΣ), is portrayed in processional line behind the prince. The Lady of the Grain is about to pour some liquid into the broad basin pictured in Triptolemus's right hand. If it's the *kukeon* or a *kukeon*-like sacrament, does the gesture indicate that Demeter's actual potion found its way to Ancient Greek colonists separated from the motherland, perhaps as far afield as Italy or sites even farther west? Would they have risked the goddess's wrath by observing her holy rites outside the Eleusinian sanctuary?[4] Either way, the grain silo on-site confirms Eleusis as the hub of a wheel that enclosed the entire Greek-speaking world. The first fruits of every harvest would always find their way back here, to the unique plot of soil that held "the entire human race together."

The next lesson in pagan continuity came a minute later, as Papangeli indicated the small boulder embedded in the ground on the very last steps of the Sacred Road that took initiates up a slight gradient to the now-vanished Temple of Demeter. "Maybe this is the Mirthless Rock," the excavator instructed, referring to the so-called *agelastos petra* (ἀγέλαστος πέτρα), where Demeter was said to have sat in mourning, waiting for Persephone to return from the depths of hell. "We know that there was an enactment during the Mysteries. So we can imagine that the priestess of Demeter sat here, very sad at the loss of her daughter, and some other priestess of Persephone came from over there," she signaled to the rock shelter known as the Ploutonion we had just inspected, twenty paces away.

Gesturing to the hollowed-out slope that rises above the archaeological site and looks down into Demeter's temple, Papangeli showed me where Persephone was resurrected from the subterranean gloom every year. A group of neo-pagans had recently left some offerings for the Queen of the Dead in a narrow crevice: a pomegranate, a sesame-seed cake, almonds, walnuts, and several sprigs of olive branches. "And here before the eyes of the initiates," Papangeli continued, "we have the reunion of mother and daughter. It's like we Christians have the Virgin Mother who lost her child."

"*Mater Dolorosa.*" I was hoping to convince the guardian of the secrets that I was a trustworthy member of the dying species of ancient linguists. It's the Latin phrase for the "grieving mother" motif in Christian devotion, Our Lady of Sorrows. The fifteenth-century oil panel from the early Netherlandish painter Dieric Bouts, currently in the Art Institute of Chicago, is one of the more famous examples of the teary Mary with bloodshot eyes.[5]

"*Mater Dolorosa.* Exactly!" confirmed Papangeli. "Mary also had an only child who went to the underworld, and then came back."

"It's interesting, isn't it? The whole pagan continuity hypothesis. These universal themes that Christianity seems to have absorbed from Eleusis. You could say *stole.*"

"Yes, many things they stole from Eleusis."

"Perhaps even *recycled*?"

"Yes," Papangeli doubled down. "Whatever they cannot extinguish . . . they keep. It's a very clever technique."

The ancient Mediterranean of the first century AD was a total melting pot. No faith is born in a vacuum. The Gospel writers and Saint Paul, perhaps even Jesus himself, would have found inspiration in the spiritual landscape of the time. In some conservative religious circles, however, the theory still smacks of heresy. It undercuts the uniqueness and originality of what is supposed to be Jesus's singular intervention into human history, with a new and unprecedented covenant that binds humanity to God through, among other things, the sacrament of the Eucharist. If the Church simply stole everything from the Greeks, it could be argued that the whole Christian enterprise is fatally flawed. And its one-of-a-kind mandate to save the human species from eternal damnation goes from something quite exceptional to something quite ordinary.

So the debate between religious authorities and secular scholars about the true origins of the rites and practices of early Christianity is an important one, with huge implications. The very first line of American historian Preserved Smith's contribution to the April 1918 issue of the philosophical journal *The Monist* is an excellent case in point. "Those who have attended the celebration of a mass have witnessed the most ancient survival from a

hoary antiquity," he wrote. Smith put particular emphasis on the word "sacrament" (from the Latin *sacramentum*), which originally meant an "oath" or
"solemn obligation." By the early decades after Jesus's death, however, it had
already become the go-to translation for the Greek *musterion* (μυστήριον):
"the initiation into holy secrets and magical practices characteristic of all the
'mystery-religions,' including Christianity."[6]

Like the Greek Mysteries, therefore, whatever the earliest followers of Jesus were doing behind closed doors at their original Eucharistic celebrations
appears to have included mystical hidden rites and revealed truths. Smith
identified an especially pagan influence on the so-called Gnostic churches
of the time—the esoteric Christian sects that thrived in the second and third
centuries AD, only to be condemned as heretical and erased from the history of the faith. "Gnostic" is derived from the Greek word *gnosis* (γνῶσις),
meaning "knowledge." But this is no ordinary learning. These Christians
were after something far more profound than the rational, down-to-earth
knowledge too often made synonymous with our Greek ancestors.

Today's foremost authority on this lost tradition is Princeton scholar
Elaine Pagels. Her definition of *gnosis* from 1979 remains the best:

> *The Greek language distinguishes between scientific or reflective*
> *knowledge ("He knows mathematics") and knowing through observa-*
> *tion or experience ("He knows me"), which is gnosis. As the Gnostics*
> *use the term, we could translate it as "insight," for gnosis involves an*
> *intuitive process of knowing oneself. And to know oneself, they [the*
> *Gnostics] claimed, is to know human nature and human destiny . . . to*
> *know oneself, at the deepest level, is simultaneously to know God; this*
> *is the secret of gnosis. . . . Orthodox Jews and Christians insist that a*
> *chasm separates humanity from its creator: God is wholly other. But*
> *some of the [G]nostics who wrote these gospels contradict this: self-*
> *knowledge is knowledge of God; the self and the divine are identical.*[7]

In *The Gnostic Gospels*, Pagels references many of the fifty-two Gnostic
texts that were unearthed in Nag Hammadi, Egypt, like a massive time-
bomb in 1945. Written in the Coptic language, a late form of Egyptian
rendered in the Greek alphabet, the first full translations of the recovered

"gospels" were not published until 1977.[8] Since then the Church has been forced to defend Archbishop Athenasius of Alexandria's rabid call in AD 367 to "cleanse the church from every defilement" by rejecting these "apocryphal books" that are "filled with myths."[9] A reactionary move, itself based on the conclusion of Irenaeus two hundred years earlier. The bishop of what is now Lyon in southeastern France had determined in AD 170 that only four Gospels—Matthew, Mark, Luke, and John—were worthy of inclusion in the final New Testament. It was hard to argue with his unassailable logic: "there are only four principal winds, and four corners of the universe, and four pillars holding up the sky, so there can only be four gospels."[10] According to Pagels, however, it was the "potentially subversive" impact of the Gnostic worldview that troubled Irenaeus and the other Church Fathers: "it claimed to offer to every initiate direct access to God of which the bishops and priests themselves might be ignorant."[11] Indeed "all who had received *gnosis*, they say, had gone beyond the church's teaching and had transcended the authority of its hierarchy."[12]

In fact that's exactly how one such Gnostic text, the *Gospel of Thomas*, opens its alternative account of Christianity's founder: "whoever discovers the interpretation of these sayings shall not taste death."[13] Like something out of the Greek Mysteries, the ancient author makes no mention whatsoever of an all-male priesthood, or their stranglehold on the Church's defining sacrament of bread and wine. Instead the Gnostics are invited to what Pagels calls "a state of transformed consciousness," in which they gain unmediated, personal entry to the Kingdom of Heaven that is ordinarily denied to the uninitiated. By simply changing their perception, they discover the cosmos to be infused with new meaning. The invisible becomes visible. "Recognize what is before your eyes," says the *Gospel of Thomas*, "and what is hidden will be revealed to you."[14] Like the priestesses here at Eleusis, the Gnostic Jesus was encountered as a mentor on the path of self-discovery that Pagels compares to psychotherapy: "both acknowledge the need for guidance, but only as a provisional measure. The purpose of accepting authority is to learn to outgrow it."

Clearly this decentralized, freewheeling brand of Christianity didn't survive very long. It's one of the many aspects of the Greek Mysteries that the Church Fathers managed to "extinguish," as Papangeli put it. But they didn't throw the baby out with the bathwater. There was still plenty of room in Jesus's cult for secrets, so long as the priesthood was there to shield them from any unworthy outsiders. After all, the very canonical, straitlaced Gospel of Mark reveals in no uncertain terms why Jesus chose to fill his public ministry with so many of the enigmatic parables recorded in the New Testament—the Prodigal Son, the Rich Fool, the Mustard Seed. Why not speak plainly? "Because the knowledge of the secrets of the Kingdom of Heaven has been given to you, but not to them [the uninitiated]." The word Mark uses for "secrets" is *musteria* (μυστήρια), the Mysteries. Thayer's *Greek-English Lexicon of the New Testament*, first published in 1889, gives an even better definition: "religious secrets, confided only to the initiated and not to be communicated by them to ordinary mortals."[15]

And just like what Demeter's temple served up only feet away, the real Christian initiation was incomplete without a sublime vision. Pagels describes how Saint Paul, for example, surpassed the "ordinary mortals" to become one of the select immortals like Jesus:

> *Following the crucifixion, they [the Gnostics] allege that the risen Christ continued to reveal himself to certain disciples, opening to them, through visions, new insights into divine mysteries. Paul, referring to himself obliquely in the third person, says that he was "caught up to the third heaven—whether in the body or out of the body I do not know." There, in an ecstatic trance, he heard "things that cannot be told, which man may not utter." Through his spiritual communication with Christ, Paul says he discovered "hidden mysteries" and "secret wisdom," which, he explains, he shares only with those Christians he considers "mature," but not with everyone.*[16]

There's little doubt that Christianity was born with all the trappings of a mystery cult. As the religion grew, however, the relationship between the initiated and uninitiated became a serious point of contention. Who should benefit from the young faith's deepest secrets—the people or the priests? As Papangeli and I approached Demeter's temple, and I finally set eyes on the 52-by-52-square-meter sanctuary where Plato spied "the holiest of Mysteries," the disconnect between the Ancient Greek and Christian initiation hit me in a visceral way. It was the last thing I expected to find here. But there it was, dominating the precipice that looked out over the entire site, with the Ploutonion far below.

"What the hell is that?"

"Ah, this is interesting." The archaeologist lit up. "A little Christian church, post-Byzantine, dedicated to our Virgin Mother. *Mater Dolorosa* also."

"Really? Isn't that a little bizarre?"

"Yes," Papangeli agreed. But there was more. "Her festival is also in the autumn. And the women of Eleusis come here bringing loaves of bread for the priest to bless."

"Just like Demeter, the Grain Mother? It's the same story . . . just a different name. For two thousand years."

"For two thousand years, yes!" Papangeli went on to explain how the chapel's patroness, Panagia Mesosporitissa, literally means "Our Virgin of the Mid-Sowing." In the Greek Orthodox Church the biography of the Virgin closely resembles the traditional growing season, making this specific Virgin the godmother of farmers. Mary is said to have died on August 15 and been buried on August 23, which coincides with the end of both the agricultural and liturgical calendars in Greece. It is then that "the Mother of God descends into the underworld, only to return in early autumn, when a new agrarian cycle begins."[17] With the arrival of the fall rains, the laborers get to work seeding and tending the land. They finish half the job by November 21, when the festival that Papangeli mentioned takes place at this humble rectangular building standing over the primitive entrance to hell.

"And they just parade through the archaeological site?" I asked about the participants in the Christian festival.

"Yes. It's the custom."

In the early evening, on the steps of the chapel across from the nineteenth-century bell tower topped by a cross, the faithful—mainly women—present their round loaves of *prosphoro,* or "holy bread," in twenty-first-century *cista mystica* for the clerical benediction. They also boil up a mixture of grain seeds and legumes known as *polysporia,* or "varied seed." The officiating priest has been reported standing "before a sea of bread and lighted candles."[18] He symbolically blesses one loaf, after which the women distribute the grain products to all assembled for a tasty Communion and, hopefully, a prosperous second half of the growing season. Many elements of the Mysteries remain. But gone is the vision, the inner transformation, and the personal responsibility for one's own spiritual development. The fate of the soul has been placed in the hands of the priest. Just as in the other 9,792 parish or monastery churches throughout Greece, or any of the myriad Roman Catholic basilicas and cathedrals across the planet, the priest calls the shots here and commands the blessing.[19]

At the climax of the Greek Orthodox ordination ceremony—when the magical, sacramental power is bestowed on the freshly ordained priest—the bishop will hold up his new sacred vestments one by one, while proclaiming "Axios!" (Ἄξιός) in Greek, which means "worthy." The congregation returns with a booming "Axios!" Indeed, only the priest is deserving of the "secrets," or *musteria* (μυστήρια), of initiation. To close the service the bishop places the consecrated Eucharist in the hands of the properly admitted priest, saying, "Receive this Divine Trust, and guard it until the Second Coming of our Lord Jesus Christ, at which time He will demand It from you."[20]

It's the longest-running old boys' club in Western civilization. Blood brothers, sworn together as God's bouncers, until the end of time. What cherished secrets have they been protecting for two thousand years? Potentially the same ones Papangeli would like to shelter from curious minds that might not fully appreciate the sanctity of this site, or the genuine spiritual legacy that continues to draw people here from all over the globe.

Tourists and pilgrims are two very different categories of visitors. Much as I tried to paint myself as the latter, Papangeli wasn't having it. I brought up the fact that I had wanted to explore this place since I was a teenager. And that I purposely chose the fall equinox for this mission, just when the ancient initiates themselves would have shown up on the Greater Propylaea. I even correctly identified her name, Kalliope, as the Muse of epic poetry and rattled off the first line of *The Odyssey* in Ancient Greek, where Homer invokes the same goddess. But in the end Papangeli seemed to disagree with the very premise of my investigation.

"I wish you luck," she teased me earlier on, "but let's keep the Mysteries mysteries."

Here under the shade of the pergola, at the tail end of our tour, the archaeologist is nevertheless indulging my probing questions about drugs. And finally we're having the conversation about Ruck's scholarship that brought me here in the first place. I have just shown her my copy of *The Road to Eleusis*, with which she's very familiar. When Ruck's book was translated into modern Greek about a decade ago, Papangeli was the one who oversaw the translation. She has reviewed the old professor's arguments in detail. And she's proudly unconvinced.

"I don't agree," she states flatly, examining the cover. "Modern people find it hard to believe that the ancients could go to a higher spiritual condition without drinking some psychedelic."

"Of course. There are many paths to the divine." I'm thinking of Fritz Graf's "endogenously produced ecstatic experience," which can't be ignored. The initiates *did* arrive here hungry, thirsty, and exhausted—whipped up by all the frenzy and excitement of the thirteen-mile parade. Not to mention the year and a half of preparation and anticipation. Plus, the anthropological record is full of countless, sometimes cruel, methods for achieving altered states of consciousness in the absence of psychoactive compounds. Consider the ritual ordeals so often present in traditional rites of passage: fasting, scarification, tattooing, body-piercing, fire-walking, beating, sleep and light deprivation, suspension in the air, amputation of fingers.[21] Romanian scholar Mircea Eliade referred to them as the "archaic techniques of ecstasy," employed since time immemorial in "tribal initiation rites" or "admission to a secret society."[22] Aside from the rougher austerities, naturally occurring sicknesses, epileptic attacks, and hallucinations can also "determine a shaman's career in a very short time."[23]

Other procedures are even more bizarre. Consider the initiation rite of the Iglulik Inuit, which is open to any "ordinary mortals" willing to undergo psychic surgery. The *angakok,* or master shaman, somehow "extracts" the candidate's soul from his eyes, brains, and intestines, separating it from the body. In Eliade's opinion "these experiences of ritual death and resurrection" are "ecstatic" rituals.[24] After "long hours of waiting" and "sitting on a bench in his hut," the future shaman is then endowed with the kind of vision alluded to in the *Gospel of Thomas*, so that the invisible becomes visible. This newfound sight is called "lighting" or "enlightenment." It's described as an "inexplicable searchlight" or "luminous fire" within the brain:

Even with closed eyes, [the initiate can] see through the darkness and perceive things and coming events which are hidden from others; thus

they look into the future and into the secrets of others. . . . He sees far
ahead of him, through mountains, exactly as if the earth were one
great plain, and his eyes could reach to the end of the earth. Nothing is
hidden from him any longer; not only can he see things far, far away,
but he can also discover souls, stolen souls, which are either kept con-
cealed in far, strange lands or have been taken up or down to the Land
of the Dead.[25]

Something along these lines was happening right here for almost two
thousand years, until Emperor Theodosius outlawed the Mysteries at the
end of the fourth century AD. In 1962 Kerenyi called it the *visio beatifica,*
or "beatific vision." He borrowed the term that was "coined to designate
the supreme goal" of Christianity: "those who obtain this vision are transported into a state of eternal beatitude."[26] Kerenyi was comfortable with
the comparison, however, given "the undeniable evidence that the *epopteia*
conferred happiness." And just like the Christian mystics blessed with "the
immediate sight of God" in the long history of the Church, the esteemed
scholar felt the Eleusinian vision was something truly miraculous. Something to be witnessed "with closed or with open eyes."[27] Unbelievable as it

The Eukrates votive
relief is said to record
the beatific vision of
the Eleusinian
Mysteries. Where
even the blind might
learn to see.
Courtesy of the National
Archaeological Museum
(© Hellenic Ministry of
Culture and Sports)

sounds, the *visio beatifica* was so exceptional, and so very different from ordinary seeing, that even the blind might take part.

In the National Archaeological Museum of Athens, there is a marble plaque known as the Eukrates votive relief. Dating to the fifth century BC, it was found right here in Demeter's temple. In the upper portion a goddess is depicted from the neck up, burnished rays of light emanating from her face. Below, two eerie, almond-shaped eyes stare back at us from across the millennia. Aside from a nose and eyebrows, the rest of the initiate's face is completely missing. The Greek inscription at the bottom reads, "To Demeter, [from] Eukrates." When its owner contemplated the head of the goddess, says Kerenyi, "he was probably reminded of the epiphany of Persephone" that cured his blindness.[28] Her name was not supposed to be written down, so Eukrates replaced it with "Demeter" to safely record his *visio beatifica* for posterity.

Kerenyi's interpretation is provocative, if unprovable. But it's worth noting an obscure paper published in the *Journal of Near-Death Studies* in 1997, "Near-Death and Out-of-Body Experiences in the Blind: A Study of Apparent Eyeless Vision." The authors, Kenneth Ring and Sharon Cooper, surveyed thirty-one blind respondents, including those blind from birth. The vast majority reported crisp, detailed visual awareness during their moment of crisis. Astonishingly, the narratives of the blind were found to be

> *indistinguishable from those of sighted persons with respect to the elements that serve to define the classic NDE [near-death experience] pattern, such as the feelings of great peace and well-being that attend the experience, the sense of separation from the physical body, the experience of traveling through a tunnel or dark space, the encounter with the light, the life review, and so forth.*[29]

One interviewee, who lost his sight in a car accident when he was nineteen, spoke of "a comforting vision of his deceased grandmother across a valley" during his NDE. Though he can't explain how it happened, he knows what he saw: "Of course I had no sight because I had total destruction of my eyes in the accident, but [my vision] was very clear and distinct. . . . I had perfect vision in that experience."[30] Given similar testimony from the other respondents, the authors conclude that "coming close to death appears to restore their sight to normal, and perhaps even superior, acuity."[31]

The phenomenon is almost identical to the *visio beatifica* witnessed by Gordon Wasson during his psilocybin trip in Mexico back in 1955: "the visions came whether our eyes were open or closed." And just like the near-death X-ray vision of the Inuit shamans who could "see through the darkness" and plumb "the Land of the Dead," the hyper-realistic mental images unleashed by the psilocybin gave Wasson the distinct impression that he had been liberated from the physical body: "a disembodied eye, invisible, incorporeal, seeing but not seen."[32]

The many decades of controlled psychedelic experiments are replete with similar tales, including "complex hallucinations" in the blind and unexpected encounters with "loved ones and ancestors."[33] In his book *Sacred Knowledge: Psychedelics and Religious Experiences*, Hopkins researcher William Richards takes note of the obvious:

> *The literature on near-death experiences, reports of those who have entered into the physical processes of death and have been resuscitated, contains many intriguing stories to ponder that are often very similar to psychedelic experiences, complete with reports of moving through tunnels, encountering visionary beings, and being drawn toward sacred realms of light.*[34]

Dismissing the apparent connections between ecstatic, near-death, and psychedelic experiences is as productive as ignoring the continuity between the pagan and Christian traditions that continue to overlap at this ancient site. Rather than pitting Albert Hofmann and Fritz Graf against each other, isn't it possible they're both right? The Eleusinian initiates could have *both* suffered through the physical demands of a traditional rite of passage, *and* received a carefully dosed psychedelic potion to amplify whatever they experienced inside Demeter's temple. The two theories aren't mutually exclusive.

I want Papangeli to appreciate my own tentative approach to Wasson, Hofmann, and Ruck, whom I've spent a decade trying to fact-check. I tell her, transparently, that I have my own reservations about their hypothesis.

And that I'm constantly appealing to the reasonable voices in the room, like Graf's mentor and Classics icon Walter Burkert. I read her a few lines from his 1985 English edition of *Greek Religion* that I captured on my phone just before the flight to Athens. A stunning passage from his chapter on "Mysteries and Asceticism" that too many historians have glossed over too quickly:

> *Demeter and Dionysus are gods of important mysteries; the drinking of the barley potion or the drinking of wine are central ceremonies. Yet to derive mysteries from agrarian magic is at best a conjecture about prehistory. . . . It may rather be asked, even without the prospect of a certain answer, whether at the basis of the mysteries there were prehistoric drug rituals, some festival of immortality which, through the expansion of consciousness, seemed to guarantee some psychedelic Beyond. . . . A ritual can persist when the original drug has long been forgotten and replaced by harmless substances. Perhaps the night of the mysteries was not so very different from an Orthodox Easter festival or a Western Christmas.*[35]

Papangeli's interest is piqued. "I've read all his books."

"Me too. But for some reason, I'd never noticed that passage before. When I read it a second time, Professor Burkert opened my mind to a possibility. A possibility I soon discovered *this* guy was sympathetic to as well." From my squatting position on the ground, I extend a copy of Kerenyi's *Eleusis: Archetypal Image of Mother and Daughter*, originally written in German, like Burkert's masterpiece.

"Ah, Kerenyi!" exclaims Papangeli, as if she just bumped into an old friend.

"Did you know there's an appendix in this edition dedicated to what Kerenyi calls 'the pharmacological question'?"

The archaeologist seems surprised. When I first spotted it, so was I. The last name I expected to find in Kerenyi's authoritative text on this sanctuary was Albert Hofmann's. Years before he teamed up with Wasson and Ruck, the Swiss chemist shared some interdisciplinary insight with his European colleague. Instead of ergot, Kerenyi was focused on the *kukeon*'s third ingredient from the *Hymn to Demeter*, mint. Today it's called *Mentha pulegium.* What species the Greeks had in mind with *blechon* (βλήχων), we're not entirely sure. So the Teutonic scholar looked to a modern-day equivalent, with broad application from North Africa to Central Europe. He believed a form of pennyroyal could have been involved in the Mysteries; its oil and leaves known to possess medicinal properties. Kerenyi quotes a personal letter he received from Hofmann at some point in the mid-1960s: "The principal ingredient of the poley oil (*Oleum pulegii*), prepared as an aromatic in southern Europe and obtained in distilling the wild plant [*Mentha pulegium*] is the aromatic substance pulegone. . . . In large doses it induces delirium, loss of consciousness, and spasms."[36]

Kerenyi's willingness to entertain the psychedelic hypothesis may have paved the way for Burkert's above speculation about the "psychedelic Beyond" in 1977, a year before *The Road to Eleusis* hit the shelves. Before psychedelics became controversial and taboo, Kerenyi's early collaboration with the discoverer of LSD reads like a fair compromise:

> It is possible that the kykeon at Eleusis conferred not only the "initial thrust" but also the necessary inner peace and perhaps still other prerequisites of the vision. Dr. Hofmann's words are: "The volatile oils contained in poley oil (Oleum pulegii) might very well, added to the alcoholic content of the kykeon, have produced hallucinations in persons whose sensibility was heightened by fasting."[37]

As I summarize their findings, Papangeli is stone-faced. When read in the context of the Classics elite that preceded him, Ruck doesn't actually seem all that crazy. "Do you think Eleusis could have started as a 'prehistoric drug ritual,' as Burkert calls it?" I ask.

"Yes," she replies with no hesitation. "Maybe it started as an agrarian festival, and then later it begins to have these eschatological meanings for the afterlife."

"But by the time that prehistoric festival came here to Eleusis, it lost the drug? So the *kukeon* was nothing more than a harmless potion?"

"Yes," she agrees again.

"Just like the Communion?" The instant the word "Communion" comes out of my mouth, as if God were listening in, the bell on the nineteenth-century tower a hundred yards away begins tolling. Twelve rhythmic clangs marking the noontime hour, right next to the chapel of Panagia Mesosporitissa.

"Exactly. A Communion."

"So that's where we are." I decide not to press my luck with the psychedelic hypothesis. Like Burkert, the archaeologist is at least willing to entertain the notion that potent hallucinogens once played their part in some Stone Age version of the Mysteries. Wherever they were practiced in remote prehistory, long before the Greeks, Papangeli can imagine those mind-altering rites descending on this now-deserted complex in some watered-down form. And that's good enough for me. Because in the forty years that have elapsed since *The Road to Eleusis* fleshed out Burkert's and Kerenyi's early speculation about the active ingredients of the *kukeon*, a new field of science has developed to confirm or deny the formerly untestable hypothesis once and for all.

As we will see in the next chapter, no longer do stuffy classicists need to fumble around in the dark "without the prospect of a certain answer," as Burkert wrote. The limitations of traditional archaeology—especially in deciphering the drinking, feasting, and other ritual habits of ancient cultures—have become all too apparent. Pioneering excavators are increasingly looking to other specialties to support their craft, resulting in the rapid growth of a scrappy, young discipline called archaeological chemistry.

Over the past couple decades, state-of-the-art technologies like Fourier transform infrared spectroscopy (FTIR), high-performance liquid chromatography (HPLC), and gas chromatography-mass spectrometry (GC-MS) have become more readily available. And scientists are now able to identify what our ancient ancestors were drinking by extracting the chemical signatures from organic residue that has either survived intact within excavated vessels, or been absorbed into the porous matrices of their ceramic pottery.[38] Some incredible finds have been announced by the few researchers dedicating their careers to this cutting-edge hunt for intoxicants, with discoveries reaching back as much as thirteen thousand years.[39]

The age of speculation is over.

As I pack up my things and prepare to leave, I recall the many chalices that were unearthed from the ground below. Papangeli just walked me through a dozen samples protected behind glass, right here in the final room of the Archaeological Museum of Eleusis.

"About those vessels. Would you be open to having them scientifically tested?"

"We have the ambition to find a *kernos* with something inside, so we can really have an experiment," she answers, referring to the earthenware or metal vessel ordinarily associated with the Mysteries. Here on-site a number have been found featuring a central bowl ringed by several smaller cups.

Ceremonial vessels excavated on-site and arranged for display in the Archaeological Museum of Eleusis. Chalices like these were used to mix or consume the *kukeon* during the Mysteries. *Courtesy of the Archaeological Museum of Eleusis, Ephorate of Antiquities—Western Attica (© Hellenic Ministry of Culture and Sports)*

Quoting an ancient author, Kerenyi lists the produce that may have once filled the peripheral containers: "sage, white poppy-seeds, grains of wheat and barley, peas, vetches, okraseeds, lentils, beans, rice-wheat, oats, compressed fruit, honey, oil, wine, milk, egg, and unwashed wool."[40] An unruly mix that provides much more detail than the *Hymn to Demeter*, though Ruck thinks the *kernos* was largely symbolic. Its shape, moreover, would have made it "ungainly as a drinking vessel."[41] More probably it was used as a "chalice containing some important ingredient for the mixing ceremony" that took place in the temple below, perhaps ergotized barley or magic mint. Once the vessel was consecrated, the hierophant performed the initiation by "raising his *kernos* aloft" and tasting the contents.[42] The initiates followed suit, sipping from vessels that more likely resembled the other containers all neatly assembled within the museum behind us. Just waiting for their ancient, microscopic contents to be flown off to any number of laboratories that would jump at the opportunity to solve the best-kept secret in the history of Western civilization. I'm shocked that Papangeli, as a skeptic of Ruck's work, is on board.

"So why haven't you tested them yet?"

"Because they were treated . . . cleaned. This is why. Of course, we have more in the storerooms," she adds. "But they were also treated for conservation." Reminding me of Eleusis's peculiar archaeological history, she informs me the vessels "were all found at the end of the nineteenth or early twentieth century."

"They were all excavated a hundred years ago? And you haven't found any since?"

"I don't excavate inside the site any longer. We excavate outside, within the modern city of Eleusis, which sits over the ancient city. We find graves and such things."

"But no vessels?"

"No ceremonial vessels."

"So is it possible there are still some vessels under *here* then?" I sweep my hand toward the ruins below.

"I think they have explored the whole thing."

"Really? You think all the ceremonial vessels were recovered by those crazy archaeologists at the turn of the century? They didn't know what they were doing." I'm exaggerating, but one of the principal credos in archaeology could not go unmentioned: to dig is to destroy. The modern excavations that began here in 1882 may have been methodical compared to what came before, but any poking around the site is inherently destructive. Like anywhere else, incomplete excavation records and find registries are a problem at Eleusis.[43] "We may never know the answer, if we can't test one of those vessels, right?"

"Yes." Papangeli nods her head pensively.

"So the Mystery continues."

"Yes . . . I hope!" she snickers. We both erupt into laughter as our chess match reaches the same stalemate that has been in place for thousands of years.

"Why don't you want to solve this thing?"

"We have different aims, Brian."

"You like the mystery being kept alive. Why is that?"

"Everybody likes a mystery. It was the mystery that attracted *you* to this story, wasn't it? So let the next generations be attracted to the mystery as well," Papangeli counsels me. With that, the archaeologist disappears into the museum.

Like the great Walter Burkert, Papangeli may be right that "a ritual can persist when the original drug has long been forgotten and replaced by harmless substances." That said, all the ancient testimony from Plato, Pindar, Sophocles, Cicero, and Praetextatus indicates that two millennia's worth of initiates flocked here for a compelling reason. And whatever happened inside Demeter's temple a few yards away was anything but the kind of empty bread-blessing ritual that takes place every November up there at Panagia Mesosporitissa. There's no doubt the modern-day Eucharist is a "harmless," un-psychedelic affair. But, once again, it tells us nothing about the sacrament that may have accompanied the Church's infancy two thousand years ago. In the Greek and Christian Mysteries alike, perhaps the classical practitioners did not want to abandon the spiked potion of their prehistoric ancestors for a mere placebo.

If we can't test the ritual chalices from Eleusis, we have to look elsewhere for clues. Fortunately my long-awaited rendezvous with the elusive Papangeli has at least narrowed the scope of this investigation. Perhaps the question is no longer *whether* mind-altering potions were used in the kinds of rituals that preceded Eleusis. But *when*, if ever, Burkert's "original drug" had been "forgotten and replaced" by a placebo.

To the dismay of many fine classicists and historians, it looks as if civilization began with a toast. And the party never stopped. Just east of the place where democracy first came to life, a prehistoric ritual was born in a country so entangled with the history of Greece that an epic battle between its people became Homer's founding poem about Western civilization. Toward the end of the last Ice Age, long before the Trojan War, the ancient land now known as Turkey was famous for something else.

The birth of religion itself.

And the religion with no name that sprang from its soil just may have been the drunken, hallucinogenic religion that made the Mysteries possible.

6

Graveyard Beer

As I pull up to the oldest working brewery in the world, the bearded giant is waiting for me in the gray Bavarian drizzle. Dr. Martin Zarnkow is head of research and development at the Weihenstephan Research Center for Brewing and Food Quality at the Technische Universität München. His laboratory marks the nexus of the beer universe here in Freising, Germany, only minutes from the Munich International Airport. In operation since AD 1040, prior to the Crusades, the first kegs that came out of this former monastery were cooked up by the Benedictines. And right here on Weihenstephan's doorstep in 1516, Duke Wilhelm IV of Bavaria issued the Purity Law that forever memorialized beer's three principal ingredients: barley, water, and hops.[1] Anything else, and it couldn't be called "beer," a complicated beverage with a complicated past going all the way back to the Stone Age. In fact the initial results of some recent archaeobotanical and archaeochemical finds point to a prehistoric connection between religion and psychoactive brews as the real driving force behind modern civilization. Once the domain of mere speculation among scholars like Walter Burkert and others, there is now hard evidence for rituals of intoxication preceding Eleusis by many thousands of years. Rituals complete with a sacrament much like the *kukeon*.

Few can tell the story quite like Zarnkow, the world's preeminent beer scientist. I've caught him on a cold Friday afternoon in November 2018, in between trips to Turkey, India, and Brazil, where the master brewer is wildly sought after to teach the high-tech methods he has brought to the original Bavarian art. Whether it's culturing the perfect brewer's yeast or developing a gluten-free beer, Zarnkow is the fixer. And he also happens to be an incredible historian. Once we escape the rain and settle into his relaxing, spacious office, the proud German directs me straight to the overflowing bookshelves lining the back wall. I spot an entire section dedicated to the early editions of some antique gems: Johann Coler's *Oeconomia Ruralis Et Domestica* (1645), Wolf Helmhardt von Hohberg's *Georgica Curiosa* (1687), the *Monumenta Boica* (1767).

In a navy blue button-down shirt and olive pants, the hefty scientist sinks into his ergonomic chair and folds his arms over his chest. We've exchanged a few emails, so he knows I'm interested in the origins of the beverage that consumes his life. But he's unsure why I've flown all the way to Munich just to speak with him. So he begins with a question.

"What is in your mind if you think about the brewing process?"

"I don't know." I hesitate, sensing I'm being set up. I flash to my refrigerator in Washington, D.C., stocked with a dozen IPAs from local breweries: Nanticoke Nectar, Double Duckpin, Surrender Dorothy. My favorite, Nimble Giant, has a cartoon hop drawn on the sixteen-ounce can. "I envision big copper vats of liquid. I think about malting and mashing and fermenting. I think about heat."

"Yes, that's what most people are thinking about. But that's modern. That's only since medieval times, when we started to brew beer—to *boil* beer," the expert begins, offering a quick tutorial on ancient brewing. He launches headfirst into the prehistory of the golden elixir occupying brightly colored bottles placed all around his office. And he stakes out a clear position on the long-running beer vs. bread debate that has been circling in the archaeological community for over six decades. Which one deserves the title of humanity's oldest biotechnology?

In 1953, J. D. Sauer from the University of Wisconsin's Department of Botany proposed the only sensible answer: beer. Unlike his colleague and leading scholar of Middle East prehistory, Robert Braidwood of the University of Chicago, Sauer believed that the Natufians—who lived in what is now Syria, Israel, and Jordan from about 13,000 to 9500 BC—brewed a primitive beer before they ever baked the first loaf of bread. The then recently unearthed sickles, mortars, and pestles had to be evidence of the Natufians' beer-making abilities.[2] Contrary to the prevailing view at the time, it was not man who domesticated wild grain, but the other way around. And according to Sauer, the first farmers did not lure the passing hunters and gatherers into their risky agricultural endeavor with a dry piece of stale bread. It must have been a mind-altering potion.

Zarnkow agrees, explaining why brewing is so much easier than baking. Turning unprocessed grain into bread takes a little bit of work. First, the grain has to be crushed in order to produce enough dough. Second, its hard protective coating has to be removed, because the kernels won't naturally break free of their casings during the harvest. And third, baking demands high temperatures. "That is one of the major mistakes people are making if they think about former beer-making. It doesn't necessarily have anything to do with heat. Just take the cereal and put it in water. That's it."

"And that will ferment?"

"Yes, the yeast is coming from your hand," replies the brewer.

"And there's really enough to kick-start the fermentation process?"

"Yeah, you have enough. If the yeast is active and vital enough, then fermentation will start. Because our body has an entire microbiome on the skin."

The beer vs. bread debate is highly charged, because it has implications for the very foundations of the world today. If beer really is the oldest biotechnology, it could very well be responsible for what archaeologists call "one of the most significant turning points in the history of mankind."[3] That sudden shift from hunting and gathering to a sedentary, community-based lifestyle known as the Neolithic or Agricultural Revolution.

We know the movement to domesticate our plants and animals began in the vicinity of the Fertile Crescent, sometime around 10,200 BC, as the Old Stone Age (Paleolithic) gave way to the New Stone Age (Neolithic). But we don't know why it happened. The transition to farming may have allowed us to pool knowledge and resources, leading the human family into the great urban civilizations that have flourished ever since, but it wasn't without some serious flaws. As the diet became less diverse and balanced, reduced to just "a few starchy crops," our overall health deteriorated. We grew noticeably shorter. And because of the crowded, unsanitary conditions that brought the former foragers into extended contact with each other and their filthy animals for the first time, parasites and infectious disease ran amok. Which is why historian Jared Diamond has referred to the Agricultural Revolution as "the worst mistake in the history of the human race."[4] For the tens of thousands of years of the Upper Paleolithic preceding it, we were tall, resilient, happy, and healthy. Why give that up?

For a steady supply of beer, of course. As Zarnkow has just argued, all you had to do was rip the crop out of the ground and steep it in some water. No crushing, no de-husking, no heat. If the brewing of beer really preceded the baking of bread, then the mysterious origins of the poorly understood Agricultural Revolution would be rewritten as the Beer Revolution. And for purposes of this investigation, it would finally put a barley-based potion like the *kukeon* in proper context. If prehistoric humans were drinking beer over twelve thousand years ago, then altered states of consciousness have played a much bigger role in the development of our species than previously acknowledged. And the beer of yesterday, we need to realize, was very different from the beer of today. Whatever made us abandon the caves for the cities would almost certainly have carried religious meaning, promoting beer from an everyday beverage to a sacrament. A sacrament that, by the time it got to Eleusis as a minty beer around 1500 BC, would have had an astoundingly long history behind it. Longer than ever thought possible.

The debate continues, but at least one reason why Zarnkow sides with Sauer over Braidwood is the recent scholarship of Brian Hayden, professor emeritus at Simon Fraser University.[5] In a twenty-first-century spin on Sauer's reasoning, Hayden highlights the "unusual efforts" expended by the Natufians to cultivate wild grains like einkorn and emmer wheat, some of the earliest domesticated crops in the Near East. Paleobotanical samples have been recovered from several Natufian sites that were located a good distance from the original source of the grains—in some cases, up to a hundred kilometers.[6] So the plants evidently held some kind of special value. According to Hayden's "feasting model," as the earliest agrarian settlements grew and competed for the manual labor needed to sustain them, whoever threw the best keg parties stood to gain a loyal following. Those who drink together, stick together. But not all prehistoric drinking was a recreational event.

Recently a team of researchers led by Stanford University lent some hard data to Sauer and Hayden's favorite theory. But in the process, they may have also unearthed the mysterious reason why our ancestors converted to the religion of brewing in the first place. As described in "Fermented beverage and food storage in 13,000 y-old stone mortars at Raqefet Cave, Israel: Investigating Natufian ritual feasting," published in the *Journal of Archaeological Science* in October 2018, archaeologist Li Liu examined three limestone mortars from a Natufian burial chamber in modern-day Mt. Carmel, just outside Haifa, Israel. Between 11,700 and 9700 BC, about thirty individuals were interred in the Raqefet Cave. The site features "clear indications" of ritual activity, complete with flower-lined graves and animal bones consumed during "funerary feasts."[7]

After collecting and analyzing the botanical residue from the mortars, Liu and her team identified a number of plants, including wild wheat and/ or barley (*Triticeae*), oats (*Avena* spp.), sedge (*Cyperus* sp.*)*, lily (*Lilium* sp.), flax (*Linum usitatissimum*), and various legumes. Some of the microremains were found to "exhibit distinctive damage features typical of malting," when the raw grain receives enough moisture to germinate, producing the enzymes needed for the brewing process. Others appeared hollowed out and

Field photo of a 13,000-year-old boulder mortar, apparently used to brew prehistoric beer at the Natufian burial site within the Raqefet Cave in Israel. *Dror Maayan. Courtesy of Dani Nadel, Zinman Institute of Archaeology, University of Haifa, Israel*

swollen, telltale signs of "gelatinization due to mashing," when the starch chains in the malt are broken down and the fermentable sugars released. For the Stanford team, the results are conclusive evidence that the stone mortars were used for brewing beer, "the earliest known experiment in making fermented beverages in the world."[8]

But at the Raqefet Cave this Stone Age brew was a craft recipe, "probably with legumes and other plants as additive ingredients." And instead of being passed around during a Natufian happy hour, the potion appears to have been something of a sacrament. Interestingly Liu says that the Natufians consciously incorporated this graveyard beer into their "mortuary rituals to venerate the dead," demonstrating "the emotional ties the hunter-gatherers had with their ancestors."[9]

Zarnkow hands me a hard copy of Liu's paper. He was reading it before I arrived. He notes the critical, missing piece of data. Evidence of malting and mashing is not necessarily evidence of fermentation. For that there are certain chemical signatures outside the paleobotanists' wheelhouse that are better detected by archaeological chemists. The primary indication of beer fermentation is a tough precipitate known as calcium oxalate, or beerstone. In modern brewing the residue is mainly just a headache, requiring intensive cleaning of aging tanks. But for an archaeological sleuth like Zarnkow, finding beerstone on sufficiently ancient brewing equipment could be the smoking gun that finally vindicates Sauer, proving that beer really is the oldest biotechnology in the world. And if calcium oxalate were discovered in a deeply spiritual setting like the Raqefet Cave, it would also establish a sacramental link, however delicate, between prehistoric beer and the psychoactive *kukeon* at Eleusis.

That's exactly what's happening at the site now famously referred to by the Smithsonian as "the world's first temple."[10] And Zarnkow is smack in the middle of a colossal mystery that is baffling archaeologists and historians the world over. Of all the extraordinary things about Göbekli Tepe in southeastern Turkey, the most extraordinary is the fact that it even exists. Nestled discreetly by the Syrian border, the massive stone sanctuary is just not supposed to be there. Rediscovered by the late Klaus Schmidt of the German Archaeological Institute in 1994, the temple has been confidently dated to the end of the last Ice Age—a stunning twelve thousand years ago, contemporaneous with the Natufians. But dozens of T-shaped pillars were erected at Göbekli Tepe, unlike the prehistoric sites in Israel. It is the earliest megalithic architecture in the world.

Some of the pillars weigh fifty tons and rise more than twenty feet in the air. They are arranged in circles referred to as "enclosures," with two central monoliths surrounded by rings of equally gigantic, freestanding limestone. While four such enclosures have been excavated to date, geophysical surveys have confirmed at least another sixteen still hidden underfoot. The main T-shaped pillars have been described by the current archaeological team as "positively human-like," with the T's representing shoulders or heads.[11] In low relief, spindly arms wrap around the sides of the stones; human hands with tapering fingers meet on the front, frozen above decorative belts. Schmidt once called them "very powerful beings," possibly ancestors or deities: "if gods existed in the minds of early Neolithic people, there is an overwhelming probability that the T-shape is the first known monumental depiction of gods."[12]

Sometime after 8000 BC, the entire complex was backfilled with gravel, flint tools, and bones—a prehistoric message in a bottle—which is why the site and its intricately carved pillars were so flawlessly preserved. And why Göbekli Tepe is now challenging all our assumptions about the hunters and gatherers who spearheaded the Agricultural Revolution, once thought incapable of such incredible feats of engineering. To put Göbekli Tepe in context, its megaliths predate Stonehenge by at least six thousand years. They predate the first literate civilizations of Egypt, Sumer, India, and Crete by even more. Unearthing this kind of Stone Age sophistication so deep in our past is like finding out your great-grandparents have been secretly coding apps and trading cryptocurrency behind everyone's back.

This once-in-a-century dig has turned the world of archaeology on its head. It was once thought that farming preceded the city, which in turn preceded the temple. God was supposed to come last, once our archaic ancestors had enough time on their hands to contemplate such impractical things. Schmidt's "cathedral on a hill," however, demonstrates the exact opposite.[13] Religion wasn't a by-product of civilization. It was the engine. And because of its location in that region of Upper Mesopotamia known as the "cradle of agriculture," Göbekli Tepe emerges as the catalyst of both farming and urbanization, the very things that drive the world today.[14] Oddly, the holy place shows no signs of permanent settlement itself. It was a pilgrimage destination. So if the architects of the temple didn't come to put down roots, why did they invest all their time and energy into the construction of this immense twenty-two-acre site in the first place? And why come back, on a seasonal basis, over the course of the sixteen hundred years that Göbekli Tepe was in use during the tenth and ninth millennia BC?

Like the Raqefet Cave, it has something to do with the afterlife. For his part Schmidt believed Göbekli Tepe was a sacred burial ground for a lost society of hunters—"the center of a death cult." The location, which means "Potbelly Hill" in Turkish and soars fifty feet above its environs, may have been consciously chosen. "From here the dead are looking out at the ideal view," Schmidt once remarked. "They're looking out over a hunter's dream."[15] In addition to the humanoid ancestors or gods, the pillars of the enclosures are carved with an array of realistic images in both high and low relief: foxes, boars, aurochs, snakes, scorpions, and hyenas. There are vultures, human heads, and decapitated bodies as well. It's the kind of iconography that is elsewhere associated with the de-fleshing of corpses and other bizarre burial rites from the Neolithic period.

At Göbekli Tepe the archaeological team sees unique evidence of a "skull cult": human crania with "repeated and substantial cutting" performed just after death. One such skull had a hole drilled into its left parietal bone, "the position of which was carefully chosen so that the skull might hang vertically and face forward when suspended."[16] The incised grooves may have

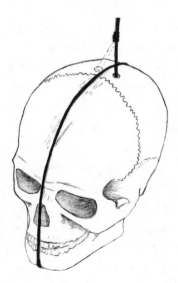

Reconstruction of how the skulls at Göbekli Tepe may have been displayed for ritual use. A cord would be inserted into the hole drilled into the top of the cranium, and then wrapped lengthwise around the skull along grooves of chiseled bone to stabilize the religious artifact.
Courtesy of Juliane Haelm (© Deutsches Archäologisches Institut, DAI)

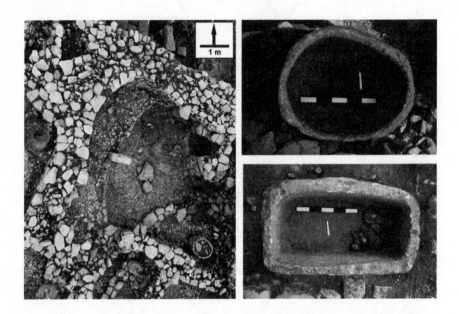

Two of the six limestone basins excavated from the archaeological site at Göbekli Tepe in Turkey. Vessels like this barrel (upper right) and trough (lower right) could have once accommodated up to 42 gallons of prehistoric beer. *K. Schmidt, N. Becker. Courtesy of Jens Notroff (© Deutsches Archäologisches Institut, DAI)*

prevented the cord that stabilized the skull from slipping, suggesting its use as an icon in what the team refers to as "ancestor veneration." And in keeping with the graveyard beer at the Raqefet Cave, "the world's first temple" may have also been the world's first bar.

In "The role of cult and feasting in the emergence of Neolithic communities. New evidence from Göbekli Tepe, south-eastern Turkey," published in the journal *Antiquity* in 2012, Zarnkow and the team from the German Archaeological Institute unveiled the results of their chemical analysis on the "grayish-black residues" found in six enormous limestone basins scattered throughout the site. Some are rounded like barrels, others more square like troughs. Dating to the ninth millennium and considered "static, integral parts of particular rooms," the barrels and troughs could accommodate forty-two gallons of liquid. Fragments of similar vessels have been found in all strata of Göbekli Tepe, testifying to their broad use in "large-scale feasting" with a "strong cultic significance."[17]

The archaeological team notes the "surprisingly large amount of animal bones" used to backfill the site, as well as the abundant grinders, mortars, and pestles dedicated to plant processing. Echoing Hayden's "feasting model," the excavators envision the sanctuary hosting "collective work events," complete with ritual dancing that might induce an "altered state of consciousness." And, of course, a graveyard beer to match the potion at the Raqefet Cave, perhaps allowing "ecstatic" communion with the ancestors.[18] Was Göbekli Tepe the scene of a drunken, skull-worshipping funeral feast? Was the whole point of humanity's first ritual beverage to facilitate what Julia Gresky of the German Archaeological Institute refers to as "the interaction of the living with the dead"?[19]

"I would say it's inconclusive," Zarnkow tells me, alluding to the promising but mixed results of his laboratory analysis. Using what's known as a Feigl spot test, the beer scientist added a drop of chemical reagent to various samples taken by the field team at Göbekli Tepe. When calcium oxalate is present, the residue changes color. In the first round, none of the samples tested positive. In the second, there was one signal indicating beerstone, followed by another two signals in the third round. "That's why we want to go there again," continues Zarnkow. Next time he wants to retrieve the residue for himself, just to be sure of no contamination within the limestone barrels and troughs. "You need really sterile conditions—absolutely sterile—when you take these samples. And this is ten thousand years ago! So it's really not that easy. But we just have to repeat the tests."

In the meantime the early results from the Raqefet Cave and Göbekli Tepe have introduced some state-of-the-art science to the beer versus bread debate. If further chemical analysis confirms the fermentation of beer in the Fertile Crescent, then it means the Agricultural Revolution was, in fact, the Beer Revolution. And civilization itself may have begun with a ritual potion. A sacrament fit for the first community-wide celebrations of the dead. Its intoxicating effects could have created a sense of cohesion among the living while establishing a mind-altering link to their ancestors. With a spiritual devotion to the grain, a shared notion of pilgrimage, and an apparent obsession with the afterlife, this prehistoric tradition from Anatolia in modern-day Turkey could very well have laid the groundwork for Eleusis, just west across the Aegean Sea. If this religion with no name really was the Stone Age inspiration for the Ancient Mysteries, it certainly wouldn't have had to travel very far.

All this raises the fascinating possibility that the graveyard beer of the Raqefet Cave and Göbekli Tepe was some kind of Stone Age precursor to the barley-based *kukeon*. Before the rediscovery by Klaus Schmidt, was Göbekli Tepe and its otherworldly ceremonies what Walter Burkert had in mind as the "prehistoric drug rituals" at the basis of Eleusis? Was this the "festival of immortality which, through the expansion of consciousness, seemed to guarantee some psychedelic Beyond"? If so, that leaves us with two burning questions: how did it survive thousands of years—in the total absence of the written word—from Neolithic Anatolia to Ancient Greece? And more important, where are the drugs?

Thanks to recent DNA analysis, an international team from the University of Washington, Harvard Medical School, and the Max Planck Institute for the Science of Human History may have actually answered the first question. The Stone Age inhabitants of Turkey did not just *influence* the Stone Age inhabitants of Greece. They *became* the Greeks. And the DNA evidence that now shows the biological relationship between the two people also suggests why the Anatolians were so popular with their immediate neighbors to the west. The age of the DNA signal happens to coincide with the very moment when the descendants of the first farmers in the Fertile Crescent started taking the family business overseas—not just into Greece, but into all of Europe.

It brings us right back to those mysterious Proto-Indo-Europeans I was discussing with Director Adam-Veleni in Athens. As we saw in chapter 3, Harvard's Calvert Watkins traced the striking similarities between the Eleusinian and Vedic rituals to a Proto-Indo-European source, all convincingly argued in his 1978 paper "Let Us Now Praise Famous Grains." If anybody was going to smuggle drugs into Europe, it was the Proto-Indo-Europeans who exported the *soma* to India—that Vedic elixir explicitly characterized by Watkins as "hallucinogenic." For some reason Western scholars are not so scandalized by the prospect of ancient Indians doing drugs. The eastern branch of our Indo-European family seems exotic and far-off, unconnected to our Greek foundations. But dig deeper, and the issue remains: where did *soma* come from? Why would the original sacrament of Western civilization make the long journey to the Himalayas, but somehow

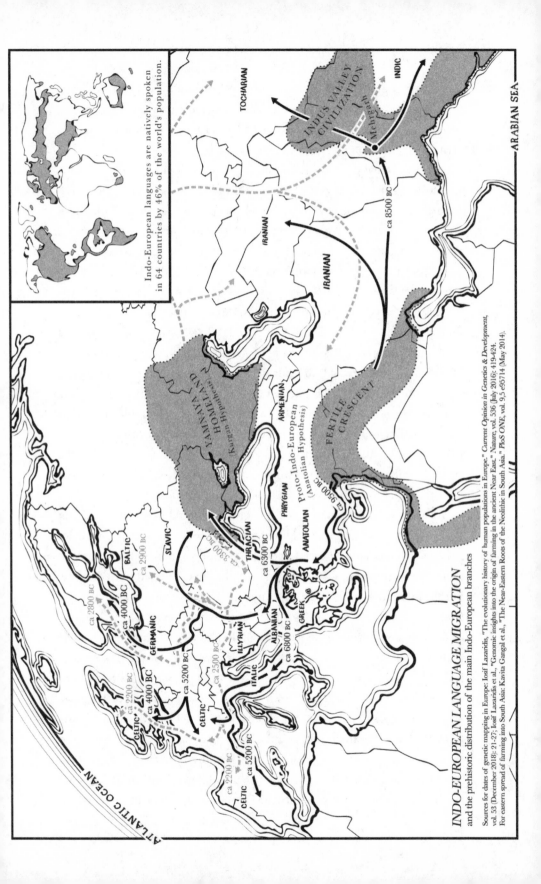

INDO-EUROPEAN LANGUAGE MIGRATION
and the prehistoric distribution of the main Indo-European branches

Indo-European languages are natively spoken in 64 countries by 46% of the world's population.

ATLANTIC OCEAN

ARABIAN SEA

INDUS VALLEY CIVILIZATION

INDIC

Mehrgarh

ca 8500 BC

TOCHARIAN

IRANIAN

IRANIAN

YAMNAYA LAND HOMELAND
Kurgan Hypothesis

FERTILE CRESCENT

ca 9500 BC

ARMENIAN

Proto-Indo-European
(Anatolian Hypothesis)

PHRYGIAN

ANATOLIAN

THRACIAN
ca 6300 BC

ca 3300 BC

SLAVIC

BALTIC
ca 2900 BC

GERMANIC
ca 4000 BC

ca 2800 BC

CELTIC*
ca 2200 BC
ca 4000 BC

CELTIC
ca 5200 BC

ca 2500 BC

ITALIC
ca 5200 BC

ILLYRIAN

ALBANIAN
ca 6800 BC

GREEK

CELTIC
ca 2200 BC
ca 5200 BC

Sources for dates of genetic mapping in Europe: Iosif Lazaridis, "The evolutionary history of human populations in Europe." *Current Opinion in Genetics & Development*,
vol. 53 (December 2018): 21-27; Iosif Lazaridis et al., "Genomic insights into the origin of farming in the ancient Near East," *Nature*, vol. 536 (July 2016): 419-424.
For eastern spread of farming into South Asia: Kavita Gangal et al., "The Near-Eastern Roots of the Neolithic in South Asia." *PloS ONE*, vol. 9,5 e95714 (May 2014).

get lost en route to Eleusis? If half of the Proto-Indo-European tradition went east into India, and the other half went west into Greece, then the common source of both could contain the answer to the whole psychedelic affair.

Everything hangs on the homeland.

Most linguists support the theory that places the genesis of the Proto-Indo-Europeans somewhere in the prehistoric steppes north of the Black and Caspian Seas, where southern Russia separates modern-day Ukraine and Kazakhstan. The nomadic tribe of pastoralists is thought to have broken away from this supposed homeland sometime after 4000 BC, very slowly sending waves of migrants east across Asia and west across Europe.[20] Another school of thought has spent the past three decades collecting evidence for a competing homeland, and a much older date for the diaspora. As part of his Anatolian Hypothesis, first published in 1987, the respected archaeologist Colin Renfrew of Cambridge University tried to pinpoint the actual mechanism that would have allowed the earliest Indo-Europeans to replace existing languages so successfully over such a wide geographic area, from Iceland to Siberia to Sri Lanka.[21] For Renfrew there had to be something in the earlier Neolithic period that sparked the initial, western spread of the richest family of languages in human history. There had to be a hook. His answer is what the British archaeologist terms "agricultural dispersal."

As early as 7000 BC the Stone Age growers would have begun sharing their expertise outside the only logical Proto-Indo-European homeland, Anatolia, where the wild and domesticated plants first met in the cradle of agriculture surrounding Göbekli Tepe. Rather than violently invading the European continent, these earliest Indo-Europeans may have fanned out from the Fertile Crescent with valuable knowledge to share. The technology of farming could have prompted a smoother, more sustainable process of acculturation. Wherever that technology was adopted in each "new ecological niche," according to the hypothesis, the mother tongue of Proto-Indo-European would have followed.[22] Perhaps that's how this extinct ur-language and its native death cult made the short hop over to the Lady of the Grain's territory, far earlier than most linguists are willing to accept.[23]

Greece has long boasted "the earliest farming settlements" in Europe, dating to about 6500 BC. Beyond that, however, not much was known about its prehistoric farmers. Until the DNA evidence came through, with a shocking result. In "Genetic origins of the Minoans and Mycenaeans," published in the prestigious journal *Nature* in 2017, an interdisciplinary team of thirty-four scientists and archaeologists across a range of specialties debuted the first genome-wide DNA sequence of Greece's Bronze Age inhabitants. As the first literate Europeans, the earliest Minoans are typically dated to the third millennium BC. Before the Mycenaeans followed them onto mainland Greece, the archaic residents of Crete have always been regarded as the oldest ancestors of the Greeks and Europeans at large. As it turns out, they're very old indeed. More than 75 percent of the DNA retrieved from nineteen ancient Minoan and Mycenaean specimens belonged to "the first Neolithic farmers" from Anatolia, who apparently began seeding Greece in the seventh millennium BC—four thousand years *earlier* than the traditional dating of the Minoans. The data matches Renfrew's Anatolian Hypothesis with amazing accuracy.[24] From their first stop in Greece, the Anatolians would then travel farther west. And by about 4000 BC, their DNA would be all over Europe.[25]

If the Proto-Indo-European homeland has been spotted at long last, then whatever sacrament came from Anatolia could be regarded as the likely source, however distant, for both the Greek *kukeon* and the Indian *soma*. Implausible as it seems, the Anatolian graveyard beer just might be the secret inspiration behind European civilization. If brewing was the cause of the Agricultural Revolution itself, then it also could have spawned the movement that forever replaced the hunters and gatherers of Europe with the city folk of today. It all happened between the seventh and fourth millennia BC. But why? In addition to the new technology of farming in general, maybe brewing was the *specific* mechanism by which the Proto-Indo-Europeans were able to entrance the entire European continent during the Neolithic period. As far as Ancient Greece is concerned, the latest archaeochemical evidence is crystal clear. Death cult potions were a bona fide reality. And they were being consumed in Greece exactly when the Mysteries landed in Eleusis.

A few weeks ago I had a long, productive phone call with Patrick McGovern, the director of the Biomolecular Archaeology Project at the University of Pennsylvania. Perhaps the most famous archaeological chemist in the world, McGovern was the one who recommended I catch the plane to Munich in the first place. The affable, bearded scientist has certainly earned his reputation as the "Indiana Jones of Extreme Beverages" and the "Lazarus of Libations." He still holds the record for the oldest undisputed identification of calcium oxalate.[26] That find came in the early 1990s, from a wide-mouthed fifty-liter jug unearthed at the Neolithic site of Godin Tepe in Iran, an historically significant trading post with links to the west among the Mesopotamian city-states of the Tigris-Euphrates Valley. The beerstone dated to as early as 3500 BC. The equivalent chemical signature for wine fermentation is tartaric acid. In 2017 McGovern would spot the earliest Eurasian evidence for that compound in Georgia, from around 6000 BC.[27] The chemistry doesn't get us back to Göbekli Tepe just yet, but it does confirm the general coordinates of what McGovern calls a Stone Age "hotbed of experimentation" in the area surrounding Göbekli Tepe.[28]

Beer can certainly ferment on its own, as Zarnkow just taught me. But it's quicker and easier in the presence of *Saccharomyces cerevisiae*, the yeast that commonly attaches to fruit and honey. As it evolved the graveyard beer

The pottery beer mug that once contained a Minoan ritual cocktail (left). The Golden Cup of Nestor unearthed from Grave Circle A at Mycenae (right). Both date to the sixteenth century BC, and testify to the prevalence of graveyard beer and other extreme beverages in the religious cults of the Minoans and Mycenaeans, the Bronze Age ancestors of the classical Greeks. LEFT: *Courtesy of the National Archaeological Museum, Ephorate of Antiquities—Argolid (© Hellenic Ministry of Culture and Sports)* RIGHT: *Courtesy of the National Archaeological Museum (© Hellenic Ministry of Culture and Sports)*

of the Raqefet Cave and Göbekli Tepe would have likely been combined with wine or mead, making for a stronger, and tastier, drink. Whenever the sacrament migrated from Anatolia, the archaeological chemistry has now proven that the Minoans and Mycenaeans definitely had a special brew on their hands, one with "a clear ceremonial and/or religious significance." And even if the Stone Age beer picked up some wine and mead along the way, it never left the graveyard behind.

In two experiments from the late 1990s, McGovern's laboratory proved there was a graveyard beer on both sides of the Aegean during the historical period, after writing finally entered Europe in the form of Linear B, the oldest deciphered evidence of written Greek.[29] First McGovern analyzed a "pottery beer mug," discovered along with the so-called Golden Cup of Nestor in Grave Circle A at Mycenae. Situated on the northeastern Peloponnese across the Saronic Gulf from Eleusis, the archaeological site excavated by Heinrich Schliemann dates to the sixteenth century BC, contemporaneous with the very beginning of the Mysteries. The mug was unearthed close to the citadel that is considered the palace of the legendary Agamemnon from Homer's epics. It tested positive for elements of a blended grog consisting of barley beer, grape wine, and honey mead. Because of a similar beverage he had recently identified on Crete in "incredibly large numbers" within "cultic contexts," McGovern called it a "Minoan ritual cocktail."[30]

Next McGovern spent two years testing a quarter of the 160 bronze vessels that had been recovered from a royal tomb in Gordium, the ancient capital of Phrygia in the Proto-Indo-Europeans' apparent homeland of Anatolia. The cauldrons, jugs, and drinking bowls were used in the eighth century BC as part of a ceremonial farewell, likely for King Midas's father, Gordias. The "intensely yellow" residues on the interior of the vessels were the remains of a ritual potion by which the deceased "was royally ushered into the afterlife," says McGovern, "to sustain him for eternity."[31]

In a first-of-its-kind analysis for a discipline that the archaeological chemist says "was still in its infancy," McGovern subjected sixteen samples to a battery of high-tech tools, including liquid chromatography tandem mass spectrometry (LC-MS/MS) and gas chromatography (GC), "using a thermal-desorption unit that captured low-molecular-weight volatile compounds." The results were a somewhat predictable mix of calcium oxalate (beer), tartaric acid (wine), and potassium gluconate (mead)—the same

"Minoan ritual cocktail" enjoyed by the Mycenaeans centuries earlier on the other side of the Aegean. In September 2000 McGovern teamed up with Sam Calagione of the Dogfish Head Brewery to resurrect the graveyard beer for mass consumption. Their re-creation, still available for purchase as Midas Touch, was unveiled at a drunken Anatolian funeral feast that the University of Pennsylvania hosted in Philadelphia at their Museum of Archaeology and Anthropology. The *kukeon* flowed through the evening, leaving my hometown with an ancient hangover.

Are these archaeochemical finds from Crete, Mycenae, and Anatolia the long-sought evidence that the same Proto-Indo-Europeans who birthed *soma* also exported a visionary drink west to Greece? Although he has not yet found an overt psychedelic signal in these samples, even McGovern himself has to wonder about the mind-altering punch of the Greek graveyard beer:

> *The pharmacological properties of this brew—whether analgesic or psychoactive is unclear, but certainly exceeding what can be attributed to a high alcohol content—is implied in the Nestor account, as well as elsewhere in Homer (e.g., when Circe changed Odysseus' companions into pigs with kykeon and a pharmaka in Odyssey 10:229-43). . . . The main point is that the mixed fermented beverage or "Minoan ritual cocktail," which has now been identified chemically, probably bears some relationship to the kykeon of Greek heroic times.[32]*

It's impossible to draw a straight line from Göbekli Tepe to Crete to Mycenae to Eleusis. Ten thousand years of labyrinthine history are not so easily resolved. But the chemical confirmation of a beer-based potion within a funerary context does potentially connect "the world's first temple" in Stone Age Anatolia to the "ritual cocktail" of the Minoans and Mycenaeans, not to mention King Midas—a staggering eight thousand years later. And the DNA data does establish some kind of continuity over the prehistoric millennia, with Renfrew's Anatolian Hypothesis as a strong candidate for the descendants of Göbekli Tepe's death cult spreading their Proto-Indo-European language on the backs of their botanical expertise and purported sacrament to Europe's oldest cities in Neolithic Greece.

But the million-dollar question I flew all the way to Munich just to ask Zarnkow remains to be discussed. Where are the drugs?

Was a low-alcohol, lukewarm Budweiser really to credit for the Agricultural Revolution? If the first farmers were drinking their crop instead of eating it, they probably had a good reason. The Stanford researchers determined that the brew at the Raqefet Cave was laced with other "additive ingredients." Is it possible one of the original graveyard beers in the Fertile Crescent was infused with a psychedelic secret? Or that it later developed, at some point in the many thousands of years separating the founders of the Eleusinian Mysteries from their Proto-Indo-European, Anatolian ancestors?

I show Zarnkow *The Road to Eleusis*. He's not familiar with it, so I introduce the psychedelic hypothesis as best I can, emphasizing the vision universally attested at the site. I relate how the Lady of the Grain turns down wine when Queen Metaneira offers a refreshment to the parched goddess. Despite the "ritual cocktail" of beer, wine, and mead thriving among the Minoans and Mycenaeans, Demeter was a purist. The *Hymn to Demeter* has the goddess demanding a drink whose ingredients—barley, water, and mint—read like a simple recipe for beer. The scientist agrees.

"The more I read your and McGovern's research," I disclose, "the more I started seeing alcohol as a potential vehicle for keeping alive these prehistoric mystery traditions, in the sense of a religious sacrament. So whether or not the beer existed at Göbekli Tepe, we know a brewing tradition enters Greece at a very early date, maybe even before wine. And that it came from the east.[33] The hypothesis from Wasson, Hofmann, and Ruck is that the naturally occurring fungus ergot, derived from barley, would have potentiated the *kukeon*."

I have a hard time translating "ergot"—a funny word, even in English. So Zarnkow googles the term on his desktop computer and starts scrolling through the first images on the screen. "Ah, yeah," he groans, instantly recognizing the infestation. "That's LSD."

"Wow. How do you know that?"

"It's *purpureum*," adds Zarnkow, citing the Latin word for "purple" or "blackish" and the color of ergot's darkened sclerotium, the slender, hardened mass that protrudes from the grain like a horn or spur. Hence the fungus's modern classification: *Claviceps purpurea*. "That's dangerous for us. We have to really look out for that. It's a good thing that it's black, and has another density and size. So we can separate it from the grain in the brewing.

If we steep it in the beginning of the malting process, it will float. Ergot is *absolutely* common. In German, we call it *Mutterkorn* (mother corn)."

Zarnkow reminds me that here in the beer capital of the world, there are actually a lot of words for ergot in German. Albert Hofmann, the father of LSD, included several in *The Road to Eleusis*, testifying to the parasite's age-old relationship with grains: *Rockenmutter, Afterkorn, Todtenkorn,* and *Tollkorn.* Even as a young boy the Swiss chemist would have been exposed to the rich legends about ergot that survived in Central Europe. As it turns out, his ergot hypothesis wasn't so far-fetched for someone whose native language has multiple words for the deadly fungus that no brewer can afford to ignore. "In German folklore, there was a belief that, when the corn waved in the wind," Hofmann once wrote, "the corn mother (a demon) was passing through the field, her children were the rye wolves (ergot)." Hofmann thought the word *Tollkorn* (mad grain), in particular, demonstrated a "folk awareness" of the "psychotropic effects of ergot"—"deeply rooted in European traditions."[34]

"Do you think there's a possibility that ancient beer contained some of the bad stuff you don't want in there, the LSD?" I ask Zarnkow. "What if the people at Eleusis, and their prehistoric ancestors, included it on purpose . . . to induce this famous vision?"

"In principle, I would believe that. Because it is impossible to have sterile conditions on the fields. *Mutterkorn* still happens. Today it's easy to separate. But before it was not so easy. And in addition to the *Mutterkorn,* we have these micro-organisms on the surface of the cereals as well. They have an influence on *every* attribute of the grain. These things are producing vitamins, inhibitors, acids, and enzymes. For example, in Egypt they found a skeleton with lots of antibiotics in the bones. One theory is they were coming from the beer, from barley, which was contaminated by different fungi."

Zarnkow is referring to the study published in the *American Journal of Physical Anthropology* in 2010 and reported in the popular media under such entertaining headlines as "Ancient Brewmasters Tapped Drug Secrets" and "Take Two Beers and Call Me in 1,600 Years."[35] Under fluorescent microscopy the ancient Nubian bones dating from AD 350 to 500 revealed the presence of tetracycline, which is produced by the fungi-resembling bacteria Streptomyces (which means "twisted mushroom" in Greek). Way before the discovery of streptomycin, the first antibiotic used to treat tuberculosis in the 1940s, lead researcher George Armelagos from Emory University tied the Nubians' use of tetracycline to their uniquely crafted beer: "Streptomyces produce a golden colony of bacteria, and if it was floating on a batch of beer, it must have looked pretty impressive to ancient people who revered gold."[36] Believing "the complex art of fermenting antibiotics was probably widespread in ancient times, and handed down through generations," Armelagos added, "I have no doubt that they knew what they were doing."[37]

But Zarnkow is convinced, of course, that the biotechnology associated with brewing goes back a lot further than Egypt. "And that's why I say the oldest pets of human beings are not dogs, but the lactic acid bacteria in the yeasts," he informs me. "We domesticated a lot of things by accident in former times. But we did not know there was a very, very small organism. It was Louis Pasteur, only a hundred fifty years ago, who told us. And it's not only an enzyme, or a group of enzymes. There's a cell wall surrounding it, making it an organism. And this organism is called yeast."

The same ingenuity that managed to develop any number of yeasts and antibiotics in our deep past could have also fashioned a hallucinogenic beer. It was perhaps no different from the psychedelic beers known as gruit ales that were being cooked up under the auspices of the Catholic Church in the many years preceding the Protestant Reformation. The Purity Law that was promulgated right here at the Weihenstephan brewery in 1516 was not about what to *include* in the beer, but what to *exclude*.

Up until the sixteenth century, the local beer was a complex blend of plants, herbs, and spices—"its composition being a mystery for the common people, and in any event a trade secret for the privileged manufacturer."[38] Before being strictly limited to its three essential parts—barley, water, and hops—beer of the era was a "highly intoxicating" recipe, "narcotic, aphrodisiacal, and psychotropic when consumed in sufficient quantity." Some have used the word "hallucinogenic."[39] The gruit trade meant big money, and the Catholic Church enforced "a veritable ecclesiastical monopoly" on its taxable cash cow.[40] It is probably no coincidence that the Purity Law came into being just before the German theologian Martin Luther was excommunicated by the Catholic Church in 1520, further inciting the Reformation. At its core the Bavarian push for tax-free hops was a spiritual protest against the perceived greed and self-indulgence of the Vatican's clergy and their drugged beer.[41] Eventually the Bavarian revolt won the day, making the innocent hop (*Humulus lupulus*) the only socially acceptable additive now servicing the global beer industry. But before that, perhaps as far back as the Stone Age, beer was a wild ride.

"I never tasted *Mutterkorn*," admits the scientist, "but I know it's very, very dangerous. And you can get really crazy. We had a lot of problems with that in medieval times."

"Right—the ergot poisoning of St. Anthony's Fire. They called it the *ignis sacer*: the 'holy fire' that caused the seizures and hallucinations."

"But these guys were professionals," continues Zarnkow, referring to the prehistoric brewers, "and the ones who knew about medicines and such things could do a controlled contamination of *Mutterkorn*. So if we've had beers for feasting, and beers for medicine, why not this special type of drink? I totally believe we've had beers like that before."

He goes on to compare the ergot of a psychedelic *kukeon* to modern-day koji, the *Aspergillus oryzae* fungus used in Japan to ferment soybeans and rice, producing soy sauce and the alcoholic *sake*. When properly monitored and harvested, the creative applications of fungi, antibiotics, and other micro-organisms—humanity's "first pets"—are seemingly endless. Their symbiotic relationship with grain was already locked in place from the very beginning of the apparent Beer Revolution thirteen thousand years ago.

Ever since the Anatolian funeral feast at the University of Pennsylvania in 2000, we have gained unprecedented insight into the extreme beverages of Ancient Greece and the prehistoric reach of the graveyard beer that may have inspired the Mysteries, or perhaps Western civilization at large. We know for a chemical fact that a Greek brew was circulating around the ancient Aegean. Because of recent analyses at the Raqefet Cave and Göbekli Tepe, there is strong data to suggest that elixir had Stone Age roots. And I now have it on good authority from the world's preeminent beer scientist, here in the heart of Bavaria, that ancient brewmasters could very well have concocted a psychedelic potion spiked with ergot. But it's gotten us no closer to a definitive answer at Eleusis. If none of Kalliope Papangeli's vessels at the archaeological site in Greece can be tested, we may never know the actual contents of the *kukeon*.

With the sky blackening and the rain unchanged from when I arrived, Zarnkow kindly drops me off at the Freising train station. He directs me straight to Augustiner-Bräu, the oldest independent brewery in Munich, founded in 1328, where I've been instructed to try the Edelstoff lager. About an hour later, I'm plopped onto the wooden barstool in the packed dining room, still shivering from the bitter cold. As I sip the golden helles from a fat German beer stein, one name keeps coming to my mind.

Triptolemus.

The royal demigod, personally dispatched by the Lady of the Grain to civilize the Mediterranean. According to the *Hymn to Demeter*, he was supposed to teach the art of agriculture to all humankind. But we know from the DNA and material evidence that farming had already spread across Europe thousands of years before the erection of Demeter's temple at Eleusis. People already knew how to tend the land. So what was his real job?

The Eumolpids and Kerykes, the hereditary officiants who controlled the Mysteries and collected their clerical dues from the start, probably didn't like it, but Triptolemus took off on his flying dragon cart for what Ruck calls a "proselytizing mission." For those pilgrims who could afford it, the journey to Eleusis could always happen over the two thousand years of the site's activity. But for those who could not, there had to be alternatives. After the conquests of Alexander the Great, the Hellenic influence over the ancient world stretched from modern-day Spain in the west to Afghanistan in the east. Any Greek speaker would have been welcomed into the Mysteries, but the distance for some was simply prohibitive. So maybe it wasn't the grain that was the focus of Triptolemus's roaming lesson, but what *grows* on the grain. And how the ergot and humanity's "first pets" could be manipulated through Zarnkow's "controlled contamination" to deliver a potion that promised immortality. If brewing really is the oldest biotechnology on the planet, and if potentially fatal hallucinogens were in the mix, then it would have taken highly trained specialists to pass that skill along.

If the *kukeon* made it outside the sacred precinct in Eleusis, then hard archaeobotanical evidence of the ritual drink should have survived somewhere in the vast Greek-speaking world of the ancient Mediterranean. And if Wasson, Hofmann, and Ruck were right about ergot as the active ingredient, then there should be evidence of that too. Nothing less will settle the vicious debate about the best-kept secret in the history of Western civilization. For centuries all the professionals on the relentless hunt for the *kukeon* have come up empty-handed. No stone left unturned. But if Heinrich Schliemann, Milman Parry, or Michael Ventris left any legacy with their brilliant, paradigm-changing discoveries, it's that the professionals aren't always looking in the right place.

Or speaking the right language.

No matter how advanced your Ancient Greek, if something turns up at an archaeological site in a remote corner of the Mediterranean with a shunned modern language, the professionals might never hear about it. Nor the public, for that matter. Sometimes the evidence has to just sit there, waiting twenty years for somebody to take notice.

7

The *Kukeon* of Catalonia

As I approach the Benedictine Abbey of Sant Pere de Galligants, I pause to enjoy the February sun breaching the cypress trees and reflecting off the bright limestone ashlars of the rectangular façade. Under a grand rosette the church's main entrance features five archivolts that recess into the medieval darkness. Where they meet spiraling columns a few feet overhead, stone gargoyles beckon me into the chilly, damp interior. Here in Girona, an hour and a half up the Spanish coast from Barcelona, construction of this Romanesque building began in 1131.[1] The local branch of the Archaeological Museum of Catalonia chose this picturesque landmark as its home in 1857. I would later learn that a scene from *Game of Thrones* was shot here, which makes sense in retrospect.[2] The whole monastery looks like something out of a fable—the perfect venue to come face-to-face with some very old secrets.

It is excruciatingly difficult to track down hard, undisputed evidence of hallucinogenic beer in the Mediterranean during the life of the Mysteries (ca. 1500 BC to AD 392). But after years of searching, and months of poring over a neglected monograph in the world's largest library back home in Washington, D.C., I'm finally closing in on the mother lode.

Ever since my meeting with Martin Zarnkow in Germany, I've been emailing with Dr. Enriqueta Pons, the former head of this museum and longtime director of excavations at an archaeological site thirty minutes to the north called Mas Castellar de Pontós. From 450 to 400 BC, Greek colonists built the oldest structures on the ancient complex that rises above the Empordá Plain on a grassy plateau, seventeen kilometers from the coast of modern-day Empúries. The Ancient Greeks called it Emporion, founded in 575 BC by pioneers from the Anatolian port city of Phocaea in Ionia, the western coast of modern-day Turkey. Experts in long-distance trade, these same Phocaeans—the so-called "Vikings of Antiquity"—first established Massalia (now Marseille in France) around 600 BC.[3] And after Emporion, they would move on to Elea (now Velia in southern Italy) around 530 BC.

The Greek Vikings appear to have gotten along well with the indigenous Iberian community, the Indigetes, who liked the exotic goods that their new, seafaring friends brought from the east. For their part the Phocaeans won another, important foothold in the ever-growing network of colonies here in the western Mediterranean.[4] They were an intensely spiritual people. Not surprisingly, religion shows up in Emporion from the very beginning.

In antiquity the city was known for its temple dedicated to Artemis of Ephesus, which has yet to be excavated. A cult statue of Asclepius, the Greek god of healing and drugs, has survived from his ancient sanctuary. The Pentelic and Parian marble, which could only have been imported from the Greek homeland, stands proudly in the Archaeological Museum of Empúries. Several *drachma,* or Greek coins, have been recovered from the area as well. From the third century BC, they show the head of Persephone.

A drachma found in the Greek colony of Emporion, dating to the third century BC. Surrounded by dolphins, the head of Persephone (left) and a Pegasus (right), emblematic of ecstatic flight. The symbols held sacred meaning for the seafaring Phocaeans, the Vikings of Antiquity from Anatolia, and their main trading partners in Carthage in North Africa. *Anna Hervera. Courtesy of Soler y Llach SL*

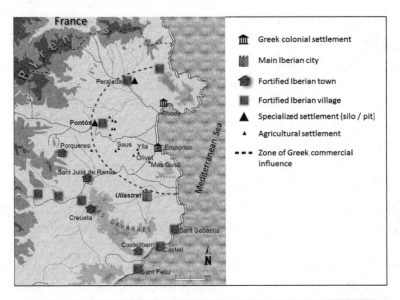

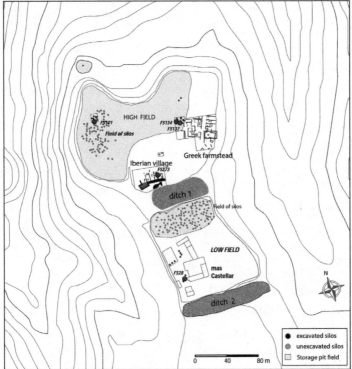

Map of Greek influence in Catalonia, radiating from the main Ancient Greek colonies of Emporion and Rhodes in northeastern Spain (above). Site plan of the archaeological works at Mas Castellar de Pontós (below). *Courtesy of Enriqueta Pons*

In 2008 a ceramic *kernos* was unearthed during ongoing excavations. It is a colonial variation of the very same vessels that were used to mix the *kukeon*, now on display in the Archaeological Museum of Eleusis. The Empúries *kernos* has three cups topping a circular base and dates back to the fifth century BC. The curators believe the discovery of many such vessels in this region of Spain is intriguing evidence of an ancient mystery cult linked to Demeter and Persephone.[5]

At some point, elements of this Phocaean religion traveled inland to Mas Castellar de Pontós, where echoes of the Eleusinian Mysteries intensify. Following the original Greek settlement in the fifth century BC, the indigenous Iberians added a fortified outpost in the early fourth century. Thereafter, what Pons calls a "Hellenistic farmstead" dominated the site under heavy Greek influence, flourishing from about 250 to 180 BC, when it was likely destroyed by the Romans. The three phases of occupation—Greek colonists, Iberian villagers, and Hellenistic farmers—are clear from Pons's systematic excavations that began in 1990.[6]

Over the past thirty years she has unearthed a number of subterranean grain silos framing a "densely urbanized" housing complex that sits at the top of a large, open field surrounded by woods. Though much of the six-acre site remains unexplored, Pons's surveys indicate as many as twenty-five hundred silos still underground. She concludes "the settlement acted as a place for the concentration, distribution, and trading of agricultural surpluses."[7] Like the bustling import-export business over at Emporion, or the massive grain silo that Kalliope Papangeli showed me on the archaeological site of Eleusis fifteen hundred miles to the east, Mas Castellar de Pontós made a fitting home for the Lady of the Grain and her daughter, the Queen of the Dead.

As a matter of fact, the links between the Greek farm and Eleusis are hard to avoid. In one of the excavated silos, numbered 101, Pons discovered the disembodied terra-cotta head of a female deity.[8] The face is cocked slightly to the right, her hair pulled back in a bun. Deposited with her was an *unguentarium,* or oil container, which is elsewhere associated with graveyards. The vestiges of a firepit were identified, with three different types of wood: silver fir, oak, and Scotch pine. Each of the species grows in the mountains, some distance from the archaeological site. Mixed in with the trees were the remains of olive, millet, and barley. Together with the ritual items, Pons

Terra-cotta head of Demeter or Perse-phone (top left); field photo of nine Greco-Italic amphoras (bottom left); and ceramic incense burner (*thymiateria*) of a Greek goddess (top right). *Courtesy of M. Solé.* All were excavated from the archaeological site at Mas Castellar de Pontós, and all date to the third century BC. *Courtesy of Enriqueta Pons and Museu de Arqueologia de Catalunya-Girona*

found a treasure trove of artifacts, all dating to the third century BC, includ-ing nine Greco-Italic amphoras. The terra-cotta goddess and oil container appear to have been intentionally buried in the silo as an offering to the underworld, leading Pons to identify the head as Demeter or Persephone (sometimes called Kore). The archaeologist says the cave-like silo, once used to stockpile grain, had been converted into a sacred subterranean chamber. It is strangely reminiscent of the hollowed-out rock shelter below the Greek Orthodox Church overlooking the ruins of Eleusis, where Persephone was said to emerge from Hades during the reenactment of the Mysteries.

Two related finds only further confirm the connection to Eleusis. In another silo, numbered 28, five ceramic *thymiateria,* or incense burners, were unearthed in 1979. One of them has been perfectly restored, showing the bust of a female deity. Dated to the third century BC, the artifact shows a woman's face centered between fins on either side of the vessel, the top of which is a shallow basket for capturing incense.[9] Pons identifies the goddess as Demeter, though Persephone cannot be ruled out. In addition, some relationship between Mas Castellar de Pontós and the Mysteries seems all but certain from the discovery of a *kalathos,* or Greek storage vessel, at the nearby site of Sant Julià de Ramis, just north of Girona. Dating from 225 to 175 BC, the ceramic is cracked and damaged, but the iconographic relief projecting from its surface is well preserved. Under a handle on the right, a woman's head emerges from the side of the vessel. She too is likened to Demeter or Persephone, mainly because of the figure who straddles a flying dragon cart to her left.

It's the same Triptolemus on the same winged, snake-drawn chariot that I saw during my visit to the Archaeological Museum of Eleusis. No different

Ceramic storage vessel (*kalathos*) showing the divine missionary of the Mysteries, Triptolemus, riding his winged chariot of flying serpents. Compare with the marble relief of Triptolemus from Eleusis (page 86) and the red-figure *skyphos* of Triptolemus from Capua, Italy (page 87). *Courtesy of Museu de Arqueologia de Catalunya-Girona*

from the Triptolemus pictured on the British Museum *skyphos* from Capua, Italy. What is he doing here in Spain?

Images of Demeter's royal missionary are, of course, common in Greece. And relics of Greek mystery cults in that part of southern Italy known as Magna Graecia (Great Greece) are not unusual at all. Ever since the eighth century BC, the region was the main target of Ancient Greek colonization.[10] But Spain? That's another thing altogether. If Kalliope Papangeli hung this Iberian Triptolemus next to her Greek Triptolemus in Eleusis, no one would believe it came from a world away. How did the vessel end up here, on the secluded shores of the Greek-speaking world? Does it mean the Mysteries, or some local interpretation thereof, were really celebrated this far from Eleusis?

It's a question most classicists aren't even trained to ask. Aside from Magna Graecia, the Ancient Greek frontier settlements are woefully neglected in the traditional curriculum. I never even heard of Emporion or Mas Castellar de Pontós until I picked up the hunt for Greek-inspired graveyard beers around the Mediterranean. Why look beyond Greece when you could spend a lifetime reading the overwhelming amount of literature produced during the Golden Age of Athens? Understandably, that's where the focus of education and scholarship lands. But it comes at a terrible cost. For a secret as intractable as Eleusis, we need to think outside the box and explore every nook and cranny of the ancient world. Fortunately a handful of classicists are at least open to the possibility that southern Italy wasn't the only rich environment for potential initiates of the Mysteries.

Though she doesn't write about Mas Castellar de Pontós in any detail, Dr. Denise Demetriou at the University of California, San Diego, does describe Emporion as both a "major economic center" and a "multiethnic environment," whose "very existence stimulated cross-cultural interactions with the indigenous populations."[11] As with other axes of trade and commercial activity across the former Greek-speaking Mediterranean, a "peculiar mixture" of religious influences in Catalonia was only natural. Far from Athens, it would make the ideal home for experimentation and, just maybe, the revelation of the *kukeon*'s psychedelic recipe that the officials in Eleusis tried so hard to protect. According to Demetriou, religion in a cosmopolitan capital like Emporion was "more flexible" than back home in Greece, which meant the "usual exclusivity of cult" wasn't always so strictly enforced. She points to Delphi and Olympia as examples of "open-access sanctuaries," where visits by the inexperienced would be facilitated by special liaisons.[12]

If Mas Castellar de Pontós was an open-access sanctuary, then the Mysteries of Eleusis would have been the most logical rites over which the Greeks and the locals would have found common ground. According to classicist François de Polignac, underworld cults like Demeter's, with her "agrarian or even funerary connotations," had a universal quality. Like the prehistoric skull cult from Anatolia, the Mysteries promised "a temporary return to a more primitive life and a period before the establishment of the city." For their part, the mother-daughter duo of Demeter and Persephone offered "a familiar face" to the locals who might have known them by another name.[13] In order to initiate the homesick Greeks or the curious Cat-

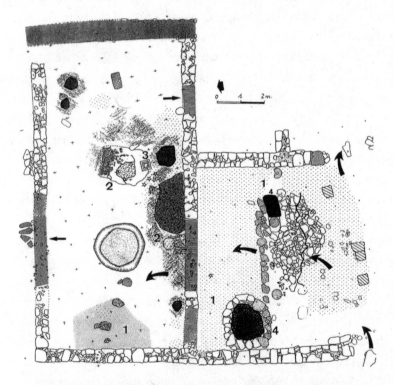

Detail of the domestic chapel (Room 3) and adjoining rooms at Mas Castellar de Pontós. 1. Areas for domestic activity, including grain processing and beer brewing. 2. Areas for ritual activity. 3. Location of the altar of Pentelic marble. 4. Homemade oven. *Courtesy of Enriqueta Pons*

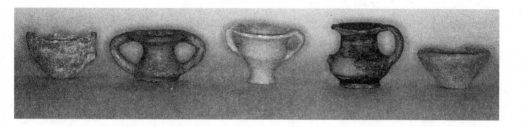

Five miniature vessels unearthed at Mas Castellar de Pontós. *Courtesy of Enriqueta Pons and Museu de Arqueologia de Catalunya-Girona*

alonians into the secrets of Eleusis, however, a dedicated sanctuary would have been integral to the ritual experience.

As it turns out, that's exactly what Dr. Enriqueta Pons uncovered.

By 1997 she had already made excellent progress on the residential area of the Greek farm. A main street cuts down the middle, separating two living quarters on either side. One of the larger units measures almost 250 square feet and is described by Pons as a "domestic chapel" for an "agrarian cult." Located in a private home, the chamber was managed by women and equipped for domestic activities. But it was also designed to become the scene of initiation rituals, where Demeter or Persephone might appear to the devotees, along with their departed ancestors. The archaeologist calls it a "shared space" for the human to come into contact with the divine, or the dead to speak to the living. The methods by which this lost mystery cult would communicate with the underworld can be fairly well reconstructed from the material finds.

In the very center of the room Pons discovered a large, rectangular hearth. She uses the Greek word *eschara* (ἐσχάρα). The burnt bones of three female dogs were found in a circular clay-coated ditch, over six feet in diameter. Pieces of an elegantly carved column of Pentelic marble, complete with an Ionic capital, were reassembled to form a two-foot altar. On top, a rectangular cavity, charred by flames, showed signs of knife and axe cuttings— evidence of "bloody sacrifice." Like the statue of Asclepius in Empúries, the expensive marble was proven by petrographic analysis to have originated at the Mount Pentelicus quarry outside Athens.[14] Interestingly, ten miniature chalices were scattered all over the chapel and adjoining rooms.[15] And two mills were unearthed along with crockery, not only for the grinding and cooking of grain, but also for the brewing of a very special beer.

All together, Pons interprets the "domestic chapel" as a holy place where dog sacrifice was combined with ceremonial purifications and ritual drinking. Elsewhere in Bronze Age Iberia, the archaeologist notes that "dogs were often buried in graves as part of the grave goods."[16] In Ancient Greece, dogs were also associated with the afterlife, where they marked the three distinct phases of the immortal journey: "the passage from life to death," "the time spent in the Underworld," and "the return to life as a spirit."[17] The most famous hellhound was Cerberus, the three-headed dog who belonged to Hecate.[18] As the mother of Circe and patron goddess of witchcraft, Hecate had a number of canine epithets: the "dog consumer" (kunosphages/κυνοσφαγής), the "dog leader" (kunegetis/κυνηγέτης), the "dog lover" (philoskulax/φιλοσκύλαξ), and the "black bitch" (kuon melaina/κύων μέλαινα). Canine sacrifices in her honor were common in Ancient Greece.[19] But Hecate also had a profound relationship to the Mysteries. In the *Hymn to Demeter*, Hecate, with her "blazing torches," is the only goddess who aids Demeter on the desperate search for her missing daughter. And she alone can accompany Persephone through the land of the dead.[20]

Trying to figure out what it all meant, Pons continued her rigorous work on the peculiar "domestic chapel" for years. She is a native Catalan speaker, so most of her finds are first published in the language that is a source of great pride among the fiercely autonomous Catalonians. The people who gave the world Antoni Gaudí and Salvador Dalí unilaterally declared their independence from Spain in a 2017 referendum that landed a dozen Catalonian political leaders in jail. As their public trial gets under way during my visit, protests and demonstrations are erupting all over Spain.[21] Throughout her career, Pons's unwavering decision to write in Catalan has been a rebellious act that puts her scholarship at serious risk of being ignored by the global academic community, where the *lingua franca* in Classics, history, and archaeology is English, French, or German. Even among the Romance languages, Catalan is only the sixth most spoken, trailing behind Spanish, Portuguese, French, Italian, and Romanian.

In an effort to bring some attention to this Greek colony in the backcountry of Catalonia, Pons finally relented. In 2010 she published a brief article about the dog sacrifice in a French journal, followed in 2016 by a longer treatment in English, which became one chapter in a book organized by the State University of New York (SUNY). There the archaeologist details

Bell-shaped *krater* excavated from silo 137 at Mas Castellar de Pontós, dating to the end of the fifth century BC. Four male figures are marching along in the mystical parade dedicated to Dionysus known as the *komos*. Several carry magical staffs and torches. A bearded man (second from left) with a garland of ivy is playing the lyre. *Courtesy of Enriqueta Pons and Museu de Arqueologia de Catalunya-Girona*

the results of excavations on additional underground silos. In one case (silo 137) "numerous drinking vessels" were unearthed, suggesting a "celebration consisting of a collective banquet."[22] It harkens back to Brian Hayden's "feasting model" from the last chapter. Ever since the Stone Age, those who drink together, stick together. But there's also a spiritual aspect here. Mixed in with the charred barley and animal remains was a spectacular bell-shaped *krater,* or vase, featuring a *komos:* the ritualistic nocturnal procession named after the son and cupbearer of Dionysus. More appropriate for an Athenian dining room than a subterranean chamber in ancient Catalonia, this *krater* shows the God of Ecstasy as the guest of honor at this drunken parade.

Looking back over the past thirty years of Pons's excavations, the intersection of the Eleusinian Mysteries and Mas Castellar de Pontós is overpowering: the twenty-five hundred grain silos; the terra-cotta head and incense burner depicting Demeter/Persephone; the ceramic vessel of their chief missionary,

Triptolemus; the drunken symposium on the Dionysian vase; abundant evidence of underworld offerings and dog sacrifice within the "domestic chapel" and subterranean pits, all closely related to the goddesses' sidekick, Hecate. The entire Eleusinian cast of characters is in attendance. Strangely, I didn't know about any of it when I reached out to Pons in November 2018. The only reason I contacted her in the first place was to make sure my Catalan wasn't playing tricks on me. Did she really find archaeobotanical evidence of a psychedelic beer? And why did no one else who was supposed to know such things ever hear about it? Not Zarnkow or McGovern. Not Fritz Graf or any of the top-notch classicists I had been consulting for years. Not even Ruck.

Unlike her work on the canine ritual, Pons's potential bombshell was never published in any of the mainstream academic journals for English, French, or German speakers. Many months before landing here in Catalonia, I came across her obscure discovery only by accident, in the course of my slow, tedious, and often discouraging hunt for hard data on hallucinogenic graveyard beers in the ancient Mediterranean. *That* research took years in itself, and always felt like a blind alley. But I pressed on. Because just when I was about to lose hope, the faintest pattern began to emerge. And for some inexplicable reason, all the clues kept leading in the same direction.

Spain.

There was the intriguing find at Eberdingen-Hochdorf, a Celtic settlement southeast of Stuttgart dating to the fifth and fourth centuries BC. From soil samples, the eminent archaeobotanist Hans-Peter Stika, of the University of Hohenheim, identified seeds of the vision-inducing henbane (*Hyoscyamus niger*), together with germinated hulled barley grains. It suggested a psychedelic brew, especially since the same henbane would later be used in the pre-Reformation hallucinogenic gruit ales in the same region of Germany. But the combination and consumption of the two ingredients, barley and henbane, could not necessarily be proven. Writing in 2010, Stika ultimately thought a henbane-infused beer was pure speculation.[23] But it's a reasonable avenue of pursuit.

Pliny credited the appearance of henbane to Hecate's pet, Cerberus, from whose urine the plant first sprung from the earth. The Greek naturalist referred to the plant as "Herba Apollinaris" (herb of Apollo), claiming that the Pythia

priestesses at Delphi inhaled the smoke of smoldering henbane seeds to produce their oracular visions. Another ancient term for the species, Pythonion,
cements the connection.[24] So add henbane to the barley meal and laurel leaves
discussed earlier as one more psychedelic candidate for the magic at Delphi.

Henbane is a member of the Solanaceae family, which, in addition to
the more familiar tomato, potato, and tobacco, also includes mandrake
(*Mandragora officinarum*), deadly nightshade (*Atropa belladonna*), and black
nightshade (*Solanum nigrum*). The so-called nightshades are among the most
poisonous plants in Europe. Starting with Hecate and the Pythia in Ancient
Greece, they became so synonymous with black magic in the Middle Ages
and Renaissance that, even through the nineteenth century, the nightshades
were still "easily anthropomorphized as witches and whores."[25] They were
also regarded as the key psychedelic ingredients of the witches' flying ointments that we will review in the next part of this investigation.

After the henbane lead, I came across three intriguing reports from
Spain, all from the early 2000s, and all published in either Spanish or Catalan. First, a ritual pit at Prats in Andorra, the tiny country between France
and Spain, turned up archaeochemical evidence of calcium oxalate, or beerstone, in several ceramic pots. In addition the researchers discovered an unidentifiable species of "mushroom wrapped in fern fronds" and eight seeds
of jimson weed (*Datura stramonium*).[26] Like its sister nightshades, jimson
weed contains a number of visionary and potentially fatal tropane alkaloids:
atropine, scopolamine, and hyoscyamine.[27] An intriguing find, but the site
dated far too early (1600 BC) for Greek colonization.[28]

The second report pushed the clock back even further. The alkaloid hyoscyamine and traces of barley beer were recovered from the undisturbed
burial cave at Calvari d'Amposta in Tarragona, south of Barcelona. The hyoscyamine could have come from any of the sinister nightshades. Dating to
2340 BC, the remains were interpreted as "a hallucinogenic beer that was
consumed during the mortuary ceremonies."[29]

The third report was the most exciting. As part of a similar barley-based
mixture, the same witchy hyoscyamine was again detected in a luxurious
tomb at the Necropolis of Las Ruedas in north-central Spain, outside Valladolid. Unlike the others, these remains dated to the pre-Roman, Celtic
population known as the Vacceans from the second century BC.[30] The depth
of contact between the Greek coastal colonies in Spain and the local tribe

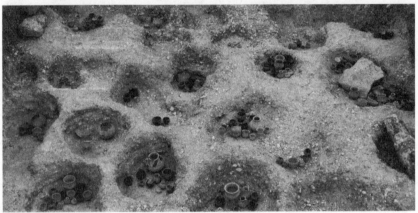

The Necropolis of Las Ruedas at the Pintia archaeological site in north-central Spain. Some 300 graves have been identified thus far, dating from the fifth century BC to the second century AD. Dozens of sacred vessels placed in their tombs of origin during the 2009 excavations (below); a recently unearthed *kernos* (above), similar to the Greek chalice that tested positive for a psychedelic beer consumed during the Vaccean funerary rituals. *Courtesy of Centro de Estudios Vacceos Federico Wattenberg, Universidad de Valladolid, Spain*

at the Pintia archaeological site, so far inland, is unknown. But for some reason the special brew was hiding out in yet another Iberian version of the Eleusinian *kernos*.[31] It wasn't the only *kernos* recovered from the site, but it was the only one that tested positive for the psychedelic graveyard beer. Just like the Empúries *kernos* unearthed in 2008, the vessels at Pintia instantly point to the Mysteries.[32]

Years of searching for an ancient specimen of hallucinogenic beer had finally paid off. When I pinpointed the evidence at the Necropolis of Las Ruedas, sporting an explicit Greek connection, I set my sights on Spain. With the archaeobotanical and archaeochemical data from Prats and Tarragona establishing a couple thousand years of extreme brewing in this part of the ancient world, my interest skyrocketed. The excavators of the Necropolis of Las Ruedas didn't mince words in the 2003 publication of their organic residue analysis: the "psychotropic" beer was consumed by an "elite class of warriors" during a funeral feast, with the "clear intent" of propelling an otherworldly journey "to the Beyond."[33] The team interprets the specific tomb where the psychedelic *kernos* was used as the site of an Iberian *devotio,* a bizarre ritual whereby soldiers took their own lives in a mystical tradition that guaranteed "the divine protection of their chief or general."[34]

Western Indo-Europeans with a death cult and psychedelic graveyard beer, contemporaneous with Eleusis. What an amazing confluence of ideas! It's tempting to recognize a Stone Age precedent for the sacrament at the Necropolis of Las Ruedas. The trail could stretch, if not all the way back to the Raqefet Cave and Göbekli Tepe, then at least to the unknown botanical experts of prehistoric Anatolia. Perhaps the same ones who inspired the "Minoan ritual cocktail" that Patrick McGovern chemically confirmed at Grave Circle A in Mycenae, or the potion he resurrected from the Phrygian tomb at Gordium, by which the deceased king was "royally ushered into the afterlife" with a psychoactive Midas Touch. The Ancient Greeks weren't the only Indo-Europeans who would have inherited the unique brew, after all. Any of the Indo-European Celts, such as the Vacceans, would have made equally good stewards of the tradition.[35]

Interestingly, recent DNA studies have proven that the Catalonians can trace their roots to "the arrival of Anatolian Neolithic–associated ancestry," a "pioneer colonization" of farmers from the east who settled the peninsula as early as 5475 BC.[36] Modern Spaniards derive about half of their genetics from these Stone Age agriculturists.[37] Even more interesting, the oldest archaeobotanical and archaeochemical evidence of beer consumption in all of Europe was discovered in 2006 at the very same place this Anatolian signal appeared in the ancient Iberian DNA: the Neolithic burial cave of Can Sadurní, just southwest of Barcelona. Together with malted grain on a stone hammer and anvil, calcium oxalate was recovered from a jar on site that dated to about 3470 BC.[38]

The beer from Can Sadurní rivals some of the earliest beer finds in Ancient Egypt and Mesopotamia, the same period that coincides with the development of the written word around 3200 BC, when history as we know it begins. Did the Iberian beer come with those Anatolian farmers whose DNA is recorded in Western Europe two millennia earlier? If so, why wouldn't their craft brew survive another few thousand years? Under Colin Renfrew's Anatolian Hypothesis, the Vaccean Celts at the Necropolis of Las Ruedas could have inherited not only the language, but also the biotechnology and peculiar religion that the Proto-Indo-Europeans had perfected in their prehistoric homeland of Stone Age Turkey.[39]

When Triptolemus showed up on the shores of Catalonia after the founding of the Eleusinian Mysteries, he may have been surprised to learn that his services weren't needed. The locals already knew how to brew beer and spike it with the kind of magical plants that might allow them to accompany their deceased loved ones to the Other Side, albeit temporarily. Aside from Magna Graecia, if ever there were a captive audience for the Mysteries on the European continent, it was in northeastern Spain. All the raw material was already there. Like long-lost cousins swapping recipes passed down by a common great-ancestor, the Indo-European Greek colonists from Phocaea who made landfall at Emporion in the sixth century BC—and infiltrated Catalonia for centuries—may have reintroduced the Indo-European Iberians to a very delicate technique. What Ruck calls the "Secret of Secrets" and what Martin Zarnkow refers to as the "controlled contamination" of a volatile fungal parasite that turns healthy grain into "mad grain" (*Tollkorn* in German) to produce LSD beer. A welcome addition to all the nightshade beers in the region. In the process, the reunited relatives appear to have constructed the Eleusis of the West for any locals who couldn't afford the trip to Athens.

In all the relevant studies from the early 2000s, the name of one young archaeobotanist kept popping up: Jordi Juan-Tresserras from the University of Barcelona.[40] In the summer of 2018, I started reading everything he ever wrote, and eventually came across a paper from 2000 in the peer-reviewed Spanish-language journal *Complutum*.[41] It was a summary of his and other drug-related archaeological findings across Iberia. Stuffed into the middle of the nine-page article was a single paragraph about an apparently unremarkable discovery, "the remains of ergot sclerotia" at Mas Castellar de Pontós in not one, but two different artifacts connected to Pons's iconic "domestic chapel."

The fungus was found embedded between several teeth of a human jawbone. Microscopic evidence of the same organism was additionally identified in one of the miniature chalices that once contained a "special beer." Given the "cultic" context of the area where both relics were unearthed in 1997, Juan-Tresserras linked whatever potion filled the tiny cup to "the consumption of the *kykeon*" during the Mysteries of Eleusis. After all, ergot played a "fundamental role" in the Ancient Greek rites according to Gordon Wasson. And no less a scientific expert than Albert Hofmann had explained how the "entheogenic alkaloids" in ergot, like the water-soluble ergine and ergonovine, could have easily been separated from the toxic alkaloids. In his bibliography Juan-Tresserras listed a Spanish version of *The Road to Eleusis* published in Mexico in 1980 that I didn't even know existed.

Given all the leads for psychedelic graveyard beer emerging from ancient Iberia over the past twenty years, I wasn't necessarily surprised. But the scientific identification of ergot was absolutely unique, and almost too good to be true. So I followed the trail of bread crumbs to the only published material that ever presented the full archaeological background of the Catalonian *kukeon*: a massive 635-page tome published in 2002 as a complete record of Enriqueta Pons's tenacious work at Pontós from 1990 to 1998. To this day, the monograph has been published only in Catalan. I was able to find a copy at the Library of Congress, where I dove into one of Indo-European's most distinctive tongues for days.

Next to the altar of Pentelic marble, amid the charred skeletons of sacrificed dogs, Pons's team chanced upon the lower-right jawbone of an adult male between the ages of twenty and twenty-five. Four teeth were intact, three were missing. They dated from between 200 and 175 BC. Juan-Tresserras analyzed two samples of tartar for any microscopic vegetal remains. Together with minerals like quartz and basalt, the silica phytoliths, calcium oxalate crystals, starch grains, and microcarbons all indicated a cereal-based diet.[42]

But more intriguing for the archaeobotanist was the presence in both samples of ergot (*Claviceps* spp.), which is *sègol banyut* in Catalan. How to explain this out-of-place jawbone in a ceremonial chamber that Juan-Tresserras calls "a sanctuary dedicated to Demeter and Kore-Persephone"?[43] That the ergot was ingested seems clear, leading the scientist to only two possible interpretations: accidental or intentional consumption. The former would have occurred in the wake of an infected harvest, just as in the frequent bouts of ergotism or St. Anthony's Fire throughout the Middle Ages. The latter would, of course, make sense as part of "a ritual associated with entheogenic drinks like the *kykeon*."[44]

Interestingly, Juan-Tresserras did not detect any ergot in the two mills where Pons believes the grain was prepared and the beer was brewed. So there doesn't appear to have been an accidental ergot outbreak. The intentional consumption hypothesis gains traction from the very existence of the jawbone in a "sacred enclosure," where no other human remains were recovered. Whenever a skull shows up, some very ancient religion is at play. Over a couple of dense pages in the Catalan monograph, Juan-Tresserras charts the various death cults that have been archaeologically catalogued across the Celtic strongholds of the British Isles, Belgium, France, and Spain—where de-fleshing of corpses, ritual decapitation, and decorative skulls are all attested.[45] He entertains the possibility that the jawbone from the "domestic chapel" belonged to an "exceptional person," an "initiate," whose skull had some special significance to the members of the cult. Likewise Pons believes the jawbone was used in rituals for making contact with dead ancestors. Whatever took place in the sanctuary, she discerns a mix of Greek, Celtic, and indigenous Iberian influences.[46]

As a meeting place for distant Indo-European cousins, could Mas Castellar de Pontós be evidence of the same skull cult discovered at Göbekli Tepe? The German Archaeological Institute believes the crania at "the world's first temple" were deliberately manipulated for ritual display. Dated some eight to nine thousand years before Pons's excavations in Catalonia, the prehistoric skulls are thought to represent a primitive version of ancestor veneration and "the interaction of the living with the dead."[47] Exactly what Pons sees in Iberia. Under Colin Renfrew's Anatolian Hypothesis, did elements of the Stone Age religion really survive for thousands of years by means of a missing Proto-Indo-European language, only to wind up on the other side of the European continent? And is the graveyard beer the elusive cipher that finally unlocks the deepest mysteries and real purpose of ancient sites as diverse as Göbekli Tepe, Eleusis, and Mas Castellar de Pontós?

It all comes down to that miniature chalice and its "special beer." Under the radar of all the professional academics who basically ignore anything published in Catalan, Juan-Tresserras was able to dissect an archaeobotanical clue that just may vindicate a scorned hypothesis from 1978 about the original contents of the Ancient Greek *kukeon* and the best-kept secret in the history of Western civilization. Martin Zarnkow's intuition that prehistoric brewers could have created an ergot-infused beer for special occasions seemed well supported. Informed speculation, but speculation nonetheless. When I finally read Juan-Tresserras's analysis of the ancient contents of the tiny cup unearthed near the jawbone, however, everything changed. On the gilded dome of the main reading room in the Library of Congress, the lantern's female figure—a symbol of Human Understanding—is depicted lifting the veil of ignorance from her face. I could feel her glaring down at me, as the first hard evidence for the hypothesis that tanked Ruck's career hit me right in the chest.

At the tail end of his Ph.D. studies, Juan-Tresserras had access to one of the most equipped research and development laboratories in Europe at the University of Barcelona. Now called the Science and Technology Centers (Centros Científicos y Tecnológicos or CCiTUB), the facilities, spread across four campuses, specialize in chemistry, material science, and biosciences. They just celebrated their thirtieth anniversary in 2018. Using both optical microscopy and a scanning electron microscope, the archaeobotanist unveils the results of his 1997 study in poetic Catalan:

Residues associated with a type of beer have been detected in good amounts: remains of gelatinized starches, starches with signs of enzymatic attack, yeasts, frustules of diatoms—something rather strange in such a small vessel. This find can be interpreted as either an offering of beer sediment or as the residue of a product that was used and/or consumed. . . . Regardless, the element to highlight is the presence of the remains of ergot sclerotia (Claviceps sp.), *also identified in one of the human jawbones. . . . This purple-colored mushroom has been associated with Demeter as well, especially because the color is associated with the goddess, and also because this fungus undergoes a cycle similar to the myth of Demeter and Persephone. After infecting the grain plant with ascospores, the purple-colored sclerotia that envelop the ears of the mature grain begin forming. At first, the sclerotia fall to the ground, where they pass the winter and fruit with the first spring rains, forming little purple-colored mushrooms that release ascospores that, using the wind to intercede, wind up infecting the ears. The harvest of the ears infected with sclerotia and their later processing contaminate the grain with toxic alkaloids. The psychoactive alkaloids of ergot are basically derivatives of lysergic acid and have hallucinogenic effects.*[48]

I immediately reached out to both Enriqueta Pons and Jordi Juan-Tresserras. Both were equally taken aback by my interest in a twenty-year-old discovery that had received only passing reference during a bygone moment of their careers. Right where she started in 1990, Pons was still leading the excavations at Mas Castellar de Pontós. And she welcomed my visit to the Benedictine Abbey of Sant Pere de Galligants. I had to see the miniature chalice and other artifacts for myself. But there was really only one person in the world who deserved a blind date with his potential smoking gun. So I called up a crazy old professor at Boston University and asked him to join me on a road trip.

I step under the gargoyles to greet the squat, white-haired Pons and the current director of Girona's archaeological museum, Ramon Buxó. We communicate in Spanish, though I can hear the Catalan accent behind most syllables. A few minutes later Ruck approaches the entrance with his long-time collaborator, Mark Hoffman, who has just escorted the eighty-three-year-old classicist from the only parking spot we could find, a good mile from the cramped streets surrounding the medieval monastery. I introduce Ruck to the humble excavator who unearthed the twenty-year-old evidence to support a forty-year-old theory in the last place anyone expected to find it. The now-aged scholar and Pons exchange a warm hug. At six foot three, Ruck towers over the archaeologist.

The five of us exit the soaring nave of the Romanesque basilica and head for the rectangular cloister on the right. We ascend into the second story above the sacristy, where the archaeological museum is housed, and set up camp in a windowless conference room. There on an unassuming desk with a navy tablecloth, waiting for our visit, are the goddesses: the incense burner and the disembodied terra-cotta head with the upswept hair—both rescued from the underworld grain silos and both identified as Demeter/Persephone. Beside them, a miniature chalice only a couple inches high, with a handle sticking out of either side. The Greeks would call it a *kantharos,* the ritual cup carried by Dionysus to induce his ecstasy.

Pons clutters the table with three decades' worth of data on the Greek farm twenty miles to our north. In page after page of carefully prepared color printouts, she walks me, Ruck, and Mark through every conceivable aspect of the site's topography: schematics, field surveys, aerial photographs. She even slips me a USB drive with drone footage for later viewing. The excavator points out the hundreds of subterranean silos to the west of the residential area on the high plateau. And then she takes us on a virtual tour of the "domestic chapel," explaining exactly where the miniature chalice and jawbone were uncovered, and where the grain was brewed for the sacrament of beer. She kindly gives me a copy of the 635-page monograph I'll no longer have to storm the Library of Congress to consult. Within a half hour, my brain is about to explode from the nonstop, real-time translation to keep Ruck up to speed.

Buxó snaps on a pair of blue latex gloves and delicately places the tiny vessel in the palm of his hand. He offers it for Ruck's inspection the way a sommelier would present the cellar's most expensive vintage. As far as the

The Director of the Archaeological Museum of Girona, Ramón Buxó, revealing the miniature Greek vessel (*kantharos*) unearthed at Mas Castellar de Pontós for inspection by Carl Ruck. Under Jordi Juan-Tresserras's optical microscopy and scanning electron microscope, this vessel tested positive for traces of ergotized beer in 1997. *Courtesy of Ramón Buxó and Museu de Arqueologia de Catalunya-Girona*

archaeological fieldwork and scientific analysis conducted thus far is concerned, Ruck is staring at the ancient container for a psychedelic graveyard beer that was brewed in the early second century BC by displaced Greek witches or their pupils. Initiates of the Mysteries of Eleusis? Perhaps. Magicians, healers, and prophets with a noble Greek pedigree? As we're about to find out, absolutely.

Ruck is withdrawn. I want to know what he thinks of the solitary cup he traveled an ocean and four decades to see. But I decide to let him process for a few minutes.

We stretch our legs and amble into the museum proper to examine the altar of Pentelic marble, quarried outside Athens and shipped all the way here to prepare Hecate's canine victims. To its left, in a display case dedicated to religion, I see the one artifact more than any other that screams the Mysteries: Triptolemus. As I study the artifact, I recall Dr. Denise Demetriou's insight that commercial centers like Emporion or Mas Castellar de Pontós could very well have served as open-access sanctuaries, promising a rare glimpse of the Eleusinian secrets in the Ancient Greek hinterland. If Demeter's missionary was here, it almost certainly means the *kukeon* came with him.

From the archaeobotanical and archaeochemical data in Prats, Tarragona, and the Necropolis of Las Ruedas, the ancient Iberians seem to have preferred the hallucinogenic nightshades to commune with the Lady of the Grain and their departed ancestors. In that case, was a Greek hand to blame for the presence of ergot in that tiny Greek vessel unearthed on the Greek farm? Did Pons and Juan-Tresserras stumble upon hard evidence of the elusive ingredient that the initiates of the Mysteries were forbidden from talking about under penalty of death for close to two millennia? In the absence of any analysis of the many vessels recovered from Eleusis itself, is this how history's longest game of hide-and-seek comes to a close?

I turn to the crazy old professor and usher him back into the windowless conference room for some alone time with the miniature chalice. We've all peppered Pons with questions over the past hour, so Ruck's reaction is long overdue. I hand him my copy of *The Road to Eleusis* and dive in. "Okay, Professor. What do you make of all this?"

The gears had been spinning in Ruck's head since the moment we set foot inside the dank monastery. His answer came out in a long run-on sentence, as if it were 1978, and the still-respected professor were back at his home office in Hull, Massachusetts, typing up a finishing thought for the prize manuscript that would rewrite history.

"Well, the most important part is where it was found," begins Ruck in that New England baritone, peering down into the chalice. "It was a sacred place for ritual. The shape of the vessel is only used for the shape of the cup drunk by the god Dionysus himself. And considering where they were found"— he refers to the other chalices scattered around the domestic chapel —"they're not toys. They are drinking vessels. And the minuscule size of the vessels would indicate that what was drunk was a very powerful potion of some kind. The size makes it clear: a tablespoon was all you needed. This was not a dinner party of wine and hors d'oeuvres. And considering the fact that residue of ergot was found, it would seem to substantiate the idea that some kind of visionary ceremony for the Grain Goddess or Persephone was being celebrated in a household shrine."

"If this all shakes out, how do we face the fact that some Greek colonists in an important cult center of the ancient world, contemporaneous with the classical Mysteries, were using drugs to find God?"

"We should have no trouble with that," Ruck responds. "It's time that we acknowledge our heritage."

And that was it. No malice or hard feelings. Just a slight tweak to the theory that Walter Burkert proposed a year before *The Road to Eleusis* scandalized the most senior discipline in the academy. The same theory echoed by Fritz Graf and Kalliope Papangeli in recent months as a drug-free Eleusis. In 1977, when Burkert speculated about "prehistoric drug rituals" at the basis of the Mysteries, he wasn't stepping out on a limb. If the Neolithic Revolution really was the Beer Revolution, then humanity's oldest biotechnology could have existed almost ten thousand years before the Greek Mysteries. Exactly when, we still don't know, but the initial findings from the Raqefet Cave and Göbekli Tepe keep pushing the dates closer and closer to the last Ice Age. It's the kind of antiquity that was unthinkable to Burkert's generation. Even without the benefit of today's archaeobotany and archaeochemistry, however, the esteemed German was still willing to attribute advanced botanical expertise to the archaic ancestors of the Greeks, whoever they turned out to be, and whenever their creative recipes transformed ordinary brewing into a psychedelic event.

By definition, the spread of agriculture had to involve a profound relationship with the natural world. But familiarity with the flora that alter human consciousness was all but assured much earlier in the protracted history of our species, which is at least three hundred thousand years old and counting.[49] "This is not necessarily surprising," says archaeologist Scott M. Fitzpatrick, "given that we have been hunters and gatherers for 99 percent of human history and would have come into contact with, consumed, and experimented with a wide array of plants."[50] But we weren't the first on the scene.

We now know for a fact that mastery over the Paleolithic pharmacopeia transcended even our species. Our closest extinct relatives, the Neanderthals, lived from about 430,000 to 40,000 years ago. In 2012 the teeth of five such individuals, discovered at El Sidrón Cave in northwest Spain, were subjected to sequential thermal desorption-gas chromatography-mass spectrometry (TD-GC-MS) and pyrolysis-gas chromatography-mass spectrometry (Py-GC-MS). The teeth provided molecular data for cooking and smoke inhalation over a wood-burning fire, as well as "the first evidence for the use of medicinal plants by a Neanderthal." The chemical signatures of yarrow and chamomile were dated to a stunning fifty thousand years ago.[51]

This new dental calculus evidence tends to support earlier suppositions about the use of medicinal, or at least hygienic, if not spiritually motivated, psychoactive plants by Neanderthals well back into the Pleistocene [2.58 million years ago to 9,700 BC]. . . . "It is extremely likely that, as practicing naturalists (and early-day ecologists?), the Neanderthals must have known and appreciated all of their environment, since their very existence depended on it" . . . and as such, positive and negative "experiences with various plants would have been passed down as part of Neanderthal ecological knowledge."[52]

According to Burkert, the expertise transferred for tens of thousands of years from Neanderthal to Neanderthal, and Stone Age *homo sapiens* to Stone Age *homo sapiens*, somehow came to a dead stop at the temple of Demeter. Without ever explaining how, the German scholar suggested that by the time these primitive rites arrived in Eleusis, the drugs had somehow vanished from the "festival of immortality" that "seemed to guarantee some psychedelic Beyond." That "expansion of consciousness"—a decadent escape from reality—was simply an embarrassing episode from the pre-Hellenic past. As John Silber would tell Ruck in 1978, "The Greeks just wouldn't have done that sort of thing."

The hard data of hallucinogenic beer at Mas Castellar de Pontós says otherwise. Rather than being replaced by one of Burkert's "harmless substances," the original, Stone Age sacrament seems to have survived well into the historical period within certain Indo-European traditions. Not just the eastern branch, among the exotic Indians with their psychedelic *soma*. Not just the western branch, among the bloodthirsty Vaccean Celts with their graveyard beer at the Necropolis of Las Ruedas. But among bona fide Greeks who hailed from Phocaea as the Vikings of Antiquity with a well-defined lineage.

Some scholars may come along and object that the ergot-infused beer at Pons's Greek farm has nothing to do with Greece. Like Prats, Tarragona, and the Necropolis of Las Ruedas, it's just another example of Celtic and Iberian extravagance—hardly emblematic of the architects of Western civilization. The Greeks had gotten mixed up with the wrong crowd. But on top of the archaeological finds that show Mas Castellar de Pontós to be immersed in an undeniably Greek context, it would be wise to recall the spiritual sophistication of the colonists who founded Emporion in the first place.

They were far from merchants or traders in the ordinary sense. The Phocaeans embossed Persephone on their coins for a reason. They spent many centuries seeding Catalonia with very Greek ideas about her underworld and, much more important, how to access it. But Spain wasn't their only offshore venture. At the beginning of this chapter, Massalia was flagged as the Phocaeans' first colony around 600 BC. Emporion soon followed, around 575 BC. Before their home on the Anatolian coast was taken over by the invading Persians, Herodotus says the Phocaeans packed up "all the votive offerings from the temples" and set sail.[53] Their final headquarters would eventually take root in the heart of Magna Graecia. The now-defunct settlement of Velia, Italy, dates to 530 BC.

There the Phocaeans would give birth to a philosopher. But not just any philosopher. He was a magician, a healer, and a prophet. According to the scholar Peter Kingsley, one of the few classicists worth reading aside from Ruck, the Greek genius known as Parmenides "was among the first generation of children brought up by Phocaean parents in Velia, with the memories of Phocaea and of the journey from Phocaea still running fresh in their blood."[54] Why does that matter? Because the region known as Ionia, where Phocaea was located, left an indelible mark on the modern world: what astrophysicist Carl Sagan once described as the "glorious awakening" into the laws of nature that happened between 600 and 400 BC in "the remote islands and inlets of the Eastern Mediterranean."[55] Thales, Anaximander, Theodorus of Samos: "the earliest pioneers of science" were all the children of merchants. "The enduring legacy of the Ionians are the tools and techniques they developed," said Sagan, "which remain the basis of modern technology."

But the legacy of the so-called pre-Socratics didn't stop there. Perhaps no single individual has done more for Greek branding over the past twenty-five hundred years than Parmenides. Plato claimed the wizard from Velia as his personal guru. For Kingsley there is no such thing as hyperbole when it comes to Parmenides:

> And there's no coming to grips with the history of philosophy or wis-
> dom in the West without understanding him. He lies at the central
> nerve of our culture. Touch him, and indirectly you're in touch with
> everything else. He's said to have created the idea of metaphysics. It's
> said that he invented logic: the basis of our reasoning, the foundation
> of every single discipline that has come into existence in the West. His
> influence on Plato was immense. There's a well-known saying that
> the whole history of western philosophy is just a series of footnotes to
> Plato. With the same justification Plato's philosophy in its developed
> form could be called a series of footnotes to that man.[56]

Without Parmenides, there is no Socrates, Plato, or Aristotle. But like the first scientists from Ionia and the founders of Emporion, the man born to Phocaean parents in southern Italy didn't come from Athens. That's simply not how Greece came to inflame the imagination of Western civilization. Maybe that's what Ruck means when he says it's high time to "acknowledge our heritage." The same people who invented science also invented techniques for entering the underworld and communing with the immortals, whether gods, goddesses, or ancestors. Techniques, that is, for becoming immortals themselves.

The great religions of antiquity all converged in Ionia, where the Phocaeans were the beneficiaries of humanity's collective wisdom. They sat right on the end of the so-called Royal Road that led through Anatolia and Syria into the Persian Gulf—the "caravan route" that Kingsley calls "a key point in the contact between ancient East and West."[57] The Phocaeans were on the doorstep of history. They absorbed ideas from both of the proposed Indo-European homelands—the scions of the Neolithic agriculturists, as well as the nomadic, Central Asian shamans. They had regular contact with the high cultures of Egypt, Babylonia, Persia, and India. In the roiling Ionian marketplace of ideas, the Phocaeans seem to have perfected one essential trick for cheating the afterlife. A trick they tried to carry to the rest of the world, breaching the Strait of Gibraltar, according to legend. "It was colonists from Phocaea," writes Kingsley, "who sailed down the west coast of Africa, and then up to France and England, to Scotland and beyond." But as far as we know, only three Mediterranean colonies were lucky enough to receive the trick: Massalia, Emporion, and Velia.

At the conclusion of this investigation, we will return to the Velians. In a strange twist to an already strange story, the Phocaean community in Magna Graecia survived intact for hundreds of years after Parmenides. When the earliest Christians began celebrating their Eucharist up the coast in Rome, the Velians would insinuate themselves into the very foundations of the latest mystery religion. Where the precious secret of how to die before you die was practiced by the first generations of Christians, the so-called paleo-Christians, and later suppressed by the growing bureaucracy of a faith that chose to deny its Greek heritage.

Ruck knows that, of course. Raised Catholic, he has been researching the origins of Christianity his entire career and writing about it since the early 2000s. The evidence at Emporion doesn't just implicate the Ancient Greeks. It implicates their Phocaean sister city in Velia. And by a documented line of succession that we will explore, it implicates Rome. For the devotees of Jesus and the Catholic Church especially, the notion that their religion was midwifed by Greek-speaking Italian mystics with a spiked Eucharist could prove a very hard pill to swallow. But Ruck has been down this road before.

So even if it takes a little while for the evidence to come to light, the old professor is confidant that a new generation of archaeochemists will be able to scientifically confirm the true nature of the original Eucharist in the years to come. And in the process, explain why the paleo-Christians in southern Italy and other Greek-speaking pockets of the ancient Mediterranean would have embraced the religion of Jesus. Not as something unfamiliar or unique, but a convenient take on the same Mysteries that had coaxed their Greek ancestors to Eleusis for two thousand years. And the same Mysteries that had inspired their Greek cousins at Mas Castellar de Pontós to create their very own house temple with their very own home brew. More than two hundred years before Jesus and his Last Supper brought the Mysteries into the dining room, the Greeks in Iberia beat him to the punch. They and their fellow witches in southern Italy were paving the way for the world's biggest religion to find easy converts in every kitchen across the Roman Empire.

In 1978, a lone classicist at Boston University tried to tell the world about this whole "perverse" idea. But the world wasn't quite ready. Before we leave the Benedictine Abbey of Sant Pere de Galligants, I have to ask Ruck one final question.

"Do you think this vindicates the past forty years of your tortured life?"

He grinned. "Well, it will certainly make some people unhappy, won't it?"

Epilogue to Part One

No lawyer ends his twelve-year hunt for evidence without calling in the expert witnesses. In May 2020, when this book had already been written and we found ourselves in the midst of a global experiment in social distancing, I called up the godfather. Aside from being one of the smartest human beings I've ever known, Greg Nagy is also one of the kindest. Ordinarily, I would just drop by the world's leading institution for the study of Ancient Greece right here in Washington, DC. But COVID-19 had us in uncharted waters. So there would be no twenty-minute drive down Massachusetts Avenue, past the Vatican Embassy and the Clintons' neo-Georgian mansion on Whitehaven Street, to see Harvard University's most esteemed professor of classical Greek literature. Since 2000, Nagy has been the director of the Center for Hellenic Studies, which sits on a spectacular plot of land that was donated to Harvard by the Mellon family in 1961. And since we first met in 2015, whenever he wasn't teaching up in Boston, Nagy would be there to answer rambling questions from a one-time aspiring classicist, breathlessly knocking on the door with each new discovery.

When I approached the legendary professor with my idea of putting Ruck's absurd hypothesis to the twenty-first-century test, Nagy was immediately receptive. It was news to me, but he and the Harvard-educated Ruck were actually dear friends back in the day. Nagy's wife was even once a student of Ruck. Boston was a smaller world in the 1970s and '80s. In the wake of *The Road to Eleusis*, however, the two classicists parted ways and lost touch. Nagy would soar to the very height of the profession. Ruck, for his original sin, would drift into obscurity. As a "card-carrying Indo-Europeanist," Nagy had always been sympathetic to Wasson's work on *soma*. And from the start, he had little problem—at least conceptually—with a similar sacrament at work among the Ancient Greeks. Open-minded though he was, Nagy had no tolerance for bad scholarship. So to aid the investigation, he generously gave me access to the 65,000-volume private library at the Center for Hellenic Studies. And he arranged for me to obtain borrowing privileges from Harvard's equally exclusive mini campus at Dumbarton Oaks in Georgetown.

After years of following my progress, the call with Nagy was a long time in the making. I'd already sent him all the updates from Spain, including the archaeobotanical data on the 2,200-year-old ergotized beer. The Hellenic presence at Mas Castellar de Pontós was self-evident. And to my relief, Enriqueta Pons's meticulous fieldwork allowed for an interdisciplinary reading of those Greco-Iberian Mysteries as a curious echo of the Eleusinian Mysteries that Nagy found generally convincing. But the tougher question was whether Jordi Juan-Tresserras had gotten the science right. For that, Nagy preferred another witness take the stand.

So I made a quarantine date with Patrick McGovern, who was sheltering in place up in Philadelphia. I needed the opinion of the archaeochemist whose recreation of the "Minoan ritual cocktail" and Midas Touch made this whole pursuit for the original *kukeon* seem like not a complete waste of my adult life. He knew many of the specifics already. When I first alerted him to Jordi's analysis in April 2019, McGovern was keen to review a "detailed archaeobotanical report" and the original photomicrographs that Jordi had taken of the ergot under optical microscopy and scanning electron microscope over twenty years ago. The road to archaeochemical glory is littered with the carcasses of false positives and misinterpretations, McGovern reminded me.[1] And I needed to proceed cautiously.

As just one example among many, consider the lack of consensus on Shakespeare's drug habit. In 2015, when the chemical signature of cannabis was reported on pipe fragments excavated from the garden of the most celebrated writer in the English language, the headlines went all-in: "Was William Shakespeare high when he penned his plays?"[2] Most media ignored the fact that the original identification of cannabinoids by gas chromatography-mass spectrometry (GC-MS) dated back to 2001, and was merely "suggestive" of cannabis. The more definitive results, which largely went unannounced, were nicotine, cocaine, and myristic acid (likely derived from nutmeg, which is psychedelic in high doses)—supporting the view that "at least one halluci-nogen was accessible" to Shakespeare in the seventeenth century.[3] Short of exhuming the Bard of Avon's body, however, proving he actually smoked the spiked tobacco is hard to do with 100 percent confidence.

For the next year, I professionally harassed Jordi to scour his physical archives and computer for every scrap of paper and kilobyte of data that had anything to do with the ergotized beer at Mas Castellar de Pontós. In the mid-2000s, Jordi left archaeochemistry for a career in cultural heritage management, so asking him to drop everything for a stubborn American took some major arm-twisting. But to his credit, on the infrequent visits to the beach house that held Jordi's scientific records, he would rip into that mountain of dusty boxes hoping to turn up something of value.

In the meantime, I reached out to Jordi's old mentor, the respected ar-chaeologist Dr. Josep Maria Fullola, as well as the staff at the University of Barcelona's Science and Technology Centers, where the original analysis was performed. Fullola sent me a hard copy of Jordi's unpublished thesis from 1997, in which the young archaeochemist included a breakdown of the two samples taken from the jawbone of the "initiate." The presence of ergot is clearly documented in the domestic chapel where the Mysteries are believed to have taken place. But it wasn't enough. So as 2019 gave way to 2020, I begged Jordi to do one last search for McGovern's "detailed archaeobotani-cal report" over the holidays.

A couple of weeks later, eureka! After more than two decades in a buried stack of notes, Jordi sent me his full analysis of both the jawbone and the miniature chalice, including a nice description of his methodology, instru-mentation, and results. Once again, the presence of ergot is clearly doc-umented. Not only in the vessel itself, like Shakespeare's pipe, but in the human skull. It all points to some kind of hallucinogenic beer being not only prepared but consumed. What neither Jordi nor the University of Barcelona could find were those photomicrographs—images of the microscopic ergot that would allow us to see what he saw, and to confirm the hit. Then again, how could the Mysteries end without a mystery?

On the quarantine call, McGovern said the absence of those original pictures adds an element of uncertainty to Jordi's identification of ergot. McGovern has written elsewhere that a botanist or chemist by definition will always demand "ever-more definitive" proof.[4] But he also acknowledged that despite technological advances, archaeochemistry remains a discipline still very much "trying to find its feet." And to this day, it is not entirely unusual for samples and data to go missing, including at the University of Pennsylvania and the most accredited institutions in Europe. It was also comforting to hear that McGovern takes no issue with Jordi's bona fides. From the mid-1990s to the mid-2000s, the Spanish archaeochemist was prolific. He contributed to dozens of scholarly and peer-reviewed publications, including a few that mention the graveyard beer from Mas Castellar de Pontós in passing.[5] Jordi was a known entity. As McGovern himself records in his book *Uncorking the Past*, the two of them even enjoyed a few drinks together at the first International Congress on Beer in Prehistory and Antiquity, which took place in Barcelona in 2004.[6]

Aside from bad scholarship, if there's one thing Greg Nagy has no tolerance for, it's sloppy language. So in deference to Harvard's classicist par excellence, I want to be exacting but fair. The archaeobotanical find in Catalonia doesn't automatically mean that Plato and the millions of initiates trekked to Eleusis for two thousand years to drink beer laced with ergot. But given all the material recovered from Mas Castellar de Pontós and its environs over the past thirty years by a dedicated and responsible archaeologist in Enriqueta Pons, I do see underworld cult activity that reeks of the Greek Mysteries. And given the intrepid work by Jordi Juan-Tresserras of good repute, I have no reason to doubt his data. I don't think he's lying, and I don't think someone of his caliber mistook the ergot for something else. With complete confidence, can we say the Greek farm was founded by magicians, healers, and prophets as the Eleusis of the West with the stated goal of drinking hallucinogenic beer on a regular basis? Not any more than we can say *Macbeth* was written on a psychedelic vision quest. That's not really how the historical sciences work. But *somebody* got high in Shakespeare's backyard. And it's not crazy to suggest that Mas Castellar de Pontós was a back door into Demeter's temple at Eleusis.

If we're lucky, the Mysteries could always decide to drop more clues. As this book was going to print, Jordi had a final surprise in store: the original ergot samples may in fact be stashed away at the University of Barcelona, he told me, awaiting fresh analysis by today's most advanced lab equipment. As soon as things settle down in Spain, one of the countries hit hardest by the pandemic thus far, the hunt will resume. And the saga will continue.

In the meantime, Ruck is convinced that Pons and Jordi found the smoking gun. Aside from the archaeological context itself, the discovery of ergot-infused beer at Mas Castellar de Pontós fits an overall pattern of extreme brewing in Europe—already evident from the nightshade beers that were detected elsewhere in Spain and Andorra without controversy. The data from Tarragona (2340 BC), Prats (1600 BC), and the Necropolis of Las Ruedas (second century BC) shows that ancient beer was combined with visionary alkaloids over thousands of years. To the best of my knowledge and until proven otherwise, the graveyard beers from Mas Castellar de Pontós and the Necropolis of Las Ruedas represent the first scientific data for the ritual use of psychedelic drugs in classical antiquity.[7]

While similar data from the rest of the continent appears to be lacking, it's important to remember that the beer of yesterday was very different from the beer of today. In the absence of fermentable sugars from the grapes that were more abundant in the east, the old brewers in the north and west of Europe turned to honey, berries, and other fruits. They were constantly experimenting with different ingredients to create more intoxicating drinks. So in addition to the nightshades, why not other mind-altering compounds? In a personal email, Hans-Peter Stika from the University of Hohenheim's Institute of Botany assured me that "the analyses of ceramic vessels is quite young." As the archaeochemical remains of beer continue to be found and tested outside Spain, he says, "we might expect new results." Psychedelic results.

Throughout most of Europe, the beer culture lasted from the Neolithic period—when the Stone Age, Indo-European sacrament first arrived, likely from Anatolia—all the way until the rise of Christianity. In fact, the Roman conquest of places like modern-day Spain and France in the two centuries before the birth of Jesus was just as much cultural as political—where the wine of the Romans was regarded as the only civilized "drink of choice."[8] And a powerful tool. Perhaps the best way to educate those savage, western Europeans like the Celts was to get rid of all their archaic, barbarian beer.

The Romans inherited their taste for wine from the Greeks.[9] And the Greeks had picked it up from the Canaanites and Phoenicians, who managed an active wine trade across the eastern half of the Mediterranean in the first and second millennia BC. From its home in the Fertile Crescent and the Near East, wine-making may have followed the beer-making we traced to sites like the Raqefet Cave and Göbekli Tepe. But already by the Bronze Age with the Mycenaeans and their "Minoan ritual cocktail," wine drinking was on the rise. As the Greeks started colonizing Italy in the eighth century BC, and classical Athens later came into its own, wine outpaced its prehistoric rival in those parts of the grape-friendly Mediterranean that are still famous for their vineyards today.[10] In Anatolia, Greece, and Italy beer slowly disappeared. And wine became the new sacrament for a new millennium. Just like the visionary beers to its west, even the *kukeon* couldn't escape the trend.

No religion lasts very long without reformers and revolutionaries coming along to stir things up a bit. If an open-access sanctuary like Mas Castellar de Pontós is evidence of anything, it's that the secret recipe couldn't be bottled up in Eleusis forever. Much as the Eumolpids and Kerykes wanted to maintain their monopoly over the primordial rites in Eleusis, the drugs were bound to leak out eventually. As the two lines of hereditary officiants faced competition from abroad, they also faced it at home. There were Ancient Greeks who didn't necessarily want to put their life on hold for a couple years to endure the long initiation into the Mysteries.

Why make the expensive journey to taste a graveyard beer from the Stone Age, when another sacrament was readily available at the Theater of Dionysus in downtown Athens? And not just there, but any mountain or forest where the wine god's devotees gathered to drink the grape potion. That's probably how Dionysus snuck his way into the Eleusinian proceedings in the first place.[11] In my conversations with the Swiss classicist Fritz Graf, he confirmed how the sanctuary that had always belonged to the prehistoric goddesses suddenly assumed a Dionysian flair in the fifth century BC. If the God of Ecstasy became the Holy Child born of Persephone only to keep his antiestablishment fans from abandoning Demeter's temple, it was a clever move. But it wasn't enough.

Over time, the pilgrims realized they didn't have to trek all the way to Eleusis. Eleusis could come to them. And the active ingredients that apparently fueled the Mysteries for millennia could just as easily be dissolved into their preferred sacrament. According to Ruck, the so-called Profanation of the Mysteries is clear evidence of the movement that would replace beer with wine as the vehicle for the drugs. In a series of incidents that occurred in 414 BC, several patrons of the Mysteries were caught initiating their dinner guests into the holiest secrets. Each ceremony was considered a blatant copy of Eleusis, and a sacrilege worthy of death. The details of the accounts reveal that some kind of sacrament was being consumed in wealthy homes across Athens. Whatever it was, wine was essential to the mix.[12] One of Socrates's most famous disciples, Alcibiades, was implicated in the scandal. Like some Ancient Greek Edward Snowden, he was forced into exile following the confiscation of all his property. Had he returned to Athens, Alcibiades would have risked execution for disclosing Demeter and Persephone's big secret. The Greek state came down hard on these heretics. Once the love of Dionysus and his wine was set in motion, however, it couldn't be stopped.

After all, there's a reason why beer isn't served in any Catholic, Orthodox, or Protestant church today. Had Jesus been born a few thousand years earlier, the Christians of the world would be throwing back a Christianized version of the *kukeon* every Sunday. But it wasn't meant to be. As we are about to explore in Part Two of this book, Jesus was born into the wine country of Galilee during the wine millennium. And no less influenced by the historical accident that made wine the premier beverage of the day, the first Christians in Anatolia, Greece, and Italy had already ditched their grain for the vine at a time when—just like the prehistoric beer we've managed to unearth so far—wine was a very different animal.

If Ruck is right about the drugged beer at Eleusis, then his scholarship on drugged wine in Ancient Greece takes on entirely new meaning. Because it was precisely this wine, he argues, that was used in the earliest and most authentic celebrations of the Christian Eucharist by people just like Alcibiades. People with no patience for Eleusis, who were nevertheless in the market for real religious experience—no matter the cost. If the beer lovers at Mas Castellar de Pontós could brew their very own craft sacrament, then wine lovers everywhere could mix their very own nectar of the gods. According to Ruck, it was the same audience targeted by the Gospel writers and Saint Paul across the eastern half of the Greek-speaking Mediterranean in the first century AD. And especially groomed by the Greek-speaking Gnostics whose holy texts never made it into the New Testament, and whose oral tradition apparently carried a pharmacological secret. They all used the Greek language to create a new religion that—now as then—lives and dies on the ability to convince its believers that Christian wine is no ordinary wine. It is the blood of God that opens the gates of eternity, promising instant immortality.

How did it do that? How did Christianity succeed in a Mediterranean world that was already full of magic wine? By tapping into some of the magic, Ruck believes. If there's any proof that the original Eucharist was actually psychedelic, then the hard evidence should be out there—lurking somewhere in the attics and basements of the Old World, where no one even bothers to look anymore.

So I'm off to Paris and Rome to find it.

Or get lost in the archives trying.

Part Two

MIXING THE PSYCHEDELIC WINE

8

The Drug of Immortality

I'm in the shadow of the shimmering glass-and-metal pyramid occupying eleven thousand square feet of the sprawling Cour Napoléon. I begin wading through far fewer visitors than I expected for such a picture-perfect Friday in Paris. Then I remember it's mid-February, and the recent bout of "yellow vest" protests hasn't exactly been doing wonders for the tourism sector here in 2019. The antigovernment movement that started over fuel prices has seen the country's most violent demonstrations since the 1960s, evoking comparisons to the French Revolution. Just a few weeks ago the authorities deployed eighty-nine thousand security personnel across the country.[1] In a rare precautionary move, the largest art museum in the world was actually ordered to shut this iconic entrance. Today, however, the streets are quiet. And we're in luck. Dr. Alexandra Kardianou, the curator of Greek ceramics for the Louvre, has graciously invited me and a special guest to examine two red-figure vases from the fifth century BC. For years I've been waiting to see them up close and personal.

If the earliest, Greek-speaking Christians really did inherit a psychedelic sacrament from the initiates of the Mysteries, the relationship had to start somewhere. So to put that pagan continuity hypothesis to the ultimate test, we're looking for anything that connects the Ancient Greeks of the final centuries BC to the paleo-Christians of the early centuries AD. The obvious link is wine. If Christianity really did base the Eucharist on a mind-altering drink that existed in the classical world at the time of Jesus, then our first task in this part of the investigation is to identify that original Ancient Greek potion. We know the first Christians didn't traffic in beer. But the discovery of an ergot-infused brew at Mas Castellar de Pontós does show the incredible longevity of graveyard beers on the European continent. If they survived from the Stone Age to the birth of Christianity, and the whole concept of drugged beverages is not just a figment of Ruck's imagination, then the long tradition of secret ingredients and hidden recipes could have easily found a home among the fans of Dionysus. If Demeter and Persephone's *kukeon* was spiked with psychedelic alkaloids, then any wine circulating in the eastern half of the Mediterranean in the centuries leading up to Jesus could have contained any number of plants, herbs, and fungi as well.

But this time around, we're not necessarily looking for ergot, which has such a unique relationship with grain. We're looking for *anything* psychoactive. Because the simple fact is that Greek wine of the era did not remotely resemble anything we would call "wine." As we'll soon see, Ruck spends about ten pages of *The Road to Eleusis* quoting a laundry list of ancient sources to rekindle the very mysterious reputation of the potion that replaced beer as the default sacrament of Western civilization. Among the Ancient Greeks, wine is routinely described as unusually intoxicating, seriously mind-altering, occasionally hallucinogenic, and potentially lethal. In an age before distilled liquor, how was any of that possible? Why was Greek wine so strong? It's well established that fermentation comes to a sudden halt when the alcoholic content of wine or beer approaches about 15 percent by volume. Most yeast can no longer survive past that natural barrier; they just die off, blocking any further production of the heady ethanol. So something else had to give ancient wine its infamous kick.

According to Ruck, the elixir known as *trimma*, that special wine mixed for the audience at the Theater of Dionysus we visited on the Acropolis, was only one such example of the Greeks' psychedelic know-how. "The Greek language did not distinguish between madness and inebriation," he writes in *The Road to Eleusis*, "because Dionysus was the god of all inebriants and not of wine alone."[2] Indeed, if the Greeks had been so obsessed with alcohol, surely they would have invented a word for it. But they did not. Unlike the other 60 percent of the English language borrowed from Greek and Latin, our word "alcohol" comes from the Arabic *al-kuhl* (الْكُحْل). The root, *kahala*, can mean to "enliven" or "refresh." Like the drinkers of the graveyard beer at Mas Castellar de Pontós, however, the Greeks wanted more than a light buzz. As mentioned earlier, the objective of the maenads or female devotees of Dionysus was the state of "divine frenzy" or "god-possessed inspiration." Having been "filled with the spirit" of the God of Ecstasy and "acquired his divine powers," the priestesses became "identified with the god himself."[3] Now that's some kick-ass wine.

In order to share in the divinity of Dionysus and become immortals themselves, the maenads could have mixed any number of psychedelic additives into their grape potion. From the textual evidence, it's clear they had an arsenal of drugs up their sleeves. But it was one of Ruck's classic unreadable footnotes that always haunted me. In that minuscule font from his 1978 bombshell, the old professor briefly mentions some ancient pottery depicting the ritual mixing of sacred wine. Every January in Athens, another elixir like *trimma* would be prepared for the midwinter celebration known as the Lenaia festival. It marked the nativity of Dionysus and the beginning of his party season. As with all such Mysteries, details are sketchy, but Ruck

Line drawing of G 409. From *Lenäenvasen*, by August Frickenhaus, published in 1912.

thought tantalizing clues were recorded on the better-preserved examples
of Greek pottery:

> *These vases show the female devotees of the god in ecstatic or mad-*
> *dened states of mind as they mix the wine in a krater or "mixing bowl"*
> *on a table behind which stands the masked pillar of the god. On the*
> *table or strung beneath it are various plants and herbs. One vase actu-*
> *ally shows a woman adding a sprig of some herb to the krater.*[4]

And that's where the pre-internet footnote ends. No pictures, no graph-
ics, no hyperlinks. Without indicating a specific page, Ruck did cite the German scholar August Frickenhaus's *Lenaevasen*, published in Berlin in 1912.
At some point the University of Heidelberg made a digitized copy freely
available online.[5] I can still clearly remember spending an entire Sunday,
several years ago, studying every single image reproduced by Frickenhaus
and hoping to track down whatever Ruck was talking about. All the pottery
is disappointingly reproduced in black and white. Some are photographs of
the actual vases in question; others, the esteemed German's best attempt at
re-creating the Lenaia scenes by hand.

There was one illustration by Frickenhaus that really grabbed my attention: three women in profile, flanking two *kraters* on a mixing table. Two
of the women are standing, gazing intently into the vessel on the left. The
central figure extends her right hand palm up to the *krater*'s open lip, while
her accomplice delicately stirs the contents with an elongated dipper. Some
unknown ingredient has just been tossed into the still-fermenting wine. The
likely additive: whatever the third woman, seated to the right, rigidly bran-
dishes in both hands. She's holding two different species. Neither is readily
identifiable, but either could fit the "sprig of some herb," exactly as Ruck
described. Under his careful line drawing, Frickenhaus included the phrase
"Louvre G 409" in parentheses, which I guessed was a hundred-year-old
inventory number that probably didn't mean anything in the twenty-first
century. After an exhaustive, weeks-long search of the internet and every
hard-copy textbook or journal I could get my hands on, no photographs of
G 409 came to light. A strange void in the literature for something of this
potential significance.

While the ancient artist could have completely invented the ritual that was painted onto G 409, what if it preserves the finer points of an *actual* wine mixing ceremony? What if G 409 is as close as we ever get to witnessing the real thing, just as it was performed twenty-five hundred years ago? And what if the two species in the hands of the seated maenad are the secret ingredients that spiked the original, Ancient Greek sacrament of holy wine? After reaching a dead end, I stowed Frickenhaus's image away on my laptop, trusting it would someday come in handy.

As it turns out, today's the day. Just before Christmas, I wrote a blind email in French to several members of the Louvre's Département des Antiquités Grecques Etrusques et Romaines. I included a photo of G 409, not fully convinced the vase hadn't found its way to some other museum or gone missing entirely. And almost certain that Frickenhaus's reference, in any event, was completely worthless. On Monday, January 7, Dionysus sprang to life. The Greek-born Dr. Kardianou wrote me back, confirming that G 409 was still, in fact, G 409. And that it very much had pride of place among the Louvre's close to fifteen thousand Greek vases. She also said I would be interested in another piece labeled G 408, which is "également décoré d'une scène dionysiaque de culte" (also decorated with another Dionysian cult scene). When I opened Kardianou's G 408 attachment, the rest of Ruck's forty-year-old footnote fell seamlessly into place.[6] In the photograph of the vase, two women are ladling wine from *kraters* into smaller drinking vessels; between them, the "masked pillar of the god," again exactly as Ruck described. Shoots of leafy creepers sprout curiously from the head of the bearded effigy of Dionysus. Another great clue, but the resolution of the attachment was too low to ferret out any detail.

Why no one has ever published a decent color photograph of G 408 or G 409, I'm not sure. But a good look at whatever those maenads are up to could finally help explain how Greek wine got its mind-altering reputation. So Kardianou and I arranged a date for a private viewing of her artifacts. And I immediately reached out to my herb expert.

To decipher G 408 and G 409 once and for all, it would take someone with an uncanny profile. If you dig deep enough, however, you'll find Francis Tiso off the beaten path in Colle Croce, a quaint town in the foothills of the Matese mountain chain in the Italian province of Isernia, just a couple hours southeast of Rome. The sixty-nine-year-old polymath is an ancient linguist and historian of comparative religion, trained at Cornell and Columbia, with a Master of Divinity degree from Harvard. He's a card-carrying, licensed mushroom hunter; an avid gardener; and a homeopathic herbalist all in one. For extra credit, he used to run Santa Ildegarda, a bed-and-breakfast even further off the beaten path in Cantalupo nel Sannio. It's dedicated to the mystical legacy of the twelfth-century Benedictine prophetess and early feminist, Saint Hildegard of Bingen. She was once Europe's premier authority on herbal remedies.

Francis seemed to check all the boxes, but his day job checked the biggest box of all. When he's not meditating or talking to plants, the alchemist gets paid to transform ordinary wine into magical wine as part of an ancient ritual whose origins remain shrouded in mystery.

I think I spot my weary friend lugging his suitcase across the courtyard. Under the neatly trimmed salt-and-pepper beard, he's not immediately recognizable without the collar.

"Ciao, Father Francis! Good to see you."

The Roman Catholic priest is fresh in from Nepal, where he has just spent the past three weeks translating a medieval Tibetan manuscript written by a disciple of Milarepa, the black magician who later became a devout Buddhist. I find the traveler in good spirits, as always, if a bit worse for wear. With a few minutes to kill before our 2:30 p.m. appointment with Kardianou, we take a seat on the rounded granite ledge fencing the fountain that surrounds the seventy-one-foot pyramid. Fortunately, Father Francis has known about my investigation for some time, so catching him up on the latest adventures in Greece, Germany, and Spain is painless.

Our first contact was back in 2015. Unsure how the priest would respond to my questions, I soon learned that he took the pagan continuity hypothesis seriously enough to read my initial notes on *terra sacra*. I'll never forget that first email:

> Hi Brian,
>
> I was able to read, pen in hand, your article while waiting for the Pope to appear in the Sala Nervi at the Vatican on Saturday. I was with the diocese of Isernia-Venafro, we had a special audience that day. I like the article overall, but have a few minor criticisms (maybe some not so minor!), but it is late, and tomorrow morning I have a funeral. Will get back to you soon. The text is next to my laptop here in exotic Colle

Croce, somewhere near the end of the universe! But maybe not so far from Eleusis and its heirs.

ciao, Francis

Keeping me honest from the very beginning. I knew I'd found my guy. Then again, if any man of God was going to sign up for this heretic's quest, I figured "the world's most controversial priest" was a safe bet.[7] It's a nickname Father Francis earned for suggesting Jesus's death and resurrection were not, in fact, a unique event—contradicting two thousand years of Church dogma. In *Rainbow Body and Resurrection* from 2016, the intrepid priest published the results of his decades-long inquiry into the so-called "rainbow body" phenomenon of Tibetan Buddhism. He schlepped all over the Indian subcontinent and the Himalayas, tracking down eyewitness accounts of spiritual gurus whose physical bodies were said to shrink or disappear after death, often transforming into radiant displays of multicolored light.[8]

"It is no longer possible to dismiss the phenomenon as folklore," says

Father Francis's kitchen, taken during the author's visit to Colle Croce, Italy, May 2018.

Father Francis.[9] He also doesn't see any point in denying the parallels to the so-called Transfiguration scene of the Gospels, when the face of Jesus suddenly "shone like the sun" and "his clothes became as bright as a flash of lightning," apparently cementing his true identity as the only Son of God. This miraculous body of light is considered a preview of the superhuman form the resurrected Jesus would later assume before his ascension into heaven.[10] However enlightened they may have been, none of the lamas interviewed by Father Francis ever claimed to be the Son of God. So if they really disappeared into the ether in a burst of rainbows, it means *each* of us is capable of the same divine feat.

As far as Father Francis is concerned, it's a perfectly commonsense reading of the New Testament—the essential message of Jesus being less about *his* abilities, and more about *ours*. Rather than looking to an external God, far off in the clouds, the atypical priest might counsel forward-thinking Christians to focus on their own, hidden potential deep within. For the Buddhists in training, that means a lifetime of meditation up in the mountains. For the rest of us, maybe there's a shortcut. One that the first Christians could have picked up from crafty women who spoke the language of Homer and who always had a pocket full of magical herbs.

Like the contents of Father Francis's garden back in Colle Croce.

The heretic's resumé spoke for itself, but I had to see the laboratory to complete my due diligence. So several months earlier I took a train to southern Italy for a botany lesson near the end of the universe. The lush backyard of the pre-Roman compound was overgrown with fig, olive, hazelnut, apple, and pear trees. Next to the artichoke, wild orchids, and thistle, Father Francis showed off his ragweed, lavender, and black-skinned Tintilia grapevines. In a different patch, the immune boosters: yarrow, nettle rhizome, echinacea, licorice, and ginger. Barely visible, a handful of slippery jack bolete mushrooms.

The kitchen in the priest's stone cottage looked like a proving ground for wizards and warlocks. Drying on a clothesline strung the length of the ceiling were two dozen distinct herbs, arranged by size. Mortars and pestles all stacked neatly by the oven. The roots, stems, leaves, flowers, and fruits of whatever surged from the earth just outside made their way into glass droppers and spray bottles for natural tinctures. Hand-scribbled notes marked the latest batch: angelica, chamomile, burdock, artemisia absinthium, and mugwort. The next batch: nutmeg, allspice, cloves, cypress, and boragine. I can't see a stack of books and not jot down the titles: *Gray's School and Field Book of Botany, The Practical Handbook of Plant Alchemy, The Practical Mushroom Encyclopedia, The Illustrated Herbal*. And my favorite, *Segreti e virtù delle piante medicinali* (Secrets and Virtues of Medicinal Plants). Merlin himself couldn't have scraped together a better operation.

"How's your Greek these days?" I kid the cleric, knowing full well the extent of his skills. From our sun-drenched seat in the Cour Napoléon, I extract the Loeb edition of Euripides's *The Bacchae* from the same brown leather pouch that has accompanied me to Athens, Eleusis, Munich, and Girona. And I point to line 274, where the blind seer Tiresias is explaining to a skeptical King Pentheus of Thebes why he ought to allow the city's women to properly celebrate the rites of Dionysus. And why this "new god" will put Greece on the map for generations to come. Euripides's chorus puts it all on the line: "There is no god greater than Dionysus."[11]

When it debuted in 405 BC, the whole play was Euripides's way of dramatizing the revolutionary movement of the time, and its stark challenge to a state-administered cult like the Mysteries of Eleusis. With the beer-based *kukeon* facing increasing competition from the more fashionable, more sophisticated sacrament of wine, Demeter and Persephone's days were numbered. And the God of Ecstasy was calling more and more to Athenians like Alcibiades, who had profaned the goddesses only a few years earlier by apparently serving spiked wine in his homemade imitation of Eleusis. But outside the cities, the real audience of the wine god was women, who were fleeing to the wild mountains and forests that would form the open-air churches of Dionysus all over Greece.

Out loud Father Francis begins chanting the text that preceded the New Testament by about four and a half centuries. His pronunciation is a bit ecclesiastical, but he nails the rhythm and cadence of the classical Greek that would have been performed to intoxicated applause at the Theater of Dionysus:

> Two things are chief among mortals, young man: the goddess Demeter—she is Mother Earth but call her either name you like— nourishes mortals with dry food. But he who came next, the son of Semele [Dionysus], discovered as its counterpart the drink that flows

from the grape cluster and introduced it to mortals. It is this that frees
trouble-laden mortals from their pain—when they fill themselves with
the juice of the vine—this that gives sleep to make one forget the day's
troubles: there is no other treatment for misery. Himself a god, he is
poured out in libations to the gods.[12]

"They always get it wrong," I tell Father Francis, referring to the Loeb's English translation of the Greek passage we just read. "There is no other *'treatment'* for misery," I read from the right-hand page. "They might say 'remedy,' or 'medicine,' or 'treatment.' But they never just say what it is. Look at the actual Greek word for 'treatment.'"

Father Francis scans the Greek on the left-hand page and notices exactly what I'm referring to. He squints through his glasses and exhales the ancient syllables, *"Pharmakon!"*

Euripides's intentional inclusion of the word *pharmakon* here signals a rich, established tradition in the Greek language, one that would not be lost on the classical audience in Athens. It certainly wasn't lost on Director Polyxeni Adam-Veleni last September, back at the Ministry of Antiquities in Athens, when we read about the "evil drugs" or *pharmaka lugra* (φάρμακα λύγρ᾽) that Circe "mixed" or *anemisge* (ἀνέμισγε) into the food of Odysseus's men to turn them into pigs. Remember that the base of Circe's magical *kukeon* was Pramnian wine from the Greek island of Ikaria.[13] From the very beginning of Greek literary culture in the eighth century BC, we find evidence of an advanced pharmacology. An understanding of the powerful combination of wine and drugs that Adam-Veleni referred to as "common knowledge" among the Greeks, "natural" to her people. It certainly didn't end with Homer.

In an obscure article from 1980, the Harvard-trained classicist Ruth Scodel took note of a thousand-year tradition that connected Homer to later thinkers like Plato, Plutarch, and Nonnus—all of whom used the word *pharmakon* to describe wine. She matter-of-factly acknowledges that "wine is conventionally praised as a good *pharmakon*" across Greek literature, calling it a "ritual formula."[14] Wine's reputation as a complex elixir traveled all the way from the Greek Dark Ages to the fall of the Roman Empire because *that's* what it was—a versatile substance ranging from what Scodel calls a "drug against grief," to a perilous, sometimes fatal "medicine," to a tool for invoking wine gods both old and new.[15]

If ever you find yourself in a game of connect the ancient dots, you want Father Francis on your team. Sensing where I'm headed with this passage from Euripides, he gets another mischievous twinkle in his eye. "You know . . . *we* call the Eucharist the *pharmakon athanasias*," he beams, using the Ancient Greek phrase for the "Drug of Immortality." The priest had first mentioned it during my visit to Italy last May. But before that, I had honestly never heard the expression. Until I found the original Greek source, I thought the brainy Catholic was just pulling my leg.

Now that we finished *The Bacchae*, I was just about to show Father Francis one of the many printouts I had stuffed into my leather pouch back in Washington, D.C. I sift through the two-inch stack and locate the Greek letter that Saint Ignatius of Antioch wrote to the church in Ephesus on the coast of what today is Turkey in the early second century AD. Though he may have wanted to distinguish the Christian Eucharist from its pagan past, the Greco-Syrian Ignatius drops a loaded phrase that seems custom-tailored for those Greco-Ephesians who weren't quite ready to leave Dionysus behind. In his little-known letter Ignatius unambiguously refers to the Eucharist as the "Drug of Immortality" (*pharmakon athanasias*)—an "antidote" or "remedy" (*antidotos*) for death, capable of generating eternal life.

It was not a random choice of words. By this tiny example we gain tremendous insight into the very Hellenized world of the eastern Mediterranean into which Jesus and his early followers were born. From Greece to North Africa to the Near East, a new generation of classicists is now referring to this melting pot of religious ideas as the "ancient cultural internet" that linked a diverse network of Greek speakers "in multi-voiced conversation."[16] From its initial discovery and ritual attachment to Greek life, wine was perceived as nothing less than a powerhouse *drug* with the potential to either slay or sanctify, at once toxic and miraculous. And in this one interconnected neighborhood, whether you were in Athens or Alexandria or Antioch—Dionysus was its dealer.

Before, during, and after the life of Jesus.

So if Greek wine was an actual *pharmakon*, does that mean Christian wine was an actual *pharmakon* as well? Or was Ignatius just using a little poetic license? Before pursuing the pagan continuity hypothesis any further, I need to see how the original sacrament was made. Time to fact-check a forty-year-old footnote.

Father Francis and I find the western façade of the massive pyramid. Rather than queuing up in the maze of crowd-control stanchions, which is the closest thing to my living nightmare, we trek farther south along the Cour Napoléon toward the Pavillon Mollien. At the end of a tranquil portico framed by seven stone arches, we were told by Dr. Kardianou to present ourselves at the Mollien's security desk with passports in hand. We're shuffled through the checkpoint and given our special "out-of-area" *(hors zone)* backstage passes, which is my first clue that we're in for a treat. In pops an astute silver-haired woman in glasses, wearing a lightweight, purple puffer jacket and printed scarf.

Dr. Kardianou explains how she scoured her nearly fifteen-thousand-piece catalogue for additional examples of wine-mixing scenes, but came up empty-handed. Not to worry: G 408 and G 409 have been off-limits to the public and remain well conserved. She had just fished them out of storage and placed them on an examining table in the "stockroom."

After stashing the priest's luggage in her office, Kardianou leads us into the Salle du Manège, with larger-than-life statues of Alexander the Great and Antinous framing the entrance. She takes off at a furious pace, buzzing through the thicket of tourists like our fairy godmother through a labyrinth of antique marble. Out of the corner of my eye, I notice a grape-crowned Bacchus to my right; the Roman Dionysus raises a cup whose potion has long since vanished. As we exit the hall up a flight of stairs, the atrium serves up a cinematic shot of the pyramid dominating the courtyard. But there's no time to take it in.

We hang an immediate right into the Galerie Daru and head toward the fifty-three steps bowing before what art historian H. W. Janson called "the greatest masterpiece of Hellenistic sculpture."[17] The eight-foot *Winged Victory of Samothrace*, cut from Thasian and Parian marble, once graced the Sanctuary of the Great Gods on the island of Samothrace in the northern Aegean. Rendered with craftsmanship from the third century BC that doesn't appear again until Michelangelo's *David*, the goddess has just touched down on the prow of a Greek ship, the folds of her tunic still fluttering in the breeze. Again, no time to dawdle.

We thread the tourists, up another level to the left of *Winged Victory*, fly past the Salle des Verres, and come to a dead stop. A velvet rope and jaded security guard seem to be blocking the way. Until Kardianou charges through unmolested and bids the priest and I do the same. She fist-bumps the wall at eye level, opening a secret wooden compartment. The curator picks up a landline. After her mumbled conversation in French, we're standing in front of Room 659.

A small plaque reveals why the public is barred from this section of the Louvre: "Following our 'flood risk' prevention campaign, this room is temporarily closed in order to protect the art works that are normally conserved in the basement." That explains our little marathon, I suppose. Kardianou stuffs her keys into the gold-trimmed portal and ushers us into the most breathtaking warehouse I have ever seen.

"This is the 'stockroom'?" My neck automatically cranes to soak in the twenty-five-foot ceilings. Father Francis is grinning from ear to ear. In sensory overload I roughly survey the wall-to-wall glass display cabinets, every one of them stuffed with Greek ceramics: bell and scroll-shaped *kraters* for mixing the wine, amphoras for transporting it, *stamnoi* for storing it, and every shallow-bodied *kylix* conceivable for gulping it down.

"We got our work cut out for us. How many pieces are in here, Dr. Kardianou?"

"In this room, we have about a thousand."

"Amazing. So this stuff is never on exhibit?"

"No. It *was* an exhibit room. But now it's our stockroom," she restates, alluding to the flood-risk policy. "And we have *another* stockroom," she adds, motioning for us to bend a corner to the left, into what I believe is Room 658. It seems twice the size of its neighbor. The dappled sunlight from an unexpectedly early spring day is streaming through the palatial window overlooking Quai François Mitterand and the River Seine. A thousand more vessels fill the ornate twelve-foot cases that line the perimeter of the room. And there on an examining table, just as Kardianou promised, are G 408 and G 409.

The whole setup seems too good to be true. It's February after all. It should be cold, rainy, and miserable. Everyone should be in an atrocious

Alexandra Kardianou pointing out the details of the seated maenad on G 409. The ancient pottery is chipped over the priestess's right hand (left and bottom left); the plant, herb or fungus in her left hand remains intact (bottom right). *Courtesy of Musée du Louvre*

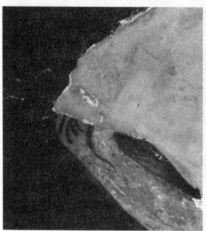

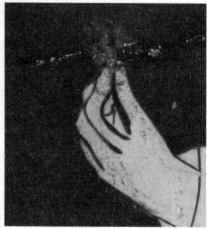

mood. And right now we should be stuck in a basement. This is not at all what I expected. As I approach the vases, however, my heart skips a beat. The line drawing from *Lenaevasen,* the century-old German monograph, flashes in my mind. I had always wondered why there wasn't a photograph of G 409. Frickenhaus, you son of a bitch.

"What happened?" I ask.

"At the end of nineteenth century, the problem is, they imagined something," Kardianou begins, gesturing to the large triangular divot on G 409 where the painted surface of the ancient ceramic had chipped away at some point in its twenty-five-hundred-year history. The apex of the triangle lands just where the right hand of the seated maenad is displaying the second of her two unidentified ingredients. What are the odds of that? Whatever floral object Frickenhaus drew in the woman's right hand, he just plain invented. The curator tries to console me, "Sometimes, they just made a reconstruction to create a beautiful image."

"But we still have *that* one," I reassure myself, pointing to the woman's left hand. Fortunately, the mystery cargo is completely intact.

"Yes, in this one . . . there *is* something." Kardianou motions to the fully preserved "sprig of some herb" that Ruck footnoted in 1978. "And here," she continues, referring back to the missing item in the right hand, "I suppose there was a flower, because here I can see something."

"What do you see there?"

"Ah, I see three red lines going like that." The curator traces three separate arcs with her index finger, just where the paint disappears into the damaged pottery. When I lean forward, to within six inches of the vase, I can detect the faintest of markings.

"You think it was a flower?"

"I don't think," Kardianou laughs. "I'm not sure. I see three little lines. *C'est juste mon interprétation.* I can't explain it."

With that, the examining table is all ours. The curator gives us the green light to snoop around as much as we like, so long as we don't take any photographs of the unexhibited stock. I guess I should have seen that coming, but I convince Kardianou to let me snap a few close-up shots of the two vases in question. She disappears next door, into yet another former exhibit room, farther east along this private square of the Sully Wing. Reeling from our good fortune, Father Francis and I give each other knowing smiles. The priest adjusts his glasses and nabs the solitary chair in front of G 409.

With a heavy sigh, I start the proceedings on a glum note: "I can't believe it, man. I mean, *that's* how a mystery stays a mystery."

A glass-half-full guy, Father Francis ignores my grumbling and grabs the retractable magnifying glass with the built-in lamp. He flicks it on and takes aim at the remaining piece of evidence we *do* have: the seated maenad's left hand. He is unusually pensive for half a minute. As the distinctive wail of a French police siren floats by, I wait. Until I can't wait any longer.

"So what do you think it is?" I impatiently prod the priest.

"It looks like a morel or some kind of mushroom."

"No way, c'mon."

"Here, look at it," Father Francis bites back. "It's about the size of a mushroom too."

"I don't know . . . maybe." I gaze through the magnifier. "It has a kind of fungal shape, and what almost looks like a stipe. It could be an herb, I guess. But look how thick that stem is. It's a bit strange, isn't it?"

For what it's worth, Frickenhaus apparently thought it was a fungus too. If you examine the original line drawing, you see a defined stipe jutting up between the maenad's thumb and forefinger. It's topped by what could hardly be anything but a mushroom cap. The specimen is very different from whatever the German tried to depict in the devotee's right hand. On that Father Francis has an additional insight: "The broken portion has a very similar kind of paint on it. Same as the mushroom down

The bearded mask of the Dionysus hangs from a leafed tree on G 408, surrounded by maenads ladling wine. *Brian C. Muraresku; courtesy of Musée du Louvre*

below, here you can see some kind of glazing, a painted color, baked into the vase."

"There was certainly something there, right?" I point to the three red lines that Kardianou noticed.

"Yeah. What she's holding here," continues the priest, indicating his mushroom, "and what she's holding here," moving to the absent plant, herb, or fungus up above, "are painted in the same way. Very differently, for example, from the rod for stirring. I don't see *anything* else painted this way."

Another fifteen minutes of intense scrutiny and debate leaves us where we started. In the left hand: a blob of crimson that could very well be a mushroom. In the right: who knows? Either way, the priest agrees that the maenad's ingredients were definitely destined for the wine, and the way the botanicals were painted accentuates their unique role in the mixing ritual.

The herbalist jumps to G 408. He's fascinated by the mass of foliage pouring from the head of "the masked pillar of the god." The branches are bending under the weight of several dozen heart-shaped leaves. Any one could easily fall or be plucked into the *kraters*, perfectly positioned on either side of the God of Ecstasy. The leaves are difficult to pin down. Father Francis thinks that Cornelian cherry dogwood (*Cornus mas*) is a possibility. But they could belong to any number of species, which is probably the point.

Across Greece the wine god was also known as the "tree god." While he was especially associated with pine, fig, and myrtle trees, the spirit of Dionysus was thought to occupy all plants, herbs, and fungi. According to the German classicist Walter Otto, his "theater of operation" was not just vegetation in general, but "a mysteriously aroused element of life which appears in an unusually clear focus in certain plants."[18] So does that mean the God of Ecstasy was also the God of Psychedelics?

As far as G 408 and G 409 are concerned, it's inconclusive. Our examination has not revealed which drugs, if any, were worthy of adding to the sacred potion of Dionysus. But I find Father Francis's mushroom theory intriguing. It calls to mind the more obvious-looking mushrooms Ruck has identified on other Greek pottery. It's clear from these artifacts that *something* was going on with Greek wine. Whatever the maenads are mixing up in front of us, it's more than just fermented grape juice. Where Kardianou's collection falls short, Ancient Greek literature fills the gaps. If you know where to look, that is. After all, the universe of ancient additives to wine hardly stops with mushrooms. And the priest and I didn't slog our way to Paris from opposite sites of the globe to be defeated by a couple of vases.[19]

I had planned to discuss my additional research with Father Francis outside by the pyramid, but there just wasn't enough time. Although our visit to the Louvre's secret warehouse is about to come to an end, I can't imagine a better classroom to go sifting through the classical texts with a true expert. As long as I have the priest on call, I'm going to tap his brain for all it's worth. I reach for my leather pouch on the examining table. Somewhere in this two-inch stack of papers are some answers to the puzzle of Greek wine.

With Father Francis glued to the magnifier, I find the laundry list of Greek authors once compiled by Ruck to remind his colleagues that ancient wine packed a punch. The thing is, the professor never reproduced the actual language of the original Greek sources in *The Road to Eleusis*— only cryptic citations buried in the footnotes, leaving the hunt for ancient testimony to some inquisitive future reader. So before hopping the plane to France, I spent a month at the dining room table doing exactly that. In the process, I happily murdered two ink cartridges, printing out the Greek of every single reference from 1978.

"What we have here, Father Francis, is a genuine ritual," I begin, pointing to the vases. "*This* is how the Greeks got in touch with the irrational. *This* is how they connected to the wine god. But as we read in *The Bacchae* just outside: *their* 'wine' is not *our* 'wine'. *Their* wine is a *pharmakon*. Ancient Greek wine was ritually mixed with all kinds of stuff: whether deadly toxins, or spices and perfumes, or magical plants, herbs, and fungi."

"Mm-hmm," nods the priest, humored by my opening salvo.

"Because of that, ancient wine was unusually intoxicating and potentially lethal. And we have the written proof." I hand Father Francis an excerpt from the *Deipnosophistae* (Banquet of the Learned). Written by Athenaeus of Naucratis in the third century AD, it is considered the oldest surviving cookbook from antiquity. I introduce the bizarre story of the Indian philosopher Kalanos, who journeyed through Persia with Alexander the Great in the fourth century BC. Upon the sage's death, Alexander decides to host a drinking contest to honor his departed comrade. But there's a catch. The wine has to be "pure" or *akratos* (ἄκρατος), meaning not watered down. *Akratos* is a very common expression in Ancient Greek, though surprisingly few classicists ever stop to ask why this "uncut wine" had to be diluted to avoid the kind of disaster that happens next.

I read Athenaeus's report out loud in the original language: "Thirty-five of those who drank the wine died on the spot from a chill, and another six did so after hanging on briefly in their tents. The man who drank the most, and took the prize, consumed four pitchers of pure wine." He evidently survived another four days before kicking the bucket as well. I turn to the priest. "All told, how do forty-two people die from drinking wine?"

Stumped for a moment, Father Francis furrows his brow. But I don't want him to think that binge drinking was to blame for these deaths. So I quickly flip to a completely different passage from the *Deipnosophistae* and lead my friend through the Greek, stopping on individual words to parse out the literal meaning. The priest takes pleasure in reciting along with me: "Because Erasixenus was not a serious drinker, two cups in a row of pure wine patently did away with him." The verb for "did away with" is *oichomai* (οἴχομαι), which means to leave someone "ruined" or "dead."

I smack the page with the back of my hand. "Now how the hell can two cups of wine kill somebody, Father Francis? The Greeks didn't have distilled liquor, right?"

"As far as we know," agrees the priest. Hard alcohol isn't generally documented in Europe until the twelfth century AD.[20] Before then, there was no way to increase the ethanol content of wine without risking exposure to methanol. "That's the problem with grappa, for example. When the woody bits of the vine are left behind, some of it ferments and becomes methanol, which is poisonous. But *here*"—Father Francis looks down at the Greek—"we're not talking about that, so why was the wine so potent?"

"If we go to Theophrastus, the mystery begins to unravel." I flip to my excerpts of the Greek naturalist from the fourth century BC. In his *Historia Plantarum*, the so-called Father of Botany takes a moment to consider *aconiton* (ἀκόνιτον). Aconite—variously referred to as the queen of poisons, the devil's helmet, monkshood, and wolf's bane—is extraordinarily deadly. Theophrastus leaves no doubt that the Greeks knew how to manipulate the poison. And no doubt that wine was a preferred method of delivery. In the hands of a true master, says the Father of Botany, the spiked wine could be mixed in such a way that death came knocking anytime between two months and two years after the drug's administration: "the longer the time, the more painful the death, since the body then wastes away."

Maybe *that's* what took down Erasixenus and Alexander's forty-two contestants. But an overdose on something that was meant to heighten the wine's psychoactivity seems more likely. If drugged wine was such a common practice in Ancient Greece, what would make it mind-altering or hallucinogenic, so much so that it convinced the maenads they had shed their mortality, escaped death, and become one with Dionysus? What were the vase painters hinting at with these mysterious ingredients on G 408 and G 409? Some kind of psychedelic mushroom is a fair guess, but the Greek world was full of other candidates.

From the two-inch stack I locate a bundle of carefully selected pages that are freely available on the internet.[21] They come from a medical manuscript dated to 1598, containing the extant works of Dioscorides. The Greek physician and pharmacologist lived from about AD 40 to 90—the exact period when the Gospels themselves were being written. His five-volume *De Materia Medica* (On Medical Material), a Greek-language encyclopedia of herbal medicine, became the basis for all modern pharmacopeias.[22] Without Dioscorides, no druggist or pharmacy would be in business today. Hippocrates may have been the Father of Medicine, but it was Dioscorides, the Father of Drugs, who proved more popular as time went on. For two millennia without interruption, the *Materia Medica* somehow *never* went out of circulation, providing a crucial bridge to the ancient world.[23] Singlehandedly Dioscorides ensured a consistent system of botanical knowledge across Europe "for generation after generation despite social and cultural changes," and huge leaps in medical theory and practice.[24]

And just like Theophrastus, the Greek genius left compelling proof that the maenads on G 408 and G 409 probably knew a thing or two about drugging wine. Book 5 of Dioscorides's magnum opus is dedicated to "vines and wines." Name your favorite magical substance, and the Father of Drugs had a wine-based cocktail just for you: absinthe wine, salvia wine, hellebore wine, betony wine. In this one section of Dioscorides alone, there are fifty-six detailed recipes, including a number of wines mixed with different members of the nightshade family, the same plants detected in the archaeobotanical and archaeochemical remains of the graveyard beers from Spain.

I raise the stapled packet—one column of the original Greek, one column of Latin translation—and pass it over to Father Francis. He noses through the ancient instruction manual that could very well hold the key to cracking the Mysteries of both Dionysus and Jesus. The alchemist is in his element, paging through the founding text of every drug prescription ever written as though he's casually perusing the hand-scribbled notes in his *cucina* back in Isernia. He smiles at the recipes for frankincense and myrrh wine, the perfumed resins used in the Catholic Mass to this day. Pretty soon the priest hits upon the vision-inducing nightshade wines.

Dioscorides describes in detail how henbane seeds of the white variety (*Hyoscyamus albus*) can be pounded into wine to soothe "inflated genitals" and "swollen breasts."[25] Unless you know what you're doing, avoid black henbane (*Hyoscyamus niger*) at all costs, however, since it "causes delirium and sleep." A similar warning creeps up for mandrake wine (*Mandragora officinarum*), which relieves pain and induces a "heavy, deep sleep" at the proper dosage. Get the measurements wrong, and just one "winecupful" of the mandrake brew is fatal.[26] More entertaining is wine mixed with black nightshade (*Solanum nigrum*). Dioscorides specifically characterizes it as psychedelic, saying a decoction of its root taken with wine produces "not unpleasant visions" or *phantasias ou aedeis* (φαντασίας οὐ ἀηδεῖς).[27]

None of this is *wine* as understood today. We simply do not have any vocabulary for these infused potions, so mainstream historians like Philip Mayerson are left inventing creative euphemisms for *drugs*. In his standard reference textbook *Classical Mythology in Literature, Art and Music*, Mayerson says, "Wine, thus, has a religious value: the worshiper of Dionysus who drinks it—or any other sacramental drink associated with the god—has taken the god within himself."[28]

I leave Father Francis to page through Dioscorides and his "sacramental drinks" in peace, while I catch my breath and meander around the stockroom. I could spend weeks here, inspecting the treasure trove of *kraters, amphora, stamnoi,* and *kylixes.* There's just too much for one visit. As Father Francis finishes with the *Materia Medica* a few minutes later, he has a light-bulb moment.

For the Greeks to be mixing the dangerous nightshades into their wine, just as the ancient Iberians mixed it into their beer, they must have been incredibly knowledgeable about the many plants, herbs, and fungi at their

disposal. The priest looks up and reminds me of an old saying from his studies: "the real secret to pharmacology is posology." Which means that when
it comes to drugs, nothing is more important than getting the dose right.
In strict measurements, a mushroom or nightshade wine could very well
be therapeutic—what the classicist Ruth Scodel might call a "drug against
grief." At higher doses the same ingredients could quickly turn medicinal
wine into hallucinogenic wine. At still higher doses just one cup laced with
too many alkaloids could be fatal. The *Materia Medica* is proof positive that
the Greeks not only spiked their wine with drugs, but had a keen eye for
dosing. Dioscorides stands in the center of a Greco-Roman tradition that
not only preceded Jesus by many centuries—the concept of drugged wine
having been documented by Homer as far back as the eighth century BC—
but followed Jesus for several centuries more, until the fall of the Roman
Empire in the fifth century AD.

So if I came to the Louvre looking for a vision-inducing Greek sacrament that could replace the *kukeon* and potentially infiltrate Christianity,
I think we're on the right track. My long-awaited face-to-face with G 408
and G 409 has convinced me that *something* was added to the wine during
the Dionysian rituals in Ancient Greece. Even if we can't pinpoint the secret
sauce, Father Francis agrees that the vase painters tried to leave a lasting
lesson about wine of the era. A lesson we have long since forgotten, despite
Dioscorides's best efforts to record the recipes for posterity. It doesn't mean
that all ancient wine was spiked, of course. At least not for everyday use. But
if the occasion called for a medicinal or religious elixir, or something more
nefarious, the biotechnology was certainly there.

The priest would later admit he found the "wine formulas" from the Father of Drugs to be "extremely persuasive evidence," not only of the Greeks'
expertise with psychedelic wine but its potential use among the early Christians as well. After all, Dioscorides was held in especially high regard by
the monks of southern Italy, who kept his manuscripts in circulation for
centuries. And with them, a written tradition of pharmacology as old as
Christianity itself.

So the next question is whether the Greek *pharmakon* really did influence the Drug of Immortality of paleo-Christianity. Did the drugged wine
of Dionysus become the drugged wine of Jesus? And if so, how? By making
its way into the Gospels, of course. G 408 and G 409 are not the only depic-

tions of magical wines to be inspected in the Louvre. Just around the corner, there's another wine-mixing scene that could very well make the definitive link between the Greek and Christian Mysteries. As the largest painting in the largest art museum in the world, you'd think more people would look up and take notice.

But some secrets are best hidden in plain sight.

9

Vineyards of Heaven

An hour and a half since the opening bell, we're back at the double security doors in the foyer beneath the Salle du Manège. Dr. Kardianou exits with Father Francis, still grinning like the Cheshire Cat. He's off to a scheduled meeting with the Mind and Life Institute, an organization founded by the Dalai Lama. The curator lets me off the leash to spend the rest of the afternoon in the museum by myself. So with the *hors zone* badge still pinned to the collar of my shirt, I head straight for the mother lode. In the ancient world the fact that wine was drugged may have made it unusually intoxicating, seriously mind-altering, occasionally hallucinogenic, and potentially lethal. But for those who believed this wine would make them immortal, it was something much more than chemical witchcraft. It was nothing less than a miracle. And the Greeks told fabulous legends about the sacrament that helped them cheat death.

Every year in the district of Elis on the western Peloponnese, for example, three empty water basins would be sealed up overnight in the Dionysian shrine at the appointed hour.[1] As the Greek travel writer Pausanias relates: "in the morning [the priests] are allowed to examine the seals, and on going into the building, they find the pots filled with wine. I did not myself arrive at the time of the festival, but the most respected Eleian citizens, and foreigners as well, swore that what I have said is the truth."[2] So too on the island of Andros, just off the mainland, Dionysus's "appearance" or *epiph-*

aneia (ἐπιφάνεια) came in the form of a particular miracle every year on January 5. A spring inside the god's temple would suddenly transform into wine, said to flow continuously for seven days.[3] According to the naturalist Pliny, this unbelievable event was still occurring in the first century AD. And he interrupts his Latin text to record the name of this special holiday in Greek: the God's Gift Day (*dies theodosia*/Θεοδοσία). By design, January 6 is now celebrated by Christians around the world as *their* Epiphany—the day when the Three Wise Men legendarily descended on Bethlehem bearing gold, frankincense, and myrrh for the newly incarnate infant Jesus.

The nativity of Dionysus himself was also something out of this world. In addition to his epiphany as the Holy Child of Persephone at Eleusis, the Greeks had a separate myth about the God of Ecstasy's strange birth by an ordinary woman named Semele. She was impregnated by Zeus in the form of an eagle, but later incinerated when the King of the Gods showed his true form, killing the mere mortal with his lightning bolt. In order to bring baby Dionysus to term, Zeus decided to sew the fetus up in his thigh, later giving birth to his own son in Anatolia—where Dionysus found his very first female followers. Semele's own sisters don't believe a word of the alleged affair with Zeus. Mortals don't mix with immortals. They think she made the whole thing up, but the wine god won't stand for it. To save Semele's good name, the whole plot of Euripides's *The Bacchae* tracks the return of this exotic eastern Dionysus to his real motherland, Greece.

The first two lines of the play stress the unusual bond between the wine god and his father in heaven. Dionysus calls himself the "Son of God" or *Dios pais* (Διὸς παῖς), and refers to his earthly mother as the "young girl" or *kore* (κόρη), which could also be "maiden" or "virgin." Yes, mortals *do* mix with immortals. And as the ultimate hybrid, the God of Ecstasy is the miraculous result, both human and divine. As *The Bacchae* proceeds, these two sides of Dionysus are in constant tension. He wants to introduce the Greeks to a new sacrament for a new millennium, but he doesn't want to repeat Zeus's lightning mishap. So in order to avoid scaring everybody to death with the full force of his godhood, the shape-shifter "exchanges his divine form for a mortal one." And a funny one at that: a long-haired wizard. He is ridiculed as "effeminate," with hair "tumbling all the way down his cheeks." Just like the "luxurious locks" of Dionysus himself, who blurs the boundary between male and female.[4] Only then is the incognito wine god able to uncork his magic potion, initiating the women of Greece into his Mysteries.

The biggest painting in the Louvre is an outstanding interpretation of the supernatural phenomena that surround the epiphany of Dionysus. And it's the only stop on my solo tour before calling it a day. At a noticeably slower pace, I retrace our steps through the Galerie Daru, until I find myself winded once again before the *Winged Victory of Samothrace*. That staircase is no joke. Instead of heading left toward the secret warehouse, I hang a right for the *Peintures Italiennes*. Past the understated Botticellis and Fra Angelico's *Crucifixion*, things get awfully Christian awfully fast. The supernova of Virgins that begins in this corner of the Denon Wing streams into the Louvre's magnificent Grand Gallery. It's hard to find an Italian Renaissance painter without a *Madonna and Child* in their portfolio. I swim past all the mom-and-son duets toward Leonardo da Vinci's *Virgin of the Rocks* and hang a hard right into the Salle des États.

It looks better fit for an aircraft hangar than an exhibition hall. Before this lofty space became part of the Louvre in 1878, it hosted legislative sessions under French Emperor Napoleon III. In 2005 the entire room was remodeled by Peruvian architect Lorenzo Piqueras. The $3.6-million project integrated a glass checkerboard roof that now showers natural light onto the museum's pride and joy.[5] I can barely see Leonardo's Muse over the gaggle of selfie sticks. There must be a hundred tourists clustered together in a frothing semicircle, all vying for their tedious shot of *La Gioconda*. That's how da Vinci's people refer to the "Florentine gentlewoman" with the "gently supercilious grin" on the thin panel of poplar about thirty yards away.[6] I prefer not to get any closer to the mosh pit. And I don't need to. Because I didn't come for the *Mona Lisa*.

I steadily twist my neck along the invisible arc leaping from the "most written about, most sung about" pair of eyes in the history of Western iconography. And I land on a sixteenth-century canvas by the Venetian artist Paolo Veronese. Overshadowing da Vinci's petite showpiece, this two-hundred-twenty-square-foot beast is the reason I'm here. Aside from *La Gioconda* and Veronese's *Jupiter Hurling Thunderbolts at the Vices* to my right, it's the only piece of art in the otherwise bare Salle des États. But no one seems to notice. With the mob at my back, I soon realize I'm the only person in Room 711 of the Louvre taking part in this sumptuous, super-sized banquet. I laugh at the absurdity of my private audience with the wine god.

I'd recognize that drunkard anywhere.

In this version of the myth, the virgin mother has somehow survived her divine pregnancy. She has dragged her adult son to a wedding party against his wishes. He has just turned thirty years old, after all, and probably had other plans for this cool evening in January. Plus, the God of Ecstasy is trying to keep a low profile. He's well aware that the wild, hallucinatory Mysteries he'll soon be introducing to civilized folk are not for everybody. With heroic patience, he has waited his entire life for just the right moment to unveil his divine intoxicant to the world. Tonight is not the night. But his mother has a reputation to worry about as well. For three decades she has endured the rumors and ridicule that plague any woman who claims to have birthed the Son of God. If only her gifted boy, disguised as an ordinary human all these years, could finally make his godhood known. Just one little miracle.

Right on cue, the wine runs out, and the party is in crisis. Had his mother planned this all along? When she apprises him of the situation, the wine god feels totally set up. In the old story that inspired this scene before me, the God of Ecstasy angrily reminds his mother in Ancient Greek, "My time has not yet come!" (*oupo ekei e ora mou*/οὔπω ἥκει ἡ ὥρα μου).

But the virgin is undeterred, instructing the hapless waiters to simply follow her son's lead. The God of Ecstasy notices six enormous stone water jars off to the side and, against his better judgment, decides it's time to shine. He digs into his bag of tricks and whips out a combination of the annual Epiphany miracles from the Greek district of Elis and the island of Andros. The God of Ecstasy takes one look at the waiters, motions to the jars, and uses a great Greek verb, *gemisate* (Γεμίσατε): "Fill 'em up to the brim."

To keep the party going the attendants are told to take an immediate sample to the chief steward. Veronese paints him in an emerald cloak and turban, his meaty hand caressing a purple pouch next to a dagger. He takes one sip of the incredible potion and is left dumbstruck. Not because the water has just inexplicably turned to wine, which the steward knows nothing about. He simply cannot believe what's being uncorked this late in the evening.

The Wedding at Cana, painted by Paolo Veronese around 1563, currently in the Louvre.

Unaware where the vintage came from, he jokes to the groom something to the effect of: "Dude, most people don't serve the good shit when everybody's already drunk."

Frozen in time, this is the ancient moment captured by Veronese, but it's all anachronistically set in sixteenth-century Venice. The guests are oblivious to the miracle taking place around them. At the bottom right of the canvas, a single servant pours the magical wine from one of the stone water jars into a golden amphora. Wide-eyed and baffled, the chief steward has just sent the first chalice of the new sacrament over to the groom for tasting. For the initiates who have unwittingly gathered for this Epiphany, things will never be the same.

And there, at the center of the gargantuan table in front of me, is the long-haired wizard orchestrating the whole affair. But it's not Dionysus.

It's the most famous human being in recorded history.

Jesus of Nazareth.

His bearded face is glowing. Beams of light explode around his head in a refulgent ring. As he stares into mid-distance from the bull's-eye of Veronese's *The Wedding Feast at Cana*, Jesus's flesh begins to morph into the divine light that signals his immortality. If he were here, Father Francis would note that only Jesus and the Virgin Mary, seated to his right, are painted with those shining halos. Of the roughly 125 figures on the busy canvas, only *they* have conquered death. Only *they* have activated the rainbow body that will transport them through the cosmos when they leave their physical bodies here on earth. Right now in remote parts of the Himalayas, the priest would remind me, Buddhist monks are actively engaged in the same pursuit.

And I'd remind him, as I often do, that the Greeks were, too. Except they figured out how to bypass a lifetime of meditation and preserved it in the Eleusinian Mysteries. What Cicero called the most "exceptional and divine thing" Athens ever produced. And what Praetextatus said was crucial to the future of our species. Eleusis held "the entire human race together." Without it, life would be "unlivable." Dionysus would eventually make his Epiphany in Demeter's temple as the Holy Child of Persephone. But it wasn't enough for his fanatics. They wanted him all the time. And so, for those who did not want to spend their time and money on the long initiation into the Eleusinian Mysteries, secret networks started popping up all over the Greek countryside, where the wine god and his immortality potion suddenly became much more accessible.

The English classicist and theologian A. D. Nock, Harvard's leading authority on ancient religion in the mid-twentieth century, summed it up best in his influential article from 1952, "Hellenistic Mysteries and Christian Sacraments." Nock understood the *real* draw of the God of Ecstasy:

Zeus and Semele, painted by Jacques Blanchard about
1632, currently in the Dallas Museum of Art.

*In spite of early institutionalization, his worship retained or could
recapture an element of choice, movement and individual enthusiasm. . . . Apart from the devotion of the sick to Asclepius, Dionysus
provided the single strongest focus for private spontaneous pagan piety
using ceremonial forms. Dionysiac initiations did not only, like those
of Eleusis and Samothrace, confer a new status on the initiate: they
also admitted him to groups of likeminded persons, possessed of the
same status and often a similar hope for the hereafter—not exactly to a
Church, but to congregations which used the same symbols and spoke
the same language.[7]*

Nock acknowledges Euripides's *The Bacchae* as our main classical source
for the Mysteries of Dionysus. Its rich, descriptive vocabulary offers unique
access to the nocturnal "congregations" of god-filled spiritual seekers. In *The*

The Annunciation, painted by Fra Angelico about 1426, currently in the Prado Museum in Madrid, Spain.

Dionysian Gospel, published in 2017, Dennis MacDonald of the Claremont School of Theology compares the Ancient Greek of *The Bacchae* with the Ancient Greek of the Gospel of John to prove that the Evangelist was intimately familiar with these Dionysian "symbols" and "language." In order to portray Jesus as the consummate Son of God, John knew all the loaded terms that would appeal to any Greek speaker of the time. And he used them throughout his Gospel to depict Jesus as the second coming of Dionysus.

The divine birth is just one example among many. As mentioned earlier, Dionysus refers to himself as the "Son of God" in the very first line of *The Bacchae*, using a phrase that is repeated later in the play. But there are many ways to communicate that in Greek. In three different places Euripides uses the unique word *gonos* (γόνος), which literally means "begotten," alluding to Dionysus's emergence from Zeus's thigh after the death of his virgin mother, Semele.[8] In the very first chapter of John, the Evangelist uses the similar-sounding word *genos* (γένος), not once but twice. He is the only Gospel writer who describes the nativity of Jesus this way. When John includes the Greek phrase *monogenes theos* (μονογενὴς Θεὸς) in 1:18, he means the "only begotten" or "unique offspring" of God. But in case it weren't obvious enough, John then goes on to say that Jesus is so close to God the Father, he resides in God's "lap." The Greek *kolpon* (κόλπον), "the region of the body extending from the breast to the legs, especially when a person is in a seated position," could not be clearer.[9]

For a Greek speaker of the time, an immediate connection to Dionysus's one-of-a-kind birth from Zeus is almost guaranteed. The only thing that is unclear about this passage is the English translation, which ignores the word *kolpon* entirely, putting Jesus "in closest relationship with the Father."[10] Without the Ancient Greek, the explicit reference to Dionysus has been entirely lost. And today, all we're left with are weird stories about humans mating with gods. In one of the most frequently depicted scenes in Christian art, the Annunciation tells of an immaculate young girl who conceives the Son of God following unusual relations with a bird. Instead of Zeus's eagle, God the Father manifests himself as a dove, the Holy Spirit sailing on golden rays of light to impregnate the Virgin Mary.

In *The Dionysian Gospel*, Dennis MacDonald goes on to examine all the key "symbols" and "language" from John's Gospel that have been lost in translation. But the scholar pays special attention to the one thing that really defined the God of Ecstasy in the centuries before Jesus: his sacrament. Without the wine, there is no Dionysus. And without the Eucharist, there is no Christianity. The potion that would become the calling card of the new Church begins right here on Veronese's sixteenth-century version of the water-to-wine miracle at Cana. *This* is how Dionysus enters Christianity. And *this* is how the Ancient Greek *pharmakon* is transformed into the *pharmakon athanasias,* the Drug of Immortality. It all started with this very scene from the Gospel of John. Here in the Louvre, across from the *Mona Lisa* sucking up all the air in the room, this is ground zero for the pagan continuity hypothesis. It places the Greek Mysteries at the very foundation of Christianity.

John's is the *only* Gospel that records this event—the first miracle that launches Jesus's public mission. In Matthew, Jesus starts his career by healing a leper.[11] In Mark and Luke, it's an exorcism.[12] From the very beginning, however, John wanted *his* Greek-speaking audience to immediately associate Jesus with the God of Ecstasy. As MacDonald states, "the changing of water into wine was Dionysus's signature miracle."[13] He goes on to quote the German scholar Michael Labahn: "The supernatural, miraculous transformation denotes the epiphany of Jesus according to the pattern of Dionysus. . . . The juxtaposition of Jesus and Dionysus depicts Jesus as a god." Just as the Greek speakers of the time could hardly hear about the "only-begotten" Son of God in the "lap" of the Father and not think of Dionysus, so they could hardly hear about Jesus's first miracle and not think of the annual miracles from the Greek district of Elis and the island of Andros. Whenever wine appears out of nowhere on the Epiphany, only one god comes to mind.

As far as we can tell, John did not want to leave any room for misinterpretation. The Greek word he uses for those enormous stone water jars is a very specific one: *hudria* (ὑδρία). We know from the material evidence that there was a bustling industry producing these soft limestone vessels. At the time their manufacture was centered in Jerusalem, where they were used for ritual purification. Each *hudria* that Jesus ordered filled with water could have held twenty to thirty gallons. It may not be the river of wine that the Andrians drank from every year, but that's still a pretty obscene amount of alcohol to take down in one night. As much as 180 gallons, or a thousand bottles.[14] Talk about the God's Gift Day! And because the wedding in Cana was said to take place in January, on the same day as the Epiphany miracle on Andros and around the same time as the Lenaia ritual that launched the festival season of Dionysus, John's Greek speakers may have wondered what was happening behind the scenes.[15] Like the maenads on G 408 and G 409, could the latest wine god have added something to the wine to make it a little more miraculous? What kind of wine was this?

I'm not the first to question the true nature of that evening's concoction. Aside from the Gospel of John, art historian Philip Fehl identified an alternative source for Veronese's banquet scene: Pietro Aretino's *Humanity of Christ*, published in Venice in 1535. Aretino dramatically captures the chief steward's physical reaction to the first sample of Christianity's magical new elixir:

> As he smelled the bouquet of wine which was made from grapes gathered in the vineyards of Heaven he was revived like a man who awak-

ens from a faint when his wrists are bathed in vinegar. Tasting the
wine he felt the trickle of its sharp sweetness down to his very toes. In
filling a glass of crystal, one could have sworn it was bubbling with
distilled rubies.[16]

In the Ancient Greek tradition the "vineyards of Heaven" could be traced back to the miraculous wine from Elis and Andros. Every year they had the honor of churning out the Dionysian sacrament. What was it about the wine in Cana that inspired John the Evangelist to pen *his* legend, pasting Dionysus onto the first page of the Christian origin story for all time? As it turns out, John's choice wasn't so arbitrary. Jesus's coming-out party in Cana was perfectly positioned, and perfectly timed, to pick up where Dionysus left off.

Typing "Cana" into Google Maps won't get you very far, but the coordinates of the Biblical town might well lead to the Christian pilgrimage site of Kafr Kanna in Galilee. Throughout the Hellenistic period leading up to the birth of Jesus, the whole region in the north of modern-day Israel remained an "important commercial center for the production and marketing" of wine.[17] Wine that would nicely serve the maenads in the area, whom the God of Ecstasy had already converted long before Mary's son came on the scene. On that drunken Epiphany in Cana around AD 30, the new wine god wasn't playing to a random crowd. Jesus's long-awaited appearance (*epiphaneia*) in Galilee came with home-field advantage.

Only slightly to the south and east, the ancient city of Scythopolis was the legendary birthplace of Dionysus himself. For that reason it was also called Nysa, providing a coherent solution for the unknown etymology of the wine god's name: "the god" (*Dio*) "from Nysa" (*Nysus*). During Jesus's lifetime, Scythopolis/Nysa was the largest of the urban centers that formed the so-called Decapolis (Greek for "ten cities") on the eastern frontier of the Roman Empire.[18] The God of Ecstasy remained the city's patron deity, appearing all over its statues, altars, inscriptions, and coins.[19] Today the place is called Beit She'an, lying just west of the Jordan River. Door to door from Jesus's hometown of Nazareth, that's about forty minutes.

Like Jesus, Dionysus liked to roam these parts. And he left his mark. The appropriately titled "Mona Lisa of Galilee" can be found in the Greek-speaking capital of Sepphoris (modern-day Tzippori), a mere twenty minutes from Nazareth.[20] The spectacular fifty-four-square-foot mosaic shows

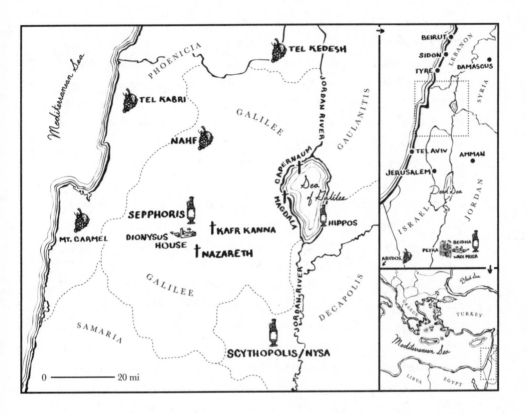

a woman with the same hypnotic sideways glance as the Mona Lisa at my back. In one of eleven surviving scenes on the floor of the banquet room, she adorns a second-century AD Roman mansion known as the "Dionysus House." The other mosaics are vignettes from the life and cult of the God of Ecstasy.[21] Several deal with ritual inebriation, including a drinking contest between Dionysus and Herakles, where the Greek word for "drunkenness" or *methe* (μέθη) appears.[22] When these explicitly pagan images surfaced for the first time in 1987, Eric Meyers of Duke University shared the consensus of the archaeological community: their surprise discovery in a Jewish town, squarely in Jesus territory, "certainly blew most everyone's mind."[23] The pagan and Judeo-Christian worlds weren't supposed to intersect, especially in a post-Jesus Galilee. But the evidence was mounting that Dionysus and Jesus could very much coexist.

Years later, minds would continue to be blown as another team sifted through the dirt on the other side of the Dead Sea, due south in modern-day Jordan. In 2005 the remains of an elaborate hall were unearthed in Beidha, just a couple miles north of the Petra archaeological site, the famed cosmo-politan capital of the Nabataean Kingdom that stretched into the Arabian Peninsula during the Roman Empire. The colonnaded structure, complete with a courtyard, was dated to the reign of Malichos I, a mere three decades before the birth of Jesus. The Greek influence over the shrine that survived into the first century AD is overpowering: "the architecture and sculpture demonstrate how well the Nabataeans had absorbed Hellenistic motifs and blended them with Nabataean traditions, including the tradition of ritual dining."[24]

The presence of the "Dionysian cosmos," including images of grapes and vines, led the team from the American Center of Oriental Research in Am-man to envision a unique role for this sanctuary in the "transformational process that culminates in communion with the god."[25] Beidha's "rural land-scape," overlooking "extensive vineyards," would have made an ideal "cult center" for the Nabataean royal family, who could seek a "transcendent" experience with Dionysus as their "role model and putative ancestor." Cut from Phrygian marble sometime in the late second century AD, a *kantharos* was discovered in the nearby Petra Church, the same kind of vessel recov-ered by Enriqueta Pons from the domestic chapel at Mas Castellar de Pontós in Spain. Contemporaneous with Jesus, the Beidha complex confirms the "abundantly attested" presence of Dionysus in the founder of Christianity's backyard. The elder wine god could be spotted all across the southern Le-vant, from the Nabataeans' stronghold in Petra, up through the Hellenized quarters of Scythopolis and Sepphoris in Galilee.

The God of Ecstasy would never stray far from his sacrament, after all. In the first century AD, the area that is now Syria, Lebanon, Israel, Palestine, and Jordan made a perfectly logical home for Dionysus, who usually hails from North Africa or the Near East in the many versions of his myth.[26] The likely reason? This is where the Canaanite and Phoenician sailors kicked off the Mediterranean wine trade in the two millennia before Jesus. If we target points farther east, it's also where the first signs of the cultivated grape were detected by Patrick McGovern, the Indiana Jones of Extreme Beverages from the University of Pennsylvania. Several sites in the area between the Taurus Mountains in eastern Turkey and the Zagros Mountains in north-western Iran have yielded grape seeds of the domesticated variety (*Vitis vi-nifera*). According to Biblical tradition, interestingly enough, this is also the same terrain that inspired Noah to plant the first vineyard on Mount Ararat, where eastern Turkey now meets Armenia (the country that boasts the earliest wine-making facility in the world at Areni, dating to about 4000 BC).[27]

From the very beginning, however, this cradle of viticulture is stocking the Mediterranean with something more than the ordinary stuff. I scrutinize all the wine in Veronese's soaring canvas: sloshing into the golden amphora, twinkling in the groom's chalice. Even the Virgin Mary cups an empty hand on the table, eager for her first taste. What was this long-haired wizard about to unleash on these people?

By making Jesus's first miracle a wine miracle, the Gospel of John undoubtedly tried to establish Jesus as the new Dionysus, turning Cana into the new Elis and Andros: the place where miracles happen. But by setting his scene in the wine country of Galilee, John wasn't actually saying anything new at all. He was merely offering a reminder about the history of wine in a region that was already intimately familiar with Dionysus and his extraordinary sacrament. Before, during, and after the life of Jesus in Nazareth, the God of Ecstasy enjoyed a loyal following in the neighborhood. The archaeological finds from Scythopolis to Sepphoris to Petra are clear about that. But precisely how long before Jesus did the wine get there? And what kind of wine was it?

John's audience would have understood that the Wedding at Cana wasn't just a party trick, and that the wine wasn't just party wine. It was a liquid *pharmakon*, with a rich heritage behind it. The use of drugged wine didn't just accidentally creep its way into Galilee in the first century AD. A couple of thousand years before the Greeks, and long before Jesus and the Gospel of John, the sacrament that would turn eastern Mediterraneans from beer drinkers into wine drinkers didn't just make a passing visit to the vineyards of Galilee.

It started there. And stayed there.

10

Holy Elixirs in the Holy Land

The wine formulas of Dioscorides from the first century AD are compelling proof of a psychedelic tradition in the Greek world. But like the spiked beer of prehistoric Europe, the physical evidence can often be elusive. At the moment, no sites in Greece have yielded any hard data for the Drug of Immortality. For the archaic origins of spiked wine, we have to look to the Near East, the place where it all began. In the distant past, far earlier than anyone else, the Canaanites and Phoenicians who occupied the Holy Land were ritually mixing psychoactive material into their wine. When the Greeks took control of the area in the centuries before Jesus, the old tradition was still alive. Thanks to freshly unearthed vessels and archaeochemical analyses, we now know for a fact that if ancient Galilee was good for anything, it was the kind of wine that would make Dioscorides proud.

In recent years the emerging discipline of archaeochemistry has not only rewritten the history of ancient beer, it has also rewritten the history of ancient wine. Like the nightshade beers from Spain, and perhaps even the prehistoric graveyard beers from the Raqefet Cave and Göbekli Tepe, the wine of yesterday has emerged as a far more complex and mysterious beverage than previously thought. Once again the star of the show is Patrick McGovern. In 2017, as mentioned earlier, he was the one who found the oldest Eurasian evidence for grape fermentation, dated to about 6000 BC,

Carl Ruck, overlooking Hingham Bay near his longtime residence
in Hull, Massachusetts, May 2018.

The author in the massive courtyard at the entrance to the archaeological site of
Eleusis in September 2018. *Ilias Monacholias*

Dr., Dr. h.c. ALBERT HOFMANN　　　　　CH-4149　Burg i.L., 2.IV.1976

Rittimatte

Dear Gordon,

I shall follow your suggestions, made in your letter of March 6, concerning our inquiry in Greece. I shall try to get the information we need for our trip in order to collect ergot samples.

The first point in our programm, the question wether Ergobasin is hallucinogenic, is al ready cleared up. Yesterday I have made a self-experiment with 1,6 mg Ergobasin. It elicited pronounced psychotropic effects, which lastened about 10 hours. The side effects were the same which I experience after taking LSD or Psilocybin, i.e. slight nausea and a strange feeling in the spinal cord. These side effects of psychedelic drugs differ from individual to individual. With my eyes closed I saw colored figures, mainly abstract geometrical forms but sometimes also organic elements, animals, plants. The feeling of my ego and its connection with the outer world was changed. I felt the need to lay down and to dream. Late in the evening just after the beginning of sleep I woke up like after an inner explosion. This happened two times.

Now we know: the watter soluble constituent of ergot is a strong psychotropic agent. It is about 5 to 10 times more effective than Psilocybin. As you know, Ergobasin is used in obstetrics to stop hemmorhage. It is injected intramuscularly to women just after the birth of the child in a dosage of 0,1 mg to 0,25 mg. I am surprised that the psychic effects of Ergobasin have not been observed until now. This may be explained by the low dosage used and by the fact that women just after the birth are anyway in an extraordinary state of mind. I foresee the implications when we publish our findings that hippies may use pharmaceutical preparations like"Ergotrate" Lilly, or "Ergonovine" etc. containing Ergobasin as oxytocic (= unterus contracting) agent, in order to get"high".

I enclose two samples of Ergobasin for your personal use, if you like to test it yourself, which I would suggest. One sample contains 2,0 mg, the other 3,0 mg Ergobasin in the form of a water soluble salt. You dissolve the content in a glass of water or fruit juice, just as you do it with Psilocybin. I have not checked the influence of Ergobasin on my bood pressure. Could you carry out the first experiment with Ergobasin under medical supervision? - in order to get absolutely save.

I shall inform you as soon as possible about the right period of time for our trip to Greece.

Cordially

PS.- I am in correspondence with Dr. St. Grof.
What is your impression from Esalen
Institute, Big Sur?

Albert.

During the author's search of the Tina & R. Gordon Wasson Ethnomycological Collection Archives at the Botany Libraries of Harvard University, this letter surfaced. From his home in Rittimatte, Switzerland, Albert Hofmann sent some "Ergobasin" (ergonovine) in the mail to Wasson for self-experimentation. Hofmann suspected that ergonovine, one of the many ergot alkaloids, was responsible for the beatific vision reported by the ancient initiates at Eleusis. His 1976 experiment with the compound proved successful: "5 to 10 times more effective than psilocybin." Carl Ruck, who acted the part of guinea pig once the psychedelic arrived in the United States, reported mixed results. The hunt for the exact chemical recipe of the original *kukeon* continues. *Courtesy of Andreas Hofmann, Beatrix Hofmann, and Simon Duttwyler*

Carl Ruck's chess set, featuring satyrs as pawns. Beside them, an Aztec mushroom stone that once belonged to Ruck's friend, collaborator, and ethnobotanical pioneer, R. Gordon Wasson.

The chief excavator of Eleusis, Kalliope Papangeli, under the wooden pergola beside the Archaeological 0Museum, September 2018.

The National Archaeological Museum in Athens, Greece. The office of the country's General Director of Antiquities and Cultural Heritage, Dr. Polyxeni Adam-Veleni, sits just around the corner.

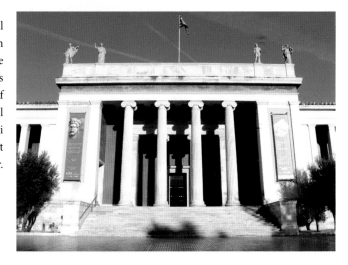

Chunks of LEGO-like marble under the shade of an olive tree at the archaeological site of Eleusis. In the background to the right, the Greek Orthodox Church of Panagia Mesosporitissa (Our Virgin of the Mid-Sowing) dominates the precipice overlooking the former pagan capital of the ancient Mediterranean world.

From inside the Ploutonion cave at the archaeological site of Eleusis, the mouth of Hell. More than 1,600 years after the Mysteries were obliterated by the newly Christianized Roman Empire, pilgrims still flock to this sanctuary to leave offerings for the Queen of the Dead, Persephone. Among the cache: pomegranate, walnuts, almonds, olive branches, and sesame cake.

Dr. Martin Zarnkow at his office next to the world's oldest working brewery, at the Weihenstephan Research Center for Brewing and Food Quality at the Technical University, Munich, Germany.

Patrick E. McGovern stands beside one of the three cauldrons from the Midas tomb at Gordion (Turkey), ca. 740–700 BC, holding a replica large drinking-bowl. *Courtesy of Thomas A. Stanley; courtesy of the University of Pennsylvania Museum ofArchaeology and Anthropology*

Mark Hoffman (left), Ramón Buxó (center), and Carl Ruck (right) transiting the nave of the twelfth-century Romanesque basilica at the Benedictine Abbey of Sant Pere de Galligants, Girona, Spain. *Courtesy of Museu de Arqueologia de Catalunya-Girona*

The medieval cloisters of the Benedictine Abbey of Sant Pere de Galligants, Girona, Spain, just below the Archaeological Museum of Girona. *Courtesy of Museu de Arqueologia de Catalunya- Girona*

Carl Ruck inspecting the ceramic incense burner (thymiateria) of a Greek goddess (left); the chalice (kantharos) that tested positive for ergotized beer (center); and the terra-cotta head of Demeter or Persephone (right). *Courtesy of Museu de Arqueologia de Catalunya-Girona*

Carl Ruck and the chief archaeologist of Mas Castellar de Pontós, Enriqueta Pons, outside the Archaeological Museum of Girona, February 2019.

Reconstruction of the Greek Mysteries dedicated to Demeter and Persephone inside the domestic chapel at Mas Castellar de Pontós in Catalonia, Spain. Two priestesses lead the ceremonial journey into the underworld: double torches are held aloft by one, sheaves of grain by the other. The ritual elements of the Mysteries are all on display: on the left, the hand mill for grinding the grain of the sacred beer; in the center, the incense burners stationed around a third priestess pouring an offering; on the back wall, the Greco-Italic amphoras; and to the right, a dog being sacrificed on the altar of Pentelic marble by two elderly witches in honor of Hecate, the patron goddess of witchcraft. Musicians fill the chapel with a haunting melody to welcome the goddesses. A young girl holds the skull of the ancestor whose teeth revealed traces of ergot, awaiting his return. And throughout, female initiates consume the home- made kukeon in miniature vessels. The psychedelic graveyard beer is being ladled by a chief witch from the bell-shaped vase that was unearthed in one of the subterranean silos outside. The Ancient Greek krater of the drunken, Dionysian parade dated to the fifth century BC, only a few generations after the Phocaeans first founded the colony of Emporion to the east. © *Cesc Pujol*

in what is now modern-day Georgia. But his scientific love affair with Stone Age wine started a couple decades earlier.

In 1996 McGovern's analysis of two ceramic vessels from the Hajji Firuz Tepe site (ca. 5400–5000 BC) in far west Iran, near the border with Turkey and Iraq, proved that Neolithic wine was resinated with terebinth or pine resin, "added as a preservative and medical agent."[1] In its archaic form wine was not the polished, moderately psychoactive product coming out of today's vineyards. McGovern says the wine enthusiasm that consolidated in this area of the Fertile Crescent "might be better dubbed a mixed fermented beverage or extreme beverage culture," making use of "a wide assortment" of fruit, grains, honey, and plant additives to their grape juice.[2] Pertinent to our investigation is what McGovern calls "special brews" with a ritualistic purpose, "perhaps laced with a flavorful or mind-altering herb."[3] Exactly what you'd need to navigate that mysterious barrier between life and death on your journey to the imperishable stars.

In "Ancient Egyptian Herbal Wines," published in the prestigious *Proceedings of the National Academy of Sciences* in May 2009, McGovern details his analysis of the tomb treasure from Abydos belonging to the protodynastic ruler Scorpion I. It was unearthed in 1988 by the Cairo branch of the German Archaeological Institute and dated to 3150 BC, at the very beginning of the pharaonic line that would govern the Egyptian kingdom for the next three thousand years. Some seven hundred pottery jars of a "foreign type" were found perfectly intact, amounting to about twelve hundred gallons of a royal potion. After isolating tartaric acid, the key biomarker for wine and grape products, McGovern decided to search the "yellowish flaky residue" within the jars for any herbal additives. His high-tech analysis, using solid phase microextraction (SPME) and gas chromatography-mass spectrometry (GC-MS), revealed a series of complex monoterpenes that naturally occur in a number of different plants and herbs.[4] Among other chemical compounds, camphor, borneol, carvone, and thymol were extracted from the ancient residue. They are all found in yarrow (*Achillea*), which McGovern has elsewhere described as "highly suggestive of a ritual involving psychoactive plants."[5]

Using these biomolecular fingerprints, McGovern was also able to pinpoint the ancient geographic source of the additives to this special brew:

Nearly all were domesticated or cultivated in the southern Levant in advance of their introduction into Egypt. . . . Beginning ca. 3000 B.C., as the domesticated grapevine was transplanted to the Nile Delta, one may reasonably hypothesize that some southern Levantine herbs accompanied or soon followed it into the gardens and fields of the country. These developments considerably expanded the Egyptian pharmacopeia.

As for the seven hundred jars themselves, McGovern's analysis of thirty-five chemical elements concluded "to a 99 percent probability" that the jars "were made of the same clays as those found in the Jordan Valley, the Hill Country of the West Bank and Transjordan, and the Gaza region."[6] In other words, they originated in the territory that would later belong to Dionysus and Jesus in the first century AD. Why did Scorpion I stockpile so much foreign wine on his deathbed? McGovern calls it "elite emulation"

Wine jars unearthed in chamber 10 of Scorpion I's royal tomb from Abydos, Egypt, dating to ca. 3150 BC. The infused wine was spiked with plants and herbs from Jesus's future home in the southern Levant. *(© Deutsches Archäologisches Institut Kairo, DAI Cairo)*

or "conspicuous consumption." Like importing "liquid gold," these wine-based elixirs from the southern Levant "were regularly exchanged between Near Eastern kings as gifts to seal treaties," or to simply "create goodwill and lend prestige to their rule."[7] In addition, McGovern supports Ruck's basic notion that "ancient wine and other alcoholic beverages are known to be an excellent means to dissolve and administer herbal concoctions externally and internally." Before the easy availability of modern synthetic medicines, McGovern says "alcoholic beverages were the universal palliative."

Because the divine intoxicant was meant to accompany the Egyptian pharaoh into the underworld, however, its use as an advanced religious bio-technology cannot be overlooked. Just like the beer from Mas Castellar de Pontós, the special brew may have fueled the visionary states that allowed Scorpion I and later Egyptian kings to both witness and become one with the gods. Although priestesses are thought to have been the original enologists, and "lore surrounding the vine personified it as a female entity," Osiris likely predated Dionysus as the first male wine god.[8]

According to the oldest surviving illustrated papyrus roll, which preserves the ancient Egyptian coronation ceremony in amazing detail, wine would be presented as an "Eye of Horus" in order to cure the king of his "spiritual blindness."[9] A ritual meal was then ingested as part of the "secret rites" engineered to transform Osiris's earthly representative into the wine god himself. In this supreme act of "mystical conjunction"—drinking the god to *become* the god—the human king sought to merge with Osiris as the Lord of Death. In preparation for his eternal sleep, the royal initiate is said to have traveled to and actually *experienced* the cosmic underworld, receiving "the awesome knowledge of what lies beyond the threshold of death."[10] Thousands of years before Jesus or the lamas interviewed by Father Francis, the Egyptian pharaohs are said to have acquired the light body of a "shining spirit" (*akh* in Egyptian) that allowed them to traverse the starry afterlife.[11]

Did psychedelic wine, first imported from the southern Levant, really provide the means, motive, and opportunity for this three-thousand-year-long religious enterprise? According to the late archaeologist and anthropologist Dr. Andrew Sherratt, the "vast quantities of wine" consumed in weeklong Dionysian festivals at the Temple of Karnak seemed worthy of a closer look. He noticed the same blue water lilies (*Nymphaea caerulea*) depicted on Karnak's pillars were also found as a garland around the golden neck of Tutankhamun, when the pharaoh's tomb was first opened in 1922.[12] Another incarnation of Osiris, the blue water lily is now extremely rare in the wild, but once grew abundantly on the shallow banks of the Nile. It was considered Ancient Egypt's most sacred plant. And with the active compounds, apomorphine and nuciferin, it was full of psychoactive possibility.[13]

As part of the *Sacred Weeds* series that aired on the UK's Channel 4 in 1998, Sherratt and his colleagues (an Egyptologist, an ethnobotanist, and a pharmacologist) enlisted two courageous volunteers to drink some wine-soaked flower concoction in the first televised re-creation of the ancient sacrament. After a nice fit of the giggles, the restless duo is seen frolicking through the rainy gardens of Hammerwood Park in East Sussex. Though no visions of Osiris were recorded, the blue water lily was shown to have undeniable mind-altering effects, even at relatively low dosage. The whole trippy experiment makes for excellent YouTube viewing at https://www.youtube .com/watch?v=Vx2AIBgnakI.

As we move closer to Christianity's home turf, the plot thickens. Some of the best evidence for ancient spiked wine just happens to come from modern-day Galilee. Where the magical appeal of the drink that would later show up in the Wedding at Cana and Christianity's founding event, the Last Supper, extended far beyond its alcohol content.

The homeland of Jesus was praised in antiquity for its wine production, going all the way back to the Canaanites. In 2013 murky hearsay met hard fact when the Tel Kabri site, an hour north of Nazareth, made international headlines. Forty jars of herbal wine were unearthed in what became known as the "world's oldest wine cellar," dating to about 1700 BC.[14] Organic residue from each of the jars was subjected to thorough testing at the Brandeis University Department of Chemistry. The results of the GC-MS analyses showed remarkable consistency across the entire batch, indicating "a sophisticated understanding of the botanical landscape and the pharmacopeic skills necessary to produce a complex beverage that balanced preservation, palatability, and psychoactivity."[15]

In their peer-reviewed paper published in the open-source journal *PLoS ONE* in August 2014, the interdisciplinary team identified a number of organic compounds in the wine. Andrew Koh (senior research fellow at the

Massachusetts Institute of Technology's Center for Materials Research in Archaeology and Ethnology), Assaf Yasur-Landau (professor of archaeology at the University of Haifa), and Eric Cline (professor of Classics, anthropology and history at George Washington University) noted the challenge in trying to pair these freshly captured biomarkers with their ancient organic sources. Like McGovern, they acknowledge that the compounds are present at varying concentrations in many different plants and herbs. Nevertheless they can still piece together an accurate match based on "the natural distribution of ancient commodities" and "surviving documentary accounts" from ancient Galilee and the surrounding area.

Aside from Greek, many ancient Near Eastern languages like Egyptian, Sumerian, Akkadian, Elamite, Hittite, Hebrew, and Aramaic have preserved the names of a dizzying number of plants, herbs, and fungi. By some estimates, however, only 20 percent of those species referenced in the dusty texts "have been definitively identified by genus."[16] That's why, for example, the debate over the kind of "laurel" employed by the Pythian priestesses at Delphi can rage on, because the ancient plant may not quite correspond to our modern scientific classification of the *Laurus* genus, let alone the *Laurus nobilis* species. But the written ethnobotanical evidence, such as the wine formulas of Dioscorides, are only half the puzzle. Completing it demands the rigorous collection of organic residue from ancient vessels, which can then be paired with paleoecological maps that plot where each of the analyzed species actually grew in antiquity. While this interdisciplinary effort was not part of the archaeological mind-set until quite recently, the combination of ancient texts, chemical data, and habitat maps is finally shedding much-needed light on the art and science of ancient wine-making. And the results from places like Tel Kabri show exactly where the Greeks inherited their taste for infused, mind-altering wine.

In addition to tartaric acid, the GC-MS readings at Tel Kabri included cinnamic acid, oleanolic acid, cineole, caryophyllene, and methyl syringate. According to the team, the most likely candidates that would have spiked the palatial red wine at Tel Kabri include honey, storax resin (*Liquidambar orientalis*), terebinth resin (*Pistacia palaestina* or *terebinthus*), cyperus roots (*Cyperus rotundus*), cedar oil (*Cedrus libani*), juniper berries (*Juniperus communis* or *phoenicea*), mint (*Mentha*), myrtle (*Myrtus communis*), and cinnamon bark (*Cinnamomum*). The many ingredients of this "luxurious ancient concoction" are attested as wine additives in the so-called Mari Let-ters, a collection of Mesopotamian tablets written in Akkadian in the eigh-teenth century BC. Evidence of a similar herbal kick appears in the widely published Egyptian recipes for *kyphi* (temple incense) that began circulating in the fifteenth century BC.

Nothing like the blue water lily was identified in the regal cellar, but the adjoining banquet hall hints at the religious nature of this special brew.[17] As does the *Juniperus* genus, certain species of which are revered for their psychoactivity. Juniper berries contain rich, volatile oils with "antiviral, an-tibiotic, and antifungal properties," which may explain their superstitious use for protection in traditional rites and ceremonies.[18] Historically shamans in Central Asia have resorted to juniper for "ritual, magical and medicinal purposes," making it "likely one of the oldest fumigants of humankind."[19] The Hunza people of the Hindu Kush in northern Pakistan, for example, say juniper is directly responsible for the "supernatural powers" of their *bitaiyos* (the magicians, healers and prophets):

> *They manifest their abilities only after inhaling the smoke of burn-ing juniper branches and drinking warm goat's blood. After this, they danced to rhythmic drum beats until they had attained the trance state. When asked about the future, they passed on the messages of the fairies in the form of songs.*[20]

For the Canaanites the wine additives identified at Tel Kabri could have come in handy during their far-reaching but understudied *marzeah* ritual, a drunken funerary feast or memorial banquet for the dead that could last up to a week.[21] The *marzeah* was reserved exclusively for the upper class of Near Eastern society. As a kind of guild or drinking club, it has earned comparisons to the more well-known wine banquet in Ancient Greece, the symposium. McGovern says, "music, dance and the recital of Canaanite myths accompanied the merriment, along with bouts of sexual intercourse to match any Roman bacchanal."[22] But the main purpose of the *marzeah*, as with the skull cults and graveyard beers we tracked over ten thousand years from Stone Age Israel and Turkey to Ancient Greece and classical Iberia, was to acquaint its participants with the afterlife and "to secure their beatification after death."[23]

Particularly fascinating about the *marzeah* is the possibility that it acted as the bridge between the more archaic drinking ceremonies from Egypt and the Near East, including Tel Kabri, and the later Mysteries belonging to both Dionysus and Jesus. Common to all these rituals is the concept of ingesting a special potion for a singular purpose: to transcend ordinary time and space, reaching a state of consciousness where the ancestors still live and breathe, and the gods and goddesses are made real. For lack of vocabulary, scholars often refer to this place as the "underworld." And maybe the initiates of the *marzeah* truly believed they went somewhere, just like the initiates of the Greek and Christian Mysteries in the centuries that followed. But at the end of the day, we're only trying to get hold of the mechanism that created the *sensation* of otherworldly travel, and the conviction that creates whole religions in the wake of these unforgettable mystical experiences. The data from Mas Castellar de Pontós show that ordinary beer could hardly take credit for the survival of a graveyard tradition that likely reaches far back into the Stone Age. For the *marzeah* ordinary wine doesn't seem to be responsible for its long history either.

Clues to the bizarre Canaanite ritual were embedded in one of the cuneiform tablets of Ugarit (modern-day Syria), composed just a few centuries after the royalty at Tel Kabri hatched their psychoactive wine. Despite many failed attempts to decipher the ceremony of the dead, a leading scholar of Canaanite religion and mysticism may have finally figured it out. In "The Marzeah and the Ugaritic Magical Ritual System," published in 2015, Gregorio del Olmo Lete deconstructs the text known as *The Divine Feast of El*, referring to the chief Near Eastern deity of this period. For del Olmo Lete, professor emeritus at the University of Barcelona, the literal translation of *marzeah* is "descent," implying a journey to the underworld. Alternatively it could mean "a tool that makes [one] fall" or collapse in ecstasy, or simply lie down dead.[24]

In a reading that parallels the Indo-European graveyard beers, del Olmo Lete sees evidence for hallucinogenic wine as advanced religious biotechnology, calling *The Divine Feast of El* a "handbook" or "recipe" for "intoxication praxis" that induces a "cataleptic state of trance."[25] In this "altered state of consciousness reached by drunkenness," the initiate is permitted "terrifying entry" into the mysterious "Other World" of "infernal ghosts," where a skilled explorer can secure divinatory answers to life's existential questions from the godlike spirits.[26] Or maybe it's the "fairies" talking. To awaken from this near-death experience, the Ugaritic text orders the paralyzed body of the initiate to be anointed from forehead to navel with an unidentifiable wild plant.

Every GOVERNMENT WARNING label on every bottle of Pinot in the United States cautions against a series of risks: birth defects, car accidents, machinery disaster. Not a single one mentions the possibility of dead relatives showing up at the door. Like the written wine formulas of Dioscorides, nothing about the *marzeah*'s special brew even remotely resembles anything we would call "wine." McGovern's "extreme beverage culture" of the eastern Mediterranean had crafted an extreme drinking ritual to accompany their extreme drink, perhaps providing the optimal setting to showcase their "sophisticated understanding of the botanical landscape" and "pharmacopeic skills." The active ingredients that may have potentiated the mixture remain an absolute mystery. But given the hard, archaeochemical data of the herbal blends from Egyptian Abydos and Canaanite Tel Kabri, it's a safe bet that someone like Andrew Koh at the Massachusetts Institute of Technology may crack the *marzeah* code in the years to come.

At forty-four years old, Koh is part of the younger generation that benefited from the work of McGovern and other pioneers such as Richard Evershed at the University of Bristol. But unlike most of his colleagues in the still-maturing discipline of archaeological chemistry, Koh has an additional background in Classics. It gives him a unique transdisciplinary perspective on the search for ancient beverages. Because of his familiarity with the tradition of drugged wine from Homer to Dioscorides and beyond, Koh is rather open-minded about the possibility of the *marzeah* linking the Galilee of the Canaanites in 1700 BC to the Galilee of the Ancient Greeks and Christians in the first century AD. As a sanity check after my trip to Paris, I called his office in Boston to make sure Ruck's scholarship on psychedelic wine was actually supported by the latest evidence.

Koh told me about the recent discovery of yet more luxury liquids at another site in Upper Galilee. Soon to be published in the *Bulletin of the American Schools of Oriental Research,* his organic-residue analysis of small vessels from a Hellenistic administrative building in Tel Kedesh, on the border with Lebanon, revealed oil from the iconic Phoenician cedar (*Cedrus libani*) was spiked with the same imported storax resin (*Liquidambar orientalis*) from the same region of Rhodes that was found fifteen hundred years earlier in the Cannanite wine of Tel Kabri. Dating to the second century BC, it shows the continuity of psychotropic infusions in the region, well into the period when Greek influence was at its height. So even if he hasn't found it yet, the odds of Koh eventually securing the hard evidence for overtly psychedelic wine seem good. The chemical answer to the *marzeah* mystery is within reach.

"I think you're absolutely right," Koh said into the phone. "When we're talking about ancient wine, we tend to have a one-size-fits-all approach. But think about beer these days, for example: it's not just for drinking and watching football. We have some really complex beers with different alcohol and flavor profiles. Ancient wine was no different. If you look carefully at the historical record, there was wine for very casual settings, all the way to very formal events like the Mysteries. But like everything else in life, it's probably not so binary. Maybe it's our puritanical background, but we want to separate the two—the casual, mundane drinking from the sacred, religious drinking. Back then, however, the lines were more blurred, and things more intertwined."

"Like at Tel Kabri or Tel Kedesh?" I asked. "And maybe even the earliest Christian communities, who could have been influenced by the *marzeah* or Dionysian Mysteries that we know were active in Galilee at the time of Jesus?"

"Right. At first glance, the wine cellar at Kabri seems like wealthy elites getting hammered and having a good time. But then you look more closely, and I think that's too simplistic of an answer. Because they're adding things to the wine, and those ingredients are not just for preservation. It's not solely to get a buzz from the alcohol. When you look at the literature from the time, there are festivals in Egypt and the Levant like the *marzeah* that are just rife with ritualistic meaning. They are literally communing with the gods and so forth. So I think Kabri *does* connect to the later Hellenistic and Roman periods, where the Mystery or cultic aspect only intensifies. I think what we in the archaeological community have been missing for a while now, is that wine is such a perfect beverage—once the right ingredients are added to it—to have a profound religious experience, with a psychotropic effect. So I call that kind of wine a potion, because it's not just a drink. It's a sacrament."

Koh is confident that the smoking-gun evidence for psychedelic wine is out there in the birthplace of Christianity, patiently waiting just underfoot. For many centuries, right up until the Wedding at Cana and the Last Supper, the *marzeah* documented in *The Divine Feast of El* remained a staple across the region, uniting ancient Israel, Judah, and Babylon in El's "wine-god cult." Like the Egyptians, Canaanites, and Phoenicians before them, the Israelites and their neighbors were just as interested in the cult of the dead and its special wine that put the Holy Land on the map in the first place.

The pagan ritual is actually mentioned twice in the Old Testament, disparagingly, of course—confirming the survival of this rather primordial tradition into Biblical times.[27] Despite the Jewish high priests' opposition to the wine-fueled séance, pilgrim flasks, wine decanters, and amphoras have been unearthed from the ancient tombs in and around Jerusalem.[28] And farther south, more death-cult remains have come to the surface. In September 2009 a sandstone block accidentally turned up in Wadi Musa, near the Dionysian temple in Petra. Its partly legible inscription confirms that the hallucinatory *marzeah* ritual was still alive and well during Jesus's lifetime. The text is "clearly dated" to the reign of the high-profile Nabataean king Aretas IV Philopatris (9 BC–AD 40). His daughter, Phasaelis, married King Herod Antipas, the infamous ruler of Galilee. To please his second wife after divorcing Phasaelis, Herod famously served the head of John the Baptist on a platter.[29]

Where the *marzeah* ends and the Dionysian banquet begins, nobody really knows.[30] The God of Ecstasy had slowly taken root in the "ancient cultural internet" of North Africa and the Levant that Osiris and El had been seeding with their magic for millennia. Eventually, part of the wine god would head west to Greece as Dionysus, debuting on Euripides's stage in the fifth century BC with his Asian maenads after a tour through Anatolia. Over in Athens, Dionysus would become the Lord of Death like his Egyptian and Near Eastern counterparts, leading an annual train of ghosts into the city during the springtime Anthesteria festival. Similar to our Halloween, it was the time of year when, "attracted by the smell of the wine that rose from the opened *pithoi* [earthen pots] and spread throughout the city, the souls emerged from the underworld."[31] But another part of the wine god would simply stay put, right where it all began over three thousand years before Jesus, who would become the latest God of Ecstasy to overcome death. The Nazarene was well acquainted with the underworld from the Harrowing of Hell episode that supposedly took place in the three days between Jesus's death and resurrection, when "the Gospel was proclaimed to those who are now dead."[32]

It's a neat line of succession: Osiris to El to Dionysus to Jesus. The critical thing that unites them all is extraordinary wine that blurs the boundary between life and death. Immortality potions. But there's a major difference between Dionysus and Jesus on the one hand, and their divine predecessors

White-figure vessel (*lekuthos*) from Attica, Greece, dating to 470 BC. Containers like this were frequently deposited in ancient graves as part of Greek funerary rituals. The god Hermes is depicted wielding his magic wand in the sacred role of psychopomp, escorting the recently deceased into the afterlife (left). From the mouth of the half-buried earthen pot (*pithos*) to Hermes's right, the souls of the dead can be seen emerging from the wine (right). Some fly off to the underworld on angelic wings. Others, more demonic, are being crammed back into the holy wine from which they came. The Halloween-like Anthesteria festival has come to end. And so too, the drinking of the drugged elixir in honor of Dionysus, the Lord of Death. *Courtesy of Dennis Graen, Friedrich-Schiller-Universität Jena, Germany*

on the other: a political disagreement. Did this wine belong to the 1 percent or the 99 percent? Was it meant for the pharaohs, royalty, and elite? Or was it meant for everybody? Who should have access to the nectar of the gods?

Religious revolution was afoot in pre-Christian Galilee. The intoxicant had begun leaking from the Near Eastern palaces and mansions the same way the *kukeon* had slipped from Eleusis, traveling to wealthy homes across Athens during the scandalous imitation of the sacred rites known as the Profanation of the Mysteries. As A. D. Nock insightfully remarked in the last chapter, the spiritually curious were being drawn to a kind of "private spontaneous pagan piety," where elements of "choice, movement, and individual enthusiasm" were preferable to whatever soul-crushing boredom the local temples had to offer the pagan and Jewish residents of the area. By the time of Jesus, a democratizing trend led by ecstatic women had revamped sacred wine into what Euripides, four centuries earlier, had called a sacrament for "simple folk" or *phauloteron* (φαυλότερον): "equally to the rich and to the lowly has [Dionysus] given the painless joy of wine."[33]

So forget the Egyptian pharaohs. Forget the royal families at Tel Kabri, Petra, and everywhere in between. Forget the *marzeah*, reserved only for the vineyard-owning aristocrats with nothing but time and money to waste on their spooky, sometimes decadent ritual.[34] Forget the Jewish high priests who banned the *marzeah*, with all its "occult" implications.[35] And forget the buzzkill Pharisees, who later in the Gospels would call Jesus a "drunk" or *oinopotes* (οἰνοπότης).[36] People were aching for their own little taste of that miraculous wine. And for the already-smashed wedding guests at Cana, where the only way for the Jesus of John's Gospel to prove his divinity was to perform the "signature miracle" of Dionysus, that's exactly what they got: 180 gallons' worth.

By bringing the oldest trick in the Dionysian book back home to the Near East, where the sacrament itself was born in the distant past and where the God of Ecstasy had reestablished a foothold thanks to the regional acceptance of Greek culture, the Gospel of John was issuing a stark challenge to the 1 percent of the first century AD. From the beginning, the Christian potion was destined for mass consumption, just like the Dionysian potion that had been working its magic in Greece and Greek-speaking hubs of the eastern Mediterranean for centuries, including parts of Galilee. Unlike the ritual beverages that preceded it, the wine at Cana was meant to travel all over the ancient world, into the hands of humble people with humble hopes for the afterlife. And into humble parts of the Roman Empire, still farther west of Greece, where the wine god that Jesus would soon replace was in desperate need of a revival. All thanks to the politicians in Rome.

As I exit the Salle des États, I take one last look at the *Mona Lisa*'s patronizing smirk. All night long, when she is blanketed in moonlight, da Vinci's masterpiece is stuck here staring at a complete and total fantasy. Not through any fault of Veronese. *The Wedding Feast at Cana* is a fair interpretation of John's Gospel, but the scene almost certainly never happened. Why is the raucous episode from ancient Galilee recorded in John and nowhere else? And why the shameless infringement of the Dionysian epiphanies from Elis and Andros? Scholars like Dennis MacDonald have concluded that John cast Jesus in the same mold as the God of Ecstasy to emphasize his godhood. Fair enough. John gets zero points for originality. But a god without wine in the southern Levant was like a car without wheels, so perhaps John had little choice but to incorporate the "extreme beverage" into that particular Epiphany around AD 30. Nevertheless, the question remains. What's the *real* relationship between Jesus and Dionysus? And what's the *real* message here?

For those Greek speakers who could recognize the secret "symbols" and "language," as A. D. Nock put it, John had many more surprises in store. Cana was just the opening act. A sneak peek of the real dinner, three years later, that would forever alter the course of human history, putting Jesus at the top of our species' virtual Twitter feed with 2.42 billion followers. The biggest religion on the planet today. The biggest religion ever. It all started at the Last Supper, a more intimate affair among friends. Where the wine became blood, and Jesus introduced part two of the trademark Dionysian sacrament: the raw flesh.

In John's poetic treatment of the event, the sacred combination of bread and wine, flesh and blood, represents the most advanced biotechnology in all of antiquity. What Saint Ignatius would later call the *pharmakon athanasias,* the Drug of Immortality that guaranteed instant divinity and life everlasting. To the Greeks this magical procedure was known as apotheosis, or deification. Anyone who ate and drank the god *became* the god. Once the exclusive property of Egyptian pharaohs and Near Eastern elite, the sacrament had been dribbling over the mountains and forests of the Mediterranean ever since Euripides. But civilizations rise and fall, and the Mysteries have a way of getting caught in the cross fire. Once obsessed with the wine god whom they inherited from their predecessors, especially in that Greek-speaking part of southern Italy known as Magna Graecia, a moral panic had swept through the Roman Empire when men started joining in the debauched festivals previously restricted to women.[37] The Roman senate prohibited the full-blown Bacchanalia in 186 BC, creating an uncertain future for the God of Ecstasy.

Around 20 BC the conservative historian Livy wrote his dramatic retelling of the scandal, portraying it "as a reaction against the sudden infiltration of too many Greek elements into Roman worship."[38] The final straw for the Roman senate was the Italian witch, Paculla Annia, the scandalous high priestess of Bacchus in Campania—the heartland of Magna Graecia, home to Naples and Pompeii.[39] In the years leading up to the mass crackdown on the Dionysian Mysteries in 186 BC, Paculla Annia refused to initiate any men over the age of twenty.[40] "Rather than having women in the control of men," says Dr. Fiachra Mac Góráin, a classicist at University College London, "this cult is putting young, impressionable men under the control of women."[41] In a staunchly patriarchal society like Rome, that was an act of war. So the authorities made the flood of magical wine slow to a trickle.

By the time of Jesus the world was ready for another injection of holy madness. At long last, the faithful may have cheered, the Son of God had come home to Galilee. Call him Jesus, if you like. But when John's Gospel called him the "only-begotten" or "unique offspring" of God, residing in the "lap" of the Father, his audience knew what he meant. After all, where else but Nazareth would Jesus grow up? Only minutes from Dionysian country in Scythopolis. And just down the road from the Mona Lisa of Galilee in Sepphoris. Of all the places for Jesus to call home, the drug-riddled Napa Valley of the ancient world just happened to be the one. Where wine was a sacrament for the cult of the dead that found inspiration in both the long-running *marzeah* and the Dionysian Mysteries. And where the magician from Nazareth and his earliest followers could have sourced an endless supply of those mind-altering substances the southern Levant had been pumping into the area for three millennia. The same drugs that would soon be encyclopedically catalogued in the most consulted, most durable manuscript of the next two thousand years: the *Materia Medica*.

Less than a decade after Jesus's death, Dioscorides was born in Cilicia in Asia Minor (near the modern Turkish-Syrian border). He studied in nearby Tarsus, the birthplace of Paul, who before becoming Saint Paul was simply Saul of Tarsus. The plants, herbs, and fungi documented by the Father of Drugs on his extensive travels with the Roman army under Emperor Nero are "overwhelmingly concentrated on the Greek-speaking world of the Aegean and the Levant."[42] It was the epicenter of experimental wine mixing, where a heavy pagan population squeezed every drop of psychoactive potential from its ancient cash crop. And where the new Dionysus had miraculously returned for one final mission.

Even if they didn't feel it on the eastern frontier of the Roman Empire, the would-be Christians knew the Dionysian Mysteries had faced an existential crisis in Italy, where as many as six thousand followers of the God of Ecstasy were executed in one fell swoop during the Roman senate's bloody campaign in 186 BC.[43] There was no predicting the next moral panic. The most powerful empire in the world, an all-male enterprise, was clamping down on a female-led religion that promised immortality to its initiates. With only a few ounces of its secret potion, this religion with no name had finally broken the spiritual exclusivity of Egypt and the Near East, and the monopoly of the Greek families in Eleusis. And for largely political reasons the Romans wanted this dangerous religion, what Euripides once called "an immoral trick aimed at women," to simply go away.[44] But the Dionysian Mysteries couldn't just disappear. Everyone deserved a taste of divinity. So perhaps the only way to keep the magical wine alive was to fill the ancient world with more Paculla Annias than the Roman Empire could ever possibly control. But the wilderness wasn't the safest or most convenient place to win new converts to the Greek death cult.

The God of Ecstasy had to come indoors.

And Christianity had the answer. On the eastern coast of the Mediterranean, everything was up for grabs in the first century AD, when the latest Son of God, born of a virgin, stepped into the spotlight. In the Gospel of John, the Wedding at Cana may have set the Drug of Immortality loose on the streets of Galilee. But it was the Last Supper that brought the Christian Eucharist into people's homes. Even Dionysus himself never managed to pull that off.

Aside from the public festivals, and the few Athenians who blasphemed Eleusis during the Profanation of the Mysteries, Dionysus's churches were kept off the grid, in the open air of the Greek countryside. So as far as John's audience was concerned, this new Dionysus had just upstaged the old Dionysus. And their interpretation of John's Gospel would have been very different from today's. The Jesus they would have seen was a Jesus who didn't come to start a new religion. But a Jesus who came to save the fragile

Mysteries with an epic, encore performance. A Jesus who came to open source the magical wine for the masses, and to finish the populist movement he started in Greece.

When his name was Dionysus.

It is impossible to understand the roots of Christianity without understanding the world in which it appeared. For roughly the first three hundred years of its existence, Christianity was an illegal cult. Just like the cult of Dionysus. By appealing to poor folks, and especially women, Jesus was simply picking up where the Dionysian Mysteries left off. Politically he posed the same threat to the Roman establishment as Dionysus. Anything that directed attention and loyalty away from by the public cult of the emperor and the traditional Roman gods was considered dangerous. Because at the time, separating young, eligible men from their military service and busy mothers from their family obligations upset the chain of command. Neither belonged in the wilderness, getting high with the God of Drugs. And they didn't belong at the wedding party where Jesus unveiled Dionysus's "signature miracle" either. John makes the general paranoia pretty explicit when he records the reaction of the Jewish high priests to Jesus's string of magic acts following Cana: "If we let him go on like this, everyone will believe in him, and the Romans will come and take away both our place and our nation."[45]

But the politics and legality were only part of the concern. At stake was the entire social order. Jesus and Dionysus were two peas in a pod. They both stood for the revolutionary principle that everybody deserved the nectar of the gods, regardless of class. While the Greeks and southern Italians had many centuries to manage the uncomfortable balancing act between the 1 percent and the 99 percent, Jesus's open invitation to an immortality potion like the Eucharist would have shocked the wealthy pagans of Galilee, as well as the influential Jewish families of Jerusalem. Magical wine was supposed to be *their* prerogative, just the way it had been for thousands of years. Salvation didn't belong in the hands of commoners. After his success in classical Athens, Dionysus was the first monopoly-buster in the Near East. For an extra kick in the pants, Jesus showed up a few centuries later with an even more convenient solution for anyone dissatisfied with the old-time religions. A solution the home brewers at Mas Castellar de Pontós had already discovered. Simply invite some friends over, and cook the sacrament up at home.

In the end Dionysus and Jesus were both really bad for the status quo. There's a reason the crackdown on the Bacchanalia by the Roman senate in 186 BC was the first large-scale religious persecution in European history.[46] And there's a reason Christianity followed suit. In the eyes of the ruling class, the idea of continuity between the Greek and Christian Mysteries was pretty darn clear. Barbaric to the core, they both offered direct access to the Lord of Death following the consumption of the god himself in the form of fortified wine. With their exotic sacraments Dionysians and Christians fit the same vile narrative. According to Mary Beard, John North, and Simon Price, the leading historians of Roman religion, "The issue was exacerbated by the appeal of Christianity to women. The combination of stereotypes of foreign and female, which had been deployed by classical Greeks of eastern women out of control, has always been especially potent."[47]

This is the political and spiritual backdrop of the pagan continuity hypothesis. And it can't be dismissed. The same people who were attracted to the radical cult of Dionysus were the same people who were attracted to the cult of Jesus. They were not so different from the spiritual-but-not-religious of today, seekers on the hunt for transcendence. A real experience with real meaning, where the key to that Dionysian experience was the kind of wine that was universally regarded as a *pharmakon*. It drove the witches like Paculla Annia and their covens mad. It made them delirious. It provoked visions. And in addition to the religious conservatives in Athens who didn't want their Eleusinian Mysteries profaned, it also pissed off the authorities in Rome—the same authorities who would later accuse the Christians of cannibalism and throw them to the lions.

The immortality potion is what unites the Ancient Greeks of the final centuries BC with the paleo-Christians of the early centuries AD. As we will see in detail in the next chapter, the more the Gospel of John could convince potential recruits that the Christian Eucharist was indeed the same *pharmakon*, the greater the chances of the young faith's success in a world where the Dionysian sacrament still dominated the ancient Mediterranean. Where, with every drink from the sacred cup, the maenads risked being branded as criminals. The early Christians ran the same risk, of course. But for some, the price of religious liberty has always been worth the cost.

The way the Greek and Christian Mysteries were targeted by the Roman Empire is well documented in the historical record. Largely ignored by modern scholars, however, is the degree to which the common sacrament of wine motivated the harsh suppression of these revolutionary movements. And whether the great secret of Dionysus and Jesus alike—the secret that unlocked the key to immortality—was, in fact, drugged wine.

It has been a long afternoon, and the Louvre is about to close. I just need a few minutes of peace and quiet to wrap my mind around everything I've seen today. I know exactly where to go to escape the tourists. I make a bee-line for the *Winged Victory of Samothrace* and descend the grand staircase to the museum's Greek collection on the lower level of the Sully Wing. I sneak past the crowd admiring the armless Venus de Milo and duck into my oasis, the Salle des Caryatides. Intentionally or not, the Louvre has constructed a pretty incredible tribute to the God of Ecstasy.

Most of the marble to be found in Room 348 is Roman, based on Greek originals. Like the Italian head of Dionysus from the second century AD, with those "luxurious locks" twisting their way down the god's neck and

Marble head of Dionysus from the second century AD, based on Greek statuary from ca. 500 BC, currently in the Salle des Caryatides in the Louvre. The feminine, flowing hair of the God of Ecstasy inspired early portrayals of Jesus that have persisted ever since. Compare with the Good Shepherd in the Hypogeum of the Aurelii from the third century AD (page 268) or the head of Jesus in Veronese's *The Wedding at Cana* from the sixteenth century AD (page 194). *Stéphane Maréchalle; (© RMN-Grand Palais / Art Resource, NY)*

Dating to ca. 40 BC, the Borghese Vase was discovered in Rome around 1566 and is now a prime attraction of the Salle des Caryatides in the Louvre. The devotee is completely lost in the kind of trance, ecstasy, and madness that defined the holy wine of Dionysus. When the sacrament was properly prepared and consumed, we can imagine divine communion with the god looking something like this. *Hervé Lewandowski;* *(© RMN-Grand Palais / Art Resource, NY)*

shoulders. If you ever wondered why Jesus was the only Jewish man of first-century Galilee to get the Jim Morrison look, this is why.[48] Across the hall, the woodland god Pan, straight out of Narnia, is clutching a bunch of grapes. After leading choirs of nymphs through the hills of Greece, the wine god's confidante would always take a midday nap. Whenever startled by a passing shepherd, Pan would wake with a terrifying shout, giving us the word "panic." The goat-man was the illiterate peasantry's last refuge against an encroaching Christianity. As a result, our popular image of Satan likely comes from this horned, lustful deity—the "rustic one" (*paganus* in Latin, whence the word "pagan").[49]

I circle the Borghese Vase. Standing five and a half feet tall, it boasts an incredible parade of bacchants, carved into the marble. Dazed and confused, one has just lost consciousness. Slumped over in ecstasy, a shaggy-tailed satyr carries him along with *thyrsos* in hand—the long, hollow wand used to carry the wine god's plant additives, according to Ruck.[50] From the celebrant's grasp has just slipped the *kantharos* that knocked him out. I wonder what was in it. The museum's didactic label says this piece "is widely admired for the fine craftsmanship of the figures shown in a trance typical of Dionysian processions." The English plaque calls Dionysus the "god of wine and revelry." In French he's the "god of wine and intoxication" (*dieu du vin et de l'ivresse*). The language barriers never stop.

But the meaning is clear. Behind the Dionysian Mysteries was no ordinary wine. And the Borghese Vase is one of the best representations of the madness that overtook the initiates of this religion. Madness that did

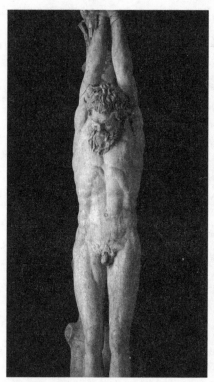

Hanging Marsyas (left), based on an original group of Hellenistic marbles from the third century BC, currently in the Salle des Caryatides in the Louvre. *Daniel Lebée / Carine Déambrosis; (© Musée du Louvre, Dist. RMN-Grand Palais / Daniel Lebée / Carine Déambrosis / Art Resource, NY)* Crucifixion, painted by Jacob Jordaens (1593–1678) (right), currently in St. Andrew's Cathedral. *Philippe Lissac*

not come from *wine* as we know it, but an infused *potion* spiked with any number of drugs. What G 408 and G 409 tried to communicate, and what Dioscorides later recorded with his wine formulas, is now a scientific fact. The latest archaeochemical data from the Near East show that herbs, resins, and other plant additives were mixed into wine for at least three thousand years before the birth of Christianity to increase its psychoactive profile. Why would that time-honored tradition suddenly stop at Jesus?

As I navigate the Salle des Caryatides, I see a bench. But not just any bench. A private retreat, nestled snugly in a secluded alcove. I plop into place, close my eyes, and cast a steady exhale into the Dionysian sanctuary. I open my eyes to a crucifixion scene. A poor figure hanging from a pine tree, about to be put to death. It's not the wine god from Nazareth.

This is the silenus Marsyas, another close companion of Dionysus. The eight-foot *Marsyas supplicié*, sometimes called the *Torment of Marsyas* or *Hanging Marsyas*, was originally cut around 200 BC. It memorializes the legend of the cocky satyr who challenged the god Apollo to a flute contest, and lost. His punishment was to be flayed alive. Plato tells us Marsyas's shaggy hide was later made into a wineskin.[51] Philostratus goes a step further and says the satyr sentenced *himself* to death for playing out of tune. Marsyas "looks forward to the slaughter" so he can be reborn as a container for Dionysus's potion, our liquid salvation.[52] Dying so that we may live, this self-sacrifice on the tree for the good of humanity occurs centuries before Jesus died on the cross.[53] If the naked Marsyas were given a loincloth and hung in a church, I wonder how long it would take the faithful to realize it wasn't Jesus.

Right here for all to see, a statue like this brings the pagan continuity hypothesis into full focus. But how far can we take it? John's Gospel certainly pulled the God of Ecstasy into Christianity. Did the sex, drugs, and rock 'n' roll really come along for the ride?

Father Francis is an open-minded guy, but how do I even start down this road? Looking at twenty-five-hundred-year-old Greek pottery is one thing. Suggesting the religion to which the priest has dedicated his life was chiseled from Greek stone and ripped from the pages of *The Bacchae* is another thing altogether. Such things are best discussed over drinks.

Drunk with the Nectar of Eternity

Just as surprisingly warm as yesterday, the sun is setting on a gorgeous Saturday in Paris. I bounce down from my Airbnb on the Île de la Cité and cross the Pont d'Arcole into the cobweb of streets in the fourth arrondissement. I'm heading for the watering hole that sprang to mind from my final moments in the Louvre, as I sat across from Marsyas gazing at the marble statue of *Apollo the Lizard Slayer*. After a brisk walk, I arrive at the bustling bar to claim the only remaining mini-table in the eye of the storm. Metallic reptiles scurry across the brickwork and mutate into tiled mosaics on the bathroom walls, assuring me I've landed in the Lizard Lounge. In the din of clanking glasses and drunken French conversation, I rummage through my stack of notes in preparation for the next face-off.

A few minutes later, my Roman Catholic friend joins me. Still no collar.

First things first. We order a blue cheese and mushroom burger and two sorely needed Scottish Brown Ales. Father Francis fills me in on the day's Mind and Life meetings; I show him some of my photos from the Salle des Caryatides. By the time the food arrives, I've tried my best to convince the mild-mannered cleric that my investigation is no less heretical than his own. The Renaissance man across from me in the purple-collared shirt, peeking out from a charcoal sweater, is already entertained. But I can't tell if he's laughing at me or with me.

The theme of tonight's dinner is apotheosis. What does it mean to become God? If Father Francis has no problem with lesser mortals like ourselves bursting into kaleidoscopic rainbows after decades of intense meditation, then why not simply drink the sacred potion and cut to the chase? At the end of the day, aren't we both talking about that cryptic promise from Eleusis: overcoming the limitations of the physical body and cheating death? That "moment of intense rapture" sought by the maenads of Dionysus, until they "became identified with the god himself." And aren't he and Ruck both committing the same arch-heresy by suggesting that the original, obscured truth of Christianity has nothing to do with *worshipping* Jesus, and everything to do with *becoming* Jesus? Aren't we all just gods and goddesses in the making?

Maybe the concept of apotheosis doesn't sound particularly heretical today. But a few hundred years ago, it got the likes of Giovanni Pico della Mirandola into a load of trouble. In 1484 the upstart Italian was only twenty-one years old when he met Lorenzo de' Medici, who promptly invited him into the Florentine Academy that was about to punch the Renaissance into high gear. Already a student of Greek, as well as Latin, Hebrew, and Arabic, the newest Florentine got to work writing *Oratio de hominis dignitate* (*Oration on the Dignity of Man*): the so-called Manifesto of the Renaissance. He wanted to publicly debut the *Oratio*, together with his *900 Theses*, in Rome on the Epiphany of 1487, the God's Gift Day. But Pope Innocent VIII was not impressed. He put a halt to the spectacle and condemned every one of Pico della Mirandola's theses for "renovating the errors of pagan philosophers."

All for the young man's simple but revolutionary act of applauding the infinite goodness and unlimited potential of every man, woman, and child on this planet. Under the principle of *ad fontes* ("back to the source"), the humanists were just beginning to tap the wisdom of the founders of Western civilization in their original language. Whenever you do that, a nagging question inevitably surfaces: if the Greeks didn't need Jesus to find salvation, why do we? In his search for answers, Pico della Mirandola went far beyond the "Mosaic and Christian mysteries," giving a neo-pagan endorsement of Eleusis:

> *Who would not long to be admitted to such mysteries? Who would not desire, putting all human concerns behind him, holding the goods of*

fortune in contempt and little minding the goods of the body, thus to
become, while still a denizen of earth, a guest at the table of the gods,
and, drunk with the nectar of eternity, receive, while still a mortal, the
gift of immortality?

The Vatican's intervention was "the first case in history of a printed book universally banned by the Church."[1] And Pico della Mirandola was soon arrested on the Pope's orders. Only after Lorenzo pulled some major strings was the young heretic freed into the protective custody of the influential Medicis back in Florence. So when I say this stuff is heretical, I mean it. Maybe no one goes to jail anymore for claiming to be God, but the doors of the psych ward are always wide open. Besides, it's pretty well established in Catholicism that the only infallible human being is the Pope. And even then, he never lets it go to his head. As the mere successor to Saint Peter, the Supreme Pontiff would *never* equate himself with Christ, let alone God.

This conversation is full of land mines. And especially uncomfortable in the company of someone who once taught at the Pontificia Università Gregoriana (the Pope's university in Rome). But I need Father Francis to weigh in on the pagan continuity hypothesis once and for all. If drugged wine was the Greeks' path to immortality, did a drugged Eucharist offer the first Christians the kind of experience reported by the participants of the psilocybin experiments at Hopkins and NYU? If that original Eucharist could cause the "dissolution of the self" and "melting away of barriers" mentioned by Dinah Bazer—as well as by the Jewish, Christian, and Islamic mystics throughout history—then it all makes sense. But without the genuine psychedelic sacrament inherited from the Greeks, how could a placebo Eucharist convince anyone to drop paganism and the entrenched religion of their ancestors? In just four centuries, how did Christianity go from being an obscure cult of "twenty or so illiterate day laborers" in a neglected part of the Mediterranean to the official religion of Rome, converting half the empire, perhaps some thirty million people, in the process?[2] What was the secret to Christianity's success?

After the waiter sets the plates on the table, the priest invites the Holy Spirit to join us. No meal begins without a blessing. He recites the same prayer my classmates and I would drone in the cafeteria, just before every lunch at the Maternity of the Blessed Virgin Mary back in Philadelphia. As Father Francis discreetly utters the invocation, not attracting too much attention from the patrons only inches away at our backs, I can hear hundreds of little Catholic voices chanting in unison, "Bless us, O Lord, and these thy gifts, which we receive through thy bounty, through Christ our Lord."

"Amen!" I proclaim. Advantage Father Francis. Helpful as he has been with my investigation thus far, I'm reminded that I'm sitting in a bar with a man of the cloth who might not appreciate the full implications of Ruck's psychedelic hypothesis, rendering Jesus just another healer in a long line of drug-dealing ancient masters.

In *The Apples of Apollo: Pagan and Christian Mysteries of the Eucharist*, published in 2001, Ruck devotes almost a hundred pages to this subject in a chapter titled "Jesus, the Drug Man." It's actually a decent translation of "Jesus," whom the Greeks knew as *Iesous* (since they never heard of the letter "j"). *Iesous*, in turn, was a spin-off of *Iesoue*, the Greek word for Joshua, the Israelites' leader following the death of Moses.[3] But according to Ruck, the true origin of Jesus's Greek name is the root for "drug" or "poison" (*ios*), which supplies the Greek words for "doctor" or *iatros* (ἰατρός). Ruck says the "drug man." Either way, it's unlikely a Greek speaker of the first century AD would have heard the name *Iesous* and not thought of *Ieso* or *Iaso,* the Greek goddess of healing and the daughter of Asclepius, who was taught the art of drugs, incantations, and love potions by the centaur Chiron.[4] It's an association that the Gospel writers didn't mind playing up a bit. Each of them uses the verb *iaomai* (ἰάομαι) to describe Jesus's healing miracles. A literal translation would be "to cure by means of drugs."[5] In Matthew 9:12, Mark 2:17, and Luke 4:23, after all, Jesus does specifically refer to himself as *iatros*, which instead of "drug man" is generically rendered as "physician."

But there's no way I'm launching headfirst into all that. The Gospel of John is all we need tonight. By the second round of beers, I figure what better venue for a little Bible study. I plunge into my leather pouch, wriggle two books from their plastic casings, and lay them on our sacrilegious desk: the hardback Loeb edition of Euripides that we read yesterday in the Cour Napoléon, and the 1829 edition of the New Testament, entirely in Greek. I've had it since college, the first and last Bible I ever purchased. Together these are our two holy books for the evening: Dionysus the Elder meets Dionysus the Younger.

"The more you read the Greek," I start off, "the weirder it gets." Though Father Francis doesn't know it, I'm referring to A. D. Nock's secret system of "symbols" and "language" that John used to tip off the Greek speakers of the time who were either initiated into or at least familiar with the Mysteries. "Because the words really matter."

"There's a lot in there," the priest agrees.

"If you read the *The Bacchae* and the Gospel of John side by side, it's kind of funny. The same scenes show up, sometimes even the same words. Greek vocabulary that doesn't appear anywhere else in the three Synoptic Gospels—Matthew, Mark, or Luke."

I lead my personal tutor through a couple of the better examples. Like the 180 gallons of wine at Cana. Or the Son of God in the "lap" of the Father. Or the "crown of thorns" (*akanthinon stephanon*) and "purple cloak" (*porphuroun himation*) that the Roman governor Pontius Pilate throws on Jesus in John 19:5, publicly mocking him as the "King of the Jews." In *The Bacchae*, the pointy crown fashioned from the fruit of nature is the definitive way of identifying the God of Ecstasy and his disciples.[6] And in Greek art Dionysus himself is frequently seen wearing such a crown, along with his trademark purple cloak.[7] In *The Dionysian Gospel*, Dennis MacDonald asserts that Pilate's overt presentation of Jesus, bearing his characteristic color for all to see, is yet another conscious clue to Greek speakers that both wine gods were cut from the same cloth (pun intended).

With a dozen more examples from MacDonald's study to discuss, I pause and admit that none of these similarities are particularly breaking news. In fact, the early Church Fathers were well aware of the disconcerting relationship between Dionysus and Jesus.

"Well, they knew Greek!" interjects Father Francis. "Of course they could read Euripides. How could anyone possibly think they didn't understand their own language?"

So the question is not whether these parallels exist, but how to interpret them. Or as far as the ancient theologians were concerned, how to explain them away. In the second century AD, Justin Martyr's defense was to blame Satan for duping the Greeks into believing that Dionysus was the real Messiah, not Jesus. Even though Dionysus was reportedly born of a virgin, discovered the vine, and later "introduced wine into his Mysteries"—just like Jesus—the "Devil" apparently used the god from Scythopolis to obscure "the prophecy announced by the patriarch Jacob and recorded by Moses."[8] Justin conveniently sidesteps the fact that Dionysus, or some form of the wine god, predates the Biblical prophets by a couple thousand years.[9] But again, this entire debate is lost on those today who can't follow the Greek. As are the many secret "symbols" and "language" in the Gospel of John.

There is no better example than John 6:53–56, the Evangelist's bizarre take on the Eucharist. It is the most explicit and intentional Dionysian reference in all of John's Gospel. In English Jesus's fascinating words at the synanogue in Capernaum go something like this:

> Very truly I tell you, unless you eat the flesh of the Son of Man and drink his blood, you have no life in you. Whoever eats my flesh and drinks my blood has eternal life, and I will raise them up at the last day. For my flesh is the True Food and my blood is the True Drink. Whoever eats my flesh and drinks my blood remains in me, and I in them.

But the original language is a different matter. No Greek speaker of the time could have heard this passage and *not* thought of Dionysus. In those few lines of Greek, John's audience would find the key to the Christian Mysteries. The same key they already knew from the Dionysian Mysteries: apotheosis by means of what John calls the "True Food" and "True Drink" that promise "eternal life." In a populist move Jesus would invite all of humanity to do the very thing that would get Pico della Mirandola arrested by the Pope centuries later—to join "the table of the gods" and receive "the gift of immortality" by getting drunk on "the nectar of eternity." The only thing separating us from God is a glass of magical wine. And John's language is equally clear that you didn't need a priest to mix it.

As it turns out, no one was more heretical than Jesus.

But to put John's Eucharist in context, it's important to review the origins of the sacrament itself. While New Testament scholars acknowledge the Bible isn't the most accurate record of historical events, they have two general criteria for assessing authenticity: the age of the sources, and their multiplicity. The Gospels of Matthew, Mark, Luke, and John were all written between AD 65 and 100, and each presents an account of the Eucharist. The earliest written evidence of the Last Supper, Paul's Letter to the Corinthians, was probably composed two decades after Jesus's death, around AD 53. It's as close as we get to the upper room at King David's burial site in Jerusalem, where this extraordinary ritual was said to take place. And it too includes the dinner. In 1 Corinthians 11:25, Paul quotes Jesus instructing his friends to continue feasting on his body "in remembrance of me" after he's gone.

So that's where the Mass came from—a two-thousand-year-old fit of cannibalism reenacted to this day, multiple times per day, in churches on every continent for billions of faithful. The ritual, once perceived as an illegal act of human sacrifice in the Roman Empire, is now the Eucharist. What Pope Francis has referred to as the "beating heart of the Church."[10] He says the Mass is not only a "commemoration of what Jesus did at the Last Supper," a mere symbol, but the "greatest of gifts" from God to mankind, "essential" for salvation.[11] Like the advanced religious biotechnology of the ancient Near East discussed in the last chapter, the Pope explicitly identified the "precise objective" of Jesus's Eucharistic ceremony during a homily from St. Peter's Square in 2015: "that we might become one with him."[12]

Eating the god to *become* the god. Drinking the god to *become* the god.

Long predating the Egyptians, Canaanites, Phoenicians, and Nabataeans, the practice has deep roots in the human psyche. Jesus must have gotten the idea from somewhere. But it certainly wasn't his Jewish upbringing, since the devouring of flesh and blood "amounts to a reinstatement of human sacrifice, which in Judaism was anathema. Indeed a large part of the Hebrew Bible constitutes a campaign against human sacrifice."[13]

So speculation began percolating in the late nineteenth century. One of the first heretics to weigh in on the pagan continuity hypothesis was Sir James George Frazer. His first edition of *The Golden Bough* (1890) scandalized the rather devout public of the time. Part of Frazer's study framed Christianity's central beliefs as unoriginal relics of a dark pagan past. He further developed this theory in the years to come, unveiling a masterful analysis of all the primitive rites of theophagy (eating of the god) that long preceded the familiar Eucharist:

> *The flesh and blood of dead men are commonly eaten and drunk to inspire bravery, wisdom, or other qualities for which the men themselves were remarkable. . . . It is now easy to understand why a savage should desire to partake of the flesh of an animal or man whom he regards as divine. By eating the body of the god he shares in the god's attributes and powers. And when the god is a corn-god, the corn is his proper*

body; when he is a vine-god, the juice of the grape is his blood; and so by eating the bread and drinking the wine the worshipper partakes of the real body and blood of his god.[14]

Frazer concluded that "the coincidences of the Christian with the heathen festivals are too close and too numerous to be accidental." The controversy has swirled ever since, pitting Church authorities against secular scholars in often-heated exchanges that would eventually include none other than the Reverend Dr. Martin Luther King Jr. The Baptist minister and future leader of the civil rights movement tried to broker some middle ground in his 1950 paper "The Influence of the Mystery Religions on Christianity."[15] For Dr. King it was pointless to deny that Christianity "was greatly influenced by the Mystery religions, both from a ritual and a doctrinal angle." But rather than "deliberate copying," he preferred "a natural and unconscious process" that placed the religion of Jesus in historical context, "conditioned by the contact with the older religions" and the "general trend of the time."

The "general trend" in the eastern Mediterranean of the first century AD was apotheosis by means of drugged wine and other intoxicants, whether in the *marzeah* or the Dionysian Mysteries. Of course the Eucharist would have found inspiration in those traditions. But in order for Dionysus to pass the baton to Jesus, there could be no room for ambiguity. So with all due respect to Dr. King, it appears that John did, in fact, deliberately copy the language of Euripides to make the greatest recruitment pitch in the history of Christianity. And perhaps the most significant point of his entire Gospel: the sacrament of Dionysus and the sacrament of Jesus are one and the same. Both of them are steeped in the same primitive rites of theophagy that had been transforming archaic humans into gods since time immemorial.

As Jesus announces the key to the Christian Mysteries in John 6:53–56, he makes crystal clear that the "True Food" and "True Drink" of his flesh and blood are nothing less than the flesh and blood of Dionysus. Not only because the words that John uses for "flesh" (*sarx*/σάρξ) and "blood" (*haima*/αἷμα) are identical to what Euripides wrote in the *The Bacchae* five hundred years earlier, but because of what Jesus asks his followers to do to that "flesh." Twice in this passage the Evangelist drops the word *trogon* (τρώγων). But to translate *trogon* as "eat," as do most English translations of John's Gospel, is at best to ignore, and at worst to suppress, the visceral act of theophagy so obviously intended to jump off the page. Yet another language barrier, stubbornly fixed in place for centuries.

I read the Greek of John's Eucharist aloud to Father Francis until I get to *trogon*. I reach into my pocket, unlock my iPhone, and open my Ancient Greek dictionary app. Yes, there's an app for that. I type in *trogon* and show the screen to my friend.

"To gnaw, to munch," affirms the priest, parsing through the dense mix of Greek and English characters on my phone.

Only in John's Eucharist does *trogon* appear. Indeed, the only other instance of the verb *trogon* in the entire New Testament is in Matthew 24:38, in reference to the pagan feasting of the pre-Flood population "in the days of Noah." Why would Jesus ask people to *gnaw* and *munch* on his *flesh* in such graphic, barbaric language? In *The Dionysian Gospel*, Dennis Mac-Donald believes the Greek of John points rather obviously to "Dionysian cult imagery," "specifically the eating of the flesh and blood of the god and the immortality that initiates gain by such activity."[16] How could any Greek speaker of the time conclude otherwise?

The God of Ecstasy lived in the wine, for sure, but there were other ways of consuming his divine blood. As Ruck made clear in *The Road to Eleusis*, "Dionysus was the god of all inebriants and not of wine alone." In addition to psychedelic plant life, the shape-shifting God of Ecstasy could come in many different animal forms. Goats were the standout favorite. As a matter of fact, the root of the English word "tragedy" that Dionysus gave birth to as the god of theater is *tragos* (τράγος), the Greek "goat" that was ritually sacrificed during competitions in Athens. So it's no surprise in *The Bacchae* when the chief priest of the Dionysian Mysteries is pictured "in pursuit of the shed blood of the slain goat." He will suck the gushing fluid straight from the carcass, gnawing and munching the uncooked meat in a gory mess. Euripides calls it "the thankful meal of raw flesh," the *omophagon charin* (ὠμοφάγον χάριν). This *charin* is the same root of the verb *eucharisteo* (εὐχαριστέω), "to be thankful." It appears fifteen times in the New Testament. And it is, of course, where we get the word "Eucharist."

But what's so psychedelic about goats? In *Entheogens and the Development of Culture: The Anthropology and Neurobiology of Ecstatic Experience*, the scholar Alan Piper wrote a thoroughly well-sourced essay exploring the mind-altering effects of flesh, blood, and other bodily fluids from animals known to forage on psychoactive plants, herbs, and fungi.[17] Piper puts particular emphasis on goats, including their love of juniper, which might explain all the guzzling of "warm goat's blood" by the Hunza people of the Hindu Kush from the last chapter. Regarding the Dionysian meal, Piper believes the ritual may have facilitated the ingestion of certain hallucinogenic but otherwise poisonous alkaloids that could be better metabolized by the sacrificial animals, it often being "necessary to consume the flesh raw to preserve or maximize its psychoactive potency."[18]

Either way, goats didn't suit Christianity for some reason. Too wild, too rustic. So instead of all the goat-men like Pan and Marsyas and the rest of the fauns and satyrs from the Louvre's Salle des Caryatides, John's Gospel opts for an adorable substitute. In his first chapter, Jesus is referred to as the "Lamb of God" or *amnos tou theou* (ὁ Ἀμνὸς τοῦ Θεοῦ). Like the Wedding at Cana, it's another of John's inventions that will echo for centuries in Christian art—in the Ghent Altarpiece, for example, which shows the holy blood draining from the chest of the still-living lamb directly into the Eucharistic chalice. It is the chalice of the Mass that holds the blood of Jesus to this day, just like the blood that once poured from the goat as the blood of Dionysus to become the Eucharist of raw flesh (*omophagon charin*) for Euripides.

Whether you gnawed and munched on the lamb, or gnawed and munched on the goat, the result was supposed to be the same. Immortality. But what does it all mean?

We have no physical evidence for the mass slaughter of psychoactive lambs across the paleo-Christian world. It looks as if the gruesome meal was left in the backcountry where it belonged. So in John 6:53–56, when Jesus says his flesh and blood are the "True Food" and "True Drink," he could have only meant the bread and wine of the Eucharist. And John could have only intended his Greek speakers to think of the blood of Dionysus. When Jesus asked his Apostles to drink it, he wasn't the first person in history to float the idea. Plutarch recorded the Egyptian belief that wine was the blood of those who had "battled against the gods." Even in the Old Testament, wine is called the "blood of grapes." But the fans of Dionysus took the image to a whole new level. The Ancient Greek musician and poet, Timotheus of Miletus (ca. 446–357 BC), explicitly refers to holy wine as the "blood of Dionysus" or *haima Bacchiou* (αἷμα Βακχίου). To drink it was to drink immortality. This ancient precedent for the magical wine of Jesus was certainly not lost on the

The Infant Bacchus, painted by the circle of Hendrik Willem Schweickhardt in the eighteenth century (above). The Ghent Altarpiece, or the *Adoration of the Mystic Lamb*, completed by Hubert and Jan van Eyck in 1432 (below), currently in St. Bavo's Cathedral in Ghent, Belgium. Over time, the barrels of wine and bunches of grapes associated with the blood of Dionysus's goats transformed into the wine/blood of the Christian sacrament pouring from the Mystic Lamb.

great Walter Burkert. It was the God of Ecstasy, the classicist openly recognized, "whose blood is represented in the sacramental drinking of the wine." Long before the Last Supper, "the drinker of the [Dionysian] wine would be drinking the god himself."[19]

For John's audience, the morbid language about drinking the blood of

Jesus was not a call to animal sacrifice. It was a dog whistle to Greek-speaking initiates everywhere that Christianity's state-of-the-art, Eucharistic meal was based on ancient Dionysian precedent. And, by extension, carried just as much of a mind-expanding kick as the *pharmakon* of Greek wine. The same *pharmakon* that Father Francis recited from *The Bacchae* in the Cour Napoléon. After all, this was the same Jesus who earlier in John performed the wine miracle at Cana, and who later in John would refer to himself as the "True Vine." The same Jesus raised among the vineyards of Galilee, where fortified wine had been a chemical reality ever since the Canaanites. The "True Drink" was no ordinary drink. It was a tool. The Drug of Immortality that might teach the first Christians how to die before they die.

The Gospel of John is full of references to the concept of death and rebirth. In John 15:13, Jesus says: "the greatest way to show love for friends is to *die* for them." In John 3:3, he adds, "I tell you for certain that you must be *born again* before you can see God's Kingdom." And the celestial visions that follow the mystical experience are emphasized time and again. In John 9:39, "I am here to give *sight* to the blind." In John 1:51, "I tell you for certain that you will *see* heaven open and God's angels going up and down." The strange, hallucinatory effect that Dionysus has on his followers is identical in *The Bacchae*. "Now you *see* as you ought to *see*," the wine god tells King Pentheus following his conversion to the wine god's new religion.

And just as in the Dionysian Mysteries, with its long tradition of the drugged wine, in the Gospel of John this new sight doesn't come about by accident. Access to the Kingdom of Heaven is not based on blind belief, or the simple act of accepting Jesus as your personal Lord and Savior, as many Christian denominations profess today. The Greek of Jesus couldn't have been more explicit in John 6:53–56, when he revealed the key to the Christian Mysteries. You had to actually *do* something. You had to sample the "True Drink." That "communion with the god, the goal of all mysticism" is best achieved through the fruit of the vine, says historian Philip Mayerson: "Once divinity had entered into the celebrant, deity and devotee became one, god and man became one."[20]

In the end John is saying that the Christian Mysteries would be as meaningless without their Eucharist as the Greek Mysteries would be without theirs. You do not become one with Dionysus by *reading* about him, or *praying* to him. You do it by *drinking* him. Even by the most mainstream interpretations of the Dionysian Mysteries, the wine of Dionysus is a *pharmakon* that results in apotheosis.

If the Dionysian drink did all that, then the "True Drink" of John's Gospel had to do the same. John 6:53–56 is how the Greek *pharmakon* became the Christian *pharmakon athanasias*. If Jesus is the new Dionysus, then *his* sacrament had to have the same effect as the Dionysian sacrament. *His* wine had to be just as unusually intoxicating, seriously mind-altering, occasionally hallucinogenic, and potentially lethal as all the holy wine from Galilee and Greece. And a shot of *his* "True Drink" had to transport you, the same way the initiate on the Borghese Vase is slumped over in ecstasy, carried along by a goat-man.

On any given Sunday, how many people leave church looking like that?

This, then, is the real relationship between Dionysus and Jesus. And the real meaning behind all the Dionysian imagery that John the Evangelist went to such great lengths to include throughout his Gospel: the 180 gallons of wine at Cana, the Son of God in the "lap" of the Father, the crown of thorns and purple cloak, the Lamb of God, the True Vine, the *gnawing* and *munching* on the *flesh* of Jesus. It was all leading to a bloody Eucharist that would actually speak to Greek-speaking pagans who had a perfectly adequate Eucharist of their own and didn't want to see it disappear under the Roman Empire. And the only way to do that is with the secret "symbols" and "language" that the initiates would actually understand.

It all makes sense to me. But I wonder if the priest reads the Greek the way I do.

Hedged in by twenty-first-century, French-speaking bacchants and maenads, I unload my burning questions on Father Francis. Why is John's Eucharist so very different from the Synoptics? Why the macabre vocabulary about *gnawing* and *munching* on the Eucharistic meal of raw flesh and blood, straight from *The Bacchae*? Why the "True Drink"?

The priest takes notes of all the similarities between Jesus and Dionysus, and the odd language in John 6:53–56. As Bob Marley's "Buffalo Solider" blares over the Lizard Lounge's speakers, and the French chatter rises to a crescendo, the priest looks me straight in the eye and cautions, "But it doesn't mean that Jesus never existed . . . or that Jesus is Dionysus. It means *this* is the version of Jesus that John chose to present. As an esthetic."

Father Francis reminds me that John's was the last Gospel to be completed, probably toward the end of the first century AD. And that he was writing for a specific community of early believers in Ephesus, the same Greco-Ephesians on the western coast of Anatolia to whom the Greco-Syrian Ignatius would soon address his letter about the *pharmakon athanasias*.[21] "Just think about Ephesus," insists the priest. "It's one of the largest cities in Asia Minor. And here's this tiny Christian community. So their mystical experiences are those of a minority group that's completely surrounded and swallowed up by the gigantic pagan community, right?"

In that environment the words that come out of Jesus's mouth in John 6:53–56 don't actually belong to Jesus. They don't even belong to John. "They were said as homilies of ecstatic individuals channeling Christ in the liturgy," Father Francis continues, pointing to the Greek of the weathered Bible lying open on the table. "John's Last Supper scene is poetic theology that doesn't correspond at all to the Last Supper of the Synoptics, because it's all coming out of a much later tradition of ecstatic, prophetic speech. Where the followers of John's community are channeling the voice of Christ in *their* time. Because Christ is just as much present in the Eucharist as he is in Galilee in the year 30. In the year 90, he's still risen. He's still *there*."

When it comes to the pagan continuity hypothesis, Father Francis is a believer, I'm pleased to learn. He doesn't deny the similarities between the Dionysian and Christian Mysteries. And fluent in the Greek, he can't dismiss the secret "symbols" and "language" that seem to be intentionally included in John's Gospel. But more pressing for both of us is why John would have presented a very Dionysian Jesus to the Greek mystics in Ephesus. The obvious answer is to communicate on their level, to convince the Greek speakers that they could find in Christianity everything they loved about the Dionysian Mysteries.

But what made the earliest Christians believe that Jesus could come back from the dead to share in their ritual meal? Was it really a psychedelic Eucharist? Father Francis's notion of paleo-Christians possessed by Jesus and prophesying in the language of Euripides makes me think of Apollo's priestesses at Delphi, or a coven of maenads overtaken by Dionysus. In addition to the *marzeah*, it also sounds eerily like the skull cults and graveyard beers that were in existence for thousands of years in Anatolia before the Christians came along. There the whole point was to enter the underworld, making contact with the departed ancestors and the otherwise invisible gods and goddesses. I can't help but think of the Phocaeans, who left their homeland in Ionia just a couple hours north of Ephesus to found the Greek settlement in Massalia, France, before moving on to Emporion, Spain, and Velia, Italy. If John was looking for Greek-speaking mystics, Ionia was the place.

The Ephesians were just the kind of audience that wanted to see their Greek Mysteries survive. The very people who would have understood all the "symbols" and "language" about the *gnawing* and *munching* on the raw flesh and blood for the one thing John was really trying to say. The Dionysian sacrament and the Christian sacrament were one and the same. If anybody could have recognized the incredible innovation taking place in John 6:53–56, it was the Ephesians. In defiance of all tradition, the outdoor churches of Dionysus were being domesticated. After centuries in the wild mountains and forests of the eastern Mediterranean, John was offering a safe haven for the magical wine, inviting it into people's homes. What was once a sacrilegious act worthy of the death penalty in classical Athens was becoming a new way, perhaps the only way, of keeping the Greek Mysteries alive in the Roman Empire. But that awesome responsibility fell on one, very specific gender.

Women were the main beneficiaries of the primordial rite of communion that brought the living into contact with the dead, and turned mere mortals into goddesses. In her 1979 article "Ecstasy and Possession: the Attraction of Women to the Cult of Dionysus," Ross Kraemer (professor of religious studies at Brown University) accumulates all the evidence "for levels of cultic initiation" that separated men and women in the ancient world. Reviewing the many texts, inscriptions, and tomb epigrams that prove these Dionysian rituals actually existed in the real world—and not just Euripides's or John's imagination—Kraemer concludes that men may have taken part in only the "lesser activities," while "initiation with its practices of possession and sacrifice [were] denied to them."[22] Except, of course, for the occasional chief priest. In their case Kraemer notes a "clear suggestion of identification of the male celebrant with Dionysus . . . who at certain times during the ritual identified with the god himself" by joining in the women's Eucharist of raw flesh and blood (*omophagon charin*).[23]

If Jesus as the Lamb of God is an alternate Dionysus, as John went to extraordinary lengths to demonstrate throughout his Gospel, what about those twelve men traditionally assembled around the table of the Last Supper? Are they witnessing the birth of a bloody, Eucharistic ritual that was otherwise largely designed for women?

Father Francis reminds me of the demographics in Ephesus, where women were accorded special honor from its earliest days. One of the Seven Wonders of the Ancient World, the Temple of Artemis in Ephesus was, of course, renowned in antiquity. The original site was sacred to the Amazons, the ferocious tribe of female warriors considered the legendary founders of the ancient city who once upon a time performed rituals there.[24] When John's Gospel started making the rounds, women played a prominent role in Ephesian affairs, occupying privileged positions in sacred institutions, including the fifteen women who served as the high priestesses of the imperial Roman cult. It was the largest group of female religious leaders anywhere in the region.[25] What better place for women to feel welcome and the maenads to set up shop?[26] In Plutarch's biography of Cleopatra's lover, Mark Antony, he describes Ephesus as a place "full of ivy and *thyrsos*-wands and harps and pipes and flutes," where the Roman general was once greeted as an honorary Dionysus by women "going into Bacchic frenzy."[27] So the Mysteries were clearly present in Ephesus. Initiation into their deepest secrets, however, was not for everyone.

As I dart through the unsettling language in John 6:53–56 one more time, it all clicks. Finally.

Was John writing for women?

"If John is addressing a group of female visionaries getting high in Ephesus, then I think I finally understand his Gospel," I tell the priest. Father Francis chuckles. And once again, I can't tell if he's laughing at me or with me. But with his insight on the pagan mystics who dominated Ephesus, and the cults of Artemis and Dionysus that made women particularly welcome in the ancient city, my friend has just unwittingly answered the biggest question I had about the secret "symbols" and "language" of John's Gospel. It is the crux of the pagan continuity hypothesis. If the earliest Greek-speaking Christians really did inherit a psychedelic sacrament from the initiates of the Dionysian Mysteries, there was only one way it was going to happen. Women.

More precisely, women with serious pharmacological expertise.

Who else was going to cook up the Eucharist?

As far as we know, women were usually in charge of the procedure. At Eleusis, Ruck traced the Secret of Secrets, the recipe for preparing ergotized beer, to the hereditary priestesses of Demeter and Persephone. For the brewing of the graveyard beer in the domestic chapel at Mas Castellar de Pontós, Enriqueta Pons points to women as well. In his office outside Munich, the world's preeminent beer scientist, Martin Zarnkow, reminded me that women also landed the job among the Ancient Egyptians and Sumerians, a specialty that may date to the Stone Age death cults from the Raqefet Cave and Göbekli Tepe.[28] It was not until the industrialization of brewing after the Protestant Reformation that men took over the trade.

And it's the same story with wine. The maenads on G 408 and G 409 were just the tip of the iceberg. Calvert Watkins traced the preparation of all the Indo-European sacraments—the *soma, kukeon,* and even Dionysian wine—to a "liturgical act" in deep prehistory, a ritual "by women for women." Based on the archaeological evidence, Patrick McGovern agrees that women likely prepared the "Minoan ritual cocktail" and Midas Touch of beer, wine, and mead that he detected in Ancient Greece and Turkey, respectively. He posits a "long tradition" of women as beverage makers that could very well stretch back to the Upper Paleolithic. In many indigenous societies today, after all, it is still women who "generally take the lead in gathering the fruit, honey, and herbs for alcoholic drinks used to mark burials, deaths [and] rites of passage."[29] Why would paleo-Christianity have been any different?

And yet, as I learned from thirteen years of Catholic school, there's only one thing the Vatican finds more suspicious than drugs. And that's women. For both of them to have been integral to a pagan ritual that turned humans into God is pretty much the most heretical thing you could ever discuss with a priest. So it's time for a break.

I excuse myself to the lizard-infested bathroom to stitch some of these puzzle pieces together. I leave Father Francis with *The Bacchae* and the New

Testament to keep him company. As I splash some cold water on my face, I think of the prostitute. The nuns always had mixed feelings about her, but why else would John make Mary Magdalene the star closer of his Dionysian Gospel? In the Gospels of Matthew, Mark, and Luke, a group of women led by Mary Magdalene are the first to witness Jesus's impossible resurrection three days after his death and burial. Only in John does the risen Jesus appear to Mary Magdalene all by herself.

And as Karen Jo Torjesen makes clear in her book *When Women Were Priests,* "She was not only the first witness to the resurrection but was directly commissioned to carry the message that Jesus had risen from the dead." Information entrusted to a visionary woman, perhaps intended for visionary women in Ephesus and elsewhere. John knew his audience, and apparently wanted his Gospel to end there. But a later copyist added an additional, final chapter where Jesus appears separately to Peter, the first Pope, and the other male disciples—instructing them to "feed my lambs" for the rest of human history. It's a pretty clear mandate. So even if Mary Magdalene was first on the scene, that's how men came to lead the early Church. Nothing much has changed in two thousand years.

But I never understood John's conflicting ending until now. In antiquity women were universally the leaders of the Dionysian faith. Euripides had described the Dionysian Mysteries as "an immoral trick aimed at women." And it was the Italian witch Paculla Annia who was blamed for the Roman Empire's prohibition of the Mysteries. In the first century AD women were the ones who had the most to lose from the Roman Empire's crackdown on their religion. So why wouldn't John's Gospel speak to *them*? And why wouldn't a woman like Mary Magdalene be tasked to lead the new movement? If his Gospel had ended as John intended, does that mean Mary Magdalene was destined to be the first Pope instead of Peter? And that women were supposed to be consecrating the Eucharist from the very beginning, the way they had been brewing the mind-altering beer and mixing the psychoactive wine for thousands of years before Jesus? Has the entire patriarchal history of Christianity been a misreading of John?

No less an authority than Raymond E. Brown, the late Catholic priest and onetime premier scholar of John in the English-speaking world, endorsed a reading of the Gospel that did indeed make women heirs to Jesus. If not to the exclusion of men, then certainly their equals as "first-class disciples."[30] His groundbreaking study from 1975, "Roles of Women in the Fourth Gospel," describes how Mary Magdalene was considered "the apostle to the apostles" in a biography as late as the ninth century AD. Even if the scribes tried to bury the lede, it could hardly be ignored that a woman was the first in John's Gospel to witness the resurrected Jesus. For a brief moment in time, Mary Magdalene *was* the Church. There was nobody else. And it could only have meant that women like her were absolutely essential to Christianity's enterprise. The female mystics in Ephesus and elsewhere in Ionia would not have missed the point.

Where John's Gospel was censored, others simply disappeared. In 1896, about fifty years before the discovery of the Nag Hammadi codices that I mentioned during our tour through the ruins of Eleusis, another secret book came to light in Egypt. Like all Gnostic literature, the Gospel of Mary Magdalene never made it into the New Testament. Because it didn't fit the Church Fathers' agenda. This precious text preserves a Jesus who came not to be idolized as an external God, but to reveal the divine spark that lives in us. And to unlock our own "innate capacity to know God," says Princeton scholar Elaine Pagels—to actually experience that divinity here and now.[31]

In her own Gospel, Mary is presented as the disciple whom Jesus "loved" more than any other, and with whom Jesus shared hidden teachings and techniques that were intentionally withheld from his male followers. It is Mary who receives personal instruction from Jesus in vivid hallucinations. And it is *she* who explains to Peter how such visions can be experienced as a normal (if untapped) part of human consciousness. Like something out of the Egyptian or Tibetan Books of the Dead, Mary goes on to reveal privileged information about the death and dying process. She is the keeper of immortality. For Pagels, the conclusion is obvious: "Without visions and revelations, then, the Christian movement would not have begun."[32]

But despite the suppression of John's perfect Dionysian ending and the entire Gospel of Mary Magdalene, women understood their vital role. An honest look through the history of paleo-Christianity leaves little doubt. For example, it was a woman named Lydia, a successful businesswoman in Philippi with influence over an extended social network in Greece, who became Saint Paul's very first convert in Europe. Importantly, she was considered the "ruler of her household." Though rare at the time, Lydia's "administrative, financial, and disciplinary responsibilities" in the domes-

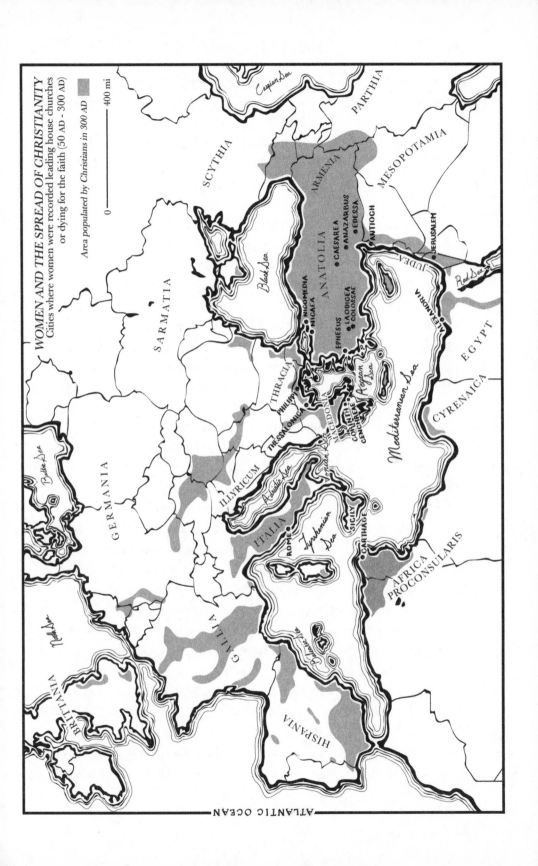

WOMEN AND THE SPREAD OF CHRISTIANITY
Cities where women were recorded leading house churches
or dying for the faith (50 AD - 300 AD)

Area populated by Christians in 300 AD

0 ——————— 400 mi

tic sphere translated into a public prestige that was ordinarily denied to women. She could afford to host Paul, making her home among the very first house churches where Christianity found refuge. And it proved successful. We learn from Paul's Letter to the Philippians that the management of the church in Philippi later passed to other women named Euodia and Syntyche.[33] They weren't the only ones carrying the torch.

"Whenever Christianity spread," says the scholar Torjesen, "women were leaders of house churches."[34] Before the religion upgraded to the more ornate buildings of worship familiar today, these house churches were one of the two primary venues where paleo-Christians gathered until the erection of basilicas in the fourth century AD.[35] Along with family tombs in the underground catacombs from Italy to Greece to North Africa, the house churches functioned as "private associations," where the "centrality of the banquet meal" perfectly suited women's entrenched authority over the home, including "receiving, storing and distributing" all the ingredients necessary for the Eucharistic ritual.[36] The New Testament is full of examples of such female luminaries.[37]

In Ephesus, it was Priscilla, who is actually mentioned in three of Paul's Letters and the Acts of the Apostles. A well-to-do tent-maker, she established a house church not only in the ecstatic territory of Artemis and Dionysus, but also later in Rome.[38] It's there we find a profusion of impressive female leadership. In addition to Priscilla, Paul mentions several by name: Mary, Tryphaena, Tryphosa, and Persis were all addressed as "coworkers." Three more—a certain Julia, the mother of Rufus, and the sister of Nereus— all enjoyed a "high profile in the community."[39] But it was Junia who was hailed as "foremost among the apostles."[40] She is thought to have belonged to a movement of Greek-speaking Jews who descended on Rome at the time in order to establish the permanent roots of the religion's future global capital.[41]

Ever since Paul's first journeys in the mid-first century AD, women like Junia embraced and nurtured their new sacrament, as well as the promise of apotheosis that would later be made so explicit in John 6:53–56. Over the previous centuries the maenad's ritual meal of raw flesh and blood paired with magical wine had been infrequently showcased in the mountains and forests of the ancient Mediterranean, perhaps only once every two years by some estimates. When they became more frequent and more organized, that's when things got tricky.

After the brutal crackdown by the Roman senate in 186 BC, their peripheral religion faced a real existential crisis in Italy.[42] The suppression could always happen again, especially during the first century AD, when the empire that had spread across the Mediterranean was hyper-conscious of promoting Roman identity in public displays of religious worship. A subversive cult dedicated to an exotic god like Dionysus, defined by secret meetings and magical sacraments, remained under constant suspicion of conspiring behind the scenes, just one step away from launching all-out revolt against Rome.[43] The emperor could tolerate the state-run Mysteries of Eleusis, with its relative order and long cultural legacy. The undying devotion of women to the God of Ecstasy, with their "inappropriate desire for knowledge" and "ritual cannibalism," according to the historians Beard, North, and Price, was another thing altogether: "fundamental breaches of the code of humanity."[44]

Witches could hardly rest easy. But hope was in the air. In the same way that Dionysus rescued his sacrament from Eleusis and brought it to the masses, Jesus was open-sourcing the wine of the Eucharist away from the palaces and mansions of the Near East. Immortality was now officially open to everyone. And not just in the rural hideouts of the Mediterranean, where the God of Ecstasy and his witches were forced into submission, but also in the comfort and secrecy of upscale homes all over the empire. So when the spiritually curious heard about a new venue for what A. D. Nock called "private spontaneous pagan piety," there would be interest. When they heard the now-domesticated ritual meal could be celebrated any time, anywhere, there would be greater interest. But when they heard the Gospel of John and realized these new Mysteries had the *identical* goal as the Dionysian Mysteries—to become one with the god by drinking him—they'd be hooked.

For the untested religion to have any chance of success, however, the Eucharist simply *had* to involve the kind of genuine mystical experiences so well documented in the Dionysian tradition. Unlike the cardboard wafer and cheap boxed wine of today's Mass, it had to actually deliver. When Pope Francis says the "precise objective" of the Eucharist is to "become one" with Jesus, I'm not sure what he means. Like many Catholics, I've taken Communion hundreds and hundreds of times in my life, and never once felt a fraction of the ecstasy reported in the art and literature of Ancient Greece.

And never once did I taste the apotheosis that was promised to me in John 6:56: "Whoever eats my flesh and drinks my blood remains in me, and I in them." For John's audience, whether the god who uttered those words came from Scythopolis or a half hour away in Nazareth, it didn't really matter. The goal of the mystical game was "the gift of immortality" by any means, as Pico della Mirandola would later risk his life to advertise across Christendom in 1487. Who cares about the god at the head of the table when the only point of the banquet is to get "drunk" with that "nectar of eternity"?

And there was plenty of nectar to be had. Fortuitously, Dioscorides published his magnum opus in the same period that Lydia and her successors were looking to stock their lavish house churches in Greece. Just like Priscilla in Anatolia. Perhaps Junia and the many women that Paul recognizes in Rome, where more females are documented than any other church in the Mediterranean, would have found the Father of Drugs especially useful. The step-by-step instructions for creating one of Ruck's hallucinogenic elixirs, doctored with any number of psychedelic plants, herbs, and fungi, were right at their fingertips. Like some corporate gimmick by Amazon Prime, the Son of God from Nazareth had just made it perfectly respectable to order the Drug of Immortality straight to your front door. If the Mysteries had any chance of making it through the unfriendly climate of the Roman Empire, maybe women and their kitchens were the last refuge for a risky sacrament that needed an insurance policy.

The witches of Dionysus could very well have passed the sacrament along to the women who ran the new religion in those three hundred years after Jesus, when paleo-Christianity survived in the house churches and catacombs before receiving Constantine's blessing in the fourth century AD. For a few generations, perhaps the witches of Dionysus and the witches of Jesus were fairly indistinguishable. Why couldn't they worship both wine gods? The women who prepared the psychedelic beer and wine in the Greek Mysteries could have been the same women who prepared the original Eucharist across the Mediterranean, where the line between pagan and Christian did not yet exist. And where it would not exist until all the men in Rome decided to exclude women from any positions of leadership in the official Church. Because if the crackdown on the Bacchanalia in 186 BC had taught the priests and bishops anything, it was that women and their sacrament were the single greatest threat to law and order.

Containment was not only possible. It was mandatory.

How was Christianity to grow without a flock? If nobody attended the new churches and basilicas to receive the Eucharist that only the male clergy had the exclusive, divine right to consecrate—transforming ordinary bread and wine into supernatural flesh and blood—there could be no future for the faith. If anyone with the right ingredients could mix up their own Eucharist at home, and meet Jesus on their own terms, Christianity never would have consolidated the wealth and power to replace the Roman Empire as Europe's central governing authority for centuries. One patriarchal institution succeeding another.

The women and their Eucharist had to go. It may have started by altering John's Gospel and getting rid of the Gospel of Mary Magdalene. But the campaign against women and drugs would last for a very long time. As we will see toward the end of this investigation, it is a war that still very much continues to this day.

As I wend my way back to Father Francis at the center of the action, he gets high marks on the heretic's test. Instead of the New Testament, I catch him poking through *The Bacchae*.

"You can't go wrong with Euripides," I salute the priest. I want to share my bathroom epiphany about Jesus's brilliant marketing scheme, and the female mystics who welcomed Dionysus with their fine china in the earliest and most authentic days of the Christian faith, but I'm pretty beat from the evening's Bible study. And honestly, I'm not sure how Father Francis will respond to the notion that his predecessors deliberately suppressed the original makers of the Eucharist. "We need another drink!"

"How about a digestif?" suggests Father Francis.

We descend into the Lizard Lounge's dimly lit basement bar, appropriately called "The Underground," and order a couple of triple-distilled Jameson Black Barrels. We stake out a nice corner by the sanguinary wall covered in gaudy Mexican-inspired Day of the Dead skulls. Beneath the snake, single eye, and pink flower-shedding lightning bolts, I notice an upside-down Christian cross. "You see a lot of strange things in the subterranean caverns of these old European cities. What a perfect appetizer for our adventure on Monday."

"*Saluti!*" cheers Father Francis, nodding his approval. He knows I'm referring to the itinerary I have spent the past nine months organizing with the
keepers of Christianity's deepest secrets. If there really was a psychedelic sacrament mixed by Greek-speaking female Jesus freaks, then there's only one
logical place to dig up the evidence. Like Junia, Paul's "foremost among the
apostles," the priest and I are heading to the Eternal City to see some things I
never heard about in Catholic school. And unless your Latin and Italian are
on point, things that might never escape the inner circle of Rome. Navigat-
ing several different branches of the Vatican bureaucracy and winning their
confidence was the least amount of fun I've had since the bar exam. Then
again, if the chemically rich Eucharist of paleo-Christianity was replaced by
the watered-down placebo of today—and the Vatican had anything to do
with it—I'd run a pretty good defense as well. It's time for Father Francis to
don that collar and smuggle me behind enemy lines.

After plotting the logistics of our next couple days, I see the priest off
in an Uber and slowly negotiate the fourth arrondissement to walk off the
whiskey. I cross the River Seine at the Pont d'Arcole, spot the building of my
Airbnb, and labor up the four flights of stairs to my cozy bedroom.

Looking south into the cool air of midnight, I lean on the open window-
sill for my last sighting of Notre Dame's three-hundred-foot spire. In less
than two months it will be gone, ravaged by the unforgiving inferno that
will be captured by legions of smartphones and zipped around the globe
in real time. The oak carpentry of the medieval roof fueled the flames that
threatened to destroy some of the cathedral's priceless treasures: the Gothic
trio of stained-glass windows dating to the thirteenth century; the more
than eight thousand pipes of the Great Organ, considered one of the most
famous musical instruments in the world; and Notre Dame's oldest bell,
the "Bumblebee," which famously tolled to mark the end of World War II.[45]
Among the smaller religious artifacts spirited away by firefighters, just in
the nick of time, were the nine-inch piece of the True Cross and the three-
inch nail, each encased in crystal and said to originate from Jesus's actual
crucifixion. But they weren't the priorities.

As I read the news reports in the days following the incident, one name
keeps reappearing: Father Jean-Marc Fournier, the fearless priest who
served in Afghanistan to later become the chaplain of the Paris Fire Bri-
gade. A man on a mission that April 15, he arrived on scene and apparently

pushed past President Emmanuel Macron and the Archbishop of Paris to salvage the cathedral's two most irreplaceable heirlooms.[46] First, the crown of thorns believed to be worn by Jesus during his passion and death. The same spiky *stephanos* donned by the God of Ecstasy centuries before the Son of God was born in Bethlehem. After purchasing the crown from Emperor Baldwin of Constantinople, the French crusader King Louis IX greeted the relic in the town of Sens in August 1239. It has been in Notre Dame ever since. Father Fournier demanded the code to the safe where the crown was deposited and had it shuffled off.

But just when the flames were licking the northern bell tower, with the spire already gone and "the ship about to collapse," there was one final object to retrieve among the "tangle of burning beams" and "droplets of molten lead." In all seriousness, the priest poker-faced to the sacristan, "It is time to take Jesus out of this burning cathedral."[47] Father Fournier approached the tabernacle at the altar of Saint George and rescued the Most Blessed Sacrament. As he later explained, "Everybody understands that the Crown of Thorns is an absolutely unique and extraordinary relic, but the Blessed Sacrament is our Lord, really present in his body, soul, divinity, and human-ity. . . . You understand that it is hard to see someone you love perish in the blaze. . . . This is why I sought to preserve above all the real presence of our Lord Jesus Christ."[48]

Rather than run for his life with the consecrated material in hand, Father Fournier did the unthinkable. He stopped for a blessing. "Here I am com-pletely alone in the cathedral, in the middle of burning debris falling down from the ceiling. I asked Jesus to fight the flames and preserve the building dedicated to his mother."[49] Evidently, the Son of God was all ears. The twin bell towers were saved, the cathedral itself left structurally intact.

Father Fournier didn't rush into a bonfire and risk his life for a *metaphor.* Though Bernard Arnault (the richest man in Europe and owner of LVMH Moët Hennessey—Louis Vuitton) may not be aware of it, his immediate pledge of $225 million to reconstruct Notre Dame in an effort that could cost $8 billion and take up the fifteen years, will not be used to house a *symbol.*[50] The "beating heart of the Church," according to the Pope, the one thing "essential" for salvation, is the *pharmakon athanasias.* But for today's otherwise ordinary bread and wine to hold this power over some of the 1.3 billion Catholics like Father Fournier, the original Drug of Immortality simply *had* to mean something. The way it meant something to the Greek-speaking mystics in the centuries preceding Christianity's rebranding of the Dionysian Mysteries in the first century AD.

When initiates ingested the raw flesh and blood of Dionysus and tasted his visionary wine, they must have experienced something profound. Enough that it made them forget all duties to family, country, and Roman society at large, escaping like addicts into the wilderness, where immortality was available in a cup. When they said they drank the God of Ecstasy and became themselves divine, they meant it. And when new initiates tasted from the same cup, they too were converted. Because the Eucharist of the Dionysian Mysteries was pure magic.

John could not possibly hope to sell Christianity to a skeptical, pagan world unless the Eucharist of the Christian Mysteries was just as magical. His entire Gospel seems engineered to make the single point that the sacrament of Dionysus and the sacrament of Jesus are one and the same. And it all seems to be uniquely addressed to women. Women who would understand the secret "symbols" and "language." And women who had the pharmacological expertise to run with the new indoor Eucharist. Before Jesus, that primitive ritual of drinking the god to *become* the god had largely survived in the wild. With John's Gospel, apotheosis came home. And it went viral.

Because *that's* how religions are born. And *that's* how religions flourish.

Until the bureaucrats come along.

But technology that time-honored and that advanced doesn't just evaporate. The witches would never allow it.

All This Was Not Just Picnicking

"*Via Luigi Luzzatti 2B, per favore,*" I instruct the taxi driver.

We race a few blocks through the Trastevere neighborhood toward our destination in back of the chic Fiat showroom on Viale Manzoni, not far from the railroad tracks that stem in all directions from the Termini station. Despite the overcast Monday morning following a sunny weekend in Paris, as soon as we cross the Tiber over the Ponte Garibaldi, it soon becomes apparent why Rome has been described as "a poem pressed into service as a city."

Dressed from head to toe in black like a born-again Johnny Cash, Father Francis is in stream-of-consciousness mode, sharing memories of the past thirty-four years he has spent exploring these storied streets. "Azienda Tessile Romana," he reads aloud from a storefront near the Torre Argentina, where Julius Caesar was assassinated. "A really terrific fabric shop, for whenever I need vestments. And then if we kept going that way"—the priest signals north toward the Pantheon—"we'd hit the ASEQ bookstore, of course." Tucked away on Via dei Sediari, the boutique business is one Father Francis recommended to me my last time in Rome, with its top-notch collection of esoteric literature. Last year I spent two hours chatting with the owner, Luca, about the survival of Greek mystery cults due south in Naples, Pompeii, and the rest of Magna Graecia. Even today an ethnic minority of Greek speakers known as the Griko can still be heard talking in a strange but unmistakably Greek dialect across pockets of Calabria and Apulia, the toe and heel of

Italy's boot. Their language and blood can be traced back to the peninsula's original Greek colonists of the eighth century BC.[1]

"Another place I want to see sometime is over here, the Crypta Balbi," announces my fellow passenger as we breeze east along Via delle Botteghe Oscure. "I'm surprised that's not on your list; I'd love to see what's down there," he adds, motioning to one of the more overlooked branches of the Museo Nazionale Romano. Leave it to Father Francis to find fault with the itinerary that has taken me the better part of a year to put together. After the Campidoglio, the hilltop square with the twelve-pointed star designed by Michelangelo, we round the Piazza Venezia and pass the Roman Forum for another favorite.

"Then you've got Saints Cosmas and Damian, with the original bronze doors." The priest points out the basilica originally dedicated to Valerius Romulus, the son of the Emperor Maxentius who underwent apotheosis and became a god upon his death in AD 309, receiving the title *Divus Romulus* (the God Romulus). The site was later Christianized on behalf of the twin Syrian brothers and patron saints of pharmacists. A fitting salute to this area of the Forum known to attract the likes of Galen, the personal physician to Marcus Aurelius who was very much the successor to Dioscorides. Much of his prolific output in Greek, like the eleven-volume *On the Mixtures and Powers of Simple Drugs*, remains untranslated.

And so, when it comes to drugs, that blind spot of the classicists continues. If even the professionals won't bother with the topic, what hope is there for the rest of us? And what hope is there of proving or disproving the pagan continuity hypothesis, and getting to the true origins of Christianity, when the potential key to the Mysteries has been ignored by both secular and religious historians for so long? Because if ever there was a missing link between the Ancient Greeks of the final centuries BC and the paleo-Christians of the early centuries AD, it's the spiked wine I have been discussing with Father Francis for the past three days straight. That long tradition of drugged potions that Aldous Huxley only roughly sketched in *The Doors of Perception* back in 1954, and that Ruck has been trying to revive since 1978.

The more I investigated the possibility of a psychedelic Eucharist over the past twelve years, the less crazy it seemed. And my time in Paris has only raised the stakes: from G 408 and G 409, to the wine formulas of Dioscorides, to the Dionysian sanctuary in the Louvre's Salle des Caryatides, to A. D. Nock's secret "symbols" and "language" in the Gospel of John.

Together with the archaeological chemistry of Andrew Koh at the Massa-chusetts Institute of Technology, it all supports the basic premise of mind-expanding wine as a five-thousand-year-old enterprise that started in the Near East with Osiris and El and later found its way to Ancient Greece with Dionysus, only to wind up back in first-century Galilee with Jesus. Where the bloody wine of Dionysus became the bloody wine of Jesus.

But the smoking gun remains elusive. As close as Patrick McGovern has gotten to finding indisputable evidence of the ancient psychedelic sacra-ment in the birthplace of the Greek Mysteries, it has not come to light just yet. At McGovern's suggestion, I even spoke with his colleague, Dr. Soultana Valamoti, at the Aristotle University of Thessaloniki. As Greece's expert on the archaeological reality of ancient plant use, she confirmed a number of prehistoric botanical finds in the north of the country that point to wine in the creation of "altered states of consciousness" on terms similar to the *marzeah,* where a "healer" could exploit their "knowledge of fermentation of grape juice" to "communicate with spirits, ancestors or gods."[2] But de-spite the discovery of diffused remains, including grapes, opium, henbane, and black nightshade, Valamoti has not yet nabbed the visionary plants all together in one ritual setting. It's the same story in Galilee, where Koh has not been able to unearth any overtly psychedelic potions amid some very promising leads. So at the moment, the two most obvious locations that might cough up a psychedelic sacrament for the Dionysian and Christian Mysteries, Greece and Galilee, have failed to deliver.

In a bit of déjà vu, the hunt for a psychedelic Eucharist reminded me very much of the hunt for hard data on graveyard beers. In the absence of testable pottery from Eleusis, I was forced to the Greek colonies, where I chanced upon the long history of nightshade beers in Spain and, eventually, the ergot potion at Mas Castellar de Pontós. In the same way, all my research in recent years has been leading to the Greek colonies in Italy, which is actually not that surprising. If the cult of Dionysus and the cult of Jesus were going to meet anywhere west of Greece and Galilee in antiquity, it was southern Italy. Right where the de-scendants of the Phocaean colony at Velia might bump into the earliest Chris-tians up the coast in Rome, or anywhere in between for that matter.

If you time-traveled to this coastal region of Magna Graecia in the centu-ries before Jesus, you'd be quickly forgiven for thinking you had just landed in Ancient Greece. The language, the temples, the city-states: they were all

Greek. As were the abundant mystery cults dedicated to Demeter, Persephone, and Dionysus that both "preceded and accompanied Christianity"
in this area.[3] The seeds of Jesus's sacrament may have been planted in Galilee
and Jerusalem, but they took root here, in the onetime capital of the Roman
Empire and home to the oldest functioning institution the planet has ever
known: the Roman Catholic Church.

Finding evidence of psychedelic wine in this part of the Mediterranean
would finally join the Greeks and Christians on the same ancient path of
death and rebirth. And it would turn the notion of pagan continuity from a
mere hypothesis into a historical and scientific fact. But before I unveil the
hard botanical data from Pompeii that brought me to Italy in the first place,
it's high time to reconstruct what Christianity actually looked like in the
period between the death of Jesus around AD 33 and Emperor Theodosius
in the fourth century AD, when the illegal cult suddenly became the official
religion of the Roman Empire.

Those three centuries of paleo-Christianity are the essence of the faith.
In a tradition that has been discarded and forgotten, Magna Graecia and
Rome are where the Dionysian and Christian Mysteries smacked into each
other and exploded into a hybrid ritual of secret meetings and magical sacraments. Where Dionysus or Bacchus was not feared as the God of Alcohol,
a word that meant nothing to the Greeks or the Greek-speaking Romans. He
was the God of Drugs—any of the plants, herbs, or fungi spiking the wine
that Euripides called a *pharmakon* in 405 BC. And where the new kid on the
block, Jesus or *Iesous*, was not feared as a happy-go-lucky wine god from the
Wedding at Cana. According to Ruck, he was the "Drug Man" (*iatros*). The
healer from Galilee whose flesh and blood became the *pharmakon athanasias,* the Drug of Immortality.

The evidence that puts Dionysus the Elder and Dionysus the Younger in
the same place at the same time is right below our feet. Where the original
Greek version of Christianity has been hiding out for a very long time. Holding its breath for a comeback. Because that's where all the magic happened.

Before the legalization of Christianity, and before the public churches
and basilicas of the fourth century AD, there were only two places the paleo-
Christians got together to celebrate their secret Eucharist. It was either in
subterranean catacombs like the one I'm about to inspect with Father Francis. Or it was in the house churches, with the doors closed and the curtains

drawn. To see how different they were from today's Mass, the ritual dinners that filled wealthy homes across the Mediterranean deserve a quick review.

Not much archaeological evidence has survived from Christianity's earliest house churches. But the textual evidence from the New Testament itself suggests the meals were not paired with the kind of wine I've been drinking since my First Communion. In the old days, the female witches of Christianity who preceded the male priests were known for serving up a deadly concoction. The kind of wine the Ancient Greeks would have had no problem calling a *pharmakon*, or Dioscorides would have easily included as one of his wine formulas in the *Materia Medica*. Judging from the Ancient Greek of Saint Paul, there's no doubt the Eucharist of yesterday was very different from the Eucharist of today.

Aboveground, the original Eucharist was being consumed as part of a larger meal, a Greek-inspired pagan banquet called an *agape* (ἀγάπη) or "love feast," that was "often marked by excessive convivial drinking."[4] Indeed the same Ignatius who coined the term *pharmakon athanasias* in the early second century seems to have regarded the Christian Eucharist and the pagan *agape* as identical. Just the kind of stealth maneuver that might protect the illegal Dionysian nature of the budding religion. According to one historian, "it is improbable that a pagan neighbor could distinguish whether the Christians who arrived in the neighboring house [in Rome] assembled for an *agape* or a eucharist."[5] While the smoke and mirrors may have kept the Roman authorities off their backs, Paul and the other Church Fathers weren't so happy about confusing sacred and profane intoxication. Eating and drinking Jesus to *become* Jesus was very different from getting smashed.

From the beginning, therefore, Paul had to contend with these out-of-control "love feasts." In 1 Corinthians 10:21, he chastises the Greek community established less than an hour's drive from Eleusis. "You cannot drink the cup of the Lord and the cup of demons; you cannot partake of the table of the Lord and the table of demons." A few paragraphs later, Paul sets the ground rules for properly celebrating the Eucharist. As mentioned in the last chapter, this is the earliest written depiction of the ritual, dating to about AD 53. And it includes one very peculiar Greek word that convinced me, more than anything, that Ruck was truly onto something. When I first read his translation of 1 Corinthians 11:30 about ten years ago, I remember being completely blown away by what instantly became, and remains to this day, my vote for the most fascinating line in the entire New Testament. It left me with little doubt that one of those unusually intoxicating, seriously mind-altering, occasionally hallucinogenic, and potentially lethal elixirs had snuck its way into paleo-Christianity.

In the middle of the first century AD, all was not well in Corinth. Paul reprimands the female-stacked church for letting their solemn Christian ceremony devolve into a mind-altering Dionysian party. Having already condemned *their* version of the Eucharist as a "cup of demons," Paul complains in 1 Corinthians 11:21 that the communal meal in the Greek house church looks more like an *agape*—a free-for-all where some overindulge, leaving others "hungry," and a predictable routine of "getting drunk" has become all too common. Which makes Paul's "I told you so" moment in 1 Corinthians 11:30 all the more understandable, once you tease out the Greek.

In English the line is usually translated, "That's why so many of you are weak and sick, and a number of you have fallen asleep." Instead of "fallen asleep," however, Ruck translates the Greek word *koimontai* (κοιμῶνται) precisely the way it's translated elsewhere in the New Testament: "That's why . . . a considerable number of you are *dying*." He further explains:

> *The congregation had fallen into rival factions, owing individual allegiance to whoever had baptized them. Paul reprimands them to do the ordinary eating at home; and reminds them of the Eucharist that Jesus instituted, the table fellowship of the bread and the cup: whoever partakes unworthily will be guilty of sinning against the body and blood of the Lord. This is clearly not the ordinary eating, for many of them have fallen sick from taking the sacrament incorrectly, and some have even died, as if it could be a poison.*[6]

My grade school could be pardoned, but how on earth did the Jesuits at St. Joe's Prep overlook this verb *koimontai*? And how is this one line from the Bible not the subject of every single Sunday Mass, church service, and televangelism spiel around the planet? Has no one ever stopped to ponder why, two thousand years ago, "a considerable number" (*hikanoi*) of Corinthians were apparently dropping like flies during the proto-Mass?

I cracked open my 1829 edition of the Greek New Testament and found *koimontai*, just where Ruck said it was, in 1 Corinthians 11:30. But his translation had to be off. How do people die from taking the Eucharist? So I checked the online Greek-English lexicon by Henry George Liddell, Robert Scott, and Henry Stuart Jones—also known as Liddell–Scott–Jones—available on the Perseus Digital Library website that had gotten me through the graduate seminars a decade earlier. Halfway down the page, there it was: "the sleep of death," "to die." To top it off, the lexicon cited an example in John's Gospel, where the same verb *koimao* (κοιμάω) is used with this *exact* meaning.[7]

As I dug deeper, I realized Ruck was not the only one who did a double take on the verb *koimontai*. The nineteenth-century English theologian Charles John Ellicott—dean of Exeter and bishop of Gloucester—compiled a sweeping commentary of the New Testament in 1878 that is still consulted by pastors and students of the faith to this day. Ellicott knew Greek, of course, and paid attention to the grammatical nuances that force an explanation of something as weird as *koimontai*. Like Ruck he preferred "and some die" as the proper translation. But the rest of his one-liner on 1 Corinthians 11:30 is priceless: "Even death sometimes resulted from their drunken orgies, either naturally, or by God's direct visitation."[8] I love the thought of God the Father descending from the clouds to slap the wineglasses from the tipsy Greeks to deliver the touch of death. What an unexpected climax to an otherwise perfectly good orgy.

Creative as Ellicott was, there are more terrestrial ways to decipher Paul's choice of words here. The plain meaning of *koimontai* could not be any clearer. The Corinthians seem to have incorporated an extreme beverage into their liturgy. The boundary between psychedelic wine and poisonous wine is razor thin, however, and fatal dosing mistakes can be made. Could the makers of the potentiated Eucharist have gotten their measurements wrong? Did the participants ingest too much of the elixir at hand? Or maybe they simply *appeared* dead, reveling in the near-death experience that brought the Corinthians closer to Jesus and the community of departed Christian saints. If Paul is to be believed, and there really was a lethal potion in Corinth, who mixed it? And why?

The answer once again points to women.

Like other house churches across the Mediterranean, the vulnerable

Christian minority in Corinth was led by charismatic prophets who "functioned as mediators of the Holy Spirit" and displayed expertise in revealing
God's messages to their brothers and sisters around the "cultic banquet."[9] In
the footsteps of the priestesses who for centuries had been communing with
Demeter in Eleusis to the east, Apollo in Delphi to the north, and Dionysus
in the nearby mountains and forests, ecstatic women grabbed the reins in
Corinth.[10] In *When Women Were Priests*, Karen Jo Torjesen depicts a typical
house church in the Greek city:

> *First one would rise and speak a blessing, a commendation, a reve-*
> *lation or a word of wisdom. Before her oracle ended, another would*
> *rise with a word of encouragement or hope or exhortation. Mingled*
> *among these voices were the ecstatic exclamations of grace, thanks or*
> *praise. For these new Christians, the presence of the Spirit dramatized*
> *the fulfillment of [Old Testament] prophecy.[11]*

Inspired by the divinity coursing through their veins, these women were
"channeling the voice of Christ in *their* time"—exactly what Father Francis
said the prophets were doing in Ephesus almost half a century later. For
Jesus to have been "present" at the consecration of the Eucharist, that sense
of possession had to come from somewhere, didn't it? As with the Greek
cult at Mas Castellar de Pontós, maybe the Corinthian witches were going
for Demeter's ergot potion, but wound up with a deadly variation instead.
Or maybe they were trying to re-create a psychoactive cocktail of whatever
put the Pythias in contact with Apollo, with good leads among the barley
meal, laurel leaves, and smoldering henbane seeds (the *Herba Apollinaris* or
Pythonion) discussed in the first part of this investigation. Or just maybe it
was the infused potion from the Lenaia and other Dionysian festivals that
nicely complemented the Eucharistic meal.

But when it comes to this murky period of paleo-Christianity, we have
way more questions than answers. If whatever happened during the Last
Supper was crystal clear, the Christian faith wouldn't have splintered into
thirty-three thousand distinct denominations over the past two millennia.[12]
Despite the relative agreement among the Gospel authors and Paul, until more material evidence surfaces from Jerusalem, it's frankly unsettled
whether the Last Supper actually took place as recorded in the New Testa-

ment, or at all.[13] No one has ever found the Holy Grail. And maybe no one ever will. Far more pertinent to our investigation is how the early Christian troops at Corinth and elsewhere chose to interpret and reenact what they *believed* had happened that evening. And as the years went by, particularly important is how the Eucharist of the Gospel of John, or the holy texts and oral traditions of the Gnostics, would have colored that interpretation.

Despite Dr. Martin Luther King Jr.'s observation in 1950 that "a natural and unconscious process" might explain the similarities between the Greek and Christian Mysteries, John appears to have quite *consciously* spoken to women in Ephesus who were predisposed to a direct mystical experience of God. There were women just like them in Corinth who came before, and there'd be women just like them in Rome who came after.[14] By deliberately copying the language of Euripides, John assured his target audience that the pagan Eucharist of raw goat flesh (*omophagon charin*) had become the Lamb of God. And the "True Drink" of Jesus's blood would carry on the illicit tradition of Dionysus in the safety of the house churches. Where, for the first time, the paleo-Christians would learn how to truly *see*—catching visions of the angels that Jesus himself promised in the first chapter of John.

If aboveground the Eucharist was being confused with the Greek *agape*, the tombs below proved to be the real melting pots of the pagan and Christian sacraments. Instead of relying on the Ancient Greek of Saint Paul, we can look at the material evidence that is still there to see. Evidence that the Vatican itself qualifies as "the most significant assets of the paleo-Christian era."[15] Where once again the original Eucharist appears to have retained its Ancient Greek flavor.

Father Francis and I chug farther east past the Colosseum until we're parked on Via Luigi Luzzatti in the Esquilino neighborhood. Here in Rome, the subterranean equivalent of the *agape* was called the *refrigerium*.

In Latin *refrigerium* literally means a "cooling," hence the English word "refrigerator." But in practice it came to describe "the commemorative rite that was intended to refresh the soul of the deceased in the afterlife and ensure its peaceful existence in the world of the dead."[16] The Church Father Tertullian, who lived from AD 160 to 220, co-opted this term to describe the "blissful state" enjoyed by the departed ancestors while they awaited the resurrection of the faithful on Jesus's return trip to Earth. Early Christianity did not have a clear idea what was supposed to happen to the deceased in the period between death and the Last Judgment at the end of time, but from the Roman cult of the dead it learned one very valuable lesson: the spirits are thirsty.[17]

Wherever they are, and whatever they're doing, the dead need constant refreshment to prevent them from haunting the living. So the Christians began celebrating the *refrigerium* meal at the gravesite burials and anniversaries of their relatives' deaths. It was believed that the dead, residing in their tombs, were actually present for the feasts.[18] Ramsay MacMullen, professor emeritus of history at Yale, has coined the best term for these intoxicated get-togethers: a "chill-out." He paints a vivid re-creation of the "traditional beliefs and rites" that "prevailed among Christians" in Rome:

> *Such loving times in the recall of the dead went on for as long as the celebrants' mood and their wine might last, even as an "all-nighter," a vigilia. The dead themselves participated. They needed such remembrances for their tranquil existence in the Beyond. They were to be offered whatever food was at hand and, most especially, a toast in wine to be tipped onto their sarcophagus or into a pipe leading down to the head-end where they rested, athirst and happy. A party mood was essential. Participants, if they were challenged to defend the bad behavior that might attend too much eating and drinking, answered indignantly that loving thoughts, respect, and the recollection of fleshly pleasures offered to ancestors whose favor was certainly of more effect than any mere human's—all this was not just picnicking. This was religion.[19]*

Like the drunken *agape* in Corinth with its lethal wine, the all-night *refrigeria* got so out of hand that the Church eventually had to put its foot down. The Roman catacombs are filled with graffiti indicating *refrigeria* were being held on sacred ground to commemorate Jesus's closest disciples, like Peter and Paul. Using the departed saints and martyrs as an excuse for Dionysian banqueting became particularly problematic in North Africa. Saint Augustine, the same theologian who earlier in our investigation reassured the Christian community in Carthage that "all superstition of pagans and heathens should be annihilated is what God wants, God commands, God proclaims," railed against the "drunken riots in cemeteries" and "social orgies" that had become a daily habit in the late fourth century in his bishopric of Hippo (the modern-day port city of Annaba, where Algerian migrants have been gathering in recent years to hitch boat rides to the Italian island of Sardinia).[20]

The Latin word Augustine uses for "drunken riot" is *comissatio*, which the Lewis and Short Latin dictionary defines as a "Bacchanalian revel, and the succeeding nocturnal procession with torches and music" that we saw on the bell-shaped *krater* excavated at Mas Castellar de Pontós and the Borghese Vase in the Salle des Caryatides. Despite the best efforts of Augustine and others to prohibit the pagan cult of the dead, it stuck around for a very long time. Cemeteries around the Mediterranean were usually maintained outside the city walls. And the celebration of the *refrigeria* kept them there. It was not until the tenth century that Christian churches, with their accompanying graveyards, moved into the centers of town, finally uprooting the rural death cult. Throughout the Middle Ages the churches and their cemeteries remained "the sacred place of the people." Where their plays, dances, revels, and "drinking-bouts" continued in full force.[21]

It's all strangely reminiscent of the excesses in Corinth that led to "a considerable number" of people dying, or appearing to die. In calling for a sober end to the intoxication, an "emergency so great and hazardous," Augustine himself quotes the First Letter to the Corinthians, where Paul rebukes the Greeks' routine of "getting drunk." If that didn't already lump the *agape* and the *refrigerium* together into one paleo-Eucharistic tradition that was slowly taking shape in the early centuries after Jesus, the *Catholic Encyclopedia* from 1907 removes any doubt. It says that the Eucharist,

> at its origin, is clearly marked as funerary in its intention, a fact attested by the most ancient testimonies that have come down to us. Our Lord, in instituting the Eucharist, used these words: "As often as you shall eat this Bread and drink this chalice, you shall show forth the Lord's Death." Nothing could be clearer. Our Lord chose the means generally used in His time, namely: the funeral banquet, to bind together those who remained faithful to the memory of Him who had gone.

It's easy to forget, even for most Catholics. But at its core, the Mass is a séance, where the living and the dead come together through the magic of the "True Food" and "True Drink." The fact that Jesus himself makes an appearance in the Eucharist is only half the story. According to the United States Conference of Catholic Bishops, that part of the liturgy known as the *Intercessions* specifically implores God to grant the departed "a place of re-freshment" in the afterlife. It signals that "the Eucharist is celebrated in com-munion with the whole Church, of both heaven and of earth, and that the oblation is made for her and for all her members, living and dead, who are called to participate in the redemption and salvation purchased by the Body and Blood of Christ."[22] Once again, we can sense bizarre survivals from the skull cults and graveyard beers of the Stone Age, as well as the *marzeah* that formed the bridge between the old beer cultures and the new wine cultures of the Near East. The same *marzeah* that could be celebrated by people who might also host a Dionysian banquet in Galilee or Petra during the first century AD.

But before these archaic traditions morphed into the Mass, there was one final bridge to cross along the way: the Roman *refrigerium*. There the wine was absolutely essential to making contact with the Other Side. Which brings us back to the same question we have been asking all along. What kind of wine was it? What kept the all-nighters alive for centuries? And why did the cult of the dead refuse to surrender to Christian orthodoxy?

I'm about to find out.

As the priest pays the cabdriver I take my first look at the unassuming wrought-iron gate with the characters "2B" etched in gray stone on the brick pillar to the right. They may as well be etched onto my brain. For months, I've been exchanging emails about this address with the Pontificia Commis-sione di Archeologia Sacra—the Vatican's Pontifical Commission for Sacred Archaeology that, at its sole and absolute discretion, controls all access to the underground chambers known as the Hypogeum of the Aurelii.

Discovered in 1919 when the Fiat shop around the corner was trying to expand into a sunken garage, this site is considered one of the most im-portant funerary monuments from the first half of the third century AD, tentatively dated from 220 to 250. While the successors of Junia and the many women applauded in Paul's Letters were busy in their house churches here in Rome, these subterranean catacombs served an equally pivotal role in the early centuries after Jesus. By the papacy of Zephyrinus (AD 199–217), they were outpacing the pagan necropolis as the preferred venue for the new religion's burial rites, soon spreading to all Christianized parts of Italy, Greece, and North Africa.[23] In Rome alone the forty or so catacombs excavated to date run underfoot for hundreds of miles along damp, darkened tunnels—an entire shadow-city hosting thousands upon thousands of ancient tombs.[24]

Only seven are open to the public.[25] For the rest, like the one I'm standing in front of, special permission has to be secured from the Vatican to examine how the paleo-Christians understood their transition to the afterlife. The prize for anyone with the credentials, patience, and €160 to cover the holy official who will chaperone your visit, is an unadulterated look at some of the very first Christian art work on record. A veritable time capsule of sub-surface frescoes that leap off the soft limestone, or *tufa* rock: a "remarkable coexistence of themes" that "demonstrates the passage from pagan to Christian imagery."[26]

According to Barbara Mazzei, the Vatican archaeologist responsible for its eleven-year restoration, the Hypogeum in particular boasts "one of the most controversial scenes of the art of the catacombs."[27] Unveiled in 2011 for the first time in high definition, this underground lair holds the key to what was really happening in the secretive Jesus cult before Constantine gave the blessing in AD 313 for Christianity to become the biggest religion in the world.

"Are you here for the Hypogeum of the Aurelii?" asks a slender young woman in a black peacoat and jeans, with designer Italian eyeglasses.

"*Sì.*"

"*Buongiorno, piacere. Sono Giovanna,*" she introduces herself.

I present Father Francis to the Vatican archaeologist, who looks nothing like the intimidating official I expected to be guarding this sequestered vault. Giovanna opens the wrought-iron gate at 2B and waves us past the lemon tree to the kind of heavy metal hatchway that belongs on a nuclear submarine. She extracts a medieval skeleton key and clangs against the lock for a minute. I snap a photo of Father Francis with the same Cheshire Cat grin he sported all through Dr. Alexandra Kardianou's stockroom. Per the written policy that the Pontifical Commission for Sacred Archaeology sent me a few weeks ago, it's the last photo I'll be taking for the next two hours.

If Giovanna catches me breaking the rules, it will result in the "immediate suspension" (*l'immediata sospensione*) of our visit.

The door snaps open with a jolt and ominously creaks open. Into the underworld we go. The initial room is at ground level, a semi-hypogeum, one flight above the two subterranean chambers down the staircase ahead. To our left are the first of the thirty-two tombs originally cut into the monument's rock. It's unknown how their inhabitants were connected to the three Aurelii who created the Hypogeum, and whose names are recorded in a mosaic inscription. Two men and a woman: Onesimus, Papirius, and Prima.

We know almost nothing about them, but the honorary "Aurelii" was typical of former slaves who had won their freedom. In the Roman system, slaves could be highly skilled and hyper-educated—for example, a *paedagogus* snatched from the sophisticated part of the empire to initiate privileged children into all the knowledge that put Greek tutors in especially high demand.[28] It was one of the great ironies of the Roman Empire that it simultaneously ruled over and bowed to the cultural supremacy of the Greek-speaking Mediterranean.[29] The lyric poet Horace (65–8 BC) once wrote about the fate that tied the Latins and Greeks together, "Greece, the captive, conquered her savage victor, and brought the arts into rustic Latium [the region of western Italy where Rome was founded, now called Lazio]."[30]

So the Greek provenance of the Aurelii is a tempting clue to unraveling the mystery of the paintings adorning the cavernous walls farther underground, some of the first Christian symbolism ever produced. A few low-quality images are available online. But until now the closest I've gotten to any detail is an oversized monograph I had to purchase from the Vatican itself. Among the many frescoes that were commissioned by the Aurelii, there are three in particular that I've come to analyze and discuss with Father Francis.

The first shows the coexistence of the pagan *refrigerium* and the Christian Eucharist. Two ghostly meals in one.

The second reveals the Greek sacrament that fueled them both.

And the third explains it all, exposing the ultimate source of the ritual activity that took place inside the Hypogeum. Where both the secret "symbols" and "language" from the Gospel of John and the very Gnostic understanding of Jesus continued to resonate with the Greek-speaking Christians in Rome.

And with one primary group of Dionysian initiates above all. Women.

13

The Holy Grail

"Do you detect a banquet scene here?" I prompt our Vatican guide, Giovanna.

We're now in the first of the two subterranean chambers proper. It's more spacious and far less claustrophobic than I expected. When we're not scrunching our feet against the dirt and pebble floor, there is an almost jarring absence of noise. Although we're many feet under the streets of Rome, this musty hole in the earth has a strangely inviting feel about it. A nice spot for a mind-bending "chill-out" with the dead. Just like the one rendered on the fresco high on the wall in front of me.

"Yes. This is the *stibadium,* the round couch at the table," answers Giovanna. "These are the men seated around it. The servants with glasses and vessels in the foreground. And a young woman in the background. These scenes are very common in the third century in the Roman tradition. And they consider her Aurelia Prima," the Vatican archaeologist motions to the female figure at the top of the painting, "just arriving for the heavenly banquet."

The color and nuance of the many figures around the table are crisp and well preserved. I can easily make out the three servants, barefoot in white tunics, approaching the dinner with refreshments in hand. The one in the middle has just raised a chalice in his right hand. It's hard to tell what they're staring at, but all the guests seem to be transfixed by the strange maneuver.

The funerary banquet fresco in the first, underground chamber of the
Hypogeum of the Aurelii. This sacred meal for the dead could alternatively be interpreted as a Roman *refrigerium* or a Christian Eucharist.
Or perhaps both. (© *Pontificia Commissione di Archeologia Sacra; courtesy
of Archivio PCAS*)

"It's being held up ceremoniously," I suggest, referring to the golden chalice. "I mean, it doesn't look like a functional pose. That's not how you serve
wine, right?"

"Right," Father Francis agrees. "He's presenting it with his fingers sticking out, and the other hand has the fingers extended as well. I think that's
intentionally some kind of ritual gesture."

"Would it be a stretch to call it a 'consecration'?" I ask, referring to the
magical procedure by which the Catholic priest is able to transform ordinary bread and wine into the body and blood of Jesus. There's a moment in
today's Mass when Father Francis holds the Eucharistic cup aloft, just like
this servant, as soon as the wine has transubstantiated into the life-giving
blood. It's called the "elevation" of the Most Blessed Sacrament.[1]

"I think it's a 'designation,'" my friend responds, mincing words. "He's
saying 'this *is* something.'"

"Sure, but that's still a ritual act. Just like in the Gospels with *touto estin*." I throw out the Greek phrase for "this is" (τοῦτό ἐστιν). In Matthew, Mark, Luke, and Paul, Jesus uses the same formula when consecrating the Eucharist for the very first time at the Last Supper: "*This is* (touto estin) my body. . . . *This is* (touto estin) my blood."[2] The fundamental meaning of that language and this arm raising, ancient and modern, is all the same: this ain't grape juice. The god is present in this liquid. And once you drink it, the god will be present inside you. So proceed cautiously.

"Yes, you're right," concedes Father Francis, sensing my reading of the fresco. "So then, how many people do we have here?" The priest begins counting the guests arranged in a semicircle around the table, laughing out loud when he gets to the final number. "Well, looks like we have twelve people all right."

Like an archaic model for da Vinci's masterpiece in Milan, the fresco conjures the sanctity of the Last Supper. Perhaps the oldest surviving example ever painted by Christian hands. But not everybody sees it this way.

"Does the Vatican have an opinion here, Giovanna?" I inquire.

"A funerary banquet scene. Just the family feasting for the deceased. *With* the deceased probably," she corrects herself. Given some of the more overt pagan motifs we're about to examine in the neighboring frescoes, the Church is hesitant to call this meal a Eucharist. But we've just spent the past half hour analyzing some of the better Christian symbols in the chamber. Behind us on the opposite wall was the bucolic landscape of a herdsman and goats, possibly John's depiction of Jesus as the "Good Shepherd." Why he's tending goats instead of lambs is not entirely clear. Whoever he is, he's definitely rocking the long-haired Jesus look. In addition, we saw the portrait of a bearded man, whom Father Francis and others have suggested is Saint Paul. And we also examined a rose-studded path leading to the gates of a vast cityscape, perhaps Jesus's entrance into Jerusalem on Palm Sunday.

"I don't think a Christian interpretation is that crazy," I disagree after a slight pause. Whenever twelve people belly up to a sacred dinner, and start drinking sacramental wine in a tomb under the Vatican's exclusive authority, what else are we supposed to think?

"But in this case, I wouldn't say it's the Last Supper," interjects Father

Francis. He doesn't see Jesus and the Apostles, but he *does* see their legacy. "Whatever group this is," he continues, "it must be celebrating a similar banquet. A ritual banquet with the Holy Grail." The priest draws my attention back to the shiny chalice he envisions holding the blood of Jesus.

Giovanna is not convinced that the Roman *refrigerium* and Christian Eucharist were so easily interchangeable. If it's really a primordial Mass, then why is a dead woman walking around? She repeats her observation about Aurelia Prima descending on the banquet from the background, and notes how the twelve men seated around the table could be her living relatives. I look back at the delicate figure of a woman, her dress painted in red and black outline that disappears into the off-white of the plaster. She is the thirteenth member of the feast, and the only female.

The Good Shepherd fresco in the first, underground chamber of the Hypogeum of the Aurelii. In John 10:11, Jesus refers to himself as the Good Shepherd who "lays down his life for the sheep." But the presence of goats here removes this imagery from the Gospels. If this scene was really meant to portray Jesus, it instantly connects him to the goats of Dionysus. (© *Pontificia Commissione di Archeologia Sacra; courtesy of Archivio*)

Fresco portrait of an unknown, bearded man in the first, underground chamber of the Hypogeum of the Aurelii. While Saint Paul is a possibility, images like this are reminiscent of the pagan philosopher, Plotinus, from the third century AD. Such portraits inspired later iconography around Saint Paul. (© *Pontificia Commissione di Archeologia Sacra; courtesy of Archivio PCAS*)

"Because you're interpreting it as some kind of *refrigerium*?" asks Father Francis.

"Yes," Giovanna answers.

"Why a *refrigerium*?" I question, trying to figure out what distinguishes this scene from a Eucharist.

"Because it's the Roman ritual during the funeral. They brought food to the tombs. They gave a banquet for the *parentalia*," she adds, referring to the nine-day celebration of the ancestors in Rome, during which the drunken night of the living dead would have been especially promoted. "For as long as the celebrants' mood and their wine might last," according to Ramsay MacMullen at Yale.

"A supernatural meal," I add. We're all getting lost in semantics and drawing boundaries where few existed in the third century: between Greek and Roman, Christian and pagan, sacred and profane. The foremost authority on this lost tradition, the secular scholar MacMullen, has no problem confirming the pagan continuity between the *refrigerium* and the Eucharist. He notes these family gatherings in a Christian context "are not imaginary," citing the "tangible testimonies" of excavations at the Papal Basilica of San Lorenzo, built to honor one of the first seven deacons of Rome who was martyred in AD 258. Several mausolea were unearthed with "bits of cooking and eating vessels," objects that MacMullen attributes to the service of "Christian *refrigeria*." All as further evidenced by inscriptions left throughout this ancient city, which record "ancestor worship" in the form of promises or debts to the Christian deceased: "Dalmatius promised a communion picnic, a *refrigerium*, as a vow"; "Tomius Coelius held a communion picnic for Peter and Paul."[3]

Establishing a channel of communication with the Other Side was mutually beneficial. On the one hand, the dead would receive the nourishment they needed while awaiting the Last Judgment; they would not go missing in limbo. On the other, the living got a little closer to their Creator, "since the martyred heroes of the congregation were believed to have special influence as petitioners at the throne of God."[4]

At St. Peter's Basilica, just a fifteen-minute drive to our west, the situation was identical. Underneath the largest Christian cathedral in the world, the seat of the papacy and the nerve center for Catholics the world over, a second-century shrine known as an *aedicula* was found, dedicated to Saint Peter himself. Around it, embedded in the earth, were heaps of bones from domestic animals. A neighboring sarcophagus was equipped with a libation tube for supplying wine to the deceased. MacMullen confirms, "The bones can only have been left from religious picnics; the tube obviously served the purposes of memorial communion."[5] The "basilica built among the dead" continued to host "chill-outs" for years after Constantine's initial construction in the fourth century, where "wine in worship flowed freely and not only on the saint's festival."[6] And why not? With "hundreds of burials beneath the floor," says MacMullen, "some family was bound to turn up for remembrance's sake on each and every day of the year."[7] It should come as no surprise that the Eucharist itself would be celebrated at St. Peter's as part of the "communion parties." One shocked cleric at the time remarked, "Their [martyrs'] tombs are seen as Christ's altars."[8] Imagine the intoxicated, all-night affair, promising an in-person appearance by your dead relatives, the holy saints, and possibly the Lord himself—all made possible by the Eucharistic funerary meal that laid the very foundations for the Catholic Mass.

For the purely pagan rituals that preceded Christianity, it was all about ancestor worship as well. The Romans designated their dead relatives as "gods" (*dii* or *divi* in Latin, sometimes adding *immortales*), much the way a Greek speaker might call them "gods" or *theoi* (θεοί).[9] The deceased were no longer limited by the physical body. They had access to cosmic information beyond time and space. They had answers. Once again I can't help but think of the Stone Age death cults from the Raqefet Cave and Göbekli Tepe. Or the mind-altering *marzeah* that survived for thousands of years in the ancient Near East—from the Canaanites all the way down to Aretas IV Philopatris, the King of the Nabataeans, whose daughter married Jesus's archenemy, Herod Antipas of Galilee.

In his decoding of the Ugaritic cuneiform, Professor Gregorio del Olmo Lete interprets the long-running ritual as a journey to the underworld. Key to the entire experience was the consumption of visionary wine, consciously manufactured under the rubric of some "handbook" or "recipe" to induce a kind of death-like trance. In the "altered state of consciousness reached by drunkenness," the living and the dead might coexist. With the drinkers' spirits temporarily dissociated from the physical body, they were essentially lifeless, free to communicate with the immortals on the Other Side. Whether his name was Osiris, El, Dionysus, or Jesus, what better way to make contact with the Lord of Death?

Was it some kind of biotechnology that allowed the ghost of Aurelia Prima to join this paleo-Eucharistic meal in the Hypogeum? A straight line can be drawn from her semi-veiled head down to Father Francis's Holy Grail. The golden chalice ties the whole fresco together. It has to mean something. Whatever is taking place here, by whatever ritual, the wine is making it happen. If it's a purely pagan *refrigerium*, then twelve relatives are summoning the dead Aurelia Prima from the underworld. If it's a Christian Eucharist, then twelve Romans who wanted to portray themselves as the twelve Apostles who attended the Last Supper are summoning a dead Christian from the Kingdom of Heaven so she can be their intermediary in the Beyond. According to Ramsay MacMullen, the pagan and Christian rituals could coexist and overlap. Christians did perform the *refrigerium*. And the wine was essential for the magic.

Here in the moldy depths of the *tufa* rock, with the Vatican archaeologist beginning to wonder what the Roman Catholic priest and his sidekick are really up to, am I looking at the first artistic rendering of the Drug of

Immortality? If so, what was in that chalice? I think the answer lies in the second fresco I came to inspect, just a couple feet to our right.

Covering much of the wall like a mural, the scene in front of me was only first unveiled in 2011, after a painstaking eleven-year restoration. By the Vatican's own admission, it quickly became one of the most controversial scenes in all the Roman catacombs. Before that, it was hard to tell what the Aurelii had in mind for the fresco, which is divided into two sections. In the lower register, I spot three nude males. They seem caught off guard. To their right, a bearded man lifts an imposing right hand, fingers splayed, toward a woman standing by a loom for weaving fabrics. The male is barefoot, seated, and wearing a tunic. The female is standing, dressed in a flowing robe that leaves the ankles exposed. In the upper register above, I notice the farm animals: sheep, cows, a donkey, a horse, and even a camel. Behind them in the background, a woman is seen in front of a rustic building with sloping roofs and canopies. By her side two male figures lie in repose on an open coffin or bier.

According to the Vatican itself, the key to unlocking this hodgepodge of

The Homeric fresco in the first, underground chamber of the Hypogeum of the Aurelii. (© *Pontificia Commissione di Archeologia Sacra; courtesy of Archivio PCAS*)

imagery lies in the loom. The Pontifical Commission for Sacred Archaeology details everything in the beautiful monograph they published in 2011, just after the fresco's restoration, complete with seventy-nine glossy plates. In it Dr. Alexia Latini dedicates an entire chapter to this one composite scene. It's the only chapter penned by the classical archaeologist from Roma Tre University, an Italian public research institution, otherwise unaffiliated with the Holy See. When I first read it in the main reading room of the Library of Congress last November (because I couldn't sit around for weeks on end, waiting for the copy I ordered directly from the Vatican), I thought it was a mistake. A serious mistake. In solving the riddle Latini drops a bombshell I had to read three times to make sure I got the Italian right.

The chapter is titled "Quadro Omerico" (Homeric Painting). For a scholar with obvious fluency in Greek and Latin, the loom was a dead giveaway.

Detail of Folio 58 from the *Vergilius Vaticanus* illuminated manuscript (left), created in Rome ca. 400 AD and currently housed in the Vatican's Apostolic Library *(© Biblioteca Apostolica Vaticana)*. Circe's loom is strikingly similar to the loom from the Homeric fresco in the Hypogeum of the Aurelii (right). For the Aurelii, and perhaps other paleo-Christians in Rome, the Ancient Greek witch and her drugs were full of hidden meaning by way of a secret doctrine known only to Greek speakers. *(© Pontificia Commissione di Archeologia Sacra; courtesy of Archivio PCAS)*

When it comes to weaving, there's only one mythical woman who instantly comes to mind. And there's only one loom in the extant manuscripts that looks exactly like the one in front of me. It's sitting peacefully in the Biblioteca Apostolica Vaticana, the Pope's personal library located right next to the Vatican Secret Archives. But if you go online to the Digital Vatican Library website and type in "Vat. Lat. 3225," you'll find a color copy of the same wonderfully preserved codex, the *Vergilius Vaticanus*, created sometime between AD 400 and 430.

It contains select vignettes from *The Aeneid*, the poet Vergil's epic adaptation of Homer's *Iliad* and *Odyssey*, written in Latin a couple decades before the birth of Jesus. Like Odysseus, the main character, Aeneas, suffers through an endless series of trials and tribulations on his fantastic voyage around the Mediterranean. At its finale Aeneas is credited with the foundation of Rome, but not before making a pit stop on Circeii. Once an island, it is now the modern-day promontory of San Felice Circeo, a couple of hours south of Rome, where Circeo Mountain and the Capo Circeo Lighthouse stand watch over the Tyrrhenian Sea. The Greeks might call it Aeaea. And as the name implies, it was believed by the Romans to house the most famous witch in antiquity, Circe.

Latini focused my attention on Folio 58 of the *Vergilius Vaticanus*, where Circe is depicted tending a giant loom that is strikingly similar to the one painted here on the wall of the Hypogeum. She notes that both are "large and equipped with massive uprights, solid feet, and two beams."[10] The restoration work of Dr. Barbara Mazzei had revealed something even more incredible, however, in the upper register of the fresco.

Ever since its discovery in 1919, the thick layer of calcium carbonate that had crystallized over the paint in the preceding centuries had prevented a clear reading of the woman in the rustic farmhouse. In her precision cleaning of the rock with laser ablation technology, Mazzei noticed the area around the ranch "appeared to be concealed by an ocher-colored layer of particular tenacity and consistency."[11] It was cinnabar, the toxic mercury-sulfide ore (HgS) once used as a red pigment. Mazzei's micro-instruments had to be specially calibrated to avoid exposing the ore to radiation, which would have destroyed the fresco. After years of careful work, however, her restoration was successful. "The laser ablation allowed us to recognize with certitude the story of Odysseus and the witch-goddess Circe ... excluding the alternative hypothesis of an episode in the life of the Prophet Job."

The distinctive pigment was another dead giveaway. Latini further explains in her chapter of the Vatican monograph that the bloodred cinnabar must have been intentionally used to indicate the same witchy scene from Book 10 of *The Odyssey*, where the Greek hero notices some "fiery smoke" rising from the halls of Circe "through the thick brush and the wood." Like the loom down below, the "thick vegetation" (*folto della vegetazione*) up above is an unmistakable Homeric clue for Latini. Together with these telltale symbols, all the animals milling about point to the "cruel goddess" Circe, who, according to Vergil, had robbed her prisoners "of their human form with potent herbs" (*potentibus herbis*).

But as the tradition goes, these weren't just any old "herbs" that Circe plucked from her garden pictured in the fresco before me. Unbelievably, Latini references the *exact* lines from Homer's *Odyssey* that I had read with Director Polyxeni Adam-Veleni at the Ministry of Antiquities in Athens. In English the Italian scholar says that the master sorceress

> gave the unfortunate [companions of Odysseus] who landed at her home the kykeón, a wine-based mixture in which goat cheese, barley flour, and honey were dissolved, to which she added extraordinary phármaka [portentosi phármaka] capable of inducing oblivion. With the aid of a rhábdos, a magic wand, she then transformed them into pigs, enclosing them in a stable.[12]

Those were the lines I had to read three times to wrap my head around them. How did the witch Circe and her magical drugged wine sneak their way into a paleo-Christian tomb under the exclusive control of the Vatican? Right next to the pagan *refrigerium* that brought Aurelia Prima back from the dead with a paleo-Christian Eucharist? Of the 27,803 lines of Homer's *Iliad* and *Odyssey* and the 9,896 lines of *The Aeneid*, why did the Aurelii include this one and only scene in their illegal underground church? Like the Holy Grail to its left, this Homeric fresco has to mean something.

It certainly explains the three nude men to the left of the loom. Latini spies their "just completed metamorphosis" (*metamorfosi appena compiuta*) from pigs back into humans a split second earlier. The bearded man next to Circe, commanding his friends to be released, must then be Odysseus. After his victory the hero is sent on yet another errand: to consult the "tribes of the dead" in "the house of Hades and dread Persephone, to seek a prophecy from the ghost of the Theban Tiresias," the same blind seer from Euripides's *The Bacchae*.[13] In order to attract the spirits in the underworld, Odysseus is instructed by Circe to offer a few libations: milk and honey, followed by "sweet wine," followed by water sprinkled with "white barley." The witch's final recipe.

It's a memorable episode in the ancient literature that obviously survived into third century Rome, where Latini characterizes Homer's epic as a "bestseller"—on a par with Vergil's *Aeneid*.[14] For an educated Greek speaker of the time, Homer was much more than a poet. He was "a divine sage with revealed knowledge of the fate of souls and of the structure of reality."[15] In *Homer the Theologian*, the Harvard- and Yale-trained classicist Robert Lamberton charts the philosophical development in the second- and third-century Roman Empire that recasts Homer's narrative as a religious allegory with a "secret doctrine." Rather than a "fixed and unchanging" teaching committed to paper, Lamberton says the tradition refers "to a mystical and privileged 'contemplation' or mode of seeing."[16]

He calls it "the bizarre realm" of neo-Pythagoreanism influenced by Plato, perhaps best represented by an enigmatic thinker like Plotinus (ca. AD 205–270), who was born in Egypt and died in the Italian region of Campania in Magna Graecia. It's still unknown if Plotinus's roots were Roman, Greek, or Hellenized Egyptian, but it doesn't matter. It's just another example of the intellectual melting pot of the time. In his introduction to the Vatican's monograph, Fabrizio Bisconti, the superintendent of Christian Catacombs, actually gives a nice shout-out to Plotinus. That bearded figure on the wall behind me, whom Father Francis and others have likened to Saint Paul? Well, Bisconti says the Aurelii must have borrowed it from the marble portraits of Plotinus that were just coming into vogue and had a major influence on all later Pauline iconography.[17]

In the last seventeen years of his life, Plotinus wrote a massive six-part treatise in Greek called *The Enneads* that repackaged the Greek genius Pythagoras for a whole new audience. In a passage that acknowledges the entire *Odyssey* as a parable of spiritual liberation, and specifically describes the Greek of Odysseus's escape from Circe's island as full of "hidden meaning," Plotinus compares our journey through life (and the afterlife) to that of Homer's main character. The real adventure, however, lies within. Our focus should be directed inward. "We must not look, but must, as it were, close our eyes and exchange our faculty of vision for another. We must awaken this faculty which everyone possesses, but few people ever use."[18]

Lamberton traces this visionary technique to "the legend of Pythagoras' own temporary death and resurrection."[19] It was said to take place in a cave on the island of Samos, where the sage reportedly discovered his well-known mathematical theorem that everyone learns in high school, $a^2 + b^2 = c^2$. What everyone doesn't learn about is the altered state of consciousness that apparently gave birth to the breakthrough in Ionia, not far from the mystics in Phocaea and Ephesus. The procedure Pythagoras would later share with the so-called Pythagorean Women, the wives, mothers, sisters, and daughters whom the philosopher-magician would meet on his extensive travels across Magna Graecia, before his death in Metapontum on the sole of Italy's boot around 495 BC.[20] So what exactly did Pythagoras teach them?

In "The Cave of Euripides," published in the peer-reviewed interdisciplinary journal *Time and Mind* in 2015, Ruck compares Pythagoras's strange practice to Euripides's own seclusion in a cave on the island of Salamis, just across the gulf from Eleusis. The second-century Roman antiquarian Aulus Gellius once visited the site where the playwright was thought to have created such works as the *The Bacchae*, confirming its draw as a place of literary pilgrimage among the refined Romans of the day, "a cultic sanctuary for hero worship."[21]

True to his forty years of scholarship on the subject, Ruck suggests that both Pythagoras and Euripides entered into "deified states of ecstasy" in their respective chambers through the "Dionysian pathway" of sacred drugs. He speculates that "the mystic rites celebrated in the cave" of Euripides, in particular, "probably involved the tragedian and his troupe of actors in a subterranean frenzy in which they communed with the god [Dionysus], who imbued their tragedian leader with his divine persona in a Eucharistic liturgy attended by an elite assemblage of his female bacchanalian devotees."[22] In his concluding remarks Ruck anticipates today's visit to the Hypogeum:

The poor early Christians of the Roman Empire customarily met in subterranean catacombs to celebrate the Eucharist. They did not do this to avoid persecution, since it was not apt to go unnoticed, nor would doing so arouse less suspicion than meeting above ground in private homes. The paintings on the catacomb walls indicate that drinking parties were celebrated there, apparently to invite the deceased to materialize and share in the banqueting. . . . This subterranean festive drinking amid the revenant spirits continued a tradition that goes back to the kinds of rites that were celebrated in the Cave of Euripides.[23]

It's an attractive theory, but I never knew what to make of it. And I never knew how Lamberton's "secret doctrine" could have possibly survived as an oral tradition in Magna Graecia from Pythagoras in the fifth century BC to Plotinus in the third century AD. Until now. Is this Homeric fresco proof that subterranean rituals of death and rebirth not only flourished in southern Italy in the centuries before and after Jesus, but also entered paleo-Christianity through Greek speakers like the Aurelii? And does it suggest that drugs were essential to the process? With countless scenes in Homer to choose from, the presence of Circe's *pharmaka* in this dank chamber could hardly be a coincidence.

I reflect back on my meeting with Director Adam-Veleni and the work of Calvert Watkins, that "towering figure" from my Sanskrit days who scoured a dozen Indo-European languages to ultimately conclude that the *soma* ritual of the Rigveda and "the ritual act of communion of the Eleusinian mysteries, by women for women," were one and the same, "just too striking for a fortuitous resemblance to be plausible." From this very passage of Homer about Circe's *kukeon* and her pigs, Watkins was able to extract the holy language "describing a religious ritual." He called it "a liturgical act" stretching back thousands of years, perhaps to the Proto-Indo-Europeans whose graveyard beers conquered Europe during the Stone Age. In the case of Circe's final underworld recipe—honeyed milk, wine, and barley water—Watkins called it a "ritual to call up the dead," with Persian influences.[24] Behind all of these Indo-European elixirs, he believed, were psychedelic drugs.

With *soma* it was the juice of a plant or fungal sacrament that Watkins explicitly characterized as "the source of the hallucinogenic agent."[25] With the Greeks he couldn't say for sure. But like Gordon Wasson, he thought the

Amanita muscaria mushroom was a good candidate. The hard data from Mas Castellar de Pontós suggests another mushroom, ergot, spiked the beer-based *kukeon* at Eleusis. As for the Dionysian wine that replaced Demeter and Persephone's beer, Watkins said, "clearly it is no ordinary wine."[26] The hard data for *that*, straight from Italy, will come later in this investigation. By the time of Jesus, the separate Greek sacraments of the grain and the vine were combined into the Most Blessed Sacrament, the Drug of Immortality. Like the *soma*, *kukeon*, and Dionysian wine before it, the Eucharist appealed to women around the Mediterranean in the *agape* meals of the female-run house churches (especially in Corinth), and the graveside *refrigeria* of paleo-Christianity (especially here in Rome and Augustine's city of Hippo).

But perhaps the drug-induced ritual found its greatest expression in a subterranean chamber just like this Hypogeum, where the legendary cave techniques of Pythagoras and Euripides could put the "secret doctrine" of Plotinus to the test. Where the "faculty of vision" that "everyone possesses, but few people ever use" could be awakened. And where the doors to the afterlife might be forced open with a big gulp of the Holy Grail. Maybe the dead Aurelia Prima would come through the portal. Maybe Dionysus, at the head of the same ghost train he conducted through Athens during the annual Anthesteria festival, the Greek Halloween. Maybe Jesus himself, fresh from the Harrowing of Hell, with a few saints and martyrs in tow. Whatever happened at the banquet scene to my left, it was not a picnic.

As Ramsay MacMullen might remind us, "this was religion."

A religion that might look like a silly little children's story about witches and pigs. But for those like Plotinus with eyes to see, Circe is here as a coded image for the *pharmaka* that offered access to the Kingdom of Heaven. If the wine that fueled this underground ritual was psychedelic, as Calvert Watkins concluded in his analysis of the very Homeric passage depicted right here, then it was not just any religion. It was the religion with no name.

This recently restored fresco might finally explain how the cult of the dead and the all-night "communion parties" refused to surrender to Christian orthodoxy. Because if life-changing visions of the afterlife were in play from Christianity's earliest days, from the house churches in Corinth to these catacombs in Rome, then the newest mystery religion would not only have found a pool of willing converts among the Greek-speaking pagan population across the Mediterranean, it would also have kept the rural

Christians glued to the graveyards of their rural churches for the next thousand years. After all, that's what the beatific vision apparently did in Eleusis. It brought the best and brightest to Demeter's temple, year after year for two millennia, on one basic principle: seeing is believing.

Was the Homeric fresco used by the Aurelii to demonstrate their intimate knowledge of the mystical Greek tradition that connected them to the likes of Pythagoras and Plotinus in Magna Graecia? And, taking a cue from both the Gospel of John and Gnosticism at large, did they try to merge the "secret doctrine" unique to this part of Italy with the Eucharist of Rome's newest mystery religion? Was that the whole point of the "True Drink" in John 6:53–56? The people of Galilee certainly didn't get it. After Jesus reveals the key to the Christian Mysteries at the synagogue in Capernaum, a number of his Jewish followers leave in disgust after hearing the cryptic instruction to drink his blood. They couldn't stomach the cannibalism. They called it too "harsh" or *skleros* (Σκληρός).[27] With that curious ending to his bizarre scene, John is clearly saying that *his* Eucharist has hidden meaning. It wasn't supposed to make sense at first blush. Only those versed in the secret "symbols" and "language" of Dionysus might understand. Only they might recognize the Greek, Gnostic Jesus.

Women like Mary Magdalene, the "apostle to the apostles," who was supposed to take Christianity to the masses as the first witness to Jesus's resurrection. And whose Gospel might reassure women everywhere that *they* were entrusted with the visionary information denied to men, and *they* were the keepers of immortality. Like Junia, the "foremost among the apostles," who made the Church in Rome a reality.

Or Aurelia Prima.

Having finished with the Holy Grail and the Homeric fresco, we ascend seven brick-and-mortar steps up to the Hypogeum's central landing and descend another seven to the second subterranean chamber. It's time to inspect the third and final fresco that called me here today. As we enter the crypt, the priest and I let out a simultaneous "Wow!"

Nearly every surface of the cramped room, slightly more cave-like than the first, is covered with imagery that stirs the imagination: peacocks, flying billy goats, cupids, genies, and nature-demons crowned with flowers. The red-and-green color scheme looks like it could have been painted yesterday. I take in the three *arcosolia,* arched recesses cut into the soft limestone to serve as tombs. In each of them twelve figures stand shoulder to shoulder. Sure, the Romans had twelve principal gods, the *Dii Consentes* memorialized in the nearby Pantheon, to match the twelve Greek Olympians. But it's hard to see twelve humans in third-century garb and not think of the banquet scene next door, or the Last Supper on which it appears to have been modeled.

The ceiling fresco in the second, underground chamber of the Hypogeum of the Aurelii. In the center of the Greek cross, the female initiate is veiled in white. Is she being welcomed into the Mysteries of Dionysus or the Mysteries of Jesus? (© *Pontificia Commissione di Archeologia Sacra; courtesy of Archivio PCAS*)

But what I'm really here for is the ceiling. A perfect circle within a perfect circle, separated by a couple feet of eggshell plaster. Connecting the inner orb to the outer orb are four rectangular spokes that give the whole scene the effect of a Greek cross, or the cruciform halo that might appear behind the head of Jesus on an Orthodox icon. In each of the four spokes, there's a single peacock feather. Between them, in each of the four wedges that form the outer orb, the same image is repeated four times: a man in a tunic and *pallium* (the long rectangular cloak traditionally worn by Greek philosophers, but now popularly featured in the papal vestments). He is holding a scroll in his right hand. Latched into a kind of holster around his waist is a long, thin object you would almost think is a sword. On closer inspection, it's more of a wand.

In a total non sequitur, the distinguished bearded man is standing on top of some kind of giant plant or fungal arrangement that branches into three pedicels. They all seem to be leafing, leading Father Francis to identify the flat, disc-shaped tops as possible *umbellifers*. But all I can think of is the hookah-smoking caterpillar from *Alice's Adventures in Wonderland* perched on a mushroom. I stare at the four carbon copies of the trippy vegetation until my neck can't take it anymore.

In the middle of the bull's-eye, the focal point of this entire chamber, two men flank a veiled woman. She is clothed from head to toe in a white robe. Only her face is visible. The males are dressed like the fungal surfers that surround them, complete with elaborate sandals. The one on the right holds the same wand clutched by each of the four men around him. He is dangling it over the lone woman's head. Aside from the five figures on the ceiling, two others are depicted on the walls, bearing the wand in exactly the same pose. They also show up elsewhere in the Hypogeum, though I hadn't even noticed them before. Like Circe's loom in the neighboring room, the wand is the key to unlocking the meaning of this scene—and perhaps the entire Hypogeum.

Leave it to one extremely obscure German monograph to crack the code. Published in 1975 by the respected classical archaeologist Nikolaus Himmelmann, *Das Hypogäum der Aurelier am Viale Manzoni: Ikonographische Beobachtungen* (The Hypogeum of the Aurelii at Viale Manzoni: Iconographic Observations) provides the answer.[28] According to the German au-

Detail of the ceiling fresco in the second, underground chamber of the Hypogeum of the Aurelii. One of the many magicians with his magic wand, standing atop a mysteriously gigantic plant or fungus. (© *Pontificia Commissione di Archeologia Sacra; courtesy of Archivio PCAS*)

thor, the purpose of the wand is unambiguous. It can easily be gleaned from the "literary record of this time," which is "filled with reports of magical practices of the popular, religiously-charged 'philosophy'":

> *The magic wand in the hands of [the male figures] shines a light on the irrational "philosophy" which is taught in the Tomb of the Aurelii. For the inexplicably numerous magicians, to the best of my knowledge, there are no certain parallels in the iconography of ancient philosophers. Even if the magic wand appears with Moses, Ezekiel, Christ and Paul, this does not suffice to interpret the figures in the tomb at the Viale Manzoni as Christian. . . . This appears to represent an initiation ritual, known mostly from Dionysian and Eleusinian contexts.*[29]

Like the Homeric fresco in the previous room, this medallion on the ceiling of the best-preserved painting in the Hypogeum takes us straight back to the Greek Mysteries. Or rather, it brings the Mysteries and the "irrational philosophy" practiced by the likes of Pythagoras, Euripides, and

Plotinus right here to the heart of Rome. And, whether they like it or not, into the custody of the Vatican. For the connection to Eleusis, Himmelmann cites the "blessing branches" (*Segenszweige*) reportedly carried by the initiates in the "oldest versions" of the rites.[30] But the Dionysian influences are really the most compelling.

The German scholar directs the reader to the so-called Villa of the Mysteries located to our south, just outside one of the main gates at Pompeii. The forty-thousand-square-foot compound somehow survived the wrath of Mt. Vesuvius in AD 79. Seventeen feet of volcanic ash once protected the spectacularly vivid dining room murals that were unearthed in 1909. Dated to the first century BC, they are widely considered to be among the best surviving depictions of an initiation into the wine god's Greco-Roman cult. All the Dionysian symbols make their way into the secret ritual sequence: the female initiate with her laurel crown, a pipe-playing satyr, a goat-suckling nymph, a bowl of the magic potion, and Bacchus himself. But it was one fresco in particular on the vermillion background that reminded Himmelmann of what is on display overhead.

The sixth scene in the Villa of the Mysteries shows four women. There is the seminude initiate in her bright purple robe, kneeling into the lap of an elder female who could be her nurse.[31] Then, to their right, a fully naked maenad clashes cymbals in the air, while the fourth woman is about to hand the initiate the *thyrsos* that symbolizes the completion of her initiation. According to Ruck, the maenads used to stash their drugs at the tips of these staffs, which is probably where our notion of the magic wand came from in the first place.[32]

To the immediate left of this scene, a winged female has just lashed the initiate, the whip arched behind her back, as if about to strike again. But as with the wand in the hand of Himmelmann's "magician" above me, literal flagellation was not the real secret to the Dionysian initiation. Rather, the long goad is the Greek *kentros,* figuratively "whipping" the initiates into ecstasy.[33] As the Harvard-trained Olga Levaniouk put it, the goad might better represent the "suddenness and unpredictability" of the madness that was the true hallmark of the rites, "manic experiences as seen through [a] visual, acoustic and emotional code."[34]

I take out my iPhone and pull up the photo album I had created specifically for this moment. I toggle back and forth between two pictures: the scene from Pompeii, where the *thyrsos* hangs over the head of the female initiate, and the relief on the Borghese Vase from the Louvre, where the dazed and confused bacchant is slumped over in ecstasy, propped up by the satyr with *thyrsos* in hand. In each case, the angle of the gesture is identical to the initiation on this ceiling.

"Yes, that angle seems to be repeated over and over again," concedes Father Francis, referring to the way the instruments appear diagonally over the initiate's head. It's no wonder Himmelmann so confidently attached this fresco to the Dionysian Mysteries. The Dionysian masks and *kantharos*, the God of Ecstasy's ritual vessel, that are painted onto the wall of the first chamber certainly don't hurt. I noticed them next to the "Good Shepherd" and his goats the minute we landed in the Hypogeum.

"It's kind of remarkable that the Vatican is preserving all this material," I announce to Giovanna. "I understand why you save this room for last."

"Yes, the *virga* is quite interesting," she responds, using the Latin word for "magic wand." She adds that all the art work of the Hypogeum, both chambers we have now analyzed, was likely meant to be read together as one combined theme. I don't dare announce it to the Vatican archaeologist,

Detail of the Borghese Vase (left); ceiling fresco of the Hypogeum of the Aurelii (center); and detail from the Villa of the Mysteries in Pompeii, Italy (right). The Dionysian initiations depicted on the Borghese Vase and the Villa of the Mysteries precede the Hypogeum of the Aurelii by at least two and a half centuries. *Courtesy of RMN (© Musée du Louvre) (left); (© Pontificia Commissione di Archeologia Sacra; courtesy of Archivio PCAS) (center)*

but I completely agree. And only two words come to mind for the theme I've noticed over the past couple hours.

Women and drugs.

For two thousand years they have been the two biggest thorns in the side of the Church. Both senselessly scrubbed from the origins of the faith, as I've now witnessed in the Hypogeum.

The first fresco shows how the Roman *refrigerium* and the Christian Eucharist could live side by side, each a drunken séance aimed at entering the underworld. In the death cults that preceded this proto-Mass by thousands of years, it was spiked beer and mixed wine that may have summoned the Lord of Death from the depths, ancestors in tow. If the Holy Grail is supposed to be the Drug of Immortality, then the second fresco adds some intrigue. The Vatican's own confirmation of Circe and her drugs implicates the "secret doctrine" from Homer that connects the Aurelii to luminaries like Pythagoras and Plotinus from nearby Magna Graecia. This one scene from the *Odyssey* also implicates the "liturgical act" that Calvert Watkins linked to a psychedelic *kukeon* and drugged Dionysian wine. Sacraments that were always prepared by women, as suggested by the third fresco. With the initiation of Aurelia Prima into the Dionysian Mysteries, the whole sequence leaves no doubt that women enjoyed a privileged position in early Christianity. Was it their ability to manufacture a mind-altering Eucharist that kept the ecstasy alive in the house churches and underground catacombs of the new faith? At a very dangerous time in the Roman Empire, when fans of both Dionysus and Jesus had to watch their backs?

As we pack our things and prepare for daylight, Father Francis offers a concluding thought on the politics of the situation. "There's little doubt that the Aurelii tried to record their self-defined elite status. But we have to remember the persecutions at this time. As Christians, they would have tried to depict their beliefs under the veil of other, more acceptable symbols. Because they couldn't just explicitly *say* they were Christian. For those who knew, the images could be interpreted as Christian: the Good Shepherd and Saint Paul and so forth. The banquet of the *refrigerium*, of course, resonates with the New Testament narratives of the Last Supper. But for those who weren't Christians, it would just look like a *refrigerium*. The whole scheme is a deliberately designed external presentation that would be acceptable in a society where Christianity was not a lawful religion. But even their

Christian friends who came here would still have to acknowledge the persistence of *this* tradition," he says, motioning to the ceiling, "this Dionysian worldview. You see, this is the whole paradox of an intercultural encounter."

Seems reasonable. The Vatican, to my Catholic-school shock, goes a step further, calling scenes like the Holy Grail, the Homeric fresco, and the ecstatic initiation of Aurelia Prima "the most explicit and concrete evidence of the origins of Christianity." That's the phrase used by Monsignor Giovanni Carrù, the secretary of the Pontifical Commission for Sacred Archaeology. In the preface to the Vatican's monograph from 2011, he explains in polished Italian prose:

> *Since the first churches disappeared, obliterated by subsequent constructions, the catacombs, already abandoned in the fifth century, constitute the most significant assets of the paleo-Christian era. . . . We are facing a border monument, where pagan thought and Christian thought are joined, giving rise to a sort of syncretism. . . . And so the monuments of the dead speak to us about the community of the people of God. With the Hypogeum of the Aurelii, the parable of "Christianization" has not yet found its final solution, it presents all the peculiarities of a cultural process in progress.*[35]

By placing the Aurelii's syncretic and peculiar brand of paleo-Christianity under its exclusive jurisdiction, however, the Vatican needs to consider the *real* reason people may have flocked to this new mystery religion in the centuries after Jesus. Maybe the earliest and most authentic Christians weren't looking forward to a "final solution," whatever that means, when the bureaucracy of the Church would stamp out the kind of private mystical experience that took place in the Hypogeum. An experience where women and drugs seem to be the driving force. Maybe paleo-Christianity was fine just the way it was—if not Jesus's original vision for the Church's defining sacrament, then at least John's. Or the Gnostics'. Their secret ceremonies and visionary techniques, all Greek to the core, would certainly fit the kind of initiation in evidence here.

When the Aurelii painted Aurelia Prima joining their Eucharistic banquet, I'm inclined to believe it actually happened, if only in their drug-soaked minds. For the intoxicated *agape* and *refrigeria* to have survived as long as they did, *something* must have made the Christian initiates believe they had ingested and become one with the Son of God.

Once you've seen the Hypogeum, it can't be unseen. If these are the true origins of Christianity, then I need to see more of "the most explicit and concrete evidence" hidden underground to make sure the Aurelii weren't the only paleo-Christians smitten by the Greek Mysteries. The frescoes I've just inspected add a lot of color to the lethal wine that Saint Paul accused the house church in Corinth of administering. Both above- and belowground, the Eucharist of yesterday appears to have been very different from the Eucharist of today. The simplest explanation is that the Christians of the first three hundred years after Jesus were caught in what Father Francis has just described as an "intercultural encounter." The witches who were attracted to the visionary "secret doctrine" and Dionysian Mysteries in Magna Graecia were the same witches attracted to the idea of the original Eucharist and its promise of instant immortality, especially as captured by the Gospel of John and the Gnostic tradition. For that crowd, drawing additional inspiration from the all-night *refrigeria* with the Roman dead, the wine of Dionysus and the wine of Jesus could have been fairly interchangeable.

Before the Church Fathers drew a sharp line between paganism and Christianity in the fourth century AD, whatever was happening in the Hypogeum of the Aurelii was far from unusual. For the paleo-Christians who vanished long ago, it was the norm. And the evidence is sitting right under the Pope's feet.

As the humanists might urge, *ad fontes*! When in doubt, go to the source.

14

A Gnostic Eucharist

The Uber speeds west across the Eternal City, skirting the Colosseum and closing in on the Tiber. Father Francis and I are off to our second appointment of the day. Just after the Rose Garden on the Aventine Hill, the priest rattles off another landmark he knows will pique my interest off Via della Greca (Greek Street). Nowadays the Greek Rite church of Santa Maria in Cosmedin is where the tourists line up to snap a trite photo of their hands entering the open stone mouth of the Bocca della Verità, the timeworn marble mask made famous by Audrey Hepburn and Gregory Peck in the 1953 film *Roman Holiday*. Originally this was the site of an old Greek-speaking parish from the sixth century AD. Since Constantine, the Greeks who cornered this part of Rome turned the whole neighborhood into the *ripa Graeca* (the Greek bank).

But the language that founded Western civilization was here much earlier, of course. After planting themselves in Magna Graecia in the eighth century BC, the Greeks and their cults traveled north to Rome centuries before the birth of Jesus. By AD 150, as the Gospel of John started circulating among Greek speakers in the capital of the empire, the mystics were still here, thirsty to keep their Mysteries alive amid opposition on all sides. The political suppression of the God of Ecstasy by the Roman senate was only part of the issue. At the time Christianity itself was already beginning to fracture. There were those like the Aurelii and the Gnostics, on the one hand, who thought initiation into Christianity's biggest secrets belonged to anybody who consumed the "True Food" and "True Drink" of the Lord of Death, just as John promised. And there were those like the Church Fathers, on the other, who thought a few men within the 1 percent were uniquely called by God to handle the Eucharist, perpetuating a tradition of elitism that had existed among the Egyptian pharaohs, Near Eastern royalty, and Jerusalem's high priests for many thousands of years.

Traces of the tangled history, where women and drugs once competed for the survival of *their* version of Christianity, have all been wonderfully preserved in the building that classicist Helen F. North once described as "the reason why Rome is still the center of the civilized world."[1]

St. Peter's Basilica.

Father Francis and I are about to meet the gatekeeper of the City of the Dead that rests under the largest church building on the planet. The foundations of Christendom were literally built on top of a death cult. Complete with a graveyard wine to match the graveyard beers that could very well have sparked the Agricultural Revolution in our deep prehistory. Was the Drug of Immortality the spark of the Christian Revolution that would turn the cult of Jesus into the religion that colonized the world? At last I've come to see the evidence for myself. Where the continuity between Dionysus and Jesus is hidden deep underground. And where all the high drama between the Greek mystics and the Greek bureaucrats is locked in place under Catholicism's highest altar, harkening back to a lost time when the sacred language of the Church was Greek.

As we motor along the eastern bank of the Tiber, the pines and cypresses guiding our way, Father Francis reminds me that the earliest Popes were, in fact, all Greek speakers, including Pope Clement I (ca. AD 88–99), who actually died in Greece; Pope Telesphorus (ca. AD 126–137), who came from a Greek family in Calabria to the south; and Pope Anicetus (ca. AD 155–160), whose name is Greek for "unconquered." After all, what good was a Pope who couldn't read the Greek of the New Testament? Or unpack the hidden teachings of Jesus that even the Gospel of Mark had plainly referred to as *musteria*, "religious secrets, confided only to the initiated and not to be communicated by them to ordinary mortals"?[2] But most important, the Popes and the emerging orthodoxy of the Church had to be able to defend against all the mystics who claimed to be the true heirs of the Dionysian

Jesus. Whether they had penetrated the "symbols" and "language" of the Gospel of John to come into possession of the *real* Eucharist, or been exposed to a Gnostic version of Jesus, the mystics wanted the *pharmakon* that would unlock the Kingdom of Heaven.

In the early centuries of the faith, there were many Christians in Rome who professed knowledge of the "True Drink." Ruck mentions several in his "Jesus, the Drug Man" chapter from *The Apples of Apollo: Pagan and Christian Mysteries of the Eucharist*. The earliest high-profile example is Simon Magus, the Samaritan sorcerer of the first century AD who traveled to Rome all the way from Jesus's neck of the woods in what today is Israel. He would establish a "rival sect" to the mainline Church, becoming "the founder of all heresies, with a religious following of Simonians who considered him a god."[3] His partner in crime was an alter–Mary Magdalene named Helena, a prostitute whom Simon Magus had picked up at a brothel in Tyre. She claimed to be the reincarnation of Helen of Troy. The Church historian Eusebius (AD 263–339) relates how Simon Magus won over "many of the inhabitants of Rome" through his "magic." Justin Martyr claimed a statue in his honor was erected on an island in the Tiber, now to my left, with the inscription: SIMONI DEO SANCTO (to Simon, a holy god).[4]

Instead of the ordinary bread and wine, wrote Eusebius, the followers of this fake "Christian philosophy" used special "incense" and "libations" in their "secret rites" that resulted in their being "thrown into marvel" or *thambothesesthai* (θαμβωθήσεσθαι) in the most Dionysian way possible, with utter "ecstasy" (*ekstaseos*/ἐκστάσεως) and "frenzy" (*manias*/μανίας).[5] The Church Father Irenaeus (ca. AD 130–202) said the Simonians' sacraments were nothing but "love charms" (*filtra*/φίλτρα) and "love potions" (*agogima*/ἀγώγιμα).[6] The *Acts of Peter*, an apocryphal Greek text from the second century AD, dramatizes the death of their spellbinding leader. When Simon Magus was levitating in the Roman Forum one day, Saint Peter prayed for God Almighty himself to stop the arch-heretic in midair. Without delay Simon Magus fell to the ground, breaking his leg at the site of the current-day Church of Santa Francesca Romana.

And so began Gnosticism. It grew particularly popular in Rome during the second and third centuries AD. As mentioned earlier, Princeton scholar Elaine Pagels has written extensively about the forbidden nature of the Greek *gnosis* (knowledge) that was the Gnostics' chief aim. "Self-knowledge is knowledge of God; the self and the divine are identical." Pagels looks to the Greek-educated Valentinus (ca. AD 100–160) as the most famous and influential of the early Gnostics, a "spiritual master" who established his school in the Eternal City around AD 140.[7] Just like Simon Magus, Valentinus was out there trying to steer Romans toward the *true* version of Christianity. He claimed to have been initiated by Theudas, a direct disciple of Saint Paul, "into a secret doctrine of God."[8] Pagels explains the position: "Paul himself taught this secret wisdom, he [Valentinus] says, not to everyone, and not publicly, but only to a select few whom he considered to be spiritually mature."[9]

It's no wonder, then, that the Gospel of John became the favorite Gospel of the Gnostics in Rome. Especially among the Valentinians, who wrote the oldest attested commentaries on John's Greek, even before the Church Fathers got around to it.[10] The record of their ritual practices adds enormous weight to Dennis MacDonald's insight about the Greek language in John 6:53–56 being designed by the Evangelist as "Dionysian cult imagery," "specifically the eating of the flesh and blood of the god and the immortality that initiates gain by such activity." In perfect accord with John's word choice— the *gnawing* and *munching* on the *flesh* of Jesus, just like the Dionysian Eucharist of raw flesh and blood (*omophagon charin*) from Euripides—part of the "secret doctrine" that apparently passed from Jesus to Paul to Theudas to Valentinus was a magical, drugged Eucharist.

And it was Valentinus's student, Marcus, who unleashed the *pharmakon* on the ancient Mediterranean in the years he was active, between AD 160 and 180. Ruck notes that "although all the heretical sects had a reputation for herbalism and sorcery, Marcus himself was apparently notorious for his expertise with drugs: thus Irenaeus accused him of pharmacological deviltry."[11] Similarly to Simon Magus, Marcus apparently seduced the wife of one of Irenaeus's deacons to become a Marcosian with a blasphemous "love potion." For some inexplicable reason, both Irenaeus and another Church Father named Hippolytus (ca. AD 170–235) went to great lengths to document the procedure by which the secret sacrament was actually made. And how the fairer sex, instead of throwing together some leftovers for the kids, was busy cooking up a healthy dose of drugged wine.

At Marcus's Mass, women were invited to perform their own solemn consecration of the holy wine. After being handed a smaller chalice by the heretic, each woman would offer up the "Eucharistic prayer," blessing the purple-reddish elixir that had been spiked with an unknown *pharmakon*. In his recounting of the Marcosian ceremony, Hippolytus uses the Greek word for "drug" no less than seven times![12] The women would then pass their cups back to Marcus, who would pour the contents into a larger chalice that seemed to miraculously overflow with more wine than had been added to it, a classic Epiphany trick worthy of both Dionysus and Jesus. Marcus would then invoke the goddess Grace or *Charis* (Χάρις) by name, the same Greek word that was used by Euripides to capture the Eucharist four hundred years before the birth of Jesus, *omophagon charin*. In the language of the Mysteries, Marcus would call Charis the one "who transcends all knowledge and speech."[13] Once the "silly women" had drunk from the central chalice and been "whipped into frenzy" and "ecstasy" like a bunch of maenads, they would then start prophesying.[14]

Echoes of the lethal wine from Corinth. And Aurelia Prima's Holy Grail.

For a time the heretical Eucharists of the Simonians, Valentinians, and Marcosians posed a genuine threat to Church. But like the Greek Mysteries themselves, Gnosticism in any robust form would not survive the fourth century AD. A movement based on underground initiation rites, intended only for the "spiritually mature," could hardly keep up with the expanding bureaucracy of Constantine's religion—those "social and political structures that identify and unite people into a common affiliation."[15] For Pagels the shadowy practices of the Gnostics simply "did not lend themselves to mass religion."[16] The Eucharist of John's Gospel may have been intended for the 99 percent, but the Greek-speaking Christian mystics ran into the same problem as their Dionysian sisters centuries earlier. It's hard to mainstream this stuff.

If drugged wine was the real secret behind the Greek and Gnostic Mysteries, then finding enough skilled women to safely and reliably produce the sacrament must have been very difficult. No wonder the Vatican went with the cardboard wafer and grape juice. Sensing their advantage, the Church Fathers did everything in their power to abolish the competition. "The framework of canon, creed and ecclesiastical hierarchy that Irenaeus and others began to forge in the crucible of persecution" during the second century, says Pagels, is what turned Christianity into the default faith of Western civilization in the fourth century and beyond.[17]

By the death of Eleusis in AD 392, the Eucharist of the female-run house churches and subterranean *refrigeria* was no more. In perfect imitation of Roman governance and law, women had been systematically excluded from the priesthood. And the bishop had come more and more to resemble a monarch, seated on his throne at the head of the new aboveground basilicas. Like loyal subjects, the parishioners lined the pews to witness the consecration of very ordinary bread and wine by very ordinary men with no particular pharmacological expertise. In a mix of misinterpreted Greek philosophy and shameful Biblical reasoning, Saint Augustine (AD 354–430) and others blamed the passions and appetites of the female body for distancing women from the religious life. Free of the chains of the menstrual cycle, childbirth, and breastfeeding, only men could properly control and tap into the rational aspect of the soul that liberated the male species from their own irrational physicality, connecting them to a spiritual heaven.

"The equation of women with sexuality," says Karen Jo Torjesen in *When Women Were Priests*, "meant she was both subordinated to man and alienated from God."[18] Nothing has changed in over sixteen hundred years. In 1976 the Sacred Congregation for the Doctrine of the Faith reaffirmed the infallible doctrine that women had been prohibited from the priesthood "in accordance with God's plan."[19] "The incarnation of the Word took place according to the male sex," it proclaimed in an official declaration that was later endorsed by Pope John Paul II in 1994 and again by Pope Francis in 2016.[20] Jesus was a man, his Apostles were men. Women can't be trusted with the Eucharist. End of story.

The 1976 declaration specifically mentions the admission of women to the priesthood by "a few heretical sects in the first centuries, especially Gnostic ones."[21] But that "innovation," notes the Vatican, was quickly condemned by the Church Fathers. With the Nag Hammadi texts, the Gospel of Mary Magdalene, and other Gnostic writings strategically banned from the final version of the New Testament that was adopted by church councils in both the Catholic West and the Orthodox East during the fourth and fifth centuries AD, all memory of the Gnostics was "excised from the history of the Church of Rome," according to Ruck.

But the clues are still out there. And we're closing in.

The Uber crosses the Ponte Vittorio Emanuele II into the majestic sector of Rome that has lured me back once again like a rare-earth magnet. As we slowly creep along Borgo Santo Spirito, and the first of the 284 Doric columns around St. Peter's Square come into view, I get that tingling sensation. The same mixed feelings that run down my spine every time I'm about to set foot into the smallest country in the world. Awe, nostalgia, and dread. No matter how warm and hospitable the Vatican staff has been when they've welcomed me here over the past year, arms open, I just can't help it. My stomach is in knots. The Catholic boy inside me is only one misstep away from excommunication.

Am I really accusing the Church that raised me of serving up a placebo for the better part of two thousand years? And suppressing the heavenly visions promised in the first chapter of John's Gospel: "I tell you for certain that you will see heaven open and God's angels going up and down"?

Whenever I haven't seen it in a while, the first sight of Michelangelo's dome on top of St. Peter's always gives me goose bumps. The most renowned example of Renaissance architecture was the model for St. Paul's in London, Les Invalides in Paris, and the United States Capitol back home in Washington, D.C. But few know why this iconic structure sits precisely where it does.

Original construction began in the fourth century under Constantine to mark the legendary tomb of Saint Peter, who was apparently crucified upside-down in the nearby Circus of Nero around AD 64. The Apostle was then reportedly interred in the existing Roman necropolis, on top of which the current basilica rises to this day. To flatten the site for his monumental church, Constantine buried some of the ancient tombs, leaving Saint Peter's intact. By the Renaissance the aging shrine needed a makeover. When he took over from Bramante and Raphael in 1547 at the age of seventy-two, Michelangelo scrapped their designs for the basilica but kept the general position of the cupola, above Saint Peter's alleged remains. After the master's death, it fell to Bernini to memorialize the exact spot where the subterranean tomb of the first Pope meets the space beneath Michelangelo's cupola. Bernini would mark the vortex in the basilica's sculpted bronze canopy known as the Baldachin.

Situated directly over the high altar where the Pope alone is authorized to transubstantiate the bread and wine during the Liturgy of the Eucharist, Bernini included balconies to warehouse precious relics—the head of Saint Andrew (Peter's brother) and fragments of the True Cross, said to date to Jesus's crucifixion like the piece in Notre Dame. At the time it was all part of Pope Urban VIII's plan. "These relics, placed within a centralized location of Peter's tomb, implicated a direct connection between the Pope, Christ, and the early martyrs, thus reinforcing his position within the church and as the medium between heaven and earth."[22] A straight vertical line welding the ancestral past not only to the present, but to the future. Because every time the Eucharist is consecrated as part of the "funeral banquet" that is the Mass, the faithful are simultaneously commemorating the Last Supper and looking forward to the end of the world—when "Christ will come again in glory to judge the living and the dead." According to the *Catechism of the Catholic Church*: "That is why Christians pray, above all in the Eucharist, to hasten Christ's return by saying to him: 'Our Lord, come!'"[23]

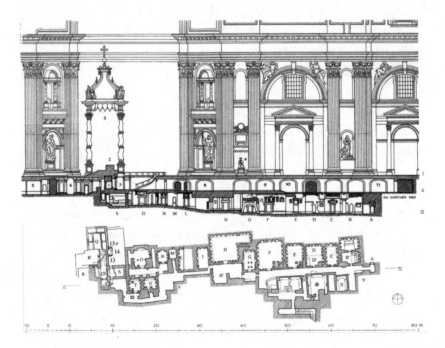

Cross section of St. Peter's Basilica, showing the relative position of the various, subterranean features of the Vatican Necropolis. *With the kind permission of the Fabbrica di San Pietro in Vaticano*

Father Francis and the author at the monastic library of the Chiesa e Convento di San Francesco in Agnone, Italy, June 2018. *Courtesy of Chiesa e Convento di San Francesco (Agnone)*

Father Francis and the Louvre's chief curator of Greek pottery, Alexandra Kardianou, examining the vast collection in the museum's stockroom. *Courtesy of Musée du Louvre*

G 408 (left) and G 409 (right) on the examining table in the restricted-access section of the Louvre. Between the vases, the Loeb edition of Euripides' *Bacchae*, together with several pages of spiked wine formulas from Dioscorides' *Materia Medica*. *Courtesy of Musée du Louvre*

Hand-colored lithograph by C. Bethmont, from Paris ca. 1850: *Plantes dangereuses*. Socrates' death by the poisonous hemlock is depicted in the center. Eight additional illustrations of toxic plants, herbs, and fungi appear on the borders, including aconite, ergot, deadly nightshade, and various hallucinogenic mushrooms. *Courtesy of the U.S. National Library of Medicine.*

Dioscorides Describing the Mandrake, painted by Ernest Board around 1912. Wine spiked with mandrake (*Mandragora officinarum*) was only one of the many hallucinogenic formulas catalogued by the Father of Drugs in his *Materia Medica*. The herbal encyclopedia was published in the second half of the first century AD, just when the Letters of St. Paul and the Gospels were being composed in the same language: Ancient Greek. *Courtesy of the Wellcome Collection*

Father Francis and the author in the Lizard Lounge, Paris, following their Ancient Greek bible study of the Gospel of John. *Courtesy of Licia Miglioli*

As Christianity developed, the sacred purple of Dionysus became the purple of Jesus, explicitly mentioned in the famous Ecce Homo (Behold the Man) scene from John 19:5.

Two details of the Villa of the Mysteries from the first century BC, with maenads showcasing the purple vestments of the God of Ecstasy (above and center). Detail of a mosaic in the Dionysus House from the second century AD, at the archaeological site of Nea Paphos on Cyprus (below).

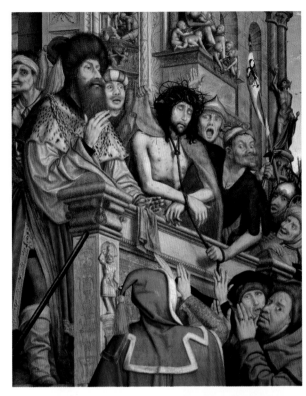

Christ Presented to the People, painted by Quinten Massys between 1518 and 1520 as an homage to John 19:5, currently in the Prado Museum, Madrid, Spain (above). Jesus carrying the cross in the Capela Mor Nossa Senhora do Espinheiro, Évora, Portugal (below).

Courtesy of Museo Nacional del Prado

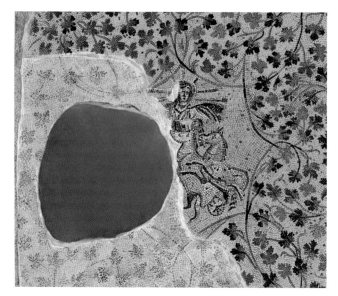

The ceiling mosaic of the so-called Tomb of the Julii (Mausoleum M) in the Vatican Necropolis. *With the kind permission of the Fabbrica di San Pietro in Vaticano*

Funerary banquet fresco from Chamber 78 of the Catacombs of Saints Marcellinus and Peter. The Latin above the priestess' head reads: "*Agape*" (To Love!), "*Misce*" (Mix it up!). © *Pontificia Commissione di Archeologia Sacra; courtesy of Archivio PCAS*

Funerary banquet fresco from Chamber 39 of the Catacombs of Saints Marcellinus and Peter. The Latin on the left reads: "*Irene*" (To Peace!), "*Da calda*" (Hand over the warm stuff!).© *Pontificia Commissione di Archeologia Sacra; courtesy of Archivio PCAS*

The Cortile della Biblioteca, separating the Vatican Secret Archives from the Biblioteca Apostolica Vaticana.

The author's access cards to the Vatican Secret Archives and the Biblioteca Apostolica Vaticana.

The senior archivist of the Vatican Secret Archives, Gianfranco Armando, emerging from the crypt-like cafeteria in the Cortile della Biblioteca

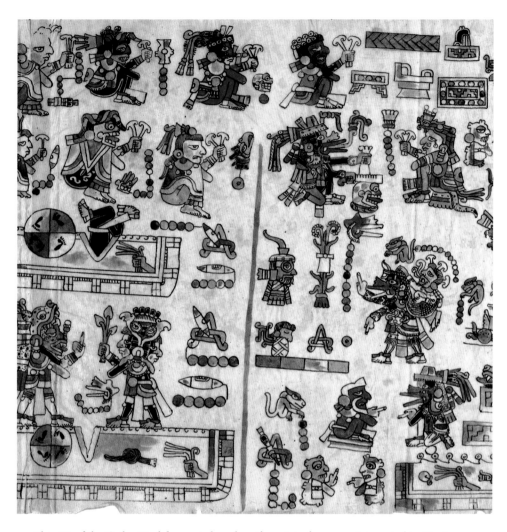

Plate 24 of the *Codex Vindobonensis*, based on the original manuscript created in Mexico ca. 1500. On the upper right, the Aztec god of visions and hallucinogenic plants, Piltzintecuhtli, is depicted with a handful of psilocybin mushrooms. They were known to the pre-Columbian population as *teonanácatl*, which literally means "the flesh of the gods" or "divine flesh." Piltzintecuhtli appears to be instructing a gathering of eight other deities in the ritual use of the sacrament that somehow escaped eradication by Hernando Ruiz de Alarcón and other missionaries during the Catholic colonization of Mexico. *Courtesy of the British Museum Images (© The Trustees of the British Museum)*

salute from the Pope's military force. On our left we pass the Sala Nervi, where Father Francis first read my proposal for this zany adventure, four years ago. After a short walk we arrive punctually at the octagonal Ufficio Scavi to our right.

In a crisp Italian suit and tie Carlo is ready with an envelope of color photographs he kindly printed prior to our appointment. Together we shuffle through the 8½-by-11-inch reproductions of the early third-century mosaics that line the interior of Mausoleum M. Father Francis marvels in particular at the shots of the ceiling, which I don't think he has seen in close detail before. Carlo stresses the strict policy of no photography and leads us toward the main entrance to the City of the Dead through Tomb Z, just beside his office.

Passing through the automatic glass doors that slide open as we approach, I can barely resist the urge to stop and soak in the kind of burial chamber that would be better placed on the Giza Plateau. Painted on the wall is a falcon-headed Horus carrying a long magical staff and the ankh, or loop-headed tau cross, that symbolizes immortality.[26] There's also an image of Thoth, the Egyptian god of magic and wisdom, often conflated with the Greek Hermes. Thoth-Hermes is pictured in profile, facing right, in the seated posture of a baboon. A marble sarcophagus that once held the inhabitant of this crypt holds a rare treat. Carved in relief, Dionysus is centered "drunk and seminude" between two fluted pillars. Just like the maenad to his right, with her back to us, the God of Ecstasy is holding his magic wand with the pine cone tip.

We head into the dank confines of the Necropolis proper, which gives off a now-familiar odor that I recognize from the Hypogeum of the Aurelii. We hang a left past Mausoleum H into a tight hallway, barely wider than our shoulders, that claustrophobes would do well to avoid. We gently maneuver around a guided-tour group, a few members of which give Father Francis the requisite nod to the collar. Within half a minute, we're halted in front of the tight entrance to Mausoleum M. Carlo undoes the double locks that ordinarily protect this tiny cage of a room from prying eyes. I get a kick out of watching Father Francis climb into the porthole, elevated a full two or three feet off the ground. Carlo remains comfortably stationed outside, choosing not to engage in the acrobatics.

Once the priest and I have both lumbered into the crypt, we can stand upright, but the ceiling is not far overhead. The whole chamber is only about thirty-five feet square. Our voices immediately begin echoing off the musty rock as we examine the three mosaics that the Vatican confidently interpreted as Christian during the initial excavations in the 1940s: a fisherman on the north wall, a shepherd on the west wall, and on the east wall two men in a boat above a third figure being swallowed by some kind of marine monster. The first is a reasonable reading of Matthew 4:19, where Jesus instructs Peter and Andrew to become "fishers of men." The Good Shepherd motif, although it's more degraded here than in the Hypogeum of the Aurelii, also fits the Gospel accounts. And the third mosaic could very well be a depiction of the Old Testament prophet Jonah, his arms raised in exasperation, entering the belly of the whale. But it's the ceiling that gives me pause.

Hundreds of tesserae, or minuscule tiles, come together to form the image of a regal charioteer partly obscured by two horses rearing on their

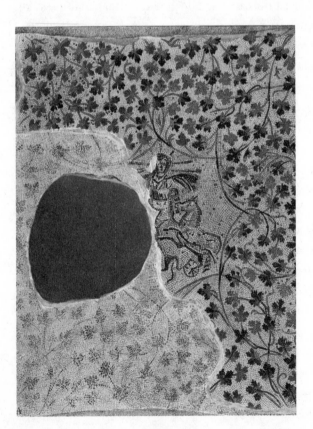

The ceiling mosaic of the so-called Tomb of the Julii (Mausoleum M) in the Vatican Necropolis. The grapevines entangle the central figure, variously interpreted as the Roman god *Sol Invictus* (the Unconquered Sun) or the Christian *Cristo-Sole* (Christ-Sun). *With the kind permission of the Fabbrica di San Pietro in Vaticano*

hind legs. He wears a white tunic and billowing cloak. Seven beams of light extend from the halo around the figure's head, suggesting the Roman god *Sol Invictus* (Unconquered Sun). Some scholars, however, make the compelling case that this is Jesus. The ancient artist may have wanted to portray the wizard from Nazareth as the "Sun of Justice" or the "New Light."[27] Like the deified emperors who would adopt the *Sol Invictus* look to signal their own apotheosis, the rider holds in his left hand a delicately assembled globe that could easily represent Jesus's "worldwide" and "eternal dominion," the supremacy of the "Christian belief in the risen God."[28] In his *Exhortation to the Greeks*, even Clement of Alexandria refers to Jesus as the "sun of righteousness," who "rides over the universe" to banish darkness and death. Surrounded by probable scenes from the Old and New Testaments, Mausoleum M could very well be the oldest Christian vault in the world, containing the oldest Christian mosaics ever discovered.

In which case, I want to know what all the vines are doing here.

Weaving in and out of the golden tesserae that make up the rich, eye-popping background of the ceiling mosaic, green tendrils wind their way on serpentine paths in every conceivable direction. Each of them sprouts brightly colored grape leaves by the dozens and dozens. Although roughly 40 percent of the tesserae from the ceiling have now disappeared, the imprint of creepers and leaves can still be seen in muted tones on the rock face. And not just around the equestrian Jesus, but on the walls too. The more I look, the more I notice the vines climbing their way down into the three scenes on all sides, engulfing the fisherman, shepherd, and sailors. Here in a cramped room only feet from Saint Peter's supposed tomb, under Michelangelo's dome that directs sunlight to Catholicism's highest altar and Baldachin up above . . . we're trapped in a subterranean vineyard.

There's a word for all these plants in Greek. I reach into my brown leather pouch and withdraw the 1829 edition of the New Testament and the Loeb edition of Euripides's *The Bacchae,* both happy to have survived the Lizard Lounge in Paris.

"Pater, why don't you read from your holy book, and I'll read from mine?" I propose, handing over the Greek of John's Gospel, already opened to the beginning of the fifteenth chapter. Father Francis squints in the dim artificial light of the catacomb while Carlo fidgets by the entrance, curious to hear what comes next.

"*Ego eimi he ampelos he alethine,*" begins the priest, bouncing the Ancient Greek around the echo chamber: "I am the True Vine." The Greek word for "vine" is *ampelos* (ἄμπελος). Like the 180 gallons of wine at Cana, the Son of God in the "lap" of the Father, the crown of thorns and purple cloak, the Lamb of God, and the *gnawing* and *munching* on the *flesh* of Jesus, the True Vine is another of John's Dionysian symbols that is unique to his Gospel. The full passage goes like this:

> I am the true vine, and my Father is the gardener. He cuts off every branch in me that bears no fruit, while every branch that does bear fruit he prunes so that it will be even more fruitful. . . . Remain in me, as I also remain in you. No branch can bear fruit by itself; it must remain in the vine. Neither can you bear fruit unless you remain in me.

For Zander, the Vatican's expert on the City of the Dead, the mass of vegetation only further supports the traditional Christian interpretation of Mausoleum M. The way the fisherman is "significantly framed by soft vine shoots" (*significativamente incorniciata da flessuori tralci di vite*) is an "obvious reference" (*evidente richiamo*) to the above passage from John's Gospel.[29] Others, however, can recognize the pagan continuity here: a motif that predates the paintings in the Hypogeum of the Aurelii by a few decades, establishing a nice precedent for Aurelia Prima's initiation into the hybrid Dionysian and Christian Mysteries. If the witch Circe in the Homeric fresco across town is evidence of a hallucinogenic Greek sacrament, are these vines subtle hints of the same? At the very epicenter of the Catholic universe?

In his analysis of Mausoleum M, art historian John Beckwith says "the luxuriant vine of Dionysus has become the True Vine of Christ."[30] Sure, but why? What does it all mean? In John's Gospel, the purpose of the secret "symbols" and "language" postulated by the eminent A. D. Nock and systematically identified by the Biblical scholar Dennis MacDonald is to connect Jesus to an intoxicating, sacramental beverage far more ancient than Christianity itself. To the Greek mind—and any Greek-speaking Romans who may have camped here overnight in the City of the Dead to commune with their ancestors and their wine god—the vine didn't just represent the God of

Ecstasy. The vine *was* the God of Ecstasy. From as early as the sixth century BC, the testimony of Greek pottery across the Mediterranean is clear: "In contrast to the god himself, his followers or worshippers are not portrayed as carrying branches of vine. The vine branch with grape clusters is thus not a general symbol of the cult or worship of Dionysus. It is rather a specific symbol of the vine tree itself, suitable only to the god."[31]

I open the *The Bacchae* to the same passage the priest and I read in the Cour Napoléon at the Louvre last Friday. I smell the paper and think of Euripides, who died before he had a chance to see his masterpiece performed at the Theater of Dionysus in 405 BC. If Homer made the long journey from Ancient Greece to the Hypogeum of the Aurelii, why couldn't Euripides wind up here? Maybe one of the paleo-Christians who descended into this gloomy cavern had a copy of the play where John sourced his language for the True Vine, and where the artist of the mosaic borrowed the green tendrils slithering over every square inch of this time capsule. It would have made for appropriate reading. Out loud I chant the Greek that brought the Eucharist here to St. Peter's Basilica in the first place:

> *It is this that frees trouble-laden mortals from their pain–*
> *when they fill themselves with the juice of the vine (ampelou)–*
> *this that gives sleep to make one forget the day's troubles:*
> *there is no other drug (pharmakon) for misery.*
> *Himself a god, he [Dionysus] is poured out in libations to the gods.*

There it is, plain as can be. The same *ampelos* or vine of John 15:1, described centuries earlier as a *pharmakon*. When an ancient Roman came here to mourn the dead with her Eucharist, which wine would she have chosen? The immortal blood of the Dionysus that I saw on the way in here with his magic wand, or the immortal blood of Jesus? During this unique period of paleo-Christianity, was there any real difference? And wasn't the Roman *refrigerium* the perfect ritual to marry the two? Isn't the all-night ceremony the glue that bound the Greek *pharmakon* to the Christian *pharmakon athanasias*? And didn't it all start right here, before Constantine built his basilica over Saint Peter's shrine, forever burying the City of the Dead and the legacy of their spiked wine?

If Mausoleum M really is Christian, as the Vatican maintains, then the telltale symbol of the True Vine signals a community uniquely dedicated to the Gnostics' favorite book, the Gospel of John. A community that could very well have inherited the same "secret doctrine" that tied Marcus to his spiritual teacher and the most famous Gnostic of the era, Valentinus. A tradition of drugged wine that apparently linked Valentinus, through Theudas and Paul, all the way back to Jesus himself. Whoever gathered in this crypt to peek into the afterlife could very well have used the same Gnostic Eucharist that was so well documented by the Church Fathers Irenaeus and Hippolytus. Just a few feet overhead, where Pope Francis blesses the watered-down grape juice that is the "beating heart of the Church," the idea of a drugged Eucharist is now called "heresy." It's been that way for eighteen hundred years. But down here in a forgotten moment, before the Vatican grew too big for its britches, it was called "Christianity." And before that, for many thousands of years, it was a religion with no name.

In this silent bunker, where the living and the dead have joined hands for more than two thousand years without interruption, I can sense the spirits huddled around the vines—riding the invisible column that leaps up toward Michelangelo's dome. If this wasn't the origin of religion in the primordial chapters of our species' history, then I'm not sure what was. The Romans didn't invent the *refrigerium* any more than the Canaanites, Phoenicians, and Nabataeans invented the *marzeah*. Or all the Indo-European speakers of the Neolithic invented their skull cults, and then passed them along to the domestic chapel at Mas Castellar de Pontós. They all inherited a common tradition that seems at least as old as the Raqefet Cave and Göbekli Tepe, and likely much, much older.

It is built into our DNA to long for the departed, and to want them back in a visceral way. But unlike the tame religions of today, the ancient mind refused to leave the mystery of death unexplored. They focused their efforts on the art and science of dying before dying, achieving that momentary glimpse of the hereafter for the sake of themselves and the ancestors. Just enough for Aurelia Prima to make an appearance at the Eucharistic banquet of the Holy Grail. Or for Saint Peter to feast with the paleo-Christians in the shrine a stone's throw to my west.

Much as Dionysus and Jesus wanted to make that experience available to everybody, the tradition didn't last. Up above, the Greek bureaucrats won the day. And the Greek mystics were left in the City of the Dead, where they belonged. Along with the original priestesses of the world's biggest religion, where the world's smallest country can pretend they never existed.

Following the visit to St. Peter's Basilica, I went on to inspect two more catacombs that had fascinated me for years. Before this jam-packed trip to Rome I had never managed to see them in person. But once I did, the subterranean clues I'd been collecting about the Greek-inspired, Gnostic brand of Christianity all came together to tell one coherent story. Like the Simonians, Valentinians, and Marcosians who preceded them, women were not just members of the underground churches that continued blurring the line between the Mass and the *refrigerium*. They were in charge. Because well into the fourth century AD, whenever a Eucharist was needed to summon the dead, only one gender could do the job.

First, there was my solo mission to the Catacombs of Priscilla, located on the Via Salaria (the Salt Road) that leads north out of Rome. Appointments, I learned the hard way, cannot really be made in advance. So just stop by during business hours, and the Benedictine Sisters who manage the property on behalf of the Vatican will happily show you around. Especially if you're wearing a Secret Archives access card, which I forgot to remove. From the look on Sister Irene's face, she thought I'd been personally dispatched by Pope Francis.

Named after the wife of a Roman senator, the catacombs were dug into an old quarry that makes the Hypogeum of the Aurelii and the Vatican Necropolis look like total child's play. The labyrinth of shafts and chambers extends for a remarkable eight miles beneath what is now the Villa Ada Savoia, a sizeable public park.[32] It was once known as the "Queen of the Catacombs" because of the number of Popes and martyrs who were buried here over the years. Plenty to explore among the forty thousand tombs, no doubt, but my only target was the Capella Greca (Greek Chapel), a square third-century enclosure featuring several scenes from the Old and New Testaments. They include frescoes depicting the sacrifice of Isaac, Daniel among the lions, and Jesus's resurrection of Lazarus. Four disembodied faces once graced the corners of the ceiling to signify the seasons; only one such pagan image remains, his Dionysian-looking head crowned with greenery. A long stone bench runs the entire length of the chamber, which would have been used for the funerary banquet meals that took place here in the "cemetery church" (*chiesa cimiteriale*).[33]

That's how the Jesuit art historian, Joseph Wilpert, referred to the ceremonial room, with its scarcity of tombs. If the Greek Chapel wasn't used to bury people, it must have been used to consume the Eucharist. For Wilpert that was the only logical conclusion in 1894, after he was able to chemically remove the thick crust of stalactites that concealed the scandalous *Fractio Panis* (Breaking of Bread) fresco on the central arch of the subterranean church.

Seven figures are seated around a typical, semicircular *stibadium,* or couch. There are four wicker baskets to their right, three to their left, reminiscent of Jesus's famous "feeding the multitude" miracle, where the Nazarene manages to feed five thousand hungry Galileans with only five loaves of bread and two measly fish. The figure on the far left is less relaxed than the others, leaning forward in the act of breaking the sacramental bread, or perhaps consecrating the nearby chalice. The other six people stretch their arms toward two platters arranged on the table, as

The *Fractio Panis* (Breaking of Bread) fresco in the Greek Chapel of the Catacombs of Priscilla. *(© Pontificia Commissione di Archeologia Sacra; courtesy of Archivio PCAS)*

a sign of joint celebration. The far-left figure is clearly the officiant of this ritual, which is why his/her gender is of monumental importance. Wilpert apparently spotted a beard. Strangely the face of the figure is now smudged, leading some to believe that the Jesuit or some Vatican colleagues may have intentionally defaced the image.

Without getting into conspiracy theory, the scholar Dorothy Irvin offered an alternative reading of the scene. In "The Ministry of Women in the Early Church: the Archeological Evidence," published in the *Duke Divinity School Review* in 1980, she micro-analyzes the seven ghostly figures in white to conclude that the whole group is "unmistakably feminine": "one wears a veil, and they are all characterized by upswept hair, slender neck with sloping shoulders, and a hint of earrings."[34] Regarding Wilpert's "male" priest, Irvin notes the "shadow of a breast below the outstretched arm." In addition she scrutinizes the length of the figure's skirt. At the time a man's tunic would never dangle below the top of the calf. Women's skirts, however, would come to within an inch of the ground. Irvin notes how the officiant's calf is completely covered by the skirt, which gathers "in a fold around the ankle."[35]

In older photos the leader's skirt can clearly be seen. In more recent ones it seems to have vanished, only adding to the mystery. During my visit to the Greek Chapel, an iron gate kept me at a safe distance to prevent any close inspection. Either way the Vatican remains unconvinced by Irvin's scholarship. In the guidebook published by the Pontifical Commission for Sacred Archaeology in 2016, Raffaella Giuliani repeats Wilpert's original interpretation, saying the person seated at the head of the table in the "position of honor" (*posto d'onore*) is unambiguously "a bearded man wearing a tunic and pallium" (*un uomo barbato indossante tunica e pallio*).[36] He would have been the "presiding bishop" (*vescovo celebrante*) at this ritual meal attended by five other men. So as not to discriminate, Giuliani recognizes one lone woman in a veil, the third figure from the right.

About Wilpert's "evocative Eucharistic reading" (*suggestiva lettura eucaristica*), the Church has since backtracked, noting that, in the course of further study, the prevailing interpretation now links this banquet to the pagan *refrigerium* tradition.[37] But even the Vatican realizes that the barrier between the pagan and paleo-Christian practice was rather porous at this critical juncture in the development of the faith. In addition to the wicker baskets, the symbolic meal arrayed on the table cannot be easily dismissed: a single chalice next to one platter loaded with five loaves of bread, and another with two fish. This tableau leads the Church to the inescapable observation that the wine, bread, and fish all point to the "Sacrament of the Eucharist" and certain Gospel passages referring to it, including the feeding of the multitude, the Wedding at Cana, and the Last Supper. Indeed the altar is filled with "Christian and Eucaristic symbols par excellence."[38]

It's an interesting concession. But for Irvin, it doesn't go far enough. As with the Holy Grail fresco in the Hypogeum of the Aurelii and the mosaic in Mausoleum M, the identity of the original Eucharist is at stake here. A proper reading of the *Fractio Panis* must explain the absence of the kind of food and drink that would have normally been consumed in the purely pagan setting of a *refrigerium*. Even the Vatican admits that the largely empty table lends a certain "liturgical quality" (*carattere liturgico*) to this banquet.[39] If the seven women aren't just picnicking, in that case, then they must be engaged in a highly charged ritual that was celebrated here, deep under the streets of Rome, for a reason.

The dedication inscribed on the wall of this chapel is written in Greek, giving the square chamber its name. It records the death of a woman named Nestoriana.[40] Like Nestor (the Peloponnesian King of Mycenaean Greece from Homer's *Odyssey*), it points to Greek worshippers. If their Eucharistic tradition was indeed imported from the Hellenized parts of the ancient Mediterranean, or due south from Magna Graecia, then the wine here depicted may be no ordinary wine. It could very well be part of the same Greek "secret doctrine" that connected Aurelia Prima to the likes of Pythagoras and Plotinus in Magna Graecia. Or the same Christian "secret doctrine" that connected the Gnostics back to Jesus and the original drugged Eucharist. Common to both were certain visionary techniques that found their highest expression in these cave-like catacombs. Where it seems women played the defining role.

By the middle of the third century, when the *Fractio Panis* likely emerged, the Greek Chapel would have made the ideal venue for both traditions, Greek and Christian, to fuse into the kind of mystery cult that would attract followers of both Dionysus and Jesus. Irvin states her case:

*This particular scene is of immense value as an extremely early testi-
mony to the eucharist, or rather, to one type of eucharist. This piece
of catacomb religious art does not show us the community agape, but
rather another usage, the eucharistic vigil. It is depicted in the catacombs because that is where this vigil was held on the anniversary of
the death of a Christian. It seems to have included passing the night
in the burial place, and celebrating the eucharist there in memory of
the deceased. It was a eucharist only, not a full meal, and that is why
there is no other food on the table.*

If seven women are really depicted here, it would perfectly fit the conclusion of the classicist Ross Kraemer, who was mentioned earlier, during my
dinner with Father Francis in Paris. Her review of the material evidence for
the Dionysian Mysteries found that "initiation with its practices of possession
and sacrifice" was ordinarily denied to men in the Greek tradition. A close
reading of all the "symbols" and "language" in the Gospel of John, and the
plain meaning of the Gospel of Mary Magdalene, both suggest the same. As
does the respected work of Raymond E. Brown, the late Catholic priest who
noted Mary Magdalene's enduring reputation as the "apostle to the apostles."
Any Greek speaker could have looked to the first witness of Jesus's resurrection as a divine figure. All the reason in the world to justify their preparation
of the kind of Eucharist that made sense to Greek-speaking Gnostics.

Not only in this Greek Chapel, but all over Rome.

For the second adventure Father Francis joined me at the Catacombs of
Saints Marcellinus and Peter. Located outside Rome's Porta Maggiore on the
Via Casilina that leads south into Magna Graecia, the tombs are way off the
typical Roman itinerary. As with the Catacombs of Priscilla, the approach
does not just gently descend a few feet into the subterranean twilight. Instead you go spelunking into sixty thousand square feet of galleries and
tunnels cut into the guts of the earth, giving life to burial chambers that
crisscross and zigzag in a dizzying display far below the surface.[41]

Of particular interest to our investigation are the eight frescoes to be
found here: banquet scenes dating to the late third or early fourth centuries, in which women very clearly command the Eucharistic cup.[42] Archaeological excavations have uncovered thirty-three *mensae*, or small tables,

complete with "fragments of glass and ceramic plates," confirming funerary meals actually took place here in the shadows.[43] In "Women Leaders in Family Funerary Banquets" from 2005, the scholar Janet Tulloch says, "It is likely that the represented action had been an accepted practice for some time in the early Christian community with the representation of the behavior lagging behind the actual practice."[44] And despite the Roman stigma against "respectable women" drinking wine to excess, Constantine's patronage of Christianity earlier in the century would have only encouraged the "visual convention" seen in these catacombs, "a practice that was already familiar to Christians in real life," and one that serves as "an index of women's status and morality in the formation of the early church."[45]

On seven of the eight banquet scenes, rather bizarrely, the Greek words *Agape* (love) and *Irene* (peace) appear in the Latin script. One prime ex-

Funerary banquet fresco from chamber 78 of the Catacombs of Saints Marcellinus and Peter (top). The Latin above the priestess' head reads: *"Agape"* (To Love!), *"Misce"* (Mix it up!). Another funerary banquet scene from chamber 76 of the Catacombs of Saints Marcellinus and Peter (bottom). The Latin reads: *"Misce mi"* (Mix it up for me!), *"Irene"* (To Peace!). (© *Pontificia Commissione di Archeologia Sacra; courtesy of Archivio PCAS*)

ample is chamber 78, off in the far reaches of the catacombs. Painted on the same kind of arched recess we saw in the Hypogeum of the Aurelii, the colors are extraordinarily well preserved. A barefoot, semi-veiled woman is standing in a long robe of damped reds and yellows; it's cinched high on the waist in the manner of a medieval friar. She ceremonially raises a cup in her right hand, delicately held between her thumb and two fingers. The four men seated around the couch take notice, some pointing to the banquet table in the middle, where a single fish seems to be placed.

The reaction is even more pronounced in chamber 45, where a very similar scene is depicted, though the fresco is a bit more damaged by time. The female officiant in a purplish robe lifts the chalice in her right hand to a party of four adults and two children. They are all stunned by the gesture, especially the wide-eyed man immediately to the woman's left, who is almost in a state of shock. I'm reminded of the twelve figures in the Holy Grail fresco who welcomed Aurelia Prima back from the dead, hypnotized by the raising of the cup. For Tulloch the exaggerated looks and gestures of the banqueters stress "the importance of this particular drinking rite," which is "the pinnacle moment of the funerary banquet." [46]

As the officiant, it was the woman who uttered the word *agape*. Tulloch reads the rest of the Latin inscription as a kind of refrain from the guests, again recalling the "liturgical quality" of these meals. So in chamber 78 the woman shouts something like "To Love!" And the men respond, "*Misce!*" or "Mix it up!" In chamber 45 the Latin is equally clear: "*Misce nobis!*" or "Mix it up for us!" Unlike the subtle consecration in the Greek Chapel, just twenty minutes to the north, the Latin here makes perfectly clear what the Greek speakers from the "cemetery church" in the Catacombs of Priscilla tried to communicate visually. The woman is in charge of not just elevating, designating, or presenting the wine, but also of *mixing* the wine. Which, like the mixing rituals we analyzed on G 408 and G 409 back at the Louvre, raises the very real possibility that no ordinary wine was being consumed in these paleo-Christian meals that gave birth to the Mass as we know it.

Indeed, Greek-speaking women in third-century Rome would have had access to a treasure trove of herbal knowledge, not only from the Father of Drugs himself, Dioscorides, but also from his successor. The Greek-writing pharmacologist Galen, who served several emperors before his death in the

Funerary banquet fresco from chamber 45 of the Catacombs of Saints Marcellinus and Peter (top). The Latin above the priestess's head to the left reads: *"Agape"* (To Love!), *"Misce nobis"* (Mix it up for us!). The Latin above the second figure from the right reads: *"Porge calda"* (Hand over the warm stuff!). A final funerary banquet scene from chamber 39 of the Catacombs of Saints Marcellinus and Peter (below). The Latin on the left reads: "Irene" (To Peace!), "Da calda" (Hand over the warm stuff!). *(© Pontificia Commissione di Archeologia Sacra; courtesy of Archivio PCAS)*

early third century, and praised the city of Rome for "its excellent supply of drugs," left a staggering amount of material that to this day—as mentioned before—remains untranslated into English.[47] His encyclopedic output could have certainly influenced a Christian Eucharist that was just as powerful as the Greek Eucharist that inspired it.

And the evidence is written right there on the wall, for anyone who wants to delve into the nether regions of the Vatican's catacombs. In chamber 39 a final Latin phrase is recorded on the left-hand side of the fresco. Nicely painted onto the wall can be discerned *"Da calda!"* or "Hand over the warm stuff!" The Latin *calda* is a curious word. Outside the catacombs, it appears on vases from this same period. Tulloch translates *calda* as "a hot mix of wine and water mixed together."[48] In Rodolfo Lanciani's *Pagan and Christian Rome*, published in 1893, we get a little more detail:

> *The meaning of the word calda is not certain. There is no doubt . . . that the ancients had something to correspond to our tea: but the calda seems to have been more than an infusion; apparently it was a mixture of hot water, wine, and drugs, that is, a sort of punch, which was drunk mostly in winter.*

Yet again, another familiar theme brings everything full circle: women and drugs. And with that, my tour of the Roman catacombs came to an end.

If the goal was to resurrect the secret meetings and magical sacraments of the earliest Christians in that crucial period between the death of Jesus around AD 33 and 380, when Theodosius turned Christianity into the official state religion of the Roman Empire, then mission accomplished.

With both the Roman state and the Church Fathers breathing down its neck, it's no wonder Christianity kept to the house churches and catacombs for over three centuries. Where the original Eucharist might flourish in the comfort and privacy of any home or cemetery that could source the magical wine, free of intrusion from the political and religious authorities. But the one question I've been trying to answer since the Louvre is whether the tradition of hallucinogenic Greek sacraments that we traced to Mas Castellar de Pontós really entered Christianity in the centuries after Jesus. And if so, how? Is there any merit to the pagan continuity hypothesis with a psychedelic twist?

Over in Greece, when Saint Paul accused the house church in Corinth of serving up a lethal potion, the charge sparked a trail of clues leading to Magna Graecia and Rome, perhaps the favorite haunt of Greek visionaries anywhere in the ancient Mediterranean. Without much archaeological evidence from the house churches themselves, we turned to the only other place a psychedelic Eucharist might show up. What the Vatican characterizes as "the most explicit and concrete evidence" for the true origins of Christianity: the subterranean crypts.

In the City of the Dead underneath St. Peter's Basilica, we saw the oldest Christian mosaics in the world. From the late second and early third centuries, the God of Ecstasy sarcophagus in Tomb Z and the "True Vine" in Mausoleum M are striking proof that the foundations of the Catholic Church are literally built on top of Dionysus, just as John's Gospel tried to communicate with all those secret "symbols" and "language" ending in the True Drink that promises immortality. Who knows what kind of potion was consumed in the Vatican Necropolis before Constantine covered it up. But if it was anything like the magical Eucharist of the Gnostics who cherished the Gospel of John above any other, then the all-night feasts between the living and the dead would have been a much more psychedelic affair than today's Mass. Where the blood of Dionysus and the blood of Jesus might be one and the same.

Across town at the Hypogeum of the Aurelii from the mid-third century, the psychedelic witch Circe leaps from the Homeric fresco—the lost symbol of a Stone Age tradition that would have spoken to initiates of the Greek Mysteries. The same initiates who might spy Aurelia Prima completing her apotheosis in the final chamber, and then returning from the dead in perhaps the oldest representation of the Last Supper as a *refrigerium*. Like the women who were initiated into the coven of Dionysus for century after century before her, from Italy to Greece and from Ephesus to Galilee, Aurelia Prima assumes her role as keeper of the Secret of Secrets. But she stood in the way of progress. Before the priests could take control of Christianity, they had to get rid of the witches.

Witches who may have revered Mary Magdalene as the "apostle to the apostles," just as the Gospel of John and the Gospel of Mary Magdalene originally intended. Witches who may have followed Junia, "the foremost among the apostles," to the Eternal City. Witches who, generations after Aurelia Prima, were still consecrating their special Eucharist for the ancestors in the "cemetery church" of the Greek Chapel, deep within the Catacombs of Priscilla. And witches who shouted prayers of "Peace" and "Love" in Ancient Greek as they mixed their drugged wine for spectators both living and dead in the Catacombs of Marcellinus and Peter.

This, then, is the overlooked story of paleo-Christianity. For almost three hundred years, it was an illegal mystery cult, with women in Greek-speaking Italy leading funerary banquets in the underworld that was said to offer access to the Other Side. But "in accordance with God's plan," as the Vatican proclaimed in 1976, the witches and their Eucharist never made it out of the City of the Dead. The Eucharist was a man's job. It still is. And just like the graveyard beer that seems to have upgraded Stone Age humanity from the caves to the cities, the graveyard wine that built Christianity is a thing of the past.

Buried perhaps.

Though miraculously preserved. Against all odds.

In the shadow of the world's most dangerous volcano.

15

Mystery Coast Highway

It was bound to turn up somewhere, I guess. But part of me found it hard to believe. If the hunt for the psychedelic *kukeon* had taught me anything, it was how to expand my narrow definition of the Greek Mysteries. Whenever I envisioned the Mysteries of Eleusis, I had always thought about the archaeological site in Eleusis. And nothing else. Until I realized that things didn't really work that way in the "ancient cultural internet" of the Mediterranean. Even if we couldn't test the vessels in Kalliope Papangeli's museum and warehouse in Greece, it didn't mean the search for a decent specimen was over.

All along I've known there was only one way to prove that the original Eucharist was, in fact, psychedelic. But locating any hard scientific data for ancient hallucinogenic wine in the Mysteries of Dionysus or Jesus was a total bust. If any such potion did attend the birth of Christianity, it certainly wasn't where I thought it would be. None of the archaeological chemists in Greece, Anatolia, or Galilee had ever been able to deliver the goods. Interesting leads, no doubt, from Andrew Koh at the Massachusetts Institute of Technology, when he announced the psychoactive blend from Tel Kabri in 2014 and shared the unpublished news about Tel Kedesh in 2019. But both preceded the rise of Christianity.

The main coordinates of my hunt were any sites where Dionysus and Jesus overlapped in the first few centuries AD. I was especially focused on places like Corinth, where an original house church might yield a Christian vessel that once held the lethal Eucharist. Or John's first audience in Ephesus, where both pagan and Christian flasks were discovered at the famed necropolis known as the Grotto of the Seven Sleepers.[1] Or Scythopolis in modern-day Israel, where Dionysian figurines have been unearthed along with Christian artifacts in the Northern Cemetery.[2] But nothing came to light.

No one is out there looking for psychedelic Christian wine, I had to remind myself. This is not a field of study. As a matter of fact, Koh is the only scholar I've ever spoken with about the topic who has the dual training in Classics and chemistry to even consider the merits of the quest. So after years of scouring the academic journals for the smoking gun, I actually gave up for a while, and just stuck to the Greek sacraments from the BC years: the *kukeon* and the Dionysian wine. The AD years went on the back burner. Until the data from Mas Castellar de Pontós in Spain reminded me to follow the Greek gods and goddesses on their journeys west. In fits and starts I trailed them to the one obvious neighborhood I had been ignoring for way too long.

Magna Graecia.

Of all the places in the ancient Mediterranean to be hiding out for centuries, just waiting for the archaeologists to come along and nose through the untouched vessels, I shouldn't have been surprised that southern Italy took the prize. It was there that I finally managed to pinpoint the most reliable data for psychedelic wine I have ever seen. Where the remains of the fabulously complex beverage were indisputably dated to the perfect moment in history, the first century AD. And where the magical potion was burrowed away in the perfect place. The region where the Greek deities made landfall in Italy's archaic past. But also the one spot that called to the one people who defined the very concept of Greek mysticism, birthing Western civilization as we know it.

The Phocaeans.

The same Phocaeans who carried the cult of Demeter and Persephone all the way from Anatolia to found the Greek colony of Emporion in Spain. The same colony that imported the Dionysian vase with the scene of a drunken wine party and left it for Enriqueta Pons to dig up in one of the many grain silos at Mas Castellar de Pontós. The same colony that seems to have introduced the classical Iberians to the graveyard beer full of ergot that opened the gates of the underworld. And the same colony that reconnected with their Indo-European cousins in a skull cult with Stone Age roots. History is seldom wrapped up in such a neat little package. But every once in a while, the God of Ecstasy comes bearing gifts.

As discussed during our visit to Girona, the Phocaeans who were the "Vikings of Antiquity" set sail from Ionia on the western coast of modern-day Turkey to found three sustainable colonies: Massalia (ca. 600 BC), Emporion (ca. 575 BC), and Velia (ca. 530 BC). Located in Magna Graecia about four hours south of Rome, Velia and its Greek mystics were always in the back of my mind. But for some reason, their potential hand in Christianity just never occurred to me. In retrospect, however, there were no better candidates to flood Rome with the immortality magic than the masters themselves.

As mentioned earlier, the classicist Peter Kingsley is the world's foremost expert on the esoteric tradition that seduced Italy in the wake of Plato's guru, Parmenides, who was born in Velia in 515 BC. It was Parmenides's relatives who introduced Magna Graecia to their cult practices from the Phocaean homeland in the east. The Greek-speaking community in Phocaea was the beneficiary of spiritual influences from the world's oldest and highest cultures—from the proposed Indo-European homelands of both Anatolia and Central Asia, to the Egyptians, Babylonians, Persians, and Indians. The melting pot that created the first scientists of Western civilization between 600 and 400 BC, laying the foundation for all the technology of the modern world, also created a secret tradition of magicians, healers, and prophets who perfected the ancient art of dying before dying.

True philosophy has nothing to do with books. The starting point for the rationality and logic too heavily associated with Western thought was anything but the witty repartee and educated arguments that fill Plato's dialogues. Behind all the mental gymnastics was a timeless teaching, mentioned only briefly by Socrates in Plato's *Phaedo*: "those who engage with philosophy in the right way are practicing nothing else but dying and being dead."[3]

And Velia was the source of it all. The epicenter of an exercise that focused on the underworld, where the whole point was to enter a "state of apparent death, of suspended animation when the pulse is so quiet you can hardly feel it."[4] In language that eerily resembles the testimony of the volunteers from the Hopkins and NYU psilocybin experiments, not to mention the *marzeah* ritual of the Near East, Kingsley describes the supreme goal of Parmenides and his disciples as a "cataleptic" state of trance in a "world beyond the senses," where "space and time mean nothing" and "past and future are as present as the present is for us."[5] Kingsley's summary of the neglected tradition that most classicists simply ignore is the playground of every Jewish, Christian, or Muslim mystic who ever dared to explore the inner core of their faith. "To go down to the underworld when you're dead is one thing," says Kingsley. "To go there while you're alive, prepared and knowingly, and then learn from the experience—that's another thing entirely."[6]

For the Phocaeans, dying before dying was the only way to get in touch with the true, underlying structure of the cosmos. As Kingsley explains,

> *Waking is a form of consciousness, dreaming is another. And yet this is what we can live for a thousand years but never discover, what we can theorize or speculate about and never even come close to— consciousness itself. It's what holds everything together and doesn't change. Once you experience this consciousness you know what it is to be neither asleep nor awake, neither alive nor dead, and to be at home not only in this world of the senses but in another reality as well.*[7]

In order to achieve this special state of consciousness, according to Kingsley, there was no need for drugs. All you had to do was enter a cave and lie down "in utter stillness without any food for several days—just like animals in a lair."[8] That's how the Ancient Greek historian Strabo (63 BC–AD 29) defined the technique known as "incubation" that took pace in the Charonium, a famous cave in the region of Caria (south of Phocaea and Ephesus) dedicated to Pluto and Persephone. Like the rock shelter amid the ruins of Eleusis, it was considered the entrance to the underworld. All over Anatolia temples to Apollo were often built over such caves, affording access to the world of the dead for the brave initiates. But Asclepius would become the most famous god of Greek incubation, which is perhaps why his statue stands in the Archaeological Museum of Empúries, not far from the Greek farm at Mas Castellar de Pontós.[9]

Kingsley believes Magna Graecia was another obvious home for the ancient practice of incubation. Even before Parmenides came to Campania, the Italian region that stretches from Naples and Pompeii in the north to Velia in the south, Pythagoras was also obsessed with Persephone. It would explain why he constructed his home in southern Italy as a literal temple, complete with "a special underground room where he'd go and stay motionless for long periods of time."[10] Was it a Phocaean love affair with the same

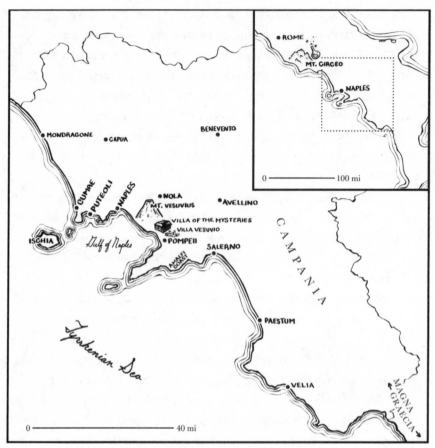

THE MYSTERY COAST HIGHWAY
Campania Region of Italy

goddess that spawned those twenty-five hundred subterranean silos across the archaeological site at Mas Castellar de Pontós? And did it also send the earliest Christians into the subterranean vineyard of Dionysus underneath St. Peter's Basilica, where the first Eucharist was celebrated in the City of the Dead? Or to the many catacombs around Rome, where Greek-speaking witches ruled the night?

If so, were the paleo-Christians merely dropping to the ground like hibernating bears, or did a magical potion occasionally lubricate the fits of incubation? To the Velians, lying down for a few days in a blackened cave may have been as natural as breathing. But maybe the Romans to their north needed a little push off the cliff. And maybe the same Phocaeans who brought the psychedelic beer to Pontós descended on Rome with just the right wine to make it happen. If there's a kernel of truth to this ancient puzzle about the secret architects of Western civilization, it has to lie on that glorious shoreline along the Tyrrhenian Sea in western Italy that is the 350 kilometers separating Velia from Rome.

It is hereby christened the Mystery Coast Highway.

Recruited from their homes in Velia, the priestesses of Persephone would indeed take the route north for hundreds of years in the wake of Parmenides. Five hundred years before Jesus, these women made generation after generation of pilgrimage to fulfill their sacred duty at the temple of Demeter and Persephone that had been built in Rome to Greek standards. Like the priestesses, the Greek gods and goddesses themselves came from Campania as well. In *The Cults of Campania*, first published in 1919, classicist Roy Merle Peterson traces the Roman reverence for Apollo and the divinely inspired Sibylline Oracles to the Greek community in Magna Graecia by way of Cumae, west of Naples.[11] Thereafter Peterson dates the introduction of the cults of Demeter, Persephone, and Dionysus into Rome by 493 BC, when grain from Campania was needed to stop a famine in Rome.[12] Once Cumae declined in influence, the sisterhoods in Naples and Velia assumed religious control of the Eternal City. By 340 BC the six gods stamped onto early Roman bronze coins "were either Greek gods whose cult had been introduced from the South or were Greek divinities who were now identified with Roman ones."[13]

Into this mystical Hellenic landscape that connected Rome to Campania came Paculla Annia, that scandalous high priestess of Bacchus whom Livy tagged as the prime reason for the prohibition of the Dionysian Mysteries in 186 BC. She refused to admit any men over the age of twenty into the all-female revels that robbed the military of eager young soldiers, provoking the Roman senate. Though Peterson is quick to note, of course, that the cult "marked by mystic devotion to the wine god did not altogether cease."[14] Indeed, by the dawn of the Christian era, Peterson chronicles a Campania where "the pagan world was at the height of its power," with "countless wayside and domestic shrines," a region "so crowded with gods that they were easier to find than men."[15]

By the second and third centuries AD, the new mystery cult devoted to the wine god from Galilee was beginning to replace the old one in Magna Graecia. It was centered in the Campanian cities of Naples and Puteoli to its west, close to the archaeological site of Cumae, where "converts of high rank especially women were not unknown from early times."[16] As Father Francis reminded me, the oldest layers of the Church in Rome are undoubtedly Greek. It was the one thing that the Greek-speaking bureaucrats like the Popes and Church Fathers had in common with the Greek-speaking mystics like the Gnostics. They may have differed wildly on their interpretation of the Gospel of John, the value of the Gnostic texts and the ultimate direction of the Church, but they all knew Greek. By AD 251 when Pope Cornelius convened a synod of sixty bishops to confirm his position as the rightful heir to Saint Peter's throne, most of the bishops came from the South. In the fourth century AD, Constantine himself erected only two basilicas outside Rome—one in Naples, and another to its north in Capua, the same city that was once home to the British Museum *skyphos* featuring Triptolemus along with Demeter, Persephone, and Dionysus.

Of all the places on earth for Peter and Paul to set up shop, and for the later Popes to rule Christendom until Martin Luther came along in the sixteenth century, they chose Rome. From its capital along the Mystery Coast Highway, this is where Christianity went into the house churches and catacombs for three hundred years before erecting the buildings that now welcome 2.42 billion Christians from every corner of the globe.

The spiritual history of Western civilization begins in Anatolia with the Proto-Indo-Europeans and, many thousands of years later, the Phocaeans. And it ends in Magna Graecia, where the Velian priestesses would travel back and forth between Rome and Campania. Where, in the decades following the death of Jesus, secret knowledge could be shared with the women in charge of the newest mystery cult. And where a polished psychedelic Eucharist might be sourced, true to the recipes that the Father of Drugs, Dioscorides (ca. AD 40–90), and Rome's leading pharmacologist, Galen (ca. AD 130–210), had preserved for the many Greek-speaking witches who went underground to lead Christianity's cave rituals. Like Aurelia Prima in the Hypogeum of the Aurelii, or all the wine sisters from the Catacombs of Priscilla and the Catacombs of Marcellinus and Peter.

On their trip from Velia to Rome, some ideal pit stops appear on the map for the Campanian priestesses. One would be Paestum, less than fifty kilometers north of Velia, with its three magnificent Greek temples. The oldest, dedicated to Hera, dates to 550 BC and is so well preserved that early archaeologists thought it was Roman. Another place for the witches to rest

their weary bones would have been Pompeii. The Greek mystics liked volcanoes. According to Peter Kingsley, they "saw volcanic fire as the light in the
depths of darkness"; it was "purifying, transforming, immortalizing." While
the eruption of Mt. Vesuvius in AD 79 was nothing but disastrous for the
ancient residents, it has given modern excavators unparalleled insight into
the past. The seventeen feet of volcanic ash kept the Villa of the Mysteries
in pristine condition, allowing the German scholar Nikolaus Himmelmann
to notice the similarities between the Dionysian frescoes in Pompeii and
the third chamber of the Hypogeum of the Aurelii, where Aurelia Prima is
being initiated into the Greek Mysteries.

For almost two thousand years the same ash from the same explosion in
the most densely populated volcanic region on the planet held tight to another
secret: hard botanical evidence for one of Ruck's unusually intoxicating, seriously mind-altering, occasionally hallucinogenic, and potentially lethal wines.

In the fall of 2018, as Enriqueta Pons and I began corresponding on a
daily basis about the ergot discovery at Mas Castellar de Pontós, I finally
started connecting the dots. If the Phocaeans really were the secret architects of Western civilization, and drugs really were involved, then Emporion wouldn't be the only place they left a trail of clues. If the Vikings of
Antiquity could seed the underworld cults of Demeter and Persephone
as far west as Iberia, why not closer to home in Magna Graecia? Or if not
them, why not any of the other Greek masters who would call Italy home
for centuries after Velia's founding. As only one example, consider Parmenides' star disciple, Empedocles (495–435 BC), who lived in the Greek
city of Akragas in Sicily. He left an enigmatic fragment about the magical
use of *pharmaka* as a "remedy for death." For a skilled shaman like Empedocles, familiarity with these unspecified drugs signals "a person capable
of descending to and returning from the underworld at will."[17] If you were
looking for a mystical experience with Demeter, Persephone, or Dionysus in the days before, during, and after the birth of Jesus, you'd be hard-
pressed to find a better spot than Magna Graecia.

From Washington, D.C., I started digging through the phenomenally
boring online archaeobotany journals I had once subscribed to and wasted a
bunch of money by not reading. Until a few days later, when that one elusive
study dropped out of the dataverse. From the dawn of Christianity on sacred
Greek territory, the psychedelic elixir was exactly where it was supposed to

be. And this time I didn't even have to leave my basement for the Library of Congress. It was all there on the internet. And strangely, it was all written in English. How did I miss this for so long?

In 1996 a 30-by-30-square-meter farmhouse named the Villa Vesuvio was excavated in Scafati on the outskirts of Pompeii by the distinguished Italian archaeologist Marisa de' Spagnolis. Because of the thick layer of pumice and *lapilli* (volcanic fragments) covering the site by the Sarno River, it was "perfectly sealed" and confidently dated to AD 79. Like other modest homes in the area, the structure featured a threshing floor, a wine press (*torcularium*), and a cellar (*cella vinaria*).[17] Seven large vessels called *dolia* were unearthed. A "thick organic deposit" was found at the bottom of each. But the "yellow, foamy matrix" from one vessel in particular contained a fascinating array of plant and animal remains.

In "Drug Preparation in Evidence? An unusual plant and bone assemblage from the Pompeian countryside, Italy," published in 2000 in the peer-reviewed journal *Vegetation History and Archaeobotany*, the archaeobotanist Marina Ciaraldi unveils the results of the analysis that found over fifty species of plants, herbs, and trees in the sample. The macroremains were in such good shape that the chemists didn't even need to get involved. The botany team was easily able to identify all the species by their seeds or fruits, including willow (*Salix* sp.), beech (*Fagus sylvatica*), peach (*Prunus persica*), and walnut (*Juglans regia*). Surprisingly, 58 percent of the botanical specimens belonged to taxa with medicinal properties. They included comfrey (*Symphytum officinale*) and vervain (*Verbena officinalis*), both long associated with magic and witchcraft.

But the real kicker was the distinctive medley of opium (*Papaver somniferum*), cannabis (*Cannabis sativa*), and two members of the nightshade family, white henbane (*Hyoscyamus albus*) and black nightshade (*Solanum nigrum*). The inclusion of the nightshades might as well have been lifted straight from the pages of Dioscorides, who specifically lauded the psychedelic properties of black nightshade with its "not unpleasant visions." The opium and cannabis, both profoundly mind-altering in high doses, are just icing on the cake. Pushing the bizarre medley even further into witch territory, however, were the skeletal remains of lizards (*Podarcis* sp.), frogs (*Rana* sp.), and toads (*Bufo* sp.). Tendrils and berries of the domesticated grape (*Vitis vinifera* L.) were found alongside a profusion of grape seeds, suggesting the combination of plants, reptiles, and amphibians was steeped in wine.

Unlike the well-documented finds in and around Mas Castellar de Pontós that place the Greek Mysteries at the Greek farm in Spain (finds that include the terra-cotta heads of Demeter/Persephone, the Triptolemus ceramic, and the Dionysian vase), the discoveries at the Villa Vesuvio are more cryptic. There simply isn't enough context to rule out more pedestrian explanations for the psychotropic blend. Ciaraldi herself believes the potion could represent either of the ancient medicinal concoctions known as the *mithridatium* or the *theriac,* compounded cure-all drugs for which countless recipes were recorded in the literature of the time.

The *mithridatium* frequently consisted of opium and lizards.[18] The *theriac* was usually mixed with the highly prized Falernian wine from Campania.[19] Though reptiles were an integral component of each, snakes and lizards were never combined in the *theriac*—which "might explain why in our assemblage we only find lizards," writes Ciaraldi.[20] In fact, no less than sixty bone fragments belonging to lizards were present in the vessel, indicating a most unusual wine. Because of a small cooker located in the Villa Vesuvio, in addition, the archaeologist sees strong evidence for "drug preparation":

> *The location of medicinal activities in the countryside was well known in the Greek world and was exported with success to the Roman world. . . . The presence of a "pharmacy" in the Pompeian country-side suggests that very specialised activities not directly connected to agricultural production may have not been limited to the city alone. Practices that involved a deep knowledge of the medicinal properties of the plants might still have been in the hands of those who lived more closely to the natural environment.[21]*

Is it too romantic to imagine the Villa Vesuvio as a laboratory for the production of a Dionysian sacrament that could have been used in the Villa of the Mysteries that was within walking distance, just west across Pompeii? Or better yet, was the humble farmhouse a supplier for the Velian priestesses and other Greek mystics who routinely made their way from Magna Graecia to the house churches and catacombs of Rome, off to initiate the devotees of the latest God of Ecstasy into an old Magna Graecian tradition with a homemade Eucharist? A sacrament guaranteed to send their paleo-Christian sisters into the same world of the dead that Empedocles apparently explored with his own *pharmaka*?

Same as I did for the ergotized beer over at Mas Castellar de Pontós, I made sure to call in my expert witnesses. During the ongoing pandemic in May 2020, I reached out to Patrick McGovern in quarantine in Philadelphia, as well as the leading archaeobotanists in Europe: Hans-Peter Stika at the University of Hohenheim in Germany, Soultana Valamoti at the Aristotle University of Thessaloniki in Greece, and Assunta Florenzano at the Università degli Studi di Modena e Reggio Emilia in Italy. Only to receive another eerie response from the professionals. None of them ever heard of the Villa Vesuvio or this extraordinary wine.

The German Stika cautioned that the seeds, in and of themselves, don't "mandatorily" make for a ritual psychedelic wine. And that the question mark in the title of Marina Ciaraldi's paper is a fair reflection of the unknowns. I pressed him on the lizards and seventeen seeds that hardly make this mix an accident: two opium seeds, nine cannabis seeds, four henbane seeds, and two black nightshade seeds. The Greek Valamoti took note and weighed in: "As an archaeologist, I am always cautious. But I would not be too cautious to say that the plants were not used for their medicinal/hallucinogenic properties." The American McGovern found some middle ground, saying the discovery was certainly "intriguing," like something out of the witches' brew in Macbeth. But he rightly suggested its credibility "hinges very much on the archaeobotanical expertise of Marina Ciaraldi," who has since disappeared from the scene. Despite my best efforts, I could never track her down.

So I reached out to the woman in charge of the dig from 1996, Marisa de' Spagnolis. Like Enriqueta Pons in Spain, de' Spagnolis is the one who actually stuck her boots in the ground. And remains the authority on the full archaeological context. Active in the field since 1973, with a full ten years in Pompeii, de' Spagnolis absolutely stands by Ciaraldi's analysis. And she had this to say over email from quarantine in Rome: "For me, the Villa Vesuvio was a small farm that was specifically designed for the production of drugs." The archaeologist then kindly shared a few details that have never before been published. Unlike other farms in the area, the Villa Vesuvio was only equipped for a "very limited production of wine." Like the home brew at Mas Castellar de Pontós, this seems to be a boutique house wine not intended for mass consumption. Piles of organic material in the yard indicate a garden for select plants and herbs. As excavations continued, de' Spagnolis would discover a V-shaped "maceration tank for cannabis" that further supports her position. And as a final touch, she also managed to decipher a lone piece of graffiti hidden under the plaster that only lends more romance to the site. In Latin, it reads *Scito: ama et aude millia.* "Know this: love and dare (to love) a thousand times." Maybe we're dealing with a love potion?

In the midst of the entertaining debate, one thing is for sure. Just as Ruck seems to have correctly predicted the ergot-infused beer at Eleusis, there is now hard data suggesting that psychedelic wine did, in fact, exist in the earliest days of Christianity, right where the Mysteries of Dionysus and Jesus came into contact. And right where the paleo-Christians would have needed it most, in the burgeoning centers of the faith—Naples, Puteoli, and Capua. In her paper, Ciaraldi can't dismiss the possibility that the strange brew in the Villa Vesuvio, if not an example of the *mithridatium* or *theriac,* could very well be one of the "aromatic or herbal wines" documented by Dioscorides, or a "spiced wine surprise" detailed by the first-century Roman gourmand Apicius.[22] Though that doesn't explain all the lizards, she openly admits, which add an altogether more magical quality to the potion.

Lizards, I would soon discover, that would continue to slither around the storied archives of the Vatican. But let's not get ahead of ourselves.

What was once informed speculation, relying purely on Greco-Roman authors like Dioscorides, Galen, and Apicius for the written support, is now a paleobotanical fact. The ancient Italians manufactured a wine with mind-bending ingredients. The solitary example that survived in the Pompeian countryside by the grace of Mt. Vesuvius is certainly not alone. There are others out there. And as more open-minded archaeologists like Andrew Koh continue digging for the evidence, more examples will come to the surface in the years ahead.

If the original Eucharist of Christianity really was psychedelic, then many of the puzzle pieces are finally coming together. The find from the Villa Vesuvio adds even more detail to the story of paleo-Christianity that we mapped out in the last chapter. The who, what, when, where, and why of the real origins of the world's biggest religion.

Who? Women. Specifically Greek-speaking women with pharmacological expertise, who may have used the portrayal of Mary Magdalene in both the Gospel of John and the Gnostic texts to justify their leading role in the newest mystery cult. Before Jesus generations of women brewed the graveyard beers and mixed the graveyard wines in the Indo-European ritual that spread east and west of Stone Age Anatolia, the "ritual act of communion" that was "by women for women." After Jesus there were the many women who dominated the house churches and catacombs that defined the faith, offering a safe haven for the old Greek sacrament that needed shelter from the wilderness. The witches of Persephone, who were the primary missionaries of the Phocaeans' secret cult, had every incentive to both influence, and in some cases even *become,* the witches of Christianity. Their sister witches of Dionysus, all across Magna Graecia, were in the same boat.

In Jesus—the wizard who died, laid for three days in a cave, and was reborn—they all may have found a brother from the East. And in the Gospel of John they may have immediately recognized the "True Drink" that guaranteed the same experience to anybody who consumed the wine god to conquer death. After all, John appears to be writing for women in Ephesus, just a short hop from Phocaea to its north. If anybody was going to understand his secret "symbols" and "language," it was Greek-speaking women whose very job was to preserve, protect, and defend the magic they had inherited from their Ionian ancestors in Phocaea. And if anybody could identify Jesus as the new God of Ecstasy, it was the maenads who had kept the cult of Dionysus alive in southern Italy for generations. And for whom Gnosticism would be a seamless transition to the new mystery religion.

What? Drugged wine. All those plants, herbs, and fungi so heavily documented by the Father of Drugs in his sophisticated wine formulas, demonstrating a profound knowledge of dosing. With such toxic, deadly species at play, Dioscorides's encyclopedia is proof of a long tradition that could induce the "not unpleasant visions" in carefully measured amounts of potent botanicals. The archaeochemical finds from Tel Kabri and Tel Kedesh were the real-life examples of spiked potions before Christianity. The paleobotanical discovery from the Villa Vesuvio is hard data of a drugged wine in the age of Jesus. And whatever *pharmakon* the Church Father Hippolytus accused Marcus and the female Valentinian Gnostics of consuming. And just maybe, the same *pharmakon* that fueled the Ancient Greek trips to the underworld in the Christian *refrigeria* that preceded and later competed with the above-ground Mass.

When? The first three hundred years after Jesus's death. Before Christianity became legal under Constantine, it was an illegal mystery religion fighting for survival in a hostile and unfriendly world. Its secret meetings and magical sacraments came under just as much suspicion as the Dionysian Mysteries that were systematically targeted by the Roman senate in 186 BC. The idea of the God of Ecstasy obliterating all loyalty to family and country was not welcome in a Roman Empire in the thick of nation building. Similarly the idea of making visionary wine available to the poor folks and women of the 99 percent was just as offensive to the 1 percent of the religious establishment who had enjoyed their monopoly on religious ecstasy for millennia. At their core Dionysus and Jesus were both absolute revolutionaries. To dismiss the real and present danger of their wine is to misunderstand the world into which the Sons of God were born. And the radical nature of their immortality potions. Because the sacrament is only a threat to the status quo if it's driving people out of their minds. No one was worried about the "alcohol" that the Greeks or Romans never even found a word to name.

Where? Magna Graecia and Rome. Southern Italy was ground zero for Greek mysticism in the centuries before and after Jesus. It was almost more Greek than Greece itself. Hence the name "Naples," the "new city" in Greek. In Pythagoras and Parmenides alone, Magna Graecia boasted the greatest prophet and the greatest philosopher the ancient world ever knew. In Empedocles, it found the greatest magician in the history of Western civilization. It was here that the "secret doctrine" of cave techniques flourished at least until the third century AD, when Plotinus died in Campania. It was here that the priestesses of Persephone practiced their death and rebirth for the Queen of the Dead, toggling between Rome and Velia along the Mystery Coast Highway. And it was here that Dionysus, the Lord of Death, found the richest soil for his vineyards, where his maenads spread out from the regional headquarters in Cumae and whirled for a thousand years between the sixth century BC and the fifth century AD.[23]

Not surprisingly Christianity's mystical coming-of-age all took place in Campania as well—Naples, Puteoli, and Capua. When they weren't summoning their own Lord of Death in the subterranean crypts of Rome, the Christian funeral banquets filled the catacombs under Naples, the so-called Valley of the Dead. And they never stopped. To this day, despite the Vatican's efforts to outlaw the fetishistic skull cult that took hold in the Fontanelle Cemetery, Neapolitans continue to consult the heads of the forty thousand "unnamed dead" displayed in the massive ossuary. If ever there were an ideal headquarters for a death cult, it was Campania.

To ignore the spiritual history of Magna Graecia and Rome is to ignore the environment that *actually* produced the first generations of Christians and made the faith what it is. Simply put, the story of paleo-Christianity is Greek-speaking mystics in southern Italy demanding personal access to the Eucharist. It wasn't the priests who attracted them to Jesus. It wasn't the Church Fathers. And it certainly wasn't the Bible or the basilicas, because neither existed. It was an experience of meeting God, free from doctrine, dogma, and any institution whatsoever. Surely that's something people today can appreciate.

Why? The only reason religions ever find an audience, the promise of an afterlife. Immortality. There are those who talk about it or read about it. And there are true philosophers who actually die for it. To repeat Peter Kingsley's single greatest insight about the Phocaeans who made Velia their new homeland: "To go down to the underworld when you're dead is one thing. To go there while you're alive, prepared and knowingly, and then learn from the experience—that's another thing entirely." If whatever was happening at Mas Castellar de Pontós was the same thing that gripped Campania as Christianity was colonizing Italy, then the death cult of the Phocaeans and other Ancient Greek mystics could not only be the answer to the best-kept secret in Ancient Greece. It could be the answer to the best-kept secret in Christianity.

Not everyone needs psychedelic drugs to die before they die. Lying down in a cave for a few days will certainly get the job done. But not everyone has the time or temerity for that kind of exercise. That's what sacraments are for. That's what they've always been for, before the bureaucracy replaced them with empty rituals and placebos. In its early days, did Christianity solve the age-old problem of delivering a life-changing mystical experience to as many people as possible by offering a chemical shortcut to enlightenment?

If so, it leaves our heretical investigation with only one final question.

If Greek-speaking witches and their drugged wine from Magna Graecia were so critical to the success of the world's biggest religion in its first three hundred years, what happened to their immortality potions? The Church Fathers could have denied women the priesthood. And prohibited the drugged Gnostic Eucharist. But that was hardly going to stop the religion with no name that had survived since the Stone Age.

Unfortunately there's only one way to silence a revolution.

Sooner or later, the bodies start burning.

And if there's one thing the Church has always been good at, it's a witch hunt.

16

The Gospel of Infinity and

the Toad Eucharist

With St. Peter's City of the Dead and the Roman catacombs checked off the itinerary, I have only one mission left in the Vatican this week. To learn the ultimate fate of the psychedelic Eucharist. If the Phocaean priestesses and the Gnostic witches helped jump-start Christianity with an injection of visionary drugs, what happened when the mystical period of paleo-Christianity came to an end? Who inherited the Ancient Greek tradition of spiked wine?

From the very beginning, when Saint Paul aired his grievances about the lethal potion in the Letter to the Corinthians, there was always a right Eucharist and a wrong Eucharist. And the Church always sided with the drug-free variety. After the fourth century AD, when the Gnostics largely went missing, Ruck charts a ping-pong battle between the Vatican and its sworn enemies. He notes "periods of suppression," followed by revivals of "renewed heresies, no doubt neo-pagan continuations of Classical rites" that culminated in the "cults of witchcraft" during the Middle Ages and Renaissance. Long disregarded by the classicists and theologians, Ruck has tried to convince his colleagues that drugs are integral to the history of Christianity. And completely failed. Because if they don't want to hear about the sober founders of Western civilization drinking beer laced with

LSD, they probably don't want to hear about devout Christians getting high on psychedelic wine.

And to be honest, twelve years ago, the idea struck me as pretty absurd too. A secret hallucinogenic Eucharist kept alive by a chain of heretics through the Dark Ages, until the grand witch hunts of the Inquisition wiped them off the map? Great stuff for late-night YouTubing. Less so for serious scholarship. How do you even start the fact-check? Not surprisingly, the hard scientific data in the thousand years between the fall of the Roman Empire and the Inquisition are incredibly sparse. If there are only a handful of archaeochemists looking for intoxicants in antiquity, there are even fewer studying medieval drugs. So I knew there was never going to be a Mas Castellar de Pontós or a Villa Vesuvio to support Ruck's wild claims. What I didn't know is that I'd wind up pacing the Vatican Museums with the world's most interesting librarian.

After weeks on the road, Father Francis has returned to Isernia, leaving me to fend for myself behind enemy lines. Since last year, however, I've made some fast friends around these parts. So I'm in no danger of lunching alone. The librarian and I started the afternoon at Taverna Bavarese Franz, just a few blocks east along the Borgio Pio. To walk off the pasta carbonara and half liter of vino, we backtrack to the northeast corner of Vatican City along the imposing brick ramparts lining the Viale Vaticano. The crowds are thin this bright, early-spring Wednesday in February 2019, so getting through museum security is painless. We check our bags into storage and make our way up the escalator to the Cortile della Pinacoteca (Courtyard of the Art Gallery) for a breathtaking view of St. Peter's dome.

To our left, the librarian points out the back wing of what has been called one of the "grandest historical collections in the world," the impenetrable haystack of thirty-five thousand volumes of catalogue spanning fifty-three miles of shelving. Some of the dusty records date back to the eighth century AD. Right next to the Sistine Chapel and barred from public view, this mysterious repository has a reputation like none other. For Catholics and non-Catholics alike, it's a total enigma. For conspiracy theorists, the site of the planet's creepiest cabals and darkest plots. For my friend and professional archivist, Gianfranco Armando, it's just the office.

The Vatican Secret Archives.

To bask a little longer in the weather, we head east into the Cortile della

Pigna, appropriately named for the humongous pine cone mounted on a marble pedestal that dominates the center of a lofty niche at the northern end of this tranquil patio. In his tan jacket, gray scarf, and plaid rain hat—because the Italians love to accessorize, even when it's not raining—Gianfranco tells me about the time he got locked in the Secret Archives' bunker. Directly beneath us a portion of the Vatican's fifty-three miles of classified material is stored in a two-story underground vault. The fireproof reinforced-concrete structure is climate and humidity controlled, and subject to constant security surveillance.[1] There's also an emergency lighting system, though I guess it was on the fritz that fateful day.

"To remain alone, without the lights, and no mobile signal," says Gianfranco, laughing in retrospect, "is not a good experience, I tell you." Though he kept his calm and eventually escaped by retracing his steps through the fixed and revolving shelving system, I don't think Gianfranco has quite forgiven the absentminded colleague who accidently left him here in the underworld. Yet another near-death trip into the subterranean chambers of the Eternal City. But it's par for the course. When you step foot inside the Secret Archives, you never know what to expect.

I had always wanted to take a look for myself, but had no idea where to begin. According to the Vatican's website, no one can access the Pope's files without first identifying the exact "archival series" of the volumes they intend to consult. A semi-impossible task, since the online Collection Index is more of a long, meaningless table of contents, available only in Italian. And it's completely unsearchable by subject matter. There are just broad, general categories of aged documents, arranged by relatively unhelpful headings like the names of centuries-old Popes, the sites of various international delegations, and lists of random religious orders. If you're looking for drugs, you're fresh out of luck.

So if I wanted to fact-check Ruck's notion that a hidden tradition of heretics trafficked in a psychedelic Eucharist for hundreds of years, long after Jesus, I needed a more creative approach. What I was really after was written evidence of the Vatican, in its own penmanship, confronting this supposed network—something that would indicate the past use of drugs in black and white. I had to identify an individual heretic whom I knew the Vatican had hunted down and snuffed out. He or she had to be particularly famous, high-profile enough to have grabbed the Church's attention in the

first place. And then historically significant enough for the Vatican to have
retained a record of the scandal. No easy task. But one obvious figure kept
dancing through my head. The occult wizard I'd been studying since my
days at Brown. The unapologetic genius who died spectacularly for his sins.

Giordano Bruno.

The Dominican monk was born in Nola in 1548, in what was then the
Kingdom of Naples in Magna Graecia. He was imprisoned by the Roman
Inquisition for seven years, before they burned him at the stake in the
Campo de' Fiori in 1600.[2] His crime? Among a long list of other heresies,
proclaiming the "gospel of infinity" that proposed the existence of multiple
earths orbiting multiple suns across the endless expanse of the cosmos.[3]
Earths that might contain other forms of human life, dethroning our species
as God's favorite. Four hundred years ahead of his time, the martyr for free
thinking somehow foresaw the discovery of the first exoplanet by NASA's
Kepler Space Telescope in 1995.[4]

Bruno wasn't the only genius who provoked the Vatican by asking big
questions, of course. A few decades after the Nolan's execution, Galileo
Galilei was sentenced to house arrest for claiming the sun, not the earth, was
the center of the solar system—something "false and contrary to the Holy
and Divine Scriptures."[5] But the funny thing about the Father of the Scientific Method, perhaps the most famous heretic of all time, is that he wasn't
considered the most dangerous. Galileo got off much easier than Bruno,
living another eleven years in the Vatican's custody until his natural death
at seventy-seven. They never sent him up in flames like the wizard from the
south who died at fifty-two. And I think I know why.

A blasphemous cosmology is one thing.

A blasphemous Eucharist is another.

In his attempt "to return to the earliest centuries of Christianity" by recovering "the monuments of classical antiquity," Bruno longed for a lost
period of history that the brilliant scholar Frances Yates calls "a pure golden
age of magic" based on Greek philosophy of supposed Egyptian origin.[6] Like
his Greek-speaking ancestors from Magna Graecia, the "Renaissance Magus" was obsessed with the same "secret doctrine" that had earlier attracted
Pythagoras, Parmenides, Empedocles, and Plotinus. Not to mention all
those witches—the Phocaean priestesses of Persephone and the Dionysian
maenads who were crushed by the Roman senate to teach Paculla Annia a

lesson. They all came from Campania. And they all seem to have been very familiar with drugs. Just like Bruno.

In *De gli eroici furori* (The Heroic Enthusiasts), published in London in 1585, Bruno overplayed his hand in a "curious episode" that Yates describes as "the culmination of the whole work." It's an allegory about nine blind men in search of the same beatific vision that beckoned the pilgrims to Eleusis for two thousand years, the "highest and final illumination" that reveals the meaning of life. The men leave the idyllic countryside of Bruno's formative years in Campania and make a three-day pilgrimage north along the Mystery Coast Highway to Mount Circeo. It's the very same place where Circe tends her loom on the *Vergilius Vaticanus* manuscript that helped Dr. Alexia Latini decipher the Homeric fresco in the Hypogeum of the Aurelii once and for all.

One of the nine cries out for Circe to brew up a "remedy" for their affliction with her "plants" (*piante*), "charms" (*incanti*), and "drugs" (*veneficii*).[7] Bruno's word for "drugs" is straight from the Latin *veneficium*, which the Lewis and Short dictionary defines as "the preparation of magic potions." The men beg for the "magic herbs" (*medicami*), but Circe stands firm. Finally, she presents them with an "elixir" (*liquor*) containing "god-like virtue" (*la virtù divina*). Sealed in a vase, the magical potion guarantees a vision of two starry objects. After another decade of travel, once their initiation is complete, the men manage to open the vase, reversing their blindness and catching the promised vision of the heavenly suns. In describing the ecstasy that results from witnessing "the fairest work of God," Bruno gets a little too close to exposing his love of the Greek Mysteries. "For a time it was like seeing so many frenzied Bacchanals (*tanti furiosi debaccanti*), inebriated with that which they saw so plainly."

Once again a familiar theme: women and drugs.

Bruno was tempting fate by calling up the Vatican's archnemeses.

If the Hypogeum of the Aurelii is evidence of the "secret doctrine," then perhaps *The Heroic Enthusiasts* is too. When he invokes Circe and her drugs, is it possible Bruno is talking about a *real* tradition? One that found its way from ancient Campania to Renaissance Rome, thanks to the Mystery Coast Highway? It's all part of a classical vocabulary that is completely lost on today's readers—the "body of knowledge" that classicists Hanson and Heath said was "virtually unrecognized" in the twenty-first century. But the

Inquisitors could certainly read between the not-so-subtle lines. They understood the implications of Bruno's work for the Church in general, and the Eucharist in particular.

Look no further than the heretic's trial records. Or the lack thereof.

The Vatican did not only want Bruno's fresh brand of neo-paganism to disappear from the face of the earth. They also wanted any evidence of his detention, torture, and death to disappear as well. Because at some point over the past four hundred years, the original records of Bruno's interrogation completely vanished, leaving only a fifty-nine-page summary of the many heresies with which he was accused. In 1817 that also went missing for several decades, until some assistant custodian in the 1880s chanced upon the actual sixteenth-century manuscript in one of the hidden cabinets of the Vatican's secretary of state. At which point Pope Leo XIII ordered the records to be immediately cut off from the public. As the scholar Maria Luisa Ambrosini once remarked, "the Church realized that burning geniuses was bad for public relations."[8]

Rather than classify the material and file it away for safekeeping, the presiding cardinal *deliberately* misplaced Bruno's trial records among the personal archives of Leo's predecessor, Pius IX. And there they sat until 1940, when then-prefect of the Vatican Secret Archives, Angelo Mercati, successfully tracked down the object of his obsession after an exhaustive fifteen-year hunt! For whatever reason, Mercati wanted the arch-heresy to be preserved, so he properly catalogued the original handwritten manuscript. Since World War II it has been quietly hiding in the Vatican Secret Archives. A needle in the haystack. As impressive as the collection is, it's also "one of the most useless," according to one recent commentator, "because it's so inaccessible."

> *Of those 53 miles, just a few millimeters' worth of pages have been scanned and made available online. Even fewer pages have been transcribed into computer text and made searchable. If you want to peruse anything else, you have to apply for special access, schlep all the way to Rome, and go through every page by hand.*

Which is exactly what I did.

But getting in wasn't easy.

My only lead was Angelo Mercati. In 1942 the former prefect published an inflammatory book, including an Italian translation of the original Bruno manuscript, complete with footnotes and commentary. After some creative googling in the spring of 2018, I was able to tease out the specific citation for Bruno's records, the "archival series" that the Secret Archives demands before they even consider granting permission for a random American to go sniffing through their dirty laundry. Appropriately Bruno's records were tucked away in some "miscellaneous" section of the so-called "Armadi" files: Misc., Arm. X, 205.

With that I was ready for the formal admissions process. Which was more like an Abbott and Costello routine. I needed a letter of recommendation from a "qualified person in the field of historical research," so I asked Ruck to pen a note on Boston University letterhead, hoping no one at the Vatican would do any creative googling of their own. Ruck kindly obliged. Under the "research topic" section of the application, I made sure to refer to Giordano Bruno as a "heretic." A few weeks later, in May 2018, cut to me and Father Francis in the shadow of Athena's statue in the main reading room of the Vatican Secret Archives. Before our visit to the Louvre and the catacombs over the last few days, it was our very first adventure together.

Under the watchful eye of the Greek goddess of Wisdom and the half-dozen all-male library custodians who did not take their eyes off us for a second, the priest and I scanned an ultraviolet light over the yellowed pages of the indictment against the most famous magician ever captured by the Catholic Church. We were lucky to even get hold of the seven-inch-thick volume that hit the desk like a sack of potatoes. At first I was given access only to a digital copy of the trial records saved onto an old-school CD-ROM. In order to see the physical manuscript itself, I had to fill out a one-page special request form that within minutes was personally reviewed by the current prefect in charge of the Secret Archives, His Excellency Sergio Pagano. Yes, his last name means "pagan" in Italian.

In another Abbott and Costello moment, the prefect and I went back and forth through one of the custodians, never actually seeing each other face-to-face. The nervous, confused intermediary had to make three separate trips to the prefect's office. After my initial request, the prefect wanted to know which specific "folios," or pages, Father Francis and I wanted to inspect. I wrote down the folios I had already reviewed in electronic form, the ones that mentioned Bruno's "gospel of infinity" and the Eucharist. But out of left field, and for no reason whatsoever, the custodian returned with a translation of Galileo's trial records from 1633. I furrowed my brow and held up both palms in the universal language of "What the hell is this?"

At that point the Vatican's senior archivist, Gianfranco Armando, graciously intervened on our behalf and finally scored the elusive manuscript in question. Whenever a couple of Americans descend on the Secret Archives looking for Giordano Bruno, it arouses interest, I suppose. When one of them is an ordained priest, hushed conversations need to take place in the crypt-like cafeteria that occupies the Cortile della Biblioteca, the lush courtyard separating the Vatican Secret Archives from the Biblioteca Apostolica Vaticana, the Pope's personal library next door.

There, over wickedly strong espresso, I let Gianfranco in on my investigation. To my astonishment God's librarian didn't bat an eye. The tall figure from the Piemonte region of northern Italy was instantly receptive to the quest for any textual evidence of the Vatican's suppression of a psychedelic Eucharist. "Any research, if done seriously," he later wrote me, "is worthy of attention." But I was barking up the wrong tree.

Through his transparent spectacles resting on an aquiline nose, and the salt-and-pepper beard that made me think he and Father Francis shared the same barber, Gianfranco told me I would have better luck in the Archive of the Congregation for the Doctrine of the Faith. In a nice twist of irony, the so-called "archives of repression"—as historian Carlo Ginzburg has referred to them—are housed in the Palazzo del Sant'Uffizio on the other side of St. Peter's Square. The same palace that was once the Vatican dungeon, where Bruno himself was detained for seven years. There I would find all the records of the Supreme Sacred Congregation of the Roman and Universal Inquisition. More popularly known as the Holy Office. It was only in 1998 that Pope John Paul II decided to open the contents of that archive to secular researchers. The final impenetrable haystack for the final chapter of this investigation.

In the meantime Gianfranco was right about the Bruno manuscript. Father Francis and I parsed through the archaic mix of Latin and Italian in the sixteenth-century trial summary for any explicit mention of drugs and came up empty-handed. That said, it was incredible to see firsthand how the Inquisitors described the Renaissance Magus's "gospel of infinity": "many worlds, many suns . . . even with human beings [on them]" (*plures mundos, plures soles . . . ac etiam homines*). In the passage on the Eucharist, Bruno is quoted by an informant making fun of the Most Blessed Sacrament, calling it a form of "bestiality, blasphemy, and idolatry" (*bestialita, bestemie et idolatria*).[9] Same as today, the sixteenth-century version of the Eucharist could hardly compete with whatever inspired the house churches and catacombs of paleo-Christianity, or the Greek Mysteries long before them. And Bruno knew it.

In the wake of the Reformation, during Bruno's lifetime, the Catholics and Protestants were actively fighting over the doctrine of transubstantiation that remains the Catholic position to this day. It says the bread and wine of the Eucharist possess some unseen and unfathomable quality that is fundamentally transformed into Jesus's literal body and blood during the Mass, even if they appear unchanged to the untrained eye.[10] According to a Pew poll from July 2019, 69 percent of self-described Catholics don't believe a word of the Church's core teaching.[11] Instead, they see the bread and wine of the Eucharist as mere *symbols* of the body and blood of Jesus, and nothing more. As the writer Flannery O'Connor pointedly quipped back in 1955, "Well, if it's a symbol. To hell with it."[12]

Bruno couldn't have agreed more.[13] As a practical mystic he wanted to get back to basics. Back to the Drug of Immortality that his Greek-speaking ancestors in Campania seemed to know all about. And the kind of psychedelic lizard potion that turned up at the Villa Vesuvio, only twenty-three kilometers from Bruno's hometown of Nola. His Eucharist was no mere *symbol*. And no placebo. It was an "elixir" of "god-like virtue," spiked with the "plants," "charms," and "drugs" of antiquity's most notorious Greek witch, Circe. Is that how Bruno gained his uncanny knowledge of the inexhaustible, starry universe that he accurately predicted by four centuries, and which modern cosmologists find hard to explain? Natural-born saints and seers have always reported experiences of cosmic awakening. As have those who spend a lifetime in meditation, like the Tibetan Buddhists that Father Francis studied up in the Himalayas. For the rest of us mere mortals, Bruno dropped some clues that ultimately contributed to his death. Clues about *his* Eucharist as a fascinating shortcut to enlightenment, the quickest way to heal our blindness to the wonder of the sublime cosmos that surrounds us. Which brings us right back to the one thing that unites every mystical tradition we have reviewed thus far.

The beatific vision.

That immediate sight of God, prompting the blind pilgrim from Eleusis to leave a timeless thank-you to Persephone for restoring his sight: the Eukrates votive relief. That strange, hallucinatory effect of Dionysus in *The Bacchae,* when he told his latest initiate, "Now you *see* as you ought to *see.*" Those words straight from Jesus's mouth in John 9:39, "I am here to give *sight* to the blind." And John 1:51, "I tell you for certain that you will *see* heaven open and God's angels going up and down." That very Greek concept of *gnosis* or intuitive knowledge that restored true sight to the Christian Gnostics. "Recognize what is before your eyes," said the *Gospel of Thomas,* "and what is hidden will be revealed to you." That "secret doctrine" that passed from Pythagoras, Parmenides, and Empedocles to Plotinus over six centuries later, when the face painted on the wall of the Hypogeum of the Aurelii wrote, "We must not look, but must, as it were, close our eyes and exchange our faculty of vision for another. We must awaken this faculty which everyone possesses, but few people ever use."

It was this same beatific vision that brought the very concept of psychedelics into the modern world. No one had ever heard of psilocybin mushrooms until Gordon Wasson reported his mind-blowing experience with Maria Sabina in the Sierra Mazateca of Mexico. In 1957 he wrote that the fungi images were "more real to me than anything I had ever seen with my own eyes." In language eerily similar to Bruno's nine blind men, "inebriated with that which they saw so plainly" under the influence of Circe's drugs, Wasson added, "I felt that I was now seeing plain, whereas ordinary vision gives us an imperfect view." Incredibly both Bruno and Wasson compared these experiences to the Greek Mysteries.

But even more amazing is the phenomenon I find myself returning to again and again in my personal notes, completely unable to provide an explanation. All that scientific research on near-death experiences mentioned in chapter 5, where the approach to the Other Side somehow miraculously offers sight to the blind, including those blind from birth. They were found to witness the same things as sighted people with "normal, and perhaps even superior, acuity." Not so different from the "complex hallucinations" of the blind that I tracked down in the psychedelic literature. In both experiences, the near-death and the psychedelic, encounters with dead loved ones are not unusual, providing a major clue to the power of the Christian funeral banquets that took place in the Roman catacombs. But if the blind are able to join in, then the beatific vision seems to be an expansion of consciousness that has nothing to do with the eyeballs. Or the intellect. Plotinus warned that this extraordinary "faculty of vision" which "everyone possesses, but few people ever use" could never be "acquired by calculations" or "constructed out of theorems."[14] True religion, as Parmenides tried to teach Plato long ago from Velia, has nothing to do with logic, reason, or reflective thought.

To get the beatific vision, you have to die for it.

The ego has to be destroyed. At least for a little while. Whether it's a few minutes or a few hours or a few days, it doesn't take very long. But everything you thought you knew about life—*everything*—has to be annihilated. It makes no sense, but it's what the mystics have been saying all along. There is no way around it. It is the sole piece of advice rendered at St. Paul's Monastery on Mt. Athos in Greece, hanging right there in the reception room: "If you die before you die; you won't die when you die." What does not go advertised in Christianity today is the important footnote that Bruno sacrificed his life to record for posterity: "To hell with placebos. Drugs welcome."

If Bruno was anything like his Greek ancestors from Campania, he earned the right to scoff at a watered-down Eucharist in those few but telling lines I read in the beaten manuscript under ultraviolet light. While the staff of the very institution that put him to death stared at me and Father Francis with utter bafflement. In 2000 Pope John Paul II issued a general apology for the use of violence against the likes of Bruno.[15] The Vatican's four-century grudge against the revolutionary was soon clarified by Cardinal Angelo Sodano, however, who ultimately defended the Inquisitors for condemning that particular heretic from Magna Graecia in an effort to "serve freedom" and "promote the common good."[16] Could the bad blood have anything to do with the fact that Bruno and his Eucharist still represent an *existing* threat? One that could render all the doctrine, dogma, and bureaucracy of the Vatican absolutely superfluous?

If Bruno's original trial records hadn't conveniently gone missing, we might know more. Then again, the Secret Archives wouldn't be the Secret Archives. If there's one thing the Vatican has learned as the longest-running institution in the world, it's how to cover its tracks. The "bishop's factory," as one journalist refers to it, knows better than to leave a paper trail. The Church of the last thousand years has been described as "a mix of bureaucracy, social mobility, and informal networks" where "not everything is written down."[17] In the deep ink-and-quill history of the Vatican, the information retention policy has always maintained a certain medieval flair. So I'm up against the world champions here.

Which is why, ever since last year, I made sure to keep in touch with God's librarian. If anybody knew how to navigate the Pope's archives, it was my new friend from Piemonte. If he could find his way out of the Secret Archives' two-story vault in the pitch black, he could help me find the original Eucharist.

Gianfranco and I saunter farther east off the Cortile della Pigna. We hang a sharp left and scale the twenty-four steps to the outdoor octagonal courtyard of the Pio Clementino collection, the best place in the Vatican Museums to see some familiar faces. On the right-hand side of the antechamber leading to the Sala delle Muse (Hall of the Muses), clear as can be, is an ivy-crowned Bacchus with a bunch of grapes dangling from his left hand. He's intently staring into the bottom of the cup in his right hand. He's wondering what the Vatican has done with his *pharmakon*.

So am I.

For the past many months, I've been obsessing over Bruno's use of the word *veneficii* (drugs) in *The Heroic Enthusiasts*. If he was talking about a real tradition from Campania, I needed to establish all the specifics. So I went back to square one and used the one piece of hard data I had uncovered as my starting point, the psychedelic lizard potion from the Villa Vesuvio. A lizard wine spiked with opium, cannabis, white henbane, and black nightshade was a great, if confusing, lead. And it soon paid off.

By the Renaissance the Latin term that Bruno used for the Greek *pharmakon* was especially associated with the kind of witch, sorceress, or medicine woman, the *venefica,* whom the Inquisition was targeting for their forbidden knowledge of psychotropic substances. Just after Bruno's birth in 1548, even the Pope's own team was talking about drugs. Trained as a pharmacologist and botanist, Andrés Laguna was the personal physician to Pope Julius III. He spent years poring over the original Greek codices of Dioscorides's *Materia Medica* that had survived since the first century

AD. His translation of antiquity's magnum opus was released in Latin and Italian in 1554 by the same publishing house in Venice that made the Father of Drugs a household name all over Europe. Laguna's *Materia Medica* was reprinted seventeen times to a large following in Italy, mainly because of his running commentary and anecdotes that accompanied the text. They provide an exceptional window onto the Renaissance experience with drugs in Bruno's lifetime. And importantly, they show that Bruno's fabulous tale about Circe and drugs was rooted in a very dangerous and apparently very real concoction: the witches' ointment.

In his discussion of the notorious unguent that witches were said to lather on their bodies and broomsticks to carry them off to satanic meetings in the woods, Laguna identified the ingredients that turned up during one of the Church's search and seizure operations:

> among other things in the abode of said witches was a jar half-filled with a certain green ointment, made of white poplar with which they anointed themselves. Its odor was heavy and offensive, proving that it was composed of herbs, cold and soporiferous in the ultimate degree, such as hemlock, black nightshade, henbane, and mandrake."[18]

Between the black nightshade (*Solanum nigrum*) and henbane (*Hyoscyamus* spp.), it's a fascinating clue that potentially connects the paleobotanical find from the Villa Vesuvio with Bruno's mention of the *veneficii* (drugs) that produced the beatific vision. But what does any of it have to do with broomsticks flying through the air?

Well, the witches never flew anywhere, of course. As discussed in our examination of the nightshade beers in ancient Iberia, the family of plants that includes black nightshade and henbane is widely known for provoking delirium, intense hallucinations, and unearthly out-of-body travel.[19] Even the early commentators knew that witches "do not leave their homes," rather, "the devil enters them and deprives them of sense, and they fall as dead and cold."[20] That's exactly what happened to one guinea pig who was prescribed the witches' ointment to cure her insomnia. Laguna recorded the woman's reaction to regaining consciousness after a full thirty-six hours: "Why did you wake me at such an inopportune time? I was surrounded by all the delights of the world."[21]

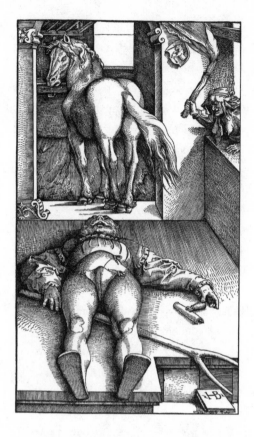

The *Bewitched Groom* woodcut by German artist Hans Baldung, created around 1544. Entranced by the witch, the central figure is "as dead and cold"—locked in a temporary state of mind-altering paralysis.

It certainly *sounds* like the beatific vision.

Indeed anyone who sampled one of the witches' magical elixirs might enjoy the same psychedelic journey, as amusingly captured by Hans Baldung's 1544 woodcut *The Bewitched Groom*. In the middle of his chores, the stable boy has fallen down "as dead and cold," overcome by whatever charm the sorceress in the window has just cooked up.[22] The art historian Walter Strauss believes the forked pole that just fell from the man's hand was used to hold a bowl or cauldron over the fire—the kind of vessel that witches customarily used for "mixing, heating, and storing potions, which were intended to be imbibed, rubbed into the skin in the manner of an ointment, or inhaled as incense."[23] Once again the motif is strangely reminiscent of the Near Eastern *marzeah*, which the scholar Gregorio del Olmo Lete described as a "cataleptic state of trance" induced by wine; or the Phocaean practice of incubation, which Peter Kingsley described as a "cataleptic" journey into a "world beyond the senses" where "space and time mean nothing."

So if Bruno was privy to a real pharmacological tradition in the sixteenth century, how did it get from ancient Campania to Renaissance Rome? To the point where it showed up on the radar of the Pope's physician? As I dug deeper the circumstantial evidence started piling up for Ruck's secret chain of heretics linking the Gnostics to the witches.

If the psychedelic lizard potion from the Villa Vesuvio is evidence of a sacrament, perhaps it was smuggled along the Mystery Coast Highway from the pharmacy in Pompeii to the house churches and catacombs of Rome to serve as the heretical Eucharist of the Simonians, Valentinians, and Marcosians during the glory days of the Gnostics. In the first three hundred years after Jesus, did the likes of Aurelia Prima sneak such a Eucharist into the Hypogeum of the Aurelii, or the Greek Chapel in the Catacombs of Priscilla, or the mixing chambers in the Catacombs of Marcellinus and Peter? Maybe even right under St. Peter's Basilica, where *refrigeria* could be held in the City of the Dead every single night of the year? The raw hallucinogenic material was certainly available. After the fourth century AD, what happened to that mysterious brand of exotic wine?

By all accounts it disappeared into the custody of anonymous heretics along the Mystery Coast Highway who are now lost to history.[24] For the next several centuries, seekers of an alternative Eucharist in Italy might find comfort in the death cults that had fled the Roman catacombs for the Neapolitan catacombs and all the cemeteries of the rural churches. It was there that the *refrigeria* would continue to be celebrated—out of sight, out of mind—until the tenth century AD, when the Christian wine parties followed the cemeteries' relocation back into the urban centers.[25] For Yale scholar Ramsay MacMullen, no pagan ritual had quite the staying power of the graveyard Eucharist, which "offered to the immortal in humans, the everlasting spark or spirit of the dead." There the Gnostic loners might find good company, "feasting, drinking, singing, dancing, and staying up through the night; the identity of joyful, even abandoned spirit."[26]

They might also take refuge in the Phocaean practice of incubation that never left Magna Graecia. Across the Mediterranean many of the sacred caves and temples of Asclepius were repurposed into *martyria*, pilgrimage sites for the consultation of Christian saints and martyrs. But in Campania specifically, MacMullen confirms that the "age-old practice of receiving visions of deities during a night's sleep at the shrine" was maintained in

Naples, "where it was customary for priests to inquire about the suppliants' dreams and to interpret them, and where sometimes the suppliants had to reside for weeks or months before obtaining relief."[27] Incredible as it seems, some kind of visionary Greek tradition *did* survive in Campania for many centuries, right where it started with Parmenides and the priestesses who succeeded him in Velia. But were women and drugs really the key to the stunning longevity of all the Christianized *refrigeria* and incubation rituals across medieval Italy?

Where the Gnostics failed to keep a low profile, the witches knew what they were doing. Some secured serious credentials to avoid the Vatican's suspicion, joining the "Women of Salerno," who would greatly influence the Medical School of Salerno along the Mystery Coast Highway south of Pompeii, just east of the Amalfi Coast on the Sorrentine Peninsula. Founded sometime in the tenth century under the guidance of Greek texts, with Latin, Hebrew, and Arabic wisdom to boot, it was the most preeminent institution of its kind. Particularly revered were the "huge collections of drug remedies."[28] It was the "only medical school in Europe that opened its doors to women," who served on the faculty and played a vital role in the history of scientific achievement.[29] Of all the places in the Old World for women with botanical expertise to redefine Western medicine, described as "a system of professional medical practice which has since prevailed in all parts of the civilized world," it happened on the Mystery Coast Highway.

But not every witch was destined for medical school. Many would stick to the old ways. That entrenched tradition of folk medicine that had survived for generations in Italy, especially among rural populations, which had learned to take care of themselves. Part of the long-standing tradition of fierce independence and self-reliance, the evidence suggests, was a homemade Eucharist. The kind that appears to have been circulating among Greek-speaking Christians since the earliest days of the faith all over the Mediterranean, including the lethal potion at the house church in Corinth.

While the Muslims in the Holy Land kept the Vatican busy overseas, the Crusades in Europe were just as distracting. Like the twenty thousand men, women, and children who were indiscriminately slaughtered in a single day in 1209 during the Church's so-called Albigensian Crusade against the Cathars, a group of Christian heretics in France.[30] All the while, a much bigger threat was brewing just down the Mystery Coast Highway. By the 1420s the nocturnal church service known as the witches' Sabbat was erupting all across the Italian peninsula. At the center of these diabolic "companies," stretching from the Alps to Sicily, were encounters with otherworldly characters known as the "ladies from the outside" (*donas de fuera*), who had cat paws or horse hooves instead of human hands and feet. Italian women young and old were said to fly through the night on billy goats with these "mysterious female beings," in order "to banquet in remote castles or on meadows."[31] The Sabbats were mainly local affairs. But they also had their headquarters, the holiest pilgrimage site in the world of witchcraft that drew women not just from Italy but all over the European continent. And not surprisingly, it was right in the heart of Campania.

The witches all came to the legendary walnut tree in the town of Benevento. There, they would frolic under the branches, which were sacred to the Greek goddess Artemis. They would link arms with a pack of Dionysian satyrs, as depicted on any bottle of Strega—a popular herbal liqueur named after the Italian word for "witch" and distilled in Benevento since 1860. And they would pay homage to a female divinity who went by many names: the Matron, the Teacher, the Wise Sibilla, the Queen of the Fairies.[32] And the one title that Bruno himself must have heard from his hometown of Nola, just an hour southwest of Benevento.

The Greek Mistress.

Like all Sabbats the ritual in Benevento was an alternative Mass with an alternative Eucharist in honor of an alternative God. A Latin treatise from the era, the *Errors of the Cathars*, records the witches mixing their own "wine" during the Sabbat for the express purpose of "vilifying the Sacrament of the Eucharist and equally to dishonor it."[33] And that's what changed everything. Because up until the 1420s the witches were just a ragtag outfit of harmless folk healers, innocently prancing naked through the forests of Italy. Pagans perhaps, but pagans the Vatican could afford to ignore when there were much bigger fish to fry, like the Muslims and the Cathars. It was only when the Eucharist got involved that the witch was promoted from nuisance to apostate, assuming the title of "Cathar," a suddenly generic term for heretics. And that's when she became a top priority, truly worthy of all the fire and fury of the witch hunts that, even by the most conservative estimates, resulted in ninety thousand prosecutions and forty-five thousand executions.[34]

"Although they pretended to be good Catholic Christians," writes historian Karen Jolly about the many women who attended the Sabbat, "they represented the most dangerous of all enemies of the human race and the Christian Church."[35] The rationale should by now be very familiar. As we saw with the Mysteries of Dionysus and Jesus, the political and religious authorities were not worried about wine as we know it today. They didn't care about alcohol, or even drugs per se, which were for the most part legal. It's what the drugs *did* to people that mattered. In 186 BC the Roman senate hunted down Paculla Annia and her maenads because their sacrament was driving good citizens out of their minds—young men dropping everything for an ancient version of the Sabbat in the woods, wives and mothers leaving their families behind. In the second to fourth centuries AD, the growing bureaucracy of the Church stamped out the Gnostics at least in part for the same reason. The women who tasted the drugged wine of the Valentinians

Two witches riding broomsticks from the *Champion of the Ladies* illuminated manuscript, written in 1451 by Martin Le Franc. The witches in question are called "Waldensians," which originally referred to a group of Christian heretics in France and northern Italy. Bilia la Castagna was a member. In the fifteenth century, the legacy of her toad Eucharist would transform from simple folk magic into the kind of demonic witchcraft and heresy that was hunted down by the Inquisition.

would never settle for the empty ritual or placebo Eucharist of the Church Fathers. They had sampled the forbidden fruit.

Just like the witches with their homemade Eucharist. In *The Witches' Ointment: The Secret History of Psychedelic Magic*, published in 2015, Thomas Hatsis dredges up an awesome piece of overlooked trivia. In the Cottian Alps of northern Italy in 1387, the torture of one heretic in the small town of Pinerolo resulted in stunning information about a certain Bilia la Castagna. It was revealed that the blasphemous witch was traveling around with a little phial that held a most unusual Eucharist, "a strange potion made from the emissions of a large toad and the ashes of burned hairs, [which she] mixes around a fire late at night on the Eve of the Epiphany."[36] The same Epiphany when Dionysus and Jesus debuted their miraculous wine. Hatsis notes the secretions of certain poisonous toads can contain such psychoactive compounds as bufotenine (5-HO-DMT), which is structurally similar to LSD. There's also 5-MeO-DMT, a chemical cousin of the dimethlytriptamine

The Witches woodcut by Hans Baldung, created around 1510. Like his *Bewitched Groom* (page 320), the forked pole or magical staff appears once again. It is carried by an airborne witch straddling a flying goat. This time, the staff cradles one of the bubbling cauldrons that was apparently used to cook up the witches' ointment, together with other hallucinogenic incenses and potions. Another steaming cauldron appears in the foreground, in the very center of the composition. It is surrounded by three naked hags, and three more staffs. Whatever gushes from the cauldron in clouds of billowing smoke, it is the secret to the witches' ecstatic flight.

(N,N-DMT) that is used in *ayahuasca*, the South American psychedelic brew sometimes referred to as the "Vine of the Dead." At the "responsible dose," anyone who drank the toad Eucharist was said to "understand all the secrets of the sect and forever question orthodox teaching."[37]

Between the witches' ointment, the heretical "wine," and the toad Eucharist, the Vatican had every reason in the world to shut down the Sabbat, even if the satanic Mass was all in the witches' heads. A fisherman's wife from Palermo, Sicily, who once completed the supposed journey to Benevento, was later cornered by the Inquisition. "All this seemed to her to be taking place in a dream, for when she awoke, she always found herself in bed, naked as when she had gone to rest."[38] Physically these women may not have gone anywhere. But spiritually they went everywhere. And like some whirlwind visit to Oz, they saw everything. Which made the Church and its Eucharist totally obsolete.

And so in the fifteenth century, with yet another wild sacrament on the loose, history was about to repeat itself. Except this time whatever had managed to survive the Dark Ages would be eradicated, with extreme prejudice. Forever silencing the religion with no name that had refused to die ever since the Stone Age.

From May to June of 1426, the itinerant Franciscan named Bernardino of Siena delivered a series of 114 sermons right here in St. Peter's Square, and across the Eternal City, turning rumors and hearsay about witches and drugs into a policy statement from the Vatican.[39] When Bernardino first alerted the crowd to the "enchantments and witches and spells" that had taken root on Italian soil, the Romans thought he was crazy. But then he threatened to charge anybody who failed to incriminate these ugly heretics with witchcraft themselves. Soon enough many a "dog-faced old woman" (*la vecchia rincagnata*), as Bernardino referred to them, found herself accused and her fate in the balance.[40] The witch hunts that would continue for another three hundred years abruptly came to life.[41] And from the very beginning the evidence is clear that drugs were a primary concern.

In consultation with the Pope, Bernardino decided that only those suspected of the most serious crimes would be brought to justice that summer, which is how the poor *venefica* named Finicella became the first victim in a war against women and their blasphemous pharmacopeia. She reportedly used the magical witches' ointment to transform herself into a cat, sneaking into people's homes at night to "suck the fresh blood" from the sixty-five children she was accused of killing.[42] The active ingredients in the unguent could well have been the magical plants that were later identified by the Pope's physician, Andrés Laguna, including the psychedelic mandrake, which Dioscorides referred to as *Circeium* because of its mythical use by Circe herself.[43] It is connections like this that made Bruno's fabulous tale about Circe and drugs so heretical.

Finicella was strangled to death and burned at the stake on the Campidoglio, the hilltop square designed by Michelangelo. It was a macabre event that "all of Rome went to see."[44] Together with Finicella another unnamed witch was sent up in flames as an exclamation point. Except she wasn't lucky enough to receive the customary strangling in advance. She was burned alive in the opening act of a gendercide that was meant to strike fear into any woman who dared to taste the heretical Eucharist and run with the Greek Mistress. The leading Italian scholar on these matters, Carlo Ginzburg, has observed, "Thanks to the preachings of San Bernardino of Siena, a sect hitherto considered peripheral was discovered in Rome at the very heart of Christianity."[45]

But is it possible this "sect" was there all along, from the Gnostics to the witches? That a psychedelic Eucharist was its deepest secret?

And that it counted Giordano Bruno among its ranks?

After a three-hour lunch break, and an unhurried waltz through the Vatican Museums, God's librarian has to head back to the office. And it's time for me to get ready for my final appointment in the Vatican at the Palazzo del Sant'Uffizio, on the other side of St. Peter's Square, where Bruno was jailed for seven years before his gruesome death.

Before we part ways, I try to summarize the above research and Ruck's master theory for Gianfranco. How psychedelics were the shortcut to enlightenment that founded Western civilization: first in the Eleusinian Mysteries, then in the Dionysian Mysteries. How paleo-Christianity inherited this tradition from the Ancient Greeks, later passing it to the witches of the Middle Ages and Renaissance. And how the Vatican would repeatedly suppress the original, psychedelic Eucharist to rob Christians of the beatific vision—first in Europe, and then around the world after the

Catholic colonization of Africa, Asia, and Latin America. A truly global conspiracy.

The archivist from Piemonte couldn't have spent fifteen years in the Secret Archives and not heard this kind of stuff before. Gianfranco, who has variously accused me of representing the CIA, Mossad, and the Freemasons, responds in Italian, *"Credo che sia una stupidaggine pazzesca."* Which roughly translates: "I think that's crazy-ass stupid."

Exactly what I thought twelve years ago too.

Of course it could all just be a dazzling coincidence that the greatest Renaissance magician who ever lived was born into the same region that lured every witch in Europe to its magical stronghold in Benevento. And that when he wrote of the *veneficii* (drugs) that could be sourced from the Greek witch Circe after a long pilgrimage to obtain the beatific vision, it had nothing to do with the *venefica* (witches) who used visionary drugs to travel in spirit with the Greek Mistress amid "all the delights of the world" in what seemed like a dream. Drugs that the Vatican perceived as a heretical imitation of its own Eucharist, which it specifically convicted both Bruno and the witches of blaspheming. Drugs that were considered so unquestionably superior to the traditional Christian Eucharist, however, that the wizard and his sisters were willing to trade their lives for the "highest and final illumination" that could only be delivered by a homemade Eucharist.

It could also be a coincidence that the man from Nola and the women from Benevento came from the same Campania that Parmenides and all their Greek-speaking ancestors settled in the ancient past. The Campania that was home to more initiates of the Mysteries than perhaps anywhere else in antiquity. And the Campania that was chosen, in the opinion of Peter Kingsley, for the sole purpose of seeding Italy with the Phocaean secret of how to die before you die. A technique of entering the same "cataleptic," death-like trance that Renaissance commentators would later ascribe to the witches who had fallen down "as dead and cold." A technique that survived as a "secret doctrine" for many centuries thereafter, until Greek-speaking Christians started mixing their own Eucharist in the house churches and crypts.

The same initiates who, once evicted from Rome by the Church Fathers, fled to the subterranean tombs and incubation temples of Naples and surrounding Campania for many centuries more to receive "visions of deities during a night's sleep," in the words of Ramsay MacMullen. And that in between all these Gnostics and the witches who followed them a thousand years later were the only group of women in the entire Mediterranean who used their "huge collections of drug remedies" to redefine the very concept of Western medicine at the Medical School of Salerno. The only place in Europe that women could actually study and practice pharmacology.

And it could be a final coincidence that the drugs unearthed in the psychedelic lizard potion from the Villa Vesuvio in the Campania of AD 79 were the very same drugs named by the Pope's drug expert in AD 1554, when Giordano Bruno was only six years old.

Yes, such coincidences are possible.

But I didn't come here for coincidences. I came here for evidence.

Evidence that the Vatican's war against women and drugs was real.

Evidence that has never before escaped this country. Because it was only in recent history made available to snooping eyes like mine. *Very* recent history, by the papal timeline. Where, in the last of the Vatican's archives to surrender its secrets and confess its sins, I'm about to discover that the lizard never went out of style.

17

Our Eyes Have Been Opened

The eyes of the world are trained on the Pope this morning. It's Thursday, February 21, 2019, and the camera crews are already in position. To my right in St. Peter's Square, I spot members of the international media dusting their collars and checking their audio feeds. It's the first day of the Vatican's much-anticipated Protection of Minors summit. Close to two hundred delegates have descended on Rome from across the planet to discuss the biggest scandal facing the Church today. Sex abuse. Because allegations of clergy misconduct are seldom referred to law enforcement, many young victims wind up entering into private settlement agreements with diocesan officials. The cost of which, by some estimates, has approached $2.6 billion since 1950.[1] In May the attorney general of California, Xavier Becerra, will launch the largest ever investigation into the global phenomenon, scrutinizing what he calls "the coverup and the conspiracy of silence at the highest levels."[2] In a recent poll 37 percent of American Catholics have considered leaving the faith because of the crisis.[3]

The future of the Vatican is on the line. But it's not the first time.

I'm standing in the Palazzo del Sant'Uffizio, staring up at the four-story saffron-bricked palace where I've spent all week investigating another conspiracy. Whenever Father Francis and I weren't spelunking through the catacombs, I've been enjoying the sedate reading room in the Archive of the Congregation for the Doctrine of the Faith, scouring the sixteenth- and seventeenth-century trial records of long-dead witches. Day after day I've been collecting whatever clues I could decipher from the challenging Tuscan dialect of the Renaissance manuscripts. With enough patience the details emerged. And the small pieces of an enormous operation snapped into place.

For any of Ruck's scholarship on Christianity to hold water, I've always wanted to see the evidence that might be hidden behind these Vatican walls. Something right here, in the Church's own handwriting, that might remove the reasonable doubt from Ruck's bold theory about a secret chain of heretics that apparently ushered the Ancient Greek legacy of drugs through the Dark Ages. Where Giordano Bruno's records at the Secret Archives came up short, these dusty tomes are telling the real story of the Vatican's life-and-death battle against the women who "represented the most dangerous of all enemies of the human race and the Christian Church." And the Inquisition that made them disappear, once and for all.

"Inquisition" is a loaded term, it's worth noting. The only documents here in Rome would have belonged to the Roman Inquisition, which began in earnest after the launch of Martin Luther's Protestant Reformation in 1517. But that was only one of several Vatican efforts to stamp out dissent over a period of some 650 years. It was preceded by the Medieval Inquisition in 1184, which was followed by the Spanish Inquisition of 1478 to 1834 and the Portuguese Inquisition of 1536 to 1821, whereby the Grand Inquisitors hand-selected by the Pope put thousands to death in Europe and the Catholic colonies of India and the New World, including many Jews, Muslims, Hindus, American Indians, and African slaves who refused to bow to Rome's definition of God.[4] An additional hundred thousand people may have died in prison as a result of torture or maltreatment.[5] It seems each phase of the Inquisition had its favorite targets. But over time there was one especially urgent threat that all the ecclesiastical and state courts would agree was worthy of a concerted attack. The witch.

As a result of this worldwide effort, the paper trail of the witch hunts is scattered in archives from Spain to Portugal to Latin America. The Roman Inquisition did enter the historical record here in Italy, but most of the evidence is housed outside Rome, where regional tribunals kept their own files. Some are in good condition, like the Vatican's archives in Udine, Florence, and Naples.[6] Others were purposely destroyed, like the archiepiscopal

archive in the witch capital of Benevento. To avoid further stoking the anti-
clerical sentiment running rampant during Italy's unification, all the documents were mysteriously spirited away in 1860.[7] If the Vatican realized that
"burning geniuses was bad for public relations," as the scholar Maria Luisa
Ambrosini remarked about the loss of Giordano Bruno's original trial records, imagine the Pope's marketing team trying to explain the persecution
of thousands of innocent Italian grandmothers.

So if I wanted to see any Inquisition records *inside* the Vatican, I had
only one shot. As my confidence man and master archivist, Gianfranco
Armando, advised me last year in the crypt-like cafeteria next to the Secret Archives, I needed to focus on the Archive of the Congregation for the
Doctrine of the Faith. Over the summer of 2018, I turned up a little-known
register published by a team of researchers at Michigan University through
Oxford University Press in 1998, *Vatican Archives: An Inventory and Guide
to Historical Documents of the Holy See*. It is apparently the only English-
language catalogue of the Vatican's full collection. I wish I'd known about
it earlier, but Gianfranco told me the higher-ups are not in the habit of
advertising this particular book to curious Americans. At the time of its release, the so-called "archives of repression" had only recently been opened to
secular scholars, so their contents couldn't even be included. In the ensuing
years the Michigan team would finally be granted access to Bruno's onetime
dungeon in the Sant'Uffizio, the Holy Office. And in 2003 they published
a tiny pamphlet specifically dedicated to all the dirty deeds of the Roman
Inquisition.[8] Bingo!

I spent weeks reviewing their notes on the Sacred Congregation of the
Index, which controlled the Index of Forbidden Books, an inventory of all
the literature that was investigated and banned by the Catholic Church. It
includes the obvious Protestant thinkers like Martin Luther and John Cal-
vin, but also weirdly censors the work of botanists like Otto Brunfels (1488–
1534) and Konrad Gesner (1516–1565).[9] Why would the Vatican be afraid
of plants and herbs, I wonder? As I continued the search for a heretical
Eucharist, however, no real leads emerged. The Vatican never makes things
easy.

I quickly learned that the story of the piecemeal collection in the Holy
Office is just as colorful as Bruno's records in the Secret Archives. Most
of whatever the Inquisitors had stockpiled through 1559 was incinerated

when a riotous crowd torched this palace now in front of me. The depot that would soon detain and torture Bruno was gutted of the documentation that might reveal all the gory details of the Vatican's constant struggle to keep the flock in check. As the witch hunts went on, even more data would evaporate when Napoleon ordered the entire archive carted off to Paris in 1810. During its partial return in 1815, incalculable losses resulted when the "papal agent charged with recovering the material had much of it burned or sold as scrap paper on the dubious ground that the cost of shipping it all back to Rome was too high."[10] Like the 99 percent of classical literature and priceless works of Greco-Roman art that went up in smoke in the fourth and fifth centuries AD, most of the Church's sins vanished without a trace. But not all of them.

There was one rare survivor that eluded Napoleon's henchmen: the *Inquisitio Senensis*. A rare collection of Inquisition files from the Tuscan city of Siena that has been described as "remarkably and exceptionally complete."[11] The whole set was transported from Tuscany to the Holy Office in 1911, making it the only regional archive now sheltered by the Holy See. If there was any evidence about witches and drugs anywhere in the Vatican, it had to be in those 255 volumes covering the sixteenth to eighteenth centuries.

But where to begin? For months I rummaged through every secondary source in the public domain that did a serious treatment of the "archives of repression." Until I finally came across one Italian scholar, Oscar di Simplicio, with an interest in Renaissance witches and their herbal expertise. He was among the first researchers who stormed the thirty-foot drawbridge-looking gate of the Holy Office when it first creaked open, champing at the bit to see what the Vatican had kept classified all these years. He went straight for the *Inquisitio Senensis* and wrote a fabulous book that was only published in Italian in 2000 as *Inquisizione Stregoneria Medicina* (Inquisition Witchcraft Medicine). More leads than I would ever have time to follow up on. So that left only one final hurdle.

Convincing the Vatican to let me in.

Before Pope John Paul II unbolted the archive, the late historian Anne Jacobson Schutte reported a shadowy operation in which "scholarly credentials and even religious affiliation carry less weight than connections."[12] Before he became Pope, Cardinal Joseph Ratzinger was prefect of the Sacred Congregation for the Doctrine of the Faith from 1981 until 2005. Under his watch the "few who obtained special permission to consult Inquisition materials were able to tap some extraordinary sources of influence."[13] All outsiders were hastily turned away. The Vatican being what it is, I wasn't entirely sure that policy had been reversed. So I picked up the phone and sent a note to my friend Gianfranco.

Ever since my first trip to the Secret Archives, we kept in regular contact via WhatsApp. When we weren't discussing the latest clues I'd tracked down, he would keep me updated on his lectures and workshops around Italy. Every day in the week leading to Christmas, he would send me a YouTube clip of the Latin devotional hymns known as the Great Antiphons. In January I'd get a shot of his snow-packed country house in San Michele di Cervasca, back home in the mountains of Piemonte. I'd counter with a pic of my wife and daughters at our winter getaway in Punta del Este, Uruguay. He may not have agreed with Ruck's scholarship, but Gianfranco sure as hell found it entertaining.

I asked him to provide an introduction to his brother librarian of God, Dr. Daniel Ponziani, who runs the Archive of the Congregation for the Doctrine of the Faith. Gianfranco kindly obliged. But I still needed a letter of recommendation from "an ecclesiastical or academic authority." So just as before, Ruck addressed a formal appeal on Boston University letterhead to the director of the archive, Monsignor Alejandro Cifres. It included the garden-variety sentence, "It is our understanding that some of the 255 volumes from the Holy Office of Siena contain rich information about the local history of the Tuscan region." In my cover note to the monsignor and Ponziani about a month earlier, I let them know I was interested in the full set of records from the *Inquisitio Senensis*. Fortunately I didn't have to specify any further than that. Together with a PDF copy of my law school diploma from Georgetown University (which I made sure to highlight as a Jesuit institution), I attached my previously issued credentials from the Secret Archives and the Biblioteca Apostolica Vaticana. One business day later, one of the twelve creaky chairs in the reading room was reserved for a good little Catholic boy with lots of questions.

Stacked one on top of the other, the thick pair of yellowed volumes hit the desk with a thud. Bound in vellum and tied together with what looks like

Renaissance shoelaces, the manuscripts I have been consulting all week match the height of the desktop monitor in front of me. I'm at the end of the long, hardy table under the fluorescent lights that has become my default position in the windowless Sala di Studio. Five other researchers join me in the reading room, hypnotized by their own imposing stacks of centuries-old paper. There is absolute silence. And if you take a minute to look around and stare impolitely as I do, a collective sense of disbelief that we actually made it in here. As if Pope Francis is at any moment going to barge in unannounced, beg our pardon, and put an end to the whole audit.

The outside world might reasonably suppose that the Vatican's worst crimes are sealed off in the Secret Archives. Everybody who has had the privilege to sit where I'm sitting right now, however, must have come to the same undeniable conclusion as me. The real dirt is right here. Yet ironically no one seems to care. Absent from the Archive of the Congregation for the Doctrine of the Faith are the closed-circuit security cameras and nosy library custodians who tracked my every move with Father Francis in the Secret Archives. Gone is the comical back-and-forth with His Excellency Sergio Pagano, the prefect of the Secret Archives, every time I want to run my greasy fingers through an original trial record. On the condition that I limit my request to two volumes at a time, I can peruse whatever I like for as long as I like, under no supervision. The chief archivist, Ponziani, occupies the airy two-story office on the other side of the closed door that separates the Sala di Studio from the rest of the Archive. The stately bald Italian with a charitable smile couldn't be less concerned about what I'm doing in here. Or more accommodating.

Earlier in the week Ponziani gave me a quick tutorial on the computerized database that can only be accessed from within these palace walls. As soon as he left my side, I tore through the "Archivum Inquisitio Senesis" subfolder on SHADES ECCLESIA (Software for Historical Archives Description), using the one thing I would have died for in the Secret Archives, a search engine. The first word I typed into the Vatican's Google was "stregoneria" (witchcraft). Immediately 120 hits came back, with beautiful summaries of the many women who were tried by the Roman Inquisition in Tuscany between 1569 and 1753.

Whose job was it to comb through 255 handwritten bundles like the ones on my desk, each six or seven inches thick, to gather up and reproduce all the charges against all these heretics? But more important, why would they do it? And why do these records even exist? The Vatican could have disposed of them a long time ago.

One by one I clicked through a fraction of the evidence of an extended campaign that would execute at least forty-five thousand witches and torture, imprison, or exile countless more across the world. Within minutes a pattern developed. And one of the Church's more sinister tactics came to light. It wasn't just trying to rid Christendom of folk healers. It was trying to erase a system of knowledge that had survived for centuries in the shadows. What Ruck might call the Secret of Secrets, a tradition of pharmacological expertise for sure, and just maybe the kind of heretical Eucharist I've been trying to fact-check for over a decade. According to the classicist from Massachusetts, the secrets were "passed on by word of mouth from herbalist to apprentice." But more precisely, they were often entrusted from older women to younger women. Because that's the only way such complex recipes and prescriptions, like the over fifty ingredients of the psychedelic lizard potion from the Villa Vesuvio, can really survive. And the only way to eliminate that multigenerational scourge is to round up mothers and daughters.

Victims of a spiritual contest that, until now, have remained anonymous.

Like Angelica di Gherardo and her daughter, Antera, whose trial and interrogation lasted five grueling years from 1583 to 1588. Or Margarita Straccioni and her daughter, Maddalena, from the same period. Another woman, Angela Mancinelli, was condemned with not one but two of her daughters, Livia di Rosato and Meca di Pietro. And then there were Angela di Cesare and her daughter, Camilla. According to the one-page summary on my screen, they were both "imprisoned and tortured" (*carcerate e torturate*) from 1595 to 1596, just a few years before Giordano Bruno himself was burned to death in the Campo de' Fiori across the Tiber.

As I scrolled through page after page of condensed trial records, the list of atrocities went on. In addition to the Roman Inquisition, imagine how many mothers and daughters were seized by the Medieval, Spanish, and Portuguese Inquisitions for centuries across Europe, India, and the New World—casualities whose names *have not* survived against all odds into a convenient database here in the Vatican. But it's not about the body count. In *God's Jury: The Inquisition and the Making of the Modern World*, journalist Cullen Murphy calls overemphasis on the numbers "pointless and distasteful."[14] He compares it to Rudolf Hess, the former commandant of Auschwitz, who, when confronted with a copy of his confession after World War II, scratched out the part where "three million" victims were mentioned and replaced it with "two million." At the end of the day, the one holy catholic and apostolic Church, a global fixture with a universal mandate to spread the love of the Gospels, went on a bloody rampage. However many lives were lost, Cullen focuses on the "deep psychological imprint" of an Inquisition that "levied penalties of some sort on hundreds of thousands of people" and generally affected millions. A campaign in which the "fear and shame instilled by any individual case, even a minor one, rippled outward to affect a wide social circle."[15]

Now *that's* how you kill the religion with no name.

Early in the week it didn't take me long to realize that part of Ruck's theory about a secret chain of heretics was absolutely correct. The Vatican waged a profound psychological war on women. No doubt the witch hunts spilled over into the state courts, and were particularly violent in Protestant jurisdictions like German-speaking Central Europe, England, and Scotland.[16] And no doubt many wizards like Bruno were targeted as well. But the Catholic Church got the ball rolling, and from the very beginning had its sights set on women. Over 150 years after Bernardino of Siena sent the cat lady Finicella to the flames here in Rome in 1426, his people back home in Tuscany were still chasing the same witches, trying to cut the infestation off at the root. The Inquisition files from Siena are clear about that. So unless the Catholic Church can provide documentation of fathers and sons being jailed and tormented with the same ferocity as mothers and daughters, then the evidence for a vicious strategy is sitting right here in the "archives of repression" for anyone to see.

So what about the other part of Ruck's scholarship? Were women really targeted by the Inquisition because they were heirs to a do-it-yourself Eucharist that came from the Gnostics? In its effort to ground the billy-goat flights to the witchcraft capital in Benevento, was the field office in Siena just trying to eradicate all those drugs in the witches' ointment, as documented by the Pope's expert, Andrés Laguna, in 1554? The kind of drugs that may have spiked the Sabbat "wine," as recorded in the previous century? Or the hallucinogens that may have fueled a toad Eucharist like Bilia la Castagna's the century before that?

I have two thick tomes on my desk—with at least *some* of the answers.

And I owe full credit to Oscar di Simplicio for getting me this far. God knows how many months he must have spent in here, hunched over the thirty-fifth volume of the trial proceedings from Siena (or P35 for short), until he stopped in his tracks at page 556. As I crack open the heavy manuscript once more, I read the Inquisitor's handwriting for the hundredth time this week. It's a wine formula from 1640, cooked up by a wizard from a small town in Tuscany called Casole. A witness testifies that this anonymous witch doctor once prescribed a special "white wine" (*vin bianco*) for an old widow who had been cursed. In order to remove the spell, the man orders the wine to be mixed with "betony, rue, dry rose and ivy" (*bettonica, la ruta, rose secche et ellera*). Betony has been described as "the most beloved of the bewitching herbs," so I'm not necessarily surprised to see it floating around the Tuscan countryside. But I *am* shocked by this level of detail in the manuscript.

And I'm particularly taken aback by the mention of ivy. Aside from the grapevine, it is the Dionysian plant par excellence. Why would anyone mix it into their wine? In the first century AD, Dioscorides specifically says that an ivy drink can "alter consciousness" or *tarassousi ten dianoian* (ταράσσουσι τήν διάνοιαν) when taken in higher doses.[17] According to the Greek naturalist Pliny, who identified twenty varieties of the plant, ivy has the power to "derange the mind."[18] And Plutarch said it could "drive out of their senses" anyone who is disposed to "spiritual exaltation," leading to "drunkenness without wine."[19] To absorb its hallucinogenic power, the maenads would apparently "rush straightaway for ivy and tear it to pieces, clutching it in their hands and biting it with their teeth."[20] It is impossible to know if this Tuscan ivy is related to the ancient ivy mentioned by Dioscorides, Pliny, and Plutarch, but it's a very strange clue.

Equally strange is the manuscript's note that this witch doctor had inherited his craft as part of a family tradition that stretched back to a notorious relative a bit west of Casole in Volterra. Her name was Lucretia. Just the kind of Tuscan witch I'm looking for. And just the kind of witch that Giordano Bruno may have crossed paths with on his many travels through Italy. The Inquisition caught up with her in 1590, a decade before Bruno's execution. For reasons that seem to only support Ruck's suspicion about a secret chain of heretics, the Pope's men in Siena put a significant amount of time and energy into taking Lucretia down. By my count, they received testimony from no less than thirty-nine accusers. And in the process, they left a fascinating record of Renaissance pharmacology.

I gently close P35 and slide it toward my fellow researcher on the right. I open the 906-page volume known as P2. Most of the handwriting is ridiculous. A note from a left-handed gastroenterologist might be more legible. But I have Oscar di Simplicio's transcription to guide my way. And fortunately, the information I'm looking for happens to be on some of the more readable pages.

Right off the bat, however, I notice something di Simplicio didn't publish. On the reverse of page 21, there's another formula for an infused "white wine" (*vin bianco*). The recipe calls for the potion to be mixed with "ivy from an olive tree" (*hellera d'ulivo*). I would later receive a PDF copy of the passage on special request from the Vatican, which I sent to Father Francis for a second opinion. He totally agreed with my reading of the sixteenth-century Italian. But neither of us can explain it. Why would Lucretia be mixing the raw madness that is ivy into a potentiated wine?

Things get more interesting as I flip the jaundiced paper to the page 47, where Lucretia is described by one of her accusers as concocting an enhanced "incense" (*incenso*) containing "the herbs of St. Cyriacus and many [other] herbs" (*erba di Santo Ciriaco et di molte erbe*). Once again neither Father Francis nor I can identify the herbs. But if this is St. Cyriacus the Martyr, the patron saint of viticulture, the botanicals take on a mystical quality, since Cyriacus was referred to as the "terror of Hell" for his intimate knowledge of the underworld and demons. What gets my attention a few lines earlier, however, is how Lucretia manages to secure the base of the incense, which she then spikes with her own witchy ingredients. The witness says Lucretia had someone steal the original bundle of incense from the church. And it's not the first time this has happened.

Yet another remarkable detail pops up on page 31 of the P2 manuscript. In pristine penmanship rendered in dark ink, the Inquisitors describe how Lucretia once asked another woman to steal a "consecrated Eucharist" (*ostia sacrata*) from the local priest in Volterra. The witch's reputation preceded her. The manuscript is clear that Lucretia had to use a covert intermediary, since the priest never would have offered the Eucharist to the herbalist herself. Lucretia is then assumed to have doctored the Eucharist for use in her healing magic, love potions, or a possible heretical sacrament. The practice was not uncommon at the time.

In 1320 a letter to the Inquisitors in France from a certain Cardinal William gave full papal permission to hunt down practitioners of the dark arts "who abuse the sacrament of the eucharist or the consecrated host and other sacraments of the Church by using them or things like them in their sorcery."[21] In *Religion and the Decline of Magic*, historian Keith Thomas notes how the Eucharist had become "an object of supernatural potency" in the Renaissance. It was believed capable of everything from curing the blind, to keeping caterpillars out of the garden. The priests fancied themselves white magicians battling black magicians, who would line up in the Church to steal the literal body and blood of Jesus, intending to repurpose it for their own nefarious ends. According to one sixteenth-century commentator, the Eucharist had fallen into the hands of not only witches like Lucretia but also "sorcerers, charmers, enchanters, dreamers, soothsayers, necromancers, conjurers, cross-diggers, devil-raisers, miracle-doers, dogleeches and bawds."[22]

Between the Dionysian ivy wine and the magical herbs, what emerges from this precious manuscript is what Oscar di Simplicio calls the "folk pharmacopeia" of a heretical witch escaping the Inquisition's grasp and passing her knowledge on to her successors, a generation or two in the future. The incredibly specific detail about the stolen Eucharist makes Lucretia a blasphemer of the Church's holiest substance. Just like Bruno. And it puts them both in the same position as the witches who mixed a custom "wine" for the Sabbat, or whipped up a toad Eucharist, for the express purpose of "vilifying the Sacrament of the Eucharist and equally to dishonor it." But no witch is complete without her ointment. So there's one final aspect to the story of Lucretia that I want to confirm with Ponziani.

In an act that would have gotten me tackled by the custodians in the Secret Archives, I pick up the leathery P2 and head for Ponziani's office, just outside the reading room. The first thing I notice is the crucifix of a dying Jesus, pinned high on the wooden paneling in the corner. Just below is a large table covered in green felt, which I'm assuming is for annoying researchers like me. So I plop the bulky volume where Jesus can get a good look. And I open it up to page 47, where the Inquisitors have recorded one very unusual ingredient for Lucretia's "unguent" (*unguento*). Surely she trafficked in the same kind of witches' ointment that was the currency of wise women all over

Italy. From the coastal town of Piombino, Tuscans with Greek names like "Olimpia" and "Artemisia" came to Lucretia seeking relief for ailments both physical and spiritual. One particular woman named "Dionisia" (a female Dionysus) approaches the witch, hoping for a miracle. Lucretia's immediate prescription is to fire up an oil pan, tossing in a bunch of unnamed "herbs" (*erbe*), together with a *lucertole*.

"Dottore Ponziani?" I address the archivist, as he shuffles back into the office from an errand. I point to the faded ink of the four-hundred-year-old paper. "Could you please help me translate this word?"

"*Lucertole . . . lucertole*," he mumbles. "It's a kind of reptile," he starts in Italian, heading for his desktop computer. He googles the animal, and shows me the images for the word he can't translate into English.

"Lizard!" I boom. "Yes, that's what I thought. Any idea why this witch would be cooking up a lizard ointment?"

"Evidently some kind of potion," responds Ponziani, not skipping a beat.

My mind immediately flashes to the psychedelic lizard potion from the Villa Vesuvio. Maybe the unnamed "herbs" in Lucretia's unguent were the black nightshade and henbane identified by Andrés Laguna in 1554 as the secret ingredients of the witches' ointment, along with hemlock and mandrake.[23] Or maybe the opium and cannabis from ancient Pompeii were still popular in Renaissance Tuscany.

As for the lizard itself, the classicist A. D. Nock had a few ideas. Harvard's greatest religious historian of the twentieth century, who postulated the secret "symbols" and "language" that bound together the followers of Dionysus, once wrote an obscure article about lizard magic, which I could only find in hard copy at Harvard's Center for Hellenic Studies in Washington, D.C. Several Ancient Greek authors, he noted, mention the lizard's association with vision. Because the reptile's own blindness could be reversed by "opening its eyes toward the rising Sun," the lizard was thought to restore human sight.[24] There's also an intriguing recipe from the so-called Greek Magical Papyri. If a sorcerer wishes "to make the god appear," they simply drown a lizard in oil.[25] Just as Lucretia did.

From one of the floor-to-ceiling bookshelves that surround us, Ponziani pulls out a thin paperback that is much younger than its neighbors, most of them bound in the same, tawny vellum as P2. It's a copy of the Oscar di Simplicio study that brought me here in the first place. I figured it would have been stacked away on the Index of Forbidden Books. But with this unexpected segue, I decide to let the archivist in on my investigation. Given all my interest in potions, incense, and unguents, Ponziani proceeds to write down another few Italian titles I should add to my library at home. Why he shares this with me, I don't know. But I get the sense that, like Gianfranco, these guys really enjoy a good mystery.

I'm not so sure their bosses agree. Then again, maybe everyone around here is just way more preoccupied with the real scandal of the day. The one the Pope is discussing with the Protection of Minors delegates at this very moment in a last-ditch effort to keep the Church from falling apart at the seams. There's nothing like a global cover-up to get people's attention. Especially when all the prosecutors are staffing up and all the cameras are rolling. Hiding sins in the twenty-first century is a tough game. It was much easier before.

If a few hundred years ago, the Vatican led a global conspiracy to suppress a psychedelic Eucharist, how would anyone ever hear about it?

Back in the fresh air I penetrate the Doric columns into St. Peter's Square and head east for the Tiber. There's only one friend left to see before my flight home. Since I started coming to Rome almost twenty years ago, I always stop by for a quick visit. But I've been too caught up in the catacombs and archives until now. It'll be good to reconnect.

As I cross the Ponte Vittorio Emanuele II, I think about everything I learned at the Archive of the Congregation for the Doctrine of the Faith. Short of taking five years off to page through each of the 255 volumes of the Siena Inquisition by hand, I'm pretty satisfied with the week that took months to plan. At the very least Lucretia's trial shows how anxious the Vatican was about pharmacology. It fought tooth and nail to keep women from acting the part of physician. Lucretia was not welcome in a world where male clerics tried to present themselves as the first line of defense against disease and death. If the use of plants and herbs as natural remedies proliferated and proved successful, everyone would begin to question the white magic of the Eucharist that was supposed to be a cure-all. And with it, the magical God on which the Most Blessed Sacrament depended.

During the Renaissance any drug aside from the Drug of Immortality, the body and blood of Jesus, was immediately suspect. Which is why so many witnesses were asked to describe Lucretia's work with the "ivy," "incense," "unguent," and "many herbs." There was a method to the Inquisitors' madness. By getting her pharmacopeia on the record, the Vatican had damning evidence that Lucretia was cooperating with the Devil, the only possible explanation for abilities that were considered supernatural.[26] Much as the Church tried to convince people otherwise, however, the fame of women like Lucretia seems well deserved from testimony as far off as Elizabethan London in 1593: "she doth more good in one yeere than all these Scripture men will doe so long as they live!"[27]

But there was something else going on with Lucretia. The detail about her underhanded scheme to repurpose the "consecrated Eucharist" is no accident. It points to far higher sorcery and far deeper heresy. In the hands of a renowned witch who knew how to mix Dionysian ivy wine, spike incense with her own magical herbs, and fry up a lizard ointment, the body and blood of Jesus was a weapon. It fits Lucretia into a long line of heretics who specifically blasphemed the Eucharist by offering a dangerous alternative, like the toad Eucharist from the 1300s, the Sabbat "wine" from the 1400s, and the witches' ointment flagged by Andrés Laguna in 1554. And it potentially fits Lucretia into an even longer line of mystics who had been trafficking in a homemade Eucharist ever since the Gnostics.

Could all this be at least part of the reason, largely unstudied by modern historians, why witches "represented the most dangerous of all enemies of the human race and the Christian Church"? What is more threatening to the institutional integrity of the Vatican than a Eucharist that provides a true beatific vision? If Lucretia and her sisters could properly "consecrate" a Eucharist for themselves, what was the point of the priest? And if they could establish a direct pipeline to God, perhaps the way it was always meant to be, what was the point of the Church? Is there really anything more worth defending than the Eucharist?

While I wish the Inquisitors in Siena were as well versed in Dioscorides as Andrés Laguna, they weren't. And while I wish they would just spell out the drugs they were targeting in Tuscany, they couldn't. Is it asking too much for the Vatican to just admit that its placebo Eucharist could never, ever compete with a visionary drug? And that it would do anything to suppress the competition?

Maybe not.

As I enter the Campo de' Fiori I round the white tents hawking flowers of every size and color and grab an outdoor table at il Nolano Bistrot. I order up a local craft beer and a glass of red wine, the two most enchanting beverages in the history of Western civilization. One of them could very well have sparked the Agricultural Revolution over twelve thousand years ago. The other helped the world's biggest religion colonize the planet, bringing Jesus to the New World. Unfortunately that side of the globe already had a Eucharist. Several, actually. And unlike the heretical Eucharist of the Old World, they weren't going anywhere.

I extract a bundle of paper from my brown leather pouch and examine the notes I've been working on for years. Hundreds of books, thousands of journal articles, and endless internet searching all distilled into one page with just a few bullet points. And one lonely phrase scribbled across the top: "The Catholic Church Started the War on Drugs."

In 1629, a couple of decades after the Inquisition managed to contain Lucretia and Giordano Bruno, a local priest named Hernando Ruiz de Alarcón wrote a long manifesto to the Archbishop of Mexico. It was meant as a guide to missionary work among the indigenous Aztec population. In his *Treatise on the Heathen Superstitions: That Today Live Among the Indians Native to This New Spain*, Ruiz de Alarcón analyzes all the pre-Columbian pagan rituals that had to be eliminated in order for the Vatican to harvest fresh souls in the New World. From the very first page none of the savages' godless habits provoke as much disgust as the sacred beverages that contained *ololiuhqui*, peyote, and tobacco. While the latter two are familiar, *ololiuhqui* was likely the most common psychedelic drug used by the Aztecs at the time. In 1960 none other than Albert Hofmann identified the plant as a species of morning glory (*Turbina corymbosa*) containing ergine, the LSD-like alkaloid that is also present in ergot.

Ruiz de Alarcón documents some of its incredible properties. "By drinking it, they consult it like an oracle for everything whatever that they want to know, even those things which are beyond human understanding."[28] As part of their "sorcery" the Aztec witches would also use *ololiuhqui* or peyote to work miraculous cures.[29] "They make themselves esteemed as almost divine," says the man of God. Little did the pagans know that these psychedelic sacraments were all part of the "ancient idolatry and cult of the

Devil."[30] While the Inquisitors may have danced around the issue in the Old World, Ruiz de Alarcón offers meticulous, detailed instructions for seizing the drugs that the locals have learned to conceal from the Roman Catholic Church. From stationing "reliable guards" at the houses of relatives (so they don't tip off the perpetrator), to letting the archbishop know where the Aztecs like to hide their stash ("in some old and dirty pot"), the priest covers all the bases.

But it wouldn't suffice just to raid the homes of the Devil worshippers. Ruiz de Alarcón had to cut off the supply. In one instance he proudly orders the fields to be cleared of "a large quantity of bushes that produce the fruit."[31] In another he torches twenty-four gallons of seed in "a large bonfire made on a day of solemn festival," which he forces all the Aztecs to come out and witness for themselves. With that kind of no-holds-barred approach, the Catholic Church won a fairly decisive victory in the overwhelmingly Catholic Mexico of today, where tens of millions might line up for a placebo Eucharist every Sunday.

But there were holdouts. Two significant holdouts who refused to forfeit their psychedelic sacrament, forever altering the course of history.

First, the American Indian. Over time peyote moved north into the territorial United States, where the Eucharist of the New World retained just as much honor as it had in the Mexico of 1629. Taking a cue from the Vatican, the Protestant missionaries and Washington, D.C., joined forces to take the very first federal action banning the use of a drug. It wasn't opium or cocaine, which were banned by the Pure Food and Drug Act of 1906 and the Harrison Narcotics Tax Act of 1914. It wasn't cannabis, which would remain unregulated until the Marihuana Tax Act of 1937. Yes, they all preceded President Nixon's official War on Drugs of the 1970s as some of the first modern prohibition laws on the planet. And they were all inspired by an American Episcopal bishop named Charles Henry Brent, who formed the so-called Brent Commission in 1901 to combat opium addiction, resulting in the first international drug control treaty in 1912. But none of those substances was the genuine priority of the Christians and the bureaucrats who invented the War on Drugs as a latter-day Inquisition for purely religious reasons. The object of their hunt was peyote.

In an effort to banish the sacrament that was making a comeback on sovereign American Indian land throughout the United States, particularly among the Kiowa and Comanche, the Bureau of Indian Affairs (BIA) issued an instruction to all federal agencies on July 31, 1890, that they "seize and destroy the mescal bean, or any preparation or decoction thereof, wherever found on the reservation."[32] Like a page out of Ruiz de Alarcón's manifesto, the operation was to be "prompt, energetic and persistent" in order "to stamp out" the "evil practice" once and for all. When the peyote cult continued to grow on the reservations, finding new converts, the commissioner of the BIA himself wrote to one of his deputies that the sacrament was "interfering quite seriously with the work of the missionaries."[33] Since 1629 had none of the Vatican's efforts in Mexico meant anything? There was no reasoning with the heathens until they abandoned the old ways.

But the American Indians didn't give up without a fight. Albert Hensley, a member of the Native American Church and the Winnebago Tribe of Nebraska, wrote an impassioned letter in 1908 to the BIA that captures the real origins of the War on Drugs. Which was nothing less than a war on the religion with no name. There were no public health and safety concerns. No issues with quality control or consumer protection. It wasn't an administrative decision. It was an act of spiritual war. Like the Inquisitors in the Old World who predated them, it was Christian missionaries trying to eradicate a homemade Eucharist that actually *worked*. Something that actually gave meaning to Jesus's words about the beatific vision in the Gospel of John: "I am here to give *sight* to the blind. . . . I tell you for certain that you will *see* heaven open and God's angels going up and down." Hensley recorded it this way:

> As you are doubtless aware, the term "Mescal" is a misnomer. The correct name for the plant is "Peyote." . . . We do not call it mescal, neither do we call it peyote. Our favorite term is "Medicine," and to us it is a portion of the body of Christ, even as the communion bread is believed to be a portion of Christ's body by other Christian denominations. We read in the Bible where Christ spoke of a Comforter who was to come. Long ago this Comforter came to the Whites, but it never came to the Indians until it was sent by God in the form of this Holy medicine. We know whereof we speak. We have tasted of God and our eyes have been opened.[34]

And that's how the War on Drugs *actually* begins. Ever since Paul yelled at the Corinthians for consuming a lethal potion, the entire history of Christianity has been one epic battle over the Eucharist. There has always been a right Eucharist and a wrong Eucharist. From the house churches and catacombs of paleo-Christianity, to the Italian graveyards and incubation temples of the Dark Ages, to the Sabbats of the Renaissance, the mystics have always tried to protect *their* version of the Drug of Immortality. And the bureaucrats have always responded with an iron fist: from the Church Fathers, to the Inquisitors, to Hernando Ruiz de Alarcón, to the Protestant missionaries, to the American federal government. When Uncle Sam got involved in 1890, and the international treaties got under way not long thereafter, this story seemed all buttoned up. Even if it took a couple thousand years, the bureaucrats had finally done away with the competition.

But there was a second holdout. The Mazatecs. While Hernando Ruiz de Alarcón was busy complaining about *ololiuhqui*, peyote, and tobacco among the Aztecs, another psychedelic sacrament was hiding out in the mountains, just a bit farther to his south. Who knows how long it had been there. As a matter of fact, were it not for one intrepid ethnomycologist, it's quite possible the "little saints" would be hiding out still. That's what the Mazatec witch Maria Sabina called them. In 1955 she let Gordon Wasson have a taste of the psilocybin mushrooms that dealt the beatific vision in no uncertain terms. Wasson instantly believed he'd cracked the code of the "Ancient Mysteries." And in 1957 he let the whole world in on a prehistoric secret that would have sent the Spanish missionaries into cardiac arrest.

By 1959 the Protestant missionaries among the Mazatecs had heard about Wasson's discovery. And they knew *exactly* what had just been unearthed. In "Mushroom Ritual versus Christianity," published in the journal *Practical Anthropology*, Eunice Pike and Florence Cowan penned the confession I've been trying to extract from the Vatican for years. A simple recognition that finally puts all my work in the Secret Archives and the Archive of the Congregation for the Doctrine of the Faith into perfect context:

> *It would appear that the eating of the mushroom has features in common with the Christian Eucharist, which are a potential source of confusion. During the mushroom ceremony the people all nibble on the*

mushroom at the same time. They make a kind of unit listening to the shaman sing and seeing visions together. In his description Wasson applied the word "agape" to the ceremony, and we have been asked (by outsiders) if the Mazatecos confuse it with the Lord's Supper. Does the eating of the divine mushroom have for the Mazateco a psychological value comparable to that which the Eucharist has for the Christian? What teaching must accompany the introduction of the Lord's Supper to the Mazatecos to prevent the Christians among them from seeking the same experience from the bread and wine that they have formerly gotten from the mushroom—and being disappointed?[35]

Well, exactly.

That disappointment was bound to creep in eventually, wasn't it? The bureaucrats couldn't possibly burn every witch, torch every plant, and throw every Indian or hippie who ever wanted a taste of God into jail, could they?

Pike and Cowan's answer to their own question was to keep the ignorant Mazatecs pounding away at their Bible study. The women instruct their fellow missionaries to have patience, since an understanding of "God's greatness" will rarely occur "after the study of a few brief passages" of Scripture. Instead they say, "It seems to take a considerable amount before a person's eyes are opened."

Round and round we go. Some prefer reading about God. Others prefer *experiencing* God. If you're in the latter camp, like the old friend I came to see in the Campo de' Fiori, then the only way to experience God is to die before you die. And one of the most reliable ways to do that, say the heretics, is with the kind of drugs that reveal the cosmos for what it truly is.

Eternal. Timeless.

Only then might the blind learn to see.

Only then might the mortal become immortal.

Because the initiate will have transcended the very concepts of past, present, and future. Or life and death. Where "every moment is an eternity of its own," as an atheist once described it to me. Why wait for death itself to experience that? If you've experienced it while still alive, even once, then the last moment of your life is a return to something familiar. Practice dying, the philosophers have been telling us for twenty-five hundred years. So that when your time comes, you won't even feel the flames that engulf everything you ever knew. This has happened before, you'll remember. This is not dying.

This is becoming God. The God you've always been.

The God the Vatican would prefer you never hear about.

The God that many, like my friend, had to be killed for. In the hope that, someday, the world might come to its senses. And the bureaucrats would stop fighting the inevitable.

I stand and toast the giant brass statue of Giordano Bruno in the center of the plaza. Today was a good day for the mystics.

Afterword

For now the journey into history's best-kept secrets comes to a close. But a lifetime of work lies ahead. Just when I've had enough of this adventure and am aching for my schedule to get back to normal, I look into my in-box and sense the cold, harsh reality.

This ain't over by a long shot.

The Old World calls. And there's a job to be done.

Because if the real origins of Christianity are to be found in the Greek Mysteries and their sacred pharmacopeia, then more of the hard scientific evidence is just waiting to be unearthed. If it hasn't been already. And the lawyer in me won't quit until that one cup, that one chalice, that one vessel comes to light. That microscopic bit of data from the site of an undeniable Christian ritual that was lost to history. Only to return when the world is in need of something that might finally heal the divide between religion and science, faith and reason. The old identity crisis that has been gnawing at the conscience of Western civilization for close to two thousand years: some days we're Christian, some days we're Greek. But the schizophrenia is getting a little old. We need some medicine.

The beauty of the pagan continuity hypothesis with a psychedelic twist is that it's either right, or it's wrong. The idea that the earliest Christians and a secret chain of heretics inherited a drugged Eucharist from their Greek-speaking and prehistoric ancestors is something very knowable.

Thanks to all the recent advances in archaeobotany and archaeochemistry, and the high-tech laboratory equipment that only gets better with each passing season, evidence of the use of psychedelics among the Stone Age Indo-Europeans, the Ancient Greeks, the paleo-Christians, and even the Renaissance witches is now observable, testable, repeatable, and falsifiable. That's how science works, after all. The residue of intoxicating substances will either continue emerging from future digs, or it won't.

In the preceding pages I've tried to establish the evidence as it exists today, particularly in southern Italy. Because in the early centuries of Christianity, that's where the Greek spiritual presence was strongest. And in Rome, at the upper limits of the Mystery Coast Highway, that's where the early converts to the ancient faith could have easy access to the mystical roots of their foremothers. And where they could hardly avoid the influence of the Phocaeans and the other Greek-speaking initiates who traveled between Velia and the Eternal City, seeding archaic techniques for peeking into the afterlife and cheating death.

Centuries before the birth of Jesus, these hidden hands behind the arc of Western civilization appear to have left the faintest of clues in ancient Iberia. The psychedelic graveyard beer at Mas Castellar de Pontós could very well be the smoking gun that proves Ruck's forty years of scholarship on the Mysteries of Eleusis absolutely correct. Only time will tell. As is, there is plenty of good material for a serious debate. But if we're lucky, Jordi Juan-Tresserras just might discover the original ergot samples stashed away in the archives at the University of Barcelona. Or Enriqueta Pons just might unearth a new vessel at the Greek farm where so much work remains to be done. In many ways the ergot sacrament that once sent the aging professor at Boston University into academic exile is really just the tip of the iceberg. It reopens the file on hallucinogens that archaeologists, classicists, and Biblical scholars have been ignoring for far too long.

As the excavations continue on the world's first temple, at Göbekli Tepe, Martin Zarnkow will be hunting down fresh, undisturbed samples from those huge limestone basins believed to contain traces of humanity's first beer. From what I gathered of our conversation on the rainy outskirts of Munich, he won't be looking only for calcium oxalate, the telltale sign of brewing, but something even more magical. Perhaps the real reason why we abandoned the caves for the cities, in search of the beatific vision of God that made civilization itself possible. If beer really preceded bread an unbelievable twelve thousand years ago, what kind of beer was it?

As in the case of Mas Castellar de Pontós, a scanning electron microscope might reveal the presence of ergot in one of Zarnkow's future samples. Evidence of what the expert referred to as a "controlled contamination" of the mushroom that, properly bioengineered, could produce LSD-like visions. Or maybe gas chromatography-mass spectrometry will detect the chemical signature of some other plant, herb, or fungus that made it into the golden elixir. Together with the initial data from the Raqefet Cave in Israel, such archaeochemical data would not only confirm beer as the catalyst for the Agricultural Revolution, something that has been debated for decades, it would also rewrite the very notion of religion, and what it means to be human.

Did God descend from Heaven in a cup? And was this the kind of technology, the Secret of Secrets, that finally explains the unrivaled success of the many Indo-European languages that are spoken by half the planet today? All of them based on that strange missing tongue that fanned out from the Fertile Crescent, east and west of Anatolia, to transform the hunters and gatherers of the Stone Age into the first farmers of Asia and Europe? Did a psychedelic graveyard beer convince our prehistoric ancestors that their loved ones never disappeared, and there was life beyond death? A few years ago these were absurd questions. Now I hope younger archaeologists will take note of Zarnkow's open-mindedness. And I hope that any time a container of any kind surfaces in the course of any fieldwork across the region, no expense is spared in the exhaustive analysis of its fragile contents.

Fortunately that interdisciplinary mentality is already being adopted on this side of the Atlantic by those who now follow in the footsteps of Patrick McGovern. The Minoan ritual cocktail of beer, wine, and mead that he resurrected from the sixteenth century BC was paired with another stunning find. Beyond the Minoans and Mycenaeans—those Bronze Age ancestors of the classical Greeks—the Anatolians across the Aegean had their own graveyard beer, the psychoactive Midas Touch of the eighth century BC. Both of the potions were identified twenty years ago, when the archaeological chemistry birthed by the Indiana Jones of Extreme Beverages was still in its infancy. Now she's a toddler. And if you listen closely enough, you can hear her stringing words together into sentences. If the rich chemical finds of all the ingredients that were added to the Scorpion I wine jars in Egypt (ca. 3150 BC) and the Tel Kabri wine cellar in Galilee (ca. 1700 BC) say anything, it's that ancient wine was not the wine of today. And the vessels of yesterday are holding on to more secrets than anyone could have suspected a generation ago.

So McGovern's inkling about the "pharmacological properties" of the *kukeon* "certainly exceeding what can be attributed to a high alcohol content" should be taken seriously. Despite looking in earnest, he hasn't yet found the elusive ingredient(s) in or around the homeland of Western civilization. Which leaves two challenges for the likes of Andrew Koh and his dedicated team at the Massachusetts Institute of Technology, some of the best and most pioneering archaeological chemists in the world. Through Koh's brainchild called OpenARCHEM—an open-source, online database and repository that seeks to better integrate archaeological fieldwork and scientific analysis—his team is systematically attacking the irritating gaps in our collective history. And, with enough funding and support, they just might be able to connect the dots.

First, from the kinds of beer that were *possibly* brewed at the Raqefet Cave and Göbekli Tepe in the Stone Age, to the herbal wines that were *definitely* mixed in the Bronze Age. In the eastern Mediterranean there are thousands of years of extreme brewing and wine-making about which we know very little. Over the millennia were prehistoric beer and wine routinely mixed with psychoactive material, as the Scorpion I and Tel Kabri caches suggest? And as wine slowly replaced beer in ceremonial drinking, did a psychedelic grape potion pick up where a psychedelic graveyard beer left off? Did hallucinogenic wine fuel the trance-like states of paralysis that offered access to the underworld for the Canaanites, Phoenicians, Nabataeans, and other Near Eastern mystics in the poorly studied *marzeah* ritual? Was that funerary feast the psychedelic bridge between prehistory and history as we know it, when writing developed among the first high civilizations in Ancient Egypt and Mesopotamia around 3200 BC? Were drugs and visionary experiences the common religious bond between the oral and literate cultures across an unbelievable expanse of time?

Second, Koh and his team could make the conclusive link from the spiked wine of the Bronze Age to the sacramental wine of the Greek and Christian Mysteries in the age of Jesus. Somewhere in Greece or the Greek-speaking parts of the Mediterranean that fell under the spell of Dionysus, I'm willing to bet, is hard botanical and chemical evidence to lend further support to the psychedelic leads that Soultana Valamoti from the Aristotle University of Thessaloniki has already uncovered in bits and pieces. It would both confirm her hunch that drugged wine was used by Ancient Greek shamans "to communicate with spirits, ancestors or gods." And it would firmly establish what our inspection of G 408 and G 409 at the Louvre Museum could not. But what no serious student of the thousand-year tradition connecting Homer to the sophisticated pharmacology of Dioscorides and Galen would, frankly, be even remotely surprised to learn. When Ancient Greek wine was described as a *pharmakon*, maybe that's exactly what it was: an unusually intoxicating, seriously mind-altering, occasionally hallucinogenic, and potentially lethal potion. And maybe Dionysus was not merely the God of Wine, but the God of Psychedelics.

I'm also willing to bet that, sooner than later, hard evidence will emerge from some house church, cemetery, or necropolis in one of those strategic sites where the Greek and Christian Mysteries overlapped in the early centuries after Jesus. It could be one of those locations that has captured my attention for years: Corinth in Greece, Ephesus on the western coast of Turkey, or Scythopolis in Galilee, near the border between Israel and Jordan. Perhaps even Antioch near the Syria-Turkey border, or Alexandria in Egypt. Aside from Rome, they were the two principal centers of Christianity before the rise of Constantinople, and the God of Ecstasy's cult gained a foothold in both.

But in Italy, Dionysus and Persephone, his mother in the Mysteries, were especially loved. And that's where the best clues have emerged thus far. For me the psychedelic lizard potion from the Villa Vesuvio in Pompeii puts the Christian catacombs of Rome and Campania at the top of the target list. Like the *marzeah* during the Bronze Age of the Near East, it's where the *refrigerium* was practiced for centuries to summon the dead back from the grave. And then, with enough exposure to the Greek Mysteries from the Phocaeans and others in Magna Graecia, to meet the Lord of Death and the Queen of the Dead. By the early centuries AD, the phenomenon was already ten thousand years old at the very least, recalling the skull cult of the forgotten clans that once gathered at Göbekli Tepe. Yet another bridge. Not only between prehistory and "history," but between the pagans and the Christians. On the very soil that the Vatican still calls home.

If ever there was a vehicle to marry the Greek and Christian Mysteries, it was the Roman *refrigerium* that Yale scholar Ramsay MacMullen has rigorously documented as a genuine "religion" in no uncertain terms. Where underground, in what the Vatican calls "the most significant assets of the paleo-Christian era," women like Aurelia Prima are seen being initiated into the deepest secrets of the illegal Jesus cult. And where, in fresco after subterranean fresco, priestesses are shown serving a Eucharist of drugged wine (*calda*) in the time-honored funerary feast. If botanical or chemical data of psychedelic wine is going to crop up anywhere, I can't help envisioning it coming from one of the dusty chalices that has been recovered by the Pontifical Commission for Sacred Archaeology. But that no one ever hears about. Because of one predictable obstacle.

The person who controls the Hypogeum of the Aurelii, the Catacombs of Priscilla, and the Catacombs of Saints Marcellinus and Peter is the same person who controls the dozens and dozens of precious catacombs all over Italy, from Tuscany to Sicily. Each of them seething with valuable, empirical evidence just waiting to be unlocked.

The Pope.

I'm not sure he or his team of archaeologists is ever going to green-light an expensive intrusion into their treasure by godless foreign chemists. Chemists with a professional interest in the kind of data that could rewrite the entire history of Christianity by confirming the existence of a visionary Eucharist. A sacrament that, as far as all the circumstantial evidence is concerned, was prepared by women with pharmacological expertise. Like the female Gnostics recorded by the Church Father Hippolytus using a drugged wine in the early third century AD. Wine that Hippolytus described as a *pharmakon* seven times, to make the extent of the heresy crystal clear. These were the same women who were excluded from the priesthood of the institutional Christianity that finally took off in the fourth century AD. And the same women who remain excluded from Church leadership to this day.

Which is why I was so surprised to hear back from Barbara Mazzei, the senior archaeologist who performed the laborious eleven-year restoration at the Hypogeum of the Aurelii. After my last visit to the Vatican in February 2019, I made sure to send a note of gratitude for the guided tour with her colleague, Giovanna. In any event I needed Mazzei's permission to publish all the catacomb photographs that appear in this book, so it gave us a good excuse to keep in touch for a while. A few emails into our correspondence, out on a limb, I asked if the Pontifical Commission for Sacred Archaeology still comes across ancient drinking vessels on their digs, and whether they'd be interested in having them tested. Surely there is scientific merit in chemically determining what the ancient followers of Jesus were consuming during the earliest Christian ceremonies. I even made an unsolicited offer to put her team in touch with Patrick McGovern, Martin Zarnkow, and Andrew Koh.

Many, many weeks passed, as my initial regret at having even sent the email soon evaporated, leaving the bipolar worlds of religion and science happily divorced. Just the way they've been for two thousand years.

Until one day in May, when I awoke to a brief email from Rome, in Italian:

> *Buongiorno Brian,*
>   *I apologize for not replying to the previous email for lack of time. I talked about the project to analyze the deposits of the containers that are in the catacomb with a colleague of mine, Dr. Matteo Braconi, who deals with the catacombs of Tuscany. In recent excavations (2017-2018) they found interesting objects with organic material that could be interesting to analyze. So we would be very pleased to collaborate on this project.*
> *Hope to hear from you soon, best regards,*
> *Barbara Mazzei*

When the shock wore off, I immediately reached out to Braconi. Then waited a month, while the silence crept in, before following up again. Then waited another six months while I finished the licensing process with Barbara Mazzei. By the end of 2019 I had successfully obtained all the legal permissions from the Vatican to publish the fresco images, a feat that was kind of remarkable in and of itself. Because in the meantime I could see from the activity on my LinkedIn and Academia.edu profiles that the Pontifical Commission for Sacred Archaeology was trying to figure out why I was so intrigued by their catacombs. And their wine vessels. I never heard back again.

By the time this book is published, the Vatican will have had every right to continue ignoring my inquiries. I'm not an archaeologist, or archaeochem-

ist. I don't represent any universities or institutions of research. And I have
no business inspecting their property. But there are credentialed scholars
with decades of experience like McGovern, Zarnkow, and Koh, who are
very interested in performing the analysis on Christianity's original sacrament. Which puts the Holy See in an uncomfortable position. In the spirit
of twenty-first-century collaboration, why not simply test the objects that
surfaced in Tuscany? Or, for that matter, any other vessels that are just sitting in undisclosed storage lockers across Italy?

It's anyone's guess how many ancient chalices are in the Vatican's possession. Vessels with long, detailed stories to tell about their use in the earliest
and most authentic versions of the Eucharist in and around Rome. Especially if, unlike the many *kernos* vessels that once held the *kukeon* in Kalliope Papangeli's warehouse in Eleusis, the Pope's containers have never been
treated for conservation purposes. Theoretically any organic residue from
the time of paleo-Christianity could still be intact, no matter when it was
excavated. In the late 1990s, for example, when Patrick McGovern decided
to test the relics of the funerary feast from Gordium, he scored his samples
of the Midas Touch from the University of Pennsylvania's very own archives.
The ritual objects that held traces of the Anatolian drink had been tucked
away for four decades, ever since they were originally collected in Turkey
by Penn archaeologist Rodney Young back in 1957 and transported to Philadelphia. After twenty-seven hundred years, against all odds, the samples
were in immaculate shape.

As this book was going to print, a final surprise proved the durability
of these samples in dramatic fashion. Published in May 2020, the very first
archaeochemical evidence for the ritual use of drugs in the Judeo-Christian
tradition made international headlines. At Tel Arad by the Dead Sea, tetra-
hydrocannabinol (THC), cannabidiol (CBD) and cannabinol (CBN) were
detected by gas chromatography-mass spectroscopy (GC-MS) in a heap of
organic remains that had survived on a limestone altar recovered from a
key shrine. Dating to the eighth century BC, the Tel Arad sanctuary has
been described as a scaled-down version of the Biblical description of King
Solomon's temple, suggesting a "similarity in cultic rituals" between the two.
Having analyzed the residue of the sacred incense, the authors conclude: "It
seems feasible to suggest that the use of cannabis on the Arad altar had a
deliberate psychoactive role." They call this the "first known evidence of [a]

hallucinogenic substance found in the Kingdom of Judah."[1] Interestingly, the altar with the cannabis remains had been excavated in the 1960s, and was just sitting in the Israel Museum in Jerusalem waiting for the right technology to come along.

The point being, this kind of data can survive. And be meticulously analyzed. If the Vatican is willing to cooperate.

What a great opportunity for a religion in the throes of a global sex-abuse crisis, at risk of losing some of the 69 percent of American Catholics who no longer believe in the doctrine of transubstantiation. If the longest-running institution on the planet has $850,000 to spend on a losing campaign to keep cannabis illegal in Massachusetts, then it has the budget to fund archaeochemical research.[2] And the results, whatever they may be, just might win back a flock that is more interested in fact over fiction. For a rising tide of Catholics like me, the placebo Eucharist has become an empty symbol. And John's language about the immortality to be gained by consuming divine flesh and blood, nothing but a fairy tale. These days, no one tastes the Eucharist and sees God. But what if the use of visionary drugs was a reality for small groups of Christians, huddled together in the house churches and catacombs of the ancient Mediterranean for the first three hundred years after Jesus? If Marisa de' Spagnolis' work at the Villa Vesuvio in Pompeii is evidence of anything, it's that the raw ingredients were available. So why not try to prove or disprove the very essence of the faith?

If the scenario sketched in the preceding pages turns out to be true, it would only confirm what we already learned from the discovery of the Gospel of Mary Magdalene in 1896, and the many Gnostic Gospels dug up in Nag Hammadi in 1945.

There was never one monolithic form of Christianity.

From the very beginning there were always competing versions of the faith. And many Christians were undoubtedly drawn to the same experience that hooked the initiates of the Greek Mysteries. The psychedelic trip to the underworld wouldn't have happened in every house church or catacomb, of course. And probably not even the majority. But the Eucharistic ritual of spiked wine could have been performed by a significant portion of the ancient Christian population from Rome to Corinth to Ephesus—a group that some scholars have estimated to be in the "hundreds of thousands" over many centuries.[3] A mystical movement that has been grossly overlooked by secular and religious authorities alike, because of nothing more than a general bias against drugs. And a general lack of the technical expertise, claimed by few aside from Andrew Koh and the team at the Massachusetts Institute of Technology, to really dissect the true botanical and chemical secrets of these ancient sacraments. But it's precisely these sacraments that could finally help explain the secret to Christianity's success in the first three centuries after Jesus.

Ever since the Stone Age, the Drug of Immortality in its many guises served a fundamental role in the development of our species. Not everyone needs a psychedelic pick-me-up to see God. But it beats lying in a cave for days on end. In short order, powerful drugs can make seers of the spiritually blind. They can turn religious idiots into religious savants. They work! Even the conservative German scholar Walter Burkert spoke of the "prehistoric drug rituals" that "through the expansion of consciousness, seemed to guarantee some psychedelic Beyond." As my investigation has proceeded over the past twelve years, the main sticking point became quite apparent. It wasn't *whether* drugs were involved in the religious exercises that preceded the Greek and Christian Mysteries. But when, if at all, they vanished, only to be "forgotten and replaced," as Burkert proposed, "by harmless substances."

The evidence I've presented suggests the drugs of the Upper Paleolithic never went anywhere. They appear to have survived the monopolies of the Near Eastern royal families and Greek hereditary officiants, the crackdown of the Roman senate, the aspersions of Saint Paul, and the united front of the Church Fathers. Until for centuries the Inquisition tenaciously went after the witches, erasing much of the Old World's pharmacological knowledge in the process. And until the Protestants followed suit, with a vengeance. Right on through to the international War on Drugs, which started as a ban on peyote by American missionaries in Indian country during the late nineteenth century, all perfectly modeled on the Vatican's campaign against the psychedelic-loving "heathens" of the New World in Mexico.

If all this is right, then the religion with no name is the oldest continuously functioning spiritual tradition the world has ever known. Twelve thousand years and counting, at the very least. It dwarfs any religion around today. The fact that it survived in the absence of the written word for thousands of years is impressive enough. Matched only by its uncanny ability to morph with the times. But the most amazing feature of this religion is that it simply refuses to die, and can pop up when and where you least expect it. As it did for me in 2007. Because the only reason I ever went down this rabbit hole in the first place was a few paragraphs in *The Economist*: "The God Pill."

Since the moment I read that article about the first modern psilocybin study out of the Johns Hopkins Psychedelic Research Unit, my first instinct hasn't changed a bit.

The religion with no name is back.

With an eye to the past, I've also been keeping one on the future.

Because something unprecedented and extraordinary is taking place.

If you take the time to comb through the fifty peer-reviewed publications on the newly launched website of the Johns Hopkins Center for Psychedelic and Consciousness Research (https://hopkinspsychedelic.org/publications), you'll learn that their proud statistic has remained incredibly stable over the past fifteen years. About 75 percent of the research volunteers consistently rate their one and only dose of psilocybin as either the single most meaningful experience of their entire lives, or among the top five. Lost in all the jargon is an insight you can glimpse only dimly. But when you sit down with William Richards at his home office in Baltimore, or grill Anthony Bossis for hours in New York City, it begins to unfold. And when you speak with someone like Dinah Bazer and listen to the tears well up, it hits you.

These people are having the beatific vision.

When you compare the testimony of the psilocybin volunteers to what little survived from the ancient initiates, it is strikingly similar. If you watch the eight-minute video posted by *The New York Times* following the historic collaboration between Hopkins and NYU in 2016, you might hear patients on the brink of death getting a new lease on life, miraculously freed from all anxiety about their mortality.[4] But what I hear are pilgrims on the long trek home from Eleusis, struggling to make sense of their life-transforming vision. I hear maenads returning from the mountains and forests, in awe of Dionysus. I hear paleo-Christians, suddenly resurrected from the under-world, thanking Jesus for restoring their sight. I hear witches groggily wak-ing up after a night's flight to the walnut tree in Benevento, having spied "all the delights of the world." And if you pay careful attention, you too might hear the impossible—Stone Age hunters and gatherers, convinced of their immortality. Hell-bent on making sure the religion they've just discovered will survive to comfort the countless generations of farmers that wait on the horizon. Farmers who must never abandon their spiritual allies in the plants, herbs, and mushrooms.

The dream would fade, of course. The religion with no name was always under threat. After the invention of writing, the Egyptian pharaohs, the Near Eastern elite, and the noble bloodlines of Eleusis would sequester the religion from the 99 percent. Until Dionysus took it to the wilderness. And then Jesus, in an act punishable by death in the Greek world, went a step further, inviting it into people's dining rooms. But the revolution never lasted. The political and religious authorities always came down hard on the visionaries and their homemade Eucharist. Little by little the "popular outbreak of mysticism" that Alan Watts likened to "setting up a democracy in the kingdom of heaven" was snuffed out.

When I take a step back and examine the psychopharmacologists and clinical psychiatrists at Hopkins and NYU through a historical lens, there's one inescapable thought that jolts a onetime aspiring classicist. And it would have astounded Gordon Wasson or Albert Hofmann, if only they were still around.

By Jove, they've done it! They've caught lightning in a bottle.

The teams at Hopkins and NYU are somehow doing what the Greek and Christian Mysteries were never able to accomplish in antiquity. And what Aldous Huxley prophesied in 1958 would result in a "revival of religion" to outdo all others in the history of the species. Today's scientists have now solved the critical flaws of the religion with no name: safety, reliability, and scalability. Delivering a profound mystical experience in the most cautious way possible, as effectively as possible, to the most number of people possible. The technology is all there: a safe, pharmaceutical-grade hallucinogen and a finely-tuned protocol that maximizes spiritual breakthrough while minimizing risk. These are the "biochemical discoveries" that Huxley predicted would "make it possible for large numbers of men and women to achieve a radical self-transcendence and a deeper understanding of the nature of things."

It all lines up. Except for the elephant in the room.

Outside the laboratory it's all illegal. In the United States and almost everywhere else. So the religion with no name will not be fully reborn until every consenting adult has the opportunity to experience something like what was happening in the Greek and Christian Mysteries, without fear of going to jail. Fortunately the prohibition of naturally occurring psychedelics is coming to an end. But I don't think we're headed back to Woodstock. From what I've picked up from Anthony Bossis in recent years, a more responsible movement is afoot. Something that could truly speak to the practical mystics by the tens of millions in this country, and eventually hundreds of millions around the world. Something that has been many thousands of years in the making. Only a Greek could spot it.

In May 2020, I have my final Zoom to finish off this book. From his home in New York City, Bossis pops onto the screen with a phenomenal salt-and-pepper quarantine beard. He looks like the stunt double for an Orthodox priest.

"So what's next in the age of COVID, Tony? Where is all this headed?"

"Well, at the moment, we have clinical trials occurring at academic medical centers all around the world, including Hopkins, NYU, UCLA, Imperial College London, and Yale. Within five to seven years perhaps, with more good findings, we are hopeful that psilocybin will be the first psychedelic prescription medicine for restricted clinical applications: addiction, PTSD, anxiety, depression, end-of-life distress. But you wouldn't just pick it up for personal use. The prescription would probably be linked to a regulated center, with a licensed team that can administer the drug in a safe, therapeutic setting."

"And then?"

"And then after nationwide FDA rescheduling of psilocybin, I can envision regulated centers all over the country—from fairly secluded to inner-city settings, and everywhere in between. Where one could visit for a week or two. There'd be a regimen of psychotherapy, of course. But there could also be adjunct modalities like mindfulness, meditation, yoga, and healthy cuisine in a comfortable, spa-like setting. There would be one or two psilocybin sessions with well-trained clinical teams. And then you go back home. Just like Eleusis."

I should have expected the comparison from a proud Greek-American whose grandparents emigrated to New York from the island of Limnos in the Aegean Sea. But it still sounds strange coming from a clinical psychologist. When I point out the irony of a Greek scientist on the cusp of resurrecting the original religion of Ancient Greece, Bossis digs around on his desk and pulls out his favorite Einstein quote: "The cosmic religious experience is the strongest and the noblest driving force behind scientific research." By referring to his colleagues as "the high priestesses of the modern era," maybe Bossis is onto something. The whole point of these psilocybin interventions, he concedes, is to trigger the same beatific vision that was reported at Eleusis for millennia. A tradition he knows very well. Because the more robust that mystical experience, the data shows, the greater the magnitude of the clinical change.[5] The clean bill of mental health comes only after a divine signature. As paradigm-changing as these regulated centers could be for those in need, however, what about otherwise "healthy" people? Couldn't we all benefit from the God Pill?

If you asked Albert Hofmann, he would say this is the technology Western civilization has been craving ever since the Mysteries were outlawed in the fourth century AD. Only something of this scale could heal the "alienation from nature and the loss of the experience of being part of the living creation" that he called "the causative reason for ecological devastation and climate change." If you asked the Roman initiate Praetextatus, he might agree. There was something about Eleusis that held "the entire human race together." Without it life has become "unlivable" (*abiotos*), just as he predicted. Would a "popular outbreak of mysticism" be able to heal our lost connection to Mother Nature and each other?

If we all died before we died, maybe we'd all discover the big secret that was known to the initiates of the Mysteries.

We are all God.

"The Son of Man is within you," said the Gospel of Mary Magdalene. But if you don't die now, you might never realize that. You might never understand that Heaven is not what happens when the physical body wastes away. And that there is no afterlife. Because there is no *after*. There's only right here, right now. "The Kingdom of the Father is spread out upon the earth," said the Gospel of Thomas, "and people do not see it." Once you enter into that "state of always being," as Dinah put it, eternity opens up. And with it, the key to immortality. Which for the mystics was never about living forever within the field of time. Just going on and on until the cosmos implodes. It was never about life *after* death. It was always about escaping into the *timelessness* of the infinite present. "There's no beginning or end," said Dinah. "Every moment is an eternity of its own."

How, in one conversation, could an atheist tell me what thirteen years of Catholic school could not? And what the mystics have been saying all along?

The God Pill, of course.

But isn't it all too convenient?

Not according to Alan Watts. In *The Joyous Cosmology: Adventures in the Chemistry of Consciousness*, published in 1962, he wrote: "The reaction of most cultured people to the idea of gaining any deep psychological or philosophical insight through a drug is that it is too simple, too artificial, and even too banal to be seriously considered. A wisdom which can be 'turned on' like the switch of a lamp seems to insult human dignity and degrade us to chemical automata."[6] After his own experiences with mescaline, LSD, and psilocybin, however, Watts could find "no essential difference between the experiences induced, under favorable conditions, by these chemicals and the states of 'cosmic consciousness'" registered in the mystical literature across the ages.

There are real-world benefits to all this supernatural mumbo jumbo. That "science of awe" with its increase in "pro-social behaviours such as kindness, self-sacrifice, co-operation and resource-sharing." After all, it's not about altered *states*, but altered *traits*, as Huston Smith once summarized the value of psychedelics. If we took the God Pill, would we really all become better people? Would we love more and hate less? Would it make any difference?

Only to the extent that the initial experience was sacred. And stayed sacred. Stayed meaningful. The Mysteries had a way of ritually ensuring the odds of that transformation from the mortal to the immortal: various stages of initiation, intense psychological preparation, a community of mentors, integration back into everyday life. The Mysteries were a machine for the making of gods and goddesses. It all disappeared with the rise of institutionalized Christianity. But I can see them coming back. And in the Reformation to end all Reformations, I can finally see my own identity crisis coming to a nice resolution.

Strange as it sounds after all this, I still consider myself a Christian. The Classics may have saved my life with a free ticket to the Ivy League and the legal profession. But not a day goes by that I don't think about the Jesuits who made it all possible. Their gift of Latin and Greek has led me to question everything about the history of Christianity. Which I'm sure wasn't the intention. But in my search for the roots of the world's biggest religion, I'd like to think I've done them proud. And I'd like to think the first Jesuit to ever lead the Catholic Church might appreciate this existential quest. Like all the spiritual mentors from my youth, Pope Francis is a warm, open-minded intellectual. In April 2020, after the previous attempt failed, he created a new commission to examine the possibility of women becoming deacons. It wouldn't give women the authority to consecrate the Eucharist, but it's a step in the right direction. I have another in mind.

For the first time in the history of the Church, the administration of the Eucharist has been suspended on a global scale. At a time when COVID-19 is forcing us to rethink everything, I think it's time to rethink the Eucharist. When I contemplate the Last Supper, and the earliest and most authentic celebrations of the Eucharist, I see one obvious theme that disappeared long ago. I see very small groups of people gathered at home. I see micro-churches. And as the initial evidence from Mas Castellar de Pontós and the Villa Vesuvio suggests, I see home brews and house wines that may have found their way into paleo-Christianity. We may never know what happened at the Last Supper, but we can now sense how the Greek speakers in the house churches and catacombs of the ancient Mediterranean interpreted it. The Mysteries had been domesticated. Well, I think the time has come to domesticate them once again.

As long as Bossis is resurrecting the Mysteries and putting all the architecture in place, I'll suggest that his regulated retreat centers and trained personnel be made available for any curious soul in search of the beatific vision. For anybody who ever wondered about the mystery of life and death, those house churches of the future could serve as the new chapels of the religion with no name. Not fun and games. As Alan Watts once said of the psychedelic initiation: "Get the message, and hang up." Ideally, you would be allowed only one visit sometime after the age of twenty-five, following an intense period of emotional and psychological preparation. The data shows that about 75 percent would leave the FDA-approved house church permanently transformed. And ready to begin a lifelong spiritual journey that could, once again, make life livable on this planet. This should begin happening by 2030, if not sooner.

In the meantime, I'm going back to the original micro-church.

On the road from Barcelona to Girona in February 2019, about to in-spect the miniature chalice that tested positive for the ergot sacrament at Mas Castellar de Pontós, I asked Ruck if it all made sense. Did he want to bring the religion with no name back into the twenty-first century?

"I hesitate, because it makes you into a campaigner. A religious prophet. Oh God, no! Let's not have any more religions."

So later on we made a pact. An agreement among fellow Catholic boys. Let's not reinvent the wheel. When the smoking gun emerges, proving be-yond any reasonable doubt that the original Eucharist was, in fact, psyche-delic, we're going to book the first flight to Rome. We're going to bust Father Francis out of his laboratory to the south. And we're all going to drink a chalice of psychedelic wine in the City of the Dead underneath St. Peter's Basilica. As it was in the beginning. With a few nuns handling the blood of Christ.

The first psychedelic experience for me and Father Francis.

Ruck's last of many.

And we're going to insist that the Pope join us.

Notes

Introduction: A New Reformation

1 S. Ross et al., "Rapid and sustained symptom reduction following psilocybin treatment for anxiety and depression in patients with life-threatening cancer: a randomized controlled trial," *Journal of Psychopharmacology*, vol. 30, no. 12 (December 2016): 1165–80, doi:10.1177/0269881116675512.

2 R. Griffiths et al., "Psilocybin produces substantial and sustained decreases in depression and anxiety in patients with life-threatening cancer: A randomized double-blind trial," *Journal of Psychopharmacology*, vol. 30, no. 12 (December 2016): 1181–97, doi:10.1177/0269881116675513.

3 "The science of psilocybin and its use to relieve suffering," https://www.youtube.com/watch?v=81-v8ePXPd4.

4 William Richards, *Sacred Knowledge: Psychedelics and Religious Experiences* (New York: Columbia University Press, 2015), 5.

5 See https://hopkinspsychedelic.org/.

6 "The science of psilocybin."

7 Richards, *Sacred Knowledge*, 4.

8 Ibid., 46.

9 A. Singer et al., "Symptom trends in the last year of life from 1998 to 2010: a cohort study," *Annals of Internal Medicine*, vol. 162, no. 3 (February 3, 2015): 175–83, doi: 10.7326/M13-1609.

10 Ashleigh Garrison, "Medicare's most indefensible fraud hotspot: Hospice care" (CNBC, August 2, 2018), www.cnbc.com/2018/08/02/medicares-most-despicable-indefensible-fraud-hotspot-hospice-care.html.

11 "Transcendence Through Psilocybin | Anthony Bossis, PhD" (YouTube, 2018), https://www.youtube.com/watch?v=jCf3h-F7apM.

12 Richards, *Sacred Knowledge*, 60–61.

13 See C. Chiron et al., "The right brain hemisphere is dominant in human infants," *Brain*, vol. 120, no. 6 (June 1997): 1057–65, doi:10.1093/brain/120.6.1057; Vinod Goel et al.,

"Asymmetrical involvement of frontal lobes in social reasoning," *Brain,* vol. 127, no. 4 (April 2004): 783–90, doi:10.1093/brain/awh086; Leonardo C. de Souza et al., "Frontal lobe neurology and the creative mind," *Frontiers in Psychology,* vol. 5, no. 761 (July 23, 2014), doi:10.3389/fpsyg.2014.00761.

14 See "'Nones' on the Rise" (Pew Research Center, October 9, 2012), http://pewrsr.ch/14gdLju. See also "Religiously Unaffiliated" (Pew Research Center, December 18, 2012), http://pewrsr .ch/13srrSd; and British Social Attitudes Report, 36th ed. (National Centre for Social Research, 2019), www.bsa.natcen.ac.uk/latest-report/british-social-attitudes-36/religion.aspx.

15 Gregory A. Smith et al., "In U.S., Decline of Christianity Continues at Rapid Pace" (Pew Research Center, October 17, 2019), https://pewrsr.ch/33zq8Hc. See also Richard Fry, "Millennials projected to overtake Baby Boomers as America's largest generation" (Pew Research Center, March 1, 2018), http://pewrsr.ch/2FgVPwv.

16 Michael Lipka and Claire Gecewicz, "More Americans now say they're spiritual but not religious" (Pew Research Center, September 6, 2017), http://pewrsr.ch/2xP0Y8w.

17 Michael Lipka, "Millennials increasingly are driving growth of 'nones'" (Pew Research Center, May 12, 2015), http://pewrsr.ch/1H1yXH3.

18 Richard A. Shweder, *Thinking Through Cultures: Expeditions in Cultural Psychology* (Cambridge, MA: Harvard University Press, 1991), 68.

19 Ahmad Shameem, *The Fascinating Story of Muhammad* (Bloomington, IN: AuthorHouse, 2014), 11.

20 "The Monk and the Rabbi—Mysticism & the Peak Experience," https://www.youtube. com/watch?v=4egjKZe4wJs.

21 David Steindl-Rast, "The Mystical Core of Organized Religion," *New Realities,* vol. X, no. 4 (March/April 1990): 35–37, https://gratefulness.org/resource/dsr-mystical-core-religion/.

22 Robert Frager and James Fadiman, eds., *Essential Sufism* (San Francisco: HarperOne, 1999), 251.

23 Ibid., 249.

24 Ibid., 244. See also Jane Ciabattari, "Why is Rumi the best-selling poet in the US?" (BBC.com, October 21, 2014), www.bbc.com/culture/story/20140414-americas-best-selling-poet.

25 Rabbi Lawrence Kushner, *The River of Light: Spirituality, Judaism, Consciousness* (Woodstock, VT: Longhill Partners, 1990), 131.

26 Ibid.

27 Reza Shah-Kazemi, *Paths to Transcendence: According to Shankara, Ibn Arabi & Meister Eckhart* (Bloomington, IN: World Wisdom, 2006), 151.

28 Ibid., 156–59.

29 Aldous Huxley, *The Doors of Perception & Heaven and Hell* (New York: Harper Perennial Modern Classics, 2004), 26.

30 Ibid., 70.

31 Aldous Huxley, "Drugs That Shape Men's Minds," *Saturday Evening Post,* October 18, 1958, available at www.hofmann.org/papers/drugstsmms.htm.

32 Alan Watts, *The Joyous Cosmology: Adventures in the Chemistry of Consciousness* (Novato, CA: New World Library, 2013), 108–09.

33 Robert Tann, "A look inside Denver's International Church of Cannabis," *CU Independent,* April 18, 2019, https://cuindependent.com/2019/04/18/inside-denvers-international -church-of-cannabis/.

34 David Roach, "How Erasmus' Greek NT changed history," *Western Recorder,* March 22, 2016, http://westernrecorder.org/825.article.

35 Huxley, *Doors of Perception,* 71.

36 Victor David Hanson and John Heath, *Who Killed Homer?: The Demise of Classical Education and the Recovery of Greek Wisdom* (New York: Encounter Books, 2001), xxiii.

37 Ibid., xxii.

38 Ibid., 11.

39 Demetrios J. Constantelos, "Thomas Jefferson and His Philhellenism," *Journal of Modern Hellenism*, nos. 12–13 (1995–96): 156.

40 Ibid., 160.

41 "Classical Heroes & Villains of the Founders" https://www.youtube.com/watch?v=FbW 20OhpGDo.

42 Hanson and Heath, *Who Killed Homer?*, 12.

43 Ibid., 16, 19.

44 Ibid., 83.

45 Ibid., 84.

46 Hanson and Heath have received no shortage of criticism for their blunt take on this phenomenon, melodrama and all. But there's no arguing with the numbers. Between 1971 and 1991, the number of Classics majors fell by about 30 percent. There were over a million bachelor's degrees awarded in 1994; only 600 were for the Classics. That's .06 percent. A few centuries ago, it was closer to 100 percent. Between 2009 and 2013, enrollments in Ancient Greek plunged a whopping 35 percent, from 20,040 to 12,917 students. The bottom of the barrel, this was by far the biggest swing of all fifteen languages surveyed by the Modern Language Association (MLA) in its 2016 comprehensive report on language programs at American universities. For comparison, 712,240 students were majoring in Spanish at the last count. And enrollments in Korean, Chinese, and American Sign Language were on the rise. See www.mla.org/content/download/83540/2197676/2016-Enrollments-Short-Report.pdf, 27.

47 Hanson and Heath, *Who Killed Homer?*, xxi.

48 "The God pill: Hallucinogens induce lasting spiritual highs in the religious," *Economist*, July 13, 2006, www.economist.com/science-and-technology/2006/07/13/the-god-pill.

Chapter 1: Identity Crisis

1 George E. Mylonas, *Eleusis and the Eleusinian Mysteries* (Elefsina, Greece: Cyceon Tales, 2009), 12.

2 Carl Kerenyi, *Eleusis: Archetypal Image of Mother and Daughter* (Princeton, NJ: Princeton University Press, 1967), 20–21. Kerenyi sees initial evidence for the cult between 1580 and 1500 BC, based on the excavations by Mylonas. See George E. Mylonas, "Excavations at Eleusis, 1932 Preliminary Report," *American Journal of Archaeology*, vol. 37, no. 2 (April–June 1933): 271–86. See also Walter Burkert, *Greek Religion* (Cambridge, MA: Harvard University Press, 1985), 285: "According to Diodorus, it was the great age and the untouchable purity of the cult that constituted its special fame. The unique position of Athens in Greek literature and philosophy made this fame spread everywhere." Hugh Bowden, *Mystery Cults of the Ancient World* (Princeton, NJ: Princeton University Press, 2010), 26: "The Eleusinian Mysteries were the most revered of all ancient mystery cults."

3 See Aristotle, *Fragmenta*, ed. Valentini Rose, fr. 15. See also Regis Laurent, *An Introduction to Aristotle's Metaphysics of Time* (Paris: Villegagnons-Plaisance Editions, 2015), 122: "The initiatory rites push conceptual knowledge into the background in favour of iconic visions that lead citizens to suspend their judgments in favour of revelations that need no explanation."

4 Kerenyi, *Eleusis: Archetypal Image*, 12.

5 Ibid.

6 D. C. A. Hillman, *The Chemical Muse: Drug Use and the Roots of Western Civilization* (New York: Thomas Dunne Books, 2008), 11, 32.

7 Ibid., 19.

8 Thucydides, *History of the Peloponnesian War,* Book 6, 61.

9 Plato, *Phaedo,* 250b–c.

10 Homer, *Odyssey,* Book 11.489–490, as translated by Samuel Butler.

11 Hē En Athēnais Archaiologikē Hetaireia ed., *Ephēmeris archaiologikē,* 1883 (Athens: Carl Beck, 1884), 81, available at https://digi.ub.uni-heidelberg.de/diglit/ephemarch1883/0058/image.

12 Pindar, fragment 137, in *Nemean Odes, Isthmian Odes, Fragments.,* ed. and trans. William H. Race, Loeb Classical Library 485 (Cambridge, MA: Harvard University Press, 1997), 384–85.

13 Sophocles, fragment 837, in A. C. Pearson, ed., *The Fragments of Sophocles, edited with additional notes from the papers of Sir R.C. Jebb and W.G. Headlam* (Cambridge: 1917).

14 See Crinagoras, *Greek Anthology,* 11.42. In the first century BC the Greek ambassador to Rome from 45 to 26 BC had this to say: "Even if yours has always been a sedentary life, and you have never sailed the sea, nor walked the roads of the land, you should nevertheless go to Attica, so that you may witness those nights of the festival of great Demeter. For then your heart may be free of care while you live, and lighter when you go to the land of the dead." See also Pausanias, *Description of Greece,* 5.10.1: "Many are the sights to be seen in Greece and many are the wonders to be heard, but on nothing does heaven bestow more care than on the Eleusinian rites."

15 Marvin Meyer, ed., *The Ancient Mysteries: A Sourcebook of Sacred Texts,* (Philadelphia: University of Pennsylvania Press, 1999), 8. See Apuleius, *Metamorphoses,* 11.23: "I approached the boundary of death and treading on Persephone's threshold, I was carried through all the elements, after which I returned. At the dead of night I saw the sun flashing with bright effulgence. I approached close to the gods above and the gods below and worshipped them face to face."

16 M. Tullius Cicero, *De Legibus,* ed. Georges de Plinval, Book 2.14.36: *"Nam mihi cum multa eximia divinaque videntur Athenae tuae peperisse atque in vitam hominum attulisse, tum nihil melius illis mysteriis, quibus ex agresti immanique vita exculti ad humanitatem et mitigati sumus, initiaque ut appellantur, ita re vera principia vitae cognovimus; neque solum cum laetitia vivendi rationem accepimus, sed etiam cum spe meliore moriendi."*

17 Mylonas, *Eleusis and the Eleusinian Mysteries,* 161–62.

18 Kerenyi, *Eleusis: Archetypal Image,* 48. Here Kerenyi explains that by the middle of the fifth century BC, the noble families who administered the Eleusinian Mysteries felt the "secret ceremonies" at Agrai, which took place in February just outside the walls of Athens, "constituted a necessary preparation for their own rites. It has also come down to us that these mysteries—and this is never said expressly of the Eleusinian Mysteries—served the purpose of *instruction,* which would imply preparation for what was to occur later at Eleusis. The progression from Agrai to Eleusis developed into a strict religious law." Thus guidance and mentorship at the hands of a so-called mystagogue could have occurred from February of a given year until September of the following year—an eighteen-month process of initiation into the full secrets of Eleusis.

19 Ken Dowden, "Grades in the Eleusinian Mysteries," *Revue de l'histoire des religions,* vol. 197, no. 4 (1980): 426. Dowden argues that the prospective initiate would have participated in the sacred dances and performances outside the *telesterion* on their first pilgrimage to Eleusis. In this way "the *mystai* would be deeply affected and something of

the attraction of Eleusis might be understood." Following this ritual excitement, only the *epoptai* "would be allowed entrance to the vision in the Telesterion." In Dowden's opinion, the term "Lesser Mysteries" might refer to the initial visit to Eleusis rather than the rites at Agrai, with the Greater Mysteries being used to refer to the advanced initiation guaranteed to the *epoptai* alone. That would still entail a full year of initiation.

20 Mylonas, *Eleusis and the Eleusinian Mysteries,* 161–62.

21 Catherine Nixey, *The Darkening Age: The Christian Destruction of the Classical World* (New York: Houghton Mifflin Harcourt, 2018), xxvii–xxix. See also Troels Myrup Kristensen, *Making and Breaking the Gods: Christian Responses to Pagan Sculpture in Late Antiquity,* Aarhus Studies in Mediterranean Antiquity (Aarus, DK: Aarhus University Press, 2013).

22 Nixey, *Darkening Age,* 221.

23 Reginald Horsman, *Race and Manifest Destiny: the Origins of American Racial Anglo-Saxonism* (Cambridge, MA: Harvard University Press, 1981), 2.

24 William C. Allen, *History of the United States Capitol* (Honolulu: University Press of the Pacific, 2005), 19: "The dome and portico were both reminiscent of the great Roman temple known as the Pantheon built in the second century A.D. by the emperor Hadrian. Thornton's adaptation of the Pantheon for his United States Capitol linked the new republic to the classical world and to its ideas of civic virtue and self-government."

25 According to the National Park Service: "The individual responsible for this design was architect Henry Bacon who modeled the memorial after the Greek temple known as the Parthenon. Bacon felt that a memorial to a man who defended democracy, should be based on a structure found in the birthplace of democracy." Available at www.nps.gov/linc /learn/historyculture/lincoln-memorial-design-and-symbolism.htm.

26 Robert Grudin, "Humanism," *Encyclopedia Britannica,* last updated Nov. 29, 2019, www .britannica.com/topic/humanism.

27 *International Bulletin of Missionary Research,* vol. 39, no. 1 (January 2015): 28–29: www .internationalbulletin.org/issues/2015-01/2015-01-029-table.html.

Chapter 2: Fall from Grace

1 P. Walcott et al., "Brief reviews," *Greece and Rome,* vol. 26, no. 1 (1979): 104.

2 "President Nixon Declares Drug Abuse 'Public Enemy Number One'" (YouTube, 2016), https://youtu.be/y8TGLLQlD9M.

3 Laura Mansnerus, "Timothy Leary, Pied Piper of Psychedelic 60s, Dies at 75," *New York Times,* June 1, 1996, www.nytimes.com/1996/06/01/us/timothy-leary-pied-piper-of -psychedelic-60-s-dies-at-75.html.

4 Leigh A. Henderson and William J. Glass, *LSD: Still With Us After All These Years* (San Francisco: Jossey-Bass, 1998), 4.

5 Ibid., 69.

6 R. Gordon Wasson, "Seeking the Magic Mushroom", *Life,* May 13, 1957, available at www .psychedelic-library.org/lifep6.htm.

7 Michael Pollan, *How to Change Your Mind* (New York: Penguin Press, 2018), 113. See also Stephen Siff, *Acid Hype: American News Media and the Psychedelic Experience* (Champaign, IL: University of Illinois Press, 2015).

8 Benjamin Feinberg, *The Devil's Book of Culture: History, Mushrooms, and Caves in Southern Mexico* (Austin: University of Texas Press, 2003), 151.

9 Percy Gardner, *New Chapters in Greek History* (London: John Murray, 1892), 394, available at https://archive.org/stream/newchaptersingr01gardgoog.

10 Jane Ellen Harrison, *Prolegomena to the Study of Greek Religion* (Cambridge, UK: Cambridge University Press, 1908), 162, available at https://archive.org/stream/prolegomenatostu00harr.

11 Ibid., 83.

12 Ibid., 453.

13 R. Gordon Wasson, Albert Hofmann, and Carl A. P. Ruck, *The Road to Eleusis: Unveiling the Secret of the Mysteries* (Berkeley, CA: North Atlantic Books, 2008), 82.

14 Ibid., 74.

15 Dieter Hagenbach and Lucius Werthmüller, "Turn On, Tune In, Drop Out—and Accidentally Discover LSD," *Scientific American*, May 17, 2013, www.scientificamerican.com/article/lsd-finds-its-discoverer/?amp.

16 Wasson, Hofmann, and Ruck, *Road to Eleusis*, 37.

17 Ibid., 42.

18 Ibid., 44.

19 John R. Silber, *Straight Shooting: What's Wrong with America and How to Fix It* (New York: HarperCollins, 1989).

20 Wasson, Hofmann, and Ruck, *Road to Eleusis*, 61.

21 Bowden, *Mystery Cults*, 43.

22 See www.bu.edu/classics/files/2011/01/CV_Ruck913_web.pdf.

23 Harrison, *Prolegomena*, 151.

24 Geoffrey W. Bromiley, *The International Standard Bible Encyclopedia* (Grand Rapids, MI: Wm. B. Eerdmans Publishing, 1979), 281.

25 Roy J. Deferrari, "The Classics and the Greek Writers of the Early Church: Saint Basil," *Classical Journal*, vol. 13, no. 8 (May 1918): 579–91 at 588.

26 Victor David Hanson and John Heath, *Who Killed Homer?: The Demise of Classical Education and the Recovery of Greek Wisdom* (New York: Encounter Books, 2001), 14.

27 Ibid., 15.

28 Ibid., 18.

29 See "Psilocybin Studies: In Progress," available from the Multidisciplinary Association for Psychedelic Studies (MAPS) at https://maps.org/other-psychedelic-research/211-psilocybin-research/psilocybin-studies-in-progress/research/psilo/passiepsilocybin1.html.

30 Ryan O'Hare, "Imperial launches world's first Centre for Psychedelics Research" (Imperial College London, April 26, 2019), www.imperial.ac.uk/news/190994/imperial-launches-worlds-first-centre-psychedelics/.

Chapter 3: Barley Meal and Laurel Leaves

1 See www.theacropolismuseum.gr/en/content/eleusis-great-mysteries.

2 Catherine Nixey, *The Darkening Age: the Christian Destruction of the Classical World* (New York: Houghton Mifflin Harcourt, 2018), 93.

3 Ibid., 94.

4 Ibid., 141.

5 J. Hahn, "The Conversion of Cult Statues: The Destruction of the Serapeum 392 AD and the Transformation of Alexandria into the 'Christ-Loving' City," in *From Temple to*

Church: Destruction and Renewal of Local Cultic Topography in Late Antiquity, ed. J. Hahn et al. (Boston: Brill, 2008), 356–57.

6   Ibid.

7   Mubaraz Ahmed, "Why Does Isis Destroy Historic Sites?" (Tony Blair Institute for Global Change, September 1, 2015), https://institute.global/insight/co-existence/why-does-isis-destroy-historic-sites.

8   My favorite is from *Ion,* 1074 ff., which Ruck interprets as a psychedelically induced, kaleidoscopic vision: "when the starry sky of Zeus also joins in the dance, and the moon dances, and the fifty daughters of Nereus, in the sea and the swirls of ever-flowing rivers, celebrating in their dance the maiden with golden crown [Persephone] and her revered mother [Demeter]." Ruck questions why the stars and moon would start "dancing" or *choreuei* (χορεύει), and how anyone could possibly notice such a spectacle in the sky if the temple in Eleusis had a roof on it.

9   Rudolf Blum, *Kallimachos: The Alexandrian library and the origins of bibliography* (Madison, WI: University of Wisconsin Press, 1991), with the original German of *Kallimachos und die Literaturverzeichnung bei den Griechen: Untersuchungen zur Geschichte der Biobibliographie* (Frankfurt: Buchhändler-Verein GmbH, 1977), translated by Hans H. Wellisch, 8: "The small nation of the Greeks was immensely productive in art and scholarship. Although it is impossible to ascertain the total number of all works written by Greek authors, there were certainly many more than those that have been preserved or are merely known to have existed. . . . Of the Greek literature created before 250 B.C. we have only a small, even though very valuable, part. We do not even have the complete works of those authors who were included in the lists of classics compiled by the Alexandrian philologists. Of all the works of pagan Greek literature perhaps only one percent has come down to us. All others were in part already forgotten by the third century A.D., in part they perished later, either because they were not deemed worthy to be copied when a new book form, the bound book (codex), supplanted the traditional scroll in the fourth century A.D., or because they belonged to 'undesirable literature' in the opinion of certain Christian groups."

10 Ezra Pound, "Hugh Selwyn Mauberley," in Lawrence Rainey, ed., *Modernism: An Anthology* (Malden, MA: Blackwell, 2005), 51.

11 Email correspondence with Fritz Graf, July 27, 2018.

12 Walter Burkert, *Greek Religion* (Cambridge, MA: Harvard University Press, 1985), 116.

13 Ibid.

14 Ibid.

15 William J. Broad, "For Delphic Oracle, Fumes and Visions," *New York Times,* March 19, 2002, www.nytimes.com/2002/03/19/science/for-delphic-oracle-fumes-and-visions.html.

16 Ibid.

17 Ibid.

18 Ibid.

19 Plutarch, "The Oracles at Delphi," 6 / 397A; Aeschylus, *The Libation Bearers,* 1035–37. For a possible influence on Burkert, see T. K. Oesterreich, *Posssession, Demoniacal and Other, Among Primitive Races, in Antiquity, the Middle Ages and Modern Times* (London: Kegan Paul, Trench, Trübner & Co., 1930), 319, https://archive.org/details/possessiondemoni031669mbp: "Of the effect produced by the mastication of laurel-leaves there is nothing circumstantial to be said. It was a customary practice on the part of all seers." In footnote 3, Oesterreich briefly details his own self-experimentation, without necessarily explaining why he chose a Swiss resort at the base of the Alps as his test site: "I made at Locarno experiments in chewing fresh laurel-leaves, but without results of any

interest." See also H. V. Harissis, "A bittersweet story: the true nature of the laurel of the Oracle of Delphi," *Perspectives in Biology and Medicine,* vol. 57, no. 3 (Summer 2014): 351–60, doi: 10.1353/pbm.2014.0032, where the actual identification of the ancient "laurel" has been convincingly argued to be *Nerium oleander.*

20 Burkert, *Greek Religion,* 115.

21 D. C. A. Hillman, *The Chemical Muse: Drug Use and the Roots of Western Civilization* (New York: Thomas Dunne Books, 2008), 42.

22 Hillman kindly shared an unpublished article with the author: "Shattering the Victorian Lens of Classical History with Pharmaceutical Precision," in which he adds: "Galen composed works on anatomy, physiology, humoral pathology, disease, and pharmacy. The Oxford Greek Lexicon itself relies most heavily upon Galen's insanely prolific Greek to define common Classical Greek words as well as an army of technical terms associated with medicine and philosophy. The first volume of the standard modern edition of Galen—the Kuhn edition—was published in 1822. Modern Classicists tend to focus not on the translation of Galen, but on the history of his profound influence. The Kuhn edition of Galen is composed of 22 volumes of over a thousand pages in each volume. Considering that half of Kuhn's Galen is a Latin translation—and a notoriously bad one at that—it is fair to say that Classicists possess over 10,000 pages of untranslated sources. Why don't they get to work? Because they can not; nor do they want to make sense of thousands of pages of thousands of drugs, drug compounds, drug theory, and drug use."

23 See Christy Constantakopoulou, "Eparchides (437)," *Brill's New Jacoby* (Brill Online, BNJ-contributors, August 25, 2011).

24 Peter Reuell, "Calvert Watkins dies at 80: Pioneer in Indo-European linguistics and poetics, taught at Harvard for decades," *Harvard Gazette,* March 28, 2013, https://news.harvard.edu/gazette/story/2013/03/calvert-watkins-dies-at-80/.

25 Calvert Watkins, "Let Us Now Praise Famous Grains," *Proceedings of the American Philosophical Society,* vol. 122, no. 1 (February 15, 1978): 9–17, at 16.

26 Michael Balter, "Farmers vs. Nomads: Whose Lingo Spread the Farthest?" *Scientific American,* May 1, 2016, www.scientificamerican.com/article/farmers-vs-nomads-whose-lingo-spread-the-farthest/. See chapter 6 for further discussion.

27 Watkins, 17.

28 *Rigveda,* 8.48.3.

29 Watkins, 16.

Chapter 4: Secret of Secrets

1 "New Acropolis Museum Receives 2011 AIA Institute Honor Award for Architecture" (YouTube, 2011), https://youtu.be/KfaKqoEzvwM.

2 Details of the events surrounding Eleusis as the European Capital of Culture here: https://eleusis2021.eu/.

3 https://issuu.com/eleusis2021/docs/eleusis_2021-_electronic_form_ecoc_.

4 See Damian Carrington, "Earth's sixth mass extinction event under way, scientists warn," *Guardian,* July 10, 2017, www.theguardian.com/environment/2017/jul/10/earths-sixth-mass-extinction-event-already-underway-scientists-warn; and Damian Carrington, "Humanity has wiped out 60 percent of animal populations since 1970, report finds,"

Guardian, October 29, 2018, www.theguardian.com/environment/2018/oct/30/humanity -wiped-out-animals-since-1970-major-report-finds.

5 Fred Pearce, "Global Extinction Rates: Why Do Estimates Vary So Wildly?" *Yale Environment 360,* August 17, 2015, https://e360.yale.edu/features/global_extinction_rates_why _do_estimates_vary_so_wildly.

6 Carl Kerenyi, *Eleusis: Archetypal Image of Mother and Daughter* (Princeton, NJ: Princeton University Press, 1967), 11–12.

7 Ibid., 12.

8 Ibid.

9 Ibid., 63–64.

10 R. Gordon Wasson, Albert Hofmann, and Carl A. P. Ruck, *The Road to Eleusis: Unveiling the Secret of the Mysteries* (Berkeley, CA: North Atlantic Books, 2008), 109.

11 Ibid., 56.

12 Ibid.

13 Ibid., 61.

14 Ibid., 45.

15 William James, *The Varieties of Religious Experience* (London: Longmans, Green Co, 1917), 381, available at www.gutenberg.org/files/621/621-h/621-h.html.

16 Ibid.

17 See L. M. Edinger-Schons, "Oneness beliefs and their effect on life satisfaction," *Psychology of Religion and Spirituality* (advance online publication, 2019), doi.org/10.1037 /rel0000259. See also Roland R. Griffiths et al., "Psilocybin-occasioned mystical-type experience in combination with meditation and other spiritual practices produces enduring positive changes in psychological functioning and in trait measures of prosocial attitudes and behaviors," *Journal of Psychopharmacology,* vol. 32, no. 1 (2018): 49–69, doi:10.1177/0269881117731279. "The study showed robust interactive positive effects of psilocybin dose and added support for spiritual practices on a wide range of longitudinal measures at 6 months including interpersonal closeness, gratitude, life meaning/purpose, forgiveness, death transcendence, daily spiritual experiences, religious faith and coping, and rating of participants by community observers. Analyses suggest that the determinants of these effects were the intensity of the psilocybin-occasioned mystical experience and the rates of engagement with meditation and other spiritual practices."

18 Emma Stone, "The Emerging Science of Awe and Its Benefits," *Psychology Today,* April 27, 2017, www.psychologytoday.com/us/blog/understanding-awe/201704 /the-emerging-science-awe-and-its-benefits. See also Jo Marchant, "Awesome awe: The emotion that gives us superpowers," *Scientific American,* July 26, 2017, www .newscientist.com/article/mg23531360-400-awesome-awe-the-emotion-that-gives-us -superpowers/.

19 William Richards, *Sacred Knowledge: Psychedelics and Religious Experiences* (New York: Columbia University Press, 2015), 55.

20 Wasson, Hofmann, and Ruck, *Road to Eleusis,* 112–13.

21 See J. B. Connelly, *Portrait of a Priestess: Women and Ritual in Ancient Greece* (Princeton, NJ: Princeton University Press, 2007), 73. See also Diodorus Siculus, *Bibliotheca historica,* Book 16.26, in C. H. Oldfather, trans., *Diodorus of Sicily in twelve volumes with an English translation by C. H. Oldfather,* vols. 4–8 (Cambridge, MA: Harvard University Press, 1989). See also Wasson, Hofmann, and Ruck, *Road to Eleusis,* 112–13. In fact, the

Hymn to Demeter anticipates Demeter's transition from mother to grandmother, Ruck points out, with reference to her knowledge of "great herbs" and "talisman plants" that can combat sorcery.

22 Elizabeth Blair, "Why Are Old Women Often the Face of Evil in Fairy Tales and Folklore?" NPR, as heard on *Morning Edition,* October 28, 2015, www.npr.org/2015/10/28 /450657717/why-are-old-women-often-the-face-of-evil-in-fairy-tales-and-folklore.

23 Carl Kerenyi, *Dionysos: Archetypal Image of Indestructible Life* (Princeton, NJ: Princeton University Press, 1976), 315, quoting Ortega y Gasset, *Meditaciones del Quijote:* "If we are truthful, we shall admit that we do not understand it. Philology has not yet sufficiently prepared us to attend a Greek tragedy. Perhaps no product of artistic creation is so shot through with purely historical motives. It must not be forgotten that in Athens the tragedy was a religious ceremony, enacted not so much on the boards as in the souls of the spectators. Stage and audience were enveloped in an extrapoetic atmosphere: religion. What has come down to us resembles the libretto of an opera of which we have never heard the music—the reverse of a carpet, ends of multicolored thread that come through from a surface woven by faith. Greek scholars are baffled by the faith of the Athenians; they are unable to reconstruct it. Until they have done so, Greek tragedy will be a page written in a language to which we possess no dictionary."

24 K. O. Müller, *History of the Literature of Ancient Greece,* trans. George Cornwall Lewis (London: Robert Baldwin, 1840), 289.

25 Ibid., 288. Interestingly, the Greek *entheos* (ἔνθεος) also forms the basis of Ruck's preferred nomenclature for visionary drugs: entheogens. The term he coined in 1978 roughly translates as "that which generates the god(dess) within." Throughout this book, I use the more traditional "psychedelics," another fabulous Greek neologism proposed by the psychiatrist Humphrey Osmond in 1956. Combining the Greek for *psyche* (ψυχή) or "self" with *delos* (δῆλος) or "visible," psychedelic means something like "that which makes clear the contents of one's consciousness."

26 Peter Hoyle, *Delphi* (London: Cassell and Company, 1967), 76.

27 Carl Ruck, *Sacred Mushrooms of the Goddess* (Berkeley, CA: Ronin Publishing, 2006), 99.

28 Ibid., 100.

29 Kerenyi, *Eleusis: Archetypal Image,* 9. Iacchus was there at the launch of the festivities as well. A statue of this youthful torch-bearing god would conduct the parade of initiates every step of the thirteen miles along the Sacred Road that led from Athens to Eleusis. The "dances, sacrifices, libations, ritual washings, and singing of hymns accompanied by pipes" would be punctuated by rhythmic chants of "Iakchos! Iakchos!" In *The Frogs,* Aristophanes wrote that this "cry resounds in the underworld, in the abode of the blessed who in their lifetime had been initiated at Eleusis." It is believed the Greek word *Iacchus* (Ἴακχος) may have influenced the Latin *Bacchus,* the Roman version of Dionysus.

30 See Fritz Graf, *Eleusis und die orphische Dichtung Athens in vorhellenistischer Zeit* (Berlin: De Gruyter, 1974).

31 Personal communication with Fritz Graf, July 30, 2018.

32 Euripides, *The Bacchae,* ed. E. R. Dodds (London: Clarendon Press, 1987), xx.

33 Carrington, "Humanity has wiped out 60 percent of animal populations."

34 Courtney Woo, "Religion rejuvenates environmentalism," *Miami Herald,* February 18, 2010, available at http://fore.yale.edu/news/item/religion-rejuvenates -environmentalism/.

35 See the introduction in Stanislav Grof, *LSD Psychotherapy* (Santa Cruz, CA: Multidisciplinary Association for Psychedelic Studies, 2008).

36 Wasson, Hofmann, and Ruck, *Road to Eleusis,* 144–45.

Chapter 5: The Beatific Vision

 1 In the *Exhortation to the Greeks* 2.19, the Church Father Clement of Alexandria reveals what he believed was hidden away in the *cista mystica*: "Are they not sesame cakes, and pyramidal cakes, and globular and flat cakes, embossed all over, and lumps of salt, and a serpent the symbol of Dionysus Bassareus? And besides these, are they not pomegranates, and branches, and rods, and ivy leaves? And besides, round cakes and poppy seeds? And further, there are the unmentionable symbols of Themis, marjoram, a lamp, a sword, a woman's comb, which is a euphemism and mystic expression for the muliebria."

 2 Jan N. Bremmer, "Initiation into the Eleusinian Mysteries: A 'Thin' Description," in *Mystery and Secrecy in the Nag Hammadi Collection and Other Ancient Literature: Ideas and Practices,* eds. Christian H. Bull, Liv Lied, and John D. Turner (Boston: Brill, 2012), doi .org/10.1163/9789004215122_019.

 3 R. Gordon Wasson, Albert Hofmann, and Carl A. P. Ruck, *The Road to Eleusis: Unveiling the Secret of the Mysteries* (Berkeley, CA: North Atlantic Books, 2008), 123.

 4 See Hugh Bowden, "Cults of Demeter Eleusinia and the Transmission of Religious Ideas," *Mediterranean Historical Review,* vol. 22, no. 1 (2007): 71–83, doi: 10.1080/09518960701539182. Bowden notes several Eleusinian-like cults dedicated to Demeter around the Aegean, though there is little evidence to confirm a "formal connection with the sanctuary of Demeter at Eleusis."

 5 See, for example, *Mater Dolorosa (Sorrowing Virgin),* painted by Dieric Bouts between 1480 and 1500, an image of which is available here: www.artic.edu/artworks/110673/mater -dolorosa-sorrowing-virgin.

 6 Preserved Smith, "Christian Theophagy: An Historical Sketch," *The Monist,* vol. 28, no. 2 (April 1918): 161–208.

 7 Elaine Pagels, *The Gnostic Gospels* (New York: Vintage, 1989), xix-xx.

 8 Ibid., xxvii.

 9 Elaine Pagels, *Beyond Belief: The Secret Gospel of Thomas* (New York: Vintage, 2004), 177.

10 Elaine Pagels, *The Origin of Satan: How Christians Demonized Jews, Pagans, and Heretics* (New York: Vintage, 1995), 69.

11 Pagels, *Gnostic Gospels,* 27.

12 Ibid., 25.

13 Pagels, *Beyond Belief,* 227.

14 Pagels, *Gnostic Gospels,* 126.

15 The definition of *musterion* (μυστήριον) from Thayer's Greek Lexicon is available here: https://biblehub.com/greek/3466.htm. For a unique perspective on the clandestine rituals of early Christianity, see Morton Smith, *The Secret Gospel* (Middletown, CA: Dawn Horse Press, 2005), 107. In 1958, the Harvard Divinity School–trained historian was rooting around an Orthodox monastery just south of Jerusalem called Mar Saba, when he made the discovery of a lifetime. Smith miraculously unearthed the two-page fragment of a lost text that is now referred to as the Secret Gospel of Mark. It mentions a covert, nocturnal rite of initiation that Christ allegedly reserved for his closest disciples—a "secret baptism"

that offered the inner circle direct access to the Kingdom of Heaven. The Gospel doesn't provide enough detail, but Smith pointed to a "technique of ascent," likely influenced by Greek and Jewish magical practices of the time, whereby "the disciple was possessed by Jesus' spirit and so united with Jesus. One with him, he participated by hallucination in Jesus' ascent into the heavens" and "entered the kingdom of God."

16 Pagels, *Gnostic Gospels,* 15.

17 "The Virgin Mary, patroness of farmers," Pros-Eleusis, November 19, 2018, https://proseleusis.com/en/the-virgin-mary-patroness-of-farmers/.

18 Ibid.

19 Apostolos Lakasas, "Greece's many places of worship," *Kathimerini,* June 1, 2017, www.ekathimerini.com/215056/article/ekathimerini/community/greeces-many-places-of-worship.

20 The Greek Orthodox Archdiocese of America includes the ritual liturgy of The Holy Sacrament of Ordination to the Priesthood, available here: www.goarch.org/-/the-holy-sacrament-of-ordination-to-the-priesthood.

21 E. M. Lee et al., "Altered States of Consciousness during an Extreme Ritual," *PLoS ONE* vol. 11, no. 5 (2016): e0153126, doi.org/10.1371/journal.pone.0153126.

22 Mircea Eliade, *Shamanism: Archaic Techniques of Ecstasy* (Princeton, NJ: Princeton University Press, 2004), 65.

23 Ibid., 35.

24 Ibid., 59.

25 Ibid., 61.

26 Carl Kerenyi, *Eleusis: Archetypal Image of Mother and Daughter* (Princeton, NJ: Princeton University Press, 1967), 95.

27 Ibid., 96.

28 Ibid., 97.

29 Kenneth Ring and Sharon Cooper, "Near-Death and Out-of-Body Experiences in the Blind: A Study of Apparent Eyeless Vision," *Journal of Near-Death Studies,* vol. 16, no. 2 (1997): 101–47, at 108.

30 Ibid., 116.

31 Ibid., 119.

32 R. Gordon Wasson, "Seeking the Magic Mushroom," *Life,* May 13, 1957.

33 William Richards, *Sacred Knowledge: Psychedelics and Religious Experiences* (New York: Columbia University Press, 2015), 136. See Alex E. Krill et al., "Effects of a Hallucinogenic Agent in Totally Blind Subjects," *Archives of Ophthalmology,* vol. 69 (1963): 180–185, where the researchers administered LSD to twenty-four totally blind subjects. Thirteen reported "visual alterations" after LSD. Eleven volunteers qualified them as "simple," while two reported "complex hallucinations." The scientists state: "it is evident that a normal retina is not needed for the occurrence of LSD-induced visual experiences." But they are cautious to point out that all subjects confirming the experience of visions did, in fact, have "a history of previous spontaneous visual activity" unrelated to LSD.

34 Richards, *Sacred Knowledge,* 136.

35 Burkert, *Greek Religion,* 277, 289.

36 Kerenyi, *Eleusis: Archetypal Image,* 179.

37 Ibid., 180.

38 Elisa Guerra-Doce, "Psychoactive Substances in Prehistoric Times: Examining the Archaeological Evidence," *Time and Mind,* vol. 8, no. 1 (2015): 91–112, doi.org/10.1080/1751696X.2014.993244.

39 Li Liu et al., "Fermented beverage and food storage in 13,000 y-old stone mortars at Raqefet Cave, Israel: Investigating Natufian ritual feasting," *Journal of Archaeological Science: Reports*, vol. 21 (September 2018): 783–93, doi.org/10.1016/j.jasrep.2018.08.008.

40 Kerenyi, *Eleusis: Archetypal Image*, 184.

41 Wasson, Hofmann, and Ruck, *Road to Eleusis*, 93.

42 Ibid., 93-94.

43 Kevin T. Glowacki, "New Insights into Bronze Age Eleusis and the Formative Stages of the Eleusinian Cults," *American Journal of Archaeology*, vol. 120, no. 4 (October 2016): 673–77, at 674, doi:10.3764/aja.120.4.0673.

Chapter 6: Graveyard Beer

1 See a brief history of the Bavarian State Brewery Weihenstephaner here: www.weihenstephaner.de/en/our-brewery/history/.

2 Robert J. Braidwood et al, "Symposium: Did Man Once Live by Beer Alone?" *American Anthropologist*, New Series, vol. 55, no. 4 (Oct. 1953): 515–26, at 515.

3 O. Dietrich et al., "The role of cult and feasting in the emergence of Neolithic communities. New evidence from Göbekli Tepe, south-eastern Turkey," *Antiquity*, vol. 86, no. 333 (2012): 674–95, at 692, doi:10.1017/S0003598X00047840.

4 Jared Diamond, "The Worst Mistake in the History of the Human Race: The advent of agriculture was a watershed moment for the human race. It may also have been our greatest blunder," *Discover*, May 1, 1999, www.discovermagazine.com/planet-earth/the-worst-mistake-in-the-history-of-the-human-race. As Diamond explains, "One straight forward example of what paleopathologists have learned from skeletons concerns historical changes in height. Skeletons from Greece and Turkey show that the average height of hunter-gatherers toward the end of the ice ages was a generous 5′ 9″ for men, 5′ 5″ for women. With the adoption of agriculture, height crashed, and by 3000 B.C. had reached a low of only 5′ 3″ for men, 5′ for women. By classical times heights were very slowly on the rise again, but modern Greeks and Turks have still not regained the average height of their distant ancestors."

5 Brian Hayden et al., "What Was Brewing in the Natufian? An Archaeological Assessment of Brewing Technology in the Epipaleolithic," *Journal of Archaeological Method and Theory*, vol. 20, no. 1 (2013): 102–50, doi.org/10.1007/s10816-011-9127-y.

6 Ibid., 131.

7 Liu et al., "Fermented beverage and food storage in 13,000 y-old stone mortars at Raqefet Cave, Israel: Investigating Natufian ritual feasting," *Journal of Archaeological Science: Reports*, vol. 21 (September 2018): 783. See also Melissa De Witte, "An ancient thirst for beer may have inspired agriculture, Stanford archaeologists say," *Stanford News*, September 12, 2018, https://news.stanford.edu/2018/09/12/crafting-beer-lead-cereal-cultivation/.

8 Liu et al., "Fermented beverage and food storage," 792. Liu further states: "The time and effort invested in the manufacture of deep stone mortars in mortuary contexts and in acquisition of knowledge apparently required for beer brewing indicates an important ritual function played by alcohol beverages in the Natufian culture." And concerning Sauer's theory from 1953: "Beer brewing may have been, at least in part, an underlying motivation to cultivate cereals in the southern Levant, supporting the beer hypothesis proposed by archaeologists more than 60 years ago."

9 Melissa De Witte, "New evidence supports the hypothesis that beer may have been motivation to cultivate cereals," *Phys.org,* September 12, 2018, https://phys.org/news/2018-09-evidence-hypothesis-beer-cultivate-cereals.html.

10 Andrew Curry, "Gobekli Tepe: The World's First Temple?" *Smithsonian Magazine,* November 2008, www.smithsonianmag.com/history/gobekli-tepe-the-worlds-first-temple-83613665/.

11 Jens Notroff, "The Göbekli Tepe excavations—Frequently Asked Questions," *Tepe Telegrams,* May 12, 2016, https://tepetelegrams.wordpress.com/faq.

12 Klaus Schmidt, "Göbekli Tepe—the Stone Age Sanctuaries. New results of ongoing excavations with a special focus on sculptures and high reliefs," *Documenta Praehistorica,* vol. 37 (2010): 239–56, at 254, doi.org/10.4312/dp.37.21.

13 Curry, "Gobekli Tepe: The World's First Temple?"

14 See Dietrich et al., "The role of cult and feasting," 675. The cereals that would spread across the Fertile Crescent, and eventually our dinner tables, began in the rich, arable land between the Tigris and Euphrates Rivers: "The distribution areas of the wild forms of einkorn and emmer wheat, barley and the other Neolithic founder crops overlap here [around Göbekli Tepe], and the transition of the two species of wheat to domesticated crops has been pinpointed to this area." See also Curry, "Gobekli Tepe: The World's First Temple?" where Stanford archaeologist Ian Hodder adds, "You can make a good case this area is the real origin of complex Neolithic societies."

15 Ibid.

16 Julia Gresky et al., "Modified human crania from Göbekli Tepe provide evidence for a new form of Neolithic skull cult," *Science Advances,* vol. 3, no. 6 (June 28, 2017): e1700564, doi: 10.1126/sciadv.1700564.

17 Dietrich et al., "The role of cult and feasting," 690.

18 Ibid., 692.

19 Gresky et al., "Modified human crania."

20 Robert Drews, *The Coming of the Greeks: Indo-European Conquests in the Aegean and the Near East* (Princeton, NJ: Princeton University Press, 1988), 9.

21 Proponents of the Kurgan Hypothesis say the Indo-Europeans who traveled west used their horses and wheeled chariots to subdue the poorly equipped indigenous populations of Old Europe. But these military artifacts don't show up in the Greek archaeological record, for example, until much later in the Bronze Age during the second millennium BC. See Colin Renfrew, *Archaeology and Language: The Puzzle of Indo-European Origins* (Cambridge, UK: Cambridge University Press, 1987), 95–96: "The appeals of older generations to the 'warlike spirit' of the Proto-Indo-Europeans are entirely unsubstantiated: the suggestion that they were mounted warriors does not carry conviction. There is indeed the strong likelihood that the horse was intensively exploited in the steppes of south Russia at about this time and there is some evidence that it was used for riding. The story of the use of the horse is indeed a crucial one for the steppelands, but there is little evidence for westward incursions by mounted warriors at this time: that case cannot really be made before the late bronze age."

22 Ibid., 96.

23 For an outstanding overview of the Kurgan vs. Anatolian debate, see this recent lecture by Colin Renfrew: "Lord Colin Renfrew | Marija Redivia: DNA and Indo-European Origins" (YouTube, 2018), https://youtu.be/pmv3J55bdZc.

24 But it doesn't necessarily discount the Kurgan Hypothesis either. See Iosif Lazaridis et al., "Genetic origins of the Minoans and Mycenaeans," *Nature,* vol. 548 (2017): 214–18,

doi:10.1038/nature23310, where the authors note that the Mycenaeans did derive some "additional ancestry from an ultimate source related to the hunter-gatherers of eastern Europe and Siberia, introduced via a proximal source related to the inhabitants of either the Eurasian steppe or Armenia." The picture that emerges is a first wave of Proto-Indo-European agriculturalists from Anatolia, followed by another wave of nomads in the third or fourth millennium BC. But, without a doubt, the Stone Age Anatolian farmers were there first. See Renfrew, *Archaeology and Language,* 30: "The earliest farming settlements in Europe are seen by 6500 BC in Greece, and very soon after in the Western Mediterranean. By 3000 BC nearly all of Europe except the extreme north was occupied by a great diversity of communities, all of them relying on farming to a significant extent."

25 Andrew Curry, "The First Europeans Weren't Who You Might Think," *National Geographic,* August 2019, www.nationalgeographic.com/culture/2019/07/first-europeans-immigrants-genetic-testing-feature/.

26 John Noble Wilford, "Jar in Iranian Ruins Betrays Beer Drinkers of 3500 B.C.," *New York Times,* November 5, 1992, www.nytimes.com/1992/11/05/world/jar-in-iranian-ruins-betrays-beer-drinkers-of-3500-bc.html.

27 Patrick McGovern, "Early Neolithic Wine of Georgia in the South Caucasus," *Proceedings of the National Academy of Sciences,* vol. 114, no. 48 (November 2017): e10309–e10318, doi: 10.1073/pnas.1714728114.

28 Ibid. Like the initial spread of Proto-Indo-European proposed by Colin Renfrew, the original area of extreme beverage-making identified by McGovern radiates out of the Fertile Crescent, stretching "west to east from the Taurus Mountains of southeastern Anatolia through the South Caucasus and northern Mesopotamia to the Zagros Mountains of northwestern Iran."

29 Ker Than, "Ancient Tablet Found: Oldest Readable Writing in Europe," *National Geographic,* April 1, 2011, www.nationalgeographic.com/news/2011/4/110330-oldest-writing-europe-tablet-greece-science-mycenae-greek/.

30 Patrick E. McGovern, *Uncorking the Past: The Quest for Wine, Beer, and Other Alcoholic Beverages* (Oakland, CA: University of California Press, 2009), 187. See also Patrick E. McGovern, "Retsina, Mixed Fermented Beverages, and the Cuisine of Pre-Classical Greece," in Yannis Tzedakis and Holley Martlew, eds., *Minoans and Mycenaeans: Flavours of their Time* (Athens: Kapon Editions, 1999), 206–209, at 207, available at www.penn.museum/sites/biomoleculararchaeology/wp-content/uploads/2010/03/MinMycretsina.pdf.

31 Patrick E. McGovern, *Ancient Brews: Rediscovered and Re-created* (New York: W. W. Norton, 2017), 29.

32 Patrick E. McGovern et al., "The Chemical Identification of Resinated Wine and a Mixed Fermented Beverage in Bronze-Age Pottery Vessels of Greece," in Holley Martlew and Martin Jones, *Archaeology Meets Science: Biomolecular Investigations in Bronze Age Greece* (Oxford, UK: Oxbow Books, 2008), 169–218, at 202.

33 Soultana Maria Valamoti, "Brewing beer in wine country? First archaeobotanical indications for beer making in Early and Middle Bronze Age Greece," *Vegetation History and Archaeobotany,* vol. 27 (2018): 611–25, at 621–22, doi.org/10.1007/s00334-017-0661-8: "Brewing was widely known in the eastern Mediterranean and the method might have been introduced to Greece from the east at least as early as the end of the 3rd millennium BC or even earlier. . . . The date of the introduction of beer brewing in this part of Europe, the Aegean region, remains obscure at the moment as are the reasons why beer was later ostracised in the ancient Greek world as a barbarian drink. . . . Our evidence shows that

the stereotypical division between 'wine cultures' and 'beer cultures' is no longer valid for prehistoric southeastern Europe and the Aegean region." Having analyzed evidence of malting from ground cereal fragments and sprouted grains at Archondiko in western Macedonia (2135–2020 BC) and Argissa in Thessaly (2100–1700 BC), the authors conclude: "The archaeobotanical evidence for brewing from Bronze Age Greece presented here, shows that previous assumptions that wine was the main alcoholic drink there are probably out of date and the tentative earlier suggestions for beer consumption in the prehistoric Aegean are better founded than previously thought." See also Catherine Perlès, "Early seventh-millennium AMS dates from domestic seeds in the Initial Neolithic at Franchthi Cave (Argolid, Greece)," *Antiquity*, vol. 87, no. 338 (December 1, 2013): 1001–15, doi.org/10.1017/S0003598X00049826, where evidence of domesticated wheat appears in the Franchthi Cave on the Argolid southwest of Athens before 6500 BC, which precedes the earliest Neolithic occupations in Bulgaria by three to five centuries, in Italy by five to seven centuries, and in Spain by at least one millennium.

34 R. Gordon Wasson, Albert Hofmann, and Carl A. P. Ruck, *The Road to Eleusis: Unveiling the Secret of the Mysteries* (Berkeley, CA: North Atlantic Books, 2008), 36.

35 M. L. Nelson, "Brief communication: Mass spectroscopic characterization of tetracycline in the skeletal remains of an ancient population from Sudanese Nubia 350–550 CE," *American Journal of Physical Anthropology*, vol. 143, no. 1 (September 2010): 151–54, doi.org/10.1002/ajpa.21340. See also Carol Clark, "Ancient brewmasters tapped drug secrets," Emory University, August 31, 2010, www.emory.edu/EMORY_REPORT/stories/2010/09/07/beer.html; and George J. Armelagos, "Take Two Beers and Call Me in 1,600 Years—use of tetracycline by Nubians and Ancient Egyptians," *The Medical Dictionary*, http://the-medical-dictionary.com/tetracycline_article_4.htm.

36 Clark, "Ancient brewmasters tapped drug secrets."

37 Ibid.

38 Stephen Harrod Buhner, *Sacred and Herbal Healing Beers: The Secrets of Ancient Fermentation* (Denver, CO: Brewers Publications, 1998), 171.

39 Nina Martyris, "The Other Reformation: How Martin Luther Changed Our Beer, Too," NPR, October 31, 2017, www.npr.org/sections/thesalt/2017/10/31/561117731/the-other-reformation-how-martin-luther-changed-our-beer-too.

40 Ibid.

41 See John Bickerdyke, *The Curiosities of Ale & Beer: An Entertaining History* (Bloomsbury, UK: Swan Sonnenschein & Co., 1889), where a trance-inducing henbane beer is recorded as an antique anesthetic from 1753: "Take the oil pressed out of fresh Herrings, a pint, a boar's gall, juices of henbane, hemlock, arsel, lettuce, and wild catmint, each six ounces, mix, boil well, and put into a glass vessel, stoppered. Take three spoonfuls and put into a quart of warm ale, and let the person to undergo any operation drink of this by an ounce at a time, till he falls asleep, which sleep he will continue the space of three or four hours, and all that time he will be unsensible to anything done to him."

Chapter 7: The *Kukeon* of Catalonia

1 Josep Maria Llorens, *Sant Pere de Galligants. Un monestir al llarg del temps* (Girona, Spain: Museu d'Arqueologia de Catalunya–Girona, 2011), 47.

2 "Game of Thrones 6x10-Samwell Tarly Arrives at The Citadel" (YouTube, 2016), https://youtu.be/nP4nGTXiqWE?t=47.

3 Peter Kingsley, *In the Dark Places of Wisdom* (Inverness, CA: The Golden Sufi Center, 1999), 11, 13.

4 For a brief history of the various phases of the Greco-Roman colony at Emporion, see here: www.livius.org/articles/place/emporiae-ampurias/.

5 The *kernos* discovered in 2008 is housed in the Archaeological Museum of Catalonia in Empúries, as described here: www.macempuries.cat/ca/Col-leccions/Objectes-de-la-colleccio/Empuries-grega/Kernos.

6 Enriqueta Pons et al., "El yacimiento ibérico de Mas Castellà de Pontós (Girona). Análisis de algunas piezas significativas," *Saguntum*, vol. 1 (1998): 55–64, at 55.

7 Enriqueta Pons et al., "Dog Sacrifice at the Protohistoric Site of Mas Castellar (Pontós, Spain)," in Carrie Ann Murray, ed., *Diversity of Sacrifice: Form and Function of Sacrificial Practices in the Ancient World and Beyond* (Albany, NY: State University of New York Press, 2016), 191–209, at 192.

8 Enriqueta Pons et al., *El deposit d'ofrenes de la fossa 101 de Mas Castellar de Pontós: un estudi interdisciplinary*, Universitat de Girona, *Estudis Arqueològics*, vol. 4 (1997): 26.

9 M. A. Martin and N. Llavaneras, "Un conjunt de timateris de terracuita, amb representació de Demèter, procedent del Mas Castellà de Pontós," *Cypsela*, vol. 3 (1980): 153–61. For additional examples of the ancient terra-cotta goddess heads found throughout Catalonia, see Mariá José Pena, "Los 'thymiateria' en forma de cabeza femenina hallados en el N.E. de la Península Ibérica," *Revue des Études Anciennes*, vol. 89, nos. 3–4 (1987): 349–58.

10 The Greek presence in Magna Graecia is discussed in further detail in part two, especially chapter 15. For a brief history of the original Greek settlements in Italy, see chapter 10, note 39.

11 Denise Demetriou, "What is an emporion? A reassessment," *Historia: Zeitschrift für Alte Geschichte*, vol. 60, no. 3 (2011): 255–72, at 268.

12 Ibid., 269.

13 François de Polignac, *Cults, Territory, and the Origins of the Greek City-State* (Chicago: University of Chicago Press, 1995), 115: "Clearly, chthonic cults, addressed for the most part to Demeter and Kore, or even Persephone, as at Locri [in Calabria in south Italy], were one of the principal vectors through which non-Greeks other than the princely elite became familiar with Greek cults and customs and managed to integrate them into their own cultures. So much is attested by their wide diffusion in indigenous areas in the sixth century, both in Sicily and in Magna Graecia. At this time, their appearance usually coincided with a reorganization of the settlement and a transformation of the material culture indicating a general adoption of Greek models throughout the society. This particular role of the chthonic cults may have stemmed from the individual characteristics of the deities and their cults, whose agrarian or even funerary connotations and sanctuaries, open to various types of practices, may have likened them to indigenous beliefs and customs."

14 Pons et al., "Dog Sacrifice," 200.

15 Pons et al., "El yacimiento ibérico," 59.

16 Pons et al., "Dog Sacrifice," 204.

17 M. De Grossi, "Dog Sacrifice in the Ancient World: A Ritual Passage?" in L. M. Snyder and E. A. Moore, eds., *Dogs and People in Social, Working, Economic or Symbolic Interaction* (Proceedings of the 9th ICAZ Conference, Durham, NC, 2002), 62–66, at 62.

18 See Richard Cavendish, *The Powers of Evil in Western Religion, Magic and Folk Belief* (Abington-on-Thames, UK: Routledge, 1975), 62: "[t]he dog is a creature of the threshold, the guardian of doors and portals, and so it is appropriately associated with the frontier between life and death, and with demons and ghosts which move across the frontier. The

yawning gates of Hades were guarded by the monstrous watchdog Cerberus, whose function was to prevent the living from entering the underworld, and the dead from leaving it."

19 Manolis Sergis, "Dog Sacrifice in Ancient and Modern Greece: From the Sacrifice Ritual to Dog Torture (kynomartyrion)," *Folklore,* vol. 45 (July 2010): 61–88, doi:10.7592/FEJF2010.45.sergis.

20 R. Gordon Wasson, Albert Hofmann, and Carl A. P. Ruck, *The Road to Eleusis: Unveiling the Secret of the Mysteries* (Berkeley, CA: North Atlantic Books, 2008), 70. Hecate was especially feared for her mythical garden in Colchis on the far eastern shore of the Black Sea. A number of "pharmacologically potent plants" were said to grow there, including aconite (*Aconitum* spp.), juniper (*Juniperus communis* or *excelsa*), laurel (*Laurus nobilis*), mandrake (*Mandragora officinarum*), deadly nightshade (*Atropa belladonna*), and black nightshade (*Solanum nigrum*). They may have been used as part of the initiation into her own personal mysteries—what the Roman Stoic and tragedian Seneca called "illuminating rituals that are, and should be, secret." See Claudia Müller-Ebeling et al., *Witchcraft Medicine: Healing Arts, Shamanic Practices, and Forbidden Plants* (Rochester, VT: Inner Traditions, 2003), 92.

21 Sam Jones, "Thousands protest in Madrid before trial of Catalan separatists," *Guardian,* February 10, 2019, www.theguardian.com/world/2019/feb/10/thousands-protest-in -madrid-as-catalan-separatists-trial-looms.

22 Pons et al., "Dog Sacrifice," 195. On top of the skeleton of a dog, Pons unearthed 6,156 carbonized seeds (mostly millet and barley) and 404 faunal remains: sheep or goats (66.21 percent), pigs (17.93 percent), and cattle (15.86 percent).

23 Hans-Peter Stika, "Early Iron Age and Late Mediaeval malt finds from Germany—attempts at reconstruction of early Celtic brewing and the taste of Celtic beer," *Archaeological and Anthropological Sciences,* vol. 3 (2011): 41–48, at 47, doi.org/10.1007/s12520-010-0049-5: "Another beer additive well-known from mediaeval and early modern times is henbane (*Hyoscyamus niger*), which adds flavour and also makes the beverage more intoxicating. The Old English word 'beolene', once naming the plant henbane, as well as the Old High German word 'bilisa' and the modern German plant name 'Bilsenkraut' are traced back to Celtic linguistic roots and linguistic connections with the Celtic god 'Belenos' are assumed. . . . A few seeds of henbane were found in the early Iron Age Hochdorf samples but statistical correspondence analysis shows that they have no direct connection to the sprouted barley. We can only speculate that henbane may have been used for flavouring the Celtic beer of Hochdorf."

24 Margaret F. Roberts and Michael Wink, eds., *Alkaloids: biochemistry, ecology, and medicinal applications* (Berlin: Plenum Press, 1998), 31–32.

25 Elizabeth Campbell, "Flowers of Evil: Proserpina's Venomous Plants in Ruskin's Botany," *Pacific Coast Philology,* vol. 44, no. 1 (2009): 114–28, at 117. See Müller-Ebeling et al., *Witchcraft Medicine,* 96. From one witch trial in 1648, we learn how the accused gave "nine henbane buttons" to a poor farmer who'd lost his ox, so that the missing animal could be located. It is indicative of the ancient shamanic practice of "finding lost objects while in a clairvoyant trance induced by a psychoactive substance."

26 Francesc Burjachs i Casas et al., "La fossa de Prats (Andorra), un jaciment del bronze mitjà al Pirineu," *Revista d'arqueologia de Ponent,* no. 11–12 (2001–2002): 123–50, at 141–42.

27 Priyanka Soni et al., "Pharmacological properties of Datura stramonium L. as a potential medicinal tree: An overview," *Asian Pacific Journal of Tropical Biomedicine,* vol. 2, no. 12 (2012): 1002–8, doi:10.1016/S2221-1691(13)60014-3.

28 Francesc Burjachs i Casas et al., "La fossa de Prats," 137.

29 Elisa Guerra-Doce, "Psychoactive Substances in Prehistoric Times: Examining the Archaeological Evidence," *Time and Mind,* vol. 8, no. 1 (2015): 91–112, at 100, doi.org/10 .1080/1751696X.2014.993244. See Ramón Fábregas Valcarce, *Los petroglifos y su contexto: un ejemplo de la Galicia meridional* (Vigo, Spain: Instituto de Estudios Vigueses, 2001), 63–64.

30 Elisa Guerra-Doce, "The Origins of Inebriation: Archaeological Evidence of the Consumption of Fermented Beverages and Drugs in Prehistoric Eurasia," *Journal of Archaeological Method and Theory,* vol. 22, no. 3 (September 2015): 751–82, at 771.

31 C. Sanz Mínguez et al., "Escatología vaccea: nuevos datos para su comprensión a través de la analítica de residuos," in C. Sanz Mínguez and J. Velasco Vázquez, eds., *Pintia. Un oppidum en los confines orientales de la región vaccea. Investigaciones arqueológicas vacceas, romanas y visigodas (1999–2003)* (Valladolid, Spain: Universidad de Valladolid, 2003), 145–71. The full website of ongoing archaeological excavations of the remains at Pintia is worth exploring at the Centro de Estudios Vacceos Federico Wattenberg, Universidad de Valladolid, Spain: https://pintiavaccea.es/.

32 C. Sanz Mínguez, *Los Vacceos: cultura y ritos funerarios de un pueblo prerromano del valle medio del Duero. La necrópolis de Las Ruedas, Padilla de Duero (Valladolid),* (Salamanca, Spain: Junta de Castilla y León, 1998), at 349–50, notes five additional ceramics imported from Athens.

33 Mínguez et al., "Escatología vaccea," 155–57 and 316: "Todo ello nos estaría ilustrando en suma sobre un conjunto correspondiente a una elite guerrera que hace uso restringido, de manera acorde a su rango, de cierta droga que, habida cuenta el contexto funerario en el que comparece, podría estar dotada de una clara intencionalidad vehicular para el allende."

34 Fiona Greenland, "Devotio Iberica and the Manipulation of Ancient History to Suit Spain's Mythic Nationalist Past," *Greece & Rome,* vol. 53, no. 2 (October 2006): 235–51, at 237.

35 Nicholas Wade, "Celtic Found to Have Ancient Roots," *New York Times,* July 1, 2003, www.nytimes.com/2003/07/01/science/celtic-found-to-have-ancient-roots.html. The divergence of British Gaelic from continental Gaelic within the Celtic language family was roughly traced back to 3200 BC, giving much deeper roots to Celtic than previously thought—perhaps even further back to the initial arrival of its Indo-European lingustic ancestors in Europe ca. 8100 BC. See note 39 below.

36 See C. Gamba, "Ancient DNA from an Early Neolithic Iberian population supports a pioneer colonization by first farmers," *Molecular Ecology,* vol. 21, no. 1 (January 2012): 45–56, doi.org/10.1111/j.1365-294X.2011.05361.x. See also Iñigo Olalde, "The genomic history of the Iberian Peninsula over the past 8000 years," *Science,* vol. 363, issue 6432 (March 15, 2019): 1230–34, doi: 10.1126/science.aav4040, and Uppsala University, "Genetic prehistory of Iberia differs from central and northern Europe," *Phys.org,* March 12, 2018, https://phys.org/news/2018-03-genetic-prehistory-iberia-differs-central.html.

37 Paul Rincon, "Ancient migration transformed Spain's DNA" (BBC, March 15, 2019), www .bbc.com/news/science-environment-47540792. The DNA signal present in today's Spaniards was also attested on the Italian island of Sardinia, a logical stopover on the westward expansion of Indo-European across southern Europe from Turkey to Spain, according to Colin Renfrew's Anatolian Hypothesis.

38 Anna Blasco et al., "Evidencias de procesado y consumo de cerveza en la cueva de Can Sadurní (Begues, Barcelona) durante la prehistoria," in Mauro S. Hernández Pérez et al.,

eds., *Actas del IV Congreso del Neolítico Peninsular, Noviembre 27–30, 2006, vol. I* (Museo Arqueológico de Alicante, 2008): 428–31. See also Universidad de Barcelona, "Most ancient pottery prehistoric figurine of the Iberian Peninsula found in Begues" (ScienceDaily, October 26, 2012), www.sciencedaily.com/releases/2012/10/121026084641.htm. The human figurine made of pottery was found in the Sadurní Cave and dated to ca. 4500 BC.

39 Colin Renfrew, *Archaeology and Language: The Puzzle of Indo-European Origins* (Cambridge, UK: Cambridge University Press, 1987), 242–45: "The Celtic languages would all be descended from this early Indo-European language or languages. There are radiocarbon dates associated with early farming in southern France around 6000 BC, associated with the so-called 'impressed ware', which is a widespread feature of early neolithic settlement in the west Mediterranean, and there are early dates for farming in Spain around 5500 BC, but the picture there is not yet a very complete one, and earlier dates are to be expected. . . . Linguistically, however, if we follow this broad picture, it might be logical to expect some differences between this west European group and the central European. Both derived, of course, from the early farmers of Greece back around 6500 BC, but different cultural and linguistic traditions had no doubt been established. . . . I would prefer to see the development of the Celtic languages, in the sense that they are Celtic as distinct from generalized Indo-European, as taking place essentially in those areas where their speech is later attested. That implies an Indo-European-speaking population in France and in Britain and in Ireland, and probably in much of Iberia also, by before 4000 BC. Linguistic development would, of course, continue after that time."

40 Under the direction of the renowned archaeologist and prehistorian Josep M. Fullola i Pericot at the University of Barcelona, Jordi Juan-Tresserras's doctoral thesis was completed in 1997: "Procesado y preparación de alimentos vegetales para consumo humano. Aportaciones del estudio de fitolitos, almidones y lípidos en yacimientos prehistóricos y protohistóricos del cuadrante n.e. de la Península Ibérica" (Processing and preparation of plant foodstuffs for human consumption. Contributions from the study of phytoliths, starches, and lipids in prehistoric and proto-historic sites from the northeast sector of the Iberian Peninsula). A brief summary is available here: https://dialnet.unirioja.es/servlet/tesis?codigo=178760.

41 Jordi Juan-Tresserras, "La arqueología de las drogas en la Península Ibérica: una síntesis de las recientes investigaciones arqueobotánicas," *Complutum*, no. 11 (2000): 261–74.

42 E. Pons et al., *Mas Castellar de Pontós (Alt Empordà). Un complex arqueològic d'època ibèrica (Excavacions 1990–1998)* (Girona, Spain: Museu d'Arqueologia de Catalunya, 2002), 481.

43 Juan-Tresserras, "Procesado y preparación de alimentos vegetales," 386.

44 Pons et al., *Mas Castellar de Pontós*, 481, 555.

45 Ibid., 555–56. The decorative skulls could be inserted into pillar niches to embellish the porticos of a dwelling (like the French sites of Roquepertuse and Entremont, north of Marseille), or affixed onto door beams (like the Catalonian sites of Puig Castellar and Puig de Sant Andreu). In addition, several ancient authors like the Roman historian, Livy (59 BC–AD 17), mention the grotesque practice of drinking blood out of skulls. According to Scottish scholar J. A. MacCulloch in *The Religion of the Ancient Celts* (Edinburgh, UK: T. & T. Clark, 1911), at 240–41, https://archive.org/details/religionofancien00macc/, the custom had a "religious aspect" with "the intention of transferring [the deceased's] powers directly to the drinker." The tradition could equally apply to enemies killed in battle or revered ancestors, where "the blood of dead relatives was also drunk in order to obtain their virtues, or to be brought into closer *rapport* with them."

46 Pons et al., *Mas Castellar de Pontós*, 548.

47 Gresky et al., "Modified human crania."

48 Pons et al., *Mas Castellar de Pontós,* 550.

49 A brief history of the 300,000-year history of *homo sapiens* is available from the Smithsonian's National Museum of Natural History: http://humanorigins.si.edu/evidence/human-fossils/species/homo-sapiens.

50 Scott M. Fitzpatrick, ed., *Ancient Psychoactive Substances* (Gainesville, FL: University Press of Florida, 2018), 13.

51 Ibid., 77. See also Colin Barras, "Neanderthal dental tartar reveals evidence of medicine," *New Scientist,* July 18, 2012, www.newscientist.com/article/dn22075-neanderthal-dental-tartar-reveals-evidence-of-medicine/.

52 Fitzpatrick, *Ancient Psychoactive Substances,* 77.

53 Herodotus, *The Histories,* 1.164.

54 Kingsley, *Dark Places of Wisdom,* 42.

55 "Cosmos: A Personal Voyage-The Ionians and the Birth of Science," https://youtu.be/VxeNgfo9ZDs.

56 Kingsley, *Dark Places of Wisdom,* 36.

57 Ibid., 12.

Epilogue to Part One

1 Elisa Guerra-Doce, "The Origins of Inebriation: Archaeological Evidence of the Consumption of Fermented Beverages and Drugs in Prehistoric Eurasia," *Journal of Archaeological Method and Theory,* vol. 22, no. 3 (September 2015): 751–82, at 755. The organic remains inside Grooved Ware pottery from Neolithic Scotland were initially reported to contain cereal-based residues, pollen and the seeds of black henbane. As Guerra-Doce summarizes, the "henbane would have transferred hallucinogenic properties to the porridge-like substance found in that pot, and this substance would have been ingested as part of the burial rites." See G.J. Barclay and C.J. Russell-White, "Excavations in the ceremonial complex of the fourth to second millennium BC at Balfarg/Balbirnie, Glenrothes, Fife," *Proceedings of the Society of Antiquaries of Scotland,* vol. 123 (1993): 43–210. Upon re-examination of the potsherds, however, no traces of henbane or any other poisonous plants were identified. See D.J. Long et al., "The use of henbane (*Hyoscyamus niger* L.) as a hallucinogen at Neolithic 'ritual' sites: a re-evaluation," *Antiquity,* vol. 74, no. 283 (March 2000), 49–53: doi.org/10.1017/S0003598X00066138.

2 See Francis Thackeray, "Was William Shakespeare high when he penned his plays? Pipes with cannabis residue were found in the Bard's garden," *Independent,* August 8, 2015, www.independent.co.uk/arts-entertainment/theatre-dance/features/william-shakespeare-high-cannabis-marijuana-stoned-plays-hamlet-macbeth-romeo-juliet-stratford-10446510.html; and Edward Delman, "Hide Your Fires: On Shakespeare and the 'Noted Weed,' Reports spread this week that the English language's most celebrated writer might have smoked marijuana, but the fuss only reveals how little is known about the Bard of Avon," *The Atlantic,* August 12, 2015, www.theatlantic.com/entertainment/archive/2015/08/shakespeare-marijuana-nope/401087/.

3 J. F. Thackeray et al., "Chemical analysis of residues from seventeenth-century clay pipes from Stratford-upon-Avon and environs," *South African Journal of Science,* vol. 97, no. 1–2 (January 2001): 19–21, available at https://hdl.handle.net/10520/EJC97282.

4 Patrick E. McGovern et al., "Ancient Egyptian herbal wines," *Proceedings of the National Academy of Sciences,* vol. 106, no. 18 (May 5, 2009): 7361–66, doi.org/10.1073/pnas.0811578106.

5 For a full list of Jordi Juan-Tresserras's publications, see his Google Scholar page: https://scholar.google.com/citations?user=kDhR6jAAAAAJ&hl=es.

6 Patrick E. McGovern, *Uncorking the Past: The Quest for Wine, Beer, and Other Alcoholic Beverages* (Oakland: University of California Press, 2009), 141.

7 For additional archaeobotanical evidence of ritual drug use in classical antiquity, though not of a strictly psychedelic nature, see Giorgio Samorini, "The oldest archeological data evidencing the relationship of *Homo sapiens* with psychoactive plants: A worldwide overview," *Journal of Psychedelic Studies*, vol. 3 (2019): 63–80, doi.org/10.1556/2054.2019.008, where Samorini mentions the carbonized macro-remains of ephedra pollen discovered at Puntal dels Llops north of Valencia dating from the third to second centuries BC, as well as the forty-five seeds of wild lettuce (*Lactuca serriola*), together with poppy seeds, at the Heraion temple on the southeastern coast of Samos dating to the seventh century BC. In D. Kučan, "Zur Ernährung und dem Gebrauch von Pflanzen im Heraion von Samos im 7. Jahrhundert v. Chr" [On the use of plants as food in the Heraion of Samos in the seventh century BC], *Jahrbuch des Deutschen Archäologischen Instituts*, vol. 110 (1995): 1–64. At 32, Kučan notes that *Lactuca serriola* contains lactucin and lactucopicrin, which can have a "soporific and analgesic effect" that is "similar to poppy juice, which is why its juice was formerly mixed with opium." For additional archaeochemical evidence of psychedelic drug use in classical antiquity, though not of a confirmed ritual nature, see Zuzana Chovanec, "Intoxication on the wine dark sea: Investigating psychoactive substances in the eastern Mediterranean," in Scott M. Fitzpatrick, ed., *Ancient Psychoactive Substances* (Gainesville: University Press of Florida, 2018), 43–70, where Chovanec details her discovery of noscapine (derived from opium), thujone (derived from white wormwood), and artemiseole together with cis-sabinene (derived from absinthe wormwood) in various ancient containers from the island of Cyprus dating from 2400 BC to 1650 BC. For recent archaeochemical evidence of psychedelic or ritual drug use outside the ancient Mediterranean, see Melanie J. Miller et al., "Chemical evidence for the use of multiple psychotropic plants in a 1,000-year-old ritual bundle from South America," *Proceedings of the National Academy of Sciences*, vol. 116, no. 23 (June 4, 2019): 11207–12, doi.org/10.1073/pnas.1902174116 (where liquid chromatography tandem mass spectrometry (LC-MS/MS) detected cocaine, benzoylecgonine (BZE), harmine, bufotenine, dimethyltryptamine (DMT), and possibly psilocin); Meng Ren et al., "The origins of cannabis smoking: Chemical residue evidence from the first millennium BCE in the Pamirs," *Science Advances*, vol. 5, no. 6 (June 12, 2019), eaaw1391, doi.org/10.1126/sciadv.aaw1391 (where gas chromatography-mass spectrometry (GC-MS) detected several cannabinoids in wooden braziers from the Jirzankal Cemetery in Central Asia, providing evidence of "funerary rites that included flames, rhythmic music, and hallucinogen smoke, all intended to guide people into an altered state of mind"); Andrew S. Wilson et al., "Archaeological, radiological, and biological evidence offer insight into Inca child sacrifice," *Proceedings of the National Academy of Sciences*, vol. 110, no. 33 (August 13, 2013): 13322–27, doi.org/10.1073/pnas.1305117110 (where LC-MS/MS on the hair samples of three frozen mummies from about 1500 AD detected cocaine and benzoylecgonine); and H.R. El-Seedi, "Prehistoric peyote use: alkaloid analysis and radiocarbon dating of archaeological specimens of *Lophophora* from Texas," *Journal of Ethnopharmacology*, vol. 101, no. 1–3 (October 2005): 238–242, doi.org/10.1016/j.jep.2005.04.022 (where thin-layer chromatography (TLC) and gas chromatography-mass spectrometry (GC-MS) detected mescaline in two peyote buttons recovered from Shumla Cave No. 5 on the Rio Grande, Texas that dated to 3780–3660 BC).

8 Max Nelson, *The Barbarian's Beverage: A History of Beer in Ancient Europe* (New York: Routledge, 2005), 54.

9 Paulina Komar, "The Benefits of Interdisciplinary Approach—A Case of Studying the Consumption of Greek Wines in Roman Italy," *European Scientific Journal*, Special Edition no. 2 (June 2013): 45–54, at 49. Whether Italy was introduced to wine drinking by the Ancient Greeks, or the taste developed among the Etruscans and other indigenous people prior to colonization, Komar summarizes the current state of the debate: "it is possible to form a hypothesis that the inhabitants of Italy in the Bronze Age were interested in vines and could make fermented beverage from its fruits. It was, however, rather primitive and on a small scale till the arrival of the Greeks, who taught them how to take proper care of *vitis* (pruning introduced by Numa in the times of Greek colonization of the Apennine peninsula). They also spread the idea of wine drinking during the symposion (Greek wine ware dominating in archaeological evidence)."

10 Patrick E. McGovern, *Uncorking the Past: The Quest for Wine, Beer, and Other Alcoholic Beverages* (Oakland, CA: University of California Press, 2009), 192.

11 Anna Isabel Jiménez San Cristóbal, "Iacchus in Plutarch," in Lautaro Roig Lanzillotta et al., (eds.), *Plutarch in the Religious and Philosophical Discourse of Late Antiquity* (Boston: Brill, 2012), 125–36.

12 Plutarch, *Lives*, Alcibiades, 29.

Chapter 8: The Drug of Immortality

1 Reuters, "Gilets jaunes protests: Eiffel Tower and Louvre to shut amid fears of violence," *Guardian*, December 6, 2018, www.theguardian.com/world/2018/dec/06/french-government-warns-of-weekend-of-great-violence-protesters.

2 R. Gordon Wasson, Albert Hofmann, and Carl A. P. Ruck, *The Road to Eleusis: Unveiling the Secret of the Mysteries* (Berkeley, CA: North Atlantic Books, 2008), 99.

3 Hoyle, *Delphi*, 76.

4 Wasson, Hofmann, and Ruck, *Road to Eleusis*, 101.

5 August Frickenhaus, *Lenäenvasen* (Zum Winckelmannsfeste der Archäeologischen Gesellschaft Zu Berlin, 1912), doi.org/10.11588/diglit.2165#0010.

6 Several images of vases resembling G 408 can be found online. The motif depicted on G 409 is far more distinctive. The Louvre identifies the artist responsible for G 408 as the prolific Villa Giulia Painter (who was active in Athens between 470 and 440 BC). G 409 has been attributed to the Chicago Painter. This naming convention for Greek pottery begins with the British archaeologist and art historian, Sir John Beazley: "Following Beazley's system of nomenclature, deriving the artist's name from the name of a city where an important vase is located, as the Berlin Painter from the *hudria* in Berlin, our artist is known as the Chicago Painter, in spite of the anomaly of an ancient Greek artist bearing an American Indian name." Betty Grossman, *"Greek Vase by the Chicago Painter," Bulletin of the City Art Museum of St. Louis*, vol. 40, no. ½ (1955): 15–24.

7 "Father Francis Tiso: The World's Most Controversial Priest talks about Spiritual Practice" (YouTube, 2014), https://youtu.be/6NONrKLVP7I.

8 See Francis Tiso, *Rainbow Body and Resurrection: Spiritual Attainment, the Dissolution of the Material Body, and the Case of Khenpo A Chö* (Berkeley, CA: North Atlantic Books, 2016). Following the Khenpo's death in 1998, "his face became youthful" and all signs of aging melted away. Five rainbows were reported to be visible above his house for several

days. When a week had passed, the body was discovered to have completely vanished—hair, fingernails, and all. In another case, Lama A Khyung, the dharma brother of Khenpo A Chö, showed Father Francis a photograph taken of him in the dark. A glow could be seen around the master's silhouette in meditation position. When the Lama died in 2008, his corpse apparently manifested rainbows as promised, and shrank down to less than three inches in length.

9 *The Other Side of Midnight* podcast, April 1, 2018, www.theothersideofmidnight.com/3018 -04-01_tiso-francis/.

10 Erik Thunø, *Image and Relic: Mediating the Sacred in Early Medieval Rome* (Rome: L'erma di Bretschneider, 2002), 141–43.

11 Euripides, *The Bacchae,* 777.

12 Euripides, *The Bacchae,* 274–84.

13 *Odyssey,* 4.230. Homer said that a seemingly dangerous drug could also be "healing" or *esthla* (ἐσθλὰ), depending on its preparation and dosage, when added to a grape potion. As early as the eighth century BC, therefore, we have written evidence of a deep familiarity with drugs in the Ancient Greek tradition. The same substance could be manipulated to achieve a range of physical, psychological, and even spiritual effects.

14 R. Scodel, "Wine, Water, and the Anthesteria in Callimachus Fr. 178. Pf.," *Zeitschrift für Papyrologie und Epigraphik,* vol. 39 (1980): 37–40. Scodel adds: "it is unlikely to be coincidence that the mythographical sources for the story of Icarios evoke wine's dangerous potential with the same term" (*pharmakon* = drug) because, after all, "myth and ritual stand in close connection."

15 Ibid., 39.

16 Charlotte Higgins, "Ancient Greece, the Middle East and an ancient cultural internet," *Guardian,* July 11, 2013, www.theguardian.com/education/2013/jul/11/ancient-greece -cultural-hybridisation-theory.

17 H. W. Janson, *History of Art,* 5th ed., rev. by Anthony F. Janson (New York: Thames & Hudson, 1986), 157–58.

18 Walter F. Otto, *Dionysus: Myth and Cult* (Bloomington, IN: Indiana University Press, 1995), 152; see also Marvin Meyer, *The Ancient Mysteries: A Sourcebook of Ancient Texts* (Philadelphia: University of Pennsylvania Press, 1987), 5, citing Plutarch's *On Isis and Osiris,* 6.35.

19 One of the most compelling finds is the red-figure *hudria* from the fifth century BC, currently housed in the Museum of Edirne in Turkey. Unearthed in 2011 at the ancient port city of Ainos in the Evros region of eastern Macedonia, where modern-day Greece meets Turkey, the vessel depicts a *pithos* urn embedded in the ground for the fermentation of wine. Around it, two couples display botanical samples for spiking the mix. Ruck identifies the first as ivy. The second, ceremonially presented by a woman whose hand pose is similar to the maenad's on G 409, looks fascinatingly like a mushroom. See Carl Ruck, ed., *Dionysus in Thrace: Ancient Entheogenic Themes in the Mythology and Archeology of Northern Greece, Bulgaria and Turkey* (Berkeley, CA: Regent Press, 2017). The discovery of the *hudria* in the Ainos necropolis, and the funerary banquet tradition that existed at the site, suggests the otherworldly nature of the wine mix. A graveyard tradition that is explicitly connected to the God of Ecstasy. See A. Erzen, "1981 Yılı Enez Kazısı Çalışmaları," in *KST IV—1982* (Ankara: Kültür ve Turizm Bakanlığı Eski Eserler ve Müzeler Genel Müdürlüğü, 1983), 285–290: "The figurine, Satyr and Maenad paintings recovered during the 1981 campaign indicate the presence of a Dionysus cult in Ainos.

20 Robert F. Forbes, *A Short History of the Art of Distillation: From the Beginnings Up to the Death of Cellier Blumenthal* (Boston: Brill, 1970).

21 The manuscript of the *Materia Medica*, scanned from the National Central Library of
    Rome, is available here: https://archive.org/details/bub_gb_ZStFeIm9EukC/.

22 Well known to manuscript specialists, but few others, is how the Dark Ages and the Re-
    naissance actually got their names. The sixth to fourteenth centuries AD were "dark" be-
    cause most Ancient Greek documents, like Dioscorides's *Materia Medica*, went missing
    during the fall of the Roman Empire, as Europe's centers of learning shifted to the Byzan-
    tine East. When the original Greek writings of Plato, Aristotle, and others were retrieved
    from Constantinople and the Middle East in the fifteenth century, their translation into
    Latin signaled the "rebirth" of Western civilization. See Paul Oskar Kristeller, *Renaissance
    Thought: The Classic, Scholastic and Humanist Strains* (New York: Harper & Row, 1961),
    15–16: "The humanists introduced Greek into the curriculum of all universities and of the
    better secondary schools of Western Europe, and they also imported from the Byzantine
    and later Turkish East, through purchase and through less honorable means, a large num-
    ber of manuscripts containing almost the entire body of extant Greek literature, which was
    thus deposited in Western libraries and diffused through handwritten copies and printed
    editions. . . . It was an important, though not yet sufficiently appreciated, achievement of
    the Renaissance scholars that they gradually translated into Latin almost the entire body
    of Greek literature then known, and thus introduced it into the main stream of Western
    thought."

23 W. B. Turrill, "A Contribution to the Botany of Athos Peninsula," *Bulletin of Miscellaneous
    Information (Royal Botanic Gardens, Kew)*, vol. 1937, no. 4 (1937): 197–273, at 197. De-
    scribing a visit to Mt. Athos in Greece in 1934, Sir Arthur W. Hill, then director of the
    Royal Botanic Gardens, wrote about the "official Botanist Monk" who bided his time "in
    searching for plants of real or supposed medicinal importance," adding, "He was a remark-
    able old Monk with an extensive knowledge of plants and their properties. Though fully
    gowned in a long black cassock he traveled very quickly, usually on foot and sometimes
    on a mule, carrying his 'Flora' with him in a large, black, bulky bag. Such a bag was neces-
    sary since his 'Flora' was nothing less than four manuscript folio volumes of Dioscorides,
    which apparently he himself had copied out. This Flora he invariably used for determining
    any plant which he could not name at sight, and he could find his way in his books and
    identify his plants—to his own satisfaction—with remarkable rapidity." Interestingly, Hill
    notes that the monk was on the hunt for the psychedelic henbane (*Hyoscyamus*).

24 Paula De Vos, "European Materia Medica in Historical Texts: Longevity of a Tradition
    and Implications for Future Use," *Journal of Ethnopharmacology*, vol. 132, no. 1 (October
    2010): 28–47.

25 Dioscorides, *Materia Medica*, Book 4.69.

26 Dioscorides, *Materia Medica*, Book 5.81.

27 Dioscorides, *Materia Medica*, Book 4.74

28 Philip Mayerson, *Classical Mythology in Literature, Art and Music* (Indianapolis, IN: Hack-
    ett Publishing Company, 2011), 251.

Chapter 9: The Vineyards of Heaven

1 W. R. Halliday, "The Magical Vine of Nysa and the Dionysiac Wine Miracle," *Classical
    Review*, vol. 42, no. 1 (February 1928): 19, doi.org/10.1017/S0009840X00043596.

2 Pausanias, *Pausaniae Graeciae Descriptio*, 3 vols. (Suttgart: Teubner, 1903), 6.26.1–2.

3 Pliny, *The Natural History*, Book 2.106: "It is accredited by Mucianus who was three times

consul that the water flowing from a spring in the temple of Father Liber [Dionysus] on the island of Andros always has the flavour of wine on January 5th: the day is called God's Gift Day."

4   Euripides, *The Bacchae,* 150, 353, 455.

5   Maggie Owens, "'Mona Lisa' to Move to Private Room in Louvre" (ABC News, January 6, 2006), https://abcnews.go.com/International/story?id=81285&page=1.

6   "The moving of the Mona Lisa," *Independent,* April 2, 2005, www.independent.co.uk/news /world/europe/the-moving-of-the-mona-lisa-530771.html

7   A. D. Nock, "Hellenic Mysteries and Christian Sacraments," *Mnemosyne,* Fourth Series, vol. 5, fasc. 3 (1952): 177–213, at 183, www.jstor.org/stable/4427382.

8   In line 603 of Euripides's *The Bacchae,* for example, *Dios gonos* (Διὸς γόνος) means "the begotten Son of God."

9   Dennis R. MacDonald, *The Dionysian Gospel: the Fourth Gospel and Euripides* (Minneapolis, MN: Fortress Press, 2017), 31.

10 The Gospel of John 1:18, New International Version.

11 Matthew 8:1–4.

12 Mark 1:21–27; Luke 4:31–36.

13 MacDonald, *Dionysian Gospel,* 40.

14 Erik Raymond, "Why Did Jesus Make So Much Wine?" (Gospel Coalition, April 18, 2018), www.thegospelcoalition.org/blogs/erik-raymond/jesus-make-much-wine/.

15 See Epiphanius of Salamis, *Adversus Haereses,* Book 2, Sect 51, 29.7, available on p. 301 here: https://archive.org/details/epiphanius02epip/. Epiphanius places Jesus's birth on "January 5 at the dawn of January 6," precisely when the Dionysian miracle on Andros was said to take place. Epiphanus then ties Jesus's Epiphany as the wine god to the same day: "the first miracle in Cana of Galilee, when the water was made wine, was performed on about the same day [as Jesus's original Epiphany, his birth] "thirty years later." Interestingly, the Wedding at Cana passage (John 2:1–11) is still read during the Roman Catholic Mass every January, on the second Sunday following the Feast of the Epiphany on January 6. In the Eastern Orthodox Church, the Epiphany is also celebrated on January 6, which is January 19 on the Julian calendar.

16 Philipp Fehl, "Veronese's Decorum: Notes on the Marriage at Cana," in Moshe Barasch, ed., *Art, the Ape of Nature: Studies in Honor of H. W. Janson* (Upper Saddle River, NJ: Prentice-Hall, 1981) 345–46.

17 Further detail is embedded in one particularly fascinating papyrus from the Zenon Archive, a collection of Greek correspondence uncovered in the late nineteenth century. Zenon was a bureaucrat under the Ptolemaic Kingdom that ruled Hellenistic Egypt for about three hundred years from Alexander the Great until Cleopatra, when the Romans took over. Sometime in May 257 BC, one pithy letter treats the acclaimed Beth-Anath estate in the Beit HaKerem Valley in Upper Galilee. Mentioned in the Old Testament, this vast plot of land today occupies Bi'ina, just outside Karmiel, a quick drive north of Nazareth. The author of the letter, a certain Glaukias, says Beth-Anath channeled their eighty thousand vines into an exceptional wine that, upon tasting, was indistinguishable from the gold-standard wines of the Greek island of Chios. In 2001 excavations in nearby Nahf confirmed that Glaukias was spot-on. Given the "inordinate amount of storage-vessel fragments" recovered from this particular site, the Israeli Antiquities Authority has now confirmed the importance of Upper Galilee for wine production during the Hellenistic era. See Howard Smithline, "Results of Three Small Excavations at Nahf, Upper Galilee" *Atiqot,* vol. 59 (2008): 87–101, at 99.

18 See Asher Ovadiah and Sonia Mucznik, "Dionysos in the Decapolis," *Liber Annuus,* vol. 65 (2015): 387–405.

19 Patricia Maynor Bikai et al., "Beidha in Jordan: A Dionysian Hall in a Nabataean Land-scape," *American Journal of Archaeology*, vol. 112, no. 3 (July 2008): 465–507, at 495.

20 Scott D. Charlesworth, "The Use of Greek in Early Roman Galilee: The Inscriptional Ev-idence Re-examined," *Journal for the Study of the New Testament*, vol. 38, no. 3 (2016): 356–95, doi.org/10.1177/0142064X15621650: "On the basis of all of the extant evidence, knowledge of Greek was probably quite common, with most people picking it up by force of circumstance rather than through formal instruction."

21 Thomas L. Friedman, "Ancient Mosaic Shows 'Mona Lisa of Palestine,'" *New York Times*, August 18, 1987, www.nytimes.com/1987/08/18/science/ancient-mosaic-shows-mona -lisa-of-palestine.html.

22 See Rachel Hachlili, "Reviewed Work: *The Mosaics of the House of Dionysos at Sepphoris (Qedem 44)* by Rina Talgam, Zeev Weiss," *Israel Exploration Journal*, vol. 57, no. 2 (2007): 248–52. Traditionally translated as "drunkenness," the root of *methe* (μέθη) has nothing whatsoever to do with wine. It comes from the Indo-European *madhu*, which in Sanskrit means any sweet or intoxicating beverage, hence the English word "mead."

23 "The Surprises of Sepphoris: the archaeological excavations at Sepphoris are painting a new portrait of Jesus' world" (PBS Frontline series: *From Jesus to Christ*, April 1998), www .pbs.org/wgbh/pages/frontline/shows/religion/jesus/sepphoris.html.

24 Bikai et al., "Beidha in Jordan," 477. Several stone heads, wonderfully preserved, would have once topped the ornate capitals of the temple's columns. One is "easily identifiable as Dionysus, for he is singled out by the vine wreath that crowns his head." In addition to satyrs and bacchants, there are also a number of female heads with "softly modeled features," interpreted as maenads, nymphs, and Greek Muses.

25 Ibid., 495.

26 Diodorus Siculus, 3.59.2, 3.64.5, 3.65.7, and 3.66.3. Diodorus elsewhere cites additional authors who place Nysa in North Africa, while Herodotus (2.146, 3.97) says it is located in Ethiopia.

27 Patrick E. McGovern, *Ancient Brews: Rediscovered and Re-created* (New York: W. W. Nor-ton, 2017), 94. See also Patrick E. McGovern, *Ancient Wine: The Search for the Origins of Viniculture* (Princeton, NJ: Princeton University Press, 2003).

Chapter 10: Holy Elixirs in the Holy Land

1 Elisa Guerra-Doce, "The Origins of Inebriation: Archaeological Evidence of the Con-sumption of Fermented Beverages and Drugs in Prehistoric Eurasia," *Journal of Archae-ological Method and Theory*, vol. 22, no. 3 (September 2015): 760. See also Patrick E. McGovern et al., "Neolithic resinated wine," *Nature*, vol. 381 (June 6, 1996): 480–81, avail-able at www.penn.museum/sites/biomoleculararchaeology/wp-content/uploads/2009/11/ neolithicwinenature.pdf.

2 Patrick E. McGovern, *Uncorking the Past: The Quest for Wine, Beer, and Other Alcoholic Beverages* (Oakland, CA: University of California Press, 2009), 89.

3 Ibid., 100.

4 Patrick E. McGovern et al., "Ancient Egyptian herbal wines," *Proceedings of the National Academy of Sciences*, vol. 106, no. 18 (May 5, 2009): 7361–66, doi.org/10.1073/pnas .0811578106. Aside from tartaric acid, the Abydos samples yielded: linalool, camphor, borneol, L-menthol, alpha-terpineol, carvone, thymol, geranyl acetate, and other sub-stances. In pursuit of their organic ancestors, McGovern explains that these compounds

occur in the following herbal genera: savory (*Satureja*), wormwood (*Artemisia seiberi*), blue tansy (*Tanacetum annuum*), balm (*Melissa*), senna (*Cassia*), coriander (*Coriandrum*), germander (*Teucrium*), mint (*Mentha*), sage (*Salvia*), and thyme (*Thymus/Thymbra*). The Gebel Adda sample tested positive for five distinct terpenoids: fenchone, camphor, borneol, cuminaldehyde, and vanillin. The most likely herbal candidate with these unique biomarkers is rosemary (*Rosmarinus officinialis*), a member of the mint family (*Lamiaceae* or *Labiatae*).

 5 McGovern, *Uncorking the Past,* 120.

 6 McGovern, *Ancient Brews,* 94.

 7 Ibid., 95.

 8 William A. Emboden, *Narcotic Plants: hallucinogens, stimulants, inebriants and hypnotics, their origins and uses* (New York: Macmillan, 1979), 149.

 9 Jeremy Naydler, *Shamanic Wisdom in the Pyramid Texts: The Mystical Tradition of Ancient Egypt* (Rochester, VT: Inner Traditions, 2004), 193–94. The Dramatic Ramesseum Papyrus, now in the British Museum, is dated to about 1980 BC. It includes a ceremonial play reenacting the accession of Senuset I of the Twelfth Dyansty to the throne. The hieroglyphics, written in narrow columns, have been compared to a modern-day comic strip.

10 Ibid., 234.

11 Ibid., 209.

12 See F. Nigel Hepper, *Pharaoh's Flowers: The Botanical Treasures of Tutankhamun* (Chicago: KWS Publishers, 2009).

13 See William A. Emboden, "The Sacred Narcotic Lily of the Nile: Nymphaea caerulea," *Economic Botany,* vol. 32, no. 4 (October–December 1978): 395–407, at 397.

14 See Lynnsay Maynard, "What Would Jesus Drink? A Class Exploring Ancient Wines Asks" (NPR, *All Things Considered,* December 25, 2014), www.npr.org/sections/thesalt /2014/12/25/372727808/what-would-jesus-drink-a-class-exploring-ancient-wines-asks; Megan Gannon, "World's Oldest Wine Cellar Fueled Palatial Parties" (LiveScience, August 27, 2014), www.livescience.com/47577-worlds-oldest-wine-cellar-israel.html; and Doyle Rice, "World's oldest wine cellar discovered," *USA Today,* November 22, 2013, www .usatoday.com/story/news/world/2013/11/22/old-wine-cellar-israel/3667621/.

15 Andrew J. Koh et al., "Characterizing a Middle Bronze Palatial Wine Cellar from Tel Kabri, Israel," *PLoS ONE* 9 (8) (August 27, 2014): e106406, doi.org/10.1371/journal.pone.0106406.

16 The website of Andrew Koh's OpenARCHEM project is a cutting-edge resource within the field of archaeochemistry: https://openarchem.com/research-teams-at-openarchem/.

17 Ilan Ben Zion, "Canaanite wine stash found in Galilee unearths ancient flavors: Excavators at Tel Kabri find hard evidence of viniculture, seek to recreate Bronze Age beverage," *Times of Israel,* August 28, 2014, www.timesofisrael.com/canaanite-wine-stash-found-in-galilee -unearths-ancient-flavors/.

18 Stephen Harrod Buhner, *Sacred and Herbal Healing Beers: The Secrets of Ancient Fermentation* (Denver, CO: Brewers Publications, 1998), 237–41.

19 Christian Rätsch, *The Encyclopedia of Psychoactive Plants: Ethnopharmacology and Its Applications* (Paris, ME: Park Street Press, 2005). The psychoactive species of juniper available in the Hindu Kush is likely drooping juniper (*Juniperus recurva*).

20 Ibid. See M. H. Sidky, "Shamans and Mountain Spirits in Hunza," *Asian Folklore Studies,* vol. 53, no. 1 (January 1994): 67–96, doi: 10.2307/1178560. A video of the full ceremony performed by the Hunza shaman can be seen here: https://vimeo.com/51983176.

21 Bezalel Porten, *Archives from Elephantine: The Life of an Ancient Jewish Military Colony* (Oakland, CA: University of California Press, 1968), 184.

22 McGovern, *Uncorking the Past,* 179.

23 Porten, *Archives from Elephantine,* 183.

24 G. del Olmo Lete, "The Marzeaḥ and the Ugaritic Magic Ritual System: a close reading of KTU 1114," *Aula orientalis,* vol. 33, No. 2 (2015): 221–42, at 224.

25 Ibid., 231.

26 Ibid., 233. See S. Tamar Kamionkowski and Wonil Kim, eds., *Bodies, Embodiment and Theology of the Hebrew Bible* (London: T & T Clark, 2010), 165. An English translation of the full Ugaritic tale can be found here: http://inamidst.com/stuff/notes/feast.

27 See Patrick E. McGovern, *Ancient Wine: The Search for the Origins of Viniculture* (Princeton, NJ: Princeton University Press, 2003) 228–30; and Randall Heskett and Joel Butler, *Divine Vintage, Following the Wine Trail from Genesis to the Modern Age* (New York: St. Martin's Press, 2012), 93–94. Since the Canaanite deity El was known to get wasted and pass out, the participants in the *marzeah* would "imitate the gods by drinking themselves into a stupor." The "heavenly feast" therefore provided an opportunity for extreme intoxication and "direct divine-human contact." The Old Testament references to the *marzeah* include Amos 6:4–7, Jeremiah 16:5, and Numbers 13:1–33, where Moses dispatches twelve spies— one from each of the twelve Israelite tribes—to see what the narco-pagans are really up to in the Promised Land. They famously return with a cluster of grapes so gigantic, it takes two men to carry the load. Among the many artistic depictions of the event, Francesco Carabelli's bas-relief on the exterior of the Duomo in Milan gives a great sense of the back-breaking mission. The meaning, once again, is clear: whatever the successors of Tel Kabri were cooking up, it was something out of this world.

28 See Elizabeth M. Bloch-Smith, "The Cult of the Dead in Judah: Interpreting the Material Remains," *Journal of Biblical Literature,* vol. 111, no. 2 (Summer 1992): 213–24, at 214 and 219, www.jstor.org/stable/3267540. It has been suggested that women dominated the role of Jewish shaman outside the male orthodoxy of Jerusalem: "One such role was providing for and consulting the ancestors, the mediator between the generations." Women were seen as the natural intermediaries between this life and the next, but the male prophets of Yahweh also knew their way around a graveyard of the so-called "Grateful Dead." In Isaiah 8:19, when Yahweh gives Isaiah the silent treatment, the Old Testament seer is encouraged to seek guidance from the departed ancestors: "the ghosts and familiar spirits that chirp and mutter. Should not a people inquire of their divine beings, on behalf of the living inquire of the dead?" See also Earl Lee, *From the Bodies of the Gods* (Paris, ME: Park Street Press, 2012), 64–65.

29 Zeyad al-Salameen and Hani Falahat, "Two New Nabataean Inscriptions from Wadi Musa, with Discussion of Gaia and the Marzeah," *Journal of Semitic Studies,* vol. 57, no. 1 (March 2012): 37–51, at 43–45. In Luke 13:32, when he learns that Herod wants him dead too, Jesus calls the tyrant a "fox" or *alopex* (ἀλώπηξ), which in Hebrew would have meant something like "small-fry" or "jackass." See Hermann Strack and Paul Billerbeck, *Kommentar zum Neuen Testament aus Talmud und Midrasch* (Munich, Germany: C. H. Beck, 1960), 2:200–201.

30 John McLaughlin, *The Marzeah in the Prophetic Literature: References and Allusions in Light of the Extra-Biblical Evidence* (Boston: Brill, 2001), 47: "In Nabataean religion Dushara is equated with, among others, the Greek god Dionysus, whose associations with intoxication suggest that heavy drinking played a role in the association. The view is reinforced by the purpose of the stone objects themselves [four trough-shaped vessels unearthed at 'Avdat, in the Negev desert of southern Israel]. Their designation in the inscriptions, combined with the large cup mark in the bottom of each, indicates they were used for serving liquid, and in light of wine's role in marzeahs in general and in this one in particular through its dedication to

Dushara/Dionysus, it is reasonable to surmise that was the kind of liquid served. Further-more, the size of the objects indicates significant amounts of wine were used."

31 Carl Kerenyi, *Dionysos: Archetypal Image of Indestructible Life* (Princeton, NJ: Princeton University Press, 1976), 303.

32 1 Peter 4:6.

33 Euripides, *The Bacchae*, 422–30.

34 A. J. Nijboer, "Banquet, Marzeah, Symposion and Symposium during the Iron Age: Dis-parity and Mimicry," in Franco de Angelis, ed., *Regionalism and Globalism in Antiquity: Exploring Their Limits* (Walpole, MA: Peeters, 2013), 95–126, at 96. The defining attributes of the elite *marzeah* are identified as: "upper-class male practices, royal patronage, the association with specific deities, banqueting with meat and wine, the use of fine perfumed oils, ownership of vineyards and fields, banqueting houses-rooms often with reclining couches, music and a correlation with death and funerary rituals probably in combination with a fostering of descent." This eastern influence on later banqueting in Greece and Italy is especially highlighted: "the concepts of marzeah in the Levant and the Phoenician-Punic world of the western Mediterranean, symposion in Greece, including the Greek colonies in southern Italy from the 7th century BC onwards, and symposium in central Italy, signify elite male, festive banquets or drinking bouts with luxuries, fine wines, music and storytelling . . . In spite of their countless cultural differences, conflicts and haggling over trade, this course of events would have sustained bonds between the Greek and Ital-ian warrior elites and their Phoenician counterparts."

35 McGovern, *Ancient Wine*, 230.

36 Luke 7:34; Matthew 11:19.

37 See P. G. Walsh, "Making a Drama out of a Crisis: Livy on the Bacchanalia." *Greece & Rome*, vol. 43, no. 2 (October 1996): 188–203, www.jstor.org/stable/643095.

38 Eric Orlin, "Urban Religion in the Middle and Late Republic," in Jörg Rüpke, ed., *A Com-panion to Roman Religion* (Hoboken, NJ: Wiley-Blackwell, 2011), 58–70, at 64.

39 See Dan Stanislawski, "Dionysus Westward: Early Religion and the Economic Geography of Wine," *Geographical Review*, vol. 65, no. 4 (October 1975): 427–44, at 441, www.jstor .org/stable/213743. Prior to the second century BC, the cult of Dionysus found a receptive audience in Magna Graecia. Greek colonization of the western Mediterranean began on the tiny island of Ischia in the Tyrrhenian Sea before the middle of the eighth century BC. Soon thereafter, another trading post with Italy was established at Kyme, south of Naples (or Neapolis, the "new city," which was younger than these early footholds). The region between Paestum and Calabria on the west coast of the peninsula came to be known as Oenotria, a name that would eventually refer to the entirety of southern Italy. Oenotria is, of course, derived from the Greek *oinos* (οἶνος), "wine." The availability of fertile land was a strong incentive for pioneering colonists from agricultural-rich bases like Corinth, Crete, Rhodes, and Naxos. The first Sicilian colony was appropriately named Naxos, where the settlers exported their "cult practices, in which Dionysus was the most important figure. Understandable, then, is the fact that Naxos, one of the earliest Greek colonies to strike coins, put a depiction of Dionysus on one side and grapes and grape leaves on the other."

40 Livy, *History of Rome*, 39.13: "Within the last two years it had been ordained that no one beyond the age of twenty years should be initiated: boys of such age were sought for as admitted both vice and corruption" (*biennio proximo institutum esse, ne quis maior viginti annis initiaretur: captari aetates et erroris et stupri patientes*).

41 See "Bacchus Uncovered: Ancient God of Ecstasy" (BBC Four, September 26, 2019), www .bbc.co.uk/programmes/b09z8d01.

42 Vivian Nutton, *Ancient Medicine* (New York: Routledge, 2012), 232. See also Menahem
    Stern, ed., *Greek and Latin Authors on Jews and Judaism, vol. 1, From Herodotus to Plutarch*
    (Jerusalem: Israel Academy of Sciences and Humanities, 1974), 422–25, for Dioscorides's
    reference to several specimens in Judaea and Petra. In Gavin Hardy and Laurence Totelin's
    Ancient Botany (New York: Routledge, 2016), 39, the authors mention how the extent of
    Dioscorides's travels is a matter of some debate, ultimately concluding that the Father of
    Drugs did, in fact, travel to many of the locations mentioned in the *Materia Medica.*
43 See Walter Burkert, *Ancient Mystery Cults* (Cambridge, MA: Harvard University Press,
    1987), 52.
44 Euripides, *The Bacchae,* 487.
45 John 11:48.
46 Matthias Riedl, "The Containment of Dionysos: Religion and Politics in the Bacchanalia
    Affair of 186 BCE," *International Political Anthropology,* vol. 5, no.2 (2012): 113–34.
47 Mary Beard, John North, and Simon Price, *The Religions of Rome: vol. 1* (Cambridge, UK:
    Cambridge University Press, 1998), 226, fn. 49.
48 See Joan Taylor, "What did Jesus really look like?" (BBC, December 24, 2015), www.bbc.com
    /news/magazine-35120965; and Joan Taylor, "What did Jesus really look like, as a Jew in 1st-
    century Judaea?" *Irish Times,* February 9, 2018, www.irishtimes.com/culture/books/what-did
    -jesus-really-look-like-as-a-jew-in-1st-century-judaea-1.3385334. A review of men's groom-
    ing style in ancient Galilee casts doubt on the historical Jesus having a long, flowing mane.
    But that didn't stop some anonymous Christian artists from copying the "big, curly hair of
    Dionysus" in the early centuries of the faith, and passing the hippie look on to posterity.
49 Barry B. Powell, *Classical Myth,* 7th ed. (New York: Pearson, 2011), 201–02. The ubiquity
    of goats in pagan imagery calls to mind Francisco Goya's *El Aquelarre* (the Basque phrase
    for "Witches' Sabbath"), the eighteenth-century oil painting featuring a fiery-eyed goat
    crowned in oak leaves, holding court with the old crones.
50 R. Gordon Wasson, Albert Hofmann, and Carl A. P. Ruck, *The Road to Eleusis: Unveiling
    the Secret of the Mysteries* (Berkeley, CA: North Atlantic Books, 2008), 98. Ruck notes
    how Theophrastus records that "herb gatherers used to stuff their cuttings into hollow,
    fennel-like stalks to preserve their freshness."
51 Plato, *Euthydemus,* 285c.
52 Philostratus the Younger, *Imagines* 2, Marsyas (395K).
53 Werner Keller, *The Bible as History* (New York: Barnes & Noble, 1995), 352.

Chapter 11: Drunk with the Nectar of Eternity

1 Wouter J. Hanegraaff, *Esotericism and the Academy: Rejected Knowledge in Western Culture* (Cambridge, UK: Cambridge University Press, 2012), 54.
2 Bart D. Ehrman, *The Triumph of Christianity* (New York: Simon & Schuster, 2018). See
   Rodney Stark, *The Rise of Christianity: How the Obscure, Marginal Jesus Movement Became
   the Dominant Religious Force in the Western World in a Few Centuries* (San Francisco, CA:
   Harper San Francisco, 1997), 10.
3 Carl A. P. Ruck et al., *The Apples of Apollo: Pagan and Christian Mysteries of the Eucharist*
   (Durham, NC: Carolina Academic Press, 2000), 145.
4 Ruck isn't the only scholar who has gone down this blasphemous road. Consider what
   Frederic Henry Chase (1853–1925), the classicist, President of Queens' College at Cambridge University, and Bishop of Ely, had to say in *The Credibility of the Book of the Acts*

of the Apostles (London: Macmillan,1902), at 205–206, footnote 3, available at https://archive.org/details/thecredibilityof00chasuoft/: "The name Ἰησοῦς, otherwise unintelligible, would be naturally connected by the Athenians with ἴασις (Ionic ἴησις), and Ἰασώ (Ἰησώ), the goddess of healing and health. . . . The Ionic form Ἰησώ was doubtless known at Athens from such passages as Herondas vi.6 (cult of Ἰησώ in Kos)."

5 Ruck et al, 146. Ruck cites Matthew 13:15; Luke 5:17 and 13:32; John 12:40; and Acts 10:38.

6 In line 81 of Euripides's *The Bacchae,* a bacchant is depicted "having crowned" himself "with ivy"—*kisso stephanotheis* (κισσῷ στεφανωθεὶς). Later on, Pentheus is urged to welcome Dionysus into Thebes by wearing the god's unique emblem. In line 341, Pentheus's father Cadmus demands: "Come here, let me crown your head with ivy."

7 The color convention can be traced back to the *Homeric Hymn to Dionysus,* among the oldest examples of Greek literature. In the hymn that predates Euripides, the cloak is specifically described as "purple" or *porphureon* (πορφύρεον). See Athenaeus's *Deipnosophistae* 5.198c: "On it was a statue of Dionysus ten cubits high pouring libation from a gold *karchēsion* [vase] and wearing a purple tunic that stretched to its feet and a thin saffron robe over this; a purple robe with gold spangles was wrapped around its shoulders."

8 Justin Martyr, *Dialogue with Trypho,* chapter 69: "The Devil, since he emulates the truth, has invented fables about Bacchus, Herakles, and Aesclapius." See also Justin Martyr, *The First Apology,* chapter 54: "the devils, accordingly, when they heard these prophetic words [from Genesis], said that Bacchus was the son of Jupiter, and gave out that he was the discoverer of the vine, and they number wine among his mysteries; and they taught that, having been torn in pieces, he ascended into heaven."

9 In Justin's wake, Clement of Alexandria decided to put a little more effort into Christianity's argument, engaging Euripides in an ancient rap battle. He invites all of Dionysus's "drunken" and "frenzy-stricken" followers to throw away their ivy and headgear. The Church Father calls Mount Cithaeron of *The Bacchae* a fictional "subject for tragedies," encouraging his audience to discover the "wineless mountain" of the Christian Mysteries in the "dramas of truth." In a lyrical word play, Clement says no "maenads" or *mainades* (μαινάδες) can be found cavorting in the "hallowed groves" of *his* mountain, only "lambs" or *amnades* (ἀμνάδες) assembled in "sober company." In Greek the words for "maenads" and "lambs" are near-identical and—with the subtlest shift—can easily trade places.

10 Hannah Brockhaus, "Pope on Corpus Christi: Only the Eucharist satisfies hearts" (Catholic News Agency, June 3, 2018), www.catholicnewsagency.com/news/pope-on-corpus-christi-only-the-eucharist-satisfies-hearts-18847.

11 "Pope celebrates Mass for Solemnity of Corpus Christi" (Vatican Radio, June 18, 2017), www.archivioradiovaticana.va/storico/2017/06/18/pope_celebrates_mass_for_solemnity_of_corpus_christi/en-1319866.

12 "Pope Francis: The Eucharist is not a symbol, it is Jesus giving himself entirely" (YouTube, 2015), https://youtu.be/fH9Lg4SFP0M.

13 Hyam MacCoby, *The Mythmaker: Paul and the Invention of Christianity* (New York: Barnes & Noble, 1998), 110.

14 J. G. Frazer, *Spirits of the Corn and of the Wild* (New York: Macmillan, 1912), available in two volumes here: https://archive.org/details/goldenboughstudy07fraz/page/n8 and https://archive.org/details/goldenboughstudy08fraz/page/n8.

15 Martin Luther King, Jr., "The Influence of the Mystery Religions on Christianity," in Clayborne Carson, Ralph Luker, and Penny A. Russell, eds., *The Papers of Martin Luther King, Jr. Volume I: Called to Serve, January 1929–June 1951* (Oakland: University of Califor-

nia Press, 1992), available at https://kinginstitute.stanford.edu/king-papers/documents
/influence-mystery-religions-christianity.

16 Dennis R. MacDonald, *The Dionysian Gospel: the Fourth Gospel and Euripides* (Minneapolis, MN: Fortress Press, 2017), 65.

17 Alan Piper, "The Milk of Goat Heidrun: An Investigation into the Sacramental Use of Psychoactive Meat and Milk," in John Rush, ed., *Entheogens and the Development of Culture: The Anthropology and Neurobiology of Ecstatic Experience* (Berkeley, CA: North Atlantic Books, 2013), 211 ff., with the *omophagia* specifically referenced on 241. Piper notes, for example, the affinity of Nordic and Siberian reindeer for psychedelic *Amanita muscaria* mushrooms. There is a well-documented tradition of shamans drinking the deer's urine, said to preserve the chief psychoactive compound of the mushroom, muscimol, while tempering other toxins that can be unpleasant for humans. In addition there is the reported discovery of the hallucinogenic *Tabernanthe iboga* by African gorillas and wild boars. Cattle, horses, and rabbits can consume plants from the nightshade family with no ill effect, while a human who feeds on the animals' suddenly psychoactive flesh can die.

18 Ibid., 247.

19 For the Egyptian tradition of wine as blood, see Plutarch, *Moralia, Isis and Osiris,* 6. For the Old Testament, see Genesis 49:11. For the holy wine of Dionysus as the holy blood of Dionysus, see Timotheus, *Fragments,* in *Greek Lyric, Volume V: The New School of Poetry and Anonymous Songs and Hymns,* Loeb Classical Library (Cambridge, MA: Harvard University Press, 1993), 86–87, doi:10.4159/DLCL.timotheus-fragments.1993. Centuries after Timotheus, the same image is invoked by Plutarch, who refers to wine as "the rushing wine-god's dark red blood" (κελαινὸν αἷμα Διονύσου θοοῦ) in his *Moralia, Table Talk,* Book 5, 676E. See also Walter Burkert, *Homo Necans: the Anthropolgy of Ancient Greek Sacrificial Ritual and Myth* (Berkeley: University of California Press, 1983), 225.

20 Philip Mayerson, *Classical Mythology in Literature, Art and Music* (Indianapolis, IN: Hackett Publishing Company, 2011), 250. Another play by Euripides called the *The Cretans* reveals the end goal of the Dionysian religion. Compared to the almost 1,400 lines of *The Bacchae,* only 120 lines of this precious fragment have survived. An initiate is speaking about "performing the rites of the *omophagion* feasts" and "raising torches to the Mountain Mother." When all is said and done, the initiate is no longer a human being, but "consecrated" and "named" a "Bacchos" (Βάκχος). They have become Dionysus himself.

21 The author of the Fourth Gospel is usually identified as John of Patmos, a Greek island south of Samos, just off the coast of Asia Minor, and within striking distance of Ephesus. Eusebius and Irenaeus both record John's settling in Ephesus and establishing a church there. A century of scholarship has supported this view. See Carl Clemen, "The Sojourn of the Apostle John at Ephesus." *The American Journal of Theology,* vol. 9, no. 4 (October 1905): 643–76, at 674, www.jstor.org/stable/3154273: "It seems to me incontestable that the Gospel of John also had its origin in or about Ephesus. The remarkable relations with the Apocalypse, and especially those with the logos speculation which we find in Asia earlier and later than this (in the case of Justin), the polemic (though not to be exaggerated) against the followers of John the Baptist, and finally the effects which at first we notice in the case of those who lived in Asia Minor all point to the Ephesian origin of the Gospel of John." See also R. Brown, *An Introduction to the New Testament* (New York: Doubleday, 1997), 371–75; and D. A. Carson, *The Gospel According to John* (Grand Rapids, MI: Eerdmans, 1990), 86–87: "The traditional view is that the Fourth Gospel was written

in Ephesus. . . . The fact that the Montanists used John, and the Montanists were largely based in Phrygia, not too far from Ephesus, is often taken to support the case for Ephesian provenance; but again, John's Gospel could have been circulating in Phyrgia half a century and more after it was written, *regardless* of where it was first published. What must be acknowledged is that no other location has the support of the church Fathers; rightly or wrongly, they point to Ephesus."

22 Ross S. Kraemer, "Ecstasy and Possession: The Attraction of Women to the Cult of Dionysus," *The Harvard Theological Review,* vol. 72, no. ½ (January–April 1979): 55–80, at 70, www.jstor.org/stable/1509675. See also Glen W. Bowersock et al., eds., *Arktouros: Hellenic Studies Presented to Bernard M. W. Knox on the Occasion of His 65th Birthday* (New York: Walter de Gruyter, 1979), 188: "The remarkable completeness of the pattern and the fact that Euripides repeatedly uses religious terminology which evokes the sacrifice leaves little doubt that these correspondences are not accidental, nor only due to the traditional quality of the myth . . . but that Euripides deliberately and constantly calls upon the audience to see and understand the dramatic and emotional climax of his tragedy as sacrifice."

23 Kraemer, "Ecstasy and Possession," 71, 76–77. In a cross-cultural analysis of modern-day African and Caribbean possession cults, Kraemer cites the anthropological scholarship of I. M. Lewis to explain how temporary fits of ecstasy can "neutralize the potentially destructive emotions felt by oppressed individuals of a society." Something Hellenic women of the period would have known all too well: "as a multitude of historians have noted, the status of women in classical Greece ranks among the worst of women in western society at any time." As a release valve, the Dionysian ritual could have served the interests of the "weak and downtrodden" who otherwise had "few effective means to press their claims for attention and respect." By establishing an "ongoing relationship between the afflicted person and the possessing spirit"—especially in a cultic setting with "other similarly afflicted individuals"—the modern, marginalized cults keep the peace by "attracting primarily those of lower social strata and particularly women." It is self-evident to imagine the Dionysian and paleo-Christian Mysteries playing a similar role for women of the ancient Mediterranean.

24 See Pliny, *The Natural History,* Book 34, chapter 19, where Pliny references a competition among Greece's greatest sculptors, resulting in five bronze statues of the women adorning the temple. See also Margaret Mowczko, "The Prominence of Women in the Cults of Ephesus" (personal blog, September 20, 2014), https://margmowczko.com/the-prominence-of-women-in-the-cultic-life-of-ephesus/.

25 See Rick Strelan, *Paul, Artemis and the Jews in Ephesus* (New York: Walter de Gruyter, 1996), 120. See also R. A. Kearsley, "Asiarchs, Archiereis, and the Archiereiai of Asia." *Greek, Roman and Byzantine Studies,* vol. 27 (1986): 183–192, at 186.

26 Cleon L. Rogers, Jr., "The Dionysian Background of Ephesians 5:18," *Bibliotheca Sacra,* vol. 136, no. 543 (July 1979): 249–57.

27 Plutarch, *Lives,* Antony 24.3. For further evidence of the worship in Ephesus as found in inscriptions, see Martin P. Nilsson, *Geschichte der griechischen Religion,* vol. 2 (Munich, Germany: C. H. Beck, 1955), 359–62.

28 Krystal Baugher, "Women and Beer: A 4,500-Year History Is Coming Full Circle," *Atlantic,* November 11, 2013, www.theatlantic.com/business/archive/2013/11/women-and-beer-a-4-500-year-history-is-coming-full-circle/281338/.

29 Patrick E. McGovern, *Uncorking the Past: The Quest for Wine, Beer, and Other Alcoholic Beverages* (Oakland: University of California Press, 2009), 19, 190.

30 Raymond E. Brown, "Roles of Women in the Fourth Gospel," *Theological Studies,* vol. 36 (1975): 688–99, available at www.womencanbepriests.org/classic/brown2.asp.

31 Elaine Pagels, *Beyond Belief: The Secret Gospel of Thomas* (New York: Vintage, 2004), 41.

32 Ibid., 89, 98–105. Aside from the Gospel of Mary Magdalene, Pagels mentions the many other Gnostic texts that prize the revelatory nature of divine visions. In the Secret Book of James, Jesus takes James and Peter on a hallucinogenic tour of the heavens, where the disciples see "trumpets blaring" and "angels rejoicing." Through this experience, Jesus hopes to demonstrate how we might "join him not only after death but also here and now." In the Prayer of the Apostle Paul, the author prays for the sight that "no angel's eye has seen." In the Apocalypse of Peter, the future Pope has a vision of Jesus "glad and laughing on the cross;" it encourages him "to face his own death with equanimity." Even in the canonical New Testament, the author of John's Gospel is sometimes identified as the hand behind the Book of Revelation, which describes the "astonishing visions" John received "in the spirit." Pagels interprets the phrase as "in an ecstatic state."

33 Karen Jo Torjesen, *When Women Were Priests: Women's Leadership in the Early Church and the Scandal of Their Subordination in the Rise of Christianity* (San Francisco, CA: Harper San Francisco, 1995), 15–16.

34 Ibid.

35 Ibid., 127.

36 Ibid., 80.

37 Elsewhere in Colossae, it was Apphia. In Philemon 1:2, Paul refers to her as "sister" or *adelphe* (ἀδελφῇ), which is interpreted to mean she was an important partner in early missionary activity. In nearby Laodicea, east of Ephesus in Asia Minor, it was Nympha, another wealthy patron like Lydia and Priscilla, who opened her home to Christian activity. In Jerusalem, it was Mary, the mother of Peter's traveling buddy, Saint Mark. When an angel busts Peter out of jail, he heads straight for Mary's home. Over at Cenchreae, next to Corinth in Greece, it was a similarly affluent woman named Phoebe. In Romans 16:1–2, Paul specifically calls her his "patroness" or *prostatis (*προστάτις) and labels her a "deacon" or *diakonon* (διάκονον). She was tasked with personally delivering Paul's Letter to the Romans to their final destination in Italy.

38 1 Corinthians 16:19; Romans 16:3–5.

39 Bart Ehrman, *Misquoting Jesus: The Story Behind Who Changed the Bible and Why* (San Francisco: HarperOne, 2007), 180.

40 Torjesen, *When Women Were Priests,* 33.

41 M. Hengel, *Acts and the History of Earliest Christianity* (London: SCM Press, 1979), 107–08.

42 Walter Burkert, *Ancient Mystery Cults* (Cambridge, MA: Harvard University Press, 1989), 52, available here: https://archive.org/details/AncientMysteryCultsWalterBurkert1987.

43 Mary Beard, John North, and Simon Price, *The Religions of Rome, vol. 1* (Cambridge, UK: Cambridge University Press, 1998), 214, 217. See also 230: "Both Caesar and Augustus banned private societies (*collegia*), fearing their role in social or political disorder. . . . From the mid-second century A.D. no one could be a member of more than one club (thus eliminating the spectre of general conspiracy evident in the Bacchanalia affair)."

44 Ibid., 225–26. The stereotype of "illicit, foreign religions" that would eventually adhere to Christianity was "traceable in Rome at least as far back as the affair of the Bacchanalia, two centuries before Christ."

45 See Lulu Garcia-Navarro and Ned Wharton, "After The Flames, Notre Dame's Centuries-Old Organ May Never Be The Same Again" (WCRB, April 21, 2019), www.tinyurl.com /yylbzkzo; and Naomi Rea, "See 7 of the Most Precious Relics That Survived the Blaze

at Notre Dame" (*ArtNet News,* April 17, 2019), https://news.artnet.com/art-world/7
-artworks-and-relics-survived-notre-dame-fire-1518991.

46 Elian Peltier, "The Chaplain, the Cathedral Fire and the Race to Rescue Notre-Dame's Relics," *New York Times,* April 17, 2019, www.nytimes.com/2019/04/17/world/europe/statues
-notre-dame-relics.html.

47 Hugues Lefèvre, "Exclusif-Père Fournier : 'Dans Notre-Dame en feu, j'ai récupéré Jésus et
béni la cathédrale'" (*Famille Chretienne,* April 17, 2019), www.famillechretienne.fr/eglise
/vie-de-l-eglise/exclusif-pere-jean-marc-fournier-dans-notre-dame-en-feu-j-ai-sorti-les
-hosties-et-beni-la-cathedrale-253491.

48 "Incendie à Notre-Dame: témoignage de l'aumônier des pompiers de Paris" (YouTube,
2019), https://youtu.be/ULpcmCCMNTc.

49 Edward Pentin, "Notre Dame Priest: How Blessed Sacrament, Crown of Thorns Were
Saved from Fire" (*National Catholic Register,* April 18, 2019), www.ncregister.com/blog
/edward-pentin/notre-dame-hero-priest-describes-rescue-of-blessed-sacrament-crown
-of-thorn.

50 Clemente Lisi, "Why rebuilding Notre Dame Cathedral could cost billions and take over
a decade" (*GetReligion,* April 22, 2019), www.getreligion.org/getreligion/2019/4/22/why
-rebuilding-notre-dame-could-cost-billions-and-take-over-a-decade.

Chapter 12: All This Was Not Just Picnicking

1 See S. Tofanelli et al., "The Greeks in the West: Genetic signatures of the Hellenic colo-
nisation in southern Italy and Sicily," *European Journal of Human Genetics,* vol. 24, no. 3
(March 2016): 429–36, doi: 10.1038/ejhg.2015.124.

2 Soultana Maria Valamoti, "Healing With Plants in Prehistoric Northern Greece," in Claus
von Carnap-Bornheim, ed., *Von Sylt bis Kastanas, Offa,* vol. 69–70 (Kiel, Germany:
Wachholtz, 2012–2013), 479–94, at 487.

3 Giovanni Casadio and Patricia A. Johnston, eds., *Mystic Cults in Magna Graecia* (Austin:
University of Texas Press, 2009), 1.

4 Peter Lampe, *From Paul to Valentinus: Christians at Rome in the First Two Centuries* (Minneapolis, MN: Fortress Press, 2003), 375.

5 Ibid. See also Ignatius of Antioch, *Epistle to the Smyrneans,* 8.

6 Carl A. P. Ruck et al., *The Apples of Apollo: Pagan and Christian Mysteries of the Eucharist*
(Durham, NC: Carolina Academic Press, 2000), 191.

7 Jesus's raising of Lazarus from the dead is arguably his greatest miracle in the New Testament. In any event it was certainly the one that sealed the Son of God's fate. When
the Jewish high priest, Caiaphas, hears the news, he decides then and there that Jesus's
showboating must come to an end. In John 11:11, the wizard from Nazareth proclaims
he's going to "awaken" Lazarus, who has "fallen asleep" or *kekoimetai* (κεκοίμηται). In the
next verse his disciples comically tell Jesus not to worry, Lazarus will wake up soon. To
which Jesus responds by explaining what he means by the verb *koimao*: he's dead, you
idiots. Likewise in 1 Corinthians 7:39, I doubt Paul is suggesting a monogamous Christian
woman is free to remarry another man every time her husband has merely "fallen asleep"
or *koimethe* (κοιμηθῇ).

8 Ellicott's commentary on 1 Corinthians 11 is available here: www.studylight.org
/commentaries/ebc/1-corinthians-11.html.

9 Karen Jo Torjesen, *When Women Were Priests: Women's Leadership in the Early Church*

and the Scandal of Their Subordination in the Rise of Christianity (San Francisco, CA: Harper San Francisco, 1995), 22.

10 See Campbell Bonner, "A Dionysiac Miracle at Corinth," *American Journal of Archaeology,* vol. 33, no. 3 (July–September 1929): 368–75, at 373, www.jstor.org/stable/498351. Just like the Amazon-descended maenads at Ephesus, to whom John's Gospel seems to have been directed, fans of the God of Ecstasy were also present in the heartland of Greece. A tunnel and water channel were long ago excavated in Corinth's fifth-century BC Dionysian temple, a "peculiar apparatus" whose purpose is "best explained" as a device to produce an extraordinary flow of wine from the temple "on certain great occasions." See also Pausanias, *Descriptions of Greece,* vol. I, Book II.6 (Corinth). The wine god's dominion over this region came straight from Euripides's *The Bacchae.* Pausanias records the existence of several wooden images in Corinth's marketplace, legendarily cut from the tree that Pentheus climbed on Mt. Cithaeron to spy on the maenads toward the end of the play. The Pythia at Delphi had ordered the Corinthians to locate the actual tree outside Thebes to their northeast and "worship it equally with the god."

11 Torjesen, *When Women Were Priests,* 22.

12 David B. Barrett et al., eds., *World Christian Encyclopedia* (New York: Oxford University Press, 2001), 16: "World Christianity consists of 6 major ecclesiastico-cultural blocs, divided into 300 major ecclesiastical traditions, composed of over 33,000 distinct denominations in 238 countries."

13 "Did the Last Supper really take place as it is recorded?" (YouTube, 2009), https://youtu.be /9qCotTdUnn8. Bishop N. T. Wright explains the historicity of the Last Supper. Despite the uncertainties, he ultimately states, "[The Eucharist] is the thing around which my life is concentrated."

14 Paul reprimands the church in Rome for behavior that was similar to that of the Corinthians, using similar language, in Romans 13:11–14.

15 F. Bisconti, *L'ipogeo degli Aureli in Viale Manzoni. Restauri, tutela, valorizzazione e aggiornamenti interpretativi* (Vatican City: Pontificia Commissione di Archeologia Sacra, 2011).

16 Juliette Harrisson, ed., *Imagining the Afterlife in the Ancient World* (New York: Routledge, 2018).

17 In Propertius's *Elegies,* 4.5.2, the ultimate insult is for the dead's living relatives to forget to properly nourish them in the afterlife: "May the earth cover your grave with thorns, bawd / and, what you abhor, may your shade feel thirst / may your spirit find no peace with your ashes but may avenging Cerberus / terrify your vile bones with hungry howl." (Terra tuum spinis obducat, lena, sepulcrum / et tua, quod non vis, sentiat umbra sitim / nec sedeant cineri Manes, et Cerberus ultor / turpia ieiuno terreat ossa sono!)

18 Franz Cumont, *After Life in Roman Paganism* (New Haven: Yale University Press, 1922), 200–03.

19 Ramsay MacMullen, "Christian Ancestor Worship in Rome," *Journal of Biblical Literature,* vol. 129, no. 3 (Fall 2010): 603, www.jstor.org/stable/25765954.

20 Augustine, *Select Letters,* Loeb Classical Library (Cambridge, MA: Harvard University Press, 1953), 44–45, doi: 10.4159/DLCL.augustine-letters.1930. In Epistle XXII.3–6 (392), Augustine references Paul's prohibition against drunkenness from Romans 13:11–14, but falls short of completely outlawing the cult of the dead: "Rioting [*Comissationes*] and drunkenness are considered so permissible and tolerable that they are practised not only on holy days, when the blessed martyrs are honoured—a lamentable sight to anyone who looks on such festivities with more than a carnal eye—but even on any and every day. . . . But since those drunken revels in cemeteries and those social orgies are usually considered

by the carnal and ignorant laity not only to honour the martyrs but also to comfort the dead, they could, I think, be more easily prevailed upon to abandon that scandalous and vicious practice, if, besides forbidding it on Scriptural grounds, we ensure that the offerings made upon tombs for the spirits of those who have fallen asleep (and we must surely believe that they are of some avail) be not extravagant and be tendered without ostentation or reluctance to any who seek them, but be not sold."

21 Ibid., 45, fn. c: "This practice of drunkenness at the martyrs' tombs was widespread (Ps.-Cypr. Dupl. Martyr.25 'annon videmus ad martyrum memorias Christianum a Christiano cogi ad ebrietatem?' Ambr. Helia xvii. 62 'calices ad sepulchra martyrum deferunt atque illic in vesperam bibunt,' etc). It was a survival of the old pagan custom of celebrating Parentalia or Feralia on the tombs of the dead, but, as Augustine says, the Church attempted to arrest this licence, not by complete suppression, but by converting the offering of bread and wine laid on the tombs (see Conf. vi. 2) to a nobler use. The martyr's tomb was made an altar, round which was built the chapel dedicated to him and called by his name; this explains why, in the fourth century, churches were built outside the towns, for the cemeteries were there; only in the tenth century did the church reach the middle of the town. Further, the martyr's fame and sanctity encouraged burial near him; hence the habit of burial within the church, and later around it. So throughout the Middle Ages the church and the cemetery were the sacred place of the people: there they held their plays, their dances (Giraldus Cambrensis describes one in Wales in 1188, Itin. Kambr. i. 2), their revels and even their drinking-bouts, in spite of repeated prohibitions by Church Councils."

22 The text of the Liturgy of the Eucharist is available on the website of the United States Conference of Catholic Bishops: www.usccb.org/prayer-and-worship/the-mass/order-of-mass/liturgy-of-the-eucharist/.

23 Fabrizio Bisconti, "The Art of the Catacombs," in David K. Pettegrew et al., eds., *The Oxford Handbooks of Early Christian Archaeology* (New York: Oxford University Press, 2019), 209–20, at 210.

24 One of the best English-language documentaries about the Roman catacombs can be watched here: www.archaeologychannel.org/video-guide/video-guide/video-guide-list/126-the-witnesses-of-silence-discovering-romes-catacombs.

25 For a list of catacombs open to the public in Rome and elsewhere in Italy, see here: www.catacombeditalia.va/content/archeologiasacra/it/catacombe/aperte-al-pubblico.html.

26 Bisconti, "The Art of the Catacombs," 211.

27 Barbara Mazzei, "Preservation and use of the religious sites: case study of the roman catacombs," *European Journal of Science and Theology*, vol. 11, no. 2 (December 2014): 33–43, at 41.

28 See Harold Whetstone Johnston, *The Private Life of the Romans* (Glenview, IL: Scott Foresman, 1909), www.gutenberg.org/files/40549/40549-h/40549-h.htm: "The boy of good family was always attended by a trustworthy slave (paedagogus), who accompanied him to school, remained with him during the sessions, and saw him safely home again when school was out. If the boy had wealthy parents, he might have, besides, one or more slaves (pedisequi) to carry his satchel and tablets. The paedagogus was usually an elderly man, selected for his good character; he was expected to keep the boy out of all harm, moral as well as physical. He was not a teacher, despite the meaning of the English word 'pedagogue,' except that, after the learning of Greek became general, a Greek slave was usually selected for the position in order that the boy might not forget what Greek he had learned from his nurse. The scope of the duties of the paedagogus is clearly shown by the

Latin words used sometimes instead of paedagogus: comes, custos, monitor, and rector. He was addressed by the boy as dominus, and seems to have had the right to compel obedience by mild punishments. His duties ceased when the boy assumed the toga of manhood, but the same warm affection often continued between the young man and the paedagogus as between a woman and her nurse."

29 See M. Hammond, "Composition of the Senate, A.D. 68–235," *Journal of Roman Studies,* vol. 47 (1957): 74–81. "The statistics shows that since the early 2nd century C.E. the senators of provincial origin began to surpass in number those of Italian origin. Numbers ranged from 50 percent to 60 percent between the early 2nd century C.E. and the early 3rd century C.E."

30 Horatius, *Epistulae,* 2.1.156: "*Graecia capta ferum victorem cepit et artis intulit agresti Latio.*"

Chapter 13: The Holy Grail

1 Larraona, *Missale Romanum* (Rome: Sacrae Rituum Congregationis, 1962), 63: "*accipiens calicem discoopertum cum Sanguine ambabus manibus, ut prius, elevat eum, et erectum quantum commode potest, ostendit populo adorandum.*" Available here: https://sanctamissa .org/en/resources/books-1962/missale-romanum-1962.pdf.

2 See Matthew 26:26–28; Mark 14:22–24; Luke 22:19; 1 Corinthians 11:24.

3 Ramsay MacMullen, "Christian Ancestor Worship in Rome," *Journal of Biblical Literature,* vol. 129, no. 3 (Fall 2010): 605. The Roman catacombs of St. Sebastian contain a dining room with graffiti from the third and fourth centuries indicating that *refrigeria* were being held on-site to commemorate the Apostles Peter and Paul.

4 Ibid., 606.

5 Ibid., 604.

6 Ibid., 603.

7 Ibid.

8 Ibid., 612–13.

9 Ramsay MacMullen, "Roman Religion: The Best Attested Practice," *Historia,* vol. 66, no. 1 (January 2017): 111–27.

10 In addition Latini cites the relevant lines from Vergil and Homer, where Circe is "driving her shrill shuttle through the fine web (*telas*)" in Book 7 of *The Aeneid,* and "singing with sweet voice, as she went to and fro before a great imperishable loom (*histon*)" in Book 10 of *The Odyssey.*

11 Barbara Mazzei, "Quando le nuove tecnologie apportano progressi. La revisione della pulitura delle pitture murali dell'ipogeo degli Aureli," in *Lo stato dell'arte 9,* VIII Congresso Nazionale IGIIC, October 13–15, 2011: 523–29.

12 F. Bisconti, *L'ipogeo degli Aureli in Viale Manzoni. Restauri, tutela, valorizzazione e aggiornamenti interpretativi* (Rome: Pontificia Commissione di Archeologia Sacra, 2011), 178.

13 Homer, *The Odyssey,* 11.34; 10.564–565.

14 Bisconti, *L'ipogeo degli Aureli in Viale Manzoni,* 185.

15 Robert Lamberton, *Homer the Theologian: Neoplatonist Allegorical Reading and the Growth of the Epic Tradition* (Oakland, CA: University of California Press, 1989), 1.

16 Lamberton, *Homer the Theologian,* 173, fn. 36. Meghan Henning, *Educating Early Christians Through the Rhetoric of Hell: 'Weeping and Gnashing of Teeth' as Paideia in Matthew and the Early Church* (Heidelberg, Germany: Mohr Siebeck, 2014), 76, fn. 165, mentions

how the Naassenian Gnostics interpreted Homer's portrayal of Hermes the psychopomp as Jesus.

17 Bisconti, *L'ipogeo degli Aureli in Viale Manzoni,* 17: "The face of Paul—or the philosopher closest to the physiognomic canons of Plotinus among the marble portraits attributed precisely to the Plotinus style, which will prepare the Pauline iconography—represents the most incisive testimony of the imagined painters' activity [of the Hypogeum of the Aurelii], who have in their portfolio of figurative motifs the oriental tradition of the great Near-Eastern philosophical theories."

18 Plotinus, *Enneads,* I.6.8.25. See Pierre Hadot, *Plotinus or the Simplicity of Vision* (Chicago: University of Chicago Press, 1998), 30.

19 Lamberton, *Homer the Theologian,* 42.

20 See Sarah B. Pomeroy, *Pythagorean Women: Their History and Writings* (Baltimore, MD: Johns Hopkins University Press, 2013).

21 Carl A. P. Ruck, "The Cave of Euripides," *Time and Mind,* vol. 8, no. 3 (2015): 279–302, at 282, doi.org/10.1080/1751696X.2015.1066127.

22 Ibid, 292.

23 Ibid, 299.

24 Calvert Watkins, "Let Us Now Praise Famous Grains," *Proceedings of the American Philosophical Society,* vol. 122, no. 1 (February 15, 1978): 10.

25 Ibid., 14.

26 Ibid., 16.

27 John 6:60.

28 Nikolaus Himmelmann, *Das Hypogäum der Aurelier am Viale Manzoni: Ikonographische Beobachtungen* (Mainz, Germany: Akademie Der Wissenschaften Und Der Literatur, 1975).

29 Ibid., 17–20.

30 Himmelmann, citing Martin P. Nilsson, *Geschichte Der Griechischen Religion* (Munich: C.H. Beck, 1967), 663: "The participants in the Mysteries carried blessing-branches (o.S. 126); they would have worn wreaths (*Bekraenzung*), although references for this are late (10), and string would have been tied around the right hand and the left foot. (11) We don't know the age of these rites, though there is nothing to say that they did not belong to the oldest versions."

31 See R. A. S. Seaford, "The Mysteries of Dionysos at Pompeii," in H. W. Stubbs, ed., *Pegasus: Classical Essays from the University of Exeter* (Exeter, UK: University of Exeter, 1981), 52–68.

32 George Rawlinson, *The History of Herodotus,* vol. II (New York: D. Appleton, 1859), 75. As Sir J. G. Wilkinson once noted in the nineteenth century, "the adoption of the pinecone to the head of the spear of Bacchus," evident on the Borghese Vase and countless other examples from antiquity, "originated in the use of the resinous matter put into wine-skins, and afterwards into amphorae."

33 Victoria Hearnshaw, "The Dionysiac Cycle in the Villa of the Mysteries: a Re-Reading." *Mediterranean Archaeology,* vol. 12 (1999): 43–50, at 47, www.jstor.org/stable/24667847: "In Euripides *Bacchae,* for example, the devotees of Dionysus sometimes had to be goaded into action on his behalf. Lyssa was the personification specifically called upon. It was she who must spur the reluctant ones into 'madness,' after they had first let their hair down to their shoulders, like the participant on the frieze at the Villa. The ritual flagellation may be seen as a means of heightening sensation, which in turn will rouse the woman participant into a frenzy." See also Euripides, *The Bacchae,* 795, where the God of Ecstasy in disguise warns

Pentheus to stop resisting the call to wild, altered states of consciousness: "I would sacrifice to him [Dionysus] rather than kick angrily against the goad [*kentra*], man against god."

34 Olga Levaniouk, "The Toys of Dionysos," *Harvard Studies in Classical Philology*, vol. 103 (2007): 165–202, at 188–190, www.jstor.org/stable/30032222.

35 Bisconti, *L'ipogeo degli Aureli in Viale Manzoni*, 10.

Chapter 14: A Gnostic Eucharist

1 Robert Kahn et al., eds., *City Secrets: Rome* (Melbourne: The Little Bookroom, 2000), 79–80.

2 See chapter 5, note 16.

3 Carl A. P. Ruck et al., *The Apples of Apollo: Pagan and Christian Mysteries of the Eucharist* (Durham, NC: Carolina Academic Press, 2000), 151.

4 Eusebius, *Ecclesiastical History*, II.13. The existence of Simon's statute is in doubt. In AD 1574, a monument was indeed found on the Isola Tiberina, part of whose inscription reads "SEMONI SANCO DEO," not the "SIMONI DEO SANCTO" preserved by Justin Martyr. The former would refer to the Sabine god of oaths and contracts, Semo Sancus.

5 Ibid.

6 Irenaeus, *Adversus Haereses*, 1.23.4. See also Epiphanius of Salamis, *Adversus Haereses* Book 1, Sect 21, 2.1, available at https://archive.org/details/epiphanius01epip/, 239, where Simon is accused of slipping a "poison" or *deleterion* (δηλητήριον) "into the dignity of Christ's name, as though he were mixing hellebore with honey." *Deleterion* is a synonym of *pharmakon*.

7 Elaine Pagels, *The Gnostic Gospels* (New York: Vintage, 1989), 36.

8 Ibid.

9 Ibid.

10 William Christian Pinner, *Reception of the Fourth Gospel in the Second Century* (master's thesis, University of Georgia, 2007), 42–46, available at https://getd.libs.uga.edu/pdfs/pinner_william_c_201005_ma.pdf.

11 Ruck, *Apples of Apollo*, 187.

12 Hippolytus, *Refutatio Omnium Haeresium*, Book 6, 39–40, available at https://archive.org/details/origenisphilosop00hipp/, 200–201. After mentioning the *pharmakon* seven times, Hippolytus concludes his discussion of Marcus's drugged sacrament by noting how the women "proceeded to drink (the mixture), as if it were something divine, and devised by the Deity."

13 Irenaeus, *Adversus Haereses*, 1.13.2.

14 Ibid. In 1.13.2, the word Irenaeus uses to describe the method by which Marcus drives his female devotees out of their minds is *exoistresas* (ἐξοιστρήσας). The verb comes from the Greek *oistros* (οἶστρος), which literally means "gadfly," but in the context of Dionysian madness can mean "sting" or "insane passion." In 1.13.5, Irenaeus accuses the Marcosians of using the same heretical sacraments as the Simonians: "love charms" (*filtra*/φίλτρα) and "love potions" (*agogima*/ἀγώγιμα).

15 Pagels, *Gnostic Gospels*, 141.

16 Ibid.

17 Elaine Pagels, *Beyond Belief: The Secret Gospel of Thomas* (New York: Vintage, 2004), 180.

18 Karen Jo Torjesen, *When Women Were Priests: Women's Leadership in the Early Church*

and the Scandal of Their Subordination in the Rise of Christianity (San Francisco, CA: Harper San Francisco, 1995), 222.

19 Sacred Congregation for the Doctrine of the Faith, "Declaration Inter Insigniores on the Question of the Admission of Women to the Ministerial Priesthood" (Vatican City, October 15, 1976).

20 Ibid. See also Pope John Paul II, "Ordinatio Sacerdotalis" (Vatican City, May 22, 1994). See also Cardinal Luis F. Ladaria, "In Response to Certain Doubts Regarding the Definitive Character of the Doctrine of Ordinatio Sacerdotalis" (Vatican City, May 29, 2018).

21 "Declaration Inter Insigniores on the Question of the Admission of Women."

22 Letha Clair Robertson, "Saints, Shrines, and Relics: Bernini's Reliquary Balconies in St. Peter's Basilica" (seminar paper, University of Kansas, May 19, 2005), available here: http://stpetersbasilica.info/Docs/LCR/SSRelics.htm.

23 The text of the Catechism of the Catholic Church is available on the Vatican website here: www.vatican.va/archive/ccc_css/archive/catechism/p1s2c2a7.htm.

24 Bruno Bartoloni, "All the Mystery Surrounding St Peter's Tomb," *L'Osservatore Romano*, August 29, 2012, available here: www.ewtn.com/catholicism/library/all-the-mystery-surrounding-st-peters-tomb-1743.

25 The website of La Fabbrica di San Pietro is available here: www.vatican.va/various/basiliche/san_pietro/index_it.htm.

26 Pietro Zander, *La necropoli di San Pietro. Arte e fede nei sotterranei della Basilica vaticana* (Rome: Elio de Rosa, 2015), 145–151.

27 Martin Wallraff, *Christus Verus Sol. Sonnenverehrung und Christentum in der Spätantike* (Münster: Aschendorff, 2001).

28 John Beckwith, *Early Christian and Byzantine Art* (New Haven, CT: Yale University Press, 1986), 19.

29 Zander, *La necropoli di San Pietro*, 301.

30 Beckwith, *Early Christian and Byzantine Art*, 19.

31 Valdis Leinieks, *The City of Dionysos: A Study of Euripides' Bakchai* (Stuttgart and Leipzig: B. G. Teubner, 1996), 187.

32 The website of the Catacombs of Priscilla is available here: www.catacombepriscilla.com/visita_catacomba_en.html.

33 *Le Catacombe di Priscilla* (Vatican City: Pontificia Commissione di Archeologia Sacra, 2016), 40. See also Vincenzo F. Nicolai et al., *The Christian Catacombs of Rome: History, Decoration, Inscriptions* (Stuttgart: Art Stock Books, 2006). An inscription elsewhere in the Catacombs of Priscilla records a *refrigerium* taking place in March 374 or 375.

34 See Mary M. Schaefer, *Women in Pastoral Office: The Story of Santa Prassede, Rome* (New York: Oxford University Press, 2013), 187.

35 Dorothy Irvin, "The Ministry of Women in the Early Church: the Archeological Evidence," *Duke Divinity School Review*, vol. 2 (1980): 76–86, at 83.

36 *Le Catacombe di Priscilla*, 46.

37 Ibid.

38 Ibid., 47.

39 Ibid., 46.

40 Nicola Denzey, *The Bone Gatherers: The Lost Worlds of Early Christian Women* (Boston: Beacon Press, 2007), 102.

41 The website of the Catacombs of Saints Marcellinus and Peter is available here: www.santimarcellinoepietro.it/english/.

42 Janet Tulloch, "Women Leaders in Family Funerary Banquets," in Carolyn Osiek et al., *A*

Woman's Place: House Churches in Earliest Christianity (Minneapolis, MN: Fortress Press, 2005), 164–193, at 165.

43 Ibid., 173.

44 Ibid., 176.

45 Ibid., 182, 192.

46 Ibid., 186.

47 D. E. Eichholz, "Galen and His Environment." *Greece & Rome,* vol. 20, no. 59 (June 1951): 60–71, at 64, www.jstor.org/stable/640892.

48 Tulloch, "Women Leaders," 190. One vase, currently in the Rheinisches Landesmuseum in Trier, Germany, bears the phrase "Da caldum."

Chapter 15: Mystery Coast Highway

1 William Anderson, "An Archaeology of Late Antique Pilgrim Flasks," *Anatolian Studies,* vol. 54 (2004): 79–93, www.jstor.org/stable/3643040.

2 Stephanie Hagan, "Death and Eternal Life at Beth Shean," Penn Museum's *Expedition Magazine,* vol. 55, no. 1 (2013): 33–36, www.penn.museum/sites/expedition/articles/volume55-issue1/.

3 Plato, *Phaedo,* 64a.

4 Peter Kingsley, *In the Dark Places of Wisdom* (Inverness, CA: The Golden Sufi Center, 1999), 79.

5 Ibid., 112.

6 Ibid., 100.

7 Ibid., 111.

8 Ibid., 82.

9 Ibid., 84.

10 Ibid., 102–103.

11 Roy Merle Peterson, *The Cults of Campania,* vol. I (Rome: American Academy in Rome, 1919), available here: https://archive.org/details/cultsofcampania00pete/page/n6.

12 Ibid., 26.

13 Ibid., 28.

14 Ibid., 31.

15 Ibid., 36.

16 Ibid., 39.

17 Peter Kingsley, *Ancient Philosophy, Mystery, and Magic: Empedocles and Pythagorean Tradition* (Oxford: Clarendon Press, 1995), 222–227. While the precise meaning of *pharmaka* in Empedocles' fragment 111 is hotly debated, Kingsley notes that a "primary reference is, no doubt, to magical remedies extracted from plants." But he prefers the "broader connotation of 'spell' or 'charm'" implied by the word: "the incantations (ἐπωιδαί) which were recited during the gathering of the plants and during their preparation."

18 Marina Ciaraldi, "Drug preparation in evidence? An unusual plant and bone assemblage from the Pompeian countryside, Italy," *Vegetation History and Archaeobotany,* vol. 9 (2000): 91–98, at 91, doi.org/10.1007/BF01300059.

19 Ibid., 95.

20 Ibid.

21 Ibid.

22 Ibid., 97–98.

23 Ibid., 97.

24 Giovanni Casadio, "Dionysus in Campania: Cumae," in Giovanni Casadio and Patricia A. Johnston, eds., *Mystic Cults in Magna Graecia* (Austin, TX: University of Texas Press, 2009), 33–45, at 33, 35. "Gods, at least the gods of paganism, have a body. They drink, eat, copulate, and with advancing years they waste away, stricken with the infirmities of old age. The place where the most pagan of all the gods of Mediterranean paganism—Dionysus-Bacchus—might have liked to spend his third age, without renouncing his most deeply ingrained habits, can ideally be identified with Campania: a land of intrinsically orgiastic nature given the effervescence of its soil (the Vesuvius, the Flegrean Fields) and the ebullience of its inhabitants (the whirling tarantella dance, the Satyric and Phlyacic figure of Pulchinello) . . . The undulating *vitiferi colles* that enliven the coastal area from the Gulf of Gaeta to the Gulf of Naples—through Ischia, the Vesuvius, and the peninsula of Sorrento—and the ensuing *temulentia nobilis* (a state of drunkenness elevated to an almost spiritual level, as in the celebrated Horatian example) are emblems of the Campanian landscape."

Chapter 16: The Gospel of Infinity and the Toad Eucharist

1 The website of the Vatican Secret Archives is available here: www.archiviosegretovaticano .va/content/archiviosegretovaticano/en/l_archivio/ambienti/bunker-e-depositi.html.

2 Ingrid D. Rowland, *Giordano Bruno: Philosopher/Heretic* (Chicago: University of Chicago Press, 2009), 276.

3 The astrophysicist Neil deGrasse Tyson pays special tribute to Bruno in *Cosmos: A Spacetime Odyssey,* a documentary series that aired on Fox and the National Geographic Channel in 2014. The clip mentioning Bruno is available to watch here: https://vimeo.com /150392001.

4 NASA's website on exoplants is an entertaining resource: https://exoplanets.nasa.gov/the -search-for-life/exoplanets-101/.

5 An English translation of the indictment against Galileo is available here: https://hti.osu .edu/sites/hti.osu.edu/files/documents_in_the_case_of_galileo_1.pdf.

6 Frances A. Yates, *Giordano Bruno and the Hermetic Tradition* (Chicago: University of Chicago Press, 1991).

7 An English translation of *The Heroic Enthusiasts* is available here: www.gutenberg.org/files /19833/19833-h/19833-h.htm; the original Italian here: www.letteraturaitaliana.net/pdf /Volume_5/t113.pdf.

8 Maria Luisa Ambrosini, *The Secret Archives of the Vatican* (New York: Barnes & Noble Books, 1996), 195.

9 My translation of the Bruno manuscript, folio 210v: "He replies, mocking that Mass as the clerical harbor for the art of love, and about transubstantiation, I don't speak of it without getting irritated, saying that bread could not be transmuted into flesh and it was as a bestiality, blasphemy, and idolatry." (*rispondea burlandosi, che messa porto d'officio de arte amandi, e de la transubstantione me ne parlo quando ragiono de la Irirrita dicendo che non si potea transmutare pane in carne e ch'erano bestialita, bestemie et idolatria*).

10 See N. J. Walforf, "Luther and Consubstantiation," *Ministry Magazine,* November 1936, available here: www.ministrymagazine.org/archive/1936/11/luther-and -consubstantiation. Sixteenth-century reformers like Martin Luther were awfully dissatisfied with the untestable leap of faith in the Catholic Church's doctrine of transubstan-

tiation. But they didn't do much better. In a series of meetings between 1529 and 1536, the leaders of the Protestant Reformation came up with the equally confusing doctrine of *consubstantiation,* or sacramental union, where the substance of *both* the bread and wine *and* the body and blood of Jesus are always present in the consecrated Eucharist.

11 "What Americans Know About Religion" (Pew Research Center, July 23, 2019), https://pewrsr.ch/2Gh6pmo.

12 James T. Keane and Sam Sawyer, S.J., "Explainer: Why the Eucharist is confusing for many Catholics (and survey researchers)," (*America,* August 09, 2019), www.americamagazine.org/faith/2019/08/09/explainer-why-eucharist-confusing-many-catholics-and-survey-researchers.

13 Giordano Bruno, *The Ash Wednesday Supper,* edited and translated by Edward A. Gosselin and Lawrence S. Lerner (Toronto: University of Toronto Press, 1995), 50: "The Hermetic, Brunian understanding of the Eucharist, the true ceremony of the cup, involves a deeper commingling of essences than that allowed by either the Protestant or the traditional Catholic definitions of the Supper; Bruno's communion is an active, two-way process, consistent with the Brunian view of the immanence of divinity in Man. As such, it transcends the passive 'one-way' communion of the narrow believers on both sides of the Catholic-Protestant gulf . . . the earth moves, the universe is alive. So too, are men animated by the divine spark which flows from man to man and God to man through the no-longer baleful nexus of the Eucharist . . . By taking the sacrament, men can share in the same animistic forces which cause the universe to move."

14 Pierre Hadot, *Plotinus or the Simplicity of Vision* (Chicago: University of Chicago Press, 1998), 40. See also Plotinus, *Enneads,* V.8.4.36 and V.8.5.5.

15 Alessandra Stanley, "Pope Asks Forgiveness for Errors of the Church Over 2,000 Years," *New York Times,* March 13, 2000, www.nytimes.com/2000/03/13/world/pope-asks-forgiveness-for-errors-of-the-church-over-2000-years.html.

16 Charles Seife, "Vatican Regrets Burning Cosmologist," *Science,* March 1, 2000, https://web.archive.org/web/20130608054739/http://news.sciencemag.org/sciencenow/2000/03/01-04.html.

17 Massimo Faggioli, "Flirting with Schism: the Right-Wing Effort to Delegitimize Pope Francis," *Commonweal,* September 6, 2018, www.commonwealmagazine.org/flirting-schism.

18 Walter Strauss, "The Wherewithal of Witches," *Notes in the History of Art,* vol. 2, no. 2 (Winter 1983): 16–22, at 17, www.jstor.org/stable/23202279. See also A. Laguna, "Contes à la première personne (extraits des livres sérieux du docteur Laguna)," *Bulletin hispanique,* vol, 58, no. 2 (1956): 201–06, at 204, available here: www.persee.fr/doc/hispa_0007-4640_1956_num_58_2_3484.

19 A. Alizadeh et al., "Black henbane and its toxicity—a descriptive review," *Avicenna Journal of Phytomedicine,* vol. 4, no. 5 (September–October 2014): 297–311, www.ncbi.nlm.nih.gov/pubmed/25386392. Yet another episode of the *Sacred Weeds* series from the UK's Channel 4 in 1998 is a must-see: "Sacred Weeds-Henbane The Witches Brew" (YouTube, 2011), https://youtu.be/uLZiKBdMEIc.

20 Strauss, "Wherewithal of Witches," 17.

21 Ibid.

22 Linda C. Hults, "Baldung's Bewitched Groom Revisited: Artistic Temperament, Fantasy and the 'Dream of Reason,'" *Sixteenth Century Journal,* vol. 15, no. 3 (Autumn 1984): 259–79, at 265–68, www.jstor.org/stable/2540763: "In the *Malleus Maleficarum* (1486), a widely circulated witch-hunting manual, this is blatantly put: 'All witchcraft comes from carnal

lust, which is in women insatiable.' Baldung's drawings of witches . . . emphasize their carnality by their nudity and indecorous poses and gestures (note the center witch . . . who
anoints herself between the legs with the 'flying unguent'). In *De Praestigiis Daemonum*
(1563) Johann Weyer boldly suggested that drugs in their ointments caused witches to
experience sensations of flight and the erotic activities of the sabbath."

23 Strauss, "Wherewithal of Witches," 17.

24 Carl A. P. Ruck et al., *The Apples of Apollo: Pagan and Christian Mysteries of the Eucharist*
(Durham, NC: Carolina Academic Press, 2000), 144.

25 See Chapter 12, note 21.

26 Ramsay MacMullen, *Christianity and Paganism in the Fourth to Eighth Centuries* (New
Haven, CT: Yale University Press, 1999), 154.

27 Ibid., 127.

28 Zoe A. Ferraris and Victor A. Ferraris, "The Women of Salerno: Contribution to the Origins of Surgery From Medieval Italy," *Annals of Thoracic Surgery,* vol. 64 (1997): 1855–57,
available here: www.annalsthoracicsurgery.org/article/S0003-4975(97)01079-5/pdf.

29 The standout celebrity was the eleventh-century Trota or Trotula, a Magistra of Medicine.
According to Ferraris and Ferraris, her *Passionibus Mulierum Curandorum* served as "Eu-
rope's primary text on women's health until the 17th century." See also "Trotula and the
Ladies of Salerno," *Nature,* vol. 145 (March 30, 1940): 507–508.

30 Colin Tatz and Winton Higgins, *The Magnitude of Genocide* (Santa Barbara, CA: Praeger
Security International, 2016), 214.

31 Carlo Ginzburg, *Ecstasies: Deciphering the Witches' Sabbath* (Chicago: University of Chicago Press, 2004), 122.

32 Ibid.

33 Written in the 1430s in Savoy (the region that encompasses modern-day France, Switzerland, and Italy), the full title of the *Errores Gazariorum* may be translated as: "*The Heresy
of the Witches, Meaning Those Who Are Known to Ride on Brooms and Staffs.*"

34 Brian P. Levack, *The Witch-Hunt in Early Modern Europe, Third Edition* (Harlow, UK:
Pearson, 2006), 21.

35 Karen Jolly et al., *Witchcraft and Magic in Europe, vol. 3: The Middle Ages* (London: Ath-
lone Press, 2002), 233.

36 Thomas Hatsis, *The Witches' Ointment: The Secret History of Psychedelic Magic* (Paris, ME:
Park Street Press, 2015), 70.

37 Ibid.

38 Bengt Ankarloo and Gustav Henningsen, eds., *Early Modern European Witchcraft: Centres
and Peripheries* (New York: Oxford University Press, 1993), 197.

39 Franco Mormando, "Bernardino of Siena, Popular Preacher and Witch-Hunter: A 1426
Witch Trial in Rome," in *Fifteenth Century Studies,* vol. 24 (1998): 84–118, at 100–01, for
uncertain dating of Bernardino's infamous sermons in Rome. See Franco Mormando, *The
Preacher's Demons: Bernardino of Siena and the Social Underworld of Early Renaissance
Italy* (Chicago: University of Chicago Press, 1999), 235, for Mormando's date of 1426.

40 Mormando, *Preacher's Demons,* 55.

41 Ginzburg, *Ecstasies,* 298.

42 See Hatsis, *Witches' Ointment,* where Finicella is mentioned at 198: "Mandrake was called
Circeium by some, indicating its role in transformation ointments and potions (it could
have been the active additive in the potion of Finicella, the cat woman of Rome). And
there is every indication that ominous notions of poisonous potions survived in the fifteenth and sixteenth centuries. As was sometimes the case, the artists of these times told

the stories that the religious elite would not. Depictions of Circe from humanists Hart-mann Schedel (1440–1514), one of the first adepts in the use of the printing press (he reproduced the works of many of the artists of his time) and the German draftsman and printmaker Virgil Solis (1514–1562), among others, show that this magical potion was still considered the true source of her powers." See also note 22 above.

43 Dioscorides, *Materia Medica,* Book 4.76.

44 Mormando, *Preacher's Demons,* 65.

45 Ginzburg, *Ecstasies,* 299.

Chapter 17: Our Eyes Have Been Opened

1 Joe Mozingo and John Spano, "$660-million settlement in priest abuses," *Los Angeles Times,* July 15, 2007, www.latimes.com/archives/la-xpm-2007-jul-15-me-priests15-story.html.

2 Aaron Schrank, "Attorney General Launches Statewide Investigation Into Catholic Dio-ceses Handling of Sex Abuse Cases" (*LAist,* May 3, 2019), https://laist.com/2019/05/03/california_ag_investigating_catholic_dioceses.php.

3 Michelle Boorstein and Sarah Pulliam Bailey, "More U.S. Catholics are considering leaving the church over the sex abuse crisis, poll says," *Washington Post,* March 13, 2019, www.washingtonpost.com/religion/2019/03/13/more-us-catholics-are-considering-leaving-church-over-sex-abuse-crisis-poll-says/.

4 See Henry Kamen, *The Spanish Inquisition* (New Haven, CT: Yale University Press, 2014), 253: "We can in all probability accept the estimate, made on the basis of available docu-mentation, that a maximum of three thousand persons may have suffered death during the entire history of the tribunal." See also F. Almeida, ed., *História da Igreja em Portugal, vol. IV* (Oporto, PT: Coimbra, 1923), Appendix IX, 442. For African slaves, see Heather Rachelle White, "Between the Devil and the Inquisition: African Slaves and the Witchcraft Trials in Cartagena de Indies," *North Star: A Journal of African American Religious His-tory,* vol. 8, no. 2 (Spring 2005), available here: www.princeton.edu/~jweisenf/northstar/volume8/white.pdf.

5 R. J. Rummel, *Death by Government* (Piscataway, NJ: Transaction Publishers, 2011), 162.

6 Anne Jacobson Schutte, "Palazzo del Sant'Uffizio: The Opening of the Roman Inquisition's Central Archive," *Perspectives on History,* May 1, 1999, available here: www.historians.org/publications-and-directories/perspectives-on-history/may-1999/palazzo-del-santuffizio-the-opening-of-the-roman-inquisitions-central-archive.

7 A. De Blasio, *Inciarmatori, maghi e streghe di Benevento* (Naples: Luigi Pierro Tip., 1900), available here: http://asmvpiedimonte.altervista.org/Credenze_popolari/De percent-20Blasio percent20inciarmatori.html.

8 Francis X. Blouin, Jr., ed., *Vatican Archives: an Inventory and Guide to Historical Docu-ments of the Holy See, Supplement #1: The Archives of the Congregation for the Doctrine of the Faith, including the Archives of the former Congregation of the Holy Office and the Archives of the former Congregation for Forbidden Books* (Ann Arbor, MI: University of Michigan, 2003), 3. The seeds of the Holy Office date back to the twelfth century. But it wasn't until 1542 that Paul III appointed the first permanent Roman commission of car-dinals and tribunals "to defend and maintain the integrity of the faith and to examine and proscribe errors and false teaching."

9 C. B. Schmitt et al., eds., *Cambridge History of Renaissance Philosophy* (Cambridge, UK: Cambridge University Press, 1988), 46.

10 Schutte, "Palazzo del Sant'Uffizio."

11 Blouin, ed., *Vatican Archives,* 11.

12 Schutte, "Palazzo del Sant'Uffizio."

13 Ibid.

14 Cullen Murphy, *God's Jury: The Inquisition and the Making of the Modern World* (New York: Houghton Mifflin Harcourt, 2012), 20.

15 The website of Brian A. Pavlac, professor of history at King's College in Wilkes-Barre, Pennsylvania, is a wonderful resource on the witch hunts: www.brianpavlac.org /witchhunts/werrors.html.

16 Gwynn Guilford, "Germany was once the witch-burning capital of the world. Here's why" (*Quartz,* January 24, 2018), https://qz.com/1183992/why-europe-was-overrun-by-witch -hunts-in-early-modern-history/.

17 Dioscorides, *Materia Medica,* 2.210, available here: https://archive.org/details/de-materia -medica/page/n379.

18 Pliny, *The Natural History,* 24.47.75, available here: https://archive.org/stream /naturalhistory07plinuoft#page/56/mode/2up/search/ivy.

19 Plutarch, *Quaestiones Romanae,* 112

20 Ibid. See D. C. A. Hillman, *The Chemical Muse: Drug Use and the Roots of Western Civilization* (New York: Thomas Dunne Books, 2008), 85–86. See also Karl-Heinrich Horz and Jürgen Reichling, "Hedera," in *Hagers Handbuch der pharmazeutischen,* 5th ed., (Berlin: Praxis, 1993), 4:398–407, where the authors make reference to the psychedelic properties of common ivy: "In the toxicological literature, it is noted that a 3-year-old child ate a large amount and had hallucinations."

21 Edward Peters, *The Magician, the Witch, and the Law* (Philadelphia: University of Pennsylvania Press, 1982), 131.

22 Keith Thomas, *Religion and the Decline of Magic: Studies in Popular Beliefs in Sixteenth and Seventeenth-Century England* (London: Penguin UK, 2003), 38.

23 Like Giambattista della Porta, the occultist who was born and raised in Naples. In 1588 he published some additional candidates for the contents of the witches' ointment, including: aconite, hemlock, deadly nightshade, and even darnel (barley's evil stepsister, and the ideal host for ergot). See his *Natural Magick (Magia Naturalis),* a later version of which has been scanned and made available by the Library of Congress: http://hdl.loc.gov/loc.rbc/pre1801 .23451.1.

24 A. D. Nock, "The Lizard in Magic and Religion," in his *Essays on Religion and the Ancient World* (New York: Oxford University Press, 1972), 271–276, at 273.

25 Ibid., 275.

26 Rossell Hope Robbins, *The Encyclopedia of Witchcraft & Demonology* (New York: Crown Publishers, 1959), 540.

27 George Gifford, *A Dialogue Concerning Witches and Witchcraft: In Which Is Layed Open How Craftily the Divell Deceiveth Not Onely the Witches But Many Other, And So Leadeth Them Awrie Into Manie Great Errours* (London: Percy Society, 1842), 116, available here: https://archive.org/details/adialogueconcer00giffgoog/page/n8.

28 Hernando Ruiz de Alarcón, *Treatise on the Heathen Superstitions: That Today Live Among the Indians Native to This New Spain, 1629* (Norman, OK: University of Oklahoma Press, 1987), 59.

29 Ibid., 66.

30 Ibid., 62.

31 Ibid.

32 Omer C. Stewart, *Peyote Religion: A History* (Norman: University of Oklahoma Press, 1993), 129.

33 Ibid., 130.

34 Ibid., 157.

35 Eunice V. Pike and Florence H. Cowan, "Mushroom Ritual versus Christianity," *Practical Anthropology*, vol. 6 (1959): 145–50, http://en.psilosophy.info/mushroom_ritual_versus _christianity.html.

Afterword

1 Eran Arie, Baruch Rosen, and Dvory Namdar, "Cannabis and Frankincense at the Judahite Shrine of Arad," *Tel Aviv*, vol. 47, no. 1 (2020): 5–28, doi.org/10.1080/03344355.2020.1732046.

2 Jim O'Sullivan, "Archdiocese gives $850,000 to fight marijuana bid," *Boston Globe*, October 28, 2016, www.bostonglobe.com/metro/2016/10/28/archdiocese-spend-against -marijuana-legalization/qtCwVY4ViWjRFwOvcyveeK/story.html.

3 Morton Smith was a Harvard Divinity School–trained historian who taught at Columbia University for thirty-three years. His *Jesus the Magician* (Newburyport, MA: Hampton Roads, 2014), originally published in 1978, continues to stir up controversy in conservative circles of the Christian faith. Recall that Dionysus was called a magician (*goes*/γόης) and enchanter (*epodos*/ἐπῳδὸς) in Euripides's *The Bacchae*. Likewise, Jesus is charged throughout the Gospels with being a "deceiver" or "illusionist" (*planos*/πλάνος). It's where we get the word "planet," which literally means "the wandering ones." As a *planos*, Jesus would be the one who "led astray" or caused the mind to wander with his magical tool kit. Smith dug into "a vast body of material testifying to the use of his name in Christian spells and exorcisms" to demonstrate Jesus's popularity among certain early Christians as a powerful magician. In a first-century curse tablet from Megara in Greece, for example, Jesus is invoked together with Hecate and Persephone. His name is also included in pagan incantations from an obscure set of formulae and rituals known as the *Papyri Graecae Magicae* (Greek Magical Papyri), largely composed in the first centuries after Jesus. According to *Jesus the Magician*, 87, it was a "side of the religion" that "was gradually driven underground" after "Christianity gained official status in the fourth century"—even if "the change was slow." Smith believes that, like the death cults that proved impossible to extricate from the rural cemeteries up through the Middle Ages, an occult version of Christianity was "accepted by hundreds of thousands of believing Christians through the first millennium, and more, of Christian history."

4 Jan Hoffman, "A Dose of a Hallucinogen From a 'Magic Mushroom,' and Then Lasting Peace." *New York Times*, December 1, 2016), www.nytimes.com/2016/12/01/health /hallucinogenic-mushrooms-psilocybin-cancer-anxiety-depression.html.

5 Frederick S. Barrett and Roland R. Griffiths, "Classic Hallucinogens and Mystical Experiences: Phenomenology and Neural Correlates," Current Topics in Behavioral Neurosciences, vol. 36 (2018), 393–430, doi:10.1007/7854_2017_474.

6 Alan Watts, *The Joyous Cosmology: Adventures in the Chemistry of Consciousness* (Novato, CA: New World Library, 2013), 14.

Index

Abydos, Egypt, 205–6, *206*
aconite, 185–86
Acropolis Museum, 55, 69
Acts of Peter, 293
Adams, John, 16
Adam-Veleni, Polyxeni, 54–62, 67–68, 176
addiction to drugs, curing, xvi
Aeaea, 63, 276
Aeneid (Vergil), 276–78
Aeschylus, 58, 77
afterlife, Greco-Roman view of, 27
agape (love), 313, *314*
agape banquet, 257
Age of Discovery, 33
Agricultural Revolution, 108–9, 115, 119, 378
agriculture
  in Anatolia and Greece, 118–19
  beginning of, 108, 112, 404*n*
  dispersion of, 118, 152
  a mistake, according to some historians, 403*n*
  Triptolemus spreading the art of, 87–88
akratos (not watered down), 184
Albigensian Crusade, 348

Alcibiades, 163
alcohol, 123, 168–69, 185
  no Greek word for, 169
Alexander the Great, 127, 184
Alexandria, 380. *See also* Great Library of Alexandria
alkaloids, 44
Allen, Thomas W., 63
Amanita muscaria mushroom, 67, 281
Amazonian shamans, xv
Ambrosini, Maria Luisa, 358
American Indians, 371–73
Americas, 33, 370–74
Anatolian Hypothesis, 118–19
Anatolians
  farming by, 118
  influence on Ancient Greece, 116
  spread throughout Europe, 119, 143
ancestor worship, 272–73
Ancient Greece. *See* Greece/Greeks
Andros, 190–91, 199
Angelico, Fra, *The Annunciation,* 197
Anicetus, Pope, 292
Anthesteria festival, 214, *215*
antibiotics, 124–25
  in Egyptian skeleton, 124–25

anticlericalism, 358

Antioch, 380

anxiety, visualization of, 4

Apicius, 329

Apollo, 323

apotheosis, 217, 226

The Apples of Apollo: Pagan and Christian Mysteries of the Eucharist (Ruck), 229, 293

archaeobotany, 325–29

archaeochemistry, 101, 158–59, 204, 212

Aretino, Pietro, *Humanity of Christ,* 199

Aristophanes, 77

Aristotle, 26

Armando, Gianfranco, 334–35, 340, 344, 358, 360

Armelagos, George, 125

Arnault, Bernard, 251

Artemis, 349

Artemis, Temple of, 241

ASEQ bookstore, Rome, 253–54

atheists, 1
    and mystics, 11

Athenaeus of Naucratis, 184–85

Athanasius of Alexandria, Archbishop, 91

attachment, non-, 5

Attar (Persian), 10

Augustine, Saint, 32, 262, 296

Augustiner-Bräu, 127

Aulus Gellius, 279

Aurelii family, 266, 267–90, 381

Ayahuasca, xiv
    drinking it, xv
    sessions, xiv

Ayin (Nothingness), 10

Aztecs, 370–71

Bacchae (Euripides), 78, 175–77, 191, 196–97, 230–31, 261, 305, 342, 421*n*, 429*n*

Bacchanalia, prohibited by Romans, 218, 221, 247

Bacchus, 178

Baldung, Hans, 346, *351*

barley, 40–43, 73

Bazer, Dinah, 1–2, 3–5, 8, 12, 75, 386, 388

Beard, Mary, 221

beatific vision, 342–43, 369

Becerra, Xavier, 356

Beckwith, John, 304

beer, 106–28
    basins for, *114*
    brewing of, 107–8, 122–27, 137, 242, 379, 405*n*
    culture of, suppressed by Romans, 161
    fermentation of, 120
    hallucinogenic, 19, 125, 156, 163
    history of, 107, 119, 405*n*
    homemade, 163
    not served in Christian churches, 163
    Purity Law of 1516, 106, 125–26
    women brewers, 242, 329–30

beer mug, *120,* 121

beerstone (calcium oxalate), 111, 115, 120

Beidha complex, 201–2

being born in a human body, privilege of, xvi

Benevento, 349

Bernardino of Siena, 352–53

Bernini, Lorenzo, 296–97

betony, 364

beverages
    drugged, 168
    ritual, 205

The Bewitched Groom (Baldung), 346, *346*

Bible, translation of, 13

Big Science and Big Technology, 35

Bilia la Castagna, 350, 351

Bisconti, Fabrizio, 278

Blanchard, Jacques, *Zeus and Semele,* 196

blechon (mint), 42, 100

blind
    sight to the, 342–43
    visions of the, 97–98

blue water lily, 208

Bolte Taylor, Jill, 7–8

books, destruction of, 57

Borghese Vase, 223–25, *223, 287*

Bossis, Anthony, 5–6, 8, 386, 387
Boston University, 45–48
Bouts, Dieric, 89
Braconi, Matteo, 382
Braidwood, Robert, 107
Bramante, Donato, 296
bread, 107–8
  blessing of, 93
Brent, Charles Henry, 371
Brent Commission, 371
breweries, 106–8
  home, 220
  medieval, 161
Bronze Age, 119
Brown, Raymond E., 243–44, 311
Brown University, 18
Bruno, Giordano, 336–43
  records of his interrogation, 338
  statue of, 375
  writings, 336, 337
bucranium, 84
bureaucrats (of the Church, the
    government), 373
burial grounds, 113
Burkert, Walter, 59, 60–61, 99, 151–52,
    236, 384, 386
burning bush, 9
Buzó, Ramon, 148–49

caffeine, 44
Calagione, Sam, 122
calda (hot brew), 314–15, 381
Calvari d'Amposta, Spain, 141
Campania, 321–32, 322 (map), 348, 354,
    433*n*
Cana, 200, 216
Canaanites, 161, 204, 210, 379
cancer, fear of, 1–2
Canfora, Luciano, 57
cannabis, 326, 371
  legalization of, 13
Can Sadurni, 143–44
Capernaum, 282
Carrù, Giovanni, 289
Carthage, 262–63

catacombs
  Christians meeting in, 256, 280, 315,
      384
  funerary banquets in, *268,* 269–73,
      312, 314, 342–43
  Naples, 331
  Rome, 67, 248, 262, 264–65, 267–90,
      307–16, 380
Catacombs of Priscilla, Rome, 307–11, 316
  Capella Greca, 307–11
Catacombs of Saints Marcellinus and
    Peter, Rome, 311–15, *312,* 316
Catalan language, 138
Catalonia, 129–56
Catalonians, ancestry of, 143
Cathars, 348
Catholic Church. *See* Roman Catholic
    Church
Catholic Encyclopedia (from 1907), 263
cave art, xiv
caves, entrances to underworld, 321
Celtic language, 409*n*
Celts, 410*n*
cemeteries, reveling in, 263
Center for Hellenic Studies, Harvard,
    157–58
Centros Científicos y Tecnológicos
    (CCiTUB), University of Barcelona,
    147
Cerberus, 138, 140
cerebral hemorrhage (stroke), 7
chalice (*kernos*)
  cleaned and not tested, 103
  at Eleusis, 101–3, *102*
  not cleaned, testable, 383
  in Spain, 132, 142
chalice (of Christian Mass), 235
  elevation of, 268–70, 313
Champion of the Ladies (Martin Le
    Franc), 350
chaos, 73
Charlemagne, 33
*The Chemical Muse: Drug Use and
    the Roots of Western Civilization*
    (Hillman)G, 62

Christian church
  all members, living and dead, 264
  destruction of pagan art by, 32–33, 56
    in Rome, 324
  view of women, 288, 363
  war on women, 363
  See also Roman Catholic Church
Christianity
  conflict with Greek religion, 72
  Eucharist central to, 198
  Greeks in, 292
  heresies in, 291–96
  an illegal cult, 220, 288, 330–31
  medieval, 11
  a mystery cult, 92, 198
  not unique, 89
  official religion of Roman Empire (AD
    380), 25, 27, 32, 315
  origins of, 9, 48–51, 155–56, 289
  and pagan rites and festivals, 13–14
  primitive, xviii
  secret of its success, 228, 281–82
  and Western civilization, 14–15
  and women, 76, 296, 381
  women excluded from leadership,
    248–49
Christian literature, 49
Christians
  Greek-speaking, 167
  persecution of, 288, 315
chthonic cults, 407n
churches
  in cities, with graveyards, 263
  house. See house churches
  outdoor and indoor, 240
Ciaraldi, Marina, 326, 328–29
Cicero, 30, 104
Cifres, Alejandro, 360
Circe (goddess), 63–65, 275, 276–78, 280,
  337, 435n
Circeii, 276
cista mystica (sacred basket), 84–85, 87
cities, beginning of, 112
Classical Mythology in Literature, Art and
  Music (Mayerson), 187

classicists, 45–52
  political stance of, 56
  and study of drugs in the ancient
    world, 62
classics, dying of, 15–18, 393n
Clement I, Pope, 292
Clement of Alexandria, 303
Cline, Eric, 209
cocaine, 44, 371
college subjects
  the classics, 15–18
  "utilitarian," 16
Colonna, Carlo, 300
Colorado, 13
comissatio (Bacchanalian revel), 263
Congregation for the Doctrine of the
    Faith, 340
  Archive of, 358
consciousness
  altered states of, 109, 321, 389
  expansion of, 384
  not confined to the body, xviii
  psychedelics as aid to, 81, 95
  surviving bodily death, 6
Controlled Substances Act of 1970, 12
Cooper, Sharon, 97
Corinth, 258, 260, 319, 380
1 Corinthians (Paul), 231, 257, 263
cosmos, 73
Counter-Reformation, 33
Cowan, Florence, 373–74
crone, 76
crucifixion, 33
Crusades, 33
cults, in Greco-Roman world, 14, 220
The Cults of Campania (Peterson), 323
Cumae, 323
curandera (Mexican healer), 39
Cyriacus the Martyr, Saint, 365

Dark Ages, 414n
The Darkening Age: The Christian
    Destruction of the Classical World
    (Nixey), 32, 56
darnel, 73

death, fear of, 6, xviii
death cults
    early European, 146, 306
    early Middle Eastern, 214, 273
    survival in Christian times, 263–64,
        281, 331, 347
Deferrari, Roy J., 49, 56
*De gli eroici furori (The Heroic
    Enthusiasts)* (Bruno), 337
Deipnosophistae (Banquet of the
    Learned), 184–85
deities, disbelief in, xii
del Olmo Lete, Gregorio, 211, 273
Delphi, Oracle of, 59–62, 76
De Materia Medica (Dioscorides), 186–88
Demeter
    in Catalonia, *133*
    at Eleusis, *70*
    myth of, 41–44, 48, 76, 79, 88, 136
    and Persephone, 76
Demetriou, Denise, 135
Denver, 13
depression, end-of-life, 5
de' Spagnolis, Marisa, 326, 328–29, 384
The Devine Feast of El, 211
devotio ritual, 143
Diamond, Jared, 109, 403*n*
die before you die, 7, 10, 11, 155, 306,
    320–21, 343
diet, less diverse and balanced, with
    farming, 108
digging and destroying (by
    archaeologists), 103–4
dii, divi (ancestors), 273
dimethyltryptamine (DMT), xiv
Diodorus Siculus, 76
Dionysian bacchanals, 49–50, 214
The Dionysian Gospel (MacDonald),
    197–99, 230, 234
Dionysian Mysteries, 240, 287
    banned by Romans, 219, 323
    and Christian rituals, 247
    men excluded from, 311
    a trick aimed at women (Euripides),
        243

Dionysus, 190–203
    birth of, 79, 191, 200
    cult of, 221
    frenzied devotees of, 169
    future research on, 379–80
    god of ecstasy, 139, *222*, 236, *300, 301*
    god of inebriants, 234, 380
    god of theaters, 234
    in Greece, 214
    and Jesus, similarities, 203, 230–31,
        233, 236–40, 247, 292–93
    and Marsyas, 225
    myth of, 79, 183
    open-air churches of, 175
    as a revolutionary, 331, 386
    in wine, 77
    wine of, 49, 163
    witches of, 247–48
Dioscorides, 186–88, 218, 248, 313, 324,
    329, 380, 420*n*
disease, 108–9
di Simplicio, Oscar, 359, 364–65, 366
DNA sequencing, 119
Dodds, E. R., 79
Dogfish Head Brewery, 122
dog sacrifice, 138
domestic chapel, *136*, 137–38
The Doors of Perception (Huxley), 11, 13,
    254
dreams, 352
Drug of Immortality, 177, 292, 341, 368,
    384
"Drug Preparation in Evidence?"
    (Ciaraldi), 326
drugs
    in the ancient world, 62–68
    curing addiction to, xvi
    See also pharmakon

Eberdingen-Hochdorf, 140
Eckhart, Meister, 11
The Economist, 18
ecstasy
    biologically normal, 3
    drug-induced, 3

ecstasy (*continued*)
  endogenously produced, 95
  methods of achieving, 95
  in women's experience, 423*n*
ecstatic speech, 239
Edelstoff lager, 127
ego, 6–7
Egypt, 378
  herbal wines of, 205–6
El (god), 211, 418*n*
Eleusinian vision, 96
Eleusis, 19, 25–28, 83–105
  alternative sites, 127
  Archaeological Museum of, 83, *102*
  drug-free claim, 151
  festival to be held in 2021, 70–71
  influence of, in Catalonia, 132–34
  nearly destroyed by barbarians, and
    rebuilt, 31
  in Persephone myth, 41
  predecessors of (Göbekli Tepe), 115
  See also Mysteries of Eleusis
*Eleusis: Archetypal Image of Mother and
  Daughter* (Kerenyi), 99
Eleusis: the Great Mysteries (exhibition),
  69–70, 76
Eliade, Mircea, 95
Ellicott, Charles John, 259
Empedocles, 325, 331
Emporion (Empúries, Spain), 130, 135–36,
  144, 153, 155
The Enneads (Plotinus), 278–79
*Entheogens and the Development of
  Culture* (Piper), 234–35
environmental problems, 80
Ephesus, 239–41, 246, 319, 380
Ephyra, 61
Epiphany, 195, 415*n*
epoptes, 27
Erasmus, 13–14
ergot (*Claviceps purpurea*), *43*
  in Catalonia, 145–46, 147–48, 150, 281
  detection of, in a skull, 159
  in German beers, 123–26
  in *kukeon* drink, 73, 281

LSD extracted from, 40
  poisonous effects, 43–44
  psychedelic property of, 44, 61–62
  spread of, through Europe, 127
ergotism, 43
ethylene, 60–61
Eucharist
  beatific vision provided by, 369
  central to Christianity, 198
  drugged and drug-free, 333
  drug of immortality, 177, 217, 238–39
  feast on body of Jesus, 232
  magic power of consecrated host, 366
  mushrooms' competition with, 373–74
  nonpsychedelic, 75, 340, 368
  of paleo-Christians, 49–50, 254
  placebo, 383
  psychedelic, 36, 156, 164, 228, 254,
    306, 335, 340, 368
  right and wrong types of, 373
  sacrament of, performed by women,
    310–11
  sacrament originated by Jesus, 33
  transubstantiation of, 341
  at witches' Sabbat, alternative type of,
    349
eucharistic vigil, 311
Eukrates votive relief, *96*, 97
Eunapius, 57
Euripides, 58, 77, 78, 175–76, 219, 229,
  243, 279, 285, 422*n*
Eusebius, 293
experiences, xiii
  spiritually significant, 2–3
Eyck, Hubert and Jan, 236
Eye of Horus, 207

farming. *See* agriculture
Fathers of the Church, 292
fear, 1–2
  visualization of, 4
feasting
  funeral, 143
  ritual, 110, 114
feeding the multitude miracle, 308

Fehl, Philip, 199
fermentation, 111, 120, 126, 204
Fertile Crescent, 108, 162, 378
festivals, restricted to women, 217
Finicella, 352–53
Fitzpatrick, Scott M., 152
flesh and blood, raw meals of, 246
Florenzano, Assunta, 328
forbidden substances, research on, 2
Fournier, Jean-Marc, 250–51
Fractio Panis (Breaking of Bread) fresco,
    308–11, *308*
Francis, Pope, 232, 247, 296
Frazer, James George, 232–33
Freising, Germany, 106
Frickenhaus, August, 170
frogs, 326
Fullola, Josep Maria, 159
funerary banquets
    in catacombs, *268*, 269–73, *312, 314,*
        342–43
    Eucharist celebrated at, 272
    in graveyards, 426*n*, 427*n*
    the Mass as, 263
    in Middle East, 210
    women depicted in scenes of, 311
funerary rites, 113–15
    pot depicting, *215*

G 408 and 409 pots, *168,* 170–71, 180–83,
    180, 182, 380
Gabriel, Angel, 9
Galen, 62, 254, 313–14, 324, 329, 380, 398*n*
Galilee, 200–201, 201 (map), 212, 379
    wine production of, 208, 415*n*
Galileo Galilei, 336
Gardner, Percy, 40
Gatsos, Nikos, 71
General Directorate of Antiquities and
    Cultural Heritage, Greece, 54–55
Germany, brewing in, 123–26
Ghent Altarpiece, 235, *236*
Ginzburg, Carlo, 340, 353
Giuliani, Raffaella, 309
gnosis (knowledge), 90, 293

Gnostic churches, 90
Gnostic Gospels, 384
The Gnostic Gospels (Pagels), 90
Gnosticism, 293–96
Gnostic literature, 244
Gnostics, 163–64, 291, 333
    persecution of, 350
goats, *270*
    psychedelic flesh of, 234–35, 421*n*
Göbekli Tepe, 111–16, *114,* 151, 377, 379
God
    appealed to by an atheist, 3–4
    reading about, 10
Godin Tepe, Iran, 120
God Pill, 388–89
gods
    Greek, 29–30, 323
    Latin, 323
    monumental depiction of, 112
    See also Roman religion
*God's Jury: The Inquisition and the Making
    of the Modern World* (Murphy), 362
The Golden Bough (Frazer), 232–33
Golden Cup of Nestor, 120, 121
Good Shepherd fresco, *270*
Gordium, 121, 383
Gospel of Infinity (Bruno), 336
Gospels (the Four)
    audience for, 163
    included in New Testament, 91
    Last Supper passages, 231
    Marriage at Cana passage, only in
        John, 217
    Resurrection passages, 243
    See also John, Gospel of
Graf, Fritz, 59, 79, 81, 95, 162
grain, 73, 84, 87, 108
grapes
    cultivation of, 202–3
    fermentation of, 204
grapevines, in a mosaic in Vatican
    Necropolis, 303–5
graveyard beer, 119–22, 142, 145, 146,
    168, 255, 329, 378
    hallucinogenic, 150

graveyard wine, 330

Great Dionysia, 77–78

Great Library of Alexandria, destruction of (A.D. 392), 56–57, 397n

Greco-Roman world

cults in, 14

violence and diseases of, 26

Greece/Greeks

characterized as rational, not drug users, 47

farming, 118–19

festivals, 49

predecessors in Anatolia, 116

psychedelics used by, 58–62, 153

religion, 29–30, 72, 323

Romans taught by, 266

in Rome, 291–92

sacrament of, 14–15

science and technology of, 154

study of, 53

and Western civilization, 25, 28–30

and wine, 167, 254

wine preferred to beer, 161–62

Greek colonists, in Southern Italy, 129–35, 131, 254, 255

Greek language, 13, 16–18, 66, 163, 167, 246, 324

of New Testament (koine), 49, 78

Greek Magical Papyri, 367

Greek Mistress, 349

Greek mythology, 28

Greek Orthodox Church, 93–94

Greek Religion (Burkert), 59, 60–61, 99

Grey, Alex, xix

Griffiths, Roland, 3, 5

gruit ale, 125

Hades, 27

Hajji Firuz Tepe, 205

hallucinations, Christian, 244

hallucinogenic beer, 19–20, 49, 67, 125, 156, 163, 214

evidence of, 129, 143, 145–47, 153, 161

hallucinogenic wine, 19–20, 49, 67, 214

evidence of, 318–32, 334

Hanson, Victor David, 15–18

Harbor-UCLA Medical Center, 52

Harrison, Jane Ellen, 40–41

Harrowing of Hell, 214

Hatsis, Thomas, 351

Hayden, Brian, 109

Heath, John Robert, 15–18

Hecate, 138, 408n

Helena (partner of Simon Magus), 293

hemispheres, left and right, 7

henbane (Hyoscyamus niger), 140–41, 326, 345, 408n

Hensley, Albert, 372

heretics, 291–96, 335, 381

persecution of, 349

secret chain of, 357, 363–64, 376

Herod, 214

Hillman, David, 62

Himmelmann, Nikolaus, 284–87, 325

Hippolytus, 294, 381

Hoffman, Mark, 148

Hofmann, Albert, 19, 38, 40–46, 45, 48, 81–82, 99–100, 124

Holy Communion, xi, xix, 33, 100–101

ecstasy of taking, 247–48

Holy Grail. See chalice (of Christian Mass)

Holy Roman Empire, 33

Homer, 51–52, 67, 278–79

Homeric fresco, 274

Homer the Theologian (Lamberton), 278

Horace, 266

house churches, 246, 248, 256, 260, 315, 384

Hoyle, Peter, 77

human body, privilege of being born in a, xvi

human sacrifice, Mass taken to be a ritual form of, 232

hunter-gatherer cultures, xiv

Hunza people, 210

Huxley, Aldous, 11–12, 13, 35, 40, 387

Hymn to Demeter, 41–44, 61, 87, 127, 138

Hypogäum der Aurelier (Himmelmann), 284

Hypogeum of the Aurelii, Rome, 265, 267–90, *268, 270, 271, 274, 283, 285, 287,* 316

Iacchus, 79, 400*n*
Ibn Ishaq, 9
Iglulik Inuit, 95–96
Ignatius of Antioch, Saint, 177, 257
immortality
    gift of, 248
    wine of, 214
immortals, 154
Imperial Center for Psychedelic Research, 52
incubation, 321, 347–48
Index of Forbidden Books, 358
India, 66
Indigetes, 130
Indo-Europeans, 118, 378. *See also* Proto-Indo-Europeans
inebriation, origins of, 411*n*
"The Influence of the Mystery Religions on Christianity" (King), 14, 233
Innocent VIII, Pope, 227
Inquisition, 340, 357–71, 385
internal and external concepts, dissolution of, 4
International Church of Cannabis, 13
Inuit shamans, 95–96
Ionia, 154–55, 240
Irenaeus, 91, 293, 294
Irvin, Dorothy, 309–11
ISIS, destruction of cultural heritage by, 57
Islam, 9, 10
Israelites, 213–14
Italy
    mystics in, 291
    southern, 255–56
    unification of, 358
    wine in, 412*n*
ivy, 364

James, William, 74
Japan, 126
Jefferson, Thomas, 16

Jesus
    accepting as your personal Lord and Savior, 237
    born in a wine culture, 163
    cult of, 84, 221
    and Dionysus, similarities, 195, 203, 230–31, 233, 236–40, 247, 292–93
    drugged wine of, 188
    Gnostic, 91
    as Greek philosopher-magician, 36
    image of, 33
    long hair style of, 223, 420*n*
    as magical healer, 78
    message of, 48–49
    mystery cult of, 323–24
    name of, 229
    raising of Lazarus miracle, 425*n*
    resurrection of, 173
    as revolutionary, 331, 386
Jews
    Greek-speaking, 246
    women, religious role of, 418*n*
John, Gospel of, 197–99
    death and rebirth passages, 237–38
    and Gnostics, 294
    Greek language of, 49
    Last Supper passage, 233–34
    Marriage at Cana passage, 203, 216–17
    Resurrection passage, 243–44
    sight to the blind passage, 342
    similarity to *Bacchae,* 230–31, 261
    Son of God passages, 218
    True Drink passage, 282, 330
    True Vine passage, 304–6
    written for women, 241–43
John Chrysostom, Saint, 33
John of Patmos, 422*n*
John Paul II, Pope, 296, 340, 343
Johns Hopkins Center for Psychedelic and Consciousness Research, xvii, 3, 19, 52, 385–87
    research into psilocybin, 1–3
John the Baptist, 214
Jolly, Karen, 350
Jones, William, 66

Jordaens, Jacob, *Crucifixion, 224*
The Joyous Cosmology: Adventures in the Chemistry of Consciousness (Watts), 388
Juan-Tresserras, Jordi, 144–48, 150, 158–61, 377
Judaism, 9, 10–11, 232
Junia of Rome, 246
juniper, 210
Justin Martyr, 230

Kabbalists, 10
kantharos (ritual cup), 149, *149*
Kardianou, Alexandra, 167, 171, 178–81
Karnak, Temple of, 207–8
Kerenyi, Carl, 72, 96–97, 99–100
kernos, 142
King, Martin Luther, Jr., 14, 233, 261
Kingsley, Peter, 153–55, 320–21
Koh, Andrew, 208, 212–13, 255, 318–19, 379–80, 384
koimontai (sleep of death), 258–59
koine. See Greek language
koji (*Aspergillus oryzae*), 126
komos procession, 139, *139*
Kostovok barbarians, 31
Kraemer, Ross, 240–41, 311
krater, 139
kukeon (drink)
  in Catalonia, 129–56
  drunk at Eleusis, 27, 100–101
  escaped from Eleusis, 215
  as harvest drink, 40–41
  origin in Anatolia, 119
  psychedelic contents of, 73, 126, 281
  tradition of manufacture of, 73
  visionary brew, claim, 35
  wine competition to, 175
Kurgan Hypothesis, 404*n*
Kushner, Lawrence, 11

Labahn, Michael, 199
Laguna, Andrés, 344–45
Lamberton, Robert, 278
Lamb of God, 235

lambs, 235
Las Ruedas, Necropolis of, 141–43, *142*
Last Supper, 217, 219, 231–34, 260–61, 269, 288
Last Supper (Leonardo), 33, *34*
Latini, Alexia, 275–78
Latin language, 16–18, 66
Latin Mass, 17
Latins
  learned from Greeks, 266
  See also Romans
laurel, 59
Lazarus, 425*n*
Leary, Timothy, 38, 46
Le Franc, Martin, 350
legomena, dromena, deiknumena, 42
Lenaevasen (Frickenhaus), 170
Leonardo da Vinci, 33
Leo XIII, Pope, 338
Levaniouk, Olga, 286
Lewis-Williams, David, xiv
liberal arts education, 17
Liddell-Scott-Jones Greek-English lexicon, 259
light body, 207
Linear B, 51
literature, ancient, loss of, 58, 62, 397*n*
Liu Li, 110
lizard/s, 326
lizard ointment, 367
lizard potion, psychedelic, 347, 380
lizard wine, 344
looms, 275–76, *275*
Louvre Museum, Paris, 167–89, 190–92, 216, 222
LSD, xiii, 40, 123
  discovery of, 43–44
Lucretia (a witch), 364–69
Luke, Gospel of, Greek language of, 49
Luther, Martin, 13–14, 125
Lydia of Philippi, 244–46

Mabit, Jacques, xvi
MacDonald, Dennis, 197–99, 230, 294, 355

Mac Góráin, Fiachra, 218
MacMullen, Ramsay, 262, 271, 299, 347, 380
maenads, 77, 80, 169, 246–47, 426n
magicians, healers, and prophets, 78, 320
Magna Graecia, 319–32, 322 (map)
    Greek colonies in, 291, 419n
    Greek religion in (Bacchanalia), 217
    mystery cults in, 135, 256, 380
Manifest Destiny, 33
Marcosians, 294
Marcus, 294
Marcus Aurelius, 30–31
    bust of, 31–32, 31
Maria, Josep, 159
marijuana. See cannabis
Mark, Gospel of, Greek language of, 49
Mark, Secret Gospel of, 401n
Marriage at Cana, 203, 216–17
Marsyas, 224, 225
martyria (pilgrimage sites), 347
Mary
    godmother of farmers, 93
    in Orthodox Church, 93
    Virgin Mother, 76, 89
Maryland Psychiatric Research Center, 3
Mary Magdalene, 243–44, 311
Mary Magdalene, Gospel of, 244, 384, 388
marzeah ritual, 210–12, 213, 273, 379, 418n, 419n
Mas Castellar de Pontós, 129, 131, 132–39, 136, 153, 158, 242, 377
    objects from, 133, 139
Mass, the, 86, 232, 263
    alternative (witches' Sabbat), 349–50
    as a séance, 264
Massalia (Marseille, France), 130, 153, 155
Mate, Gabor, xvii
Mater Dolorosa, 89
materialist-reductionism, xvii
Materia Medica, 218, 344–45
Matthew, Gospel of, Greek language of, 49
Mayerson, Philip, 187, 237
Mazatec shamans, xx, 373–74
Mazzei, Barbara, 265, 276, 381, 382

McGovern, Patrick, 119–22, 158, 202, 204–7, 242, 255, 328, 378–79, 383
Medici, Lorenzo de', 227–28
medicine, women in, 348
megaliths, 112
men/male sex, in religious life, 296
Mercati, Angelo, 338–39
mescaline, 11
Mexico, 39, 370–71
    shamans, 373–74
Meyers, Eric, 201
Michelangelo, 296
microbiome, 108
Midas, 121
Midas Touch, 378, 383
Middle Ages, 11, 161, 333
Middle East, 201 (map), 210
Milarepa, 172
mind-expanding wine, 255
miniature vessels, 137
Minoans, 119, 120, 121, 378
mint (Mentha pulegium), 99–100
misce (mix it), 313, 314
missionaries, xi, 33, 372
mithridatium medical concoction, 327
mortars, 110–11, 110
Moses, 9
Mother Ayahuasca, xv
Mother Nature, 80
Mount Athos, 11, 343
Mount Vesuvius, 325
Muhammad, 9
Murphy, Cullen, 362–63
mushrooms, 373–74
    Amanita muscaria, 67, 281
    magic, 38–40
    psilocybin, xx, 373
musteria (mysteries), 92
Mutterkorn, 124
Myceneans, 119, 120, 121, 162, 378
Mysterien von Eleusis (Kerenyi), 72
Mysteries of Eleusis, 72–74
    age and reputation of, 393n
    copied in Catalonia, 136
    expense of visiting, 162, 195

Mysteries of Eleusis (*continued*)
   experience of, 26–28
   exported by Triptolemus, 144
   exported to Catalonia, 139–40
   fame of, 394*n*
   official toleration of, 247
   predecessors of, 152
   Renaissance awareness of, 227
   secrecy of, 26, 394*n*
   theories about, 37–38, 40, 377
   women priestesses of, 242
   See also Eleusis
mystery, derivation of word, 27
"Mystery Coast Highway" (Campania
   region of Italy), 322 (map), 323, 337,
   347
mystery cults, 70, 135, 256, 380
Mystical Experience Questionnaire, 3
mysticism, popular, 386
mystics
   experience of, 74
   in Italy, 291
   persecution of, 12, 373
My Stroke of Insight (Bolte Taylor), 7

Nabataean Kingdom, 202, 214, 379
Nag Hammadi, Egypt, 90, 384
Nagy, Greg, 157–58, 159
Naples, 323, 331
Napoleon, 359
Native American Church, 372
Natufians, 107–8, 110–11
   burial site, *110*
Nazareth, 200, 218
Neanderthals, 152
near-death-experience (NDE), 97–98, 342
Neolithic Revolution, 108, 151
neo-pagans, 88
neo-Pythagoreanism, 278
New Testament, 13, 49, 78, 91, 229
New York University, psychedelic
   research at, 52, 386–87
nicotine, 44
nightshades, 141, 150, 326, 345
   in beer, 161

nightshade wines, 187
Nixey, Catherine, 32, 56–57
Nixon, Richard, 38
Nock, A. D., 195–96, 215, 217, 229, 367
North, Helen F., 292
North, John, 221
Nothingness, 10
Notre Dame, Paris, fire in, 250–51
Nysa, 200

Oakland, 13
O'Connor, Flannery, 341
Odysseus, 27, 278
Odyssey, Book 10, 63–65, 277
ointment, witch's, 141, 366–68
ololiuhqui (a psychedelic drug), 370–71
Olympian gods, 29–30
OpenARCHEM, 379
opium, 326, 371
Oracle. *See* Delphi, Oracle of
*Oratio de hominis dignitate (Oration
   on the Dignity of Man)* (Pico della
   Mirandola), 227
Orthodox Christianity, 11, 33, 93
Osiris, 207–8
Otto, Walter, 183

Paculla Annia, priestess, 218, 243, 323, 350
paedagogus (tutor), 427*n*
Paestum, 324
pagan continuity hypothesis
   belief in, 228, 239, 271
   doubts about, 172
   at Eleusis, 84, 88–89
   evidence for, 20, 167, 254, 256, 315, 376
   at Marriage at Cana, 198
   origin of, 14–15, 232
   Ruck's contribution to, 35
Pagano, Sergio, 339, 361
pagan rites and festivals, Christianity and,
   13–14
Pagels, Elaine, 90–92, 244, 293–95
paleo-Christianity
   connection to pagan cults, 13, 36
   Eucharist of, 49–50, 254

an illegal mystery cult, 316–17
literature of, 49
rites and practices of, 89, 155
paleo-Christians
connection to Greeks through wine, 167, 254
gatherings of, 49–50
motivation for becoming, 240, 289–90
women's role, 244–49, 245 (map)
paleoecological maps, 209
Paleolithic era, 152
palliative care, 5
Pan, 223
Panagia Mesosporitissa, 93
Pandermalis, Demetrios, 70
Papangeli, Kalliope, 68, 69, 83–86, 88, 93–95, 98–104
parables, 92
Parmenides, 153–55, 320, 331
Parry, Milman, 51, 63
Parthenon, 77
Paul, Saint, *271*
audience for, 163
and Gnostics, 294
Greek language of, 49
Last Supper passages, 231
position in early Church, 92
road to Damascus, 9
warns against drugged wine, 257–59, 263
Pausanius, 190
Pegasus, *130*
Perlmutter Cancer Center, New York University, 1
Persephone
in Catalonia, 130, *130, 133*
cult of, 380
and Demeter, 76
meeting pilgrims at Eleusis, 74
myth of, 41, 79, 88, 136
priestesses of, 323
witches of, 330
Peter, Saint, 271
tomb of, 296, 299
Peterson, Roy Merle, 323

peyote, 11, 370, 371–72, 385
pharmaceutical industry, 2
ancient, 327
pharmacopeia, Paleolithic and Neolithic, 152
pharmakon (drugs, medicine)
Circe's, 64–65
Greek, 176, 221, 237
of heretics, 381
pharmakon athanasias (drug of immortality)
Eucharist as, 177, 217, 238–39
at Marriage at Cana, 198
Philippi, 246
Phocaea, 330
Phocaeans, 153–55, 240, 319–32
Phoenicians, 161, 204, 379
Phrygia, 121
Pico della Mirandola, Giovanni, 227–28
Pike, Eunice, 373–74
Pindar, 28, 104
Pintia archaeological site, 142, *142*
Piper, Alan, 234–35
Pius IX, Pope, 338
Pius XII, Pope, 299
Plato, 27, 104, 154
Pliny, 140
Plotinus, *271*, 278–79, 286, 331
Polignac, François de, 136
polysporia, 93
Pompeii, 286, 325
Pons, Enriqueta, 129, 132–34, 137–40, 145, 148–50, 377
Pontifical Commission for Sacred Archaeology, 20, 382
Ponziani, Daniel, 360, 361, 367
Pope, 381, 389
poppy, 59
pottery, Greek, 169–71, 179
Pound, Ezra, 58
Praetextatus, Vettius Agorius, 72–73, 75, 79–82, 104
Prats, Andorra, 141
Preller, Ludwig, 40
Presbyterians, xi

prescriptions, renewable, 2
President, U.S., swearing in of, 34
Price, Simon, 221
priesthood, Christian, 92, 94
Priscilla of Ephesus, 246
private societies (*collegia*), banned,
    424*n*
Profanation of the Mysteries scandal,
    162–63, 215
Protestants, 385, 434*n*
Proto-Indo-Europeans, 116, 404*n*,
    409*n*
    language of, 66–67, 116–18, 117 (map)
psilocybe mushrooms, xx
psilocybin, xvii, 373, 385
    research on, banned, 1–3, 19
    research resumed in 2000, 3
    visions on a trip, 98
psychedelic plants and fungi, xiv
psychedelic potions
    components of, 280–81
    equally accessible to all, 220
    theories about, 37–38
psychedelics
    banning of, 12, 35–36, 52
    future promise of, 81
    Greeks' use of, 58–62, 151, 153
    legalization of, 13, 52
    research on, 1–3, 19, 35, 52, 386–87
    and Western civilization, 353
"psychedelic slapdowns," xix
psychedelic wine, 49, 207–15, 259, 379,
    381
    research on, 212–13
psychoactive beverages
    and civilization, 106
    and religion, 106
Puteoli, 323
Pythagoras, 278–79, 285, 321, 331
Pythias (Delphi priestesses), 60, 76

Qur'an, dictated to Muhammad, 9

rainbow body, 173, 195, 413*n*
Raphael, 29, 296

Raqefet Cave, Israel, 110–11, 115, 151,
    378, 379
Rarian plain, near Eleusis, 41–42
Ratzinger, Joseph (later Pope Benedict
    XVI), 359
Reagan administration, 38
reality, nature of, 3
rebirth, 11
Reformation, 13, 33, 125
refrigerium (funeral banquet), 261–64,
    270–72, 288, 347–48, 380
relics, 298
religion
    convergence of many religions in Ionia,
        155
    mystical core of, 9–10
    organized, 8–10, 12
    origin of, 105, 112
    psychoactive beverages and, 106
    revival of, 13, 35–36, 387
    vs. science, 35
    with no name, 387
Religion and the Decline of Magic
    (Thomas), 366
religious experience, in medical setting, 8
religiously unaffiliated people, 8
Renaissance, 227, 414*n*
Renfrew, Colin, 118
research, on forbidden substances, 2
Resurrection, 173, 243–44
rice, fermentation of, 126
Richard, Carl, 16
Richards, William, 3, 5–6, 8, 75, 98
Rigveda, 66
Ring, Kenneth, 97
The Road to Eleusis (Wasson et al.), 19,
    35, 38, 45–47, 58, 81, 95, 123, 151,
    168–69, 184, 234
Roman Catholic Church, xi
    beer monopoly of, 125–26
    confronting primitive Christianity,
        xviii
    Mass, 86
    "not everything is written down,"
        343–44

origins of, 155–56
papal leadership of, 228
sex abuse scandals, 356
See also Vatican
Roman Empire
banning of Dionysian Mysteries, 219, 323
Christianized, 25, 27
Roman religion
cults, 220
official, 217, 247
six Greek gods of, 323
twelve principal gods of, 283
Romans
borrowings from Greeks, 30, 266
wine preferred to beer, 161–62
Rome
banning of Bacchanalia, 218, 221, 247
Christian Church in, 324
Christian women in, 246
a religious melting pot, 256
rosette, 84
Royal Road (a caravan route), 155
Ruck, Carl, 45–53, *45*, 148–51, 157–59, 339, 389
on Church origins, 155–56
on Jesus's name, 229
and pagan continuity hypothesis, 35
on psychedelic potions, 38, 161
reputation of, 58
theories of, 76, 78, 84, 162–64, 168–69, 279–80, 333–34, 347, 357, 377
writings, 19, 95, 293
Ruiz de Alarcón, Hernando, 370–71
Rumi, 10

Sabina, Maria, 39–40, 373
sacraments
preparation of, by women, 242
psychedelic, xviii, 20, 153, 167, 315
Sacred Knowledge: Psychedelics and Religious Experiences (Richards), 3, 6, 98
Sacred Road, *85*
St. Anthony's Fire, 43, 126

St. Joe's Prep, Philadelphia, 18
St. Paul's Monastery, Mount Athos, 343
St. Peter's Basilica, 20, 271, 292, 296–99, *298*
Salerno, Medical School of, 348
sanctuary, open-access, 136, 150, 162
Sandoz Laboratories, 46
San Lorenzo, Papal Basilica of, 271
Sanskrit language, 66
Santa Cruz, 13
Sant Pere de Galligants, Abbey of, 129
sarcophagus in Vatican Necropolis, *300, 301*
satyrs, 349
Sauer, J. D., 107–9
Schedule I drugs, 12–13
Schism of 1054, 33
Schliemann, Heinrich, 51, 121
Schmidt, Klaus, 111–13
School of Athens (Raphael), 29, *29*, 33
Schutte, Anne Jacobson, 359
Schweickhardt, Hendrik Willem, *The Infant Bacchus*, 236
science and technology, 35
of Greeks, 154
Science and Technology Centers, Barcelona, 147, 159
Scodel, Ruth, 176–77
Scorpion I of Abydos, 205–6, 378
wine jars in tomb of, *206*
Scythopolis, 319, 380
"Seeking the Magic Mushroom" (Wasson, in *Life* magazine), 39
self, dissolution of, 4
Semele, 191
Sepphoris (Tzippori) mosaic, 200–201
Serapis, statue of, 56
serpents, xv
sex abuse scandals of Roman Catholic Church, 356
SHADES ECCLESIA (Software for Historical Archives Description), 361
Shakespeare, xvii
pipe found in yard of, 158–59

shamans, xiv
  Inuit, 95–96
  Mexican, xx, 373–74
Sherratt, Andrew, 207–8
Sibylline Oracles, 323
Siena, 359
Sierra Mazateca, 39
Silber, John, 46–47, 153
Simon Magus, 293
sixth mass extinction event, 71
skull cult, 113–15, *113*, 146, 331
Smith, Huston, 14, 37, 389
Smith, Morton, 438*n*
Smith, Preserved, 89–90
Socrates, 320
Sodano, Angelo, 343
soma, 66–67, 116, 119
Soma: Divine Mushroom of Immortality
    (Wasson), 67
Son of God, 197, 218
Sophocles, 28, 58, 77, 104
soybeans, fermentation of, 126
Spain. *See* Catalonia
Speth, Gus, 80
spiritual-but-not-religious (SBNR), 9, 52
Staples, Danny, *45*
Steindl-Ras, David, 9
Stika, Hans-Peter, 140, 161, 328
stimulants, 44
Strabo, 321
Strauss, Walter, 346
stregoneria (witchcraft), 361
Streptomyces, 124
Sufism, 10
Supernatural: Meetings with the Ancient
    Teachers of Mankind (Graham
    Hancock), xiv
symposium, 210

Takiwasi clinic, xvi
tartaric acid, 120
Tatar, Maria, 76
Telesphorus, Pope, 292
Tel Kabri, 208–10, 212–13, 379
Tel Kedesh, 212–13

temples, earliest, 112
Tertullian, 261
Thayer Lexicon, 92
Theater of Dionysus, Athens, 162
theaters
    Dionysus god of, 234
    Greek, 77–78, 400*n*
Theodosius, Emperor, 27, 32, 96
theophagy, 232–33
Theophilus, Bishop of Alexandria, 56–57
Theophrastus, 185
theriac medical concoction, 327
therianthropes, xv
Theudas, 294
Thomas, Gospel of, 91, 342, 388
Thomas, Keith, 366
Tibetan Buddhists, 172–74
Timotheus of Miletus, 235
Tiso, Francis, 171–89, 226–42, 249–50,
    253, 269, 287, 291, 334, 339, 389
    kitchen of, *173*
toad Eucharist, 351
toads, 326
    poisonous and psychedelic, 351
tobacco, 370
Torjesen, Karen Jo, 243, 246
touto estin (this is), 269
Transfiguration, 174
transubstantiation, 341, 434*n*
travels while dreaming or hallucinating,
    352
trimma (wine), 78, 168
Triptolemus, *86,* 87–88, 127, 134, *134,*
    144, 150
trogon (eat, gnaw, munch), 233–34
Troy, discovery of site of, 51
True Food and True Drink, 233, 235, 282,
    330
True Vine, 304–6
Tsoukalas, Giorgos, 71
Tulloch, Janet, 311–13
Turkey, 105, 116

Ugarit, 211–12
un-churching of America, 8

underworld
    entrances to, 321
    visits to, 211
underworld cults, 136
"utilitarian" college subjects, 16

Valamoti, Soultana, 255, 328, 380
Valentinian, emperor, 72
Valentinians, 294
Valentinus, 294
The Varieties of Religious Experience
    (James), 74
Vatican
    bureaucracy of, 250
    research at, 20–21, 382–83
    war against women and drugs, 355
    See also Roman Catholic Church
Vatican Necropolis, 299, 315–16
    Mausoleum M, Tomb of the Julii,
        299–306, *302*
    Tomb of the Egyptians, *300*, 301
Vatican Secret Archives, 334–35, 338–44,
    361
Vedic rituals, 116
Velia, Italy, 153, 155, 255, 320–32
venefica (witch), 354
veneficii (drugs), 337, 345, 354
Ventris, Michael, 51
Vergilius Vaticanus, 275, 276–78
Veronese, Paolo, *The Wedding at Cana*,
    192–96, *194*, 203, 217
Villa of the Mysteries, Pompeii, 286,
    287
Villa Vesuvio, Scafati, 326–29, 380, 384
vines. *See* grapevines
Visigoths, 32
visio beatifica, 96–97, 98
visions
    divine, 424n
    seen by Greeks, 59
volcanoes, 325

Waldensians, 350
wand, magic (*virga, thyrsos*), 285–87,
    300

War on Drugs, xvii, xix, 2, 35, 38, 372–73,
    385
    by the Church, 370
Wasson, R. Gordon, 19, 38–46, *45*, 48, 67,
    74, 98, 280, 342, 373
Wasson-Ruck theory, 59
Watkins, Calvert, 65, 67, 116, 242, 280–81
Watts, Alan, 12, 386, 388
Webster, Noah, 16
Weihenstephan, 106
Western civilization
    beginning of, 14–15, 25, 28–30
    Christianity and, 14–15
    psychedelics and, 353
    war for the soul of, 15
When Women Were Priests (Torjesen),
    243, 260, 296
Who Killed Homer? (Hanson and Heath),
    15, 51
Wilhelm IV of Bavaria, Duke, 106
Wilpert, Joseph, 308–9
wine
    as blood of grapes, 235, 421n
    Christian use of, 167
    competition with *kukeon* (drink), 175,
        421n
    Dionysian, 49, 77, 163, 281
    as drug (*pharmakon*), 176–77
    drugged, 186–88, 233, 294, 330, 381
    equally for rich and lowly, 216
    fermentation of, 120
    formula for, in Inquisition records,
        364
    in Galilee, 208, 415n
    hallucinogenic, of immortality, 19, 49,
        214
    history of, 204
    of immortality, 214
    magical, 220
    mixing, by women, 259, 313
    not watered down, 184
    poisonous, 259
    preferred to beer, 161–62
    psychedelic, 49, 207–15, 259, 379
    sacramental, 379

wine (*continued*)
  spiked, 204, 209, 254, 333
  strong, 168
  visionary, 273
  water changed to, 190–94, 198–99, 203
wine banquet, Greek, 210
winemaking, history pf, 162
Winged Victory of Samothrace, 178–79
witchcraft
  in Greek myth, 138
  in Middle Ages and Renaissance, 333
witches
  burning of, xi
  carnality of, 434*n*
  Eucharist potion found on a, 351
  number executed or tortured, 362–63
  ointment of, 141
  witch hunts, 21, 349, 352, 357–58
witches, Greek
  of Demeter, at Eleusis, 48
  of Dionysus, 247, 248
  paleo-Christian, 290
  of Persephone, 330
  in Rome, 324–25
The Witches (Baldung), *351*
*The Witches' Ointment: The Secret History
    of Psychedelic Magic* (Hatsis), 351
witches' Sabbat, 349
women
  beer brewing of, 242, 329–30
  Christian church's view of, 288, 363
  cult initiation of, excluding men, 240

and drugs, 288, 313
in early Christianity, 240–49, 245
    (map)
and ecstasy, 423*n*
and Eucharist, 311
excluded from Christian priesthood,
    76, 248–49, 296, 381
Greek, 423*n*
Jewish, 418*n*
in medicine, 348
pharmacological expertise of, 329–30
priestesses of Eleusis, 242
religious activity of, 308–11
sexuality of, making them ineligible for
    religious life, 296
spiritual leaders, xix, 424*n*
war on, 355, 363
wine mixing by, 259, 313
The World's Religions (Smith), 14

Yahweh, 9
Yale University, 52
Yasur-Landau, Assaf, 209
Yates, Frances, 336
yeast (*Saccharomyces cerevisiae*), 108, 120
Young, Rodney, 383

Zander, Pietro, 299–300, 304
Zarnkow, Martin, 106–11, 114–15, 122–26,
    242, 377–78
Zinn, Howard, 46–47
Zosimus, 72